THE
ARTISTS'
YEARBOOK
2008/9

EDITOR: OSSIAN WARD

THE
ARTISTS'
YEARBOOK
2008/9

'Required reading for every aspiring artist or student'
RA Magazine

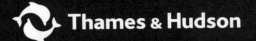
Thames & Hudson

On the cover Photo Jonathan Stephenson, from his book *Paint with the Watercolour Masters*, Thames & Hudson, 1998

First published in the United Kingdom in 2007 by
Thames & Hudson Ltd, 181A High Holborn, London WC1V 7QX

www.thamesandhudson.com

British Library Cataloguing-in-Publication Data
A catalogue record for this book is available from the British Library

ISBN 978-0-500-28692-0

Printed and bound in Germany by Bercker

Contents

00

Introduction

Introduction to
The Artists' Yearbook 2008/9

Ossian Ward

As *The Artists' Yearbook* expands and filters through to the farthest reaches of the country, so the art world itself keeps growing and attracting an ever-wider audience. Most of the talk has been of the mushrooming market for contemporary art and for the obscene amounts of money being realized at auctions or art fairs for work by living artists, many of which can now outstrip the asking prices for minor Old Master works. While the stratospheric top-end of the market will forever mystify many involved in the making and appreciation of art, the recent buoyancy and growth in the sales of art can benefit the lower echelons of the art world too. There are more galleries opening all the time and consequently more opportunities to exhibit and sell work than ever before. A young gallery owner, Niru Ratnam, has contributed a new essay on the different support structures that this network of small exhibition spaces provides; from merely being places to hang out and drink coffee, to looking after the 'necessary evils' of showing, interpreting and selling an artist's work to the wider world.

Nowhere is the market for art more open than on the internet and Rebecca Wilson, the editor of Charles Saatchi's popular online meeting place for artists, Your Gallery, writes of the unprecedented levels of communication and collaboration available to artists nowadays, as well as how such democratic websites can also attract the odd appreciative buyer (like Saatchi himself).

There is still room for those who don't want to rush headlong into a commercial career, especially away from London, the acknowledged centre of all things market-related in this country. Artist duo Heather and Ivan Morison left the capital to settle down and make art in Birmingham, buying an allotment that became the focus of some of their practice. In her essay on the benefits of living outside the conventional hub of art activity, Heather

Morison describes how they then moved to a remote spot in Snowdonia and continued to flourish and succeed as artists, but under different terms from their colleagues in the capital.

Some artists choose to go further afield to set up their studios. Restless artists will find inspiration in the section devoted to competitions, residencies, awards, prizes and other funding opportunities that facilitate travel in pursuit of personal and artistic betterment. In a guide to what to expect, Tim Braden recalls the initial bewilderment, followed by his occasionally demanding but happy years spent studying in Amsterdam at the prestigious Rijksakademie.

Just as location shouldn't matter, *The Artists' Yearbook* tries not to differentiate between the amateur and the professional artist. It is designed to be useful for everyone, from the undecided undergraduate looking for the right degree or the best college to the hobbyist painter in search of a local supplier of canvas and paints, as well as the established artist urgently needing to organize safe passage for their work to an exhibition in a Berlin gallery.

Also new to this edition of *The Artists' Yearbook* is a preface by one of Britain's most consistently original artists, Gavin Turk. When asked to respond to the provocation: 'Why be an artist?' he travels back in time to find out just how useful the endeavour of creative thinking and doing can be. His break-neck survey of the history of art is one beamed clearly through the lens of the artist – the view of the passionate maker rather than the detached art academic.

Andy Warhol, an idol of Turk's and the artist who shaped the role of the contemporary artist more than anyone in the last century, once said with typical irony, 'Why do people think artists are special? It's just another job.' But is it possible to measure professionalism in a wholly self-motivated occupation that has no job description or chances of promotion? Susan Jones, Director of Programmes at a-n, The Artists Information Company based in Newcastle-upon-Tyne, believes there is a code of professionalism that artists should constantly refer to in order to aid their progress and keep their affairs in order. As she discusses, a confident, open and aspirational frame of mind is more important than following any rigid guidelines and will give you an edge over some of the other 60,000 artists currently working in the UK and the 3,700 who finish various art degrees and courses across the country every year.

If those numbers cause dismay, depression or doubts along the lines of 'To be or not to be an artist', then fear not. Just as there is no orthodoxy governing what an artist should be, do or make, neither is there a secret to success in the art world – rather there are simultaneously many and none. Any quest for success as an artist only elicits more questions and all but the most arrogant artists share these crises of confidence and purpose. What actually qualifies as success in an endeavour such as art that demands only that you be creative, original, passionate and dedicated to what you do? Add some persistence, self-belief and a bit of luck and you have the elements of one success story contained in *The Artists' Yearbook*, that of young artist Zöe Mendelson. In her contribution to this edition, she charts the highs and lows of her career after art school, from the icy plunge into the harsh unknown of the 'real world', through periods of uncertainty and poverty to a gradual influx of exhibitions, gallery shows and new horizons.

The likelihood of making it as an artist is greatly increased by spending time at art school and many courses offer the kind of vocational training that is essential for developing and sustaining an artistic career. Whether you are looking for part-time study, a place on an art foundation or degree course, or even a post-graduate qualification, the essay by Janet Hand and Gerard Hemsworth of Goldsmiths College in London should be required reading: it offers a step-by-step guide to choosing the right course.

The stereotypical image of the starving artist toiling away in a grotty garret may be a hundred years out of date, but graduate artists often need to supplement their earnings in order to maintain a studio and their own production.

Practical information is provided by the Arts Council's Head of Visual Artists Development, Tim Eastop, in the chapter devoted to securing funding for your practice or a commission to create new work.

Sourcing the right materials can also be a pursuit all of its own and the Mike Smith Studio has spent the past two decades designing and fabricating complex works of art for other artists, not least building Damien Hirst's famous shark tank, Rachel Whiteread's Trafalgar Square plinth and Michael Landy's replica house at Tate Britain. Mike Smith urges artists to explore the full diversity of materials and technologies available, even if this means seeking expert advice or enlisting the help of others in a work's manufacture. He also reveals a few secrets of the trade as well as some strategic guidance on budget, transportation and installation for anyone planning an ambitious work of art.

Creativity does not just apply to the conception and creation of your work, but also to its distribution. Career-minded artists hoping to sell and exhibit widely may need to learn the basics of self-publicity, taking helpful hints from the team at Brunswick Arts in London, who specialize in providing press coverage for major events in the art world and have written an introduction on how to conduct your own public relations campaign.

You may not see art as a competitive activity, but a recent boom in art prizes has added significantly to the number of opportunities for emerging artists to be seen by the wider public. However, with so many and varied awards it is worthwhile reading the foreword to the section on competitions, residencies, awards and prizes by Sacha Craddock, the chair of an annually selected prize for recent art school leavers called New Contemporaries, originally set up in 1949. She offers help on how to apply for prizes or residencies, how they function, who selects the entrants and what a place on the shortlist can mean for an artist's curriculum vitae.

Further outlets for artists' work include the UK's numerous art fairs and festivals.

Contemporary art author and expert Louisa Buck surveys the contemporary art market, now estimated to be worth over £500 million annually – a heartening figure for artists and the industry alike – and a few of the ways that artists can hope to be seen either at one of the high profile, international contemporary art gatherings such as the Frieze Art Fair in London or at localized events in the UK's many vibrant cities for art such as Bristol, Glasgow, Edinburgh, Liverpool, Manchester, Newcastle-upon-Tyne and Sheffield.

As the cycle of making, exhibiting, selling and appreciating art is such a restless process, it naturally follows that the art world itself is a moveable feast. We update this book every year to account for this constant flux, weeding out the dead wood, adding in the new shoots and supplementing the current categories of information wherever possible. Whether you see being an artist as your calling in life, a professional vocation or just a pastime, then hopefully this book will provide a shortcut to success, allowing you more time to make more work.

A Note on Using The Artists' Yearbook

The Artists' Yearbook is divided into ten sections of listings, each preceded by at least one essay written by an authority on the topic. There are subdivisions within some of these sections, for instance, the chapters on COMMERCIAL GALLERIES, DEALERS AND EXHIBITION SPACES or PUBLIC MUSEUMS AND GALLERIES are divided by region and each venue is listed alphabetically within the appropriate geographical area. The large section SUPPLIERS AND SERVICES is broken down into sub-categories, including art insurance, consultants, conservators, packers and shippers, printmakers and so on. ART EDUCATION is divided into two sections: degree-giving institutions and foundation courses; within these two sections listings are alphabetical. The smaller sections, such as ART FAIRS AND FESTIVALS and ART MAGAZINES, are not regionalized, but simply arranged alphabetically by company or event name. While this directory focuses on England, Wales, Scotland and Northern Ireland, some of the sections, such as COMPETITIONS, RESIDENCIES, AWARDS AND PRIZES and SOCIETIES AND OTHER ARTISTS' ORGANIZATIONS, list a number of overseas artists' groups and opportunities for artists looking to work outside of the UK.

If you want to find an organization whose name you already know, turn to the General index. If you know what kind of material, service or style of art you are interested in, but do not know where to find it, use the Subject index. This index is designed to group specialist categories of art, working practices or media together and includes such general terms as painting and sculpture, as well as more particular kinds of medium such as ceramics, photography and watercolours. As many galleries and museums cater to multimedia forms of art and do not actively distinguish between them or specialize in one field, this Subject index will by and large *not* refer you to the listings of non-specialist venues or services.

The listings are generally self-explanatory, but where categories of information are missing – perhaps a website address or a gallery's submission criteria – it is because either the information does not exist or it has not been provided. However, while we have made every effort to confirm that the correct contact details have been included for every entry within *The Artists' Yearbook*, as with all such directories, addresses, contact numbers and email addresses are subject to change. To account for the art world's comings and goings, the book will be updated annually.

If you would like us to add a new entry, wish to update or correct an existing entry, or have a suggestion for improvement, please write to:

Ossian Ward
Editor
The Artists' Yearbook
Thames & Hudson Ltd
181A High Holborn
London WC1V 7QX

E artistsyearbook@thameshudson.co.uk

Why be an artist?

By Gavin Turk

This simple question is very complex. Being an artist in 2008 is greatly motivated by an analysis of this question. The answers could seem simple:
Because you can...
Why not?
Because I like making pictures.
Because I can't think of anything better to do...
Instead of answering in these obtuse ways, I have gone on a little meander: wondering about art's purpose, tracing the *use* of art within the landscape of art history.

One, Two, Skip-a-Few, Ninety-Nine, a Hundred...

The first artists
The earliest forms of representation referred to as art are cave paintings: dream-like hieroglyphs of cattle made schematically with purpose-built tools. Were the people who made them spending time just grinding up coloured rocks and acquiring esoteric skills while others were doing the necessary jobs to sustain life?

The cave walls became not windows to the outside world, but some form of testament to the inside one, in both senses of dwelling and mind. These pictures were made to last, made to remember something. The author was making something for the community to use as a thinking space.

Turning their hand to god
As this philosophical space grew, so the community created what might be called gods: 'special forces' that explained the presence of certain unfathomable phenomena. These gods needed to find some earthly stasis and certain characters in the community had the provision and vision to create forms that could represent these life-affirming powers. These people were simultaneously in contact with the gods while being servants of the social group – producing objects and images for people to use in the act of worship. History was conceptually initiated and continued, growing in breadth and depth.

The Emperor's new painting
Eventually powerful parties in societies started to employ the services of artists to represent not just the gods, but also themselves as some historic marker of their existence. The images of kings, queens and men of the cloth gave way to nobles, lords, barons and businessmen, in fact anyone who had the *wasta* or finances to employ artists to depict the subject of their desires. Artists (as they had begun to be known) were employed to record aspects of the way the world looked and by the middle of the 16th century an art market was in existence.

Art as storytelling (with codes and messages)
Art was not only a space for acting in an objective or political way, but also a means of storytelling in a more passive narrative sense. In 1638 Nicolas Poussin painted *The Shepherds of Arcadia* as a commission for Cardinal Richelieu. It shows three shepherds standing in a romantic landscape pointing out an old sarcophagus with the Latin inscription 'et in arcadia ego'. Even in utopia, death existed. Allegedly the picture also contained secret messages hidden in the composition, so it may serve as a kind of map to those who know how to read it.

The artist paints himself into the picture...
In 1656 the artist Diego Velázquez painted his masterpiece *Las Meninas* (the Maids of Honour). In the picture he is in the process of painting a portrait of King Philip IV of Spain and his wife Mariana. Standing beside the artist is the young Princess Margarita surrounded by her various servants. In the presence of the work, the audience is flattered to be in the place of the monarchs (reflected in the mirror) as they look up at the painting, but they also find themselves looking at the artist and have to think of his lifestyle and his ego. Art starts to take the audience on some sort of Mobius

journey travelling out from and arriving back at the artist.

Social politics
The use of the art platform for social commentary was already an artistic tradition when William Hogarth made his series of eight paintings collectively named *A Rake's Progress* in 1735. This moralizing tale designed to entertain and educate the audience depicted the rich merchant's son, Tom Rakewell, frittering his wealth away in brothels and gambling dens, only to end his days in Bedlam.

The art goes public
Artists were soon being collected like anthropological artefacts from distant lands. Museums and galleries were being constructed and art was becoming public property, causing the audiences for art exhibitions to swell.

Artists who wanted to change the world
In the 1920s a collective group of artists formed and called themselves Surrealists. Headed by André Breton, they wrote manifestos claiming that through art a radical shift in political reason could be achieved. Culture was the life-affirming glue between people and art was a major part of its political make up. Like the Dada artists (1916–20) before them, who refused all accepted or existent forms of art, the Surrealists believed that the truth was to be found in Sigmund Freud's notion of the murkier recesses of the subconscious. Cathartic, freed-up experiences lay in wait for those who came in contact with it, much like a dream being seen as a sorting of unprocessed, unfiled thoughts. The effect these artists had in changing the visual fabric of the western world is still in evidence today, although as usual not perhaps in ways that they intended.

More politics, less dreams
In the 1960s the Situationists, another collective of politicized artists, began remixing ideas from Dada and Surrealism, adding in Karl Marx. For them, art was primarily propaganda: a means of disseminating revolutionary socialist ideas about how to, or how not to, think, which was ironic given the prescriptive art coming out of the Soviet Union at the time. Daily life was a political scenario and so was art. Art was made to express community ideals; it was part of a discussion, which in the case of the Situationists revolved around driving a critical wedge into the heart of the bourgeoisie. After meetings in shady cafés or bars in Paris members would jump into cars and drive around defacing posters and advertisements put up in prominent communal sites. By adding or removing bits of material, satirical social comments were inadvertently exposed to the audience in much the same way that some graffiti art functions today.

The artist addresses the audience
By the mid-1970s the notion of a culture travelling full steam ahead for progress started coming up against issues of gender and race. This coupled together with new technologies gave rise to artists choosing to work with new media such as video or film, avoiding the historically male and colonialist forms of painting and sculpture. New forms of democratic art production ensued, most memorably when the artist Joseph Beuys claimed in a 1973 lecture that 'civilization is an art work and everybody is an artist'.

Colour and marketing
Colour itself has been used to express certain meanings in art. The use of ultramarine blue (Lapis Lazurite) in religious paintings of the Middle Ages became synonymous with depictions of the Virgin Mary. It also increased the value and status of the work, as Lapis was more expensive than gold at the time. In 1964 Yves Klein created his own blue, which he termed 'International Klein Blue' or IKB, making several series of works using the colour as a kind of signature or worldview. In 1961 Johannes Itten wrote *The Art of Color: The Subjective Experience and Objective Rationale of*

Color where he tried to outline how particular colours make people feel.

Art makes you feel better

The simple activity of 'creating art' has been understood to have therapeutic properties as seen in institutions using art therapy; this also has roots in outsider art or Art Brut, a sub-category of art from around the beginning of the last century. One of the earliest and most prolific exponents was the Swiss psychiatric patient Adolf Wölfli who produced over 2,000 super-intricate and elaborate drawings at the beginning of the 20th century.

Art as self expression: the need for originality

A history of expressing ideas and emotions through art is a complex thread culminating in the image of Jackson Pollock wildly and energetically throwing paint onto his canvas to enter the new virgin territory of art as pure emotion.

Knowing your place in the world

The process of making art puts the author in direct contact with the artistic context; art history and cultural background surround the work and all act on it in a discursive way. So new art is always in some form of synergetic relationship with both the past and the present as well as its cultural context. As China opens up its trade routes to the West so Chinese artists are beginning to be able to communicate across cultural boundaries through museums and galleries of the western world.

The last frontier of the real

Recently, art has become a kind of last bastion to the real. Its contemporary status has been cast by former challenges to 'the perceived reality of things'. Art is always a picture making, once an object is situated in an artistic context it is fated to be an artistic version of its former self, for instance, the clichéd image of *Fountain*, the 1917 sculpture by Marcel Duchamp. But situated in the image-flooded, mass-marketed culture of today, ironically art is probably more than ever a confirmation of time, space and actual object.

Photography as alchemy

Sam Taylor-Wood

Sam Taylor-Wood is a photographer, film and video artist who explores emotional and physical extremes through carefully crafted and choreographed scenarios. Since graduating from Goldsmiths College in 1990, she has produced some of the most complex and cinematic photographs in British art, especially in two early series involving 360-degree panoramas – *Five Revolutionary Seconds* of 1996 and *Soliloquies,* begun in 1998. Her self-portraiture ranges from the intensely personal and confrontational images of *Slut* or *Self Portrait in a Single Breasted Suit with Hare* to the acrobatic and physically demanding theatrics of her *Self Portrait Suspended* and *Bram Stoker's Chair* series of 2004–05. She has continued to explore the boundaries between art and artifice in her depictions of over two dozen Hollywood movie stars in various degrees of acted or induced breakdown for *Crying Men* 2002–04. In addition to solo shows in 2006 at BALTIC, Gateshead and the Museum of Contemporary Art in Sydney, she was the first woman to be granted a retrospective at the Hayward Gallery in 2002 and is represented by White Cube in London. Taylor-Wood discusses the role of photography in her practice, revealing the secrets behind her first photograph, her influences and inspirations.

When did you first pick up a camera?
I took my first picture at around five years of age, of my parents together in Belgium. It's small and square with a yellowing border depicting their feet at an angle, but is a spectacular picture that holds a lot of memory for me. From there I didn't focus much on photography until school when I took an O' level in it.

What specific features of the medium first appealed to you?
The magic of it – the alchemy and the unexpected.

Were your peers or inspirations also photographers?
Not really. Most of my friends were painters, which made photography more special as a medium. I take most inspiration from painting and life.

Which painters have inspired you, and are there any tangible similarities between your practice and painting?
Caravaggio is one artist that springs to mind and I spend a lot of time at the National Gallery looking at religious painting for its sense of pathos, theatre and extreme humanness. As for similarities, I look to painting for the way it represents ideas, thoughts and emotions.

Did you study photography formally? Was it widely or well taught in your opinion?
I studied sculpture at Goldsmiths until 1990, but it wasn't until over a year after leaving before I quietly began to investigate photography. It suddenly gave me the voice I was looking for. I realized that all my thoughts were images and that sculpture was just a process for me that held limited ideas.

Would you advise young artists to take a course in practical photography (developing techniques, etc.)?
I guess so, although I believe that knowing too much technically can ruin an artist, as you know the tricks without the experiment and adventure.

Is photography more integrated into the art world now, and what is its status relative to other media?
Yes, it is totally integrated now and with equal status.

How does the photography scene in London and the UK seem to you, say in comparison with other major centres such as New York or Paris?
New York has a stronger emphasis on photography as an important medium. There are a lot more dedicated photography galleries there.

Do you see a distinction between photography and fine art?
I look at it this way, art is about ideas – not ideas to promote or sell a product – but ideas or thoughts that can form a conversation within yourself about your deepest psychological feelings. In this way you work with only yourself in mind, no one else matters. The medium of those ideas is specific to the artist but the sphere of commercial photography involves an entirely other world.

How does your appreciation of journalistic or commercial photography differ from that of the photographic work you encounter in a gallery?
I don't see the distinctions as that clear-cut, because one of the most powerful photographs I have ever seen was taken by a journalist in Armenia, of a woman crying next to a wall. It had so many painterly qualities as well – which I am sure he was aware of – with the woman's red shroud recalling images of the Virgin Mary.

Do you have much experience of commercial photography and is it something that struggling artists can take up in order to fund their private work? Would you recommend this to young artists as a valid means of subsistence?
Being commissioned to do other photography work apart from your own is great. It makes you think constantly, it keeps you in motion. Obviously, you have to be discerning, you have to choose work you are interested in and that it is someone or somewhere genuinely interesting to photograph. You may find you can be just as influenced by these people or places as you can by other art or artists. I don't necessarily see commercial work as a sell-out or a compromise.

How important is reality in photography?
The whole notion is questionable. Does photography really depict reality or does it represent an invented reality?

How does your video work relate to your photography? Do you view the two media in parallel or completely separately?
Strangely, I view them completely separately. It's almost as though I use two different parts of my brain and work in two contrasting speeds. Film is more meditative and the process is much more constructed but also terribly frustrating. Photography is all over too quickly.

When, if ever, is scale important or relevant for photography? Should artists avoid going big?
It is tempting to go big, but big is not necessarily better; you have to balance the idea with the scale. The first series I went big with was *Soliloquies*, which all had additional captions running below the main images. These totally distinct elements meant that the upper portions had to be large-scale in order to be able to read the texts. On the other hand, I made a series called the *Passion Cycle* that was photographs of two people having sex, but in this case, I felt the flesh needed to be made small and intimate.

When to use black-and-white and when to use colour?
That is just instinct.

How important is finding a good printer?
Essential. If you aren't going to do it yourself you need someone who cares as you do.

Has digital technology endangered or enhanced photography?
Not really, it's just another process – although it is making it harder to get specific film and papers.

Are technological advancements in art-making of any concern to your work?
They are not a concern so much as a means to enable you to do amazing things. Without Photoshop for example, I wouldn't be able to make a series of images in which I am seemingly suspended in mid-air above my studio floor.

What, in your opinion, elevates the everyday snapshot to a work of art?
Nothing elevates it in that way. It's about the artist, their work and their social context, the context it is made in. Then it comes down to the idea behind the piece and whether it can hold its own or whether it needs to be part of a larger body of work to give it significance.

How do you take pictures? Are you an impulsive photographer or a meticulous controller of your images?
A meticulous controller. I also spend a long time going through my contact sheets.

Can you learn artistry in photography? Is the skill more important than the concept or vice versa?
Skill in conveying your idea is the most succinct way to enable the idea to be understood or at least appreciated.

What other photographers do you admire (contemporary or historical) and why?
Diane Arbus for her ability to be courageous and make images you'll never forget. Cindy Sherman for making the path easier to walk. Dorothea Lange for making my all-time favourite photograph, *Migrant Mother*, 1936. When I first saw it, I remember wishing that I had taken the picture and that she was the same age as me, 32, when she took it.

Do you (have you) used elaborate set-ups and techniques for your work (I am thinking here of your 360-degree images *Five Revolutionary Seconds*)?
I've been working a lot with a bondage expert who comes in and dangles me from the ceiling of my studio for hours on end to produce two recent major bodies of work, the first being *Self Portrait Suspended* and then *Bram Stoker's Chair*, both of which were pretty elaborate.

Should artists be aware of how much their photographs are going to sell for, i.e. taking into account the number of prints or the size of an edition, or are these concerns best left up to a gallery?
I get freaked out by thinking about prices or my work in those terms; besides I have no head for numbers. It really is best left up to the gallery, but I have always stuck to the same edition of six for all my prints.

Do you suggest artists employ a traditional photographer's assistant?
It helps if you are technically challenged, but obviously depends on your budget.

Where do you see the art of photography going next?
I'm not sure but the digital revolution scares me.

01

Commercial galleries, dealers and exhibition spaces

Dealing with the galleries: How to build your own community

Nicholas Logsdail

There is no single pathway to being an artist. If there were it would be much like any other industry such as medicine, accountancy or the legal profession, where there is a structured and ordered process. By its very nature, the art world is both straightforward and yet also quite baffling until you have acquired 'the knowledge' (to use the analogy of the apprenticeship undertaken by every London taxi driver). For anyone who aspires to be an artist with a capital A, this is the only way.

Know your gallery

There is an extraordinary naivety among certain artists who believe that their lack of success is simply because they do not have a good gallery. This has nothing to do with it; the gallery does not make the difference, nor will a good gallery take on an artist unless the work and studio practice are sufficiently interesting.

There is no single system or specific way of discovering new artists. Good galleries are always trying to find the best interface with new art, but it is a complicated process; one can only be enquiring, open-minded and knowing, and hopefully make a decent judgment. You feel it when someone is really interesting, when you can envision the work carving out a place in history. This comes not only from the work itself but from the combination of your knowledge and an original mind. I have seldom encountered a talented artist who subsequently becomes important who was not knowledgeable or clever – not necessarily in the conventional sense, but a degree of artistic intelligence is necessary to any kind of creativity.

Artists are in a difficult position, but generally if they fit the criteria mentioned above they will find the path through their own skill. Just putting a foot in the door doesn't work because there are hundreds of people trying to

do that. Neither does cold-calling galleries, especially if you haven't been there or don't know the names of some of the artists they exhibit.

There is a great resentment among young artists who see galleries as snooty and uncaring, but it is not a closed world – go to openings, know your galleries. This is where knowledge and education come in. Artists should be informed and aware of what is happening. It must be a passion, an obsession.

Know your history

All young artists, particularly students and those in the formative phase of their careers, should immerse themselves in the art history of the past fifty years and come to terms with general art history. This way they can position and judge themselves against the best art out there, which has already been validated. My experience of students is that they are full of the arrogant, intellectual blossom of youth – which is very attractive and can be turned to great advantage – but as often as not, it is merely an excuse not to learn or inform themselves. An ignorant artist is not likely to go very far, because you need to be able to discuss your own work with a breadth and depth of reference that makes such a conversation interesting. There is an enormous difference between being able to talk about your work well and just being pushy or opportunistic.

Being able to convey artistic or intellectual information, and question it, forms part of the mechanics of becoming an artist, but the other part is doing the right thing, at the right time and in the right place, as well as meeting the right people. It is important to foster professional friendships, and building a community around you does this.

Create your own scene

Good art does not come without community. This community is built in many ways and begins, for most artists, when they join the art school system. The conceptual artists of the

1960s and 1970s, the British sculptors Cragg, Deacon, Kapoor et al, the YBAs or the Royal College situation before that – these were all small, intense young communities of like-minded artists.

My early history was about creating my own community. The Minimal/Conceptual art movement of the late 1960s, when I started, was a particular way of thinking about art that was specific to my generation. When one group forms and becomes powerful it takes a kind of insider control over the international contemporary art world, gaining the support of the serious critics, museums and collectors. Each subsequent generation takes a position that is contrary in some way to the previous one, and this engenders what we call 'movements' in art. Often these are not consciously created, they just happen, but they always happen through the formation of community.

Artists at heart

If you cannot create your own community, you can always look for a community to which you feel you belong. A gallery is one such place.

There is a major distinction between a gallery and an art dealer. Many dealers only manage to sustain their contemporary art programme through backroom sales of secondary-market material. On the other hand, galleries such as the Lisson Gallery aim to develop the careers of emerging or living artists – they are not dealers as such – and this sense of purpose was characteristic of many of the more serious galleries of the past. Clearly, conventional art dealing is the more profitable activity (even if you are only taking ten per cent) because the margins are smaller and all you need are knowledge and contacts. However, galleries whose prime preoccupation is dealing have less time to service or look after the interests of their artists.

Neither of these two different models is right or wrong. When I started the Lisson Gallery thirty-seven years or so ago, it began as an artist-curated space; that was always my idea of what a gallery should be. I came to the field with no formal training or preconceptions: in fact, I was just over twenty years old when I got thrown out of art school for doing this, which is one of the reasons why I did not continue as an artist myself. Many people who enter the gallery scene come from the business side, the auction houses or the high-powered commercial galleries, and because of their experience and education they have a very different viewpoint.

The challenge or ideal of a gallery that sustains itself through its living artists should be self-fulfilling: if the central focus is on the quality of the artists, then they should be good enough to sustain the gallery economically. This is by no means the easiest path, but it fosters loyalty with artists. The other side of the business is when the gallery becomes a selling operation, rather than a nurturing one; any gallery can enter the scene once an artist has become well known or commercially viable. Loyalty of artist to gallery and vice versa is the only way to build a solid history with the right gallery or community.

Commerce and other dirty words

Unfortunately, the art world has changed so much in the past twenty years that the economic pressures are now greater than ever – everything costs more. Although we have to project ourselves as affluent organizations, galleries are not such profitable enterprises. We turn over relatively vast sums of money – many millions of pounds – but if you look at what we have to pay for, there is often not much surplus. A gallery runs essentially on its cash flow, so even as artists become more ambitious and grow with the gallery, we can afford only to share major fabrication costs and generally work to the international art world standard of fifty per cent commission on works of art.

Tying up vital capital in the long term can be problematic, but it is sometimes essential. Galleries' problems are thus linked to artists', because they are part of the same world; if a gallery's artists all have big commercial and financial worries, then so will the gallery.

Lisson is not commercial in the sense that it does not encourage artists to make work whose significance is only to supply the market. Inevitably, if an artist sells one piece of work they will then make two more – that is how the system works – but artists who continue to churn out their work like a product line, even if it is selling well, can be committing artistic suicide. The art world is full of exceptions and contradictions, of course: take Pablo Picasso, who made thousands of works without undermining his market.

Art, language and vision

Strategically, artists should begin with some vision of the end in mind – perhaps of where they want to be in five or ten years' time. The contemporary art world has become quite black and white, with not a lot of middle ground, so by the time an artist is in their late twenties they really need to be honest with themselves about how they feel about the quality of their work. Artists who blame others for their lack of success are very unlikely ever to do well.

Having said all of this, great artists are not overly concerned about how the world sees them and so make art for themselves rather than the marketplace. Success should not be the only reason why you want to be an artist

in the first place, and maybe you should start out with the idea that there is no such thing as success or failure. For example, some artists with MA qualifications choose to teach one or two days a week, even though they could make more money and be more productive, prolific and successful making art. This doesn't mean they have failed; some teach out of necessity, while others want to put something back into their community. It simply means they have taken a different pathway and understand the journey they have chosen to embark upon.

Instead of seeking 'success', an artist should make it their life's work to develop an original and personal language. It is then the job of the gallery to interpret that language so that it transcends everything the artist does. Although the chances of rising from art-school graduate to top international artist are depressingly small, if you want to be a serious artist then there is no point in aspiring to be something less than the best, at least until you find a level you are satisfied with.

Nicholas Logsdail is director of the Lisson Gallery in London, which he founded in 1967. He represents international and British artists, including Douglas Gordon, Anish Kapoor and Julian Opie.

Commercial galleries, dealers and exhibition spaces

East Anglia

Ann Jarman
The Old Fire Engine House,
25 St Mary's Street, Ely, CB7 4ER
T 01353 662582
F 01353 668364
E ofeh65@hotmail.com
W www.theoldfireenginehouse.co.uk
Contact Alice Johnson
Founded in 1968. All media shown. Artists
represented include Julia Ball, Anthony Day,
David Remfry, Terence Harjula, Richard Sell
and Simon Beer.
Submission Policy No specific entry requirements
except gallery's approval of the work.
Price range £50–£2,000.
No of exhibitions annually 20

Big Blue Sky
Warham Road, Wells-next-the-Sea, NR23 1QA
T 01328 712023
F 01328 712024
E shop@bigbluesky.uk.com
W www.bigbluesky.uk.com
Opened in 2003, selling an eclectic mix of
contemporary art, craft and design by artists and
crafts people from Norfolk. Work includes
painting, photographs, print-making, jewellery,
glass, ceramics, furniture, wood-turning, fashion
accessories and home accessories. Artists include
Vanessa Vargo, Simon Cass, Sarah Horton, Peter
Lely, Stephen Parry and Claire Robertson.
Submission Policy Artists must live and work in
Norfolk or their work must represent something
of Norfolk.
Price range £5–£4,500
No of exhibitions annually 6–8

Bircham Gallery
14 Market Place, Holt, NR25 6BW
T 01263 713312
E birchamgal@aol.com
W www.birchamgallery.co.uk
Contact Deborah Harrison or Gail Richardson
Specializes in contemporary British paintings,
original prints, Modern British graphic works,
ceramics, glass, sculpture and jewellery. Artists
include Ros Loveday, Elaine Pamphilon, Nicholas
Homoky, Walter Keeler, Disa Allsopp and Elaine

Cox. Approved for Arts Council England's Own
Art scheme.
Submission Policy Invites applications from artists
in any medium (UK only). Include images,
statement, CV and sae for return.
Price range £10–£10,000
No of exhibitions annually 10

Broughton House Gallery
98 King Street, Cambridge, CB1 1LN
T 01223 314960
E bhgallery@btconnect.com
W www.broughtonhousegallery.co.uk
Founded in 1987 exhibiting mainly living artists.
Holds the archive of the work of Gwen Raverat
(prints made by her for sale) and work by G.D.
Aked, Ceri Richards, Jack Hellewell and Norman
Mommens.
Submission Policy Initial approach by email or
disc (not by personal visit). No large sculptures
or pop art.
Price range £50–£2,500
No of exhibitions annually 6

Buckenham Galleries
81 High Street, Southwold
IP18 6DS
T 01502 725418
F 01502 722002
E becky@buckenham-galleries.co.uk
W www.buckenham-galleries.co.uk
Contact Becky Munting
Founded in 1999 with the aim of showing
contemporary fine and applied art from local,
national and international artists. Seeks to
maintain a friendly atmosphere in which clients
and artists can relax and discuss the work. There
are five galleries on two floors.
Submission Policy Any living artist considered.
Price range Usually up to £2,500
No of exhibitions annually 9

Byard Art
4 St Mary's Passage, Cambridge, CB2 3PQ
T 01223 464646
F 01223 464655
E info@byardart.co.uk
W www.byardart.co.uk
Contact Juliet Bowmaker or Ros Cleevely
Established in 1993. Runs an exhibition
programme of contemporary fine and applied art
in a series of solo and group shows throughout the
year. Exhibits figurative and abstract art ranging
from established names to young emerging artists.

Maintains a strong presence at selected art fairs in London and New York.
Submission Policy See website for details.
Price range From £100
No of exhibitions annually 8

Chappel Galleries

15 Colchester Road, Chappel, Colchester
CO6 2DE
T 01206 240326
F 01206 240326
E chappelgalleries@btinternet.com
W www.chappelgalleries.co.uk
Contact Edna Mirecka
Founded in 1986. Sells contemporary painting and sculpture of predominantly East Anglian artists or those with a strong regional connection. Artists represented include Roderic Barrett, Mory Griffiths, Jonathan Clarke, Bernard Meadows, Wlodyslow Mirecki and Paul Rumsey.
Submission Policy By invitation only.
Price range Up to £30,000
No of exhibitions annually 13

Choyce Gallery

26A George Street, St Albans, AL3 4ES
T 01727 739931
F 01920 463003
E kaleemwalden@bt.co.uk
W www.choycegallery.co.uk
Housed in a building dating back to the fifteenth century. Exhibits glass art produced by contemporary artists mainly from Britain and Europe. Also contains a designer jewellery and fine-art section.

Darryl Nantais Gallery

59 High Street, Linton, Cambridge, CB1 6HS
T 01223 891289
E enquiries@nantais-gallery.co.uk
W www.nantais-gallery.co.uk
Sells oils, pastels, watercolours, acrylics, charcoals and coloured pencil work. Exhibits works covering a range of styles, from traditional to contemporary, and subjects, including landscapes, seascapes, flowers and animals and abstract work.
Also sells prints.

Harleston Gallery

37–39 The Thoroughfare, Harleston
IP20 9AS
T 01379 855366
F 01379 855366
E challis@harlestongallery.fsnet.co.uk

Founded in 2001, with the addition of a coffee shop in 2003. Aims to promote an enjoyment and understanding of the visual arts within the community. Areas of specialization include paintings, prints and contemporary crafts (ceramics, glass, jewellery, sculpture, textiles, wood, etc.)
Submission Policy Artists residing in East Anglia are welcome to submit a CV and images of recent work by post.
Price range £5–£1,000
No of exhibitions annually 6

Head Street Gallery

Halstead, CO9 2AT
T 01787 472705
E information@headstreetgallery.co.uk
W www.headstreetgallery.co.uk
Mainly shows contemporary work. Exhibitions throughout the year last seven to eight weeks, with a private view during the first week. Two artists are featured each time, each occupying one room. A third room hosts an ongoing display by various local artists. There is also an art library. The gallery sells paintings, sculpture, glass, ceramics, jewellery, handmade gifts, toys and cards.
Submission Policy Submissions from artists are welcome. A CV, statement and at least three images of work should be sent via post or email.
No of exhibitions annually 7

Hertfordshire Gallery

6 St Andrew Street, Hertford, SG14 1JE
T 01992 503636
F 01992 503244
E info@hertfordshiregallery.com
W www.hertfordshiregallery.com
Contact Colin Gardner
Founded in 2003. Showcases original works by Hertfordshire artists and craftspeople, including paintings, ceramics and glass. Sponsors the Hertford Art Society, Welwyn Garden City Art Club and Enfield Art Circle Exhibitions. Based in Hertfordshire Graphics' Art Shop.

Hunter Gallery

Coconut House, Hall Street, Long Melford
CO10 9JQ
T 01787 466117
E info@thehuntergallery.com
W www.thehuntergallery.com
Contact Camilla Rodwell
Founded in 2001. Represents painters including Stephen Brown RBA, Andrew King ROI NS, John

Lowrie Morrison, Caroline Bailey, Edward Noott and John Tookey PS. Also shows sculpture by Kate Denton, woodturned vases by Richard Chapman and fine contemporary furniture. The gallery is spread over four rooms and there is a large sculpture garden. Also offers bespoke picture framing.
Submission Policy Applications by email to camillarodwell@thehuntergallery.com or by post, including photos or CD.
Price range £40–£10,000
No of exhibitions annually 6

ICAS–Vilas Fine Art
8–10 Leys Avenue, Letchworth Garden City SG6 3EU
T 01462 677455
E info@vilascollection.co.uk
W www.vilasart.co.uk
Contact Bipin Vilas
More than twenty years' experience in international contemporary fine art. Gallery artists include John W. Mills (British sculptor), Domy Reiter-Soffer (modern oil painter), Anne Sudworth (British landscape artist), Sally Rutherford (equestrian artist and sculptor), Angela Bishop (bronze figurative sculptor), Lara Alridge (British glass sculptor), Mark Clark (figurative artist), Rob Ford (British landscape painter) and Gabriel Ellison (Zambian landscape and wildlife artist).
Submission Policy Portfolio includes established and emerging British and international artists, sculptors and potters. New artists' enquiries welcome at BipinVilas@vilascollection.co.uk.
Price range £500–£65,000+
No of exhibitions annually 6

Letter 'A' Gallery
40 Whitmore Street, Whittlesey, Peterborough, PE7 1HE
T 01733 203595
W www.justfineart.net
Contact Caesar Smith
Founded in 1972, specializing in paintings by the owner Caesar Smith, whose work is published in limited editions only by the gallery.
Price range £150 for limited editions; up to £16,000 for originals.

Lynne Strover Gallery
High Street, Fen Ditton, Cambridge CB5 8ST
T 01223 295264
W www.strovergallery.co.uk

Opened in the early 1990s. Exhibits range of prints, paintings and sculptures. Many shows have strong Cornish flavour.

McNeill Gallery
112 Watling Street, Radlett, WD7 7AB
T 01923 859594
E info@mcneillgallery.com
W www.mcneillgallery.com
Contact B. McNeill
Since opening in 1996 the gallery has nurtured talented unknowns as well as established artists. Over 80 artists represented, including Alex Rennie, Lawrie Williamson, Leszek Blyszczynski, Georgie Young, Sara Hill, Alain Magallon, Anton Psak, Sara Barrow, Rob Selkirk, Enzo Marra, John Holmes and Inge Clayton.
Submission Policy Quality figurative landscape and representational landscape artists who wish to be represented are welcome to approach the gallery.
Price range from £500–£12,000
No of exhibitions annually 7

Patrick Davies Contemporary Art
Barley House, The Old Brewery
Furneux Pelham, Buntingford, SG9 0TS
T 01279 777070
E gallery@patrickdaviesca.com
W www.patrickdaviesca.com
Promotes the work of both emerging and established artists. Offers a consultancy service to corporate and private clients. Digital library with examples of work from over two thousand artists.
Submission Policy Application by email with CV and no more than six digital images.
Price range £1,000–£25,000
No of exhibitions annually 6

Peterborough Art House Ltd
245 St Paul's Road, Peterborough PE1 3RJ
T 01733 349024
E helen.mould@btinternet.com
W www.peterborougharthouse.com
Contact Helen Mould
Founded in 1996, an independent gallery specializing in large Abstract Expressionist paintings by Helen Mould. Also has a collectors' room with nineteenth- and twentieth-century artists such as Alexander Graham Munro, Ainsley Bean, John Bellany, Mary Fedden and Anthony Green. Provides consultancy, art-search and advisory services.

Submission Policy Artists represented by invitation or stock only.
Price range £100–£12,000
No of exhibitions annually 5

Picturecraft Gallery Ltd
23 Lees Courtyard, off Bull Street, Holt, NR25 6HS
T 01263 711040
F 01263 711040
E info@picturecraftgallery.com
W www.picturecraftgallery.com
Contact Adrian Hill
Totally refurbished art gallery and exhibition centre that reopened in 2003. Offers thirty-two display spaces for artists to rent on a three-weekly, no-commission basis.
Submission Policy All artists welcome.
No of exhibitions annually Fourteen mixed and five specialist major exhibitions.
Cost to hire or rent Rental from £30 per week.

Primavera
10 King's Parade, Cambridge, CB2 1SJ
T 01223 357708
E infoprimavera@aol.com
W www.primaverauk.com
Gallery and shop located over three floors, presenting fine contemporary British arts and crafts.

Regency Gallery
39 Fitzroy Street, Cambridge, CB1 1ER
T 01223 365454
F 01223 364515
E info@regencygallery.co.uk
W www.regencygallery.co.uk
Wide selection of limited edition prints. Also offers framing service.

Roar Art Gallery and Archive
9–10 Redwell Street, Norwich, NR2 4SN
T 01603 766220
E roar-art@hotmail.com
Contact Sarah Ballard
A registered charity founded in 2004 and dedicated to the work of self-taught, marginalized or 'outsider' artists.
Price range £40–£1,000
No of exhibitions annually 6–7

School House Gallery
Wighton, nr Wells-next-the-Sea, NR23 1AL
T 01328 820457
Contact Diana Cohen
Founded in 1983 in the school where Henry Moore

lived and sculpted in the 1920s when his sister was headmistress. Artists exhibiting include Norman Ackroyd, Alfred Cohen, Derrick Greaves, Alison Neville, Sula Rubens and Malcolm Weir.
Submission Policy Hosts a mixed exhibition every summer during July, August and September and considers works submitted for these shows.
Price range £250–£5,000
No of exhibitions annually 3

Skylark Studios
Hannath Road, Tydd Gote, Wisbech, PE13 5ND
T 01945 420403
E louise@skylarkstudios.co.uk
W www.skylarkstudios.co.uk
Founded in 1993. A small gallery set in quiet Fenland countryside offering monthly exhibitions by selection. Stocks original prints, photographs and paintings. Workshops held in etching and blockprinting.
Submission Policy Professional artists working in two dimensions may send slides or photographs of work for consideration.
No of exhibitions annually 11
Cost to hire or rent £100 per month.

Southwold Gallery
64A High Street, Southwold, IP18 6DN
T 01502 723888
F 01502 723888
E karen@southwoldgallery.co.uk
W www.southwoldgallery.co.uk
Exhibits work by 38 regional artists including Karen S.J. Keable, Mary Gundry, George Gill, Anthony Osler, Mandy Walden, Rosemary Cook, Matthew Garrard and Debbie Faulkner-Stevens. Exhibitions are constantly changing and works can be purchased over the phone and delivered anywhere in the UK by a courier.

Storm Fine Arts
Church Street Barns, Great Shelford, Cambridge, CB2 5EL
T 01223 844786
F 01223 847871
E info@stormfinearts.com
W www.stormfinearts.com
Specializes in British and European painting from 1550 to the present. Also deals in decorative fine arts including textiles, prints, ceramics, pottery and glass of this period.

Thompson Gallery
175 High Street, Aldeburgh, IP15 5AN

T 01728 453743
F 01728 452488
E john@thompsonsgallery.co.uk
W www.thompsonsgallery.co.uk
Established in 1982. Specializes in early twentieth-century and contemporary sculpture and paintings. Artists include Fred Cuming, Terry Frost, Mary Fedden, Edward Seags and Robert Kelsey.
Price range £500–£25,000
No of exhibitions annually 4

Waytemore Art Gallery
10–11 Florence Walk, Bishop's Stortford, CM23 2NZ
T 01279 506206
E info@waytemore-art-gallery.com
Submission Policy Will consider contemporary abstracts, landscapes and figurative works in oil, acrylic and watercolour.
Price range £500–£10,000
No of exhibitions annually 4–5

Whittlesford Gallery
Old School Lane, High Street, CB2 4YS
T 01223 836394
F 01223 290061
E johnshead@whitgallery.fsnet.co.uk
W www.whittlesfordgallery.co.uk
Shows original work, with an emphasis on East Anglian artists and local landscapes.

Wildlife Art Gallery
97 High Street, Lavenham, CO10 9PZ
T 01787 248562
F 01787 247356
E wildlifeartgallery@btinternet.com
W www.wildlifeartgallery.com
Founded in 1988, specializing in wildlife art, both twentieth-century and modern. Represents artists from Europe and the UK.
Price range Up to £10,000
No of exhibitions annually 4

Wildwood Gallery
40 Churchgate Street, Bury St Edmunds, IP33 1RG
T 01284 752938
F 01284 752938
E info@wildwoodgallery.co.uk
W www.wildwoodgallery.co.uk
Contact Mr K. Youngman
A contemporary art gallery, opened in 2002. Also sells limited-edition prints, sculptural furniture and ceramics. Offers a full picture-framing service. Exhibited artists include Francis Farmar, Samantha Toft, Anita Klein and Jenny Thompson.

Submission Policy Send photos or CD with CV and artist's statement. Include sae if you want these returned (allow 28 days for response). Artists seen by appointment only.
Price range £50–£5,000
No of exhibitions annually 4–5

Yarrow Gallery
Glapthorn Road, Oundle, PE8 4JQ
T 01832 277170
W www.oundleschool.org.uk/arts/yarrow/
Originally opened in 1918 and refurbished in the 1990s. Attached to Oundle School, offering extensive space for exhibitions.

East Midlands

Belvoir Gallery
7 Welby Street, Grantham, NG31 6DY
T 01476 579498

The Bottle Kiln
High Lane, West Hallam, Near Ilkeston, DE7 6HP
T 0115 9329442

Castle Ashby Gallery
The Byre, The Old Farmyard, NN7 1LF
T 01604 696787

Christopher Wren Gallery
St Marys Way, 40 Nottingham Street,
Melton Mowbray, LE13 1NW
T 01664 480220
Established in 1985. Stocks original paintings and fine-art, and limited-edition prints by artists such as David Weston.

Clark Galleries
215 Watling Street West, Towcester, NN12 6BX
T 01327 352957
E sales@clarkgalleries.co.uk
W www.clarkgalleries.com
Established in 1963, specializing in figurative, marine, landscape and animal pictures. Also offers a full conservation service.

Croft Wingates
Wingates Walk, 44a St Mary's Road, LE16 7DU
T 01858 465455
E shop@croftwingates.co.uk
W www.croftwingates.co.uk
Contact John Snape
Established since 1975. Stocks a wide range of images from popular artists including Mackenzie

Thorpe, John Waterhouse, Paul James and Govinder Nazran. Carries both limited-edition prints and original work.
Price range £250–£5,000
No of exhibitions annually 6

Evergreen Gallery
Sheaf Street, Daventry, NN11 4AB
T 01327 878117
E rsvp@egart.co.uk
W www.egart.co.uk
Established in 1979, dealing in contemporary original work and some limited editions. Also offers framing service.

Fermynwoods Contemporary Art
Fermyn Woods, Brigstock, Kettering, NN14 3JA
T 01536 373469
E gallery@fermynwoods.co.uk
W www.fermynwoods.co.uk
An artist-led gallery that shows work by artists of national and international standing alongside others less well known at regional level. Areas of interest include geometric abstraction, artists' prints, architecture, landscape and photography. Runs an educational programme alongside exhibitions. Fermynwoods receives public and private funding. Works are for sale.
Submission Policy Artists usually invited.
Price range Up to £20,000
No of exhibitions annually Approx. 5

Focus Gallery
NG1 5FB
T 0115 9537575
E jjames@focus-gallery.co.uk

Gallery 52
Main Road, Brailsford, Ashbourne, DE6 3DA
T 01335 360368
Stocks array of works in various media.

Gallery 93
93 Belper Road, Derby, DE1 3ER
T 01332 364574
Contact J.A. Thomas
Opened in 1990 in owner's home, showing art within a domestic environment. Artists represented include Ronald Pope, Walter Beizins, Alan Smith, Ann Ellis, Keith Hayman and James Brereton.
Submission Policy Shows mostly work by living artists, with preference for solo shows.
No of exhibitions annually 12

Gallery Top
Chatsworth Road, Rowsley, Matlock, DE4 2EH
T 01629 735580
E enquiries@gallerytop.co.uk
W www.gallerytop.co.uk
Exhibits contemporary art by emerging and established artists in painting, sculpture, ceramics, glass and jewellery.

Granby Gallery
Water Lane, Bakewell, DE45 1EU
T 01629 813050

Harley Gallery
Welbeck, Worksop, S80 3LW
T 01909 501700
F 01909 488747
E info@harley-welbeck.co.uk
W www.harleygallery.co.uk
Contact Lisa Gee and Susan Sherrit
Funded by The Harley Foundation, a charitable trust set up in 1977 to support artists and craftspeople in their chosen field. As well as the gallery, the foundation provides studio space at subsidized rental. The gallery was built in 1994 on the site of the 19th-century gasworks at Welbeck. It offers a changing programme of contemporary exhibitions which have included Euan Uglow, David Hockney and Peter Blake. Also displays objects from the Portland Collection. Craft shop sells work by established and emerging makers.
Submission Policy To apply for an exhibition or studio contact Lisa Gee (Director). To apply to stock work in the shop contact Susan Sherrit (Gallery Manager).
Price range £10–£1,000 (in shop)
No of exhibitions annually 6

Hart Gallery
23 Main Street, Linby, Nottingham, NG15 8AE
T 0115 9638707
F 0115 9640743
E info@hartgallery.co.uk
W www.hartgallery.co.uk
Represents artists, sculptors and studio ceramicists, from the emerging to those with international reputations.
Branches 113 Upper Street, Islington, London N1 1QN. **T** 020 77041131.

Henry Brewer
3 Tudor Square, West Bridgford, Nottingham, NG2 6BT
T 0115 9811623

Hope Gallery

The Courtyard, Castleton Road, Hope Valley
S33 6RD
T 01433 621111
E alanglasby@hotmail.com
Wide range of traditional and contemporary
sculpture, fine art and craft by local and national
artists.

Little London Gallery

Nightingale House, Church Street, Matlock
DE4 5AY
T 01629 534825
E info@littlelondongallery.co.uk
W www.littlelondongallery.co.uk
Established in 1991 by Chris and Krystyna Tkacz.
A small private gallery in the village of Holloway,
nestled in the hillside on the edge of the Peak
District. Shows the work of local Derbyshire artists
such as Carol Hill, Rosalind Forster, Shirley Anne
Johnson, Sandy Bartle and Ursula Newell Walker.
A picture-framing service is offered.
Submission Policy Initial submission of CV and
photographs of recent work, followed by invitation
to bring work for a private selection with the
gallery directors.
Price range From £40
No of exhibitions annually 8

Magpie Gallery

2 High Street West, Uppingham, LE15 9QD
T 01572 822212
F 01572 822212
E alan@themagpiegallery.com
W www.themagpiegallery.com
Deals in paintings, sculpture, ceramics and glass
by a range of local, national and international
artists and craftsmen.

Manhattan Galleries

8 Flying Horse Walk, Nottingham, NG1 2HN
T 0115 9418916

Mere Jelly

3rd Floor, Oldknows Factory Building,
St Anns Hill Road, Nottingham, NG3 4GP
T 0115 9413160
E denisecweston@hotmail.com
Contact Denise Weston or Simon Withers
Established in 2003 to facilitate new opportunities
for artists. Consists of a project space and gallery
space. Seeks to broker interest between the artist
and galleries, curators, critics and the public.
Focuses on contemporary avant-garde work.

Miller Fine Arts

55 Station Road, Hugglescote, Coalville
LE67 2GB
T 01530 810469
E finearts@miller-art.co.uk
W www.miller-art.co.uk
Contact Pam and Michael Miller
Founded in 1989. Specialists in fine-art animal
portraits and paintings on commission.
Price range £100–£2,000

Mosaic Gallery

10 Hall Bank, Buxton, SK17 6EW
T 01298 77557

Nest

43 Francis Street, Stoneygate, Leicester, LE2 2BE
T 0116 2709290
F 0116 2709290
A contemporary applied arts gallery founded in
2002. Aims to represent both established makers
and new designers currently making in Britain.
Permanent collections include the work of Chris
Comins, Delan Cookson, Vivienne Ross, Julia
Groundsell, Peter Davey and Roger Broady.
Submission Policy Professional artists and makers
are asked to submit CV, personal statement and
images with an sae for return. No telephone
submissions.
Price range £25–£300

Oakwood Ceramics

5 Kenmore Close, Mansfield
NG19 6RA
T 01623 635777
E oakwood.gallery@virgin.net
W www.oakwoodceramics.co.uk
Formally known as The Oakwood Gallery,
oakwoodceramics.co.uk was founded in 2003 to
exhibit and promote contemporary ceramics using
the internet. In addition to being a virtual gallery,
oakwoodceramics.co.uk has an actual exhibition
programme, details of which can be found on the
website.
Submission Policy Welcomes approaches from
potters and makers. Send CV and images of typical
work by email or post.
Price range £25–£1,500
No of exhibitions annually 2

Old Coach House

28–30 Nottingham Road, Nottingham
NG16 3NQ
T 01773 534030

Opus Gallery

34 St John's Street, Ashbourne, DE6 1GH
T 01335 348919
F 01335 348919
Contact Jill Stone
Established in 2000, offering monthly painting exhibitions and providing a showcase for British contemporary ceramics, glass, textiles, metalwork and handmade jewellery. Exhibited artists include Guilearia Lazzenni, Glyn Macey, Clare Caulfield and Peter Beard.
No of exhibitions annually 10

Patchings Art Centre

Oxton Road, Calverton, Nottingham, NG14 6NU
T 0115 9653479
F 0115 9655308
E Chas@patchingsartcentre.co.uk
W www.patchingsartcentre.co.uk
Contact Liz or Chas Wood
Founded in 1988. A family business aimed at promoting the enjoyment of art. Two exhibition galleries showing two- and three-dimensional work, framing centre, art materials shop, an art school and eight studio workshops. Annual four day Art Craft and Design Festival held each June.
No of exhibitions annually 12

Peter Robinson Fine Art

Bardney Road, Wragby, LN8 5QZ
T 01673 858600

Piet's Gallery

102 Lawrence Court, Semilong, NN1 3HD
T 01604 624351

Sally Mitchell Fine Arts

Thornlea, Askham, Newark, NG22 0RN
T 01777 838234
F 01777 838198
E info@dogart.com
W www.dogart.com
Among the largest publishers of limited-edition dog, equestrian and countryside prints and cards for over twenty-five years. Artists represented include John Trickett, Mick Cawston, Malcolm Coward, Paul Doyle and Debbie Gillingham.
Submission Policy Send a good selection of photos or low-res jpegs via email or CD.
Price range £1–£5,000
No of exhibitions annually 12

St John Street Gallery

50 St John Street, Ashbourne, DE6 1GH
T 01335 347425
E info@sjsg.co.uk
W www.sjsg.co.uk
Founded in 2000, showing sculpture, crafts and paintings by living contemporary artists, including Lewis Noble, Andrew Macara and Jiri Borsky.
Price range £500–£10,000 for paintings.
No of exhibitions annually 6

Thoresby Gallery

Thoresby Park, Ollerton, Newark, NG22 9EP
T 01623 822009
F 01623 822315
E gallery@thoresby.com
W www.thoresby.com
Founded in 1991 the gallery stocks pictures, prints, cards and crafts from leading national and regional artists and craftspeople. There is a changing exhibition programme throughout the year. Artists include Hazel Lane, Anthony Osler, Elise Savage, Alison Read and Sally Mitchell Fine Arts. There is also an annual open exhibition.
Submission Policy Photographs of work (with details of size, medium and price) for consideration by the gallery manager and the trustees.
Price range Up to £1,000
No of exhibitions annually 6

Treeline Gallery

Water Street, Bakewell, DE45 1EW

Watling Street Galleries

116 Watling Street East, Towcester, NN12 6BT
T 01327 351595
E info@picture-shop.co.uk
W www.picture-shop.co.uk
Established in 1975. Deals in the latest fine-art prints and originals. Offers an in-house framing service.

West End Gallery

4 West End, Wirksworth, Matlock, DE4 4EG
T 01629 822356
E wheeldon@westendceramics.co.uk
W www.johnwheeldonceramics.co.uk
Specializes in Raku-fired ceramics. Viewings by appointment only.

Woodbine Contemporary Arts

21 The Crescent, Spalding, PE12 0TT
T 01775 710499/01406 330693
F 01406 331004
E yorath@woodbinecontemporaryarts.co.uk

W www.woodbinecontemporaryarts.co.uk
Contact Liz or Rowan Yorath
Founded in 1996 and based in two venues in
South Lincolnshire, showing high quality fine art
and ceramics. Also represented at British and
European art fairs and regularly exhibits the work
of over thirty established and emerging artists.
Submission Policy By email or non-returnable
photographs/CD. To include at least six images of
recent work and brief CV.
Price range £6,500 maximum
No of exhibitions annually 7 gallery shows and
inclusion in 5 fairs.

London

198 Gallery
198 Railton Road, Herne Hill, London, SE24 0LU
T 020 79788309
F 020 77375315
E gallery@198gallery.co.uk
W www.198gallery.co.uk
Established in 1988 to support black artists
needing exhibition space. Now used by artists from
range of backgrounds, specializing in issues-based
exhibitions and art education.

291 Gallery
291 Hackney Road, London, E2 8NA
T 020 76135676
F 020 76135692
E admin@291gallery.com
W www.291gallery.com
The grade II-listed, deconsecrated neo-Gothic
Victorian church at 291 Hackney Road was
restored and converted into an art gallery,
restaurant and bar in 1998. Since then it has
shown everything from music, digital work and
sculpture to poetry, theatre and visual art.

96 Gillespie
96 Gillespie Road, London, N5 1LN
T 020 75033496
E info@96gillespie.com
W www.96gillespie.com
Founded in 2004. Specializes in photography and
American art. Artists represented include Gee
Vaucher, Melanie Standage, Pat Graham and
Cynthia Connolly.
Submission Policy Will accept submissions that
include artist's past press, examples of work and
ideas for the show. Directors will do their best to
respond if possible. Gallery is booked up to one
year in advance.

Price range £25–£1,000
No of exhibitions annually 6

Abbott and Holder Ltd
30 Museum Street, London, WC1A 1LH
T 020 76373981
F 020 76310575
E abbott.holder@virgin.net
W www.abbottandholder.co.uk
Contact Philip Athill
Founded in 1936 as a picture dealer and
conservator. Sells watercolours, drawings, oils and
prints from 1780 to the present. A twentieth-
century watercolour and drawings show is held
every September while the Christmas show has six
hundred works priced between £5 and £250
Submission Policy Artists should telephone and
visit the gallery to establish whether the artist's
work and the gallery are suitable for each other.
Price range £25–£10,000
No of exhibitions annually 8

Ackermann & Johnson Ltd
27 Lowndes Street, London, SW1X 9HY
T 020 72356464
F 020 7823 1057
E ackermannjohnson@btconnect.com
W www.artnet.com/ackermann-johnson.html
A two-floor gallery in the heart of Belgravia, just off
Sloane Street. Specializes in eighteenth- and
nineteenth-century British paintings, notably the
Norwich School, English landscapes, sporting
paintings, marine paintings and portraiture. Also
exhibits bronzes, watercolours and works by
contemporary artists including John King,
Douglas Anderson and Peter Howell.
Price range From £300 for watercolours.

Adonis Art
1b Coleherne Road, Earls Court, London
SW10 9BS
T 020 74603888
E stewart@adonis-art.com
W www.adonis-art.com
Contact Stewart Hardman
Opened in 1995. Specializes in antique and
contemporary art of the male form. Monthly
exhibitions, plus a large selection of individual
items – bronze figures, statues, nineteenth-
century life study drawings and male figurative art
of all types. Artists exhibited include Cornelius
McCarthy, Peter Samuelson and Duncan Grant.
Submission Policy Always interested in viewing
the work of new artists but the subject matter must

be the male form.
Price range £100–£10,000
No of exhibitions annually 12

Advanced Graphics London
32 Long Lane, London, SE1 4AY
T 020 74072055
F 020 74072066
E gallery@advancedgraphics.co.uk
W www.advancedgraphics.co.uk
Contact Louise Peck
A print studio founded in 1967, specializing in
screenprinting techniques combined, in some
cases, with woodblock printing. Moved to current
location near London Bridge in 2003. Shows
contemporary artists' prints made in the advanced
graphics studio and also paintings. Attends
selected art fairs. Artists printed at the studio
include Craigie Aitchison, Basil Beattie, Neil
Canning, Anthony Frost, Albert Irvin, Anita Klein
and Ray Richardson.
Price range £200–£20,000
No of exhibitions annually 10

The Agency
15A Cremer Street, London, E2 8HD
T 020 77296249
E info@theagencygallery.co.uk
W www.theagencygallery.co.uk
Founded in 1993 as a space for installation art and
new media with a focus on recent critical debates.
Launched 1996 as a commercial gallery.
Represents international young and mid-career
artists. The works are promoted with a longterm
view to museums and collections.
No of exhibitions annually 7

Agnew's
43 Old Bond Street, London, W1S 4BA
T 020 72909250
F 020 76294359
E agnews@agnewsgallery.co.uk
W www.agnewsgallery.co.uk
Founded in 1817, primarily as an Old Master
paintings dealership, the gallery now also
specializes in twentieth-century British art and
represents a small selection of contemporary artists.

Air Gallery
32 Dover Street, London, W1S 4NE
T 020 74091255
F 020 74091856
E adminair@airgallery.co.uk
W www.airgallery.co.uk

Contact Clare Rea
Founded in 1996, two well-equipped galleries for
hire in Mayfair. Has hosted a wide range of
exhibitions, mainly but not only of contemporary
art. Past clients include national and international
artists and dealers and also several art prizes.
Submission Policy A hire gallery. Welcomes
submissions from any interested artists.
Cost to hire or rent Upper Gallery is £4,950 + VAT
and the Lower Gallery is £2,250 + VAT.

Alan Cristea Gallery
31 Cork Street, London, W1S 3NU
T 020 74398166
F 020 77341549
E info@alancristea.com
W www.alancristea.com
Founded in 1995 and the largest publisher and dealer
of master graphics and contemporary prints in
Europe. Represents an international stable of artists
including Gillian Ayres, Ian Davenport, Richard
Hamilton, Jan Dibbets, Mimmo Paladino, Julian
Opie, Ian McKeever, Lisa Milroy, Gordon Cheung,
Boo Ritson, Paul Schütze and Howard Hodgkin.
Submission Policy Does not accept submissions
from artists.
Price range £1,000–£200,000
No of exhibitions annually 8

Albemarle Gallery
49 Albemarle Street, London, W1S 4JR
T 020 74991616
F 020 74991717
E info@albemarlegallery.com
W www.albemarlegallery.com
Focuses on contemporary figurative, still life and
trompe l'oeil work, together with urban and rural
landscapes. Presents group and solo shows of
established and emerging artists, supported by full-
colour catalogues.

Albion
8 Hester Road, London, SW11 4AX
T 020 78012480
F 020 78012488
E mhw@albion-gallery.com
W www.albion-gallery.com
Contact Michael Hue-Williams
Founded in 1993 on Cork Street and moved in
2004 to a new Norman Foster-designed space on
the banks of the Thames. Comprises 12,500 sq. ft
of exhibition space. Exhibited artists include Mark
di Suvero, James Turrell and Andy Goldsworthy.
No of exhibitions annually 5

Alison Jacques Gallery

16–18 Berners Street, London, W1X 1RB
T 020 72877675
E info@alisonjacquesgallery.com
W www.alisonjacquesgallery.com
Formerly known as Asprey Jacques when it opened in 1998, this relatively young contemporary gallery in the area around Cork Street shows international and British artists such as Ian Kiaer and Catherine Yass.

Alma Enterprises

1 Vyner Street, London, E2 9DG
T 07769 686826
E info@thisisland.net
W www.almaenterprises.com
Run by a group of artists and curators. Shows a programme of experimental and interdisciplinary exhibitions and events, foregrounding artists and curators who work critically with contemporary ideas and art forms.
Submission Policy Information on submitting a proposal can be found at www.almaenterprises.com/proposals.html
Price range From £350 upwards
No of exhibitions annually 5

Anderson Hill

St Peter's House, 6 Cambridge Road
Kingston-upon-Thames
KT1 3JY
T 020 85463800
F 020 85471227
E info@andersonhill.co.uk
W www.andersonhill.co.uk
Contact Douglas A. Hill
The gallery started in 2001 as an addition to an existing commercial framing and corporate-art business established in 1977. Framing service available to artists, as well as potential exposure to corporate clientele. Gallery space is in a converted Edwardian church-school building.
Price range £50–£10,000
No of exhibitions annually 6

Andipa Gallery

162 Walton Street, London
SW3 2JL
F 020 72250305
E art@andipa.com
W www.andipa.com
Dealers in fine art since 1593 [sic.]; London gallery since 1969. Specializes in modern and contemporary art (Picasso, Matisse, Chagall, Warhol, Lichtenstein, Damien Hirst) and Byzantine art. Offers restoration and valuation services.
Price range £500–£100,000

Andrew Coningsby Gallery

30 Tottenham Street, London, W1T 4RJ
T 020 76367478
F 020 75807017
E debutart@coningsbygallery.demon.co.uk
W www.coningsbygallery.com
Established in 1994. Specializes in exhibitions for contemporary illustrators, photographers and fine artists.
Price range £50–£10,000
No of exhibitions annually 52; one per week.

Anne Faggionato

4th Floor, 20 Dering Street, London, W1S 1AJ
T 020 7493 6732
F 020 74939693
E info@annefaggionato.com
W www.annefaggionato.com
Dealers in Impressionist, modern and contemporary paintings, sculpture and works on paper.
Submission Policy Not open to submissions.
No of exhibitions annually 3

Annely Juda Fine Art

4th Floor, 23 Dering Street, London, W1S 1AW
T 020 76297578
F 020 74912139
E ajfa@annelyjudafineart.co.uk
W www.annelyjudafineart.co.uk
An established name on the gallery scene for over forty years, showing major figures from the history of twentieth-century art from Britain, Europe and Japan, with a special interest in Russian avant-garde and Constructivist art.

Anthony Reynolds Gallery

60 Great Marlborough Street, London, W1F 7BG
T 020 74392201
F 020 74391869
E info@anthonyreynolds.com
W www.anthonyreynolds.com
Established in 1985, the gallery moved to the West End in 1990 and the current building was opened in 2002. There are twenty-two artists represented exclusively by the gallery, including the Atlas Group, David Austen, Richard Billingham, Leon Golub, Paul Graham and Mark Wallinger.
Submission Policy No submissions accepted.
No of exhibitions annually 9

AOP Gallery
81 Leonard Street, London, EC2A 4QS
T 020 77396669
F 020 77398707
E gallery@aophoto.co.uk
W www.the-aop.org
Contact Anna Roberts
Part of the Association of Photographers, the gallery has been staging exhibitions and events since 1986. Committed to heightening awareness and promoting photography, exhibition programmes represent a broad range of photography, incorporating both commercial and personal work from established and up-and-coming photographers.
Submission Policy Photography only.
Price range £70–£6,000
No of exhibitions annually 12
Cost to hire or rent £2,500 + VAT per week. Exclusive AOP Member discounts available.

The Approach
1st Floor, 47 Approach Road, London, E2 9LY
T 020 89833878
F 020 89833919
E info@theapproach.co.uk
W www.theapproach.co.uk
Located on the first floor above a traditional Victorian public house in the Bethnal Green area since 1997, the gallery shows young British artists, including recent graduates, as well as artists from Europe and the USA.

APT Gallery
6 Creekside, Deptford, London, SE8 4SA
T 020 86948344
E enquiry@aptstudios.org
Gallery of the Art in Perpetuity Trust. Available for hire, starting at £260 per week for shows that hold an educational/community event.

Archeus
3 Albemarle Street, London, W1S 4HE
T 020 74999755
F 020 74995964
E art@archeus.co.uk
W www.archeus.co.uk
Specializes in British and international contemporary art, with an emphasis on established 'blue chip' artists who have genuine influence. Exhibited artists include Yves Klein, Ed Ruscha, Donald Judd and Dan Flavin. Holds a permanent stock of over one-thousand works by the artists in which it deals.
No of exhibitions annually 10–12

Arcola Theatre
27 Arcola Street, London, E8 2DJ
T 020 75031646
E info@arcolatheatre.com
W www.arcolatheatre.com
Contact Leyla Nazli
Founded in 2001 to provide a much-needed cultural venue in Dalston, Hackney, and has become a well-respected fringe theatre. The theatre's gallery space is designed to air new and local work in need of a space.
Submission Policy Open to a wide range of work. The decision to exhibit is at the discretion of the booker.
No of exhibitions annually 10–12; exhibitions run to coincide with performance runs, which usually last four weeks.

Arndean Gallery
23 Cork Street, London, W1S 3NJ
T 020 75897742
F 020 75893888
E info@arndeangallery.com
W www.arndeangallery.com
Contact Kate Sadler
High-profile gallery for hire in Cork Street, in the heart of London's art world. Approximately 900 sq. ft over two floors. With neighbours including Flowers Central, Waddingtons, Beaux Arts and the Royal Academy, the gallery is well placed to attract serious buyers.
Cost to hire or rent £4,900 + VAT per week (discounts available at various times of the year).

Art First
1st Floor, 9 Cork Street, London, W1S 3LL
T 020 77340386
F 020 77343964
E artfirst@dircon.co.uk
W www.artfirst.co.uk
Established in 1991. A contemporary-art gallery exhibiting UK and international artists. Has a regular stable of artists, many of whom with works in public collections in the UK and worldwide.
Submission Policy Contemporary painting and drawing. No video. Photographs or CDs (with relevant CV) by post only, with sae for any returns.
Price range £500–£20,000
No of exhibitions annually 10 major exhibitions in the main gallery and regular shows in the front-room project space.

Art Space Gallery
84 St Peter's Street, London, N1 8JS

T 020 73597002
E mail@artspacegallery.co.uk
W www.artspacegallery.co.uk
Founded in 1986 by Michael and Oya Richardson to show and promote serious painting. Shows work of young artists alongside established names.

Artcadia
108 Commercial Street, London, E1 6LZ
T 020 74260733
F 020 73752601
Large stock of contemporary computer-generated art.

Arthouse Gallery
Lewisham Arthouse, 140 Lewisham Way, London, SE14 6PD
T 020 82443168
F 020 86949011
E lewishamarthouse@btconnect.com
W www.arthouse.dircon.co.uk
Contact Gallery Coordinator
Lewisham Arthouse, an artist-run studio cooperative, relocated its gallery to its current site in a listed Carnegie building in 1994. Aims to offer exhibitions to artists at the start of their careers. Not a commercial gallery and does not represent artists.
Submission Policy Welcomes applications in any medium (subject to selection) on production of images, an exhibition proposal and a completed application form.
No of exhibitions annually Approx. 12

Artist Eye Space
1st Floor, 12 All Saints Road, London, W11 1HH
T 020 77924077
E vlm@artisteye.com
W www.artisteye.com
Opened in 2003. Alongside established figures, the gallery introduces up-and-coming young artists. Runs a wide-ranging exhibition programme, including salon and corporate events. Exhibited artists include Michelle Molyneux, Paul Maffrett, Simeon Farrar, Amanda Couch, Anastasia Lewis and Jocelyn Clarke.
Submission Policy Painting, sculptures, mixed media, video, and installations all considered.
Price range £1,000–£16,000
No of exhibitions annually 6

Atlas Gallery
49 Dorset Street, London, W1U 7NF
T 020 72244192
F 020 72243351

E info@atlasgallery.com
W www.atlasgallery.com
Contact Robin Page
Founded in 1994, showing classic twentieth-century photography, contemporary photography and photo-journalism.
Submission Policy Preferred method of application is by email.
Price range £170 upwards.
No of exhibitions annually 6–8

August Art
Wharf Studios, Baldwin Terrace, London N1 7RU
T 020 7354 0677
E info@augustart.co.uk
W www.augustart.co.uk
Inaugural show held in 2004. Hosts 3–5 shows per year of contemporary art by artists the gallery represents or respects.
Submission Policy Email jpgs/tiffs with brief CV or artist statement but limit mail size to 2MB maximum. Due to volume of submissions does not always reply to all requests.
Price range £200–£5,000
No of exhibitions annually 3–6 including art fairs.

Austin/Desmond Fine Art Ltd
Pied Bull Yard, 68–69 Great Russell Street, London, WC1B 3BN
T 020 72424443
F 020 74044480
E gallery@austindesmond.com
W www.austindesmond.com
Contact Carlotta Graedel Matthai
Specializes in Modern British, Irish and international art. Established in 1979, the gallery has been located in Bloomsbury since 1988. Deals in paintings, drawings and sculpture by renowned artists including Frank Auerbach, Jean Dubuffet, Dan Flavin, Lucian Freud, Barbara Hepworth, Howard Hodgkin, David Hockney, Henry Moore, Ben Nicholson, Bridget Riley and Cy Twombly. As well as buying and selling important works, the gallery holds a comprehensive stock with a particular emphasis on twentieth-century British art. A yearly exhibition programme of classic painting and sculpture is complimented with a series of contemporary shows.
Submission Policy Painters and ceramic artists can apply either by email with jpegs or by post with images and sae enclosed.
Price range £300–£300,000
No of exhibitions annually Approximately 7

Barbara Behan Contemporary Art

50 Moreton Street, Pimlico, London, SW1V 2PB
T 020 78218793
F 020 78343933
E info@barbarabehan.com
W www.barbarabehan.com
Contact Barbara Behan
Barbara Behan opened in 2003, establishing an
international platform for an artistic scene hitherto
almost completely absent from galleries in
London. The cosmic chaos of Italy's Informale
experiences of the 1950s and movements such as
Spazialismo, Arte povera and Movimento Nucleare
opened up new artistic languages for the decades
to follow. The gallery seeks to trace the progression
of these languages in its contemporary artists,
placing them in dialogue with their British and
international contemporaries in a series of
thematic group and solo exhibitions. Painting,
sculpture, photography, graphic and installation
art all feature. Artists include Maria Morganti,
Bruna Esposito, Rossella Bellusci, Carmengloria
Morales, Giuseppe Spagnulo, Marco Gastini and
Paolo Icaro.
Submission Policy Email cover letter with artist's
statement, CV and examples of recent work. Visit
the gallery or refer to the website first to ensure
compatibility.
Price range £200–100,000
No of exhibitions annually 6

Barrett Marsden Gallery

17–18 Great Sutton Street, London, EC1V 0DN
T 020 73366396
E info@bmgallery.co.uk
W www.bmgallery.co.uk
Established in 1998. Exhibits contemporary studio
ceramics, glass, metal and wood including work by
Gordon Baldwin, Alison Britton, Caroline
Broadhead, Philip Eglin, Michael Rowe, Martin
Smith and Emma Woffenden.

Baumkotter Gallery

63a Kensington Church Street, Kensington
London, W8 4BA
T 020 79375171
E art@baumkottergallery.com
W www.baumkottergallery.com
Specializes in seventeenth- to twenty-first-century
paintings, English and European Old Master
paintings, and modern art fine oils. Subjects
include hunting, sport, shipping, seascape and
landscape. Nicholas Baumkotter has been in the
London fine-art trade for twenty-seven years and
provides restoration services for fine oil paintings
and picture frames. A bespoke framing service is
also offered.

Bearspace

152 Deptford High Street, London, SE8 3PQ
T 020 86948097
E bearspace@thebear.tv
W www.thebear.tv/bearspace
Contact Julia Alvarez
Recently established contemporary art gallery
situated on Deptford High Street in South East
London. Shows the cutting edge of emerging talent,
promoting recently established artists responding
to contemporary stimuli and topics with wit and
innovation in a range of media. Aims to produce
vibrant exhibitions while maintaining and
developing a business-like attitude towards artists
and artwork, identifying promising work by artists
and promoting this on an international scale.
Submission Policy Exhibits painting, photography,
film and occasionally three-dimensional work.
Contact the gallery for further information.
Price range £500–£5,000
No of exhibitions annually 11

Beaux Arts

22 Cork Street, London, W1S 3NA
T 020 74375799
F 020 74375798
E info@beauxartslondon.co.uk
W www.beauxartslondon.co.uk
Opened over twenty-five years ago in Bath; in 1993
expanded to Cork Street in London. Gallery policy
is to show modern and contemporary British
painting and sculpture, and to offer an opportunity
to new and dynamic artists to exhibit in the heart
of Mayfair.

Ben Brown Fine Arts

1st Floor, 21 Cork Street, London, W1S 3LZ
T 020 77348888
F 020 77348892
E info@benbrownfinearts.com
W www.benbrownfinearts.com
A newly founded gallery in Cork Street showing
mainly twentieth-century masters and recent
photography.

Bischoff/Weiss

95 Rivington Street, London, EC2A 3AY
T 020 70330309
E info@bischoffweiss.com
W www.bischoffweiss.com

Promotes young and up-and-coming artists in London and abroad. Hosting seven shows per year, the gallery encourages artists to use the space as a laboratory for experimentation, pushing the boundaries of aesthetics visually and conceptually. Artists include Nathaniel Rackowe, Ali Silverstein, Tatiana Trouve, Olivier Millagou, Hildur Margretardottir, Markus Hansen, Maya Hewitt, Michael Ajerman and Nina Gehl.
No of exhibitions annually 7

Blackheath Gallery
34A Tranquil Vale, Blackheath, London
SE3 OAX
T 020 88521802
E james@blackheath-gallery.co.uk
W www.blackheath-gallery.co.uk
Contact Sue Marshall
Established in 1975. Provides a showcase for artists from the UK, USA and Europe. Stocks fine prints by twentieth-century artists including Francis Bacon, David Hockney and Henry Moore. Exhibited artists include Graeme Wilcox, Mark Demsteader and Ray Donley.
Submission Policy Painters, sculptors, printmakers and glass blowers are invited to submit applications via email with digital attachments or send CD or photographs and CV together with an sae.
Price range £50–£15,000
No of exhibitions annually 6–7

Blink Gallery
11 Poland Street, London, W1F 8QA
T 020 74398585
E info@blinkgallery.com
W www.blinkgallery.com
Contact Daniel Hay
Opened in 2002. A contemporary photography gallery specializing in music, celebrity and fashion photography. Artists represented include Terry O'Neill, Michael Cooper, Sir Peter Blake, Gered Mankowitz and Dennis Morris.
Price range £300–£5,000
No of exhibitions annually 5

Blow de la Barra
35 Heddon Street, London, W1B 4BP
T 020 77347477
E info@blowdelabarra.com
W www.blowdelabarra.com
A West End art gallery showing the work of young international avant-garde artists, many of them previously unseen in London. Artists include

Stefan Bruggemann, Los Super Elegantes, Frederico Herrero and Marcelo Krasilcic.

Bloxham Galleries
4–5 The Parade, St Johns Hill, London
SW11 1TG
T 020 79247500
F 020 75853901
E info@bloxhamgalleries.com
W www.bloxhamgalleries.com
Contact Julia Lister
John Bloxham, a respected London dealer involved in the arts for over thirty years, opened the galleries in 1994. There are two light and airy spaces at street level with a downstairs exhibition area for smaller, more intimate pieces. Specializes in sculpture and photography and figurative, landscape and abstract pieces.
Submission Policy Welcomes all artists' submissions. Email CV and high-quality jpegs or send postal submissions (including sae) to Julia Lister.
Price range £400–£30,000
No of exhibitions annually 10–12

Boundary Gallery–Agi Katz Fine Art
98 Boundary Road, London, NW8 0RH
T 020 76241126
F 020 76241126
E agi@boundarygallery.com
W www.boundarygallery.com
Contact Agi Katz or Louise Homes
Established for twenty-one years. Specializations include: modern British artists (1900–60), mostly of Jewish origin, including David Bomberg, Horace Brodzky, Jacob Epstein, Josef Herman, Jacob Kramer, Bernard Meninsky, Morris Kestelman and Alfred Wolmark; and contemporary figurative work displaying good draughtsmanship and composition and a strong palette. Artists include Peter Prendergast, David Tress, Sonia Lawson, Anita Klein, Breuer-Weil, Paul Bloomer, Neil MacPherson and Davina Jackson.
Submission Policy Figurative work (can be representational) with good draughtsmanship, strong composition and a strong palette. Accepts paintings and works on paper. No prints.
Price range £300–£40,000
No of exhibitions annually 7–8

Brent Artist's Resource and Gallery
Willesden Green Library Centre, 95 High Road, London, NW10 2SF

T 020 8459 1421
E info@brentartistsresource.org.uk
W www.brentartistsresource.org.uk
Contact Lorenzo Belenguer
Founded in 1984, an artists-led voluntary
organization with a dedicated gallery space ideally
suited for group and individual shows. Aims to be
the leading forum for contemporary visual art in
Brent, presenting a mixture of exhibitions that
include painting, installation, video, performance,
photography and community art projects.
Price range £20–£2,000
No of exhibitions annually 10
Cost to hire or rent Can be hired for £500 for 4
weeks (no commissions taken). Artists may also
become members and exhibit in group shows.

Brick Lane Gallery
196 Brick Lane, London, E1 6SA
T 020 77299721
E tony@thebricklanegallery.com
W www.thebricklanegallery.com
Contact Danielle Horn
Contemporary art gallery showcasing new and
established artists from around the world,
presenting innovative developments in painting,
photography, sculpture and video. Has worked on
group projects with Charles Saatchi, Wolfgang
Tilmans and Bob and Roberta Smith. Gallery
artists include Bjorn Veno, Antti Laitinen, Saul
Zanolari, Eduard Bigas, Hektor Mamet, Mike
Newton and Rebecca Tabber.
Submission Policy Submissions welcome from
artists and curators.
Price range £500–5,000
No of exhibitions annually 10

Brixton Art Gallery
35 Brixton Station Road, London
SW9 8PB
T 020 77336957
E brixart@brixtonartgallery.co.uk
W www.brixtonartgallery.co.uk
Contact Ms D. Parker
Founded in 1983. Specializes in contemporary art.
Artists represented include L. Postma, Kudzanai
Chiurai, Amos Cherfil, Dubois, Sean Hasan and
Teresa Nills. Offers training scheme for artists in
schools.
Submission Policy Submit statement, CV and
images of work by post or through gallery
website.
Price range Up to £1,000
No of exhibitions annually 8

Cabinet
Apartment 6, 3rd Floor, 49–59 Old Street, London
EC1V 9HX
T 020 72516114
F 020 76082414
E art@cabinetltd.demon.co.uk
Contact Martin McGeown or Andrew Wheatley
Founded in 1992. Aims for 'informed, engaged
and critical work by artists with an international
perspective independent of art-world trends
(economic/curatorial/editorial)'. Artists
represented include Gillian Carnegie, Enrico
David, Mark Leckey, Lucy McKenzie, Paulina
Olowskan and Tariq Alvi.
Submission Policy Unsolicited applications not
sought.
No of exhibitions annually 6

Campbell Works
27 Belfast Road, London, N16 6UN
T 020 88060817
E info@campbellworks.org
W www.campbellworks.org
An independant space and art project directed by
artists Neil Taylor and Harriet Murray, providing a
gallery, project space, studios and education room.
Curates a public programme of contemporary,
visual and combined art-form practice. Fosters the
development and curation of new ventures with
artists of all disciplines. Exhibits up-and-coming
artists and experimental projects as well as
established artists. Particularly supports projects
and installations that explore ways to
communicate with audiences.
Submission Policy Applications welcome from
curators and artists. Submissions should include
up to eight 35mm slides, DVD or VHS for media-
based works, a CV and brief statement, and an sae
to the correct amount if the work needs to be
returned.
Price range £10–£10,000
No of exhibitions annually 6
Cost to hire or rent The project space is available
for hire at certain times. Call for further
information.

Capital Culture
3 Bedfordbury, Covent Garden, London
WC2N 4BP
T 020 78360824
E info@capitalculture.eu
W www.capitalculture.eu
Contact Rachael Dalzell
Opened in 2005. Primary focus is on fine art

photography, but 'we like to keep things interesting so anything is possible'. Shows both up-and-coming and established artists.

Submission Policy Reviews submissions of work and CVs on CD. Primary focus on photography but other medias considered.

Price range £500–£8,000

No of exhibitions annually 8

Cost to hire or rent By arrangement.

Centre for Recent Drawing

C4RD, Nanospace, 61–63 Cudworth Street Bethnal Green, London, E1 5QU

T 020 78717367

E info@c4rd.org.uk

W www.c4rd.org.uk

Provides a webservice and an independent non-commercial exhibition space dedicated to the exhibition of recent drawing.

Submission Policy Welcomes submissions from those with a particular interest in drawing as a core experience from within and outside the arts.

Centre of Attention

67 Clapton Common, London, E5 9AA

T 020 88805507

F 020 88805507

E on@thecentreofattention.org

W www.thecentreofattention.org

Contact Pierre Coinde

Founded in 1999. A London-based contemporary-art gallery examining the formalities of production, distribution and consumption of art. Exhibitions take place both in the UK and overseas.

Submission Policy Welcomes submissions from artists and curators. Post a small number of non-returnable slides, pictures, images or other medium that give a fair idea of the work or project. Can also view websites.

Price range £1–£10,000

No of exhibitions annually 8

Charing X Venue

121–125 Charing Cross Road, London WC2H 0EW

W www.venuereservations.co.uk/charing-x-venue.htm

Gallery space available for hire. See website for details.

Chinese Contemporary Ltd

21 Dering Street, London, W1S 1AL

T 020 74998898

F 020 74998852

E ccartuk@aol.com

W www.chinesecontemporary.com

Contact Julia Colman

Founded in London in 1996, specializing exclusively in Chinese contemporary art from artists living and working in mainland China, both established and emerging. Sister gallery in Beijing set up in 2004

Submission Policy Must be Chinese nationals living and working in mainland China.

Price range US$1,000–$100,000

No of exhibitions annually 8–10 solo shows.

Clapham Art Gallery

Unit 02, 40–48 Bromell's Road, London SW4 0BG

T 020 77200955

E direct@claphamartgallery.com

W www.claphamartgallery.com

Established in 1998 to discover and promote emerging artists. Runs a programme of five-week curated and one-person exhibitions and participates in selected art fairs and events.

Submission Policy 6–8 medium resolution jpegs sent via email with artist's CV and statement.

Price range £180–£15 000

No of exhibitions annually 8

Clarion Contemporary Art

387 King Street, Hammersmith, London, W6 9NJ

T 020 87483369

E info@clariongallery.co.uk

W www.clariongallery.co.uk

Founded in 2005, specializing in contemporary painting by artists from the UK and abroad. Aims to exhibit a varied selection of work appropriate for both domestic and business settings.

Submission Policy Submissions welcome.

Price range £500–£4,000

No of exhibitions annually 10

Collins & Hastie Ltd

62 Tournay Road, London, SW6 7UF

T 020 73814957

E caroline@collinsandhastie.co.uk

W www.collinsandhastie.co.uk

Founded in 1993, dealing in contemporary (mainly figurative) art. Specializes in the work of Paul Maze, known as 'the lost British Impressionist'. Gallery runs by appointment only. Also exhibits at the Art on Paper Fair, the Affordable Art Fair and the Chelsea Art Fair. Artists include Glen Preece, Jenny Thompson, Michael Bennallack Hart, Janet

Tod, Caroline Chariot Dayez, Jim Bradford, Alex Chamberlain, Rose Shawe-Taylor and Jill Barthorpe.
Price range £500–£30,000
No of exhibitions annually 4 solo shows, not including London art fairs.

Contemporary Applied Arts
2 Percy Street, London, W1T 1DD
T 020 74362344
F 020 74362344
W www.caa.org.uk
Among Britain's largest galleries specializing in the exhibition and sale of contemporary crafts. Founded in 1948 as the Craft Centre of Great Britain, the double-level gallery shows leading makers of ceramic, glass, jewellery, textiles, metalwork, silver, wood and furniture.
Submission Policy Professional craftpersons working in the British Isles can apply for membership of the society. Following selection, the subscription rate is £75 per year.
Price range £10–£10,000
No of exhibitions annually 7

Corvi-Mora
1a Kempsford Road, off Wincott Street, London SE11 4NU
T 020 78409111
F 020 78409112
E tcm@corvi-mora.com
W www.corvi-mora.com
Specializes in international contemporary art. Exhibited artists include Liam Gillick, Brian Calvin, Roger Hiorns, Dee Ferris, Monique Prieto, Rachel Feinstein, Richard Hawkins and Jason Meadows.
No of exhibitions annually 8

Cosa Gallery
7 Ledbury Mews North, London, W11 2AF
T 020 77270398
F 020 77929697
E info@cosalondon.com
W www.cosalondon.com
Contact Julie Pottle
Founded in 2002 to promote innovative and highly crafted work by artists working in a variety of media. Particularly interested in contemporary studio ceramics. Artists include Georgia Peskett, Ana Bianchi, Dominic Theobald, James Evans, Andy Shaw and Noel Hart. Gallery available for rent.
Submission Policy Contact by email. Check website first to determine whether work would

complement existing artists' work. Especially interested in sculptural studio ceramics.
Price range £500–£7,500
No of exhibitions annually 6

Counter Gallery
44a Charlotte Road, London, EC2A 3PD
T 020 7684 8888
F 020 7684 8889
E info@countergallery.com
W www.countergallery.com
Established in 2003. Presents exhibitions by emerging international artists. Gallery artists include Armando Andrade Tudela, Michael Fullerton, Simon Martin, Gareth McConnell, Peter Peri and Fergal Stapleton.
Submission Policy Does not accept submissions.
Price range £300–£50,000
No of exhibitions annually 7

Cubitt Gallery and Studios
8 Angel Mews, London, N1 9HH
T 020 72788226
F 020 72782544
E info@cubittartists.org.uk
W www.cubittartists.org.uk
Established in the early 1990s as an independent artist-run gallery and studios, with a focus on progressive international contemporary art projects and artist-led initiatives. Also provides an 18-month bursary for an independent curator to develop the gallery's artistic programme.
No of exhibitions annually 6

Cynthia Corbett Gallery
15 Claremont Lodge, 15 The Downs, Wimbledon SW20 8UA
T 020 89476782
F 020 89476782
E info@thecynthiacorbettgallery.com
W www.thecynthiacorbettgallery.com
Contact Odette Selva
Established in 2000 by former Christie's Education Art History graduate, Cynthia Corbett, and operated from her Victorian home. Promotes both established and emerging artists. Offers a personalized service for clients including advice on collecting, in situ viewings and installation. corbettPROJECTS was launched in 2004 to focus on young, emerging and experimental artists and art forms including photography, video, conceptual, installation and performance art.
Submission Policy Contact via email.
Price range £350–£15,000

No of exhibitions annually 6, as well as a variety of UK and international art fairs.

Danielle Arnaud Contemporary Art

123 Kennington Road, London, SE11 6SF
T 020 77358292
F 020 77358292
E danielle@daniellearnaud.com
W www.daniellearnaud.com
Founded in 1995 and located in a large Georgian house. Encourages artists with strong individuality to explore freely and present work outside the constraints of markets or trends. Also active in collaborations and temporary public art projects. Artists include David Cotterrell, Sophie Lascelles, Marie-France and Patricia Martin, Helen Maurer, Heather & Ivan Morison, Paulette Phillips and Sarah Woodfine.
Submission Policy Artists should apply via email by sending images and short statement and/or proposals for themed exhibitions. It is highly recommended that artists visit the gallery and website before applying.
Price range £250–£10,000
No of exhibitions annually 6 curated for the gallery; 2–3 touring/off-site projects.

David Risley Gallery

45 Vyner Street, Brunswick Wharf, London, E2 9DQ
T 020 76134006
F 020 77298008
E info@davidrisleygallery.com
W www.davidrisleygallery.com
Contact David Risley or Poppy Sebire
Opened in 2003, presenting exhibitions of represented artists alongside curated group shows, mixing established and emerging artists. Artists include James Aldridge, Masakatsu Kondo, Henry Krokatsis, Helen Frik, Peter Jones, John Stezaker, Jonathan Allen, John Zurier, Matt Calderwood, James Hyde and Hurvin Anderson.

DegreeArt.com

Unit 2.07, 417 Wick Lane, London, E3 2JG
T 020 89800395 or 07971 456396
E info@DegreeArt.com
W www.DegreeArt.com
Price range £30–£3,000
No of exhibitions annually 10

Dicksmith Gallery

74 Buttesland Street, Hoxton, London, N1 6BY
T 020 72530663
E dicksmithgallery@hotmail.com

W www.dicksmithgallery.co.uk
Contact Sam Porritt, Meiro Koizumi, Duncan Marquiss, Rupert Norfolk, Mauro Bonacina or Natsuki Uruma
Founded in 2003. Works with young artists to develop and present new work.
Submission Policy Accepts application on CD only; images in jpeg only. Any other information also on CD.
No of exhibitions annually 6

Dominic Guerrini Fine Art

18 Redburn Street, London, SW3 4BX
T 020 75652333
F 020 75652444
E sales@dominicguerrini.com
W www.dominicguerrini.com
Stocks original watercolours, drawings, signed and unsigned limited editions, paintings and prints. Viewing is by appointment only.

Domo Baal

3 John Street, London, WC1N 2ES
T 020 7242 9604
F 020 7831 0122
E info@domobaal.com
W www.domobaal.com
Founded in 2000, a contemporary art gallery. Artists represented include Christiane Baumgartner, Daniel Gustav Cramer, Haris Epaminonda, Ansel Krut, Jeffrey T. Y. Lee and Miho Sato. All artists exhibit internationally and the gallery exhibits at international art fairs.
No of exhibitions annually 6

Drawing Room

Brunswick Wharf, 55 Laburnum Street, London E2 8BD
T 020 77295333
F 020 77298008
E mail@drawingroom.org.uk
W www.drawingroom.org.uk
Founded in 2002, the only public gallery in the UK dedicated to the investigation and support of contemporary drawing practice, from the traditional to the experimental. Supports the production of new work and runs educational projects as well as public 'in-conversations' between artists, writers and critics. Produces publications and tours its exhibitions to regional museums and galleries.
Submission Policy No unsolicited submissions.
Price range £100–£30,000
No of exhibitions annually 3

Duncan Campbell

15 Thackeray Street, Kensington Square, London
W8 5ET
T 020 79378665
Founded in 1986. Contemporary artists include
John Gillespie, Liz Knox, Janet Freeman, Roberta
Booth, Sandra Pepys, Michael Alford, Harry
Weinberger, Allan MacDonald, John Newberry
RWS and Rowland Hilder. Modern British painters
include Paul Maze, Bernard Meninsky, Heinz
Koppel, Lamorna Birch and Leonard McComb.
Also British Wood Engravers (1900–2006).
Submission Policy Oils, watercolours and wood
engravings.
Price range £200–£50,000
No of exhibitions annually 12

Duncan R. Miller Fine Arts

6 Bury Street, London, SW1Y 6AB
T 020 78398806
F 020 78398806
E DMFineArts@aol.com
W www.duncanmiller.com
Contact Tanya R. Saunders
Founded in 1985. Dealers in nineteenth-century
European and modern British works. Specialists in
the Scottish Colourists. Artists include J.D.
Fergusson, F.C.B. Cadell, S.J. Peploe and G.L.
Hunter. Branch: 17 Flask Walk, Hampstead,
London, NW3 1HJ T/F 020 74355462.
Submission Policy Applications by email or post.
No visits.
Price range From £500
No of exhibitions annually 4–6

E&R Cyzer

33 Davies Street, London, W1K 4LR
T 020 76290100
F 020 74993697
E info@cyzerart.com
W www.cyzerart.com
Opened renovated gallery space in Mayfair in
2002. Deals in twentieth-century modern masters
and exhibits at several major international shows.
Also acquires works for collectors and institutions
both at home and internationally.

Eagle Gallery Emma Hill Fine Art

159 Farringdon Road, London, EC1R 3AL
T 020 78332674
E info@emmahilleagle.com
W www.emmahilleagle.com
Contact Christian Bonett
The gallery and its associated imprint (EMH Arts)

were founded in 1991. Promotes contemporary
British artists through exhibitions, installations
and graphics publications. Off-site projects have
included collaborations with Sadler's Wells and
Almeida Opera. Artists include Basil Beattie,
Matthew Burrows, Jane Bustin, James Fisher, Tom
Hammick and Terry Smith.
Submission Policy Very few artists are taken on by
submission. Phone the gallery for details.
Price range £50–£30,000
No of exhibitions annually 8–10

East West Gallery

8 Blenheim Crescent, London, W11 1NN
T 020 72297981
F 020 72210741
E david@eastwestgallery.co.uk
W www.eastwestgallery.co.uk
Contact David Solomon
Established in 1989. Art consultancy; valuations
and commissions undertaken. Located in west
London (Notting Hill), just off the Portobello Road.
Contemporary art, paintings and drawings (some
prints and sculpture), mainly figurative with a
strong emphasis on drawing, design and colour.
Submission Policy Submissions welcome. Send
images either as CD, slides or photos plus CV and
sae. Allow thirty days for return of material.
Price range £50–£30,000
No of exhibitions annually 10

ecArtspace

18 Temple Fortune Hill, London, NW11 7XN
T 020 84554548
F 020 84554548
E info@ecartspace.com
W www.ecartspace.com
Contact Angela Diamandidou
Founded in 1998 as a peripatetic or moving gallery.
Aims to show contemporary artists in unused
buildings and spaces, connecting the art with the
architecture of the building. Organizes and curates
exhibitions mainly in Clerkenwell (London) and in
Mitte (Berlin). The last exhibition in Berlin in 2006
was a collaboration with two other Berlin galleries,
showing young British Artists. Artists exhibited
include established painters (Basil Beattie, John
McLean, Frances Aviva Blane) as well as younger
artists such as Sarah Douglas and Laura Green.
Submission Policy Interested in site-specific work
and architectural projects, depending on type of
work and possible building or space setting.
Price range £500–£15,000
No of exhibitions annually 1–2

Elastic Residence

22 Parfett Street, London, E1 1JR
T 020 72471375
E info@elastic.org.uk
W www.elastic.org.uk
Contact Deej Fabyc
Established in 2004. A gallery space for projects
and durational performance. Run by artists, it aims
to give artists direct access to exhibition
opportunities. Showcasing the work of Micheal
Corris, Coco Fusco, Andrew Hurle, Elvis
Richardson, Viveka Marksjo and Joanna Callaghan
among others.
Submission Policy Does not accept unsolicited
applications but occasional open-call events are
advertised on the website.
No of exhibitions annually 10

Eleven

11 Eccleston Street, London
SW1W 9LX
T 020 78235540
F 020 78248383
E info@elevenfineart.com
W www.elevenfineart.com
Contact Laura Parker Bowles and Rachael Hall
Founded in 2005 by Charlie Phillips, previously
founding director of Haunch of Venison.
Committed to showing the best of international
contemporary art by established and emerging
artists. Artists include Olly & Suzi, Natasha Law,
Natasha Kissell, Jonathan Yeo, Rick Giles and
Cedric Christie.
Price range £400–£15,000
No of exhibitions annually 8

Emily Tsingou Gallery

10 Charles II Street, London
SW1Y 4AA
T 020 78395320
F 020 78395321
E info@emilytsingougallery.com
W www.emilytsingougallery.com
Founded in 1998. Focuses on international
contemporary art. Exhibition programme
concentrates on artists represented by the gallery
and includes off-site projects and publications.
Artists represented: Michael Ashkin, Henry Bond,
Kate Bright, Peter Callesen, Lukas Duwenhögger,
Paula Kane, Karen Kilimnik, Justine Kurland, Won
Ju Lim, Dietmar Lutz, Daniel Pflumm, Sophy
Rickett, Jim Shaw, Georgina Starr, Marnie Weber
and Mathew Weir.
No of exhibitions annually 7

The Empire

33a Wadeson Street, London, E2 9DR
T 020 89839310
E info@theempirestudios.co.uk
W www.theempirestudios.co.uk
Founded in 2004, putting on high-quality group
shows and beginning to represent individual
artists. Artists represented include the Council.
Submission Policy Accepts submissions from any
area or medium. Specializes in painting.
Price range £1,000–£10,000
No of exhibitions annually 12
Cost to hire or rent £1,100 per week or £850 per
week for shows of two or more weeks.

Enfield Arts Partnership

54–56 Market Square, Edmonton Green
Edmonton, N9 0TZ
T 020 88879500
F 020 88879501
E info@enfieldartspartnership.org
W www.enfieldartspartnership.org
Founded in 1999 as a provider to the creative and
cultural industries, providing business advice,
training, information and professional
development services for artists, arts professionals
and businesses in North London. Runs three
galleries, as well as a theatre space and studios.
Submission Policy Does not welcome
submissions.
No of exhibitions annually 20+
Cost to hire or rent £100 for individual artists and
£200 for groups up to 6 artists; £300 for
businesses and groups over 6; all prices for a
minimum of two weeks.

England & Co Gallery

216 Westbourne Grove, Notting Hill, London
W11 2RH
T 020 72210417
F 020 72214499
E england.gallery@virgin.net
Established in Notting Hill since 1987. Hosts
monthly shows of contemporary artists, together
with exhibitions reappraising avant-garde
twentieth-century art and artists. Also offers a
corporate consultancy service.

f a projects

1–2 Bear Gardens, Bankside, London, SE1 9ED
T 020 79283228
F 020 79285123
E info@faprojects.com
W www.faprojects.com

Founded in 2001, the gallery represents artists from both the UK and abroad, working in a variety of media. Represented artists include John Wood and Paul Harrison, David Burrows, Grazia Toderi, Jason Salavon, Neal Rock and James Ireland.
Submission Policy Submissions only considered after initial consultation with gallery directors.
Price range £500–£50,000
No of exhibitions annually 7

FarmiloFiumano
27 Connaught Street, London, W2 2AY
T 020 74026241
F 020 74026241
E info@farmilofiumano.com
W www.farmilofiumano.com
Specializes in contemporary European art, such as the Neapolitan Realismo Magico School. Constantly striving to find new artists.
Submission Policy Artists should apply to the gallery by sending good-quality images and as much information as possible either via email or by post. Enclose sae if material is to be returned.
Price range £200–£25,000
No of exhibitions annually 6

Fieldgate Gallery
T 07957 228351
E fieldgategallery@googlemail.com
W www.fieldgategallery.com
Located in Whitechapel, a 10,000 sq. ft contemporary art gallery and project space. Does not represent any of the artists who have participated in shows and is not a hire space.

Fine Art Commissions Ltd
7 Bury Street, St. James's, London, SW1Y 6AL
T 07768 864 065
E info@fineartcommissions.com
W www.fineartcommissions.com
Contact Sara Stewart or Lara Bailey
Founded in 1997, specializing in commissioned art (predominantly portraiture). Artists represented include Nick Bashall, Valery Gridnev, Marcus Hodge, Howard Morgan, Paul Benney, Nicky Philipps and Tom Leveritt. Also runs Arndean Gallery in Cork Street.
Submission Policy Interested in portrait painters who have completed a minimum of five commissions. Also interested in landscape/figurative/still life painters for exhibitions.
Price range £500–£40,000
No of exhibitions annually 10

Fine Art Society Plc
148 New Bond Street, London, W1S 2JT
T 020 76295116
F 020 74919454
E art@faslondon.com
W www.faslondon.com
Established in 1876, specializing in paintings, drawings, prints, sculpture, furniture and decorative arts of the nineteenth, twentieth and twenty-first centuries.
Submission Policy Submissions only in writing with photographs.
Price range £1,000–£500,000
No of exhibitions annually 12

Five Years
E info@fiveyears.org.uk
W www.fiveyears.org.uk
Founded in 1998, a collaborative artists' project run by Edward Dorrian, Marc Hulson and Alex Schady. Original aim was to set up an artist-run gallery where programming and curation would maintain as direct a relationship as possible to practice. Has since held 56 exhibitions and events including solo, curated and collaborative projects both by members and numerous guest participants. Projects are presented in both gallery and non-gallery spaces.

Flaca
69 Broadway Market, London, E8 4PH
T 020 72757473
F 020 72757473
E info@flaca.co.uk
W www.flaca.co.uk
Contact Kirsty Dixon
Flaca was established by the artist Tom Humphreys in 2003. The gallery is run on a non-commercial, experimental, artist-led basis. Has recently worked closely with artists including Michael Beutler, Jacob Dahl Jurgensen, Sally Osborn and Alexander Wolff.

Flowers East
82 Kingsland Road, London, E2 8DP
T 020 79207777
F 020 79207770
E gallery@flowerseast.com
W www.flowerseast.com
Founded over thirty years ago by Angela Flowers. Now has two London galleries (one on Kingsland Road, E2, and the other on Cork Street) and one on Madison Avenue in New York. Specializes in a variety of painting, sculpture, prints, photography,

installation and also owns its own publishing company, Momentum. Artists represented include Tai-Shan Schierenberg, Glenys Barton, Glen Baxter, Peter Howson, Ken Currie and John Keane.
Submission Policy Send photos, printouts or slides of work to Angela Flowers at the above address. Include CV, cover letter and sae for return of work.
No of exhibitions annually 12 per site.

Flying Colours Gallery
6 Burnsall Street, King's Road, London SW3 3ST
T 020 73515558
F 020 73515548
E art@flyingcoloursgallery.com
W www.flyingcoloursgallery.com
Founded in Edinburgh in 1986 and moved to Chelsea in 1995. Still shows contemporary Scottish artists such as Shona Barr, Stephen Mangan, Jean B. Martin RSW, Anthony Scullion and Ethel Walker. Also John Cunningham RGI (1926–98).
Submission Policy Scottish artists and sculptors may submit by email with jpegs or by post enclosing transparencies, photos or digital printouts.
Price range £500–£20,000
No of exhibitions annually 6

Fosterart
20 Rivington Street, London, EC2A 3DU
T 020 77391743
E info@fosterart.net
W www.fosterart.net
Manages a collection of artist-owned work available for placement with individuals and institutions. All work selected by a panel of experts to ensure quality contemporary art.
Submission Policy Agreements are available on the website.
Price range £1,000–£12,000
No of exhibitions annually 10, focusing on artists in the collection.

Foyles Bookshop
113–119 Charing Cross Road, London WC2H 0EB
T 020 74375660
W www.foyles.co.uk
The bookshop has been in Charing Cross Road since 1906. The gallery space on the second floor is available for hire. Recent exhibitions have included Lena Herzog and Carlos Reyes-Nanzo. Gallery also suitable for launch parties.

Fred [London] Ltd
45 Vyner Street, London, E2 9DQ
T 020 89812987
F 020 89818912
E info@fred-london.com
W www.fred-london.com
Opened in May 2005, representing twelve international artists. Artists include Mark Fairrington, Abetz/Drescher, Nayland Blake, Stuart Croft, Kate Davis, Paul Hosking, John Jodzio, Phillip Jones, Peter Jones, Jorg Lozek, Melanie Manchot and English Simon.

Frith Street Gallery
59–60 Frith Street, London, W1D 3JJ
T 020 74941550
F 020 72873733
E info@frithstreetgallery.com
W www.frithstreetgallery.com
Opened in 1989. Has developed a programme of exhibitions by international artists working in painting, photography, sculpture, film and video. Currently represents twenty artists from both Britain and abroad and also collaborates with other artists on specific projects. Artists represented include Chantal Akerman, Fiona Banner, Tacita Dean, Marlene Dumas, Craigie Horsfield, Callum Innes, Dayanita Singh, Annelies Strba and Daphne Wright.
No of exhibitions annually 6–7

Frivoli
7a Devonshire Road, London, W4 2EU
T 020 87423255
F 020 89947372
E info@frivoligallery.com
W www.DevonshireRoad.com
Contact Hazel Peiser
Founded by Hazel Peiser in 1991. Shows contemporary works in all media. Work by many artists displayed informally throughout the year in addition to summer and winter exhibitions.
Submission Policy Happy to view current work by professional artists in all permanent media.
Price range £150–£2,500
No of exhibitions annually Ongoing changing display; occasional exhibitions.

Frost & Reed Contemporary
2–4 King Street, St James's, London, SW1Y 6QP
T 020 7839 4645
F 020 7839 1166
E contemporary@frostandreed.com
W www.frostandreed.com

Contact Sandrine Janet

Frost&Reed announced the formation of Frost&Reed Contemporary in 2006 as a direct result of the acquisition of the Blue Gallery. It now operates from Frost&Reed's King Street premises, curating 4–5 shows a year in a specially refurbished inner gallery space. Participates in art fairs in both the UK and abroad. Continues to uphold the Blue Gallery ethos and principles, as well as developing and promoting the careers of its artists and sourcing new talent.

Submission Policy Suitable applications are welcome, initially by email, after which an invitation to make an appointment may be extended.

Price range Up to £20,000

No of exhibitions annually 4–5

Gagosian Gallery

6–24 Britannia Street, London, WC1X 9JD

T 020 78419960

F 020 78419961

E info@gagosian.com

W www.gagosian.com

Has expanded from its space on Heddon Street in the West End into a 12,500 sq. ft space on Britannia Street, converted by architects Caruso St John in 2004. The gallery represents some of the world's most prestigious living artists and also has branches in New York, where it was founded, and Los Angeles.

Branches 17–19 Davies Street, London, W1K 3DET 020 7493 3020

Galerie Besson

15 Royal Arcade, 28 Old Bond Street, London W1S 4SP

T 020 74911706

F 020 74953203

E enquiries@galeriebesson.co.uk

W www.galeriebesson.co.uk

Has won a worldwide reputation for exhibiting contemporary ceramics since opening in 1988. Runs mainly one-person shows and is the only London ceramic gallery showing international artists. Stock of classic artists includes Lucie Rie and Hans Coper.

Submission Policy Although opportunities for new artists to exhibit at the gallery are rare, introductions and images from ceramic artists are welcomed.

No of exhibitions annually 10

The Gallery at Willesden Green

Willesden Green Library Centre, 95 High Road,

London, NW10 2SF

T 020 84591421

E info@brentartistsresource.org.uk

W www.brentartistsresource.org.uk

Contact Lorenzo Belenguer, gallery coordinator

Aims to serve the cultural needs of the people of Brent and North West London by providing a supportive environment for artists. Offers information, professional development, opportunities to participate in exhibitions and workshops, and mentoring schemes.

Submission Policy Artist can become members by paying an annual fee which will allow them to show in the three group shows held every year.

Price range £20–£2,000

No of exhibitions annually 11

Cost to hire or rent £500 per month for the gallery; £150 per month for the wall space in the main hall of the centre.

Gallery in Cork Street Ltd and Gallery 27

28 Cork Street, London, W1S 3NG

T 020 72878408

F 020 72872018

E enquiries@galleryincorkstreet.com

W www.galleryincorkstreet.com

Contact Caroline Edwards (Manager)

One of London's leading suppliers of short-term gallery rental space. Operates two letting galleries in the centre of London's art trading area.

No of exhibitions annually 52; one per week.

Gallery Kaleidoscope

64–66 Willesden Lane, London, NW6 7SX

T 020 73285833

F 020 76242913

E info@gallerykaleidoscope.com

W www.gallerykaleidoscope.com

Established for over thirty years, with a policy of showing well-known names alongside promising newcomers. Artists represented include John Duffin, Elizabeth Taggart, Mark R. Hall, John Afflick, Chuck Monroe, Jean Cairns, Pete Mckee, Gursel Tunali and Inge Clayton.

Submission Policy Welcomes enquiries from artists, sculptors and ceramicists but insists on seeing images first via email or post.

Price range £100–£10,000

No of exhibitions annually 6–8

Gallery N. von Bartha

Contemporary Art–London, 1st Floor, London W11 1QU

T 020 79850015

F 020 79850016
E info@vonbartha.com
W www.vonbartha.com
Contact N. or D. von Bartha
Founded in 2000, dealing in minimal, conceptual and new-media art. Represents Jill Baroff, Frank Gerritz, Herbert Hamak, Julia Mangold, Eline McGeorge and Winston Roeth.
Submission Policy Does not guarantee to respond to every submission or return submitted material. Advises visiting the gallery or website prior to submitting.
Price range £80–£200,000
No of exhibitions annually 6

Gallery on the Green
33 Markham Street, London, SW3 3NR
T 020 73492917
E gallery@felixr.com
W www.galleryonthegreen.co.uk
Showcases a rolling exhibition of contemporary decorative art and accessories for collectors and interior designers. Portfolio includes original paintings, limited edition prints and individually tailored fine art prints. By working closely with artists, aims to ensure that the balance between originality, interior design and artistic integrity is met. Offers a complete service from framed artwork ready-to-hang to packaged, worldwide delivery.
Submission Policy Does not view original paintings for exhibitions but is linked to an art print and poster publishing company. Photographs or transparencies preferred. No originals.
Price range £250–£10,000
No of exhibitions annually 4

Gallery One
19 Station Road, London, SW13 0LF
T 020 84872144
E info@galleryone.ws
W www.galleryonelondon.com
Contact Teffany Tooke
Opened in 2001. Committed to sourcing and exhibiting the best of contemporary art. Includes emerging new talent and established names. Stocks and sources an extensive portfolio of original graphics, paintings and sculpture. Also provides a corporate-art consultancy service and a bespoke framing service.
Submission Policy Welcomes submissions from all artists, by email or post in the first instance.
Price range £50–£10,000
No of exhibitions annually 4–8

Gillian Jason Modern & Contemporary Art
Ormond House, 3 Duke of York Street, London SW1Y 6JP
E art@gillianjason.com
W www.gillianjason.com
In the 1980s and early 1990s the gallery in Camden Town was the focus for exhibitions by key artists of the modern British school and 1994 saw the creation of the Jason & Rhodes Gallery. In 1999 Gillian Jason began working as a private dealer, offering a personalized service to collectors and vendors, including sourcing and placing of works of art by British and European artists, consultancy and valuation.

Gimpel Fils
30 Davies Street, London, W1K 4NB
T 0207 4932488
F 0207 6295732
E info@gimpelfils.com
W www.gimpelfils.com
Founded in 1946. Modern and contemporary art, project space for installations and video. Represents Alan Davie, Pamela Golden, Albert Irvin, Peter Kennard, Antoni Malinowski and the estate of Peter Lanyon.
No of exhibitions annually 8

Greengrassi
1a Kempsford Road, London, SE11 4NU
T 020 78409101
F 020 78409102
E info@greengrassi.com
W www.greengrassi.com
Has recently moved from central London to Kennington, south of the river. The stable of international artists includes Aleksandra Mir, Pae White, Lari Pittman and Margherita Manzelli.

Grosvenor Gallery (Fine Arts) Ltd
21 Ryder Street, London, SW1Y 6PX
T 020 7484 7979
F 020 7484 7980
E art@grosvenorgallery.com
W www.grosvenorgallery.com
Specializes in twentieth-century European and British paintings and sculpture, and modern Indian painting (working in collaboration with the long-established Vadehra Gallery, based in Delhi). Limited to the representation of two contemporary artists, Mark Shields and Victor Newsome.
Submission Policy Currently not looking to take on any more living artists.
No of exhibitions annually 7

Hackelbury Fine Art

4 Launceston Place, London, W8 5RL
T 020 79378688
F 020 79378868
E katestevens@hackelbury.co.uk
W www.hackelbury.co.uk
Opened in 1998, showing twentieth- and twenty-first-century photography by stable of emerging and established artists. Exhibits each year at the AIPAD Photography Show in New York and at Photo-London.

Hales Gallery

7 Bethnal Green Road, London, E1 6LA
T 020 70331938
F 020 70331939
E info@halesgallery.com
W www.halesgallery.com
Founded in 1991 in Deptford, Hales moved to the East End in 2004. The gallery represents artists from the UK and abroad working in a variety of media. Represented artists include Tomoko Takahashi, Spencer Tunick, Hew Locke, Adam Dant, Richard Galpin, and Bob and Roberta Smith.
Submission Policy Artists' submissions not encouraged.
No of exhibitions annually 8

Hamiltons

13 Carlos Place, London, W1Y 2EU
T 020 74999493
F 020 7629 9919
E art@hamiltonsgallery.com
W www.hamiltonsgallery.com
A major European gallery for nearly twenty years, dealing in late-twentieth century and contemporary photographs. Also shows modern and contemporary paintings.

Hanina Fine Arts

180 Westbourne Grove, London
W11 2RH
T 020 72438877
F 020 72430132
E contact@haninafinearts.com
W www.haninafinearts.com
Specialists in twentieth-century European art, particularly the post-war School of Paris.
Submission Policy Contact from artists or their representatives with relevance to European art from 1900 to 1980 welcome. The gallery does not deal in works on paper or in prints.
Price range £5,000–£250,000
No of exhibitions annually 4

Harlequin Gallery

68 Greenwich High Road, London
SE10 8LF
T 020 86927170
E jr@studio-pots.com
W www.studio-pots.com
Specializes in contemporary exhibitions of work by leading British studio potters including Phil Rogers, Alan Wallwork and Aki Moriuchi, together with older work by Bernard Leach and associates. Paintings and sculpture by artists such as Denis Bowen are often shown in conjunction with the above.
Submission Policy Studio potters and artists may apply but telephone or email first.
Price range £25–£5,000
No of exhibitions annually 8

Haunch of Venison

6 Haunch of Venison Yard, off Brook Street, London, W1K 5ES
T 020 74955050
F 020 74954050
E info@haunchofvenison.com
W www.haunchofvenison.com
Contact Stephanie Camu, Jade Awdry or Ben Tufnell
Founded in 2002. Artists include Thomas Joshua Cooper, Bill Viola, Richard Long, Keith Tyson, Mark Alexander, Jorge Pardo, Anton Henning and James Rosenquist.
Submission Policy No unsolicited submissions.
Price range £5,000–£1,000,000
No of exhibitions annually 9

Hauser & Wirth

196A Piccadilly, London, W1J 9DY
T 020 72872300
F 020 72876600
E london@hauserwirth.com
W www.hauserwirth.com
Opened in 2003 just across the road from the Royal Academy of Arts in a historic building designed by Sir Edwin Lutyens in the 1920s. Swiss gallerist-collectors Ursula Hauser and Iwan Wirth, who represent important European and American artists, also have branches of their gallery in Zurich and a joint venture in New York.

Hazlitt Holland-Hibbert

38 Bury Street, St James's, London, SW1Y 6BB
T 020 78397600
F 020 78397255
E info@hh-h.com

W www.hh-h.com

Holds a selected stock of twentieth-century art works with particular emphasis on modern British painting, drawing and sculpture. Also able to offer discreet advice on the purchase and sale of modern paintings and sculpture and the acquisition of new works either for stock or for sale on a consignment basis.

No of exhibitions annually 1–2

Henry Boxer Gallery

98 Stuart Court, Richmond Hill, Richmond
TW10 6RJ

T 020 89481633

F 020 89481633

E henryboxer@aol.com

W www.henryboxergallery.com

Founded in 1980, specializing in Modern British, Visionary and Outsider art. Artists represented include Joe Coleman, Donald Pass, Laurie Lipton, Dora Holzhandler, Scottie Wilson, Madge Gill, George Widener and Austin Spare. Henry Boxer is a director of Raw Vision magazine and curates exhibitions of outsider art both in the UK and the USA.

Submission Policy Submissions welcome, from self-taught, visionary and outsider artists. Send sae and photographs or email images of work to be considered.

Price range £500–£10,000

No of exhibitions annually 4

Herald Street

2 Herald Street, London, E2 6JT

T 020 71682566

E mail@heraldst.com

W www.heraldst.com

Contemporary art gallery which has shown artists including Markus Amm, Alexandra Bircken, Pablo Bronstein, Spartacus Chetwynd, Christina Mackie, Djordje Ozbolt, Oliver Payne & Nick Relph, Klaus Weber and Nicole Wermers.

Hicks Gallery

2–4 Leopold Road, Wimbledon, SW19 7BD

T 020 89447171

E galleryhicks@aol.com

W www.hicksgallery.co.uk

Contact Jeff or Ann Hicks

Founded in 1988. Handles the work of mainly contemporary artists with an emphasis on drawing skills. Exhibits both established and up-and-coming artists. Exhibited artists include Andrea Byrne, Lawrie Williamson RBSA, Phillip James

ROI, Terry Whybrow, Linda Meaney and Jeffrey Pratt.

Submission Policy Submissions welcome either by email or, if possible, CD. Can also be contacted by telephone, but would prefer if appointments are made before making submissions.

Price range £250–£15,000

No of exhibitions annually 6

Highgate Fine Art

26 Highgate High Street, Highgate Village
London, N6 5JG

T 020 83477010 / 83407564

F 020 83407564

E sales@oddyart.com

W www.oddyart.com

Contact Laurie MacLaren

The Phoenix Gallery Highgate opened in 1988 and relaunched in 1997 as Highgate Fine Art. Over fifty twentieth-century artists represented including Frederick Gore CBE RA, Paul Demaria, Alan Hepburn, Douglas Wilson RCA, Richard Robbins RBA and Arthur Easton ROI. Runs one of the most visited gallery websites in Europe.

Submission Policy Applications reviewed by committee weekly.

Price range £150–£25,000

No of exhibitions annually 15; new shows open every three weeks.

Hiscox Art Café

Ground Floor, Hiscox Building, 1 Great St Helen's,
London, EC3A 6HX

W www.hiscox.com/artprojects.

The Café is a modern art gallery and home to Hiscox Art Projects, established in 2003. The scheme aims to bring contemporary art into the heart of the City and to support and represent talented contemporary artists by providing an exhibition space.

Hofer Printroom

43 Museum Street, London, WC1A 1LY

T 020 79301904

E info@hofer-photo.com

W www.hofer-photo.com

Stocks over 2,000 hand-finished original photographic prints and 500 limited edition prints.

Honor Oak Gallery Ltd

52 Honor Oak Park, Forest Hill, London, SE23 1DY

T 020 82916094

Founded in 1986, the gallery specializes in original

works of art on paper dating from the early twentieth-century to the present day. Artists shown include Norman Ackroyd, June Berry, Elizabeth Blackadder, Margarete Berger-Hamerschlag, Sanchia Lewis and Karolina Larusdottir. A comprehensive framing and conservation service is also offered.

Submission Policy Submissions welcome, provided they are within the area of specialization outlined above.

Price range From £25

No of exhibitions annually 1 plus 6 'features'.

Hoopers Gallery

15 Clerkenwell Close, London, EC1R 0AA

T 020 74903908

E gallery@hoopersgallery.co.uk

W www.hoopersgallery.co.uk

Opened in 2003 by photographer Roger Hooper to provide a platform for up-and-coming as well as established photographers.

Hotel

53 Old Bethnal Green Road, London, E2 6QA

T 020 77293122

F 020 77394095

E info@generalhotel.org

W www.generalhotel.org

Opened in 2003 in a spare room in the flat of Darren Flook and Christabel Stewart, before moving into a groundfloor shop space in 2005. Has held solo shows by Carol Bove, Alan Michael, Richard Kern, Alasatair MacKinven, David Noonan, Steven Claydon, Carter and Michael Bauer. Artists not located in London are invited to stay at Hotel during the production period of their project.

Submission Policy Does not accept submissions.

Price range £250–£25,000

No of exhibitions annually 6

Hothouse Gallery

Hothouse, 274 Richmond Road, London Fields E8 3QW

T 020 72493394

F 020 72498499

E contact@freeform.org.uk

W www.freeform.org.uk

An artist-led gallery and workspace for visual and new media artists, urban designers and architects working in the public realm. Opened in 2003, a flexible white space 184m2 (1,982 sq. ft) with mobile screens. Has all-round CAT 5 cabling for installations, digital and ICT media presentations,

and external digital art space. Past exhibitions include RIBA London, Ash Sakula Architects, Maggie Ellenby and Hot House Open: Applied Arts. Hosts talks, seminars and events.

Submission Policy Welcomes exhibition proposals from established and emerging visual artists, new-media artists, urban designers and architects working in the public realm.

No of exhibitions annually 3, in visual arts, photography, and architecture and urban design.

Houldsworth

50 Pall Mall Deposit, 124–128 Barlby Road, London, W10 6BL

T 020 89696166

F 020 89696209

E gallery@houldsworth.co.uk

W www.houldsworth.co.uk

Contact Ben Cranfield

Project space promoting and selling the work of contemporary artists of international importance. Focuses on solo exhibitions and external projects for its artists, whilst hosting artist curated projects and open debates to provide work with a critical and collaborative context. Recent projects include Gordon Cheung, British Art Show (2006), Laura Ford Venice Biennale (2005), Jonathan Callan Mattress Factory, Pittsburgh (2005) and Royal Art Lodge, Yerba Buena Center for the Arts, San Francisco (2006).

Submission Policy Submit a small email presentation or, ideally, a website link. Other documentation submitted cannot be returned or retained. Only successful applicants are contacted.

Price range £350–£65,000

No of exhibitions annually 6

House Gallery

70 Camberwell Church Street, London, SE5 8QZ

T 020 73584475

E info@housegallery.org

W www.housegallery.org

Contact Phil Stokes

Neighbouring Camberwell College of Arts and the South London Gallery provide a varied and professional audience. The gallery has large front windows and is an airy space with high ceilings. Exhibitions tend to be experimental in nature, from installation to performance and video work. Aims to create an independent platform for artists to respond to contemporary stimuli in a professional environment.

Submission Policy Exhibition proposals are accepted. Include a CV, short artist's statement,

images and a written proposal for the exhibition. These can be sent or emailed. Group shows are also accepted.
No of exhibitions annually 20

IBID Projects
21 Vyner St, London, E2 9DG
T 020 89834355
F 020 89834605
E info@ibidprojects.com
W www.ibidprojects.com
Contact Vita Zaman
Founded in 2003, with a programme focused on a series of solo shows by emerging British and Baltic artists as well as curated shows, off-site mobile projects and publications. Artists include Anthea Hamilton, Christopher Orr, Janis Avotins, Guillermo Caivano, William Hunt, Ross Chisholm, Anj Smith and Nedko Solakov.
Submission Policy Submissions not encouraged.
Price range £1,000–£100,000
No of exhibitions annually 10

Ieda Basualdo
8–9 Grosvenor Place, Belgravia, London SW1X 7SH
T 020 72359522
F 020 72359577
E ieda@bottaccio.co.uk
W www.bottaccio.co.uk
Particularly suitable for large exhibitions, the Grand Gallery (300m2) has hosted exhibitions for, among others, Arturo Martini, Igor Mitoraj, Giorgio Morandi, Gio Pomodoro, Marino Marini and Damien Hirst. Exhibitions last a minimum of two weeks and a maximum of four weeks.
Price range £80–£50,000
No of exhibitions annually 12

Illustration Cupboard
22 Bury Street, St. James's, London, SW1Y 6AL
T 020 79761727
E john@illustrationcupboard.com
W www.illustrationcupboard.com
Established in 1995, exhibiting for purchase original artwork by leading contemporary book illustrators. Continuous schedule of events including a winter exhibition, as well as single artist and two-man shows. Entrance to all events is free.

Ingo Fincke Gallery and Framers
24 Battersea Rise, London, SW11 1EE
T 020 72287966
F 020 76527966
E kira@ingofincke.com
W www.ingofincke.com
Contact Kira Fincke
Founded in 1958, the gallery specializes in contemporary paintings on canvas. Exhibits both new and established artists and also offers a framing service.

James Hyman Fine Art
6 Mason's Yard, Duke Street St James's, London SW1Y 6BU
T 020 78393906
F 020 78393907
E mail@jameshymanfineart.com
W www.jameshymanfineart.com
Specialists in twentieth-century British art. Represented artists include Lewis Chamberlain, Peter de Francia, Derrick Greaves and Arnold van Praag, and Estates include Michael Andrews, Robert Medley, Edward Middleditch and William Townsend.
No of exhibitions annually 6

Jerwood Space
171 Union Street, London, SE1 0LN
T 020 76540171
F 020 76540172
E space@jerwoodspace.co.uk
W www.jerwoodspace.co.uk
Contact Sarah Williams
A major initiative of the Jerwood Foundation. As well as providing rehearsal facilities for dance and theatre companies, the refurbished Victorian building houses a contemporary-art gallery. Free to visitors it offers a year-round programme of work by young artists and photographers as part of the Jerwood Visual Arts awards and prizes supported by the Jerwood Charitable Foundation. Emerging artists are shown in the café space and courtyard.
Submission Policy Visit www.jerwoodvisualarts.org for information on applying for Jerwood prizes.
No of exhibitions annually 8

Jill George Gallery
38 Lexington Street, London, W1F 0LL
T 020 74397319
F 020 72870478
E jill@jillgeorgegallery.co.uk
W www.jillgeorgegallery.co.uk
Established in 1974. Deals in paintings, drawings, small sculpture, monoprints and edition prints by contemporary British artists, from established

names to recent graduates. Participates in British and international art fairs. Member of SLAD. Organizes commissions and undertakes all ancilliary services. Artists include Martyn Brewster, Jill Frost, Alison Lambert, David Mach, Christina Niederberger, Chris Orr, Gro Thorsen and Tomas Watson.
Submission Policy Media as above. Prefers to see photographs initially.
Price range £200–£40,000
No of exhibitions annually 10

John Martin Gallery
38 Albemarle Street, London, W1S 4JG
T 020 74991314
F 020 74932842
E info@jmlondon.com
W www.jmlondon.com
Contact Tara Whelan
Two galleries in London showing the work of contemporary British and Irish artists. Opened in the West End in 1992 and exhibits at major British and American art fairs.
Submission Policy Exhibits both representational and abstract painting and sculpture and artists are always welcome to submit a selection of photographs. Send sae, brief statement and biography (no books or valuable items should be sent). No responsibility is taken for lost items.
Price range £200–£50,000
No of exhibitions annually 20

Kate MacGarry
7a Vyner Street, London, E2 9DG
T 020 8981 9100
E mail@katemacgarry.com
W www.katemacgarry.com
Contact Fabio Altamura
Opened in 2002, hosting mainly solo shows with one or two group shows per year. Artists exhibited include Tasha Amini, Matt Bryans, Josh Blackwell, Stuart Cumberland, Luke Gottelier, Dr Lakra, Goshka Macuga, Peter McDonald, Stefan Saffer, Francis Upritchard, Iain Forsyth and Jane Pollard.
No of exhibitions annually 6

Keith Talent Gallery
2–4 Tudor Road, London, E9 7SN
T 020 89862181
F 020 85332060
E keithtalent@tiscali.co.uk
W www.keithtalent.com
Established in 2001 in an industrial space in London Fields by two graduates of the Royal

Academy Schools. Shows emerging artists, collaborating and forming links with a number of artist-run project spaces and established commercial galleries both in Britain and abroad.

Kings Road Galleries
436 Kings Road, Chelsea, London, SW10 0LJ
T 020 73511367
F 020 73517007
E admin@kingsroadgallery.com
W www.kingsroadartgallery.com
Contact Tanya Baxter and Nadya Al-khusaibi
Represents contemporary painters and sculptors (predominantly figurative but some strong abstract artists such as Richard Allen), who tend to be established on the international art-fair circuit and museum front. Also has a corporate-art consultancy division. Gallery owner Tanya Baxter's ties to Hong Kong ensure a strong reciprocal exhibition programme with galleries in Hong Kong, Singapore and Shanghai. Baxter opened the Ryder Street Gallery in St James's in 2004, showcasing the same artists and acting as a host to touring international exhibitions.
Submission Policy Represents artists whose 'fervour for painting and sculpting is markedly different from the current trends, which favour shock art and conceptual works'.
Price range £350–£65,000
No of exhibitions annually 10
Cost to hire or rent The Ryder Street Gallery, St James starts from £3,500 per week.

Laura Bartlett Gallery
22 Leathermarket Street, London, SE1 3HN
T 020 74033714
F 020 74033715
E mail@laurabartlettgallery.com
W www.laurabartlettgallery.com
Contemporary art gallery. Artists include Sachiko Abe, Anna Boggon, Harrell Fletcher, Adam Humphries, Elizabeth McAlpine, Dwayne Moser, Raul Ortega Ayala, Martin Skauen and Michael Whittle.

Lena Boyle Fine Art
1 Earls Court Gardens, London, SW5 0TD
T 020 72592700
F 020 73707460
E lena.boyle@btinternet.com
W www.lenaboyle.com
A small business established in 1989 and run from a private house, with a policy of showing established artists alongside relative unknowns.

Attends several of the major London Art Fairs and also hosts 2–3 exhibitions a year.
Submission Policy Does not have scope to take on many new artists each year. Tends to specialize in contemporary figurative works with an abstract element.
Price range £200–£15,000
No of exhibitions annually 2–3

Lennox Gallery
77 Moore Park Road, London, SW6 2HH
T 01488 681379
F 01488 681379
E sally@poltimore.fsbusiness.co.uk
W www.lennoxgallery.co.uk
Founded in 1998, specializing in Scottish contemporary art. Artists include Pat Semple RSW, Leonie Gibbs, Elizabeth Cameron, Jim Neville, Allan MacDonald and Kate Slaven. Painting courses available and lectures held on past and present-day artists. Space also available for artists to put on their own exhibitions.
Submission Policy Preferably living artists working in Scotland, using a strong sense of colour.
Price range £300–£5,000
No of exhibitions annually 4

Lesley Craze Gallery
33–35a Clerkenwell Green, London, EC1R 0DU
T 020 76080393 (jewellery) or 020 7251 9200 (textiles)
E textiles@lesleycrazegallery.co.uk
W www.lesleycrazegallery.co.uk
Showcase for contemporary jewellery, metalwork and textiles, including work from a hundred artists from around the world. Varied programme shows emerging and established names across a range of techniques and materials.

Limited Edition Graphics
2 Winchester Road, London, N6 5HW
T 020 83481354
F 020 83481357
Contact Allan Wolman
Specializes in nineteenth- and twentieth-century and contemporary works.

Lisson Gallery
52–54 Bell Street, London, NW1 5DA
T 020 772 427 39
F 020 772 471 24
E contact@lisson.co.uk
W www.lisson.co.uk

Opened in 1967 by Nicholas Logsdail and later moved into current premises (designed by Tony Fretton) near Baker Street, Marylebone, in London. Now one of the world's leading galleries for contemporary art. A new gallery at 29 Bell Street opened in 2002
No of exhibitions annually Approximately 10 at each space.

Llewellyn Alexander (Fine Paintings) Ltd
124–126 The Cut, London, SE1 8LN
T 020 76201322 / 76201324
F 020 7928 9469
E gallery@llewellynalexander.com
W www.llewellynalexander.com
Contact Diana Holdsworth
Founded in 1987, specializing in figurative paintings, oils, watercolours and pastels by British artists. Other subjects include the architecture and landscapes of Italy, France and London, still lifes and animals. Among the leading galleries in Europe for contemporary miniatures.
Submission Policy Interested in figurative paintings in oils and watercolours. Submissions from living British artists welcome. Send photographs or CD with images (plus sae for return of items within the UK). Replies by post to UK only. Do not email images.
Price range £150–£6,000
No of exhibitions annually 9

London Picture Centre
723 Fulham Road, London, SW6 5HA
F 020 77367283
E info@thelondonpicturecentre.co.uk
W www.thelondonpicturecentre.co.uk
Contact Albert Williams
Established for over thirty years, with six sites.
Branches 709 Fulham Road SW6; 18 Crawford Street W1 T: 020 74872895; 75 Leather Lane, EC1 T: 020 74044110; 152 and 287 Hackney Road, E2 T: 020 74044110
Price range 020 77314883

Long & Ryle
4 John Islip Street, London, SW1P 4PX
T 020 78341434
E longandryle@btconnect.com
W www.longandryle.com
Contact Tom Juneau
Established over fifteen years ago to promote the work of emerging talents and mid-career artists in the same space. Has a bias towards bold and painterly work. Artists include Brian Sayers, John

Monks, Simon Casson, Simon Keenleyside, Balint Bolygo, Ricardo Cinalli, Mark Entwisle and Daisy Richardson.
Submission Policy Mostly painting, with an emphasis on figuration. Looking for a certain 'edge' in an artist.
Price range £500–£50,000
No of exhibitions annually 10

Lounge
28 Shacklewell Lane, London, E8 2EZ
T 020 7249 7606
E monikabobinska@onetel.com
W www.lounge-gallery.com
Lounge has been based in Dalston, east London, since 2004. The gallery has an ongoing programme of solo exhibitions by represented artists, group exhibitions and collaborative projects. Represented artists are Victoria Hall, Adam King, Gavin Maughfling, David McKeran, Jost Muenster, Gaia Persico, Kate Potter, D.J. Roberts and Greg Rook.
Submission Policy Accepts submissions from artists who are familiar with the gallery's work and feel that their work suits its aims and ethos. Artists should contact the gallery before submitting an exhibition proposal.
Price range £200–£10,000
No of exhibitions annually 6

Lucy B. Campbell Fine Art
123 Kensington Church Street, London, W8 7LP
T 020 77272205
F 020 72294252
E lucy@lucybcampbell.com
W www.lucybcampbell.com
Contact Lucy B.Campbell
Founded in 1984. Represents British, European and American artists and sculptors. Work includes both figurative and abstract, contemporary, still life, landscape, botanical and naive genres. Artists exhibited include Anna Pugh, Sophie Coryndon, Bernard McGuigan, Mia Tarney, Christine Pichette, Aly Brown, Norma Miller and Gazala.
Submission Policy Interested in still life, landscape, contemporary paintings and sculpture.
Price range £1,000–£40,000
No of exhibitions annually 2

Lupe
7 Ezra Street, London, E2 7RH
T 020 76135576
F 020 76132287
E info@lupegallery.com

W www.lupegallery.com
Contact Nicky Sims
Launched in 2002. Represents the work of some thirty of the UK's leading contemporary photographers. Artists include David King, Stuart Redler, Tim Flach, Perou, Morgan Silk and George Kavanagh. Other services include fine-art printing and scanning.
Submission Policy Photography with an emphasis on craft and innovation. Initial contact by email preferred.
Price range £150–£2,000
No of exhibitions annually 3

M-Art
88 Bevington Road, London, W10 5TW
T 020 89690800
F 020 89690801
E m-artgallery@btconnect.com
W www.m-art.co.uk
Contact Martin Brock
Opened in 2004, specializing in contemporary paintings, photography and sculpture by young, up-and-coming artists.
Submission Policy Welcomes submissions from artists.
Price range £50–£3,000
No of exhibitions annually 9

Maas Gallery
15a Clifford Street, London, W1S 4JZ
T 020 77342302
F 020 72874836
E mail@maasgallery.com
W www.maasgallery.com
Founded in 1960 by the late Jeremy Maas. Originally a 'revivalist' gallery, specializing in the then unfashionable field of Pre-Raphaelite paintings. Rupert Maas, his son, now owns and runs the gallery. Deals in major Victorian paintings and with myriad lesser-known artists of the period. Also deals in reproductive engravings and has a small stable of living artists.
Price range From £20
No of exhibitions annually 2

Manya Igel Fine Arts
21–22 Peters Court, Porchester Road, London W2 5DR
T 020 72291669 / 72298249
F 020 72296770
E paintings@manyaigelfinearts.com
W www.manyaigelfinearts.com
Gallery meets clients by appointment only.

Specializes in traditional, modern British oils by Royal Academicians, members of the New English Art Club and other well-known artists. Exhibited artists include Diana Armfield, Fred Cuming, Bernard Dunstan, Frederick Gore, Ken Howard, Geoffrey Humphries, Peter Kuhfeld and Susan Ryder.
Submission Policy Generally has long-established relationships with artists and purchases their work outright.
Price range £350–£25,000
No of exhibitions annually 3–5 fine-art fairs, including solo shows in the Channel Islands.

Mark Jason Gallery

First Floor, 1 Bell Street, London
NW1 5BY
T 020 7258 5800
F 020 7258 5801
E art@markjasongallery.com
W www.markjasongallery.com
Contact Mark Jason or Kate Jason
Opened in 2001 and showcases young emerging talent from fresh new graduates to mid-career artists. Shows mainly paintings and photography. Artists are selected from most mainstream art schools including the Royal Academy, the Slade School of Art, Goldsmiths, Chelsea School of Art and others around the UK.
Submission Policy For artist enquiries, send information in disc format to gallery address or jpeg images via email.
Price range £300–£10,000
No of exhibitions annually 8
Cost to hire or rent Call gallery for further details.

Marlborough Fine Art

6 Albemarle Street, London, W1S 4BY
T 020 76295161
E info@marlboroughfineart.com
W www.marlboroughfineart.com
Founded in 1946. One of the world's leading contemporary art dealers. In addition to being a foremost dealer and publisher of fine-art prints, the gallery deals in paintings and sculpture by prominent international artists and has branches in New York, Madrid, Monte Carlo and Santiago.
No of exhibitions annually 6–8

Matt's Gallery

42–44 Copperfield Road, London, E3 4RR
T 020 89831771
F 020 89831435
E info@mattsgallery.org

W www.mattsgallery.org
Contact Rosalind Horne
Founded in 1979. Specializes in solo exhibitions of young and established artists, especially in installation, performance, video, sculpture and painting, and has a publishing programme. Arts Council-funded. Artists represented include Imogen Stidworthy, Willie Doherty, Mike Nelson, Lucy Gunning, Nathaniel Mellors and Hayley Newman.
Submission Policy Seeks to support artists in the generation of new work, providing them with the time and space to experiment and engage audiences in a critical debate. Welcomes submissions from those familiar with the ethos of the gallery.
Price range £1,500–£100,000
No of exhibitions annually 6

Matthew Bown Gallery

First Floor, 11 Savile Row, London
W1S 3PG
T 020 7734 4790
F 020 7734 4791
E mail@matthewbown.com
W www.matthewbown.com
Shows leading contemporary artists including Oleg Kulik, Irina Zatulovskaya, Vitali Komar, Katya Arnold, Ilya Tabenkin, Arnis Balcus, Dmitri Gutov, Eduard Shteinberg, Komar & Melamid, Erik Bulatov and Geli Korzhev. Particualr focus on art from Russia and the former Soviet Union.

Maureen Paley

21 Herald Street, London, E2 6JT
T 020 77294112
F 020 77294113
E info@maureenpaley.com
W www.maureenpaley.com
Contact Susanna Chisholm or Oliver Evans
Since 1999 the gallery has been situated in Bethnal Green in premises of 5,000 sq. ft. Relocated from a Victorian terraced house in London's East End where the gallery programme began in 1984. One of the first galleries to present work in London's East End and a pioneer of the current scene, promoting and showing art from the USA and continental Europe as well as launching new talent from Great Britain. Artists exhibited include Kaye Donacie, Andrew Grassie, Paul Noble, Saskia Olde Wolbers, Seb Patane, David Thorpe, Wolfgang Tillmans, Rebecca Warren and Gillian Wearing.
No of exhibitions annually 8–10

Max Wigram Gallery
99 New Bond Street, London, W1S 1SW
T 020 74954960
E info@maxwigram.com
W www.maxwigram.com
Gallery artists include Cory Arcangel, Michael
Ashcroft, Slater Bradley, Jason Brooks, FOS
(Thomas Poulsen), James Hopkins, Barnaby
Hosking, Pearl C. Hsiung, Marine Hugonnier,
Mustafa Hulusi, Alison Moffett, John Pilson,
Julian Rosefeldt, Nigel Shafran, Joel Tomlin,
Christian Ward, Richard Wathen and James White.

Mayor Gallery
22a Cork Street, London, W1S 3NA
T 020 77343558
F 020 74941377
E mail@mayorgallery.com
W www.artnet.com/mayor.html
Founded by Fred Mayor in 1925; the first gallery to
open in Cork Street. Has exhibited many artists for
the first time in England including Bacon, Ernst
and Miró. James Mayor, Fred's son, took over the
gallery in 1973 and has since shown the work of
many leading American artists including
Lichtenstein, Oldenburg and Warhol. Continues to
show the works of leading American Pop artists
and remains London's foremost gallery for Dada
and Surrealism.
Submission Policy Deals in most fields of the
visual arts but excludes prints. More inclined
towards established artists than new submissions.
No of exhibitions annually 5

Medici Gallery
5 Cork Street, London, W1S 3LQ
T 020 74952565
E info@medicigallery.co.uk
W www.medicigallery.co.uk
Contact Jenny Kerr
Established in Mayfair for the past ninety-eight
years and and now at 5 Cork Street. Known for
contemporary figurative art and exhibiting the
work of leading British craftmakers.
Submission Policy Images should be sent,
preferably by email or via post with sae; include
medium, size, artist's CV, etc.
Price range £1,000–£60,000
No of exhibitions annually 10

Michael Hoppen Gallery
3 Jubilee Place, London, SW3 3TD
T 020 73523649
F 020 73523669

E gallery@michaelhoppengallery.com
W www.michaelhoppengallery.com
Contact Kathlene Caldwell and Lucy Chadwick
(contemporary)
Founded in 1992. Holds various exhibitions across
three floors. Specializing in photographic art, it
has one of the widest selections of nineteenth-,
twentieth- and twenty-first-century works in
Europe. The gallery's remit is to present the
broadest spectrum of photography that is judged
not only on its market value, but also on the quality
and integrity of the artist's particular vision.
Champions new artists as well as maintaining
stock of the recognized masters. Artists
represented include Jacques-Henri Lartigue,
Desiree Dolron, Daido Moriyama, Sarah Moon,
Peter Beard and Bill Brandt.
Submission Policy Works must be original and
photography-based, and the artist must have been
previously exhibited.
Price range £100–£100,000
No of exhibitions annually 6–7

Millinery Works Gallery
85–87 Southgate Road, London, N1 3JS
T 020 7359 2019
F 020 7359 5792
E jeff@millineryworks.co.uk
W www.millineryworks.co.uk
Contact Jeff Jackson
Founded in 1996 to exhibit, promote and sell
contemporary and modern British fine and applied
arts. Exhibited artists include Edward Wolfe RA,
John Bratby RA, Gerald Wilde, Hugh Mackinnon,
Eric Rimmington and Frances Newman. A leading
specialist in the British Arts & Crafts Movement.
Price range £150–£60,000
No of exhibitions annually 9

Modern Art
10 Vyner Street, London, E2 9DG
T 020 89807742
F 020 89807743
E info@modernartinc.com
W www.modernartinc.com
Formerly known as Modern Art Inc., the gallery
moved from Shoreditch to Bethnal Green in 2004.
Represents international and British contemporary
artists such as Juergen Teller, Nigel Cooke, Ricky
Swallow, Tim Noble and Sue Webster.

MOT
Unit 54, Regents Studios, London, E8 4QN
T 020 79239561

F 020 79239561
E info@motinternational.org
W www.motinternational.org
Founded in 2002. Functions as both independent space and curatorial project, exploring the different roles within art production and redefining their terms. Exhibitions have included the work of curators and critics, and have showcased new talent and more established artists, including Kelley, Kippenberger, Graham, McCarthy, Gillick, Creed, Lucas, Wallinger, Jeremy Deller and Matthew Higgs.
Submission Policy Will consider submissions from artists or curators. Up to six images (jpegs at 72dpi) or a website link should be emailed to the gallery. Include full CV and supporting statement.
Price range £500–£25,000

Multiple Store

Central St Martins College of Art & Design, 107–109 Charing Cross Road, London, WC2H 0DU
T 020 75147258
F 020 75148091
E info@themultiplestore.org
W www.themultiplestore.org
Founded in 1998. Commissions limited-edition multiples (mostly three-dimensional) by contemporary British artists, both emerging and established. Does not have a permanent exhibiting space but work can be shown to individual collectors at offices of Central St Martins.

Museum 52

52 Redchurch Street, London, E2 7DP
T 020 73665571
F 020 77396707
E admin@museum52.com
W www.museum52.com
Founded in 2003, showing emerging international talent as well as working with established artists on one-off projects. Artists include Tom Gallant, Pierre Ardouvin, Stephen Vitiello, John Issacs, Nick Waplington, Kate Atkin, Kay Harwood, Lee Maelzer, Frank Selby and Peter Macdonald.
Submission Policy Send two printed full colour images and a brief description of the work.
Price range £1,000–£50,000
No of exhibitions annually 8

Nancy Victor

Basement, 36 Charlotte Street, London
W1T 2NA
T 020 78130373
F 020 87489818

E info@nancyvictor.com
W www.nancyvictor.com
Non-commercial underground space showing new and up-and-coming artists only. No services offered to artists.
Submission Policy Artists sending applications should be proactive and display a quality of work and commitment.
Price range £20–£10,000
No of exhibitions annually 8

New Realms Limited

26 Phipp Street, London, EC2A 4NR
T 02070339721
E contact@newrealms.org.uk
W www.newrealms.org.uk
Contact Jonathan Wiggin
Founded in 2004, specializing in contemporary art from the former Soviet Republics, including paintings, prints, drawings, sculpture, installation, performance and new media. Aims to promote young artists representing the highest standards of contemporary art production in their countries of origin, bringing their work to a wider Western European audience.
Submission Policy Only natives of one of the seventeen states that formerly constituted the Soviet Union. No older than 45 years.
Price range £50–£15,000
No of exhibitions annually 8
Cost to hire or rent £500 per week

Northcote Gallery Chelsea

253 King's Road, Chelsea, London, SW3 5EL
T 020 7351 0830
E info@northcotegallery.com
W www.northcotegallery.com
Contact Ali Pettit or Alexander MacFaul
Founded in 1992 on Northcote Road, Battersea followed by expansion into large exhibition space on two floors on King's Road, Chelsea. Consultants in Los Angeles and Melbourne. Exhibits international contemporary and modern British paintings and sculpture. Painters and photographers represented include Jo Barrett, Martin Burton, Louise Butler Adams, Daisy Cook, Sean Cotter, Molly Garnier, Sarah Hillman, Tom Homewood, Katharine Horgan, James Leggat, Colette Leinman, Ffiona Lewis, Sarah Lewis, Fay Macaulay, Rebecca McLynn, Jonathan McCree, Dan McDermott, Robert McKellar, Melanie Miller, Dawn Reader, Gill Rocca, Dion Salvador Lloyd, Alice Scrutton, Oinuen Sprunt, Ann Penman Sweet, Josep Pla, Alice Von Maltzahn, Stephanie

Rogers, Ger Sweeney, Malcolm Temple and Richard Whadcock. Sculptors represented include Debi O'Hehir, Carol Peace, Benjamin Piggott, Andrew Smith, Anthony Stern and Petrina Stroud. **Submission Policy** Selection by committee. Artists are invited to submit portfolios to the committee, which meets every six weeks. Portfolio's to Selection Committee, Northcote Gallery, 110 Northcote Road, Battersea, London SW11 6QP together with sae if to be returned.
No of exhibitions annually 20 across the 2 gallery sites.

October Gallery
24 Old Gloucester Street, London, WC1N 3AL
T 020 72426367
F 020 74051851
E gallery@octobergallery.co.uk
W www.octobergallery.co.uk
Contact Elisabeth Lalouschek
Founded in 1979. A charitable trust dedicated to the advancement and appreciation of art from all cultures. To this end, the gallery is actively engaged in education and the promotion of intercultural exchange. Exhibits and promotes artists of the 'transvangarde' – the trans-cultural avant-garde. Artists represented include Aubrey Williams, William Burroughs, Brion Gysin, Kenji Yoshida, El Anatsui and Rachid Koraichi.
Submission Policy Submissions from artists from the cross-cultural exchange welcome.
Price range £250–£30,000
No of exhibitions annually 8

Offer Waterman & Co.
11 Langton Street, London, SW10 0JL
T 020 73510068
F 020 73512269
E info@waterman.co.uk
W www.waterman.co.uk
Aims to provide the best of twentieth-century British painting, drawing and sculpture, with an emphasis on the Camden Town Group, Euston Road School, 7 and 5 Society, Unit One, School of London, Neo-Romantics, St Ives Group and Pop. Can source specific European and contemporary work where required. Always looking to acquire important pieces and will buy or consign directly from private collectors. Additional services include insurance and probate valuations, research, conservation, framing and display advice. Represents Diarmuid Kelley and Celia Hegedus.
Price range £2,000–£500,000
No of exhibitions annually 2

Oliver Contemporary
17 Bellevue Road, Wandsworth Common, London, SW17 7EG
T 020 87678822
F 020 87678822
E mail@oliverart.co.uk
W www.oliverart.co.uk
Founded in 2001. Brings together new and established contemporary artists working within the modern British tradition.
Submission Policy Not looking for any new artists.
Price range £250–£5,000
No of exhibitions annually 6

One in the Other
45 Vyner Street, London, E2 9DQ
T 020 72537882
F 020 72537882
E oneintheother@blueyonder.co.uk
W www.oneintheother.com
Works with mainly young UK and International artists, with an emphasis on young radicalism
Submission Policy Does not invite submissions but encourages artists to stage their own shows and inform the gallery of them.
Price range £1,000–£20,000
No of exhibitions annually 6

Osborne Samuel
23a Bruton Street, London, W1J 6QG
T 020 74937939
F 020 74937798
E info@osbornesamuel.com
W www.osbornesamuel.com
Formed in 2004 as a partnership between Gordon Samuel (Scolar Fine Art) and Peter Osborne (Berkeley Square Gallery). Exhibition schedule includes established painters, printmakers and sculptors. Known worldwide as a dealer in modern and contemporary sculpture, in particular the work of Moore and Chadwick. Substantial inventory of masterprints by major artists of the last century, specializing in graphics by Picasso and Miró, and 1930s linocuts by artists of the Grosvenor School of Modern Art. Contemporary artists represented include Sophie Ryder, Sean Henry and Graciela Sacco.
Submission Policy Represents a number of contemporary artists and is therefore fully committed. Will look at submissions but these will only be returned if an sae is included. Does not invite email submissions.
No of exhibitions annually 10–12

Panter & Hall
9 Shepherd Market, Mayfair, London, W1J 7PF
T 020 73999999
F 020 74994449
E enquiries@panterandhall.com
W www.panterandhall.com
Specialists in contemporary Scottish and modern British paintings.
Submission Policy Only interested in looking at painters with established markets.
Price range £500–£20,000
No of exhibitions annually 12

Paradise Row
13 Hereford Street, London, E2 6EX
T 020 76133311
W www.paradiserow.com
Cutting-edge contemporary gallery. Exhibited artists include Diann Bauer, Jake & Dinos Chapman, Poppy de Villeneuve and Kirk Palmer.

Parasol Unit Foundation for Contemporary Art
14 Wharf Road, London, N1 7RW
T 020 74907373
F 020 74907775
E info@parasol-unit.org
W www.parasol-unit.org
A non-profit initiative established to showcase the work of leading international contemporary artists in various media. An 800 sq. metre space over two floors, it comprises an exhibition space, a reading area and a live/work unit to accommodate the artist-in-residence programme. Mounts four exhibitions each year and conducts a programme of events in conjunction with each exhibition. In order to encourage the widest possible access to its exhibition programme, the foundation does not charge admission fees.
Submission Policy Gallery does not welcome submissions from artists but runs an education and artist-in-residence programme.
No of exhibitions annually 4

Paul Mason Gallery
149 Sloane Street, London, SW1X 9BZ
T 020 77303683
F 020 77307359
E Paulmasonart@aol.com
Founded in 1964. Specializes in eighteenth-century through to contemporary marine, sporting and decorative paintings and prints, ship models, nautical artifacts, portfolio stands and picture easels.
Submission Policy Top-quality marine oil paintings.

Price range From £2,000
No of exhibitions annually 3

Peer
99 Hoxton Street, London, N1 6QL
T 020 77398080
E mail@peeruk.org
W www.peeruk.org
Independent arts organization and registered charity that develops and presents projects in a range of media at the gallery, at other venues and in the public realm. Since 1998 Peer has commissioned and initiated a number of important projects with artists such as Martin Creed, Mike Nelson, Hannah Collins, Siobhan, John Frankland, Juan Cruz and Bob and Roberta Smith. Also produces publications by artists, about artists and about the cultural impact of contemporary art.
Submission Policy Becuase Peer is a very small organization and must raise funds for each project, cannot accept unsolicited applications.

Photofusion
17a Electric Lane, London, SW9 8LA
T 020 77385774
F 020 77385509
E gallery@photofusion.org
W www.photofusion.org
Contact Catherine Williams
Started life in the early 1980s as a photographers' collective and now among London's most comprehensive photography and media centres. Situated in Brixton since 1991. Committed to promoting diversity within the photographic arts, encompassing both chemical and digital media. Presents a broad range of exhibitions, from emerging UK-based photographers to internationally recognized ones. Also runs artists' talks, professional-development workshops, and photography and digital training courses, as well as housing a picture library, studios, darkrooms, digital suites and a membership scheme.
Submission Policy Accepts only photographic or digital-based work. Programming by committee. Send a comprehensive written description, CV and examples (not original prints).
Price range From £300
No of exhibitions annually 8

Piano Nobile Fine Paintings Ltd
129 Portland Road, London, W11 4LW
T 020 72291099
F 020 72291099

E art@piano-nobile.com
W www.piano-nobile.com
Contact Suzy Meek
Founded in 1985, specializing in fine-quality
twentieth-century international, modern British
and post-war paintings, drawings, watercolours
and sculpture for private, corporate and museum
collections. Period work exhibited alongside shows
by leading contemporary painters and sculptors
including Adam Birtwistle, Dora Holzhandler,
Barbara van Hove, Leslie Marr, Kasey Sealy and
Nicolaus Widerberg.
Submission Policy Painting and sculpture in all
media with a preference for figurative work.
Price range £150,000–£250,000
No of exhibitions annually 4–6

Pieroni Studios
1 Dickson House, 3 Grove Road, Richmond
TW10 6SP
T 020 89488066
E lark@pieronistudio.co.uk
Contact Lark Harrison
Represents several painters and sculptors.
Submission Policy Does not want submissions
from other artists at present.
Price range £1,000–£4,000 for paintings;
£3,500–£7,500 for sculpture.
No of exhibitions annually 2 in-house; 6 off-site
(mainly London).

Plus One Gallery
91 Pimlico Road, London, SW1W 8PH
T 020 7730 7656
F 020 7730 7664
E info@plusonegallery.com
W www.plusonegallery.com
Contact Maggie Bollaert or Colin Pettit
Founded in 2001, specializing in an international
contemporary realist and photorealist art
programme. Deals exclusively in paintings and
sculptures. Artists represented include Andrew
Holmes, Barry Oretsky, John Salt, Cesar Santander,
Gus Heinze, Carl Laubin, John Beader and Ben
Johnson.
Submission Policy Living artists represented but
within all aspects of the genre of contemporary
realism.
Price range £300–£100,000
No of exhibitions annually 9–10

Pond Gallery
26 The Pavement, Clapham Old Town
London, SW4 0JA

T 020 76224051
F 020 76224051
E info@pondgalleries.co.uk
W www.pondgalleries.co.uk
Contact Dee-Michael Hutchings
Founded in 2002, dealing in contemporary
paintings, ceramics and sculpture. Represented
artists include Rochelle Andrews, Samantha
Barnes, Henrie Haldane, Ilia Petrovic, Jess
Pearson and Jason Lilley.
Submission Policy Submissions should be made
by sending CD of images or photographs by post
with sae.
Price range £500–£5,000
No of exhibitions annually 6–8, plus a summer
garden party in the sculpture garden.

Proud Galleries
5 Buckingham Street, Off the Strand, London
WC2N 6BP
T 0207 8394942
F 0207 8394947
E info@proud.co.uk
W www.proud.co.uk
Contact Astrid Merget
Photographic galleries with over 150,000 visitors a
year. Set up over 10 years ago, operates on two
sites, the one in Camden being the largest photo
gallery in the UK. Has put on over 100 major
exhibitions attended by over 1 million people,
including museum quality blockbusters like
Underexposed (a history of censorship), Vietnam
Requiem (Pulitzer prize-winning account of the
war from both sides) to exhibitions like Football
Days and Bob Dylan.
Submission Policy Applications on disk or email to
astrid@proud.co.uk. Images, biography and some
background information helpful.
Price range £50–£10,000
No of exhibitions annually 15–20
Cost to hire or rent £5,500 full day hire. For
exhibitions, £15,000 for first week and £10,000
each additional week.

Purdy Hicks Gallery
65 Hopton Street, Bankside, London, SE1 9GZ
T 020 74019229
F 020 74019595
E contact@purdyhicks.com
W www.purdyhicks.com
Represents a number of pre-eminent British and
foreign artists including Hughie O'Donoghue,
Ralph Fleck and Alice Maher. Founded in 1993,
specializing in painting and photography and also

regularly publishes prints by gallery artists.
Price range From £300 for prints; from £1,000 for paintings and photographs.
No of exhibitions annually Approx. 10

Quantum Contemporary Art
The Old Imperial Laundry, 71–73 Warriner Gardens, London, SW11 4XW
T 020 74986868
F 020 74987878
E quantum.art@virgin.net
W www.quantumart.co.uk
Contact Johnny Gorman
Founded in 1996 in a design hub called the Old Imperial Laundry in Battersea. Represents about forty artists, mainly painters whose style is representational. Participates in art fairs in the UK and USA.
Submission Policy Artists' submissions welcome, but conceptual, abstract, sculpture, photography, digital and performance art are not exhibited.
Price range £250–£10,000
No of exhibitions annually Approx. 10

Rachmaninoff's
Unit 106, Kings Wharf, 301 Kingsland Road, London, E8 4DS
T 020 72750757
E info@rachmaninoffs.com
W www.rachmaninoffs.com
Contemporary gallery. Also has a programme of publications.

Rafael Valls Ltd
6 Ryder Street, St James's, London, SW1Y 6QB
T 020 79300029
F 020 79762589
E lizzie@rafaelvalls.co.uk
W www.rafaelvalls.co.uk
Contact Caroline Valls or Lizzie Aubrey-Fletcher
Over thirty years of experience, specializing in Old Masters. Also holds a number of contemporary exhibitions each year.
Submission Policy Artists wishing to be given an exhibition should email images or send a link to a website.
Price range £500–£25,000
No of exhibitions annually 4

Rebecca Hossack Gallery
35 Windmill Street, Fitzrovia, London, W1T 2JS
T 020 74364899
F 020 73233182
E rebecca@r-h-g.co.uk
W www.r-h-g.co.uk
Contact Maria Morrow
Opened in central London by Rebecca Hossack in 1988. Programme combines non-Western art with work in the Western tradition.
Submission Policy Artists wishing to apply to the gallery should send a copy of their CV along with images of recent works (jpegs if sent via email or slides with an sae if sent via post).
Price range £50–£50,000
No of exhibitions annually 24 (12 in each gallery).

The Red Mansion Foundation
46 Portland Place, London, W1B 1NF
T 020 73233700
F 0207 323 0788
E info@redmansion.co.uk
W www.redmansion.co.uk
Contact Isabelle Chalard
A not-for-profit organization that promotes artistic exchange between China and Great Britain. Its vision is to encourage mutual cultural understanding through contemporary art. Expert staff in both China and the UK provide advice to corporate and private clients on contemporary Chinese art. Has excellent relationships with artists and galleries; represents a cross-section of significant Chinese artists and exhibits their works in Britain. All proceeds from sales and consultancy services support the foundation's programmes. Works with Zhao Bandi, Cang Xin, Shi Jing, Zhan Wang, Liu Jianhua and Weng Fen among others.
Submission Policy Represents and welcomes submissions from contemporary Chinese artists.
Price range £500–£300,000
No of exhibitions annually 6

Redfern Gallery
20 Cork Street, London
W1S 3HL
T 020 77341732
F 020 74942908
E art@redfern-gallery.com
W www.redfern-gallery.com
Founded in 1923. One of London's oldest commercial galleries, dealing mainly in modern and contemporary British and European art. Artists represented include Paul Feiler, Eileen Agar, Patrick Procktor, David Tindle, Paul Jenkins and Linda Karshan.
Submission Policy No unsolicited submissions.
Price range £500–£500,000
No of exhibitions annually 11

The Residence
Verger's Cottage, St. Mary of Eton Church
London, E9 5JA
T 020 8986 2324
F 020 8986 2324
E info@residence-gallery.com
W www.residence-gallery.com
Contact Ingrid Z
Exhibits contemporary art in a gallery 'work'
produced by artist Ingrid Z. Formerly situated in a
shop front, the gallery opened in 2007 in a church
cottage residence. Home to experimental
programming and new arrivals from local and
international artists working in a range of media.
Presents an ever-evolving social environment and
situation for artists and audience. The gallery is a
live structure to be experienced as a whole or in its
individual pieces. In addition, the gallery boutique
sells artist multiples, limited edition publications
and curiosities.
Submission Policy See website.
Price range £1–£10 000
No of exhibitions annually 12 (plus undetermined
amount of spontaneous events)

Richard Green
147 New Bond Street, London, W1S 2TS
T 020 74933939
F 020 76292609
W www.richard-green.com
Dealing in paintings for over forty years. Has three
galleries in London's West End, specializing
mainly in Old Master, Impressionist, marine and
sporting paintings, as well as twentieth-century
British art, with artists such as Sir Terry Frost RA
and Ken Howard RA.

Riflemaker
79 Beak Street, London, W1F 9SU
T 020 74390000
E info@riflemaker.org
W www.riflemaker.org
Contact Charlotte Bonham-Carter
Independent contemporary art gallery in a
boutique-sized former riflemaker's workshop in
Soho. Presents visually potent, conceptually
rigorous exhibitions by both new and established
British and international artists. Artist's
represented include Florian Balze, Christopher
Bucklow, William S. Burroughs, Cherrymead, Juan
Fontanive, Chosil Kil, Jaime Gili, Sam Kaprielov,
Francesca Lowe, John Maeda, Marta Marce, Kaori
Nakayama, Anja Niemi and Julie Verhoeven
Submission Policy The gallery accepts

submissions via email only.
Price range £1,000–£100,000
No of exhibitions annually 8

Ritter/Zamet
2 Bear Gardens, London, SE1 9ED
T 020 72619510
F 020 72619516
E info@ritterzamet.com
W www.ritterzamet.com
Founded in 2003, aims to present a cohesive
programme of emerging European and American
contemporary artists. Artists represented include
Simon Bedwell (UK), Krysten Cunningham
(USA), Nogah Engler (Israel), Paule Hammer
(Germany), Kate Hawkins (UK), Nate Lowman
(USA), Moriceau and Mrzyk (France), Danica
Phelps (USA), and Peter Stauss (Germany).
Submission Policy Does not normally work on an
artist-submission basis.
Price range £500–£30,000
No of exhibitions annually 5

Rivington Gallery
69 Rivington Street, London, EC2A 3AY
T 020 77397835
F 020 77397855
E rivingtongallery@aol.com
Founded in 1997. Shows painting, sculpture,
drawing, photography and crafts. Represented
artists include Tom Kemp, Michael Green,
Nichollas Hamper, Neave Brown and Julie Oakes.
Submission Policy Has a complete roster of artists
but will look at work by appointment.
Price range £200–£10,000
No of exhibitions annually 10–12

Robert Sandelson
5 Cork Street, London, W1S 3NY
T 020 74391001
F 020 74392299
E info@robertsandelson.com
Opened in Cork Street in 1999 and specializes in
modern and contemporary British and
international art. The gallery also presents
changing exhibitions of sculptures in the grounds
and premises of Narborough Hall in Norfolk.

Rocket
Tea Building, 56 Shoreditch High Street
London, E1 6JJ
T 020 77297594
F 020 77290079
E js.rocket@btinternet.com

W www.rocketgallery.com
Founded in 1995. Contemporary art with an emphasis on minimalism and photography. Artists include Martin Parr, Michelle Grabner, Charles Christopher Hill, Lars Wolter, David James Smith, Keld Helmer-Petersen and Paul Shambroom. Alongside the contemporary programme, Rocket also exhibits abstract artists from the 1960s and exclusively represents the Estate of Jeremy Moon.
Price range £100–£30,000
No of exhibitions annually 5

Rokeby

37 Store Street, London, WC1E 7QF
T 020 71689942
E rokeby@rokebygallery.com
W www.rokebygallery.com
Founded in 2005, an independent commercial gallery for contemporary art. Exhibits work by emerging and established artists from the UK and beyond, in a wide range of media. Presents solo shows or curated exhibitions focusing on no more than two artists. Gallery artists include Kathrine Ærtebjerg, Sam Dargan, Craig Fisher, Graham Hudson, Simon Keenleyside, Raul Ortega Ayala, Claire Pestaille and Michael Samuels.
Submission Policy Submissions by email only, with ten low-resolution jpegs, a statement and biography. Replies to email not guaranteed.
Price range £10–£20,000
No of exhibitions annually 8

Rona Gallery

1–2 Weighhouse Street, London, W1K 5LR
T 020 74913718
F 020 74914171
E info@ronagallery.com
W www.ronagallery.com
Contact Stanley Harries
Founded in 1980. Shows figurative art mostly by living artists. Particular focus on painting by 'one-off individualists'. Artists include Richard Adams, Alfred Daniels RBA, Nicola Slattery, Christopher Hall RBA, Martin Leman and Michael Kidd.
Submission Policy Paintings in oil or acrylic (figurative only). Phone or email first.
Price range £2,000–£10,000
No of exhibitions annually 8–9

Rowley Gallery Contemporary Arts

115 Kensington Church Street, London, W8 7LN
T 020 72295561
F 020 72295561
E art@rowleygallery.com
W www.rowleygallery.com
Contact David Kitchin
Exhibits a continuous mixed exhibition, with an average of fifteen to twenty artists at any one time.
Submission Policy Submissions always welcome from artists.
Price range £125–£4,500
No of exhibitions annually 2

Royal Exchange Art Gallery

7 Bury Street, St James's, London, SW1Y 6AL
T 020 78394477
F 020 78398085
E enquiries@marinepictures.com
W www.marinepictures.com
Contact Adrian Thomas
Founded in 1974. Specializes in fine marine oils, watercolours and etchings from the eighteenth century to the present day. Leading contemporary marine artists represented include Steven Dews, Martyn Mackrill and Paul Freeman. Other earlier artists include A. Briscoe, T. Buttersworth, N.M. Condy, G. Chambers, T. Luny, E. Seago, N. Wilkinson and W.L. Wyllie.
Submission Policy Always looking for fine-quality marine pictures. Send photographs and size details via email first.
Price range £650–£140,000
No of exhibitions annually 2 major shows, but a regular change of stock.

Sadie Coles HQ

35 Heddon Street, London, W1B 4BP
T 020 74342227
F 020 74342228
E sadie@sadiecoles.com
W www.sadiecoles.com
Established in 1997. Represents around thirty British and international artists working across all media. Artists include Sarah Lucas, John Currin, Wilhelm Sasnal, Urs Fischer, Elizabeth Peyton and Richard Prince.
Price range £500–£1,000,000
No of exhibitions annually Approx. 10

Sartorial Contemporary Art

101a Kensington Church Street, London W8 7LN
T 020 77925882
F 020 77925820
E art@sartorialart.com
W www.sartorialart.com
Founded in 2002 in an eighteenth-century

Georgian house in Notting Hill, London. A project-led space set up by artist/curator Gretta Sarfaty Marchant. The aim of the gallery is to present work by both emerging and established artists/curators and to promote the exchange of current ideas and practices. Artists include James Jessop, Harry Pye, Gavin Nolan, Jasper Joffe, Chris Davies and Tim Parr.
Submission Policy No submissions.
Price range £200–£10,000
No of exhibitions annually 10

Scout
1–3 Mundy Street, off Hoxton Square, London N1 6QT
T 020 77490909
F 020 77396691
E mail@scoutgallery.com
W www.scoutgallery.com
Contact Simon Pearce
Founded in 2002 as an east London gallery dedicated to international contemporary photography and associated film or video work. Artists shown so far include Ben Watts, cinematographer Christopher Doyle, Steven Klein, Royal College of Art graduate Marc Wayland, Kyoichi Tsuzuki and Magnum photographer Susan Meiselas.
Submission Policy Accepts photography proposals by email with a brief written statement accompanied by low-resolution jpegs or a website referral.
Price range £300–£10,000
No of exhibitions annually 6–7

Sesame Gallery
354 Upper Street, Islington, London, N1 0PD
T 020 72263300
E info@sesameart.com
W www.sesameart.com
Dedicated to exhibiting the work of emerging artists in the UK. Specializes mainly in painting.
Submission Policy Send CV, 6–8 images of work plus a brief statement giving insight into artist's approach.
Price range £500–£10,000
No of exhibitions annually 6–8

Seven Seven Contemporary Art
77 Broadway Market, London Fields, London E8 4PH
T 07808 166215
E info@sevenseven.org.uk
W www.sevenseven.org.uk

Founded in 2002, the gallery has evolved from a not-for-profit, artist-led organization. Works closely with international partners and affiliated artists. The gallery keeps some slots available for very high quality applications from organizations, curators and artists and continues to participate in a wide range of projects, both locally and internationally.
Submission Policy Artists and curators should refer to website for application information and to see examples of recent shows.
Price range £200–£7,000
No of exhibitions annually 10

Sheen Gallery
245 Upper Richmond Road West, London SW14 8QS
T 0208 3921662
F 0208 8760422
E info@thesheengallery.com
W www.thesheengallery.co.uk
Specializes in modern British and leading contemporary artists. Prominent contemporary artists represented include Diana Armfield, Sonia Lawson, Mick Rooney, Charles Williams, Susan Ryder and Arthur Neal.
Submission Policy Paintings and drawings.
Price range £350–£12,000
No of exhibitions annually 8

The Ship
387 Cable Street, London, E1 0AH
T 020 77900409
E TheShip@Mail.com
A non-commercial project space in the East End of London, situated in a disused pub on Cable Street with a history of the sex industry and right-wing activism. All shows are curated projects focusing on contemporary art.
Submission Policy Not currently handling any submissions.
No of exhibitions annually 7

The Showroom
44 Bonner Road, London, E2 9JS
T 020 89834115
F 020 89814112
E tellmemore@theshowroom.org
W www.theshowroom.org
The Showroom has existed as a publicly-funded, not-for-profit contemporary art gallery since 1989. It has offered many artists their first solo show in London, including Mona Hatoum, Sam Taylor-Wood, Simon Starling, Jim Lambie, Claire Barclay

and Eva Rothschild. Programmes four shows a year of newly commissioned work by individual artists or collaborative groups.
Submission Policy Does not accept unsolicited proposals.
Price range £500–£30,000
No of exhibitions annually 4

Simon Lee Gallery
12 Berkeley Street, London, W1J 8DT
T 020 74910100
E info@simonleegallery.com
W www.simonleegallery.com
Contact Lindsay Ramsay
Represents prominent and influential artists including Stephen Shore, Jenny Holzer, Cindy Sherman, George Condo, Christopher Wool, Robert Therrien, Larry Clark and Bernard Frize but has also added some younger artists to the programme such as New Yorker Gary Simmons and London-based painter Toby Ziegler.
Submission Policy The gallery is committed to its exhibition schedule for the next two years; artists are asked not to send proposals or portfolios.
No of exhibitions annually 6

Skylark Galleries
Unit 1.09 (First Floor Riverside), Oxo Tower Wharf, Barge House Street, London, SE1 9PH
T 020 7401 9666
E info@skylarkgallery.com
W www.skylarkgallery.com
Two artist-run galleries in the Oxo Tower and Gabriel's Wharf on London's South Bank. Skylark 1 (Gabriel's Wharf) was founded 1994 and Skylark 2 (Oxo Tower) in 2001. Entirely staffed by exhibiting artists.
Submission Policy Contact gallery (by email / post with sae) for joining details. Exhibiting artists work in gallery one day every three weeks.
Price range £20–£1,000
No of exhibitions annually 3–5 including Affordable Art Fairs London and Bristol.

Space Station Sixty-Five
65 North Cross Road, London, SE22 9ET
T 020 86935995
E spacestationsixtyfive@btopenworld.com
W www.spacestationsixtyfive.com
Opened in 2002. An artist-run space that works closely with artists being shown. Does not currently represent artists. A shop-front gallery in a busy street, particularly interested in live art, sculpture, video, time-based/process work and

installation. Hosts window exhibitions (viewed from the street) as well as exhibitions where the space is open to the public.
Submission Policy Proposals should be a maximum of one side of A4. Also include a CV and visuals. Artists are strongly recommended to visit the gallery before sending proposals.
Price range Prices decided by artists and directors.
No of exhibitions annually 3–6

Spectrum Fine Art
77 Great Titchfield Street, London, W1W 6RF
T 020 76377778
E anne@intelligent-pr.com
W www.spectrumlondon.co.uk
Opened in 2004, aiming to bring the work of a new generation of artists to the public and to provide a springboard for newly graduated talent. Artists include Craigie Aitchison, Marco Amura and Peter Howson.
Price range £150–£40,000
No of exhibitions annually 9

Spencer Coleman Fine Art
1 Cloisters Walk, St Katharine Docks, London E1W 1LD
T 020 74811199
Contact Spencer Coleman
Established for over ten years, specializing in a selection of oils, watercolours and pastel paintings by British, Russian and Continental artists. These include Jorge Anguilar AEA APB FRSA, Andrew White, Crin Gale, Israel Zohar (Royal Portrait Artist), Douglas Gray, Juriy Ochremovich and Pippa Chapman.
Branches 8 Gordon Road, Lincoln LN1 3AJ; 5–9 The George Mews, The George Hotel, St Martin's, Stamford, Lincolnshire PE9 2LB; 22a North Bar Without, Beverley, East Yorkshire HU17 7AB.
Submission Policy New artists welcome (local and international) in all media, covering narrative, landscape, still life, seascape and equestrian topics.
Price range £300–£15,000
No of exhibitions annually 2

Spitz Gallery
109 Commercial Street, Old Spitalfields Market, London, E1 6BG
T 020 72479747
F 020 73778915
E gallery@spitz.co.uk
W www.spitz.co.uk
Founded in 1996. Background in photography but displays other art forms including painting,

graphic design, video art, sculpture, etc.
Submission Policy Submissions accepted in June
and November only. Email image(s) in body of
email, or post on CD. Will contact if interested.
Price range £200–£3,000
No of exhibitions annually Approx. 20

SS Robin Gallery

SS Robin, West India Quay, London, E14 4AE
T 020 75380652
F 0870 1316566
E info@ssrobin.com
W www.ssrobin.com
Contact David Kampfner
Documentary photography gallery based onboard
SS *Robin*, the world's oldest complete steamship,
moored at West India Quay in the heart of Canary
Wharf in London. Founded by two photographers,
David and Nishani Kampfner, in 2002. Shows a
rolling programme of photography in the newly
restored cargo hold, open from March to
September.
Submission Policy Visit the website to download
the curation policy.
Price range £500–£5,000
No of exhibitions annually 6

Standpoint Gallery

45 Coronet Street, Hoxton, London, N1 6HD
T 020 77394921
F 020 77394921
E standpointgallery@btconnect.com
W www.standpointlondon.co.uk
Contact Fiona MacDonald (Gallery Curator)
Opened in 1992. One of the first galleries in an
area that has become a hub for the visual-art scene.
An artist run project space that acts as a platform
for emerging artists. Exhibits a range of media and
reflects the diverse nature of contemporary artistic
practice. Without commercial constraints, it
focuses on innovation and execution over
saleability and fashion. The gallery runs and hosts
the Mark Tanner Sculpture Award, a yearly award
worth £10,000 to an exceptional emerging
sculptor.
Submission Policy Submission by proposal or
invitation. See website for details on submission
and application process for the Mark Tanner
Sculpture Award.
Price range £50–£10,000
No of exhibitions annually 8

Stephen Friedman Gallery

25–28 Old Burlington Street, London, W1S 3AN

T 020 74941434
F 020 74941431
E info@stephenfriedman.com
W www.stephenfriedman.com
Founded in 1995. Specializes in contemporary art.
Artists include Mamma Andersson (Sweden),
Stephan Balkenhol (Germany), Tom Friedman
(USA), Kendell Geers (South Africa), Dryden
Goodwin (UK), Donald Moffett (USA), Yoshitomo
Nara (Japan), Rivane Neuenschwander (Brazil),
Yinka Shonibare (UK), Catherine Opie (USA) and
David Shrigley (UK).
Submission Policy Post CV and a maximum of ten
slides demonstrating work. Enclose sae for return
of material.
No of exhibitions annually 6

STORE

27 Hoxton Street, London
N1 6NH
T 020 77298171
F 020 77298171
E info@storegallery.co.uk
W www.storegallery.co.uk
Opened in 2003. Presents new work by British and
international emerging artists. Artists represented
include Chris Evans, Aurelien Froment, Ryan
Gander, Dan Holdsworth, Claire Harvey, Pamela
Rosenkrantz, Bedwyr Williams and Roman
Wolgin.
Submission Policy Does not welcome unsolicited
submissions. Details of exhibitions welcome.
Price range £400–£20,000
No of exhibitions annually 7

Studio 1.1

57a Redchurch Street, London
E2 7DJ
T 07952 986696
E studio1-1.gallery@virgin.net
W www.studio1-1.co.uk
Contact M. Keenan
Collective begun in 2003 with 'no particular battle-
plan'. Has evolved with a diverse range of shows,
presenting artists at any stage of their career, from
any country, in any discipline. Commitment is to
the work itself and to fostering the three-way
relationship between artist, artwork and viewer.
Artists shown include Phyllda Barlow, John
Summers, Cees Krijnen, Oliver Bancroft, Annie
Kevans and Craig Andrews.
Submission Policy Refer to website.
Price range £200–£10,000
No of exhibitions annually 6

Studio Glass Gallery

63 Connaught Street, Marble Arch, London
W2 2AE
T 020 77063013
E mail@studioglass.co.uk
W www.studioglass.co.uk
Contact Zaf Iqbal
Established in 1994. Represents leading English
and Czech artists working in glass including
Libensky/Brychtova, Annja Matouskova, Ivana
Sramkova, Dany Lane, Colin Reid, Max Jacquard,
Richard Jackson, Sally Fawkes and Javier Gomez.
Undertakes commissions for fabricating glass art,
conceptual and architectural.
Submission Policy Artists working in the glass
medium.
Price range £1,500–£45,000
No of exhibitions annually 4

Studio Voltaire

1a Nelson's Row, Clapham, London, SW4 7JR
T 020 76221294
F 020 76278008
E info@studiovoltaire.org
W www.studiovoltaire.org
Contact Joe Scotland
Founded in 1994. An artist-led gallery in south-
west London promoting access and participation
in contemporary art with its exhibition, education
and studio programmes. Past exhibitors have
included Pablo Bronstein, Lali Chetwynd, Liam
Gillick, Lawerence Weiner, Joanne Tatham and
Tom O'Sullivan and Allison Smith.
Submission Policy No areas excluded. Does not
represent artists but works in collaboration with
artists to achieve projects and exhibitions. Artists
and curators are encouraged to contact the gallery
to receive a copy of the artistic policy if they are
interested in submitting a proposal.
Price range £2–£20,000
No of exhibitions annually 5

Sutton Lane

1 Sutton Lane, Entrance at 25–27 Great Sutton
Street, London, EC1M 5PU
T 020 72538580
F 020 72536580
E info@suttonlane.com
W www.suttonlane.com
No of exhibitions annually 8

Terry Duffy–340 Old Street

340 Old Street, Shoreditch, London, EC1V 9DS
E terryduffy@340oldstreet.co.uk

W www.340oldstreet.co.uk
Established in 1998 as an experimental art space to
question and confront contemporary art, culture
and society.
Submission Policy Apply by email only with CV
and jpegs of images. No media, method, sex, race,
religion, nationality or beliefs excluded. No
deadlines.
Price range £1,000–£25,000
No of exhibitions annually 10

Theresa McCullough Ltd

80 Riverview Gardens, Barnes, London
SW13 8RA
T 020 85631680
E info@theresamccullough.com
W www.theresamccullough.com
Opened in 2000 and moved to current riverside
location in 2004. Dealer specializing in Indian and
South-east Asian works of art (predominantly
stone and bronze sculpture) as well as South-east
Asian gold jewellery. Exhibits at the Asian Art in
London fair in November and in New York at the
International Asian Art Fair in March.
Submission Policy Deals in antique South Asian
sculpture. Submissions welcome from
contemporary Indian artists.
No of exhibitions annually 2

Thomas Dane

11 Duke Street, St James's, London
SW1Y 6BN
T 020 79252505
F 020 79252506
E info@thomasdane.com
W www.thomasdane.com
Established in 2004 as the culmination of over a
decade of behind-the-scenes activity, including
supporting artists, hosting landmark exhibitions
and dealing privately. Closely associated from the
start with the generation of British artists whose
work grew in stature in the 1990s, the gallery has
now developed an expertise and reputation in the
international arena. Exhibitions of selected
international contemporary artists employing a
wide range of media. Artists include Paul Pfeiffer,
Michael Landy, Stefan Kürten, Anya Gallaccio,
Hurvin Anderson and Albert Oehlen.
Submission Policy No unsolicited submissions.
No of exhibitions annually 5

Timothy Taylor Gallery

24 Dering Street, London, W1S 1TT
T 020 74093344

F 020 74091316
E mail@timothytaylorgallery.com
W www.timothytaylorgallery.com
Founded in 1996, specializing in contemporary
art. Artists include Craigie Aitchison, Tim Braden,
Jean-Marc Bustamante, Marcel Dzama, Ewan
Gibbs, Susan Hiller, Fiona Rae, Bridget Riley, Sean
Scully, Alex Katz, Jonathan Lasker, James Rielly,
Kiki Smith and Miquel Barceló.
Submission Policy Submissions not welcome.
No of exhibitions annually 7–10

Tom Blau Gallery–Camera Press
21 Queen Elizabeth Street, London, SE1 2PD
T 020 73781300
F 020 72785126
E info@tomblaugallery.com
W www.tomblaugallery.com
Founded in 1993 and named after the founder of
the photographic agency Camera Press.
Specializes in vintage, modern and contemporary
photography. Exhibited artists have included
Jacques Lowe, Yousef Karsh, Jason Bell, Patrick
Lichfield, Chris Shaw, and Morten Nisson. Also
shows photographs from the Camera Press
Archives and hosts the annual Ian Parry
Scholarship Awards for young photojournalists.
Submission Policy Submissions from artists not
welcome. Exhibitions by Camera Press-
represented photographers only.
Price range From £200
No of exhibitions annually 6–10

Transition Gallery
Unit 25a / 2nd Floor Regent Studios, 8 Andrews
Road, London, E8 4QN
T 020 7254 4202
E info@transitiongallery.co.uk
W www.transitiongallery.co.uk
An artist run space founded in 2002, showing
work by emerging and established artists with a
particular interest in strong curatorial themed
projects. Transition Editions, the gallery's
publishing imprint, works in tandem with the
gallery to expand upon themes and instigate new
critical writing. Artists shown include Stella Vine,
Liz Neal, Delaine Le Bas, Rebecca Knapp, Hew
Locke and Zoë Mendelson.
Submission Policy Artists are welcome to submit
images, statements and proposals by email or post.
No of exhibitions annually 8

Trolley
73a Redchurch Street, London, E2 7DJ

T 020 77395948
E info@trolleynet.com
W www.trolleybooks.com
Specializing in art and photography books, Trolley
operates a gallery space primarily exhibiting work
linked to books projects but with exceptions.
Artists include Deirdre O'Callaghan, Adam
Broomberg and Oliver Chanarin, Chris Steele-
Perkins, Alex Majoli, Philip Jones Griffiths,
Werner Bischof, Vedovamazzei, Doris Vassmer,
Mia Enell and Stanley Greene.

The Troubadour Gallery
267 Old Brompton Road, Earls Court, London
SW5 9JA
T 020 73701434
F 020 72416329
E susie@troubadour.co.uk
W www.troubadour.co.uk/gallery.php
Opened in 2001 with the idea of creating a
dedicated space in which the many artists who
come to the associated Café could display their
work. The space is classically decorated with white
walls and a generous but plain cornice and
skirting. There is natural light from both north and
south, as well as track-mounted adjustable spot
lighting. Total gallery area is 42 m2. There are 30
linear metres of hanging space and ceiling height
is 3.3m. Each exhibition is individually tailored but
the space is ideally suited for short shows – one
week or less – with one or more private views.
Submission Policy Welcomes approaches from
artists to hire the gallery. Does not take any
commission on sales. However, for private views
does expect all food and drink to be purchased
from associated deli or café. Contact if you would
like to see the gallery or alternatively look on the
website.
No of exhibitions annually 50–60
Cost to hire or rent Single day at £200, from 2–3
days at £150 per day (with one private view), 4 days
or more at £125 per day (with one private view).
Additional private views at £50 per evening.

Tryon Galleries
7 Bury Street, St James's, London
SW1Y 6AL
T 020 78398083
F 020 78398085
E info@tryon.co.uk
W www.tryon.co.uk
Contact Liz Thorold
Founded in 1959 with a strong reputation in the
fields of sporting, wildlife and Scottish paintings,

and bronzes. Deals in nineteenth- and twentieth-century and contemporary artists, from Archibald Thorburn, George Lodge and Lionel Edwards to Rodger McPhail.
Price range £500–£50,000
No of exhibitions annually 6

Union

57 Ewer Street, London
SE1 0NR
T 020 79283388
F 020 79283389
E info@union-gallery.com
W www.union-gallery.com
Five minutes' walk from Tate Modern and established at the start of 2003. Presents group and solo shows by established and emerging international contemporary artists, many of whom are showing to a UK audience for the first time. Has an ambitious programme of exhibitions, effectively allowing museum shows previously only seen overseas to be brought to a London audience in the context of a commercial space.
Submission Policy Does not look at submissions from artists.
No of exhibitions annually 4–5

Victoria Miro Gallery

16 Wharf Road, London, N1 7RW
T 020 73368109
F 020 72515596
E info@victoria-miro.com
W www.victoria-miro.com
Established in Cork Street in 1985 and moved to the East End in 2002. Has been associated with many emerging artists and has two Turner Prize winners to date, Chris Ofili in 1998 and Grayson Perry in 2003.

Vilma Gold

6 Minerva Street, London
E2 9EH
T 020 89813344
F 020 89813355
E mail@vilmagold.com
W www.vilmagold.com
Represents international, young and mid-career contemporary artists such as Mark Titchner, Aida Ruilova, Vladimir Dubossarsky and Alexsander Vinogradov, Brian Griffiths and Josef Strau. Vilma Gold was founded in 2000 and in 2005/6 ran a one year project space in Berlin.
Submission Policy Does not accept submissions from artists.

W.H. Patterson Ltd

19 Albemarle Street, Mayfair, London
W1S 4BB
T 020 76294119
F 020 74990119
E info@whpatterson.com
W www.whpatterson.com
Founded in 1964. Deals in contemporary art and has a nineteenth-century department. Hosts an annual 'Venice in Peril' (VIP) exhibition; ten per cent of proceeds donated to the VIP Fund.
Price range £450–£60,000
No of exhibitions annually 10

Waddington Galleries

11 Cork Street, London, W1S 3LT
T 020 78512200
F 020 77344146
E mail@waddington-galleries.com
W www.waddington-galleries.com
Deals in modern and contemporary works of art (paintings, sculpture, and works on paper). A substantial inventory is held of major twentieth-century artists including Jean Dubuffet, Giorgio De Chirico, Henri Matisse, Joan Miró, Henry Moore and Pablo Picasso. Represents a number of contemporary artists from Great Britain, Europe, and North America including Craigie Aitchison, Peter Blake, Ian Davenport, Barry Flanagan, Peter Halley, Mimmo Paladino, Antoni Tàpies, William Turnbull and Bill Woodrow. Also represents the estates of Josef Albers, Milton Avery, Patrick Caulfield and Patrick Heron.

White Cube

48 Hoxton Square, London, N1 6PB
T 020 79305373
F 020 77497480
E enquiries@whitecube.com
W www.whitecube.com
Contact Susannah Hyman
Founded in 1993. Has presented solo shows of British artists such as Jake and Dinos Chapman, Tracey Emin, Lucian Freud, Gilbert & George, Antony Gormley and Damien Hirst. International artists include Franz Ackermann, Chuck Close, Ellsworth Kelly, Julie Mehretu, Doris Salcedo and Hiroshi Sugimoto. Also frequent group shows.
Branches 25–26 Mason's Yard, London, SW1Y 6BU
T 020 7930 5373
Submission Policy All works considered by any living artist.
Price range From £1,000
No of exhibitions annually 8–10

Whitechapel Project Space

20 Fordham Street, London, E1 1HS
T 020 73776289
E info@whitechapelprojectspace.org.uk
W www.whitechapelprojectspace.org.uk
Contact Maria Trimikliniotis or Richard Birkett
Founded in 2002. Aims to facilitate progressive
cultural and curatorial practice through
exhibitions, events and engagement. Artists are
invited to consider how the space can further their
work and operate as a catalyst to their practice. Has
hosted activities that both complement and
contradict the familiar notion of a contemporary
art gallery. Artists worked with include Anja
Kirschner, Craig Mulholland, Babak Ghazi, Pablo
Bronstein, Hardcore is More Than Music, and
Luke Dowd and Giles Round.
Submission Policy Aims to show contemporary art
within the broad remit of presenting current
cultural production and provoking debate.
Principally shows invited artists but, dependent on
constraints on time, will consider proposals and
submissions.
No of exhibitions annually 6–10

Whitford Fine Art

6 Duke Street, St James's, London, SW1Y 6BN
T 020 79309332
F 020 79305577
E info@whitfordfineart.com
W www.whitfordfineart.com
Opened in 1973 as Whitford & Hughes and
changed its name to Whitford Fine Art in 1991.
Stock spans the twentieth century, from
Modernism up to post-war abstraction and Pop
Art. Examples of 1960s and 1970s designer
furniture are a permanent feature of the gallery.
Price range £1,000–£500,000
No of exhibitions annually 4

Whitgift Galleries

77 South End, Croydon, CRO 1BF
T 020 86880990
F 020 87600522
E info@whitgiftgalleries.co.uk
W www.whitgiftgalleries.co.uk
Founded in 1945, showing fine-quality oil
paintings and watercolours. Artists include Brian
Davies, Ben Maile and David Smith. Limited
editions by Sir William Russsell Flint and others.
Also offers a framing and restoration service.
Price range £50–£10,000
No of exhibitions annually 2

Wilkinson Gallery

50/58 Vyner Street, London, E2 9DQ
T 020 89802662
F 020 89800028
E info@wilkinsongallery.com
W www.wilkinsongallery.com
A major gallery in the Hackney and Bethnal Green
area since 1998, showing a mixture of
international and British art by mostly young and
emerging artists including David Batchelor,
George Shaw, Ged Quinn, Robert Orchardson and
Tilo Baumgartel.

William Thuillier

14 Old Bond Street, London, W1S 4PP
T 020 74990106
F 020 72338965
E thuillart@aol.com
W www.thuillart.com
The gallery specializes in Old Master and British
Paintings 1600–1850, with an emphasis on
classical landscapes and historical portraits.
Ongoing exhibition includes *The Drowning of
Pharoah in the Red Sea* by William Kent, portraits of
Edward Gibbon attributed to Mason Chamberlain
and *Lady Anne Capel* by Sir Peter Lely. Shows some
contemporary artists (Philip Chitty, Annalisa
Catelli and Rosalind Adams).
Price range £500–£250,000
No of exhibitions annually 2
Cost to hire or rent By discussion.

Williams & Son

2 Grafton Street, London, W1S 4ED
T 020 74935751
F 020 74097363
E art@williamsandson.com
W www.williamsandson.com
Contact John R. Williams
Founded in 1932. Specializes in nineteenth- and
twentieth-century paintings. Handles the work of a
few contemporary artists who paint in the
academic and traditional styles and who can hang
with stock of nineteenth-century paintings.
Price range £1,000–£200,000
No of exhibitions annually 1

North-east

Art Cafe

18 Market Place, Corbridge, NE45 5AW
T 01434 634090
E info@theartcafe.uk.com
W www.theartcafe.uk.com

Contact Claire Bolam (Manager)
Opened in 2002. Exhibits original British
contemporary art and design. Artists include
Alexander Millar, Gavin Penn, Mary Ann Rogers,
Jan Huntley-Peace and Kate Wilkinson.
Submission Policy Viewing panel meets each
Tuesday to select new work. All details (including
contract and code of practice) on website.
Price range £5–£15,000
No of exhibitions annually Mostly open exhibition.
1 or 2 themed or individual per year
Cost to hire or rent By negotiation.

Barnard Gallery
2 Theatre Yard, Stockton-on-Tees, TS18 JZ
T 01642 616203

Biscuit Factory
Stoddart Street, Newcastle-upon-Tyne
NE2 1AN
T 0191 2611103
F 0191 2610057
E art@thebiscuitfactory.com
W www.thebiscuitfactory.com
Contact Karen Tait
One of Europe's largest commercial galleries,
exhibiting a wide range of artists (national and
international) and art forms including glass,
ceramics, sculpture and paintings. Has shown and
sold work by over a thousand artists, including
Damien Hirst and Andy Warhol.
Submission Policy Artists who feel their work is
suitable for the gallery should apply via criteria on
the website.
Price range £20–£50,000
No of exhibitions annually A rolling programme,
with four preview nights per year.

Centre Gallery
Deptford Terrace, Sunderland, SR4 6DD
T 0191 5658584

Chatton Gallery
Church House, New Road, Chatton, Alnwick
NE66 5PU
T 01668 215494

Colliers
Milburn House, Dean Street, Newcastle-upon-
Tyne, NE1 1LF
T 0191 2322819
F 0191 2302026
E anne@colliers.wanadoo.co.uk
W www.colliersgallery.co.uk

Contact Anne Collier
Founded in 1975, initially specializing in framing.
Now a contemporary gallery showing mainly local
artists. Wall space available to rent. Some in-house
publishing of mainly local images.
Submission Policy 'Not interested in Turner Prize-
type art – no installations, shockers, etc.' Well-
executed art of a professional standard always
welcome.
Price range £5–£5,000
No of exhibitions annually Varies.

Corrymella Scott Gallery
5 Tankerville Terrace, Jesmond, Newcastle-upon-
Tyne, NE8 4EL
T 0191 2818284
E corrymella@corrymella.co.uk

Crown Fine Arts
25 Selbrigg Lane, Ingleby Barwick,
Stockton-on-Tees, TS17 0XT
T 01642 761883

Crown Studio Gallery
Bridge Street, Rothbury, NE65 7SE
T 01669 622890
E info@crownstudio.co.uk
W www.crownstudio.co.uk
Founded in 2001, specializing in painting, prints,
sculpture and ceramics. Exhibits professional
(mostly regional) artists, both emerging and
established. Space is domestic in scale but
carefully arranged to show work to its best
advantage. Shows high-quality contemporary art in
a rural setting.
Submission Policy Exhibition proposals welcome.
Send photographs, prints, slides or jpegs, CV and
statement. Enclose sae for return of material.
Price range £20–£5,000
No of exhibitions annually Up to 6

Customs House
Mill Dam, South Shields, Tyne & Wear, NE33 1ES
T 0191 4541234
F 0191 4565979
E mail@customshouse.co.uk
W www.customshouse.co.uk
Contact Anna Snell
With a riverside location, the exhibition programme
incorporates a diversity of art forms by artists of
regional, national and international standing.
Submission Policy Contact Anna Snell on 0191
4278199.
No of exhibitions annually 20

Dale Gallery

Castle Gardens, Durham Dale Centre Unit 1F,
Stanhope, DL13 2FJ
T 01207 509511
The Gallery has been open for 9 years showing the
work of George Skelton. His work can be seen in
the form of original watercolours and Limited
Edition prints.
Submission Policy Only the work of George
Skelton is shown.
Price range £10–£350

Dial Gallery

5 Dial Place, Warkworth, NE05 0WR
T 01665 710822

Evergreen Gallery

3 Grainger Street, Newcastle-upon-Tyne
NE1 5DQ
T 0191 2321011

Fenwick Gallery

21 Castle Street, Morpeth, NE65 0UW
T 01665 711136
E enquiry@fenwickgallery.co.uk
W www.fenwickgallery.co.uk
Established in 1990, offering a range of paintings
and prints, ceramics, studio glass, wood pieces and
jewellery.

fifiefofum

Westside Farm, Newton Hall, Near Newcastle
NE43 7TW
T 01661 843778
E sue@fifiefofum.com
W www.fifiefofum.com
Contact Sue Moffitt
Established in 2003. A rural contemporary gallery
specializing in original fine art from established,
emerging and graduate north-eastern artists.
Artist-led, with a specific focus on supporting the
artist. Also offers art-related workshops and
courses. Venue hire is available along with light
refreshments and catering facilities.
Submission Policy All artists' work is considered
on an individual basis but it is expected that artists
have some formal relevant qualifications or have
been working as artists for many years. Aims to
support and show work from graduates from BA,
MA and PhD programmes as well as more
established artists.
Price range £65–£4,000. From £3.50 for original
hand-printed cards.

No of exhibitions annually 6
Cost to hire or rent Venue hire approx. £150 per
day (2006).

Gallagher & Turner

St Thomas Workshops, St Thomas Street,
Newcastle-upon-Tyne, NE1 4LE
T 0191 2614465
F 0191 2614465
E gallery@gallagher-turner.co.uk
W www.gallagherandturner.co.uk
Contact Clare Turner
A small, established gallery with eclectic tastes,
showing local and national artists. Mostly solo
shows but some mixed. Past exhibitions include
Ray Richardson, Albert Irvin and Norman
Ackroyd. Also show Japanese woodblock prints
and work by original printmakers. As a specialist
high quality conservation framer, is prepared to
take exhibitions unframed. Other services include
gilding, conservation and restoration.
Submission Policy Does not currently display craft
or jewellery. Welcomes submissions by email with
images or post containing slides, with CV attached.
All submissions by post will be returned safely.
Price range £40–£5,000
No of exhibitions annually Approx. 5

Gate Gallery

12 Bondgate Within, Alnwick, NE66 1TD
T 01665 602165

Glass and Art Gallery

194 Medomsley Road, Consett, County Durham
DH8 5HX
T 01207 583353
F 01207 500218
E glassdesigner@hotmail.com
W www.glassdesign.co.uk
Founded in 1999, exhibiting art from over one
hundred regional artists. The gallery also houses
three studio/workshops where stained glass is
designed and made. Weekend workshops are held
once per month.
Submission Policy All work must be unique,
original and not mass-produced. All artists must
either be regional or have some connection with
the northeast.
Price range £5–£5,000
No of exhibitions annually 8

Lime Tree Gallery

6 The Butts, Stanhope, Bishop Auckland, DL13 2UF
T 01388 526110

Macdonalds Fine Art
6 Ashburton Road, Gosforth,
Newcastle-upon-Tyne, NE3 4XN
T 0191 2844214

Newgate Gallery
6a The Bank, Barnard Castle, DL12 8PQ
T 01833 695201
E info@newgate-gallery.co.uk
W www.newgate-gallery.co.uk
Intimate gallery specializing in wildlife and
country subjects.

Norslands Gallery
The Old School, Warenford, Belford, NE70 7HY
T 01668 213465

Serendipity
10 Market Place, Wolsingham, DL13 3AF
T 01388 526800
Founded in 2003, specializing in north-eastern art
and especially Weardale artists.
Submission Policy Interested in original and
unique work (framed paintings) by north-eastern
artists. Work must be different from what is
already exhibited.
Price range £10–£5,000
No of exhibitions annually 12

Side Gallery
5 & 9 Side, Newcastle-upon-Tyne, NE1 3JE
T 0191 2322000
W www.amber-online.com
Specializes in photography.

T.B. & R. Jordan Lapada
Aslak, Eaglescliffe, Stockton-on-Tees, TS16 0QN
T 01642 782599
E info@tbrj.co.uk
W www.tbrj.co.uk
Founded in 1974. Sources works by Impressionist
artists painting in the North-east of England a
century ago, especially pictures by members of the
Staitnes Group and Cullercoats Colony. Also acts
as agents for Richard Marshall b. 1944 and the
estate of the late Robert L. Harvey 1900–1981.
Submission Policy By appointment and through
exhibitions. No facilities to show more work by
living artists.
Price range £200–£25,000
No of exhibitions annually 8

Yarm Gallery
37 High Street, Yarm, Stockton-on-Tees, TS15 9BH

T 01642 789432
F 01642 767733
E enquiries@yarmgallery.co.uk
W www.yarmgallery.co.uk
Contact Carol Byrne
Founded in 2004, a gallery of contemporary art.
Artists include Mackenzie Thorpe and Alexander
Millar. Also offers bespoke conservation level
framing and giclée printing services.
Submission Policy No requirements for formally
trained artists.
Price range £60–£5,000+
No of exhibitions annually 4

Northern Ireland

Annexe Gallery
15 Main Street, Eglinton, BT47 3AA
T 028 71810389
E aml.davidson@talk21.com
W www.annexegallery.co.uk
Stocks original paintings, many by local artists,
and a wide selection of prints and limited editions.
Also offers framing service.

Ballance House
118a Lisburn Road, Glenavy, Crumlin, BT29 4NY
T 028 92648492

Bell Gallery
13 Adelaide Park, Lisburn Road, Belfast
BT9 6FX
T 028 90662998
F 028 90381524
E bellgallery@btinternet.com
W www.bellgallery.com
Contact Pauline McLarnon
Founded in 1964, dealing in work by Irish artists
of all periods and providing exhibition space
throughout the Troubles. Specializes in modern
British paintings, drawings and sculpture, and also
nineteenth- and twentieth-century Irish sculpture.
The gallery consists of three rooms.
Submission Policy Lack of space precludes very
large exhibitions or excessively large individual
video or installation work.
Price range £500–£10,000

Collett Art Gallery
73 Dublin Road, Belfast, BT2 7HF
T 028 90319589
E marion@collettartgallery.com
W www.collettartgallery.com
Established in 1990 and moved to its current

premises in 1995. Displays and sells paintings by Irish artists to buyers all over the world.

Context Gallery
5–7 Artillery Street, Derry, BT48 6RG
T 028 71373538
E info@contextgallery.com

Eakin Gallery Armagh
Portadown Road, Armagh, BT61 8RF
T 028 38872013
E info@eakingalleryarmagh.co.uk
W www.eakingalleryarmagh.co.uk
Opened in 2004 by Harry and Carol Eakin, who have over twenty-five years' experience in the Irish art market. Artists include Tom Carr, Maurice C.Wilks, J.B.Vallely, William Cunningham, Joe Hynes, Gavin Fitzsimmons, Tom Kerr, David Jess, Tanya Smith, Denis Orme Shaw, William Conor, Frank McKelvey, Paul Henry, Hamilton Sloan, Basil Blackshaw, Sam McLarnon, J.W. Carey and Liam Reilly.
Submission Policy Leading Irish artists are welcome to show work on acceptance by the gallery.
Price range £150–£10,000
No of exhibitions annually 4

Emer Gallery
467 Antrim Road, Belfast, BT15 3BJ
T 028 90778777
F 028 90779444
E info@emergallery.com
W www.emergallery.com
Displays and sells Irish art of the nineteenth and twentieth centuries alongside contemporary artists. Has a particular interest in naive and primitive painting. Artists include Jimmy Bingham, Comhghall Casey, Sasha Harding, John McCart, Noel Murphy, Rhonda Paisley, J.B. Valley and Ross Wilson.
No of exhibitions annually 7–10

Gallery 148
148 High Street, Holywood
E mail@gallery148.com
W www.gallery148.com
Shows established and emerging contemporary Irish artists.

Gallery One
1 Brewery Lane, Cookstown, BT80 8LL
T 028 86765438
F 028 86765438
E info@galleryone.co.uk

W www.galleryone.co.uk
Stocks traditional and contemporary fine art by European, UK and Irish artists in media including oils, watercolours and acrylics and mixed media.

Laneside Gallery
5 Stable Lane, Coleraine, BT52 1DQ
T 028 70353600/ 7001 or 07816 585184
F 07816 585184
E info@lanesidegallery.com
W www.lanesidegallery.com
Contact David Green
Established in 1999 and moved to purpose-built premises in 2001. Accommodates wide range of original paintings by leading and emerging artists, as well as handmade artists prints, original drawings and sculptures. Commissions both paintings and sculpture on behalf of individual and corporate clients from most of its represented artists. Ranges from modern to traditional styles. Bespoke in-house framing service offered.
Price range £100–£20,000
No of exhibitions annually 4

Manor Fine Arts
18 Rathfriland Street, Banbridge, BT32 3LA
T 028 40623434
F 028 40623434
W www.manorfinearts.co.uk
Exhibits both emerging and established artists and offers a framing service.

Ormeau Baths Gallery
18a Ormeau Avenue, Belfast, BT2 8HS
T 028 90321402
F 028 90312232
E admin@obgonline.net
W www.ormeaubathsgallery.co.uk
Opened in 1995. An innovative exhibition and education programme features nationally- and internationally-recognized artists working across a broad range of contemporary visual-art practice.

Stables Gallery
6 Heathmount Hall, Portstewart, BT55 7RA
T 028 7083 4006
E stewart-moore@btconnect.com
W www.stablesgallery.co.uk
Founded in 1980. Deals in twentieth-century and contemporary paintings. Specializes primarily in Irish art but also represents the work of several French, Spanish and English artists.
Submission Policy The gallery is happy to look objectively at submissions by artists of quality.

Price range £500–£40,000
No of exhibitions annually 9

TailorMadeArt
2 Brookmount Road, Omagh, BT78 5HZ
T 028 82246613
F 028 82252097
E info@tailormadeart.com
W www.tailormadeart.com
A team of artists and art specialists produce
paintings and digitally created images on canvas,
board, card or premium-quality art paper to order.

Taylor Gallery
471 Lisburn Road, Belfast, BT9 7EZ
T 028 90687687
E taylorgallery@btinternet.com
W www.taylorgallery.co.uk
Contact Stephen Donnelly
Established in 1998. Generally features works by
leading Irish and contemporary artists such as
Michael Gemmell, Patsy Dan Rodgers (King of
Tory Island), Gladys Maccabe, Dennis Orme Shaw
and Joop Smits. Also specializes in original
screenprints by Andy Warhol and keeps an
extensive range of these in stock. Offers a
professional appraisal and valuation service.
Submission Policy Usually Irish artists.
Price range £195–£100,000
No of exhibitions annually 5

Throatlake
68B Rathmore Road, Dunadry, County Antrim
BT41 2HX
T 07841 506166
E info@throatlake.com
W www.throatlake.com
Deals in contemporary and traditional paintings
via an online gallery. Artists include R.B. Higgins,
Paul Holmes, Darren Paul, J.P. Rooney, Hamilton
Sloan and Maurice C. Wilks.

Tom Caldwell Gallery
429 Lisburn Road, Belfast, BT9 7EY
T 028 90661890
F 028 90681890
E info@tomcaldwellgallery.com
W www.tomcaldwellgallery.com
Contact Chris Caldwell
Founded in 1969. A two-floor gallery specializing
in Irish living art (primarily painting but also
sculpture and ceramics). Exhibited artists include
Colin Middleton, George Campbell, Gerard Dillon,
Paddy Collins, Tom Carr and Basil Blackshaw.

Currently represents fifteen to twenty artists
including Christine Bowen, Colin Davidson, Carol
Graham PRUA, Barbara Rae RA, Neil Shawcross
and Ronnie Wood.
Price range £300–£50,000
No of exhibitions annually 9

Townhouse Gallery Portrush
6 Bath Street, Portrush, BT56 8AW
T 028 70822826
E frankie@townhousegalleryportrush.com
W www.townhousegalleryportrush.com
Opened in 2003, exhibiting photographs,
paintings and prints by leading contemporary
artists as well as ceramics, textiles and jewellery.
Artists include Jonathan Aiken, Frankie Creith
Hill, Naomi Horner, John Johnson, Martin Lloyd,
Brian Magee, Anne Michael, Peter McCausland,
Patricia McCormack-French, Vincent McDonnell,
James McNulty, Ross Wilson, Simon Craig,
Stephen Duke, Andrew Hill and Alastair McCook.

WhiteImage.com
34 Lisburn Street, Hillsborough, BT26 6AB
T 028 92689896
F 028 92688433
E info@whiteimage.com
W www.whiteimage.com
Contact Bill Morrison
Founded in 1994. Specializes in contemporary
Irish art. Aims to bring affordable Irish art to the
widest possible audience. Gallery artists currently
represented include J.P. Rooney, Sue Howells,
Marie Carroll, Colin Middleton, Louis Le Brocquy
and Darren Paul.
Submission Policy Interested artists should
submit at least six works. See website for details.
Price range £75–£14,000
No of exhibitions annually 6

North-west

5+ Contemporary Ceramics
Unit A, Dixons Court, 101 Lake Road, Ambleside
LA22 0DB
T 015394 33821
E fiveplus@onetel.com
W www.fiveplus.org.uk
Contact Abigail Jacobs or Roger Bell
Founded in 2003 and run by the makers of the
work on show. Established to promote
contemporary ceramics in the north and provide a
fresh and friendly atmosphere in which to discuss
and view contemporary crafts. Artists represented

include Michael and Vicky Eden, Philamena Pretsell, Vivid Ceramics, Jonathan Garratt and Fiona Thompson.
Submission Policy Artists interested in exhibiting should send an up-to-date CV with good-quality images of work.
Price range £5–£500
No of exhibitions annually 2

Acorn Gallery

Egg Cafe, 2nd Floor, 16–18 Newington, Liverpool L1 4ED
T 0151 7072755
E egg_cafe@hotmail.com
W www.cocoon.u-net.com
Founded in 1984, an open-plan gallery within the café offering for hire 75 linear feet of hanging walls and screens and 600 sq. ft of floor space for sculpture/3-D work.

Ainscough Gallery

Hargreaves Building, 5 Chapel Street, Liverpool L3 9AG
T 0151 236 6676
F 0151 236 6870
E gallery@ainscoughs.co.uk
W www.ainscoughs.co.uk
Established 15 years ago as Merhmal gallery. The gallery has now moved to the heart of the business district in Liverpool. Selling Northern artists.
Submission Policy No conceptual installations etc.
Price range £50–£12,000
No of exhibitions annually 4

Arena Gallery

82–84 Duke Street, Liverpool, L1 5AA
T 0151 7079879
F 0151 7071667
E arenastudios@clara.co.uk
W www.arena.uk.com
Contact James Buso or Paul Luckraft
Artist-led space within walking distance of all of Liverpool's major public galleries. Aims to show the work of emerging talent and to build dialogue and exchange with other artist-led organizations, both nationally and internationally.The 9m x 9m gallery is suitable for one-person and small group exhibitions.
Submission Policy Send written proposal and CV.
No of exhibitions annually 6

Artizana

The Village, Prestbury, Cheshire, SK10 4DG
T 01625 827582
F 01625 827582
E art@artizana.co.uk
W www.artizana.co.uk
Founded in 1984 as a private gallery. Aims to promote contemporary British crafts, with a particular emphasis on one-off furniture designs. Exhibited artists include Rachel Woodman (studio glass), Magdalene Odundo (ceramics), Ahmed Moustafa (calligraphy), Alan Peters OBE (furniture), Stephen Broadbent (sculpture), Tim Stead MBE (furniture), Kevin O'Dwyer (silver), Verina Warren (embroidery) and Charles Bray (glass sculpture). Commissions undertaken for private clients and public institutions.
Submission Policy Most craft disciplines considered. Primary requirement is that work is contemporary, original and of the highest quality.
Price range £50–£15,000
No of exhibitions annually 2

Benny Browne & Co. Ltd

63 Lawton Street, Congleton, CW12 1RU
T 07765 047598
E bennybrowne@yahoo.com
W www.bennybrowne.com
Contact Vanessa Browne or William Kemp
Exclusive art boutique offering original paintings and limited-edition giclée prints by living artists and designers. Offers bespoke commissioning through on-site artists that combine traditional principles of colour, harmony and proportion with modern trends and design flair.
Submission Policy Work must display traditional principles of colour, harmony and proportion.
Price range £50–£1,000
No of exhibitions annually Regularly changing works and quarterly events.

Blyth Gallery

Amazon House, Brazil Street, Manchester M1 3PJ
T 0161 2361004
F 0161 2880633
E gallery@artmanchester.com
W www.artmanchester.com
Contact Denise Thornton (Gallery Director)
Established in 1997 and located in the Canal Street area of central Manchester. Catering for corporate and private clients, it exhibits contemporary paintings, sculpture, ceramics and glass works by both northern-based and international artists. Has an eclectic selection policy, with an associated art shop on the premises.
Submission Policy Professional/established artists

and sculptors should submit a CV, statement and captioned images with an sae. No photography, installations or video.
Price range £80–£1,800
No of exhibitions annually 12

Bureau

Ground Floor, Islington Mill, James Street, Salford, M3 5HW
T 07757 956555
E info@bureaugallery.com
W www.bureaugallery.com
Purpose-built gallery launched in 2006. Delivering four shows a year, ranging across all media, the gallery's intention is to promote dynamic and exciting new work by emerging and established artists from the UK and internationally. Also works on collaborative projects with other international galleries and institutions. Complimentary to the exhibitions programme, Bureau regularly commissions new work and critical writing, houses collections of artists' film and video and publication projects, and presents performances, screenings, symposiums and off-site events.
No of exhibitions annually 4

Castlefield Gallery

2 Hewitt Street, Knott Mill, Manchester, M15 4GB
T 0161 832 8034
F 0161 819 2295
E info@castlefieldgallery.co.uk
W www.castlefieldgallery.co.uk
Initiated by artists in 1984. Now one of the most established artist-run galleries in the UK. Curates exhibitions by both emerging and high-profile national and international contemporary artists. Runs a creative and professional-development programme for artists and curators, including residencies, seminars, debates, e-newsletters, a resource directory and assistance in new artist-led projects.
Submission Policy One annual deadline at the end of February. All media considered. Artists should provide exhibition proposal, statement, CV, professional reference and 5–10 images. See website for full details.
Price range From £80–£50,000. Operates Arts Council England's Own Art interest-free loan scheme.
No of exhibitions annually 6

Colin Jellicoe Gallery

82 Portland Street, Manchester, M1 4QX

T 0161 2362716
W www.colinjellicoe.co.uk
Opened in 1963 by Colin Jellicoe, a painter since the late 1950s. Specializes in figurative and modern drawings, paintings, graphics and sculpture. Gallery artists include Granville, Colin Gilbert, Debbie Hill, Jellicoe, Jackie Mitchell and John Picking. Acts as agent for several art competitions (Royal Academy Summer Exhibition, Singer Friedland Watercolour).
Submission Policy Only shows living artists. Send a CV and up to ten good colour prints.
Price range £50–£500
No of exhibitions annually 2–4

Comme Ca Art Gallery

24 Worsley Street, Castlefield, Manchester M15 4LD
T 0161 8397187
E info@commecaart.com
W www.commecaart.com
Established in 1994, an art and design agency with a pool of over 800 artists and designers covering a range of disciplines.

De Lacey Fine Art

15 The Colonnades, Albert Dock, Liverpool L3 4AA
T 0151 7076020
E info@delaceyfineart.co.uk
W www.delaceyfineart.co.uk
Contact Gordon or Martin Farmer
Founded in 2001, specializing in modern British and contemporary art. Deals in original works and original printed works of established artists.
Submission Policy Approachable, but does not usually welcome submissions from artists.
Price range £200–£200,000
No of exhibitions annually 6

Domino Gallery

11 Upper Newington, Liverpool, L1 2SR
T 0151 7070764 / 07775 605326
E felicity.wren@fsbdial.co.uk
W www.dominogallery.com
Founded in 1989. Shows local, national and international artists (established and new) such as John Bratby, Adrian Henri, George Jardine, Nicholas Horsfield, Jason Jones, Claire Chinnery and Lisa Cole Kronenburg. Has a wide range of work including painting, photography (both digital and traditional), prints, drawings, jewellery and small-scale ceramics.
Submission Policy Director chooses exhibitors

according to fairly strict criteria but all approaches welcomed. Advice given to new graduates regarding portfolios and presentation, etc.
Price range £75–£3,000
No of exhibitions annually Approx. 6

dot-art
Oriel Close, Water Street, Liverpool, L2 8UQ
T 0845 017 6660
F 0870 1412116
E artists@dot-art.com
W www.dot-art.com
Contact Lucy Byrne
Founded in 2005 to help local artists promote and sell their work via a city centre gallery, website, and external exhibitions, as well as providing a complete service to businesses looking to buy, rent or commission art. Holds regular social events for artists. Offers discount framing and art supplies as well as general support and guidance.
Submission Policy Artists are welcome to submit work for consideration at any time, either by email or post (on CD). All media considered. Must be based in Merseyside area.
Price range £30–£8,000
No of exhibitions annually 6

Fold Gallery
3 Walton's Yard, Market Square, Kirkby Stephen CA17 4QT
T 017683 71561
E newart@foldgallery.co.uk
W www.foldgallery.co.uk
Contact Steve or Richeldis
Founded in 2001 to provide and promote access to contemporary art in the rural environment. Small exhibition space in rural market town shows programme of work by artists from rural areas of the UK and beyond. Also runs FRED – Europe's largest festival of site-specific art – at venues across Cumbria. Commissions in 2005 included new work by Graham Rawle, Sue Flowers and Jenny Holzer.
Submission Policy Work must meet the exhibition criteria, available from the website. Work does not need to be commercially viable.
Price range £2–£10,000. Most work is not for sale.
No of exhibitions annually 6

Gallery 2000
Windle Court, Clayhill Industrial Park, Neston CH64 3UH
T 0151 3531522

The Gallery–Manchester's Art House
131 Portland Street, Manchester, M1 4PY
T 0161 2373551
F 0161 2283621
E enquiries@manchestersarthouse.com
W www.manchestersarthouse.com

Henry Donn Gallery
138–142 Bury New Road, Whitefield, Manchester M45 6TD
T 0161 7668819
F 0161 7668819
E donn@netline.uk.net
W www.henrydonngallery.com
Sells contemporary original art and prints. Runs an online gallery facility.

Howarth Gallery
134–138 St James Street, Burnley, BB11 1NR
T 01282 416079
E richard@howarth-gallery.co.uk
W www.howarth-gallery.co.uk
Established for over twenty years. Deals in both antique and contemporary art and prints. Also offers framing and valuation services.
Contemporary artists include McKenzie Thorpe, Sandra Blow RA, Sir Terry Frost RA, Alex Millar, Stephen Ormerod, Sir Peter Blake RA and Roy Fairchild-Woodard.
Submission Policy Always willing to look at new work.
Price range £20–£30,000
No of exhibitions annually 6

International 3
8 Fairfield Street, Manchester, M1 3GF
T 0161 2373336
E ll@international3.com
W www.international3.com
A non-profit gallery founded in 2000. Exhibits and commissions new work by contemporary artists, both initiating projects and working with invited curators. Artists commissioned include Andrew McDonald, Bob and Roberta Smith, Ryan Gander, Rachel Goodyear, Matt Stokes and Hayley Newman. Also represents a core group of eight artists: Brass Art, Rachel Goodyear, Josephine Flynn, Pat Flynn, David Mackintosh, Andrew McDonald, Kristin Mojsiewicz and Magnus Quaife.
Submission Policy Artists wishing to exhibit should visit the gallery and be familiar with its programme. Most exhibitions are initiated by the gallery rather than as a result of unsolicited applications.

Price range £100–£10,000
No of exhibitions annually 7

The Kif

23a Parr Street, Liverpool, L1 4JN
T 0151 7060008
E kif@livingbrain.co.uk
W www.livingbrain.co.uk
Founded in 2003 as an exhibition, workshop,
recording and rehearsal space in a disused
warehouse in Liverpool city centre. There is also a
pottery on site. Aims to assist artists young and old
within the city to become established and move
forward into self-sustainability.
Submission Policy Artists should phone or visit
the space to assess suitability.
Price range £25–£500
No of exhibitions annually 10

Liverpool History Shop

5 The Colonnades, Albert Dock,
Liverpool, L3 4AA
T 0151 7093566
E norma@liverpoolpictures.co.uk
W www.liverpoolpictures.co.uk
Contact Norma Lyons
Founded in 1991, specializing in photographs,
prints and paintings of Liverpool and surrounding
areas. Showcases many Liverpool artists.
Submission Policy Must be of local interest. Laser
prints not accepted.
Price range £120–£1,500 for original paintings;
£20–£200 for original photographs; £24.50–£125
for unframed art prints.

Lowes Court Gallery

12 Main Street, Egremont
CA22 2DW
T 01946 820693
E email@egremont-tic.fsnet.co.uk
W www.lowescourtgallery.co.uk
Contact Gallery Manager or Exhibition Organizer
Established in 1972 to promote appreciation of
visual arts in Cumbria. Aims to show a high
standard of contemporary and traditional arts and
crafts by emerging and established artists.
Exhibitions are in the main gallery; members work
in the back gallery.
Submission Policy Submissions welcome; hard
copy preferred. Limited space available. Work from
Cumbria or bordering counties only.
Price range Up to £500
No of exhibitions annually 8, at least two of which
are reserved for specific local features.

Manchester Craft & Design Centre

17 Oak Street, Northern Quarter, Manchester
M4 5JD
T 0161 8324274
F 0161 8323416
E info@craftanddesign.com
W www.craftanddesign.com
Sited in the heart of Manchester's Northern
Quarter, the hub of the city's artistic and innovative
community. Occupying the old Smithfield fish
market, it provides studio and retail space for a
wide range of contemporary applied artists
producing ceramics, jewellery, furniture and
interiors, textiles and fashion, photography and
visual arts, in workshops over two floors. Also has
a year-round programme of exhibitions; the
exhibition space can be hired when not in use.
Open to the public throughout the year. Admission
free. All work is for sale and commissions are
welcome.
Submission Policy Focuses on contemporary
crafts, both for tenant artists and temporary
exhibitions.
No of exhibitions annually 5

Mathew Street Gallery

31 Mathew Street, Liverpool, L2 6RE
T 0151 2350009
E lennonart@mathewstgallery.co.uk
W www.lennonart.co.uk
Opened in 1999 with a particular emphasis on The
Beatles and related work.

Mill House Gallery

The Old Windmill, Mill Lane, Parbold
T 01257 462333
E jb.millhousegallery@virgin.net
W www.jamesbartholomew.co.uk
Founded in 1997, specializing in work by James
Bartholomew. Also sells work of other artists
including Neville Fleetwood ROI, David Stanley
NAPA and Lawrence Isherwood. Offers a full
framing service ('Space Framing') in adjoined
premises.
Submission Policy All media considered. Apply in
the first instance with photos, slides, etc.
Price range £100–£2,000
No of exhibitions annually 4

Northern Lights Gallery

22 St John Street, Keswick, CA12 5AS
T 01768 775402
E info@northernlightsgallery.co.uk
W www.northernlightsgallery.co.uk

Contact Paul Martin
Founded in 1999, specializing in contemporary art
and crafts from the north of England and Scotland.
Artists represented include Jonathan Trotman,
Alison Critchlow, Matt Jardine and Joe Dias.
Submission Policy Artists must be resident in
Cumbria or neighbouring counties.
Price range £10–£2,000
No of exhibitions annually 4–6

Percy House Gallery
38–42 Market Place, Cockermouth, CA13 9NG
T 01900 829667
F 01900 829667
W www.percyhouse.co.uk
Established in 2002 in Cockermouth's oldest town
house, dating back to 1598 and still with many
original features. Displays unique arts and crafts.
Exhibition area upstairs.
Submission Policy Main priority of gallery is to
support living, working UK artists. Occasional
exhibitions by artists living abroad.
Price range £5–£4,000
No of exhibitions annually 12

Philips Contemporary Art
Studio 10, 10a Little Lever Street, Manchester
M1 1HR
T 0161 9414197
E philipsgallery@supanet.com
W www.philipscontemporaryart.com

Platform Gallery
Station Road, Clitheroe, BB7 2JT
T 01200 443071
F 01200 414556
E platform.gallery@ribblevalley.gov.uk
W www.ribblevalley.gov.uk/platformgallery
Contact Grace Whowell
A showcase for contemporary craft in Lancashire,
run by Ribble Valley Borough Council. Specializes
in textiles, ceramics, glass, jewellery and wood by
local and national makers. There is also a craft
shop and education space for workshops and talks.
Submission Policy Work must be craft-based,
rather than painting or photography. Send images,
CV and artist's statement.
Price range £3–£3,000
No of exhibitions annually 8

Richard Goodall Gallery
59 Thomas Street, Northern Quarter, Manchester
M4 1NA
T 0161 8323435

F 0161 8323266
E richard@richardgoodallgallery.com
W www.richardgoodallgallery.com
Stocks wide range of prints and posters.

Thornthwaite Galleries
Thornthwaite, Keswick, CA12 5SA
T 01768 778248
E enquiries@thornthwaite.net
W www.thornthwaite.net
Contact Ron Monk
Now in its thirty-fifth year, displaying over one
hundred artists. Work includes paintings (oil,
pastel, watercolour, etc.), wood-turning, wood
sculpture, metal sculpture, pottery, ceramics,
jewellery, photography and furniture.
Price range £5–£2,000

Tib Lane Gallery
14A Tib Lane, Manchester, M2 4JA
T 0161 8346928
Contact J.M. Green
Founded in 1959, dealing primarily in British
(mainly figurative) twentieth-century works.
Established and less widely known artists are
shown in both solo and mixed exhibitions from
October to June. Exhibited artists include Frink,
Herman, Valette and Vaughan.
Submission Policy Gallery exhibits oil paintings,
watercolours, drawings and pastels. No ceramics.
Price range From £200
No of exhibitions annually 5

Unicorn Gallery
1 Kings Court, Water Lane, Wilmslow, SK9 5AR
T 01625 525276
E originalpaintings@btconnect.com
W www.originalpaintings.com
Established in 1950, dealing in traditional and
contemporary original works of art. Specialists in
northern artists including L.S. Lowry, Arthur
Delany and Braag. Others include portrait artist
Robert Lenkiewicz, teddy-bear artist Deborah
Jones and landscape artist Gerhard Neswadba.
Large studio space may be available for use by
artists.
Submission Policy Always looking for talented new
artists. Both painters and sculptors are welcome to
submit work.
Price range £175–£40,000
No of exhibitions annually 2–3

Victorian Gallery
40 St John's Hill, Shrewsbury, SY1 1JQ

T 01743 356351
F 01743 356351
E victoriangallery@xln.co.uk
Founded in 1987. A specialist in antique maps and prints. Also stocks etchings, aquatints, etc. by contemporary artists, including Piers Browne and other British and Latvian etchers.
Price range £50–£300

View Two Gallery
23 Mathew Street, Liverpool, L2 6RE
T 0151 2369555

Watergate Street Gallery
60 Watergate Street, Chester, CH1 2LA
T 01244 345698
F 01244 3458837
W www.watergatestreetgallery.co.uk
Opened in 1992, offering original paintings, etchings and screenprints. Artists include Bernhard Vogel, Roy Fairchild Woodard, Willi Kissmer, Jurgen Gorg and Ian Fennelly.
Price range £250–£4,000

Wendy J. Levy Contemporary Art
17 Warburton Street, Didsbury, Manchester M20 6WA
T 0161 4464880
E wendy@wendyjlevy-art.com
W www.wendyjlevy-art.com
Specializes in paintings, drawings and sculpture by local, national and international artists. Also offers consultancy service.

Scotland

Amber Roome Contemporary Art
75–79 Cumberland Street, Edinburgh, EH3 6RD
T 0131 558 3352
E mail@amberroome.co.uk
W www.amberroome.co.uk
Based in the heart of Edinburgh's New Town. Exhibits a changing programme of contemporary art by established and emerging artists from Scotland and beyond. Includes exhibitions of work by artists such as Jackie Anderson, Michael Craik, Delia Baillie, Andrew Mackenzie, James Lumsden and Graham Flack.
Submission Policy Accepts submissions from artists in painting, photography, printmaking, drawing and mixed media. Send a CD of images in the first instance.
Price range £150–£5,000
No of exhibitions annually 9

Anthony Woodd Gallery
4 Dundas Street, Edinburgh, EH3 6HZ
T 0131 558 9544
F 0131 558 9525
E sales@anthonywoodd.com
W www.anthonywoodd.com
Specialist in Scottish, sporting, military, landscape and contemporary works. Framing, restoration, valuation and commission services undertaken.
No of exhibitions annually 4

Bourne Fine Art
6 Dundas Street, Edinburgh, EH3 6HZ
T 0131 5574050
F 0131 5578382
E art@bournefineart.com
W www.bournefineart.com
Founded in 1978, specializing in paintings and sculpture from the seventeenth century to the present day. Artists represented include Allan Ramsay, Sir Henry Raeburn, Sir David Wilkie and Alexander Nasymth as well as contemporary artists including John Boyd, John Byrne, Paul Martin and John Mclean. Also offers framing and restoration services.
Submission Policy Not currently taking on any new artists.
Price range £200–£650,000
No of exhibitions annually 8

Castle Gallery
43 Castle Street, Inverness, IV2 3DU
T 01463 729512
E info@castlegallery.co.uk
W www.castlegallery.co.uk
Contact Denise Collins
Founded in 2001. A leading contemporary art gallery in Scotland. Exhibitions feature paintings, sculpture, handmade prints, crafts and designer jewellery. Represents established artists and emerging talent including Karolina Larusdottir, Shazia Mahmood, Jonathan Shearer, Vega, Blandine Anderson and Dorothy Stirling.
Submission Policy Artists should send by post the following: ten recent images as photos, slides or jpegs; details of the images with titles, sizes and artist's prices; biographical information; an sae.
Price range £100–£5,000
No of exhibitions annually 5 solo or joint shows. Also a constantly changing mixed display throughout the year.

Cat's Moustache Gallery
54 St John's Street, Creetown, nr Newton Stewart

DG8 7JT
T 01671 820577 / 01659 50680
F 01671 820577
E rtrevanion@hotmail.com
W www.thecatsmoustachegallery.co.uk
Contact Penelope Nye
Offers original handmade arts and crafts from
Scotland, the UK and beyond. Stocks a wide range
of paintings in oils, acrylics and watercolours, silk
painting, calligraphy and lettercutting, ceramics,
jewellery, wood, glass, textiles and other handmade
gifts. Runs a regular series of exhibitions and
demonstrations throughout the year, all of which
are free. Open all year Fridays, Saturdays and
Sundays and seven days a week during July and
August, or by appointment.
Price range £1–£500
No of exhibitions annually 12

Collective Gallery
22–28 Cockburn Street, Edinburgh, EH1 1NY
T 0131 2201260
E mail@collectivegallery.org
W www.collectivegallery.org
Originally established as an artist-run space in
1984 and now an independent, publicly funded
exhibition, commissioning and development
agency. Aims to support emergent Scottish
contemporary art and artists within the context of
an international programme. Committed to
creating access to the contemporary visual arts
through a range of innovative projects and
structures. Ongoing exhibition programme in the
two galleries and project room. Increasingly
interested in inviting artists to design specific
projects operating within the framework of the
city's contemporary social, economic, political and
physical spheres.
Submission Policy Has extensive membership
scheme, costing £5 for Scottish-based artists and
£15 for all other artists. Members are entitled to
submit exhibition applications twice a year
(deadlines are in March and September).
No of exhibitions annually 8 in main gallery; 8 in
project room.

Compass Gallery
178 West Regent Street, Glasgow, G2 4RL
T 0141 2216370
F 0141 2481322
E compass@gerberfineart.co.uk
W www.compassgallery.co.uk
Contact Jill Gerber
In its thirty-seventh year, promoting young,

emerging Scottish-based artists and established
contemporary artists throughout the UK. A
registered charity and non-profit-making company.
Submission Policy By email or post (CD preferred).
Price range £50–£10,000
No of exhibitions annually 6–8

Custom House Art Gallery and Studios
Custom House, 19 High Street, Kirkcudbright
DG6 4JZ
T 01557 330585
E customhouse@btinternet.com
W www.customhousegallery.co.uk
Contact Suzanne Davies
Shows contemporary art in the traditional setting
of Kirkcudbright, an attractive coastal town in
south-west Scotland with strong links to the
Glasgow Boys and the Scottish Colourists. Painter
Suzanne Davies and printmaker-illustrator
Malcolm Davies live and work here, showing their
own work and work by other professional artists
and makers, mostly from Dumfries and Galloway.
Non-residential drawing and painting courses are
held all year.
Submission Policy CV and recent images welcome
from professional artists and makers in southern
Scotland, northern England and Northern Ireland.
Price range £20–£1,000
No of exhibitions annually 5–6

Cyril Gerber Fine Art
148 West Regent Street, Glasgow, G2 2RQ
T 0141 2213095
F 0141 2481322
E cyril@gerberfineart.co.uk
W www.gerberfineart.co.uk
Contact Jill Gerber
Established in 1983, the gallery's large stock
includes prominent nineteenth- and twentieth-
century British artists (including the Glasgow
School, Scottish Colourists and twentieth-century
Scottish masters) as well as contemporary work.
Submission Policy Apply by email or post (CDs
preferred).
Price range £100–£95,000
No of exhibitions annually 4–6

doggerfisher
11 Gayfield Square, Edinburgh, EH1 3NT
T 00 44 (131) 558 7110
F 00 44 (131) 558 7179
E mail@doggerfisher.com
W www.doggerfisher.com
Established in 2001. Exhibits and promotes new-

generation and established artists from Scotland and beyond. The 100m2 gallery in a former tyre garage was designed by architect Oliver Chapman. Has so far been selected to participate in over ten international art fairs including the Art Statements, Art Basel, Armory in New York, and Frieze in London. In addition to the programmed exhibitions, it also holds an archive of represented artists' work available to view in the gallery. Represented artists include Charles Avery, Claire Barclay, Nathan Coley, Graham Fagen, Moyna Flannigan, Louise Hopkins, Rosalind Nashashibi, Sally Osborn, Lucy Skaer and Hanneline Visnes.
Submission Policy The gallery is programmed by the director, showing exhibitions by represented and invited artists. It does not accept proposals for exhibitions. Non-returnable invites and details of exhibitions welcomed.
Price range £200–£45,000
No of exhibitions annually 6

Dundas Street Gallery
6a Dundas Street, Edinburgh, EH3 6HZ
T 0131 5589363
E carolyn@bournefineart.com
W www.bournefineart.com
Contact Carolyn Henderson
A recently refurbished gallery offering 700 sq. ft of exhibition space available for hire.

Edinburgh Printmakers
23 Union Street, Edinburgh, EH1 3LR
T 0131 5572479
F 0131 5588418
E enquiries@edinburgh-printmakers.co.uk
W www.edinburgh-printmakers.co.uk
Contact Alastair Clark Assistant Director
Established in 1967. Dedicated to promoting contemporary printmaking practice. It achieves this by providing, maintaining and staffing an entrance-free gallery and open-access print studio, where artists and members of the public can use equipment and source technical expertise to develop their printmaking skills.
Submission Policy Annually selects a set number of exhibitions from artists' proposals.
Price range £30–£3,000
No of exhibitions annually 10

English-Speaking Union Scotland
23 Atholl Crescent, Edinburgh, EH3 8HQ
T 0131 2291528
F 0131 2298620
E director@esuscotland.org.uk

W www.esuscotland.org.uk
Contact John A. Duncan
A charity founded in 1918 to promote international understanding through English. The Edinburgh gallery has provided high-quality exhibition space in the heart of the city for the last forty years.
Submission Policy No restrictions.
Price range Depends on exhibitors.
No of exhibitions annually 5–6
Cost to hire or rent £750 per week, or 30% commission on sales – whichever is higher.

Glasgow Print Studio
22 & 25 King Street, Merchant City, Glasgow G1 5QP
T 01415 520704
F 01415 522919
E gallery@gpsart.co.uk
W www.gpsart.co.uk
Active since 1972 in encouraging and promoting the art of printmaking through practice, exhibition, education and sales. One of the largest publishers of original prints in the UK. A member-led organization offering artist members open-access facilities in etching, lithography, relief print, screenprint and digital print production. Also offers introductory classes in printmaking.
Submission Policy Exhibition submissions welcome from artists specializing in printmaking.
Price range £100–£5,000
No of exhibitions annually 20

Infrared Gallery
18a Meadow Road, Glasgow Harbour, Glasgow G11 6HX
T 0141 3371283
E infraredgallery@btconnect.com
Contact James Russell
Founded in 2003, specializing in contemporary Scottish art. Artists represented include Rick Ulman, Leila Smith, Evan Sutherland, Simon Laurie, Michelle Dawn Hannah and James Russell.
Submission Policy All contemporary living artists considered. Work viewed preferably on slides or as digital photos on CD.
Price range £50–£10,000
No of exhibitions annually 12

Ingleby Gallery
6 Carlton Terrace, Edinburgh, EH7 5DD
T 0131 5564441
F 0131 5564454
E info@inglebygallery.com
W www.inglebygallery.com

Founded 1998 and has an exhibition programme of international contemporary art by established and emerging artists from Scotland and beyond. Since 2000 the gallery has also published a series of artist books, prints and editions. Artists represented include David Austen, Anna Barriball, Ian Davenport, Ian Hamilton Finlay, Howard Hodgkin, Callum Innes, Peter Liversidge, Sean Scully and Alison Watt.
Submission Policy Welcomes serious submissions from artists but recommends artists consider the gallery programme and the specific kinds of work exhibited before making a proposal. Prefers an initial submission of a CV and a small number of images by email.
Price range From £10 for prints; from £500 for original works.
No of exhibitions annually 6

The Jerdan Gallery
42 Marketgate South, Crail, Fife, KY10 3TL
T 01333 450797
E david@thejerdangallery.com
W www.thejerdangallery.com
Founded in 2002, the gallery specializes in Scottish contemporary art, woodwork, sculpture, glass and jewellery. Works regularly in stock by Duncan Macleod, Joe McIntyre, Lin Pattullo, Derek Sanderson, Pat Kramek and Tom Scott.
Price range £100–£10,000
No of exhibitions annually 8

John Green Fine Art
182 Bath Street, Glasgow
G2 4HG
T 0141 3331991
E mail@johngreenfineart.co.uk
W www.johngreenfineart.co.uk
Contact Phyllis Malcolm
Founded in 1984. Dealers in nineteenth- and twentieth-century and contemporary oils and watercolours, mostly by Scottish artists but also including British and continental artists. Current stock includes works by the Glasgow Boys and Girls, the Scottish Colourists, post-war artists Sir Robin Philipson and William Gear, and contemporary artists Blair Thompson, Jonathan Robertson and Norman Edgar. Also offers specialist framing and restoration services.
Submission Policy Welcomes submissions from artists. Initial contact should be made via email or telephone.
Price range From £100.
No of exhibitions annually 4

Lloyd Jerome Gallery
200 Bath Street, Glasgow, G2 4HG
T 0141 3310722
F 0141 3310733
E lj@dentalpractice.com
W www.dentalpractice.com
Opened in 1994 with the aim of creating a space that would show work that might not otherwise be seen in Glasgow.
Price range Up to £50,000
No of exhibitions annually 10

Marchmont Gallery and Picture Framer
56 Warrender Park Road, corner with Marchmont Road, Edinburgh, EH9 1EX
T 0131 2288228
E enquiries@marchmontgallery.com
W www.marchmontgallery.com
Contact James Sutherland
Founded in 2004. Mixed exhibitions of mainly new and up-and-coming artists including Claudia Massie, Nicola Moir, Catherine Rayner and Peter Gorrie. Professional in-house picture-framing service including mount-cutting and canvas-stretching
Submission Policy Always interested in any arts, crafts, ceramics etc. from Scotland and the UK. Email pictures of work with any relevant info to the gallery.
Price range £5–£1,500

Modern Institute/Toby Webster Ltd
Suite 6, 1st Floor, 73 Robertson Street, Glasgow G2 8QD
T 0141 2483 711
F 0141 2483280
E mail@themoderninstitute.com
W www.themoderninstitute.com
Contact Andrew Hamilton
Founded in 1998. Represents thirty artists, including Jim Lambie, Cathy Wilkes, Victoria Morton, Simon Starling, Richard Wright, Martin Boyce, Jeremy Deller, Richard Hughes, Scott Myles, Toby Paterson, Eva Rothschild, Tony Swain, Hayley Tompkins, Sue Tompkins, Urs Fischer, Mark Handforth and Monika Soswsnowska.
No of exhibitions annually 10

Open Eye Gallery and i2 Gallery
34 Abercromby Place, Edinburgh, EH3 6QE
T 0131 5571020 / 5589872
F 0131 5571020
E mail@openeyegallery.co.uk
W www.openeyegallery.co.uk

Contact Michelle Norman
Established in 1982 and situated in Edinburgh's historic New Town, the Open Eye Gallery is equidistant between the Scottish National Gallery and the Portrait Gallery. Deals with both established and young contemporary artists. Exhibitors include Alan Davie, John Bellany, Calum Colvin and Adrian Wiszniewski. In addition to paintings, the gallery exhibits applied arts. i2 focuses on British and international printmaking, exhibiting Picasso, Miró, Albers, Warhol, Lucian Freud, William Scott and David Hockney.
Price range £100–£50,000
No of exhibitions annually 16

Peacock Visual Arts
21 Castle Street, off the Castlegate, Aberdeen AB11 5BQ
T 01224 639539
F 01224 627094
E info@peacockvisualarts.co.uk
W www.peacockvisualarts.co.uk
Contact Monika Vykoukal (Assistant Curator)
Founded in 1974. An educational charity funded by Aberdeen City Council and the Scottish Arts Council. It exists to bring artists and public together to share and explore ideas and to make and present art in innovative ways. Has developed a wide range of production facilities and skills (in design, digital imaging, photography, printmaking and video) and promotes numerous artists' participatory and exhibition projects each year.
Submission Policy Artists are invited to submit exhibition or project proposals, focusing on participatory, socially-engaged practice. No areas or media are excluded.
Price range From £25
No of exhibitions annually Exhibition programme changes regularly throughout the year.

scotlandart.com
2 St Stephen's Place, Stockbridge, Edinburgh EH3 5AJ
T 0131 2256257
E edinburgh@scotlandart.com
W www.scotlandart.com
Contact Marion Ferguson
Established in 1999. Carries extensive stock of original art work (over 1,400 paintings). Has a number of leading Scottish artists, including Blair Thompson, Patsy Macarthur, Lesley Banks, Barry Mcglashan, Kirsty Whitten and Ian King. The website has a page for each artist where purchases can be made. Offers gift vouchers, wedding lists,

free art consultancy to homes or offices and a leasing service. Takes artists' work to art fairs all over the UK, arranges commissions, ships work nationally and internationally. Holds exhibitions every month of selected artists. Can also arrange framing for artists and reframes for customers.
Submission Policy Only accepts original paintings, sculptures and jewellery from living artists. Applications welcome all year round, preferably jpegs or photos.
Price range £80–£6,000
No of exhibitions annually 12 in each gallery (total of 24).

The Scottish Gallery
16 Dundas Street, Edinburgh, EH3 6HZ
T 0131 558 1200
F 0131 558 3900
E mail@scottish-gallery.co.uk
W www.scottish-gallery.co.uk
Established by Aitken Dott in 1842. Deals in contemporary and twentieth-century Scottish painting and contemporary objects by established figures and talented newcomers. A craft department was established in 1986. Work by gallery artists and makers always available. Also exhibits at major art fairs and holds an annual exhibition in London.
Submission Policy Specializes in the work of Scottish artists, artists with a strong Scottish connection through training, etc. or artists living and working in Scotland. International craft artists.
Price range £20–£300,000
No of exhibitions annually Changing monthly programme

Shoreline Studio
2 Shore Road, Aberdour, KY3 0TR
T 01383 860705
F 01383 860705
E ianmcc@shoreline.demon.co.uk
W www.shoreline.sco.fm
Contact Ian McCrorie
Founded in 1997. A compact gallery aiming to promote quality works of art primarily from artists living and/or working in Scotland. Adjacent listed buildings are intended to become nine workspaces for artists, and an exhibition and workshop space.
Submission Policy For display purposes all art work should be signed and appropriately presented and labelled.
Price range £1–£1,000
No of exhibitions annually 6

Sorcha Dallas
5–9 St Margaret's Place, Glasgow, G1 5JY
T 0141 5532662 / 07812 605745
F 0141 5532662
E info@sorchadallas.com
W www.sorchadallas.com
Contact Jo Charlton (Director's Assistant)
Founded in 2004, representing thirteen local and
international emerging artists. Develops and co-
ordinates commissioning, purchasing and
exhibiting opportunities on a local, national and
international level. Represented artists include Rob
Churm, Henry Coombes, Kate Davis, Alex Frost,
Charlie Hammond, Fiona Jardine, Sophie
Macpherson, Alan Michael, Craig Mulholland,
Alex Pollard, Gary Rough, Clare Stephenson and
Michael Stumpf.
Submission Policy Does not run an open
submissions policy. Invitation only.
Price range £300–£15,000
No of exhibitions annually 7

Stills
23 Cockburn Street, Edinburgh, EH1 1BP
E info@stills.org
W www.stills.org
Established in 1977 and now one of Scotland's
most important centres for research and for
showing works utilizing existing and developing
technologies.

Street Level Photoworks
1st Floor, 48 King Street, Glasgow, G1 5QT
T 0141 5522151
F 0141 5522323
E info@streetlevelphotoworks.org
W www.streetlevelphotoworks.org
Contact Malcolm Dickson
Founded in 1989, promoting the creative use of
photomedia. Recognized for its integrated practice,
the organization presents an ongoing series of
exhibitions and an education and open-access
programme.
Submission Policy Recently moved to a temporary
location while exhibition and workshop spaces are
being redeveloped. Not in a position to accept artist
proposals until 2009, at which stage the gallery
expects to be up-and-running in its new venue.

Torrance Gallery
36 Dundas Street, Edinburgh, EH3 6JN
T 0131 5566366
F 0131 5566366
E enquiries@torrancegallery.co.uk

W www.torrancegallery.co.uk
Contact Brian Torrance
Founded in 1970. The first contemporary art
gallery in Dundas Street, the renowned centre for
contemporary art.
Price range £100–£8,000
No of exhibitions annually 15

Tracey McNee Fine Art
47 Parnie Street, Merchant City, Glasgow, G1 5LU
T 0141 5525627
F 0141 5528207
E info@traceymcnee.com
W www.traceymcnee.com
Contact Tracey McNee
Seeks to exhibit the best in contemporary art from
Scotland and beyond. Promotes artists in the
gallery and at the major art fairs throughout the
UK. Artists represented include Gerard M. Burns,
Francis Boag, Sandra Bell and James Hawkins.
Submission Policy Artists from all media
welcomed. Preferably send CV, statement and
images by email.
Price range £200–£40,000
No of exhibitions annually 8

Westgate Gallery
39–41 Westgate, North Berwick, EH39 4AG
T 0160 894976
F 01620 890452
E admin@westgate-gallery.co.uk
W www.westgate-gallery.co.uk
A gallery and gift shop selling original and limited-
edition works by local, Scottish and UK artists.
Includes jewellery, glass and ceramics.
Submission Policy All submissions, from both
new and established artists, considered.
Price range Up to £3,000
No of exhibitions annually 4

South-east

The Afton Gallery
4 Eastcliff Road, Shanklin Old Village
Isle of Wight, PO37 6AA
T 01983 868373
F 01983 531447
W www.aftongalleryfineart.co.uk
Founded in 1988, exhibiting an extensive range of
Isle of Wight paintings and prints, limited and
signed editions of Anne Cotterill (floral) and Tim
Thompson (marine), and handpainted bone china.
Also offers picture-framing and restoration
service.

Submission Policy No further submissions wanted.
Price range Framed prints up to £200. Framed originals up to £1,500.

Alan Kluckow Fine Art

65 Chobham Road, Sunningdale, SL5 0DT
T 01344 875296
E alan@kluckow.com
W www.kluckow.com
Contact Alan Kluckow
Founded in 1999. Promotes contemporary British and international painters, sculptors and photographers. Shows styles from traditional representational through abstract and new media. Aside from regular exhibitions featuring gallery artists, it also runs collaborative shows with other national and international galleries and arts organizations. Artists include Anne Penman Sweet, Ian Rank Broadley, John Meyer, Martin Yeoman, Robbie Wraith and Susan Leyland. Other services offered include consultancy for corporate and private collectors, arts management, career advice for artists and portfolio analysis.
Submission Policy Preferably send a CD with a minimum of 6 images, including a CV and artist statement (with sae if returns necessary).
Price range £250–£30,000
No of exhibitions annually 10

Albion

Albion House, North Street, Turners Hill, Worth, RH10 4NS
T 01342 715670
E albion@fsmail.net
Art consultants founded in 1965 specializing in all aspects and mediums of international, modern and contemporary art from c.1900, with a particular interest in American and European. Undertakes complete research and administration for private collectors, artist estates and public institutions, for single items or complete collections. Artworks researched for authenticity/history particularly where an artwork's authorship or provenance may be questioned. Research and advice for art restitution. Condition/restoration reports and valuations provided. Artworks discreetly purchased and/or sold via private treaty.
Submission Policy Submissions are welcomed in writing from established international artists or executors of artists' estates/collections.
Price range £500–£5,000,000+
No of exhibitions annually None; strictly by appointment only.

Alexander-Morgan Gallery

7b Station Road, Epping, CM16 4HA
T 01992 571639
F 01992 571639
Contact Dee Alexander-Morgan
Opened in 1997. Sells original paintings, handmade prints such as etchings and silkscreens, a few sculptures, ceramics and one-off glass pieces. Mostly abstract and humorous pieces.
Submission Policy Always happy to look at new work. Usually asks to see photos or flysheets first.
Price range £10–£3,000
No of exhibitions annually 3

Alexandra Wettstein Fine Art

52 Wendover Way, Welling, DA16 2BN
T 020 83047920
E alexandra.wettstein@virgin.net
Deals in paintings, sculpture, prints and ceramics. Exhibited artists include John Piper, Charles Newington, Dale Devereux Barker and Sandy Sykes. Has arranged exhibitions of twentieth-century and contemporary British artists at museums and galleries around the country, including three major retrospectives of John Piper's work.
Price range From £100

Animal Arts

20 Orange Street, Canterbury, CT1 2JA
T 01227 451145
E info@AnimalArts.co.uk
W www.AnimalArts.co.uk
Contact Keith Williams
Founded in 2001. An independent publisher of wildlife art, producing giclée prints from artists' original work. The gallery is situated in the shadow of Canterbury Cathedral and sells throughout the world and to the fine-art trade.
Submission Policy Only sells prints (not originals). All media accepted.
Price range £45–£300

Art Connection Eton

100 High Street, Eton, Windsor, SL4 6AF
T 01753 865265
F 01753 865265
E info@theartconnectioneton.co.uk
W www.theartconnectioneton.co.uk
Contact Jon Barker and Soozy Barker
Founded in 1999. Specializes in contemporary landscape, abstract and figurative work in oils and mixed media. Light and spacious gallery offers a relaxed environment to view. Main artists include

Jon Barker, John Lawrence, George Thomas, Peter Collins, Soozy Barker and Ian Elliot.
Submission Policy Email applications preferred.
Price range £300–£7,500
No of exhibitions annually 4

Art in Action Gallery
Waterperry Gardens, Waterperry, nr Wheatley
OX33 1JZ
T 01844 338085
E art_in_action.gallery@virgin.net
Contact Wendy Farha
Founded in 1994 as a spin-off from 'Art in Action' and a haven for highly crafted decorative and fine arts. Emphasis is on excellence and originality, with work by John Leach, T. Millway, Jennie Gilbert and Laurence McGowan.
Submission Policy Highly trained and exhibited artists from all media welcome.
Price range £10–£16,500
No of exhibitions annually 4

Art@94
94 London Road, Apsley, Hemel Hempstead
HP3 9SD
T 01442 234123
F 01442 239761
E info@art4interiors.co.uk
W www.art4interiors.co.uk
Retail and trade (wholesale) outlet for abstract, contemporary, mixed media and traditional paintings on canvas. Most media are catered for. Artists include Kriss Keer, Lizzie Gregory, D. Zealey, S. Ringer, Saiqa, Edward Clarke and John Greenwell. Suppliers of blank canvases (single- and double-stretched). Trade and contract framing also undertaken. Specializes in art for homes, interior designers and businesses.
Submission Policy Requires mature artists painting contemporary seascapes and abstracts in oils on canvas (not panels). Apply by sending in photos of work or email high-resolution jpegs.
Price range Price range £35–£7,500
No of exhibitions annually 3–4

Arthouse Gallery
10 Western Road, Brighton, BN3 1AE
T 01273 770083
E info@brightonarthouse.com
W www.brightonarthouse.com
Opened in 2005. One of the largest commercial contemporary-art galleries in Brighton and Hove. Provides a retail outlet for a diverse range of artists producing paintings, prints, sculptures, ceramics,

jewellery and furniture. The integrated skylight café ensures a high level of traffic. Aims to provide a friendly, calm, non-pressured environment for people from all walks of life to enjoy and purchase art.
Submission Policy Constantly looking for new, exciting artists. Offers highly competitive commission rates and hard-working representation.
Price range £50–£5,000
No of exhibitions annually Private views every month.

artrepublic
13 Bond Street, Brighton, BN1 1RD
T 01273 724829
F 01273 746016
E info@artrepublic.com
W www.artrepublic.com
Contact Lawrence Alkin
Features thousands of art prints from hundreds of famous artists including Dali, Warhol, Lichtenstein, de Lempicka, Klee and Hockney. Also offers a high-quality mounting and framing service.
Submission Policy Although most prints are by famous artists, it occasionally features prints by local artists.
Price range £10–£2,500

Artwork Sculpture Gallery
3 The Shambles, Sevenoaks, TN13 1LJ
T 01732 450960
E info@artworksgallery.co.uk
W www.artworksgallery.co.uk
Founded in 1990. Specializes in sculptures in bronze, bronze resin, steel and stone. Artists represented include Tom Greenshields, Kate Denton, Everard Meynell, Gill Brown, Angela Bishop and Martin Roberts.
Price range £200–£15,000

Barn Galleries
Aston, Henley-on-Thames, RG9 3DX
T 01491 577786
F 01491 577786
E info@barngalleries.com
W www.barngalleries.com
Established in 1990. Hosts Artspace, an annual contemporary art extravaganza where seventy-five invited artists show in eighteenth-century timbered barns and gardens.
Submission Policy Applications invited from September to December for the following summer season.

Price range £20–£5,000. Most paintings under £1,000.
No of exhibitions annually 2–3

Barry Keene Gallery

12 Thameside, Henley-on-Thames, RG9 1BH
T 01491 577119
E barrykeene@fsbdial.co.uk
W www.barrykeenegallery.co.uk
Opened in 1971. Shows antique, modern and contemporary art including paintings, watercolours, etchings, prints, drawings and sculpture. Master frame-maker, picture restorer and conservator. Artists represented include Ronald Ossary Dunlop, RA RBA NEAC, L.G. Samuel Palmer RWS, John Martin RBA, Helen Hale ROI NS SWA FPS, David Eustace RBA and Richard Pikesley RWS NEAC.
Submission Policy Details and photos by post or email.
Price range From £50
No of exhibitions annually 2

BCA Gallery

13 The High Street, Bedford, MK40 1RN
T 01234 273580
E BCAGallery@bedfordcreativearts.org
W www.bedfordcreativearts.org.uk
Exhibits contemporary visual art with a focus on film, photography and digital media.

Bell Fine Art Ltd

67b Parchment Street, Winchester, SO23 8AT
T 01962 860439
F 01962 860439
E bellfineart@btclick.com
W www.bellfineart.co.uk
Founded in 1977, specializing in original art from 1800 to the present day. Also sells sculpture, ceramics and glass, and offers a full picture-framing service. Exhibits at 10 art and antique fairs annually.
Submission Policy No video or installations.
Price range £5–£5,000
No of exhibitions annually 2

Bluemoon Gallery

18 Camden Road, Tunbridge Wells, TN1 2PT
T 01892 540100
E info@bluemoongallery.co.uk
W www.bluemoongallery.co.uk,
Originally opened as a base for owner Iaysha Salih to show her paintings. Now also exhibits work by other artists including paintings, sculptures, vases,

textiles, scarves, bags and jewellery. Items exhibited must be individually handmade. The gallery's primary focus is to raise awareness of healing with art.
Submission Policy Original art only (no prints). Artists wishing to exhibit should send in a CD of their work.
No of exhibitions annually 4

Brian Sinfield Gallery Ltd

150 High Street, Burford, OX18 4QU
T 01993 824464
E gallery@briansinfield.com
W www.briansinfield.com
Established in 1972. Specializes in contemporary and twentieth-century painters including Fred Cuming, P.J. Crook, Peter Kuhfeld, L.S. Lowry and Alan Lowndes. Up to 8 exhibitions a year with catalogues. Also art brokers (selling higher priced paintings on behalf of clients).
Submission Policy Will consider the work of new artists in any medium, though not pure abstract or 'cutting-edge'.
Price range £500–£100,000. Most paintings sell between £1,500 and £12,000.
No of exhibitions annually 8

Brighton Artists' Gallery of Contemporary Art

108a Dyke Road, Brighton, BN1 3TE
T 01273 711016
E alicia.murphy@baggallery.co.uk
W www.baggallery.co.uk
Established in 2001 and one of the largest commercial galleries in East Sussex. Exhibited artists include Man Ray and Damien Hirst as well as local artists. Gallery restructured in 2005 to include the Bank café-bar. Solo-show, print and photographic galleries available. Framing service offered.
Submission Policy Artists looking for solo shows should send jpegs at 300 pixels high and no more than 72 dpi, plus short biography and statement. Only contemporary artists will be considered.
Price range From £50 for limited-edition prints to £2,500 for paintings.
No of exhibitions annually 12 in each gallery space.

Canon Gallery

New Street, Petworth, GU28 0AS
T 01798 344422
F 01798 344422
E enquiries@canongallery.co.uk
W www.thecanongallery.co.uk
Founded in 1985, specializing in eighteenth-,

nineteenth- and twentieth-century oils and watercolours. Also sells work by contemporary artists.
Submission Policy 'Any artist who can paint!'
Price range £400–£50,000
No of exhibitions annually 3

Chameleon Gallery
13a Prince Albert Street, Brighton, BN1 1HE
T 01273 324432
F 01273 324432
E info@chameleongallery.co.uk
W www.chameleongallery.org
Contact Mark Francis
Positioned at the heart of Brighton in the Lanes, the gallery displays work on two floors, holding over one hundred pieces. As well as showing local artists, the owner travels extensively across the country looking for new talent. The gallery's philosophy is to show art of the highest quality at affordable prices.
Submission Policy Considers all contemporary art. Artists should send examples of work via email.
Price range £100–£1,000
No of exhibitions annually 6

Chichester Gallery
8 The Hornet, Chichester, PO19 7JG
T 01243 779821
F 01243 773345
Founded to encourage interest in and acquisition of all forms of painting (contemporary and period). Aims to help encourage up-and-coming painters, often by promoting their work through exhibitions held on the premises. Gallery housed in a grade-2 Georgian building, comprising seven rooms, five of which are permanently used for displaying pictures. Cleaning and restoration of oils and watercolours also undertaken. Artists include Claude Hayes, Lennard Lewis, William Gallcott Knell, Christopher John Adams, Kenneth Child and Richard Rennie.
Price range £75–£7,000
No of exhibitions annually 2

Craftsmen's Gallery
1 Market Street, Woodstock, OX20 1SU
T 01993 811995
F 01993 811995
E richard.marriott@btclick.com
W www.craftsmensgallery.co.uk
Art and craft gallery under present ownership for over 20 years, specializing in work by contemporary British artists and craftsmen including Valerie Petts, Ken Messer, Andrea Bates, Colin Tuffrey, Isis Ceramics and Poole Pottery. Complete picture framing service. The Art and Craft Materials section provides a wide range of materials from all the major makers.
Price range £30–£1,500
No of exhibitions annually 1–2

Cranbrook Gallery
Stone Street, Cranbrook, TN17 3HF
T 01580 720720
E info@britishfineart.com
W www.britishfineart.com
Contact Paul Rodgers
Founded in 1977, specializing in watercolours by British artists working from the eighteenth to early twentieth centuries. Also UK sales agents for award-winning equestrian artist Alison Guest. Publishers of fine-art prints.
Submission Policy Submissions from living artists working in watercolour are welcome.
Price range £100–£16,000
No of exhibitions annually 2

Daniel Laurence Fine Artworks
226 and 246 Kings Road Arches, Brighton BN1 1NB
T 01273 739694 / 07780 616223
F 01273 739694
E info@daniellaurence.co.uk
W www.daniellaurence.co.uk
Contact Daniel Laurence
Seafront gallery and working studio, set within Brighton's famous Artists' Quarter, exhibiting a wide range of unique artworks, including limited-edition prints, original paintings, sculpture, furniture and home accessories.
Submission Policy Open to applications by painters, sculptors and craftspeople.
Price range £35–£255 for limited-edition prints; £250–£1,000 for original works.

Fairfax Gallery
23 The Pantiles, Tunbridge Wells, TN2 5TD
T 01892 525525
E andrew@fairfaxgallery.com
W www.fairfaxgallery.com
Founded in 1995. Exhibits established, award-winning and emerging contemporary artists including Mary Jane Ansell, Shaun Ferguson, Mark Johnston, James Naughton, Alice Scrutton and Frank To. Further branches in Chelsea, London and Burnham Market, Norfolk.
Submission Policy Work may be submitted on

slides, prints or CD, with CV and sae. May also be submitted by email.
Price range £300–£10,000
No of exhibitions annually 9

Farnham Maltings East Wing Gallery
Bridge Square, Farnham, GU9 7QR
T 01252 726234
F 01252 718177
E info@farnhammaltings.com
W www.farnhammaltings.com
Contact Kate Martin (Visual Arts Officer)
Set in one of the old kilns. Hosts a variety of exhibitions throughout the year, ranging from graduate shows to national touring exhibitions. Exhibited artists include David Hockney, Matisse and Andy Goldsworthy.
Submission Policy Space is for rental to individuals and art groups. All artists are asked to present work for selection. All media considered.
No of exhibitions annually 15–20

Four Square Fine Arts
5 Waterloo Place, Lewes, BN7 2PP
T 01273 479646
E sonia@foursquarearts.co.uk
W www.foursquarearts.co.uk
Presents a portfolio of emerging and well-established artists from a variety of disciplines including painting, printmaking, photography, ceramics and sculpture. Curates shows in hired galleries in London and Sussex and exhibits at major art fairs throughout the UK.
Submission Policy Send a CD or good transparencies with a current CV and statement about the work.
Price range £100–£5,000
No of exhibitions annually 6–8

Fourwalls
31a Hamilton Road, Brighton, BN1 5DL
T 01273 694405
E info@four-walls.co.uk
W www.four-walls.co.uk
Contact Lara Bowen
An art agency with an eclectic portfolio of quality contemporary work from artists in Brighton and the surrounding area. From portraiture to landscapes, oils to photography, there is no house style. Manages, promotes and publishes work by artists including Sophie Abbott, Becky Blair, Emma Brownjohn, Simon Dixon, Sam Hewitt, Shyama Ruffell and Adrian Talbot. Also curates group and solo shows in a range of spaces

including non-gallery settings. Does not have a set gallery space, preferring to utilize other exhibition opportunities.
Submission Policy Artists interested in working wth Fourwalls should initially send five images, a CV and statement by email or post.
Price range £100–£2,500
No of exhibitions annually 50, many rotated.

Fovea Gallery
140 Vaughan Road, Harrow, HA1 4EB
T 020 83572924
E fovea@btconnect.com
W www.foveagallery.co.uk
Contact Debbie de Beer
Founded in 2002 in an old butcher's shop, aiming to offer solo or mixed shows in a small dedicated space. Peer critique sessions for artists. Opportunities to run workshops.
Submission Policy Any medium considered. Artists should visit to view the space. Solo shows usually scheduled at least eighteen months in advance.
Price range Up to £1,000
No of exhibitions annually 10
Cost to hire or rent £250 for two weeks including coverage on website and email invite.

Francis Iles
Rutland House, 103 High Street, Rochester ME1 1LX
T 01634 843081
F 01634 846681
E nettie@francis-iles.com
W www.artycat.com
Contact Nettie Iles-North
Established in 1962. Exhibits living artists work mainly in a representative vein but there is some contemporary work as well. Handles the estates of Rowland Hilder OBE PPRI RSMA and Roland Batchelor RWS. Shows over 700 works at any one time.
Price range £60–£20,000
No of exhibitions annually 4 in-house; 4 art fairs.

Gallery 99
25 High Street, Knaphill, GU21 2PP
T 01483 797884
F 01483 797884
Sells mainly original paintings. Also offers a picture-framing service and sells artists' materials.
Submission Policy Applications welcome in person by prior arrangement. All works sold on commission (thirty per cent to the gallery, seventy

per cent to the artist). Flat art work only; no room for sculpture.
Price range £50–£500

Gallery Beckenham
71A High Street, Beckenham, BR3 1AW
T 020 86503040
E enquiries@gallerybeckenham.com
W www.gallerybeckenham.com
Family-owned gallery specializing in contemporary art from noteworthy young artists and those more established. Specializations include original canvases, sculpture, glass and art photography. Artists include Yuri Gorbachev, Sandro Negri, Anna Bocek, Susan Caines, Mark Leach, Enver Gursev, Manuel Quintanilla, Ev Meynell and Danny Green.
Submission Policy All types of art considered. Email contact details with six images of work.
Price range £200–£40,000
No of exhibitions annually 6

George Street Gallery
4 George Street, Kemptown, Brighton, BN2 1RH
T 01273 681852
E gsg@onetel.com
W www.gsfg.co.uk
300 sq. ft of gallery space available for hire from February to December, including a caretaker so artist's presence is required only on hanging and removal days. Also offers a bespoke picture framing service from a basement workshop established over 100 years ago.
Submission Policy Artists should submit images of work and CV by post or email. Most types of wall-hung art considered, including abstract and photographic.
Price range £50–£2,000
No of exhibitions annually 10
Cost to hire or rent £300 per month basic then 25% commission (VAT not charged).

Grace Barrand Design Centre
19 High Street, Nutfield, RH1 4HH
T 01737 822865
F 01737 822617
E info@gbdc.co.uk
W www.gracebarrand.co.uk
Contact Aileen Hamilton
Founded in 1996. Committed to promoting and selling the best in contemporary art and design by established and new makers. Regular exhibitors include Bob Crooks, Peter Layton, Sharon Ting, Janet Bolton and Sandra Eastwood. There is a café where wall space is rented out to artists.

Submission Policy Artists need to contact the centre initially and then submit their work, which is put before a selection committee.
Price range £25–£17,000
No of exhibitions annually 6

Greengage Gallery
21 High Street, Chalfont St Giles, HP8 4QH
T 01494 875855
Established in 2002 and located in the heart of a Chilterns village in a seventeenth-century listed building. Shows a variety of contemporary works by living artists from the south-east and Lakeland.
Submission Policy Will consider original paintings only, plus ceramics, sculptures and wrought iron designs.
No of exhibitions annually 10

Hannah Peschar Sculpture Garden
Black & White Cottage, Standon Lane, Ockley RH5 5QR
T 01306 627269
F 01306 627662
E hpeschar@easynet.co.uk
W www.hannahpescharsculpture.com
Contact Hannah Peschar
Has developed over the last twenty-five years and shows over one hundred different national and international contemporary sculptors, including Peter Randall-Page, Stephen Cox, Charlotte Mayer, Neil Wilkin and Bert Frijns.
Submission Policy Good-quality images and CV in the first instance. All work must be durable for the outdoors, i.e. frost- and storm-proof.
Price range £200–£70,000
No of exhibitions annually 1

Inspires Art Gallery
27 Little Clarendon Street, Oxford, OX1 2HU
T 01865 556555
F 01865 556555
E artgallery@inspires.co.uk
W www.inspires.co.uk
Opened in 2000. Stocks a wide range of original limited-edition prints, original canvases, ceramics, sculpture and glassware. Artists include Heidi Konig, Terry Frost, Carol Peace and Peter Layton. Also offers a framing service with full conservation framing if needed. Accepted on to the Arts Council 'Own Art' scheme in 2005.
Submission Policy The gallery requests images on slides or transparencies or by email for the owner's consideration. Does not accept jewellery or embroidery.

Price range £20–£13,000
No of exhibitions annually 10, including 5 solo exhibitions.

Island Fine Arts Ltd

53 High Street, Bembridge, Isle of Wight, PO35 5S
T 01983 875133
E gallery@islandfinearts.com
W www.islandfinearts.com
Contact Nick Fletcher, Liz Fletcher or John McLagan
Founded in 1997 and based in the seaside village of Bembridge, the gallery is split into four rooms and deals in works by twentieth- and twenty-first-century modern British painters. Artists include Ken Howard RA, L.S. Lowry RA, Mary Fedden RA, George Devlin, Trevor Chamberlain, Jo Bemis, Rod Pearce and Edward Seago RBA RWS. Exhibits throughout the year both on the Isle of Wight and in London. Has a corporate arm specifically aimed at working with companies.
Submission Policy Always interested in meeting and viewing the work of new painters.
Price range £450–£50,000
No of exhibitions annually 7

Jointure Studios

11 South Street, Ditchling, BN6 8UQ
T 01273 841244
F 01273 841244
E gallery@jointurestudios.co.uk
W www.jointurestudios.co.uk
Contact Shirley Crowther
Spacious gallery for rental created from the late Sir Frank Brangwyn's studios. Good natural daylight, modern lighting and hanging systems, high-ceilinged main hall plus balcony area.
Cost to hire or rent From £300 upwards.

Kent Potters' Gallery

22 Union Street, Maidstone
ME14 1ED
T 01622 681962
W www.kentpotters.co.uk
Contact Janet Jackson
Opened in 1994. Promotes original, exclusive and innovative work. The centre of excellence for the Kent Potters' Association (KPA) and over twelve members represented at any one time. Includes a resource centre on courses, etc. and is stewarded by members. Work is for sale and/or commission.
Submission Policy Entry is by being a member of the KPA. Applications from non-members are not accepted.
Price range £4–£400

Legra Gallery

8 The Broadway, Leigh-on-Sea, SS9 1AW
T 01702 713572
Contact Peter Vinten
Founded in 1973, specializing in marine paintings (traditional and contemporary). Also offers conservation-framing service to artists and public and an oils-restoration service. Resident artists include Colin Moore, Peter Vinten, Eric Pead, John Dawkins and Rod Brown. The gallery has also shown work by the late Vic Ellis in recent years.
Submission Policy No specific entry requirements. Preference given to local artists.
Price range £20–£500. £200–£2,000 for Vic Ellis works, when available.

Lincoln Joyce Fine Art

40 Church Road, Great Bookham, KT23 3PW
T 01372 458481
F 01372 458481
E rosemarylincolnjoyce@hotmail.com
W www.artgalleries.uk.com
Contact Rosemary Pearson
Gallery since 1987, aiming to present fine-quality paintings in a relaxed and friendly atmosphere. Focuses on watercolours and oil paintings. Subject matter (mostly representational) includes landscapes, marine scenes, figures, still lifes and genre paintings. Artists represented include Paul Banning RI RSMA, Keith Noble ARSMA, David Bellamy, Hugh Chevin, F. Donald Blake RI RSMA, Rowland Hilder OBE, PRI, RSMA, Gordon Rushmer, Sonia Robinson RSMA SWA, Anthony Flemming, George Busby MCSD RBSA FRSA, Clive Madgwick RBA, Peter Newcombe, Edward Stamp RI, Mervyn Goode, John Uht RI and Neil Spilman. Valuation and framing services also offered.
Price range £50–£20,000
No of exhibitions annually 11

Linda Blackstone Gallery

The Old Slaughterhouse, R/O 13 High Street, Pinner, HA5 5QQ
T 020 88685765
F 020 88684465
E linda@lindablackstone.com
W www.lindablackstone.com
Founded in 1985 to exhibit contemporary British artists whose work is classed as representational. Artists include Mike Bernard RI, Leo McDowell RI, Janet Ledger, Colin Kent RI, Mat Barber Kennedy RI, Ken Paine PS SPF. Shows paintings, sculpture, ceramics and studio glass. Offers a

bespoke framing service. Artists' work is exposed at many national and international art fairs as well as in-house exhibitions.

Submission Policy No print, photography, abstract or installation work. Apply by email or post with examples of work and full CV. Seen by appointment only.

Price range £150–£8,000

No of exhibitions annually 2 set exhibitions and ongoing exhibition of works.

Magic Flute Gallery

231 Swanwick Lane, Lower Swanwick, Southampton, SO31 7GT

T 01489 570283

E art@magicfluteartworks.co.uk

W www.magicfluteartworks.co.uk

Contact Bryan Dunleavy

At current location since the late 1990s. Exhibits paintings, original prints and small sculpture. Features south-coast and national artists including Russell Baker, Dorothy Brook, Bryan Dunleavy, John Horsewell, Michael Morgan and Stan Rosenthal.

Submission Policy Applications should be made in the first instance by email with low-resolution jpeg images.

Price range Up to £3,000; most under £1,000.

No of exhibitions annually 6

Modern Artists' Gallery

High Street, Whitchurch-on-Thames, Reading RG88 7EX

T 0118 9845893

E info@modernartistsgallery.com

W www.modernartistsgallery.com

Contact Olivia O'Sullivan

Founded in 2000. Aims to support professional and emerging artists. Specializes in contemporary abstract and figurative work. Artists include Anita Austwick, Stuart Buchanan, Mark Hall, Kate Kessling, Paul Kessling, Patrick John Mills, Lucy Orchard and Paul Wright.

Submission Policy Artists should submit by email or telephone, sending jpegs or directions to own website.

Price range £50–£5,000

No of exhibitions annually 6

Cost to hire or rent 6 months notice required. Costs negotiable.

Neville Pundole Gallery

8a–9 The Friars, Canterbury, CT1 2AS

T 01227 453471

F 01227 453471

E neville@pundole.co.uk

W www.pundole.co.uk

Contact Neville Pundole

Established in 1980 and moved to current premises in 1996. Artists represented include Sally Tuffin, Siddy Langley, Peter Layton, Roger Cockram, Martin Evans and the Moorcroft family. Specializes in art pottery and studio glass with pictures, textiles and sculpture. Gallery space for self-promoting artists.

Submission Policy The owner 'must like the work'.

Price range £50–£5,000

No of exhibitions annually 8

Nicholas Bowlby

Owl House, Poundgate, TN22 4DE

T 01892 667809

F 01892 667809

E info@nicholasbowlby.co.uk

W www.nicholasbowlby.co.uk

Contact Nicholas Bowlby

A direct descendant of Sir Henry Tate, Nicholas Bowlby started to deal in early English watercolours in 1976, and since then has extended his interests to include modern British paintings from the first half of the twentieth century, as well as representing a number of contemporary painters and sculptors.

Submission Policy Enquiries welcome. Send photographs in the first instance, preferably by email. All submissions answered.

Price range £100–£55,000

No of exhibitions annually 6

Nick Whistler

5 High Street, Battle, TN33 0AE

T 01424 772458

E nickwhistler@btinternet.com

W www.nickwhistler.com

Contact Nick Whistler

Established in 2000, showing contemporary paintings by British and Canadian artists including Andrew James, Alan Rankle, Heather Stuart, John Holdcroft, Bewabon and Travis Shilling, Tim Pryke, Graham Sendall, Alvaro Petritoli, Erik Addison and Paul Jackson.

Price range £50–£10,000

No of exhibitions annually Rotating exhibitions in three locations.

North Laine Photography Gallery

Upstairs at Snoopers Paradise, 7–8 Kensington Gardens, Brighton, BN1 8AR

T 01273 628794

E studio@northlainephotography.co.uk
W www.brightonphotography.com
Contact Daryl Swallow
Founded 2003. 900 sq. ft. gallery with in-house studio and print services. Uses sales of popular Brighton images and established resident photographers to draw in a wide audience. Uses these sales to fund space and studio assistance for new photographers to put on open brief exhibitions. Photographers sponsored are mainly found through a bi-annual competition and occasionally individual assessment.
Submission Policy All interpretations of the photographic medium accepted for review. Bi-annual Brighton-based competition. Otherwise email images referencing 'subject:open submission from...'
Price range From £4.50 for photo greetings cards. Exhibition pieces £75 to £5,000.
No of exhibitions annually 8
Cost to hire or rent Gallery exchanges considered internationally.

Omell Galleries

The Corner House, Course Road, Ascot, SL5 7LH
T 01344 873443
F 01344 873467
E aomell@aol.com
W www.omellgalleries.co.uk
Founded in 1947, offering fine-quality paintings at realistic prices. Specializes in traditional oil paintings. Artists include Antoine Blanchard, Pierre Bittar, David Dipnall, Raymond Campbell, John Donaldson and Ivars Jansons.
Submission Policy Traditional works by professional artists.
Price range £300–£15,000
No of exhibitions annually 6

Oxmarket Centre of Arts

St Andrew's Court, East Street, Chichester, PO19 1YH
T 01243 779103
F 01243 779103
E info@oxmarket.com
W www.oxmarket.com
Contact Sharonne Lane (Administrator)
Founded in 1971 with the aim of promoting the arts in the community. Works with music and the arts generally but has a concentration on visual arts. Exhibits paintings and drawings, sculpture and ceramics. Mainly used by artists from West Sussex and Home Counties but hosts national figures too.

Submission Policy All two- and three-dimensional work welcomed. Selection is by a panel of professional artists.
Price range Varies from exhibition to exhibition. No artist represented permanently.
No of exhibitions annually 150, in six gallery spaces.
Cost to hire or rent See website.

Paddon & Paddon

113 South Street, Eastbourne, BN21 4LU
T 01323 411887
E paddon@uk2.net
W www.paddonandpaddon.co.uk
Contact Henry Paddon
Established in 1992. Offers a diverse range of two- and three-dimensional work by leading studio makers based in the UK and Europe. Media offered include ceramics, glass, metalwork, jewellery, wood, sculpture, printmaking and furniture. A commissioning service is available. Selected by Arts Council England for participation in the Own Art scheme, which facilitates interest-free purchases of contemporary art and craft by members of the public.
Price range £10–£3,750
No of exhibitions annually Up to 4

Permanent Gallery

20 Bedford Place, Brighton, BN1 2PT
T 01273 710771
E info@permanentgallery.com
W www.permanentgallery.com
A not-for-profit space, opened in 2003. Dedicated to bringing challenging and innovative contemporary art to the public. Programme includes local, national and international artists exhibiting work of all disciplines. Houses an independent art bookshop selling artist-made books, small-press publications, magazines and multiples sourced both locally and internationally. The gallery runs a varied events programme, which has featured group drawing on the beach, live drawing in the gallery, readings, discussion forums and artists talks.
Submission Policy Accepts submissions by email or post all year round from artists creating contemporary work in any medium.
No of exhibitions annually 12

Pierrepont Fine Art

52 Vicarage Road, Oxford, OX1 4RE
T 01865 724957
E kate@pierrepontfineart.co.uk

W www.pierrepontfineart.co.uk
Specializes in British and European twentieth-century and contemporary art.

Planet Janet
86 Church Road, Hove, BN3 2EB
T 01273 738230
E richard@onehappymother.co.uk
W www.planet-janet.com
Founded in 2002. A healthy vegetarian café and therapy centre specializing in alternative therapies, complete with a changing collection of art work on display.
Submission Policy Artists' work must be shown to one of the managers.
Price range £40–£500
No of exhibitions annually 6

Red Gallery
54 North Street, Thame, OX9 3BH
T 01844 217622
E micky@redgallery.co.uk
W www.redgallery.co.uk
Founded in 1998 to showcase renowned artists and promote fresh graduates through solo gallery exhibitions and representation at international art fairs. Artists represented include Claire Boyce, Stanley Dove, Robin Eckardt, Cat James, Paul Lemmon, Garry Raymond-Peirera, Trevor Price and Alexander Smith.
Submission Policy Submissions must be hard copy only. Include photos or CD, CV and biography, plus sae for reply.
Price range £100–£12,000
No of exhibitions annually Up to 9 international art fairs along with gallery exhibitions.

Robert Phillips Gallery
Riverhouse Barn, Manor Road, Walton-on-Thames KT12 2PF
T 01932 254198
E arts@riverhousebarn.co.uk
W www.riverhousebarn.co.uk
Contact Prue Robinson, Manager
Opened in 2000 as part of the Riverhouse Arts Centre. Exhibits contemporary works by artists practising in all media, including painting, sculpture, prints, new media, video, performance and applied arts. Also hosts touring exhibitions. A designated space for applied and decorative arts exhibits three makers per month. A cafe-bar wall space is also available.
Submission Policy Send at least five images plus a CV and artist statement either by post or email.

There is 30% commission on sales.
Price range £20–£50,000
No of exhibitions annually 12

Roche Gallery
93 High Street, Rye, TN31 7JN
T 01797 222259
E timroche@onetel.com
W www.rochegallery.com
Contact Timothy Roche
Showcases the work of Marina Kim, a painter and printmaker from Tashkent, Uzbekistan. Also regularly exhibits paintings from other leading contemporary artists from the former Soviet Union including Lena Lee, Alexander Kim and Gairat Baimatov.
Submission Policy Interested in original paintings, drawings, prints and sculpture in any medium. Overseas artists preferred. No crafts or photography.
Price range £55–£1,500
No of exhibitions annually 6

Room for Art Gallery
15a Church Street, Cobham, KT11 3EG
T 01932 865825
F 01932 865825 (phone first)
E john@roomforart.co.uk
W www.roomforart.co.uk
Contact Hilary Donnelly
Opened in 2004, specializing in contemporary original British and South African art. Also specializes in Zimbabwean stone sculpture (also known as Shona sculpture), with one of the widest ongoing selections of this genre in the UK.
Submission Policy Preference for contemporary oils and acrylic work, mainly figurative or landscape.
Price range £250–£5,000
No of exhibitions annually 4–6, each of 4–5 weeks' duration. Mixed shows in between.

Royall Fine Art
52 The Pantiles, Tunbridge Wells, TN2 5TN
T 01892 536534
F 01892 536534
E royallfineart@tiscali.co.uk
W www.royallfineart.co.uk
Established in 1983. Specializes in fine-quality paintings, sculpture and studio glass by established and emerging artists. Regular exhibitors include Matthew Alexander, Raymond Campbell, Jonathan Pike, Paddy Burrow and Ronald Cameron.
Submission Policy Applications should be made by

photograph, email or appointment.
Price range £300–£20,000
No of exhibitions annually 4

Saltgrass Gallery
1 Angel Courtyard, Lymington, SO41 9AP
T 01590 678148 / 07976 830569
F 01590 678148
E info@saltgrassgallery.co.uk
W www.saltgrassgallery.co.uk
Owned and run by practising painter Jenny Sutton. Alongside her own work in oil, watercolour and acrylic, she exhibits a varied selection of paintings, prints, ceramics and glass by chosen contemporaries. The work is largely representational and mostly under £1,000
Submission Policy Telephone in the first instance to see whether submission is advisable.
Price range £10–£1,000
No of exhibitions annually 4

Simon Fairless
27 Balmoral Gardens, Windsor, SL4 3SG
T 01753 841216
E simon@simonsgallery.com
W www.simonsgallery.com
Contact Simon Fairless
Specializes in abstract, landscape and Pop Art works using acrylic on canvas. Exhibits owner's own work as well as work of other artists.
Price range £50–5,000
No of exhibitions annually 8

Six Chapel Row Contemporary Art
The Elm Coach House, Church Lane
Chipping Norton, OX7 5NS
T 01608 645258
E sixchapelrow@btinternet.com
W www.sixchapelrow.com
Contact Tim Heywood
Founded in Bath in 1995 where it became one of the leading regional art galleries in the UK, showing a wide variety of high quality contemporary fine and applied art. Now based in Oxfordshire, Six Chapel Row is open by appointment and continues to deal with a wide selection of painting, sculpture, photography, furniture, ceramics and glass.
Price range £100–£100,000

Star Gallery
Castle Ditch Lane, Lewes, BN7 1YJ
T 01273 480218
F 01273 488241

E info@stargallery.co.uk
W www.stargallery.co.uk
Contact Hayley Brown
Established in 1989 and now a centre where artists of local, national and international reputation sell their work. As well as the contemporary gallery in the old brewery building, it also features a series of creative workshops and studios for hire.
Submission Policy Welcomes artists' submissions. Work can be emailed as jpegs or posted as slides or on CD with an sae.
Price range Prices vary according to artist being shown.
No of exhibitions annually Approx. 12
Cost to hire or rent From £150 per week

Start Contemporary Gallery
8 Church Street, Brighton, BN1 1US
T 01273 233984
E email@startgallery.co.uk
W www.startgallery.co.uk
Contact Edward Milbourn
Opened in 2000. Shows and sells new work in all mediums from photpgraphy to performance. Recent exhibitors include Foxtrot Echo (Coum Transmission) and photographs by Karen Fuchs and Robert Yager.
Submission Policy Contact the gallery for an information pack (email preferred). All exhibitions considered. No unsolicited work.
Price range £40–£2,000
No of exhibitions annually 20
Cost to hire or rent Between £225–£400 a week depending on the time of year.

Sundridge Gallery
9 Church Road, Sundridge, Sevenoaks, TN14 6DT
T 01959 564104
Founded in 1986. Sells well-draughted watercolours, oil paintings and drawings in good condition. Mostly nineteenth- and twentieth-century but does sell some twenty-first-century modern and traditional work. Artists include Robert Thone Waite, David Cox Jr, F.J.Aldridge, Frank Henry Mason and Edward Wesson. Restoration service also offered.
Submission Policy Will show modern artists but traditional fine art only.
Price range £100–£5,000
No of exhibitions annually 1–2

Sussex Arts Club Ltd
7 Ship, The Laines, Brighton, BN1 1AD
T 01273 778020
E info@sussexarts.com

W www.sussexarts.com
Contact Michael Fowdrey (Events Manager)
Submission Policy Ring to arrange appointment
and viewing of portfolio.
No of exhibitions annually Monthly for
individuals; bimonthly for joint shows.

Taurus Gallery
16 North Parade, off Banbury Road, Oxford, OX2 6LX
T 01865 514870
Sells paintings, sculpture and ceramics. Also offers
framing and restoration services.

Upstairs at the Halcyon
The Halcyon Bookshop, 11 The Broadway
Haywards Heath, RH16 3AQ
T 01444 412785
F 01444 443509
E halcyonbookshop@aol.com
W www.halcyonbookshop.com
Contact Kay O'Regan
Opened in 2003, specializing in works by Sussex
artists.
Submission Policy Chooses exhibitors from
samples of their work. Encourages new talent.
Price range £50–£10,000
No of exhibitions annually 15

Verandah
13 North Parade, Oxford, OX2 6LX
T 01865 310123
Small gallery opened in 1999 by five designers and
makers. Offers jewellery, ceramics, glass, textiles,
metal and paper work and some paintings.
Contributors include James C. Cochrane, Sara
Drake, Sara Withers and Prue Cooper.
Submission Policy Welcomes submissions from
craftspeople and artists at the lower end of the size
and price scale, as the gallery is small.
Price range £8–£800
No of exhibitions annually 2, plus featured artists.

Webb Fine Arts
The Museum Room, Avington Park, Winchester
SO21 1DB
T 01962 779777
F 01962 880602
E davieswebb@hotmail.com
W www.webbfinearts.co.uk
A gallery established by Davies Webb, an
international art dealer for over forty years. Holds a
large stock of nineteenth- and twentieth-century oil
paintings.
Price range £350–£10,000

Webster Gallery
13 Pevensey Road, Eastbourne, BN21 3HH
T 01323 735753
Contact Simon Webster
Founded in 1984, dealing in twentieth-century
paintings (mainly French). Offers full restoration
and valuation service. Artists include Frank
Wootton, Pierre de Clausade, Gabriel Deschamps,
Erwin Eicheiger, Rene His, James Noble, Frank
Archer and Roland Batchelor.
Price range £500–£3,000
No of exhibitions annually 2

Whittington Fine Art
26 Hart Street, Henley-on-Thames, RG9 2AU
T 01491 410787
F 01491 410787
E barry@whittingtonfineart.com
W www.whittingtonfineart.com
Contact Barry Whittington
Opened in 1992 and relocated to Henley-on-
Thames in 2001. Specializes in contemporary
paintings and bronze sculpture. Has a large stock
of traditional watercolours and oil paintings dating
from 1796 to 1940, as well as works by
approximately thirty contemporary artists
including Peter Graham VPROI, Jeremy Barlow
ROI, Jacqueline Rizvi RBA RWS NEAC, Nick
Hebditch and Aldo Balding. Other artists include
Mary Fedden RA, Donald Hamilton Fraser RA,
Ceri Richards, Sir William Russell Flint RA,
Jonathan Wylder, Adrian Sorrell, Anne Smith and
Peter Knapton.
Submission Policy Portfolios welcomed for
viewing. Time and advice will always be given,
although wall space is limited.
Price range £400–£52,000
No of exhibitions annually 6

Wiseman Gallery
40–41 South Parade, Summertown, Oxford
OX2 7JL
T 01865 515123
E sarahjane@wisegal.com
W www.wisegal.com
Almost a decade's experience of selling original
contemporary art from established and emerging
names.
No of exhibitions annually 6

Wren Gallery
Bear Court, 34 Lower High Street, Burford
OX18 4RR
T 01993 823495

F 01993 823247
E enquiries@wrenfineart.com
W www.wrenfineart.com
Specializes in contemporary British and Irish art.
Price range £500–£10,000
No of exhibitions annually 11

Zimmer Stewart Gallery
29 Tarrant Street, Arundel, BN18 9DG
T 01903 885867
E james@zimmerstewart.co.uk
W www.zimmerstewart.co.uk
Contact James Stewart
Founded in 2003, specializing in contemporary art
in all media by living artists. Represented artists
include Felix Anaut, Nick Bodimeade, Ann Sutton
MBE, Keith Milow and Richard Walker. Works
directly with artists and aims to show work to both
buyers and as many other visitors to the gallery as
possible. Licensed to offer Own Art loans in
conjunction with the Arts Council. Also in
Teddington near London.
Submission Policy Send details of training,
exhibitions and examples of current work via email
or on disc.
Price range £100–£7,000
No of exhibitions annually 10

South-west

Alexander Gallery
122 Whiteladies Road, Bristol, BS8 2RP
T 0117 9734692
F 0117 9466991
W www.alexander-gallery.co.uk
Established for over 30 years. Artists include John
Yardley RI, Michael Barnfather, Edward Wesson
RI, Beryl Cook, Sir William Russell Flint RA, David
Shepherd, Karl Taylor, Peter Graham and Richard
Thorn. Also offers conservation, restoration and
consultancy services.

Anthony Hepworth Fine Art Dealers Ltd
3 Margarets Buildings, Brock Street, Bath
BA1 2LP
T 01225 447480
F 01225 442917
E anthony.hepworth@btinternet.com
Founded 1989. Dealers in twentieth-century and
contemporary British painting, sculpture and
drawings, specializing in post-war British pictures.
Artists represented include Peter Lanyon, Keith
Vaughan, Christopher Wood, Roger Hilton, Ben
Nicholson and Barbara Hepworth. Offers services

to executors of deceased estates regarding the
dispersal of collections on their behalf.
Submission Policy Artists are invited to send slides
of their work for consideration if they feel their
work would fit in with the gallery's ethos.
Price range £500–£400,000
No of exhibitions annually 2

Art Space Gallery
The Wharf, St Ives, TR26 1PU
T 01736 799744
E lesley@artspace-cornwall.co.uk
W www.artspace-cornwall.co.uk
Contact Lesley Ninnes
A seven-member cooperative gallery established in
2000. An offshoot of Taking Space, a local group
of women artists formed ten years ago to find
venues for regular exhibitions. Founding members
took the next logical step and acquired permanent
exhibiting space.
Submission Policy Artists can submit contact
details for when a vacancy arises. Members pay a
share of rent/rates, spend one day per week in the
gallery and attend a monthly meeting/rehanging.
Price range £45–£750
No of exhibitions annually Monthly rotation of
work, with an optional monthly theme.

ArtFrame Galleries
61 Cornwall Street, Plymouth, PL1 1NS
T 01752 227127
F 01752 672235
E artframegallery@supanet.com
W www.artframegallery.co.uk
Contact Harry or Sally Eves
Founded in 1984. Exhibits 'special and different'
art and craft work. With an emphasis on quality
and affordability, the gallery stocks a wide selection
of artists and makers working in diverse media.
Bespoke picture-framers, with discounts to
exhibiting artists. Painters include Ben Maile, Lee
Woods and James Martin. Makers include Rudge
Ceramics, Jennie Hale and Suzie Marsh.

Astley House Contemporary
Astley House, London Road, Moreton-in-Marsh
GL56 0LL
T 01608 650601 / 652896
F 01608 651777
E astart333@aol.com
W www.contemporaryart-uk.com
Family business opened in 1973. Contemporary
gallery opened in 1997. Artists include Charles
Neal, Daniel Van der Putten, Chris Bruce, Michael

Kitchen-Hurle, Helen Haywood and Kay Elliott. Ceramics by Peter Beard and Ashraf and Sue Hanna. Jewellery by Guen Palmer and Gordon Yates.
Submission Policy Happy to look at artists' original work to decide if it is suitable.
Price range £250–£12,000.
No of exhibitions annually 3

Atishoo Designs
71 Charlestown Road, Charlestown, St. Austell PL25 3NL
T 01726 65900
E enquiries@atishoodesigns.co.uk
W www.atishoodesigns.co.uk
Established in 2003. Contemporary gallery mainly featuring West Country artists including David Wheeler, Paul Clark, Lamorna Penrose, Alan Arthurs, Keith Bunt and Sue Bryant. Hand-made ceramics and glassware. Picture-framing workshop on site.
Submission Policy Mainly West Country artists. Common theme is 'Vibrant'.
Price range £100–£1,000
No of exhibitions annually 2

Atrium Gallery
Units 2 & 3, The Podium, Northgate Street, Bath BA1 5AL
T 01225 443446
F 01225 422910
E framing@theframingworkshop.com
W www.theframingworkshop.com
Recently expanded, having been established for five years selling both limited-edition prints and originals by artists including Doug Hyde, David Cobley, Jonathan Shaw, Fletcher Sibthorpe and Michael Austin. Also sources poster prints. A specialist framing service is available from the workshop at 80 Walcot Street in Bath, which stocks a selection of art work by local artists depicting local scenes.
Submission Policy
framing@theframingworkshop.com

Baytree Gallery
48 St Margaret's Street, Bradford on Avon BA15 1DE
T 01225 864918
E jane.gibson@ukonline.co.uk
Situated in the centre of town, has exhibitions of two or three complementary artists' work lasting for about three weeks. Artists showing include David Cox, Diana Heeks, Jackie Morins, Estienne

Sheppard, Lizzie Macrae and Amanda Backhouse.
No of exhibitions annually 8

Beaux Arts
12–13 York Street, Bath, BA1 1NG
T 01225 464850
F 01225 422256
E info@beauxartsbath.co.uk
W www.beauxartsbath.co.uk
Contact Aidan Quinn
Has exhibited the work of contemporary and modern British painters, sculptors and ceramicists since 1980 including Dame Elisabeth Frink, the post-war St Ives School and Lynn Chadwick. Current exhibitors include Akash Bhatt, Nathan Ford and Roxana Halls and other young British artists working in a mainly figurative style.
Submission Policy Does not accept email applications from artists. Slides, photos or CDs with sae will be returned after viewing.
Price range £60–£30,000
No of exhibitions annually 8, including a selected summer exhibition of painting, sculpture and ceramics.

Bettles Gallery
82 Christchurch Road, Ringwood, BH24 1DR
T 01425 470410
W www.bettles.net
Founded in 1989, specializing in original contemporary paintings and studio ceramics by British artists and makers. Work in stock from leading established potters and painters, plus some from promising newcomers. Painters include Brian Graham, Martyn Brewster and Paul Jones. Ceramicists include Peter Hayes, William Marshall, Jim Malone, Ian Gregory and Walter Keeler.
Submission Policy Original paintings and individual one-off ceramics considered. First approach with photographs (not slides or CD) accompanied by CV.
Price range Up to £2,500
No of exhibitions annually 8

Bi-Hand
121 St George's Road, Hotwells, Bristol, BS1 5UW
T 0117 9210053
E joandsimon@bihand.co.uk
W www.bihand.co.uk

Black Swan Arts
2 Bridge Street, Frome, BA11 1BB
T 01373 473980
F 01373 473980

E office@blackswan.org.uk
W www.blackswan.org.uk
Set up in 1986. Has three exhibition spaces, Gallery One, Gallery Two in the Round Tower, and the Arts Café. Shows a variety of both two- and three-dimensional visual art and holds an open competition biannually (next scheduled for February 2008)
Submission Policy Submissions accepted. Send images and artist information (CV, statement).
No of exhibitions annually 8–10

Blue Dot Gallery

14 Regent Street, Clifton, Bristol, BS8 4HG
T 0117 9467777
E lee.purvis@bluedotgallery.com
W www.bluedotgallery.com
Showcases wide range of original paintings, limited editions, sculptures and glassware. Artists include Charlotte Atkinson, Doug Hyde, Jonathan Shaw and Peter Wileman.

Blue Lias Gallery

47 Coombe Street, Lyme Regis, DT7 3PY
T 01297 444919
E office@bluelias.co.uk
W www.bluelias.co.uk
Contact Jennie Pearson
Founded in 1996 and under present ownership since 2002. Specializes in contemporary art and craft works celebrating especially the Jurassic Coast (sea, cliffs, beaches, fish, etc). Particular emphasis on artists from the locality and south-west region. Commissioning actively undertaken. Artists include David Potter, Cath Read, Rebecca Stidson, Joy White, Rachel Jennings and Albert Duplock.
Submission Policy All artists considered whose work is compatible with the ambience of the gallery.
Price range Up to £2,000. Works of higher value considered.
No of exhibitions annually 6

Bristol Guild

68–70 Park Street, Bristol, BS1 5JY
T 0117 9265548
F 0117 9255659
E info@bristolguild.co.uk
W www.bristolguild.co.uk
Contact Simone Andre (Manager)
The gallery is on the second floor of the Bristol Guild shop, which was founded in 1908 as a guild of craftsmen.
Submission Policy Exhibitors are selected for the high standard of their work. Paintings, prints, ceramics and glass are the main exhibits.
Price range Up to £2,000
No of exhibitions annually 12

Chagford Galleries

20 The Square, Chagford, TQ13 8AB
T 01647 433287
F 01647 433287
E sales@chagfordgalleries.fsnet.co.uk
In existence for over thirty-five years and under present ownership for fifteen years. Specializes in West Country artists and craftspeople, with Dartmoor providing a lot of inspiration. Sells original paintings, prints, ceramics, jewellery, glass and woodwork.
Submission Policy West Country artists only, preferably from Devon or Cornwall.
No of exhibitions annually 2

Chapel Gallery

Saltram House, Plympton, Plymouth, PL7 1UH
T 01752 347852
F 01752 347852
E kirsty.eales@nationaltrust.org.uk
Shows local arts and crafts from Devon and Cornwall. Work on display includes pottery, ceramics, original paintings, prints, jewellery, glass and woodturning. Holds three large art-and-craft fairs every year.
Submission Policy Artists need to live in Devon or Cornwall.
Price range £1–£4,000
No of exhibitions annually 6 solo exhibitions in the upper gallery; 4 exhibitions in the lower gallery.

Church House Designs

Church House, Broad Street, Congresbury
BS49 5DG
T 01934 833660
F 01934 833660
E robert-coles@btconnect.com
W www.churchhousedesigns.co.uk
Established for over twenty years. Specializes in quality handmade British crafts (ceramics, glass, textiles, jewellery and woodware). Artists include Lucy Willis (prints), John Leach (ceramics), Peter Layton (glass), Nick Rees (ceramics), Richard Dewar (ceramics) and Clive Bowen (ceramics).

Clifton Gallery

18 Princess Victoria Street, Clifton, Bristol
BS8 4BP
T 0117 9706650

E info@cliftonart.co.uk
W www.cliftonart.co.uk
Opened in 1992 in an exclusive area of Clifton Village. Specializing in original-only, contemporary fine art, mainly paintings with some sculpture. Showing artists from all around the world. Represented artists include Shen Ming Cun, Les Matthews, Stephen Brown and Hennie De Korte.
Submission Policy Only original work will be considered. Does not show abstract and conceptual work. Artists must have minimum of ten years' experience.
Price range £500–£25,000
No of exhibitions annually 6

Contemporary Art
1 John Street, Stroud, GL5 2HA
T 01453 758829
Contact Wendy Drake
Founded in 2002, specializing in contemporary art, including paintings, prints, ceramics, glass, sculpture, textiles and jewellery. Artists include Lawson Rudge, Paul Jenkins, Ralph Bayer, Dorothy Brooks and Alister Malcolm.
Submission Policy All areas and media covered. Send images in the first instance, together with statement and CV.
Price range £1–£1,500
No of exhibitions annually 5

Contemporary Studio Pottery
6 Mill Street, Chagford, TQ13 8AW
T 01647 432900
W www.contemporarystudiopottery.co.uk
Contact B. Chivers
Founded in 1999, specializing in studio ceramics. Artists include Clive Bowen, Bruce Chivers, Nic Collins, Penny Simpson, Ross Emerson and Svend Bayer.
Submission Policy National and international potters invited.
Price range £20–£3,000
No of exhibitions annually 4

Coombe Gallery
20 Foss Street, Dartmouth, TQ6 9DR
T 01803 835 820
F 01803 722275
E mark@coombegallery.com
W www.coombegallery.com
Contact Mark Riley
Opened in 2004 as an extension of Coombe Farm Gallery, which was established in 1989. Exhibits

fine and applied arts from predominantly UK-based artists. Exhibitors include Mary Stork, David Leach OBE, Gerry Dudgeon, Paul Riley, Tom Rickman and Diane Nevitt. Displays work from recent graduates alongside artists and makers with international reputations.
Submission Policy Living artists whose work displays skill, integrity and imagination.
Price range £100–£10,000
No of exhibitions annually 4

Cornwall Galleries
4 Bank Street, Newquay, TR7 1JF
T 01637 873678
E enquiries@cornwallgalleries.co.uk
W www.cornwallgalleries.co.uk
Founded in 1960 by Leonard Charles Rollason and run as a family business since the early 1990s. Aims to provide quality oil paintings that anybody can afford. Exhibited artists include Josephine Wall, Deborah Jones, Joel Kirk, Graham Petley, Peter Cosslett and John Bampfield.
Price range £16–£6,000

Courtenays Fine Art
11 Westbourne Arcade, Bournemouth, BH4 9AY
T 01202 764884
E info@courtenaysfineart.com
W www.courtenaysfineart.com
Gallery opened in 1998. Shows originals, limited editions and prints. Over fifty artists, including Josephine Wall, Bill Tolley and David Danbey-Wood.
Submission Policy Initial contact by photographs then, if interested, four originals required.
Price range £50–£5,000

Cowdy Gallery
31 Culver Street, Newent, GL18 1DB
T 01531 821173
F 01531 821173
E info@cowdygallery.co.uk
W www.cowdygallery.co.uk
Contact Harry Cowdy
Established in 1990. A 125m2 private glass gallery showing leading established artists alongside notable emerging makers. Selection is based on quality, integrity and craftsmanship. A permanent collection is displayed between exhibitions. Exhibited artists include Keith Cummings, Sally Fawkes, Ronald Pennell, Pauline Solven, Colin Reid and Rachael Woodman.
Submission Policy Applicants should have an art or craft degree. Submissions should include CV

and illustrations (CD, slides or prints). Interested in glass only.
Price range £100–£3,000
No of exhibitions annually 2

Crescent Galleries Ltd
9 Bath Place, Taunton, TA1 4ER
T 01823 335050
F 01278 663317
E ian@crescentgallery.co.uk
W www.crescentgallery.co.uk
Under current ownership since 2001. Two galleries in Somerset actively supporting local artists with shows and free hangings. Open policy, with work encompassing the traditional to contemporary abstract.
Submission Policy Only considers artists from the West Country.
Price range £150–£2,500
No of exhibitions annually 6

Croft Gallery
22 Devizes Road, Old Town, Swindon, SN21 4BH
T 01793 615821
F 01793 615821
E info@thecroftgallery.co.uk
W www.thecroftgallery.co.uk
Opened in 2000. Promotes up-and-coming and established artists, and sells variety of original art work (oils, acrylics, pastel, watercolours, limited editions). Specialist framing service available. Artists include Carl Scanes, Ken White, Henderson Cisz, Victoria Stewart, William Tolley and Alex Jawdokimov. Offers to sell art work (featured on website) on commission basis.
Submission Policy Submissions from artists always welcome.
Price range £100–£2,500

Crown Gallery
7 Winchcombe Street, Cheltenham, GL52 2LZ
T 01242 515716
E paul-bott@tiscali.co.uk
W www.crowngallery.co.uk
Contact Paul or Donald Bott
Opened in 1984. Offers a framing service and discount plans for artists and repeat clients.
Price range £30–£2,500
No of exhibitions annually 2–3

Cube Gallery
12 Perry Road, Bristol, BS1 5BG
T 0117 3771470
E info@cube-gallery.co.uk

W www.cube-gallery.co.uk
Opened in 2002, showing original works in oil, acrylic or pastel plus some sculpture, from local artists and names from further afield. Recently moved to larger premises to better promote its artists' work in numerous exhibitions throughout the year. Mostly Bristol-based artists, including Barrington Tabb, Karen Edwards, Rachel Nee, Dawn Sidoli, Margaret Gregory and Melissa Kiernan.
Submission Policy Submissions by appointment only.
Price range £250–£10,000
No of exhibitions annually 4

Delamore Arts
Delamore, Cornwood, Ivybridge, PL21 9QT
T 01752 837711
F 01752 837888
E admin@delamore.com
W www.delamore-art.co.uk
Contact Gavin Dollard or Rebecca Prince
An art and sculpture park promoting the work of artists through several shows, including an annual exhibition of more than 100 painters and sculptors each May (now in its fifth year). Also represents artists at other exhibitions and has interests in publishing. New purpose built gallery opened in Autumn/Winter 2007.
Submission Policy Send details and samples of work.
No of exhibitions annually 2+

Dolphin House Gallery
Dolphin House, Dolphin Street, Colyton, EX24 6NA
T 01297 553805
E art@dolphinhousegallery.co.uk
W www.dolphinhousegallery.co.uk
Founded in 1990, specializing in the works of etcher Roger St Barbe, with guest exhibitions several times a year (e.g. the late Mary Shields). Ceramics by Nicholas Hillyard. Framing service offered.
Submission Policy Original works or handmade original prints only (no reproductions or photographs exhibited). Small works preferred due to limited space.
Price range £50–£800
No of exhibitions annually 5

Elliott Gallery
Hillsview, Braunton, EX33 2LA
T 01271 812100 / 863539
W www.elliottartgallery.co.uk
Contact Walter A. Elliott
Founded in 1984. Aims to encourage local and

West Country arts (especially painting and sculpture) and crafts. Strives to be a valuable amenity for the local community and visitors to the region.
Submission Policy Artists are invited to send photographs of their paintings, craft works or sculpture and, if considered suitable, to submit art work for exhibition.
No of exhibitions annually 2–8 one-person exhibitions in the two smaller halls. Continuously changing displays in the two large galleries.

Exmouth Gallery

46 Exeter Road, Exmouth, EX8 1PY
T 01395 273155
E info@exmouthgallery.co.uk
W www.exmouthgallery.co.uk
The main room shows changing exhibitions; a second room shows prints and illustrated books; a third shows botanical illustrations by Royal Horticultural Society Medallists; and a fourth shows gallery artists including Bob Clement, Alan Richards, Michael Buckland, Jean Esther Brook, Rob Ritchie, Pat Johnn, Mark Abdey, John Stone and Tim Hogben.
Submission Policy No pottery or jewellery, but outdoor sculpture can be displayed in the enclosed garden.
Price range £50–£2,000
No of exhibitions annually 8

Farrington Gallery

Bristol Road, Farrington Gurney, BS39 6TG
T 01761 453880
E email@farringtongallery.freeserve.co.uk

Fisherton Mill–Galleries Cafe Studios

Fisherton Mill, 108 Fisherton Street, Salisbury SP2 7QY
T 01722 415121
E thegallery@fishertonmill.co.uk
W www.fishertonmill.co.uk
Set within an 1880s converted grain mill, Fisherton Mill is one of the region's largest independent galleries. Work exhibited is predominantly from artists in the south-west. Artists include Nick Andrew (painting), Michael Peckitt (jewellery), Stephanie Wooster (textiles), Stuart Akroyd (glass), Eric French (furniture) and Kim Norton (ceramics). There are studio workshops and a cafe.
Submission Policy Applications should be made with images of the work in the first instance. No specific entry requirements or restrictions.

Price range £3–£4,000
Cost to hire or rent Beams Gallery available to hire. £250 per week including an evening private view and access to mailing list. Reductions for longer run.

Frances Roden Fine Art Ltd

Beacon House, New Street, Painswick, GL6 6UN
T 01452 814877
E info@francesrodenfineart.com
W www.francesrodenfineart.com
Founded in 2004. Specializes in contemporary art. Artists represented include Stephen Goddard, Sally Trueman, Alan Thornhill and Jon Edgar.
Price range £1,000–£40,000
No of exhibitions annually 2

Gallerie Marin

31 Market Street, Appledore, nr Bideford, EX39 1PP
T 01237 473679
F 01237 421655
E galleriemarine@btopenworld.com
Established in 1972, specializing in contemporary marine art. Artists include Mark E. Myers PP RSMA, Michael Les, David Brackman, Tim Thompson, Steven Thor Johanneson RSMA and Jenny Morgan.
Price range £200–£6,000
No of exhibitions annually 1

The Gallery

Silver Street House, South Cerney, Cirencester GL7 5TP
T 01285 869469
E gallery.cirencester@virgin.net
W www.cirencester-galleries.com
Founded in 1997, specializing in colourful watercolours. Expanded to display themed exhibitions and group exhibitors. Now specializing in renting art works to businesses that need to impress both staff and sales prospects.
Submission Policy Shows works that are representational, colourful and peaceful.
Price range £500–£2,500

Glass House Gallery

Kenwyn Street, Truro, TR1 3DJ
T 01872 262376
E theteam@glasshousegallery.co.uk
W www.glasshousegallery.co.uk
Founded in 1995 to represent the work of established and rising Cornish artists, sculptors, ceramicists, jewellers and printmakers. Exhibitions have included the first solo shows of

artists such as Naomi Frears and Sasha Harding. Other artists represented include David Briggs, Jason Lilley, John Middlemiss and Colin Orchard. The gallery undertakes commissions.
Price range £100–£2,000
No of exhibitions annually 2

Goldfish Contemporary Fine Art
56 Chapel Street, Penzance, TR18 4AE
T 01736 360573
E mail@goldfishfineart.co.uk
W www.goldfishfineart.co.uk
Contact Joseph Clarke
Founded in 2000 in St Ives and relocated to the current multiple-floor space in 2003. Specializes in the best of Cornish contemporary painting and sculpture, from figurative to abstract with an emphasis on originality and personal expression. Gallery artists include Kenneth Spooner, Nicola Bealing, Zoe Cameron, David Briggs, Andrew Litten, Nicola Bealing, Tim Shaw, Simon Allen and Joy Wolfenden Brown.
Price range £300–£30,000
No of exhibitions annually 9 solo shows alongside mixed exhibitions.

Great Atlantic Map Works Gallery
St Just, Penzance, TR19 7JB
T 01736 788911 / 786016
F 01736 786005
E gallery@greatatlantic.co.uk
W www.greatatlantic.co.uk
Contact Sarah Brittain
Founded in 1995, specializing in painting, sculpture, printmaking and ceramics from both Cornwall and Wales where its galleries are situated. Travelling exhibitions are staged annually around the UK and also in Canada and America.
Submission Policy Submissions welcome (no textiles, jewellery or photography). In the first instance approach in writing to Sarah Brittain.
Price range £100–£10,000
No of exhibitions annually Exhibitions change fortnightly.

Hartworks Contemporary Art
12 Foss Street, Dartmouth, TQ6 9DR
T 01803 839000
F 01803 839000
E art@hartworks.co.uk
W www.hartworks.co.uk
Contact Theresa or Simon Hart
Established in 1999 and features work by many renowned contemporary artists from the West

Country, as well as prominent British artists, printmakers and ceramicists. Artists include Simon Hart, Sue McDonald, Gerry Plumb, Louise Braithwaite, Michael Turner and Glyn Macey.
Submission Policy Submissions by slide, photographs or email invited from contemporary makers and artists (excluding photography, jewellery and watercolour).
Price range £20–£2,000
No of exhibitions annually 4

Here Gallery
108 Stokes Croft, Bristol, BS1 3RU
T 01179422222
E heregallery@yahoo.co.uk
W www.thingsfromhere.co.uk
Originally opened to house an exhibition as part of Ladyfest in 2003 for two weeks and never left. An entirely unfunded not-for-profit workers coop. Open to humour and experimentation, showing everything from illustration to graffiti to sound art. Hosted Peskimo's Monster Mash and has collaborated with gHOSTbOY and 'obsessive consumption'. The shop specializes in comics/zines/books/artist-made/limited edition/prints and things that you wouldn't necessarily find elsewhere.
Submission Policy Proposals should include one A4 page about the artist and their aims plus 4–6 images via post or email
Price range £10–£300
No of exhibitions annually 12
Cost to hire or rent £100+

Hind Street Gallery and Frame Makers
Hind Street, Ottery St Mary, EX11 1BW
T 01404 815641
E info@therealart.co.uk
W www.therealart.co.uk
Established in 1978, showing original art works from local and international atists. Bespoke frame-making service offered.
Price range £50–£5,000
No of exhibitions annually 4

Innocent Fine Art
7A Boyces Avenue, Bristol, BS8 4AA
T 0117 9732614
F 0117 9741425
E enquiries@innocentfineart.co.uk
W www.innocentfineart.co.uk
Founded in 1997, specializing in contemporary West Country art with particular emphasis on Cornish artists. Has a large collection of twentieth-

century Cornish artists including Sir Terry Frost, Barbara Hepworth and Sandra Blow. Contemporary artists include Paul Lewin, Mary Stork, Gerry Plumb, Neil Pinkett and Elaine Jones. Also has one show a year of School of Paris, Picasso, Miro, Chagall and others.

Submission Policy Prints and paintings only. Send slides or photos, or email first.

Price range £250–£4,000

No of exhibitions annually About 4 one-person or themed exhibitions; the rest are mixed shows.

John Davies Gallery

Church Street, Stow-on-the-Wold, GL54 1BB

T 01451 831698

F 01451 870750

E daviesart@aol.com

W www.johndaviesgallery.com

Contact John Davies

Established in 1977, showing European Post-Impressionist paintings (1890–1950), nineteenth- and twentieth-century British art, including Scottish and Welsh painters past and present. Works from the studios of Alexander Goudie and Will Roberts. Contemporary painters include Lionel Aggett, Malcolm Edwards, Peter Evans, Philip Hicks, John Kingsley, Sandy Murphy, Gareth Parry, David Prentice and William Selby

Submission Policy The gallery is always interested in seeing new work. Send photos or images on disc. Do not email images. Telephone first. Interested in finding a good modern equestrian artist.

Price range £250–£100,000

No of exhibitions annually 8

Jonathan Poole Gallery

Compton Cassey House, nr Withington, Cheltenham, GL54 4DE

T 01242 890224

F 01242 890479

Established for over thirty years, specializing in contemporary sculpture and exhibition-organizing throughout the world. Represents the art estates of John Lennon and Miles Davis. Exhibited artists include Lucy Kinsella, Jonathan Poole, Bobby Plisnier, Vicky Wallis, Dennis Westwood, Jill Sanders and Ronnie Wood.

Jordan & Chard Fine Art

c/o Bridge House, Truro, TR1 1ER

T 01872 262202

F 01872 266199

E taraphysick@jordanchard.com

W www.jordanchard.com

Contact Tara Physick

Specializes in the plein air painting of the Newlyn and early St Ives Schools (1880–1940). Based in Cornwall, the gallery presents an ever-changing selection of these paintings, many sourced from private local collections. Works are offered by the leading and lesser names from the schools, including Stanhope and Elizabeth Forbes, Walter Langley, Harold Harvey, Henry Scott Tuke, Lamorna Birch, Laura Knight, Dorothea Sharp and Newlyn Copper. Viewing is by appointment. Telephone or visit the website to view paintings, reference material and artists' biographies.

Submission Policy Interested in contemporary, impressionist and realist painters, particularly those working in Cornwall. Subjects of interest include figurative, seascape, marine/nautical subjects and local landscape.

Price range £450–£100,000

No of exhibitions annually 3–4

Kangaroo Kourt

68 Thornleigh Rd, Horfield, Bristol, BS7 8PJ

T 01179080485

E kangarookourt@blueyonder.co.uk

W www.kangarookourt.pwp.blueyonder.co.uk

Began as a domestic/alternative artspace in 2002 concentrating on stencil graffiti hosting local names such as gHOSTbOY, Nick Walker and Kid Carpet. Has since shown a wide range of experimental and conceptual sculpture, installation and performance. Open to artist/curators who are keen on interacting directly with their audience.

Submission Policy Artist/curators with ideas to challenge preconceived ideas of a domestic artspace. Contact via email.

Lander Gallery

Lemon Street Market, Truro, TR1 2PN

T 01872 275578

F 01872 275578

E landergallery@btconnect.com

W www.landergallery.co.uk

Contact Viv Hendra

Housed in an award-winning new building, making the gallery one of the largest in the south-west. Shows fine art from four centuries, with a rich Cornish flavour. Contemporary artists share Cornish inspiration with the more traditional Classics, from all periods and styles including Newlyn, Lamorna, St Ives and Falmouth.

Submission Policy Particularly interested in work

with a Cornish connection. New and established artists shown; new artists are welcome to make an appointment.

Price range From £100–£50,000

No of exhibitions annually 10 featured exhibitions (solo or mixed) and a large permanent show of artists working today. Also Lander Classics, a display of historic works.

Cost to hire or rent Open to discussion

Market House Gallery

Market House, Marazion, TR17 0AR

T 01736 710252

Specializes in post-war West Country artists such as Sir Terry Frost, Alfred Wallis and Ben Nicholson, and potters such as Leach and Troike.

Submission Policy Applications welcome from living local artists in any media.

Price range £120–£20,000

No of exhibitions annually 8

Martin's Gallery

Imperial House, Montpellier Parade, Cheltenham GL50 1UA

T 01242 526044

E ian@martinsgallery.co.uk

W www.martinsgallery.co.uk

Started in 1987 to present art in the home environment. Concentration on Modern British, Vietnamese contemporary and west European. Also sculpture in stainless steel, stone, bronze, glass and porcelain. Exhibited artists include Thomas Bush Hardy (Victorian watercolours), Sir William Russell Flint (Modern British), Dan Llywelyn Hall, Inge Clayton, Sophie Raine, Míla Judge-Fürstová, Michael B. Edwards and Ray Hedger (contemporary), and Thanh Binh, Dinh Quan, Ng Dieu Thuy and Van Ngoc (Vietnamese).

Submission Policy Artists should submit a CV and some photos of their work initially (preferably by email and including contact details). If the gallery is interested, artists will then be contacted.

Price range £300–£20,000

No of exhibitions annually 12–15

Mayfield Gallery

907 Wimborne Road, Moordown, BH9 2BJ

E mayfield.gallery@tiscali.co.uk

W www.juliestooksart.com

Contact Julie Stooks

Opened in 1987. Attracts well-known artists who exhibit regularly, both contemporary (Simon Stooks, James Preston) and traditional (David Dipnall, Josephine Wall, Sally Winter). Solo and group exhibitions held. Commissions accepted for portrait and animal studies.

Submission Policy Always interested in seeing new artists.

Price range £100–£5,000; gallery commission applies.

No of exhibitions annually 4

Michael Wood Fine Art

The Gallery, 17 The Parade, The Barbican, Plymouth, PL1 2JW

T 01752 225533

F 01752 225770

E michael@michaelwoodfineart.com

W www.michaelwoodfineart.com

Contact Michael Wood

Established in 1967, offering an eclectic selection of work from 1800 to the present day. Over 3,500 works in stock at any time including paintings, watercolours, original prints, sculptures, ceramics and studio glass. Exhibited artists include local, national and international artists of the Newlyn School, St Ives Society of Artists and Royal Academicians. Notable past exhibitions include works by Sir Terry Frost, Justin Knowles and Robert Oscar Lenkiewicz.

Price range £100–£250,000

No of exhibitions annually 1

Mid Cornwall Galleries

St Blazey Gate, Par, PL24 2EG

T 01726 812131

E info@midcornwallgalleries.co.uk

W www.midcornwallgalleries.co.uk

Opened in 1980 and housed in a Victorian school 3 miles east of St Austell. Regularly shows new collections of fine contemporary arts and crafts. Artists include Jo March, Glyn Macey, Ray Balkwill, Amanda Hoskin, Trevor Price and Arthur Homeshaw.

Submission Policy New submissions welcome either on CD, by post (with return postage) or via email.

Price range £100–£2,500

No of exhibitions annually 6

New Art Centre Sculpture Park & Gallery

Roche Court, East Winterslow, Salisbury SP5 1BG

T 01980 862244

F 01980 862447

E nac@globalnet.co.uk

W www.sculpture.uk.com

Contact Helen Waters (Curator)

Founded in 1957 in London and relocated to Roche Court in Wiltshire in 1993. Represents the Estates of Barbara Hepworth and Kenneth Armitage and shows sculpture from 1950 to the present day in an art-historical context, including works by Antony Gormley, Richard Long, Gavin Turk and Rachel Whiteread. In two contemporary buildings there is a changing exhibition programme and there is an active education programme. All works are for sale.
Submission Policy Sculptors are welcome to send CVs and images of their work, although space is limited.
Price range From £100
No of exhibitions annually 6–8

New Craftsman
24 Fore Street, St Ives, TR26 1HE
T 01736 795652
F 01736 795652
E stella.redgrave@btinternet.com
W www.newcraftsmanstives.com
Contact Stella Redgrave
The oldest established craft shop in St Ives, established in the 1960s. Stocks paintings, prints, ceramics and crafts, mostly modern and contemporary. Artists represented include Peter Lanyon, Tony O'Malley, Bryan Pearce, John Miller and John Piper.
Submission Policy Artists must be living and working in Cornwall. Craftmakers from throughout the UK. Submissions welcome in any form.
Price range £10–£10,000
No of exhibitions annually 2

New Gallery
Portscatho, nr Truro
TR2 5HW
T 01872 580445
F 01736 793121
E a.insoll@virgin.net
W www.newmillenniumgallery.co.uk
Contact Lynn Golden
Founded in 1984. An artist-run gallery, showroom and studio. Artists include Chris Insoll, Lynn Golden, Trevor Felcey, Eric Ward, Endel White and Grace Gardner.
Submission Policy Submissions from painters welcome. New artists would be required to help existing cooperative in some way. The gallery is an established 'society of artists'.
Price range £60–£6,000
No of exhibitions annually 12

Organized Gallery
Churchill House, Olveston, Bristol, BS35 4DP
T 01454 613788
F 01454 202606
E gallery@organized.com
W www.organizedgallery.co.uk
Opened in 2002 to show quality glass art from Seattle. Paintings and furniture added in 2003 but specialization remains glass. Glass artists exhibited include Mel Munsen, Sabine Lintzen, Yosuke Otsuki and James Minson. Painters exhibited include Richard Howell and Anne Mieke Van Ogtrop.
Submission Policy Will look at submissions.
Price range £200–£3,000

Plan 9
PO Box 2590, Bristol' BS6 9BJ
T 07811 428 381
E info@plan9.org.uk
W www.plan9.org.uk
Founded in 2005 as an artist-led experimental project space. Originally sited in a disused retail space in Bristol's Broadmead shopping area, Plan 9 now has no fixed location and operates as an independent curating/commissioning body. In the first year it ran 10 shows/events including works by Matt Stokes, Mike Stubbs, the Caravan Gallery, Chris Barr and Martin Parr. In 2006 it was scheduled to run four main events with the likes of Marcus Coates, Claire Barclay and Simon Morrissey.
No of exhibitions annually 4–10

Rainyday Gallery
116 Market Jew Street, Penzance, TR18 2LD
T 01736 366077
E info@rainydaygallery.co.uk
W www.rainydaygallery.co.uk
Started in 1992 and shows mostly Cornwall-based artists. Abstract, landscape, seascape and naive. Monthly exhibition is complemented by about one hundred other works. Artists include Matthew Lanyon, Chris Hankey, Phil Whiting, Anthony Frost, Jo March and Nick Williams.
Submission Policy Cornwall/Devon-based artists mainly. Paintings only. Send photos (and sae) or indicate website if useful.
Price range £100–£5,000
No of exhibitions annually 12

Red Rag Gallery
Church Street, Stow-on-the-Wold, GL54 1BB
T 01451 832563
E mail@redraggallery.co.uk

W www.redraggallery.co.uk
Contact Carole Teagle
Originally the studio of influential British artist
John Blockley, the building has operated as a
gallery for twenty years. Specializes in the original
art works of present-day British artists, including
Davy Brown, Andrew Macara, Romeo di Girolamo,
Charles Hardaker, Joe Hargan, Louis McNally,
David Cobley and Dawn Sidoli.
Price range £300–£20,000
No of exhibitions annually 10

Rooksmoor Gallery
31 Brock Street, Bath, BA1 2LN
T 01225 420495
E info@rooksmoorgallery.com
Contact Verity James (Manager)
Founded in 1985, specializing in traditional
contemporary paintings, sculpture and ceramics.
Permanent artists include Colin Vincent, Allan
Morgan, Walter Awlson and the Rudge family.
Submission Policy Artists' work must show
traditional skills, quality of execution and
composition.
Price range £100–£2,000
No of exhibitions annually 6

Ropestore
The Shambles, Stroud, GL5 1AS
T 01453 753799
F 01453 753799
E lizzi@ropestoregallery.co.uk
W www.ropestoregallery.co.uk
Shows contemporary fine and applied arts from
national and local designers and makers.
Submission Policy The gallery prefers to source its
own work.
Price range £10–£5,000
No of exhibitions annually 4

Rostra Gallery
5 George Street, Bath, BA1 2EH
T 01225 448121
F 01225 447421
E info@rostragallery.co.uk
W www.rostragallery.co.uk
Contact Amy Kennedy, Emma Birts or Verity James
Opened in 1997. Has developed a reputation for
showcasing a diverse range of sculpture, ceramics,
paintings, jewellery, glass and giftware. Specialists
in limited-edition prints. Exhibited artists include
Sir Terry Frost, Sonia Rollo, Caroline Pedler, Joe
Cooke and Anna Danielle.
Submission Policy Contact the gallery for specific

dates and requirements. Maximum of four
submission dates throughout the year.
Price range £2.75–£5,000
No of exhibitions annually 12+

Sadler Street Gallery
23 Market Place, Wells, BA5 2RF
T 01749 670220
E jillswale@thesadlerstreetgallery.co.uk
W www.thesadlerstreetgallery.co.uk
Contact Jill Swale
Founded in 1993 and moved to present location in
2003 (one minute from Wells Cathedral).
Specializes in watercolours and etchings from
1750 to 1950, some oils, small bronzes and
contemporary work in all media. Particular focus
on work by West Country artists. Artists include
John Yardley RI and David Sawyer RI.
Submission Policy Landscape, marines, figure
studies, etc.
Price range £50–£10,000
No of exhibitions annually 8

Salar Gallery
20 Bridge Street, Hatherleigh, EX20 3HY
T 01837 810940
W www.salargallery.co.uk
Founded in 1991. Exhibits paintings, sculpture,
crafts, photography and multimedia prints in
contemporary and traditional styles by living West
Country artists. Subject matter largely inspired by
the land, animals and rural subjects. Featured
artists include Pam Cox, Hermione Dunn,
Adrienne Fryer, Ken Hildrew, Jo Seccombe and
Maryjane Carruthers.
Submission Policy Send photos/disc of work,
details of work and career history to the gallery.
Chosen work is usually taken on consignment.
Price range Up to £1,000
No of exhibitions annually 6

Salisbury Playhouse Gallery
Malthouse Lane, Salisbury, SP2 7RA
T 01722 320117 / 320333
F 01722 421991
E marketing2@salisburyplayhouse.com
W www.salisburyplayhouse.com
Contact Jane Wilkinson (Gallery Officer)
Founded in 1977. A large space within a well-
attended theatre, with room for sixty to eighty
paintings or photographs from new and
established artists. Design and distribution of
preview invitations, preview organization, and all
sales, publicity, etc. catered for by the gallery.

Exhibiting artists include Elisabeth Frink, Bill Toop, Hugh Casson, Mary Feddon and Julian Barrow.
Submission Policy Selection by gallery committee based on suitability to venue. No fee; thirty-five per cent commission plus VAT. No facility for three-dimensional work.
Price range £95–£2,500
No of exhibitions annually 10, approximately three weeks each (January to June and September to December).

Somerville Gallery
25 Mayflower Street, Plymouth, PL1 1QJ
T 01752 221600
E lenkiewicz@btconnect.com
W www.somervillegallery.com
Contact Ben Somerville
Established in 1995 to represent the best of West Country painters. Specialists in Robert Lemkiewicz, Sir Terry Frost, Anthony Frost, Luke Frost, Henrietta Dybrey and Bob Crossley.
Submission Policy Local established artists welcome. Gifted newcomers need to work their passage through established means.
Price range Up to £50,000
No of exhibitions annually 5

St Ives Society of Artists Gallery
Norway Quare, St Ives, TR26 1NA
T 01736 795582
E gallery@stisa.co.uk
W www.stisa.co.uk
Contact April Brooks
Founded in 1927. Aims to provide an independent exhibition space for the visual arts in St Ives for members and other groups and individuals. Judges work on artistic worth, regardless of commercial appeal. Prominent members include Ken Howard RA, Lionel Aggett, Nicholas St John Rosse, Ken Symonds, Raymund M. Rogers and Sonia Robinson. The Mariners Gallery in the former crypt of the old Church (which houses the society) is also available for artists to hire for individual separate exhibitions.
Submission Policy Membership is currently about sixty living artists and applications are welcomed from all good artists in any medium.
Price range £120–£20,000 for framed work and sculptures. Unframed etchings, prints and cards also available.
No of exhibitions annually 3 members' exhibitions and 2 invited exhibitions in the main gallery as well as 2 open exhibitions; 20 exhibitions in the Mariners Gallery.

Cost to hire or rent Mariners Gallery is available for hire at about £175 per week.

Steam Pottery
Pendeen, Penzance, TR19 7DN
E patrick@steampottery.co.uk
W www.steampottery.co.uk
Established in the late 1990s, showing high-quality ceramics in stoneware and porcelain by Patrick Lester. Has now broadened its range to include work by a number of known and emerging potters including Walter Keeler, Emma Johnstone, Daniel Boyle, Richard Henham, Simon Rich and Georgina Dunkley.
Price range £10–£800

Steps Gallery
15 Christmas Steps, City Centre, Bristol, BS1 5BG
T 0117 9304137
E enquiries@stepsgallery.co.uk
W www.stepsgallery.co.uk
Contact Tamsin Bates
Founded in 2004, aiming to provide a platform for both unknowns (including recent graduates) and those more established but unshown in the south-west. Specializes in cutting-edge contemporary and modern work (in terms of style and new techniques). Exhibited artists include Klari Reis, Mandy Wilkinson, Juliet Rose, David Stanley and Robert Belderson.
Submission Policy Interested in modern contemporary work, including paintings and sculptures. Corporate art portfolio includes digital work/computer generated images. Exhibitions can be arranged in spaces outside the gallery. Gallery space includes outdoor sculpture garden created in 2005.
Price range £1–£10,000
No of exhibitions annually 5

Steve Farnsworth
Grimes House Fine Art, High Street, Moreton in Marsh, GL56 0AT
T 01608 651029
E grimes_house@cix.co.uk
W www.grimeshouse.co.uk
Contact Steve or Val Farnsworth
Founded in 1978, representing many nationally known living artists with a traditional rather than contemporary style. Artists featured include Edward Hersey, Gordon King, Brian Jull and John Trickett.
Submission Policy Gallery owners must 'personally like the artist and their work'.

Price range £100–£7,000
No of exhibitions annually 1 ongoing exhibition; 2 additional specialist exhibitions.

Strand Art Gallery

2 The Strand, Brixham Harbourside, Brixham TQ5 8EH
T 01803 854762
E strandartgallerybrixham@hotmail.com
W www.strandartgallery.com
Contact Andrew Stockman and Tina Stockman
A marine gallery with a strong West Country flavour, with the emphasis on original paintings by living artists. Founded in 1972. Artists-in-residence with studios open to the public all year round. Artists include Gordon Allen, Bill Stockman, Terry Burke, David Deakins, Bob Tucker, Karen Chapman, Peter Duffield, Donald Ayres and 'Alicia'.
Submission Policy Submissions considered from local (South Devon area), professional fine art artists only. Acrylics, oils or watercolours preferred.
Price range £25–£5,000
No of exhibitions annually Ever-changing exhibition runs for fifty weeks per year. As work is sold, a 'rolling' exhibition takes place, with new works being added daily.

Street Gallery

1 The Bayliss Centre, 147 High Street
BA16 0EX
T 01458 447722
E andrew@street-gallery.co.uk
W www.street-gallery.co.uk
Specialists of Edward Wesson, Archibald Thorburn and Rolf Harris. Stockists of signed prints by Sir Peter Scott, L.S. Lowry, David Shepherd, Robert Taylor, Alan Fearnley, Nick Eatts, Govinder, Mackenzie Thorpe and E.R. Sturgeon. Originals by Richard Thorn, Cecil Rice and Edward Wesson.
Price range £100–£10,000
No of exhibitions annually Annual Edward Wesson and Rolf Harris exhibitions.

Stroud House Gallery

Station Road, Stroud, GL5 3AP
T 01453 750575
E info@stroudhousegallery.co.uk
W www.stroudhousegallery.co.uk
Founded in 1997, specializing in conceptual, contemporary works of art (including fine art, installation, performance and film). Work is curated around a theme from artists selected throughout the UK.
No of exhibitions annually 8–10

Summerleaze Gallery

East Knoyle, Salisbury, SP3 6BY
T 01747 830790
F 01747 830790
E kelly@summerleazegallery.co.uk
W www.summerleazegallery.co.uk
Contact Kelly Ross
Founded in 1991, exhibiting the work of contemporary and modern British painters and sculptors. Exhibited artists include Charlie Baird, Ursula Leach, Paul Macdermot, Tobit Roche, Tim Scott Bolton and Henrietta Young.
Price range £150–£20,000
No of exhibitions annually 4

Susan Megson Gallery

Digbeth Street, Stow-on-the-Wold, GL54 1BN
T 01451 870484
F 01451 831051
E SueMegsonGallery@aol.com
Founded in 2000, showing unique examples of creative glass art from around the world. Exhibited artists include Bob Crooks, Amanda Brisbane, Jonathan Harris, Isle of Wight Glass, Vandermark-Merrit and French artists such as Lohe, Loumani, Mallemouche and Didier Saba.
Submission Policy Pieces must be unique and handblown.
Price range £50–£2,000
No of exhibitions annually 4

Swan Gallery

51 Cheap Street, Sherborne, DT9 3AX
T 01935 814465
F 01308 8868195
E L4949@aol.com
W www.swangallery.co.uk
Founded in 1982. Specializations include fine eighteenth-, nineteenth- and twentieth-century watercolours and oil paintings, and antique maps and prints. Artists represented include Myles Birkett-Foster, Harry Sutton Palmer, John Varley, W. Tatton Winter, Henry Alken and T.B. Hardy. Other services offered include restoration, framing and valuation.
Submission Policy Occasional exhibitions by living artists.
Price range £15–£20,000
No of exhibitions annually 3

The Toll House Gallery

The Beach, Clevedon, BS21 YQU
T 01275 878846
F 01275 790077

E clevedonpier@zoom.co.uk
W www.clevedonpier.com
Contact Tamsin Welch
Each month different local artists display their
work, including oils, watercolours, mixed media,
acrylics, photography, ceramics and wooden
sculpture.
No of exhibitions annually 12
Cost to hire or rent Approx. £200 per month.

Tregony Gallery
58 Fore Street, Tregony, Truro, TR2 5RW
T 01872 530505
F 01872 530505
W www.tregonygallery.co.uk
Established in 1998, selling fine contemporary
Cornish art. All original work, predominantly
seascapes. Hosts a constantly changing display of
paintings, sculpture, ceramics, jewellery and
glassware. Artists represented include John
Brenton, David Rust, Josep Pla, John Piper, Paul
Lewin and Robert Jones.
Price range £100–£6,000
No of exhibitions annually 1

Turn of the Tide Gallery
7 The Triangle, Teignmouth, TQ14 8AU
T 01626 777455
E sal@andersons5.fsnet.co.uk
W www.turnofthetide.net
Opened in 2000, showing mainly Cornish and
Devon painters. Shows etchings, collographs,
ceramics, handmade jewellery and open prints.
Most work has connections to the sea. Artists
include Robert Jones, Michael Praed, Judy
Hempstead, Andrea Stokes, and Norman and
Lesley Stuart Clarke. Originals, prints and cards by
Sally Anderson.
Submission Policy Existing work includes boats,
beaches and the Devon countryside painted on
board, canvas and driftwood. Gallery looking for
work with vibrant colours and a 'slightly quirky
and naive style'.
Price range £1.50–£1,500
No of exhibitions annually 1, mixed.

Turner Gallery
88 Queen Street, Exeter, EX4 3RP
T 01392 273673
E turnergallery@yahoo.com
W www.thebarnardturnergallery.co.uk
Founded in 1997 with the aim of showing
paintings of quality by artists dedicated to the
traditions of painting (landscape, figurative,

abstract and idiosyncratic, in acrylic, oil and
watercolour). Artists include Brian J.Turner, Philip
James ROI, Richard Slater RI and Julian Anniss.
Tutorial scheme with artists offered.
Submission Policy Applications welcome but from
professional artists only. Send hard-copy examples
of work with CV, letter of introduction and sae.
Price range £150–£5,000
No of exhibitions annually Continually changing
with occasional keynote exhibitions.

Vitreous Contemporary Art
7 Mitchell Hill, Truro, TR1 1ED
T 01872 274288
E info@vitreous.biz
W www.vitreous.biz
Contact Jake Bose
Founded in 2004. Specializes in contemporary
living artists and aims to represent both
established and up-and-coming artists. Exhibitions
change every month. Most media and styles
shown, including sculpture, ceramics and fine art.
Hosts solo and joint shows, and small themed
group exhibitions.
Submission Policy Always looking to introduce
new artists to the exhibition programme and is
committed to considering all applications. Initially
provide at least four images either by email or on
CD, slides or hard copy.
Price range £300–£2,000
No of exhibitions annually 10

Wharf Gallery
The Wharf Arts Centre, Canal Road, Tavistock
PL19 8AT
T 01822 611166 (box office) / 613928 (office)
F 01822 613974
E enquiries@tavistockwharf.com
W www.tavistockwharf.com
Contact Chris Burchell
Founded in 1996. One of West Devon's leading
arts and entertainment centres. Aims to promote
local artists, arts groups, schools and
photographers.
Submission Policy Interested in well-presented
work in any medium (limited sculpture). West
Country artists welcome.
Price range From £25
No of exhibitions annually 12

Widcombe Studios Gallery
The Old Malthouse, Comfortable Place, Bath
BA1 3AJ
T 01225 482480

E admin@widcombestudios.co.uk
W www.widcombestudios.co.uk
Founded in 1996 to provide studio
accommodation, gallery and exhibition space and a
programme of courses and talks. Moved to new
premises in 2004.
Submission Policy Applications for hiring the
gallery should be made to the studios'
administrator. There is a selection process.

Wales

Art 2 By Ltd

Harbour Lights Gallery, Porthgain, Haverfordwest
SA62 5BW
T 01348 831549
F 01348 831549 (phone first)
E info@art2by.com
W www.art2by.com
Founded in 1995 to promote the art of
Pembrokeshire and Welsh artists. Artists include
Bernard Green, Sheils Knapp Fisher, Wendy Yeo,
Gillian McDonald, Cherry Pickles and Graham
Hurd-Wood.
Submission Policy Artists' work is viewed strictly
by appointment.
Price range £19.50–£20,000
No of exhibitions annually 4

Art Matters Gallery

South Parade, Tenby, SA70 7DG
T 01834 843375
E Info@artmatters.org.uk
W www.artmatters.org.uk
Contact John Faulkner or Margaret Welsh
Established in 2001. A large gallery with an
eclectic and changing mix of work. More than fifty
current artists including Leonard Beard, Andrew
Douglas Forbes, Elizabeth Haines, Hilary Paynter
and Derek Williams. Mostly paintings but also
shows sculpture, ceramics, wood (carved and
turned) and wood engravings.
Submission Policy Application by post or email
with CV and images, prior to possible
appointment for viewing.
Price range £100–£2,000
No of exhibitions annually 15, plus continuously
changing exhibition in other parts of the gallery.

Attic Gallery

14 Cambrian Place, Swansea, SA1 1RG
T 01792 653387
E roe@atticgallery.co.uk
W www.atticgallery.co.uk

Contact David Roe
Founded in 1962 and among Wales's longest
established private galleries. Aims to highlight the
work of contemporary artists working in Wales.
Runs a full exhibition programme of solo and
mixed shows with a changing display of new
paintings, graphics and sculpture.
Submission Policy Initial approach by post
(include sae) with photos and CV, or by email.
Price range £50–£10,000
No of exhibitions annually 8

Black Mountain Gallery

The Square, Cwmllynfell, Swansea, SA9 2FJ
T 01639 830920
E sales@blackmountaingallery.com
W www.blackmountaingallery.com
Contact Mark Williams
Publishing the work of contemporary commercial
artists Muriel Williams and Mark Williams.

Bowie & Hulbert

5 Market Street, Hay-on-Wye, HR3 5AF
T 01497 821026
F 01497 821801
E info@hayclay.co.uk
W www.hayclay.co.uk
Partner gallery to Brook Street Pottery (also in Hay-
on-Wye), founded in 1994. Specializes in applied
arts (ceramics and jewellery) and some fine-art
prints. Artists include Walter Keeler, Jane Hamlyn,
Peter Beard and Catherine Mannheim. Only shows
UK artists and makers.
Submission Policy Apply only by letter with slides
or photographs and other relevant information.
Price range £50–£2,000
No of exhibitions annually 3–4

Brooklyn Art Gallery

52 Birchgrove Road, Birchgrove, Cardiff
CF14 1RS
T 029 20529950
E info@brooklynartgallery.co.uk
W www.brooklynartgallery.co.uk
Founded in 1999 by artist Nasir Shiraz.
Continuously exhibits new works by resident
artists including Nasir Shiraz, Rob Lee, Babette
Edwards, Huw Walters and Victoria Stewart. Art
works are presented on large canvas to suit the
modern interior.
Submission Policy Artists should send a CV and
photos of work by email.
Price range £100–£5,000
No of exhibitions annually 8

Capsule
48 Charles Street, Cardiff, CF10 2GF
T 029 20382882
E info@acidcasuals.com
W www.acidcasuals.com
Owned and run by Acid Casuals. Represents Ruth
Mclees, Mark Cadwallader and R. Mer.
Submission Policy All applications welcome.
Price range £36–£2,000
No of exhibitions annually 8–10
Cost to hire or rent £1,000 per week

Celf
85 Newton Road, Mumbles, Swansea, SA3 4BN
T 01792 366800
E info@celfdesign.co.uk
W www.celfdesign.co.uk
Celf was set up in 2002 to exhibit paintings by
Michelle Scragg and architectural decorative glass
designed by Caroline Rees
Price range £100–£2,000
No of exhibitions annually 1

Chapel of Art–Capel Celfyddyd
8 Marine Crescent, Criccieth, LL52 0EA
T 01766 523570
E mail@the-coa.org.uk
W www.the-coa.org.uk
Contact Eckhard or Janet Kaiser
Established in 1995. Exhibits contemporary fine
art and selected crafts by local, regional and
international artists and makers. A specialist
ceramic gallery and home of the International
Potters' Path, made by potters and ceramic artists
from around the world.
Submission Policy Artists are required to submit
work appropriate to the exhibition titles as
published on the website and are advised to
contact Janet Kaiser about size and weight
restrictions. Textiles and jewellery are only
accepted in exceptional circumstances.
Price range £25–£2,000
No of exhibitions annually 6

Chepstow Ceramics Workshop Gallery
13 Lower Church Street, Chepstow, NP16 5HJ
T 01291 624836
F 01291 624836
E nedheywood@aol.com
W www.nedheywood.com
Founded in 1982, specializing in studio ceramics.
Exhibited artists include Walter Keeler, Julia Land
and Ned Heywood.
Submission Policy Ceramics only.

Price range £20–£1,000
No of exhibitions annually 6

Coed Hills Rural Artspace
St Hilary, Cowbridge, CF71 7DP
T 01446 774084
E mail@coedhills.co.uk
W www.coedhills.co.uk
An arts venue based on a philosophy of positive
living in environmental and social contexts. Has
workshops, galleries and a woodland sculpture
trail, among other facilities.
Submission Policy Welcomes proposals of all types.

Craftsman Gallery
58 St Helen Road, Swansea, SA1 4BE
T 01792 642043
F 01792 642043
E bowden@craftsmangallery.co.uk
W www.craftsmangallery.co.uk
Established since 1978, specializing in works by
Welsh artists or artists working in Wales.

GPF Gallery
18 George Street, Newport, NP20 1EN
T 01633 264581
E gpfgallery@aol.com
Contact Janet Martin
Established for over twenty-five years. The
associated GPF Gallery opened in the late 1990s.
Artists represented include Philip Muirden, John
Selway, Sarah Ball and Michael Organ. Opened
Robbins Lane Studios in 2004, housing eight
studios and an artist's studio-flat, as well as
providing exhibition space and meeting-room hire.
Submission Policy Any living artist is welcome to
contact the gallery to make an appointment to
show work.
Price range £100–£3,000
No of exhibitions annually 6

Green Gallery
The Green, Rhossili, Swansea, SA3 1PL
T 01792 391190
E GreenGalRhossili@aol.com
W www.thegreengallery.co.uk
Contact Fiona Ryall
Founded in 2001. Specializes in fine art, mainly
traditional twentieth-century paintings. Also
stocks a broad spectrum of modern work including
sculptures in bronze and stone. Artists
represented include Helen Sinclair, Kevin Ryall,
Stuart Mulligan, James Selway and Janet Bligh.
Submission Policy Welcomes applications and

keen to represent new talent.
Price range £60–£3,000
No of exhibitions annually 2

Kilvert Gallery

Ashbrook House, Clyro, nr Hay-on-Wye, HR3 5RZ
T 01497 820831
F 01497 820831
E art@clyro.co.uk
W www.kilvertgallery.co.uk, www.clyro.co.uk
Founded in 1986 by the painter Elizabeth Organ to
promote recent graduates in fine art and specialist
crafts. The gallery's artist-in-residence is portrait
painter Eugene Fisk. Other artists represented
include Peter Bishop, Roger Cecil, Maryclare Foa,
Sally Matthews, Kate Milsom Hawkins, Betty
Pennell, Ronald Pennell, Charles Shearer and
Alfred Stockham.
Submission Policy Not currently taking any more
artists.
Price range £50–£5,000
No of exhibitions annually 2

Kooywood Gallery

8 Museum Place, Cardiff, CF10 3BF
T 021 20235093
E enquiries@kooywoodgallery.com
W www.kooywoodgallery.com
Opened in 2004 to provide a forum for established
and new artists to show and sell work. Exhibits and
exhibitions cover a wide range of contemporary
visual art, including painting, sculpture, ceramics,
glass, photography and prints.
Price range £85–£15,000
No of exhibitions annually 12

La Mostra Gallery

Mermaid Quay, Cardiff Bay, Cardiff, CF10 5BZ
T 029 20492225
F 029 20492226
E enquiries@lamostragallery.com
W www.lamostragallery.com
Cardiff's first commercial art gallery to exhibit
international paintings, sculpture and objets d'art
exclusively. Periodically holds group and personal
exhibitions, with special evening openings and
private viewings. International artists represented
include Julian Murphy (UK), Andrew Buryah
(Belarus), Sandro Soravia (Italy) and Rebecca
Adams (UK).
Submission Policy Send CV, exhibition history and
images of work, plus sae if you wish images to be
returned.
Price range From £150

The Makers Guild in Wales

Craft in the Bay, The Flourish, Lloyd George
Avenue, Cardiff Bay, Cardiff, CF10 4QH
T 029 20484611
F 029 20491136
E admin@makersguildinwales.org.uk
W www.makersguildinwales.org.uk
Contact Exhibitions Officer
Founded in 1984, with a permanent exhibition
venue at Craft in the Bay in Cardiff. All work is for
sale. There are 74 members of the guild and the
work exhibited includes ceramics, jewellery,
textiles, woodwork and metalwork. Also shows
temporary exhibitions of contemporary designs
created by artists throughout the UK and abroad. A
comprehensive education programme provides
opportunities for young people and adults to
participate in practical courses, demonstrations
and talks.
Submission Policy Artists living and working in
Wales wishing to apply for membership should
contact the manager at Craft in the Bay for further
details. Artists interested in showing work in the
temporary exhibitions area should contact the
exhibitions officer at Craft in the Bay.
No of exhibitions annually 7, temporary. Guild
members have permanent displays of their work.

manorhaus

10 Well Street, Ruthin, LL15 1AH
T 01824 704830
F 01824 707333
E post@manorhaus.com
W www.manorhaus.com
Contact Christopher Frost
Founded in 2001 and housed within a listed
Georgian townhouse hotel and restaurant. Artists
include Ann Bridges RCA, Ian Williams, Dave
Merrills RCA, Meurig Watkins, Terry Duffy and
Alan Baynes.
Submission Policy Preference for contemporary
works and wall-hung pieces; no space for sculpture
or display cabinets. Solo exhibitions require
approximately twenty to forty pieces, depending on
size.
Price range £100–£1,000
No of exhibitions annually 6

Martin Tinney Gallery

18 St Andrew's Crescent, Cardiff, CF10 3DD
T 029 20641411
E mtg@artwales.com
W www.artwales.com
Contact Myfanwy Shorey

Founded in 1990, promoting the best of twentieth-century and contemporary Welsh art in Cardiff, London and abroad. Clients include Tate Gallery and National Museum of Wales. Artists include Augustus John, Gwen John, Ceri Richards, Harry Holland, Gwilym Prichard, Shani Rhys James, Peter Prendergast, Kevin Sinnott, Evelyn Williams and Sir Kyffin Williams.
Submission Policy Welsh or Wales-based artists. Submit a portfolio of images (digital, photograph or slide format) and current CV with sae.
Price range £100–£250,000
No of exhibitions annually 12

Mission Gallery
Gloucester Place, Maritime Quarter, Swansea SA1 1TY
T 01792 652016
F 01792 652016
E missiongallery@btconnect.com
W www.missiongallery.co.uk
Founded in 1977. Hosts a changing exhibition programme of contemporary visual art, photography, film, installation, painting and craft. The gallery's Craft Space shows work by established and emerging makers and designers.
Submission Policy Contact the gallery for application procedure.
No of exhibitions annually 8

Number 15
15 Victoria Road, Penrith, CA11 8HN
T 01768 867453
E number15@btinternet.com
Contact Andy Askins or Kat Thomas
Exhibits contemporary national and international artists working in mixed media, paintings, prints, photography and film. A spacious exhibition room is connected by double doors to Number 15 Café.
Submission Policy Wall-hung work only. Submit photographs to Andy Askins. Artists must have their own insurance.
Price range £30–£10,000

Oriel
2 Tyn-Y-Coed Buildings, High Street, Barmouth, Gwynedd, LL42 1DS
T 01341 280285
E info@orielgallery.com
W www.orielgallery.com
Founded in 1992. Offers a broad selection of contemporary work, as well as more traditional work. Apart from work by Valerie McArdell and Sue Moore (both working full-time at the gallery),

also promotes the work of Keith Davis, Alex McArdell and Janet Bell. Offers giclée printing services in-house, as well as bespoke framing.
Submission Policy Considers other artists' work. However, it has to fit in well with other work being exhibited at that time. If the gallery rejects, it may well reconsider at a later date.
Price range £50–£1,500

Oriel Canfas Gallery
44a Glamorgan Street, Cardiff, CF5 1QS
T 029 20666455
F 029 20666455
E info@olacanfas.co.uk
W www.olacanfas.co.uk
Contact Old Library Artists Ltd
An artists' cooperative formed in 1994. In 1996, with the help of Lottery funding, it secured the present building, studios and education space. Exhibits a wide variety of visual art including painting, sculpture and photography, as well as mixed and multimedia.
Price range £50–£5,000
No of exhibitions annually 10

Phillip Davies Fine Art
130 Overland Road, Mumbles, Swansea, SA3 4EU
T 01792 361766

St Anthony Fine Art
30A St Anthony Road, Heath, Cardiff, CF11 6JZ
T 029 20400160
E keith@stanthonyfineart.co.uk
W www.stanthonyfineart.co.uk
Founded in 2004, representing established and emerging artists. Previous exhibitors include Jack Crabtree, Peter Nicholas and John Selway.
Price range From £50
No of exhibitions annually 8

Washington Gallery
1–3 Washington Buildings, Stanwell Road, Penarth CF64 2AD
T 029 20712100
F 029 20708047
E info@washingtongallery.co.uk
W www.washingtongallery.co.uk
Founded in 1998, specializing in Welsh contemporary art. Artists include Dan Llywelyn Hall, John Selway, James Charlton, Arthur Giardelli, Aneurin Jones, Iwan Lewis, Laurie Williams, and 2005 Artes Mundi finalist, Sue Williams.
Submission Policy Entry open to contemporary artists in all media (but restricted for video or

photographic artists). Send examples of work.
Enquiries welcome from Welsh artists (based in
Wales or working elsewhere).
Price range £100–£6,000
No of exhibitions annually 30, over two levels.
Cost to hire or rent Special hire from £500 per
week: Upper Gallery (2,000 sq ft).

West Wales Arts Centre
16 West Street, Fishguard, SA65 9AE
T 01348 873867
E westwalesarts@btconnect.com
W www.westwalesartscentre.com
Contact Myles Pepper
Established for over twenty years, exhibiting
contemporary paintings, sculpture and ceramics
and featuring established and emerging artists
including David Tress, James MacKeown, Ross
Loveday, Brendan Stuart Burns, Sonya Dawn
Flewitt and James Campbell. Lectures, seminars
and music performances throughout the year.
Price range £100–£5,000
No of exhibitions annually 5

Workshop Wales Gallery
Manorowen, Fishguard, SA65 9QA
T 01348 891619
F 01348 891619
E alicecleal@hotmail.com
Contact Alice Cleal
Founded in 1970. Currently exhibits about forty
contemporary artists, including Daniel Backhouse,
Mitchell Cleal, Jack Crabtree, David Humphreys,
Barbara Stewart and Alice Tennant.
Submission Policy Only original works accepted.
No prints, photography, jewellery or craft items.
Price range £100–£5,000
No of exhibitions annually 2

West Midlands

Acanthus Gallery
326 Kenilworth Road, Balsall Common,
Warwickshire, CV7 7ER
T 01676 535792
F 01676 535792
E acanthusart@btconnect.com
W www.acanthusart.co.uk
Contact Sandra Tattersall
Founded in 1976 as trade framer (artists'
exhibitions and retail). Artists include Ian
Warwick-King, Laurence Hayfield, Nancy Wood
SFP, Geoff Birks YWS, Stuart Ellis and Roger
Cockram (ceramics).

Submission Policy Gallery area available for artists'
exhibitions free of charge, subject to conditions.
Price range £50–£5,000
No of exhibitions annually 4, but none for the past
two years.

Artist's Gallery
373 Bearwood Road, Smethwick, Birmingham
B66 4DL
T 0121 4292298
E support@artistsgallery.co.uk
W www.artistsgallery.co.uk
Founded in 1990, specializing in Italian oil
paintings and contemporary art. Artists
represented include Sue Canonico, Mario
Sanzone, Franco Casalloni and Nino D'Amore.
Submission Policy All artists welcome to exhibit
work after prior agreement.
Price range £100–£2,000
No of exhibitions annually 1, permanent.

Birties of Worcester
46 Friar Street, Worcester, WR1 2NA
T 01905 28836
F 01905 339418
E linda.birtwhistle@birties.fsnet.co.uk
W www.birtiesofworcester.com
Contact Linda Birtwhistle
Founded in 1979 to promote contemporary fine art
by local and nationally-known artists. Artists
include David Birtwhistle (watercolours), Graham
Clarke (etchings), Martin Caulkin RI
(watercolours), Tom Greenshields (sculpture),
Howard Coles (mixed media) and Nancy Turnbull
(oils).
Submission Policy By appointment only. Gallery
requires to see at least six original recent works.
Decisions cannot be made based solely on slides or
photographs. Work exhibited must be framed to
conservation standard.
Price range £100–£5,000
No of exhibitions annually 6

Bond Gallery
180–182 Fazeley Street, Digbeth, Birmingham
B5 5SE
T 0121 7532065
Specializes in contemporary art.

Broadway Modern
10 The Green, Broadway, WR12 7AA
T 01386 858436
F 01386 858957
E modern@john-noott.com

W www.broadwaymodern.com
Contact Amanda Noott
Founded in 1999, showing contemporary
painting, sculpture, ceramics and furniture.
Price range £50–£5,000
No of exhibitions annually 6

Castle Galleries
Bards Walk, Stratford-upon-Avon, CV37 6EY
T 01789 262031
F 01789 262480
E stratford@castlegalleries.com
W www.castlegalleries.co.uk
Artists include Mackenzie Thorpe, Paul Horton,
Alex Miller and Rolf Harris.
Price range £100–£20,000
No of exhibitions annually 4

Cowleigh Gallery
14 Cowleigh Road, Malvern, WR14 1QD
T 01684 560646
F 01684 560646
E cowgall@tiscali.co.uk
Contact William E. Nicholls or Caroline A. Nicholls
Has hosted six exhibitions per year for the last six
years, including the Society of Wildlife, the ROI,
the RWA and the Bath Society.
Submission Policy Encourages emerging painters
but has a large list of gallery artists who are
professional and established.
Price range £100–£5,000
No of exhibitions annually 2–3 special solo shows,
in addition to continual display.

Custard Factory
Gibbs Square, Birmingham, B9 4AA
T 0121 6047777
F 0121 6048888
E info@custardfactory.com
W www.custardfactory.com
A new arts and media quarter for Birmingham, in
development since 1990 and covering over five
acres of riverside factories built a hundred years
ago by Sir Alfred Bird, the inventor of custard.
Houses over five hundred artists and small creative
enterprises, offering not only exhibition spaces but
also affordable studio workshops and examples of
large-scale public art.

Driffold Gallery
78 Birmingham Road, Sutton Coldfield, B72 1QR
T 0121 3555433
W www.driffoldgallery.com
Established in 1983, specializing in British and

European paintings by valued artists from 1840 to
the present. Living artists include members of
British academies and societies.
Price range £300–£25,000
No of exhibitions annually 4–5

England's Gallery
Ball Haye House, 1 Ball Haye Terrace, Leek, ST13 6AP
T 01538 373451
F 01538 373451
Founded in 1967, showing mainly nineteenth- and
twentieth-century oils and watercolours. Holds
specialist exhibition of lithography, etching,
engravings and woodcuts. Offers framing,
restoration, conservation and valuation services.
Price range £45–£8,000
No of exhibitions annually 5 named exhibitions;
gallery stock on show when no featured exhibition.
Open from 2 pm to 5 pm daily (except Sunday and
Monday) throughout the year.

Eyestorm-Britart Gallery
Radio House, Swan Street, Warwick, CV34 4BJ
T 01926 495506
E alan@aeart.co.uk
W www.eyestorm.com
Founded in 1989, now specializing in modern art.
Artists exhibited include Damien Hirst, Sir Terry
Frost, Helmut Newton, Willi Kissmer and Bob
Carlos Clarke.
Submission Policy Submissions from new artists
should be sent to head office at 18 Maddox Street,
London W1S 1PL.
Price range £200–£20,000
No of exhibitions annually 6–8

Friswell's Picture Gallery Ltd
223 Albany Road, Earlsdon, Coventry, CV5 6NF
T 024 76674883
E patrick@friswells.com
W www.friswells.com
Contact Patrick Kelly
Established 1870. Offers artists the opportunity to
exhibit their work in a prominent location (subject
to approval). Holds work by artists including
Govinder, Lawrence Coulson, Mark Spain, Russell
Baker and David Morgan. A full bespoke framing
service is also available.
Submission Policy A portfolio of works needs to be
submitted by artists wishing to exhibit. If
approved, details are then discussed.
Price range From £2.50
No of exhibitions annually 10
Cost to hire or rent Starting prices from £60

The Gallery Upstairs

Torquil, 81 High Street, Henley-in-Arden, B95 5AT
T 01564 792174
E galleryupstairs@aol.com
Shows work of contemporary artists in ceramics and
fine art. Deals with leading artists in their fields but
also likes to promote those starting out. Has run two
large group exhibitions a year (November to
December and May to June) since 1985.
Price range £50–£5,000

The Gallery

17A Broad Street, Leek, ST13 5NR
T 01538 372961
F 01538 399696
E info@leekbooks.co.uk
Contact Lisa Salt
Established in 2001, specializing in paintings, art
work and crafts by local artists. Artists exhibited
include Leslie Gilbert RI, Tom Mountford and Ivan
Taylor. Framing service also offered.
Submission Policy Artists welcome to leave work
at the gallery for inspection. All work must be
framed for hanging to a reasonable standard.
Price range £50–£600
No of exhibitions annually 3, including a
Christmas exhibition in November and December.

Halcyon Gallery

The International Convention Centre, Broad
Street, Birmingham, B1 2EA
T 0121 2488484
E icc@halcyongallery.com
W www.halcyon.co.uk
Over twenty years' experience dealing in original
paintings, drawings and sculpture, master
graphics and limited editions. Changing
programme of exhibitions. Also has three London
spaces, in Mayfair and in Harrods and Selfridges.

Helios at the Spinney

The Spinney, Birmingham, Broad Lane, Tanworth-
in-Arden, Solihull, B94 5HR
T 01564 742506
E mail@heliosgallery.co.uk
W www.heliosgallery.co.uk
Established for over twenty years, selling
paintings, prints, sculpture, glass and ceramics.
Artists include Gillian Lever, Sue Howell, Angela
Palmer, Siobhan Jones and Elaine Hind. Runs
extensive art library and offers framing service.

John Noott Galleries

Dickens House, 20 High Street, Broadway

WR12 7DT
T 01386 858969
E aj@john-noott.com
W www.john-noott.com
Contact Amanda Noott
Founded in 1972, showing works of art by leading
painters and sculptors from the nineteenth
century to the present day.
Submission Policy Artists apply via website.
Price range £50–£50,000
No of exhibitions annually 10

Manser Fine Art

Coleham Head, Shrewsbury, SY3 7BJ
T 01743 240328
F 01743 270066
E info@fineartdealers.co.uk
W www.fineartdealers.co.uk
Contact Charlotte Cash
Founded in 1994 and owned and managed by the
third generation of the Manser family. Sells
eighteenth-, nineteenth- and twentieth-century
works of art, including sculpture and works with a
Russian or maritime theme. Artists include Anton
Bouvard, Alfred de Breanski, Oliver Clare, Paul
Gribble, Richard Hilder and Edgar Hunt. Also
offers restoration, valuation and framing services.
Submission Policy Contact the gallery by phone,
post or email. Send slides or jpegs of works.
Price range £500–£150,000
No of exhibitions annually 3

Montpellier Gallery

8 Chapel Street, Stratford-upon-Avon, CV37 6EP
T 01789 261161
F 01789 261161
W www.montpelliergallery.com
Contact Peter Burridge
Established in 1991, specializing in contemporary
paintings, printmaking, sculpture, studio
ceramics, glass and designer jewellery by
established and emerging artists. Annual
exhibition programmes feature group and solo
shows. Exhibited artists include John Hammond,
Brenda Hartill, Anita Klein and Peter Eugine Ball.
Submission Policy Artists should be semi-
professional or professional, showing a
consistency of style and technique.
Price range £25–£5,000
No of exhibitions annually 4

Moya Bucknall Fine Art

Barn End, Park Avenue, Solihull, B91 3EJ
T 0121 7056215

F 0121 7051699
E moya@moyabucknall.co.uk
W www.moyabucknall.co.uk
Formed over thirty years ago. Specializes in sourcing and commissioning original works of art for both companies and private individuals. Represents a wide range of established artists, including James Butler, Iestyn Davies, Peter Evans, Pam Hawkes and Terrence Millington. Always on the lookout for new artists. Works with all types of media, from paintings, drawings and etchings to ceramics, glassware, fabric installations and three-dimensional sculpture in bronze, wood and other materials.
Submission Policy Requires digital images, photographs or samples of actual work prior to a meeting to view the artist's portfolio.
Price range £100–£40,000
No of exhibitions annually 2

New Gallery
St Paul's Square, Birmingham, B3 1RL
T 0121 2330800
E info@thenewgallery.co.uk
W www.thenewgallery.co.uk
Specializes in British twentieth-century greats (John Piper, Graham Sutherland et al.), living UK-based artists of international renown (Royal Academicians, etc.) and other professional UK-based artists in all styles (Roger Oakes, John Hodgett, Sara Hayward, David John Robinson). Limited-edition prints and photographic prints, monoprints and originals available. Caters to private and corporate collectors. Offers interest-free Arts Council England Own Art loans.
Submission Policy By email with CV, images and exhibition history.
Price range £100–£5,000
No of exhibitions annually 8

Number Nine the Gallery
9 Brindley Place, Birmingham, B1 2JA
T 0121 6439099
F 0121 6439199
E noninethegallery@btclick.com
W www.numberninethegallery.com
Established in 1999, selling a diverse range of Midlands-linked international artists in painting, glass, ceramics and sculptures, original prints and rock art. Linked to Arts Council England's Own Art scheme. Artists include Ralph Brown RA, Mila Judge Furstova RCA, Glenn Badham, Kevin Pearsh, Bertil Valien and Matthew Draper.
Submission Policy Does not take published

commercial artists. Sells mainly original works of art.
Price range £100–£50,000
No of exhibitions annually 6
Cost to hire or rent Buttermarket available from £1,200 per week.

Owen Taylor Art
The Hunting Lodge, Castle Park, Warwick CV34 6SZ
T 01926 400058
F 01926 402898
E cyril@owentaylorart.com
W www.owentaylorart.com
Founded in 2002. Stocks British contemporary painting and graphics. Work is varied in style and content. Artists range from Royal Academicians and London Group to recent art-school graduates. Operates Arts Council England's Own Art purchase scheme.
Submission Policy Artists should review the gallery website to establish suitability of their work.
Price range £50–£3,000
No of exhibitions annually 4, plus a mixed stock.

Park View Gallery
70 Vicarage Road, Kings Heath, Birmingham B14 7QL
T 0121 4444851
Opened 1998 and now has three spaces. Shows solo and group exhibitions, mostly by artists with links to the local region.

Priory Gallery Broadway
34 The High Street, Broadway, WR12 7DT
T 01386 853783
F 01386 853783
E info@priorybroadway.com
W www.priorybroadway.com
Deals in twenty-first-century artists and sculptors including Dianne Flynn, Paul Hedley, Paul Gribble, Tony Sheath, Bruce Hardley and Tina Morgan.
Price range £200–£5,000
No of exhibitions annually 4–6

Retrospectives Gallery
The Minories, Rother Street, Stratford-upon-Avon CV37 6NE
T 01789 297706
E info@retrospectives.co.uk
W www.retrospectives.co.uk
In Stratford for nearly twenty years and taken over by present management in 2003. Offers modern

and contemporary art, specializing in originals and some limited editions. Exhibitions of local artists include David Collins, Tom Ashridge FRSA and Kay Elliott. International artists supplying originals include Starlie Sokol-Hohne (USA), Pinto (Portugal) and Wilfred (USA).
Submission Policy Looking for contemporary and mainly abstract art in oils, acrylic and mixed media. Also quality traditional art.
Price range £100–£800
No of exhibitions annually 1

Shell House Gallery
36 The Homend, Ledbury, HR8 1BT
T 01531 632557
E padireland@aol.com
W www.shellhousegallery.co.uk
Founded in 1979, specializing in original watercolours and mixed media by living artists. Main exhibitions are by the Royal Institute of Painters in Watercolours and the Royal Institute of Oil Painters. Also offers a framing and restoration service and publishes limited-edition prints.
Price range £50–£3,000
No of exhibitions annually 10

Spectacle
38 Freeth Street, Ladywood, Birmingham, B16 0QP
E info@spectacle-gallery.co.uk
W www.spectacle-gallery.co.uk
Contact Greg Cox
Spectacle gallery is an artist-led gallery space on the outskirts of Birmingham's centre. The programme is varied and non-specific but aims for a sense ambitiousness. Artists include Reactor, Dan Mort, Jon Lockhart, Dr Brian D Haddock, Captain Ed, Harminder Singh Judge and Matt Robinson.
Submission Policy Exhibitions run for four weeks; open 12pm–5pm at weekends and by appointment at all other times.
No of exhibitions annually 4

St Paul's Gallery
94–108 Northwood Street, Birmingham, B3 1TH
T 0121 2365800
F 0121 2360098
E info@stpaulsgallery.com
W www.stpaulsgallery.com
Sells originals and editioned pieces as well as working with other galleries to bring internationally-important shows to Birmingham.

Valentyne Dawes Gallery
Church Street, Ludlow, SY8 1AP

T 01584 874160
E sales@gallery.wyenet.co.uk
W www.maritime-paintings.com
Founded in mid-1980s, specializing in coastal and maritime paintings. Mainly nineteenth and early twentieth century. Artists include E.W. Cooke RA, David James and John Brett. Modern British artists are also represented, in particular Terrick Williams RA. Contemporary painters include Ian Cryer.
Price range £80–£80,000
No of exhibitions annually 1 – the December Maritime Exhibition continues until Christmas.

Warstone & Turner
67 Warstone Lane, Hockley, Birmingham
B18 6NG
T 0121 6936968

Warwick Gallery
14 Smith Street, Warwick, CV34 4HH
T 01926 495880
E wg@artisatart.fsnet.co.uk
W www.art-is-a-tart.com
A contemporary gallery featuring the works of over 100 artists. Continualy changing selection of arts and crafts.
Branches 82 Regent Street, Leamington Spa, CV32 4NS. A new gallery, Filthy but Georgeous, scheduled to open in Leamington Spa soon.)
Submission Policy Chooses work that appeals to the gallery.
Price range £1–£3,000
No of exhibitions annually 2

Wenlock Fine Art
3 The Square, Much Wenlock, TF13 6LX
T 01952 728232
Opened in 1991, dealing in twentieth and twenty-first century artists. Artists represented include William Gear RA, John Piper, Mich Rooney RA, Henry Inlander, John Christopherson and Adrian Ryan.
Price range £100–£15,000
No of exhibitions annually 3

Wildside Books and Gallery
Rectory House, 26 Priory Road, Great Malvern WR14 3DR
T 01684 562818
F 01684 566491
E enquire@wildsidebooks.co.uk
W www.wildsidegallery.co.uk
Founded in 1999, specializing in wildlife art with a particular interest in nineteenth and twentieth

century ornithology. Exhibits work by Keith Shackleton, Charles Tunnicliffe, George Lodge, David Rid Henry, Robert Bateman, Geoffrey Dashwood and R. Talbot Kelly.
Submission Policy Not currently accepting work by living artists
Price range £25–£15,000

Wolseley Fine Arts Ltd
Middle Hunt House, Walterstone, Hereford HR2 0DY
T 01873 860525
F 01873 860525
E info@wolseleyfinearts.com
W www.wolseleyfinearts.com
Founded in 1990. Specializes in early twentieth-century works on paper, mainly by French Post-Impressionist and modern British artists. Also shows contemporary sculpture, carved lettering and still life and landscape paintings.
Submission Policy Although the gallery shows contemporary sculpture and carved lettering, the style is so specific that applications from artists are not encouraged.
Price range £150–£50,000
No of exhibitions annually 6

Yorkshire and Humberside

108 Fine Art
108 West End Avenue, Harrogate, HG2 9BT
T 01423 819108
F 01423 525847
E andrew@108fineart.com
W www.108fineart.com
Established in 1997 to promote the work of emerging and established contemporary artists. Artists shown include Joash Woodrow, Ana Maria Pacheco, Paul Reid, Alan Davie, Peter Sedgley, Christopher P. Wood, George Rowlett and Robert MacMillan. Also stock works by twentieth century British artists. Offers a comprehensive paintings conservation service to collectors, museums and galleries.
Submission Policy Welcomes work by artists working in all media.
Price range £100–£100,000
No of exhibitions annually 6

Archipelago Art Gallery and Studio
742 Ecclesall Road, Sheffield, S11 8TB
T 0114 2686885
F 0114 2682272
E info@archipelago-art.co.uk
W www.archipelago-art.co.uk
Opened in 2002, featuring contemporary painters, printmakers and photographers. Also incorporates digital printmaking and giclée services, and a framing and making workshop. Exhibitions in 2005 included work by Heidi Konig, Charlotte Cornish, Pete McKee and flyeronthewall.com.
Submission Policy Submissions welcome from active painters, printmakers or designers. Also illustrators working in the fashion and music industries.
Price range £250–£2,500
No of exhibitions annually 10

Artco
1 Meanwood Close, Leeds, LS7 2JF
T 0113 2620056
F 0113 2628388
E info@artco.co.uk
W www.artco.co.uk
Established for over twenty years. Exhibits work from both well-established artists and emerging talent, maintaining a strong presence at selected art fairs throughout the UK. The gallery covers 2,000 sq.ft, exhibiting a diverse selection of styles of art work. Bespoke and commercial framing service offered.
Submission Policy Submissions from artists welcome. No installation or video art.

Artolicana
25 Church Street, Ilkley, LS29 9DR
T 01943 603866
E info@artolicana.org
W www.artolicana.org
Established over ten years ago, selling local artists' work. Deals in original paintings only. Artists exhibited include Giuliana Lazzerini, David Greenwood, Tamara Lawson, Judith Levin, Jane Fielder and Brian Irving.
Submission Policy Established artists with proven mailing lists considered for inclusion in the gallery's programme of exhibitions.
Price range £100–£5,500
No of exhibitions annually Every three weeks for established artists; unsold work held in stock after three weeks for further month.

Bianco Nero Gallery
14 Bridge Road, Stokesley, TS9 5AA
T 01642 714433
E info@bianconero.co.uk
W www.bianconero.co.uk
Contact Michele Bianco

Founded in 2003, showing a wide range of contemporary art. From artists prints and paintings to 3-D work, including glass, ceramics and sculpture. Exhibited artists include Emma Stothard (willow sculptures), Richard Spare (prints), Joanne Mitchell (glass), Jim Wright (painting), Malcolm Teasdale (painting) and Lorna Graves (ceramics). Bespoke picture framing service available.
Submission Policy Applications welcome and should include biographical details and sample images (slide, photo or digital only).
Price range £10–£2,500
No of exhibitions annually 9

Blake Gallery
18 Blake Street, York, YO1 8QH
T 01904 733666
F 01904 733730
E info@blakegallery.com
W www.blakegallery.com
Shows contemporary art including a permanent collection of sculpture by Sally Arnup and an extensive range of works by Piers Browne. Other artists include Mamdoh Badran, Lesley Fotherby, Roy Hammond, Tom Wanless and Walter Holmes.
Price range £50–£20,000
No of exhibitions annually 6

Bohemia Galleries
7 Gillygate, York, YO31 7EA
T 01904 466488
E info@a-r-t.co.uk
W www.a-r-t.co.uk
Opened in the mid-1990s. Has developed a reputation for innovative stock, which includes contemporary works of art, ceramics and glass of the last two centuries. Artists represented include Mark Halsey, Frank Bentley, David Baumforth, Ludmila Curilova, Giluliana Lazzerini and Emilija Pasagic.
Branch Bohemia Galleries Two, 2 Sow-Hill Road, Beverley, HU17 8BG, T 01482 881882, sheana@bohemia-galleries.com
Submission Policy Submissions welcome.

Braithwaite Gallery
42 Low Petergate, York, YO1 7HZ
T 01904 655707
F 01904 655707
E artist@yorkartist.com
W www.yorkartist.com
Located a few yards from the South Transept of York Minster in a historic, beamed, listed building belonging to York Minster. Owned by the

Braithwaite family. Resident artist Mark Braithwaite has a constant display and there are prints and originals of many other artists including Kay Boyce, John Silver, David Shepherd, Christine Comyn and Warwick Higgs. Offers an in-house giclée printing service for artists.
Submission Policy Most originals are purchased from leading publishers. Self-publishing artists can contact via email or phone (no cold-calling; contact Anne or Vicky for an informal chat).
Price range £1–£10,000
No of exhibitions annually Permanent selling exhibition.

Browns Gallery
Wesley Street Chambers, Wesley Street
Otley, LS21 1AZ
T 01943 464656 / 850404
F 01943 464328
E sales@brownsgallery.co.uk
W www.brownsgallery.co.uk
Established over fifteen years ago and situated in a building occupying the site of Chippendale's birthplace. A family company representing well-known artists such as Shepherd, Flint, Rolf Harris, Mackenzie Thorpe, Doug Hyde and Kay Boyce, in addition to established and emerging local artists.
Price range £25–£4,000
No of exhibitions annually 4

Bruton Gallery
P.O.Box 145, Holmfirth, HD9 1YU
T 0870 7471800
E art@brutongallery.co.uk
W www.brutongallery.co.uk
Over thirty years of experience, selling art and sculpture by British and international artists to individual and corporate clients.

Crescent Arts
The Crescent, Scarborough, YO11 2PW
T 01723 351461
E info@crescentarts.co.uk
W www.crescentarts.co.uk
Established in 1979, providing: studio space for up to eight resident artists; support and resources for artists across the Borough of Scarborough; a programme of contemporary exhibitions; related education workshops; open-access facilities including darkroom, kiln and printmaking facilities. Resident artists pay subsidized rent in return for their time administering the exhibition/education programme. They are expected to undertake a personal, tailormade

programme of professional training, supported by the management committee.
Submission Policy Look at website or phone for details of exhibition opportunities, studio vacancies, workshops or open-access bookings.
No of exhibitions annually 6

Cupola Contemporary Art Ltd
178a Middlewood Road, Hillsborough
Sheffield, S6 1TD
T 0114 2852665 / 2812154
F 0114 2852665
E info@cupolagallery.com
W www.cupolagallery.com
Contact Ian Gracey
Established in 1991, specializing in contemporary art. Exhibits a broad range of work from both new, emerging talent and more established artists. Covers painting, sculpture, photography, original printmaking (etching, lino cuts, mezzotint, collograph, etc.), ceramics, glass, textiles and jewellery. Installations, film, video and new media work are also occasionally exhibited. Cupola Framing offers a comprehensive bespoke framing service (contact Ben or Nix on 0114 20011023). Karen Sherwood is also the director of Cupola consultancy. Artists represented include Lyn Hodnett, Derek McQueen, John Brokenshire, Anne Penman Sweet, Anita Klein and Corinna Button.
Submission Policy For submission requirements contact the gallery.
Price range £10–£5,000
No of exhibitions annually 8–10
Cost to hire or rent Negotiable

Eyecandy
118 Trafalgar Street, Devonshire Quarter
Sheffield, S1 4JT
T 0114 2787979
F 0114 2787979
E info@eyecandyimagesuk.com
W www.eyecandyimagesuk.com
Opened in 2004, Eyecandy merges gallery, retail outlet and workshop in a loft-style setting. Offers contemporary and fine-art prints, limited editions, originals, quality greeting cards and ceramics. There is also an in-house framing service. Exhibited artists include Caroline Wood, Sheryl Lee, Alistaire Scarlett, Elvis Davis and Ben Sutcliffe.
Submission Policy Accepts submissions at any time. All works considered.
Price range £25–£600
No of exhibitions annually 4

Forge Gallery
New Road, Robin Hood's Bay, Nr Whitby
YO22 4SF
T 01947 881049
E dave@forgegallery.co.uk
W www.forgegallery.co.uk
Contact Dave Jeffery
Opened in 1998. Sells original works of art including paintings, ceramics, sculpture and jet jewellery. Specializes in work produced in Yorkshire and in particular the North Yorkshire coast area. Artists include Dave Jeffery, Janet R. Moodie ARCA, Heather Gatt, Richard Nesling and David Beven.
Submission Policy Contact Dave Jeffery by letter, phone or email. Alternatively, call in at the gallery for further information.
Price range £10–£1,500

The Gallery
24 Market Place, Masham, HG4 4EB
T 01765 689554
E enquiries@mashamgallery.co.uk
W www.mashamgallery.co.uk
Founded in 1994. Exhibits high-quality contemporary art and craft.
Submission Policy Work should be clearly labelled and include an sae if posted. Do not send original pieces. Submissions are welcomed by email but the gallery should be contacted before sending images. Restriction include no installations, photography or video art. Artists must be living and working in the UK.
Price range £5–£2,000
No of exhibitions annually 4

Gallery 42
42 St Joseph's Street, Tadcaster, LS24 9HA
T 01937 530465
F 01937 530465
E art@gallery42.com
W www.gallery42.com
Aims to take modern art into the local community and encourage local artists. Artists exhibited include Nel Whatmore, Graham Illingworth, Malcolm Cowerd and John Wilson.
Submission Policy Work taken on a commission basis.
Price range £20–£15,000
No of exhibitions annually 2–3

Gascoigne Gallery
Royal Parade, Harrogate, HG1 2JN
T 01423 525000

F 01423 525000
E info@thegascoignegallery.com
W www.thegascoignegallery.com
Founded in 1998, showing original contemporary work that is semi-abstract and marginally representational. Landscape predominates, with the aim of conveying the essence and atmosphere of a subject rather than describing each minute detail.
Price range £200–£4,000
No of exhibitions annually 12–18

Glenrhydding Gallery
38 Bondgate, Otley, LS21 1AD
T 01943 466323
E howardgcf@tiscali.co.uk
W www.glenrhydding.com
Established in 1985 and under present ownership for the last nine years. Artists include John Sibson, Graham Carver, Neil Simone, Keith Melling, Patricia Jones and Sue Howells. Framing service also offered.
Price range £20–£1,000
No of exhibitions annually 2

Godfrey & Watt
7–8 Westminster Arcade, Parliament Street
Harrogate, HG1 2RN
T 01423 525300
E mail@godfreyandwatt.co.uk
W www.godfreyandwatt.co.uk
Founded in 1985 by Alex and Mary Godfrey to show work that 'we personally love by the best artists and makers that we can find.' Constantly changing range of ceramics, jewellery, studio glass, sculpture, paintings and original prints. In addition to this, a series of exhibitions is mounted each year, usually focusing on the work of an individual artist. Artists and makers exhibited include John Maltby, Morgen Hall, Lucy Casson, Guy Taplin, Piers Browne and Elaine Pamphilon.
Submission Policy Submissions welcome from artists by post or email. Should include photos, biography and prices.
Price range £50–£2,000
No of exhibitions annually 5

Grosmont Gallery
Front Street, Grosmont, Whitby, YO22 5QE
T 01947 895007
E info@grosmontgallery.com
W www.grosmontgallery.com
Promotes and sells fine art and quality crafts. Most artists currently on show are reasonably local but not exclusively. Among current artists exhibiting

are David Baumforth, Sally Gatie, Chris Geall, Janet Moodie, Angela Chalmers and Bren Head.
Submission Policy All artists are welcome to make contact, especially those with new and challenging work.
Price range £5–£5,000
No of exhibitions annually 4

Headrow Gallery
588 Harrogate Road, Alwoodley, Leeds, LS17 8DP
T 0113 2694244
F 0113 2694244
E maxwellroberts@btconnect.com
W www.headrowgallery.com
Founded in 1900. Specializes in contemporary North American and European art work.
Submission Policy Artists' submissions always welcome.
Price range £150–£5,000
No of exhibitions annually 2–3

Jim Robison and Booth House Gallery and Pottery
3 Booth House Lane, Holmfirth, Huddersfield
HD9 2QT
T 01484 685270
E jim.robison@virgin.net
W www.jimrobison.co.uk or
www.boothhousegallery.co.uk
Began in 1975 as a studio for Jim Robison and exhibition space for invited artists. Specializes in ceramics with continuous displays of both established and emerging talent. Paintings and prints also exhibited. Commissions undertaken.
Submission Policy Exhibition by invitation only.
Price range £5–£500

London Road Gallery
100 London Road, Sheffield
S2 4LR
T 0114 201 0630
E info@londonroadgallery.co.uk
W www.londonroadgallery.co.uk
Founded in 2004 as an outlet for the work of the Hallamshire Crafts Co-operative and of other artists/makers in the Sheffield area. Stocks a wide variety of quality original art and craft items and holds regular one-day workshops.
Submission Policy Selection meetings are held regularly. Work must be made locally and is assessed on quality, originality and ability to fit within the gallery environment.
Price range £2–£600
No of exhibitions annually 12

Massarella Fine Art and Darren Baker Gallery

14 Victoria Road, Saltaire, Shipley
BD18 3LQ
T 01274 580129
E admin@dbfinearts.co.uk
Founded in 1998 to promote and raise awareness
of the local art scene as well as to represent
national artists. Artists include Darren Baker, Joe
Scarborough, Stuart Hirst, Jeremy Taylor, Chris
Wade and Steve Capper.
Submission Policy Artists should submit CV and
five examples of work (photos or CD). All media
considered.
Price range £100–£6,000
No of exhibitions annually 4

McTague of Harrogate

17–19 Cheltenham Mount, Harrogate, HG1 1DW
T 01423 567086
E paul@mctague.co.uk
W www.mctague.co.uk
A traditional art gallery established in 1974,
dealing in old watercolours, antique prints, maps
and oil paintings. Specialities include Yorkshire
and northern artists, and sporting and rural
subjects.
Price range £50–£1,500
No of exhibitions annually 1

Phoenix Fine Arts Ltd

11 Finkle Street, Richmond, DL10 4QA
T 01748 822400
Founded in 2002, exhibiting mostly local original
art. Has shown over 250 different artists including
Piers Browne, Chris Mounay, Peter Bailey, John
Degnan and Barbara Lamb. Commissions
undertaken and an art purchase plan offered.
Submission Policy New artists welcome. Work
shown on a commission basis for five weeks.
Price range £25–£3,000
No of exhibitions annually 12

Pybus Fine Arts

127 Church Street, Whitby, YO22 4DE
T 01947 820028
E enquiries@mpybusfinearts.co.uk
W www.mpybusfinearts.co.uk
Founded 1997, selling modern and antique works
including early twentieth-century works by the
Staithes group of artists. Contemporary artists
include David Curtis, Trevor Chamberlain,
David Allen, Peter Hicks, Howard Bedford and
Christine Pybus.
Submission Policy Solo shows of loosely realist

works, mainly by artists with an established
track record.
Price range £200–£6,000
No of exhibitions annually 4

Rachel Gretton Glass

Workshop 1, Dalby Courtyard, Pickering, YO18 7LT
T 01751 460174
E info@rachelgrettonglass.com
W www.rachelgrettonglass.com
Rachel Gretton Glass was established in 2004 by
artist Rachel Gretton. The working studio based in
the centre of North Yorkshires National Park,
Dalby Forest was opened in 2006 with support
from the Arts Council. A showcase gallery displays
sculptural glass alongside a selection of work from
both established and emerging local artists. Artists
include Claudia Phipps, Sarah Cilia, Rebbecca
Stoner, Alice Highet and Rachel Gretton.
Submission Policy Artists are approached by the
gallery.
Price range £20–£1,500
No of exhibitions annually 2

Reubens Gallery

83 Great George Street, Leeds, LS1 3BR
T 0113 2457771
E enquiries@reubensgallery.co.uk
W www.reubensgallery.co.uk
Representing artists who 'push the boundaries
within traditional genres'. Regularly appears at art
fairs and home viewings can be arranged.

Sculpture Lounge

11 Upperbridge Street, Huddersfield Road,
Holmfirth, HD9 2JR
T 01484 687425
F 01484 687425
E sculpture.lounge@virgin.net
W www.sculpturelounge.com
Founded in 2002, specializing in ceramics,
ceramic scupture, sculpture, paintings and
jewellery. Prominent artists represented include
Brendon Hesmondhalgh, Elizabeth Price, Mari-
Ruth-Oda, Annie Peaker, Christine Cummings
and Melanie Adkins.
Submission Policy Artist applications by post,
including photographs of works, artist statement
and CV.
Price range £20–£5,000
No of exhibitions annually 8

Smart Gallery

Redbrick Mill, 218 Bradford Road, Batley, WF17 6JF

T 01924 455445
F 01924 455425
E info@smartgallery.co.uk
W www.smartgallery.co.uk
Founded in 2002 at Redbrick Mill, followed by a second at Christopher Pratts in Leeds. Sells Washington Green limited-edition and original prints and has a craft and design centre based in Batley. Encourages local artists to exhibit.
Submission Policy Encourages work from a wide range of artists in a variety of media.
Price range £100–£5,000
No of exhibitions annually 8

Talents Fine Arts
7 Market Place, Malton, YO17 7LP
T 01653 600020
F 01653 600020
E talentsfinearts@hotmail.com
Established for almost twenty years. Contemporary artists include David Howel, John Gibson, Neil Spelman, Barry Peckham, Susan Bower and Steven Lingham. Shows glass and ceramics. Framing and restoration services offered.
Submission Policy Submissions by prior notice only.
Price range £100–£3,000
No of exhibitions annually 2

Taylor-Pick Fine Art
7 North Bar Within, Beverley, HU17 8AP
T 01482 881169
E andrew@taylor-pick.com
W www.taylor-pick.com
Founded in 1996 with the aim of presenting quality contemporary fine art by either established or up-and-coming young artists. The gallery has an established and growing regular client base. Represents artists from the UK, Spain, Ireland and the Czech Republic, including George Hainsworth, Beltran Bofill, Gordon King, Fraser King and Jan Vich.
Submission Policy Submissions should be of a professional manner by artists of a high standard. All media considered. Photographs or CD preferred.
Price range £400–£25,000
No of exhibitions annually 8

Walker Galleries Ltd
13 Montpellier Parade, Harrogate, H91 2TJ
T 01423 526366
E walkercontemp@aol.com
W www.walkerfineart.co.uk

Contact Angela Noble
Founded in 1971, presenting a wide array of styles from photographic to semi-abstract. Gallery artists include Jeremy Barlow Roi, John Mackie, John Lowrie Morrison, Peter Graham, Caroline Bailey and Mike Bernard. Branches 104 High Street Honiton, Devon.
Submission Policy Only handles living artists. Submissions welcome from established artists but will consider other artists if photographs supplied.
Price range £250–£10,000 for paintings; £200–£4,500 for bronzes; £40–£400 for ceramics.
No of exhibitions annually 10

Ireland

Access to Arts
Third Floor, The Design Tower, Trinity Centre, Grand Canal Quay, Dublin 2
T 01 6770107
E info@accesstoarts.com
W www.accesstoarts.com
Contact Patricia Clyne-Kelly
Promotes Irish contemporary applied art and fine art through exhibitions and commissions. The gallery is housed in an historic stone-built tower with brick-vaulted ceilings and white and natural stone walls, on the fringe of the Docklands area in Dublin. Exhibitions are also arranged in corporate settings.
Submission Policy Applications from all artists living in Ireland are welcomed.

Apollo Gallery
51c Dawson Street, Dublin 2
T 01 6712609
E art@apollogallery.ie
W www.apollogallery.ie
Specializes in the work of Irish artists, aiming to bring Irish paintings, sculpture and prints to an international audience.
Submission Policy The Gallery represents painters who are resident in Ireland whose work is representative of Ireland exclusively.
Price range €190–€250,000
No of exhibitions annually 1–2

Arklow Fine Art Gallery
7 Lower Main Street, Arklow, County Wicklow
E info@arklowfineartgallery.com
Opened in 2004 to showcase art by Irish artists, and especially those from County Wicklow. Hosts several exhibitions a year, showing local and

international artists, including Robert Harcus, Tony Kew and Carol-Ann Waldron.

Artselect Ireland
13 Ros Mor View, Scholarstown Road, Dublin 16
T 01 4952474
E greved@eircom.net
W www.greved.com
Contact Greville Edwards
Founded in 2000, initially as a gallery space and art provider with graphic design and photography services available.
Submission Policy Established and emerging artists are welcome to submit examples of work via the website or by email. Exhibitions will be held each year in the Dublin area depending on sponsorship and popularity. Undertakes private and corporate commissions.
Price range €300–€5,000
No of exhibitions annually 2

Bad Art Gallery
Francis Street, Dublin 8
T 01 4537588
E info@thebadartgallerydublin.com
W www.thebadartgallerydublin.com
Opened in 2005 and can exhibit over 200 pictures at a time. Work changed regularly and also available via website. Artists include Deborah Donnelly, Val Byrne B.Arch, FRIAI, Anna-Marie Dowical, Daragh Muldowney, Olgu Fitzpatrick, Tony O'Dwyer, Gareth Daly, Jim Kilgarriff and Robert Andrew Smyth.

Barn Gallery
Garranes South, Drimoleague, County Cork
T 028 31677
F 028 31677
E sheilahooks@eircom.net
W www.barngalleryireland.com
Opened in 1996. Open studio of Sheila Hooks BA ATD, specializing in Irish landscapes and life drawings.
Price range €100–€1,000
No of exhibitions annually Continuously changing exhibition.

Bin Ban Gallery & Antiques
Beech Lodge, Ballyenerghty, The Kerries
Tralee, County Kerry
T 066 7122520
E info@binbanart.com
W www.binbanart.com
Hosts major exhibitions of national and

international contemporary works and limited edition prints.

Black Cat Gallery
17 Market Street, Galway, County Galway
T 091 566422
E jvinnell@eircom.net
W www.janetvinnell.com or www.tedturton.com
Founded 1997, selling original artwork, paintings in pastel and watercolour and photo-generated artwork by artists-in-residence Janet Vinnell and Ted Turton. Also shows glass and ceramics by other artists.
Submission Policy Submissions not encouraged.
Price range €100–€2,000
No of exhibitions annually Continually rotating work on view and for sale.
Cost to hire or rent By arrangement in January or February. Negotiable.

Blue Leaf Gallery
10 marino mart, Fairview, Dublin 3
T 01 8333456
E info@blueleafgallery.com
W www.blueleafgallery.com
Contact Jane Ross
Opened on current premises in 2001, presenting work by Irish and international artists.
Submission Policy Requires a disc of 3–10 images of recent works, a biography and an artist statement.
Price range €500–€10,000
No of exhibitions annually 6

Bold Art Gallery
Merchants Road, Galway
T 091 539900
E info@boldartgallery.com
W www.boldartgallery.com
Represents 85 artists producing work in range of styles. Specializes in original fine art paintings by Irish and international artists and also displays a small selection of sculpture. Does not deal in reproductions of any kind.
Submission Policy Submit a portfolio of recent works as slides, printed photographs or digital images on CD. All illustrations should have details such as size, medium and title. Submissions should be clearly marked with contact details and include an sae. Details of previous exhibitions, gallery representation (if represented) and artist's biography should be attached.
Price range €200–€50,000
No of exhibitions annually 12

Bridge Gallery
6 Upper Ormond Quay, Dublin 7,
T 01 872 9702
F 01 872 9699
E mail@thebridgegallery.com
W www.thebridgegallery.com
Contact Deirdre Carroll
Gallery within restored eighteenth-century
Georgian building. Features work of established
and rising artists, contemporary arts and crafts,
watercolours, oils, prints, etchings, ceramics,
wood, glass and jewellery. Artists include
Frank Boag, Sheelagh Flannery, Brigit
Beemster, Sara Flynn, Leonard Sexton and
Shane Johnson.
Submission Policy Contemporary work.
New artists welcome. A little photography
and some photo intaglio prints and photo
craft.
Price range Ceramics etc. €20–€600 approx.
Paintings etc. €100–€3,000 approx.
No of exhibitions annually 12

Canvas
5 Upper Ormond Quay, Dublin 7
T 087 6339208
E info@canvas.ie
W www.canvas.ie
Established 2003, representing and promoting
contemporary, mainly emrging, artists. All gallery
artists are Irish or currently based in Ireland and
include Miriam McConnon, Beatrice O'Connell,
Cris Neumann, Cormac Healy, Neal Greig and
Naomi Sex. Artists and their work are made
accessible to a wider audience through online and
digital presentations. Commercial and private
buyers are afforded a more personal service with
works and showcases presented to them in their
own settings.
Submission Policy Submissions and enquiries are
welcome from working artists by email or phone.
Price range €100–€7,000

Catherine Hammond Gallery
Glengarriff Center, West Cork
E info@hammondgallery.com
W www.hammondgallery.com
Contemporary art gallery founded in 2004 by
Catherine Hammond, who has over 20 years
experience working with leading American
cultural organizations, including the Institute of
Contemporary Art (Boston), the MacArthur
Foundation (Chicago), and the Smithsonian
Institution (Washington, D.C.).

Cavanacor Gallery
Ballindrait, Lifford, County Donegal
T 074 9141143
E art@cavanacorgallery.ie
W www.cavanacorgallery.ie
Contact Marianne O'Kane (Curator)
Initiated in 1999, a professional private gallery
exhibiting emerging and established national
and international artists. Exhibitors to date
include Deborah Brown, Felim Egan, Sean
Fingleton, Rita Duffy, Neil Shawcross and Hughie
O'Donoghue. The gallery operates primarily
through solo and group exhibitions on relevant
themes. Consultancy is offered on private and
corporate collections.
Submission Policy Submissions are welcomed
from artists and should consist of biographical
information accompanied by a maximum of ten
images on slide or CD format.
Price range €250–€3,000
No of exhibitions annually 5

Cherrylane Fine Arts
Cherrylane, Wicklow
T 01 2875565
E michael@cherrylanefinearts.com
W www.cherrylanefinearts.com
Family-run art gallery housed in seventeenth-
century rustic buildings. Exhibits contemporary
paintings, prints and photography as well as
indoor and outdoor sculpture.

Claremorris Art Gallery
Mount Street, Claremorris, County Mayo
T 094 9371348
F 094 9372961
E drpnoone@eircom.net
Contact Brian Bourke, Jay Murphy or
Mary Kelly
Gallery established in 1988 to promote
professional Irish artists. Artists represented
include Brian Bourke, Tony O'Malley, John
Shinnors, Michael Farrell, Basil Blackshaw and
Camille Souter. Exhibitions have been toured
internatinally and an artist's studio and residence
is under construction.
Submission Policy Artists must be living and
professional. Painting, prints, mixed media,
photography, film and sculpture all accepted.
Installations and performance art generally not
accepted.
Price range €250–€50,000
No of exhibitions annually 6
Cost to hire or rent €100–€300 per week

Combridge Fine Arts Ltd
17 South William Street, Dublin 2
T 01 6774652
E artsales@cfa.ie
W www.cfa.ie
Contact Brian Sibley
Experience of selling and promoting the work of
Irish artists for over ninety years. Specialists in
Irish landscape. Current artists can be viewed on
website.

Courthouse Gallery, Ballinglen Arts Foundation
Main Street, Ballycastle, County Mayo
T 096 43184
F 096 43184
E baf@iol.ie
W www.ballinglenartsfoundation.org
Contact Una Forde
Founded in 1991 to bring serious artists from all
over the world to live and work in North Mayo to
benefit themselves and the community. The
Foundation's programmes were designed to
support serious artists making important work in
what they consider to be ideal, inspiring conditions
Submission Policy Ballinglen's programmes are by
application (form downloadable from website).
Each successful artist receives a sky-lit studio and a
full house (where friends and family can stay or
visit). In return each artist leaves a piece of work to
remain in the Archive, which now boast 349
pieces.

Courtyard Arts Limited
The Courtyard Craft & Exhibition Centre
8 Main Street, Midleton, County Cork
T 021 4634644
F 021 4630919
E thecourtyardgallery@eircom.net
W www.thecourtyardmidleton.com
Contact Anne Ahern or Sue van Coppenhagen
Founded in 2000. Two galleries for rent to
individual artists/crafters or groups, for two-week
slots. Also an Art Source Network, representing
twenty-four member artists, whose work is
promoted on an ongoing basis to buyers,
particularly those looking for commissioned work.
A craft shop displays Irish-made crafts.
Submission Policy Artists' work is vetted by
committee before being accepted for exhibition or
membership of Art Source Network.
Price range €100–€3,000
No of exhibitions annually 30
Cost to hire or rent Main gallery €520 for 2 weeks;
Studio One €450 for two weeks.

Cristeph Gallery
Port Road, Letterkenny, Donegal
T 074 26411
Established in 1982, showing paintings by local
and international names. Also offers framing and
consultancy services.

Cross Gallery
59 Francis Street, Dublin 8
T 01 4738978
F 01 454 5391
E info@crossgallery.ie
W www.crossgallery.ie
Work shown over four spaces. Artists include
David Begley, Michael Coleman, Jack Donovan,
Simon English, Bridget Flannery, Gillian Lawler,
Horace Lysaght, Ann Quinn, Ian Stuart and Clea
van der Grijn.

Cunnamore Galleries
Cunnamore Point, Skibbereen, West Cork
T 028 38483
E art@cunnamore.com
W www.cunnamore.com
Shows contemporary works by artists such as
Patrick Barker, Monica Boyle, Anthony Gross,
Majella O'Neill Collins and Ian Humphreys.

CY Gallery
Cotters Yard, Main Street, Schull, Cork
T 028 28165
F 028 28413
E freewheelin@eircom.net
Gallery of drawings, paintings and sculpture.

Cynthia O'Connor Gallery
Swords, Dublin
T 01 8405045
F 01 8401220
E ballinacorestate@eircom.net
W www.cinoa.org/gallery.cfmMID=4044
Specializing in Irish paintings and watercolours,
from the eighteenth century to the present day.

D FOUR Gallery @ The Berkeley Court
Lansdowne Road, Dublin 4
T 01 6653200
F 01 6617238
W www.jurys-dublin-
hotels.com/berkeleycourt_dublin
Housed in the Berkeley Court Hotel, dealing in
Irish fine art and antiques. Stocks work by artists
including Dorothy Smith, Celine Eagle and Doris
Houston.

Daffodil Gallery
Skerries, County Dublin
T 01 8492142
F 01 8492535
E daffodil@iol.ie
W www.daffodilgallery.com
A garden gallery, representing artists living and
working in Ireland. Shows paintings, drawings,
sculpture and prints from emerging and
established names.

Dalkey Arts
19 Railway Road, Dalkey, Dublin
T 01 2849663
E info@dalkeyarts.com
W www.dalkeyarts.com
Offers range of contemporary paintings, drawings,
prints and glass from Irish and international
artists. Also offers a full framing service.
Price range €100 to €10,000
No of exhibitions annually 4

Dyehouse Gallery
Mary Street, Waterford
T 051 844770
F 051 850399
E info@dyehouse-gallery.com
W www.dyehouse-gallery.com
Contact Liz McCay
Established in 1995 with the aim of bringing the
best of contemporary Irish and international art to
the south-east of Ireland. Moved to current
premises in 2005 and maintains a lively exhibition
programme with works by Tony O'Malley, John
Shinnors, Brian Bourke, Jane O'Malley, Rosemary
Higbee and Paddy Lennon.
No of exhibitions annually 6–7

Fado
Main Street, Dingle, County Kerry
T 066 9151452
F 066 9152530
E evahennessy@eircom.net
Contact Pat Hennessy and Eva Hennessy.
Founded in 1976, the oldest gallery, framers and
antiques shop in Dingle.

Fenton Gallery
5 Wandesford Quay, Cork
T 021 4315294
F 021 4917100
E nualafenton@eircom.net
W www.artireland.net
Contact Nuala Fenton, Ita Freeney and Helena Tobin.

Established in 2000 by Nuala Fenton, occupying
over 2,000 sq. ft. five minutes from the city centre.
Exhibition programme changes every three weeks
and includes artists such as Basil Blackshaw,
William Crozier, Hughie O'Donoghue, Tony
O'Malley, Charles Tyrrell and Patrick Scott.
Emerging, younger artists are also profiled.
Submission Policy Applications taken by post.
Include images in CD or slide format.
No of exhibitions annually 10

Form Gallery
Unit 2, Paul Street Shopping Centre
Cork
T 021 4271333
F 021 4271414
E form@affordableart-ireland.com
W www.affordableart-ireland.com
Exhibits broad range of contemporary art.

Framework Gallery
55 Upper Georges Street, Dun Laoghaire,
County Dublin
T 01 280 5756
E info@theframeworkgallery.com
W www.theframeworkgallery.com
Deals in contemporary and traditional paintings,
drawings, etchings and prints. Also offers framing
and giclée print services.

Frank Lewis Gallery
6 Bridewell Lane, Killarney, County Kerry
T 064 31108
F 064 31570
E info@franklewisgallery.com
W www.franklewisgallery.com
Presents different monthly individual and group
exhibitions of paintings and sculpture, showing
emerging and established names.

The Gallery
Dunfanaghy, County Donegal
T 074 9136224
Founded in 1968, specializing in fine watercolours
and oil paintings. Works on display by artists
including Frank Egginton, James McConnell,
Kenneth Webb, Thomas Ryan, Pat Cowley and
Robert Egginton.
Submission Policy Pleased to discuss and view
any professional work. Quality and suitability the
main criteria.
Price range €250–€12,000
No of exhibitions annually Continuous, changing,
mixed exhibitions.

Gallery 44

44 MacCurtain Street, Cork
T 021 450 1319
Set on three floors, with around six solo shows a
year. Framing services also offered.

Gallery 75

75 O'Connell Street, Limerick
T 061 315650
Deals in paintings, drawings and sculpture. Artists
include Patrick Cahill, Gerald Davis, Michael
Gemmel, Paul Quane, Thomas Ryan R.H.A and
Viale.

Gorry Gallery Ltd

20 Molesworth Street, Dublin 2
T 01 6795319
F 01 6795319
W www.gorrygallery.ie
Established 1885. Picture restorers and fine art
dealers. Specialists in eighteenth-, nineteenth- and
twentieth-century Irish art.
No of exhibitions annually 3

Graphic Studio Gallery

Through the Arch, Cope Street, Temple Bar
Dublin 2
T 01 6798021
F 01 6794575
E gsg@iol.ie
W www.graphicstudiodublin.com
Opened in Temple Bar in 1988, exhibiting and
selling fine art prints by emerging and established
names from both Ireland and abroad.
Price range From €60

Green Door Studio

Port-Na-Blagh, Dunfanaghy, County Donegal
T 07491 36864
E kandkraff@hotmail.com
Founded 2001. Presents and exhibits original
paintings by a family of three (mother, father
and daughter), who work from a purpose-built
studio. Specializing in oils, watercolours,
acrylics, handmade prints, abstract and figurative
works.
Price range £150 (€225)–£2,000 (€3,000)
No of exhibitions annually Two, one at Easter and
one at beginning of August, both ongoing until
Christmas. Studio closed Christmas until St.
Patrick's Day.

Green Gallery Dublin

Top Floor, St. Stephen's Green Centre, Dublin 2

T 01 4783122
E info@greengallerydublin.com
W www.greengallerydublin.com
Retails broad range of contemporary works from
national and international artists. Comprehensive
framing service also available.

Green On Red Gallery

26–28 Lombard Street East, Dublin 2
T 01 6713414
F 01 6727117
E info@greenonredgallery.com
W www.greenonredgallery.com
Contact Molly Sullivan
Established in 1997, occupying a nineteenth-
century converted warehouse space. Initially
developed a reputation for exhibiting more
experimental contemporary Irish and
international art, a programming policy it has
adhered to ever since. Mixture of solo exhibitions,
group exhibitions and art fairs. Programme
includes guest-curated and contemporary
international exhibitions, concerts, talks and
one-off events.
Submission Policy Cannot accept artist
submissions at this time.
Price range €500–€150,000
No of exhibitions annually 12

Greenacres

7 Selskar, Wexford
T 053 22975
F 053 24905
E info@greenacres.ie
W www.greenacres.ie
Established in 2001, selling a wide range of
paintings from artists including Eamon Colman,
Paul Kelly, Paddy Lennon, Arthur Maderson, Mary
M. O'Connor, Mark O'Neill and Molly Poencet.

Greenlane Gallery

Holy Ground, Dingle, County Kerry
T 066 9152018/9152047
E info@greenlanegallery.com
W www.greenlanegallery.com
Contact Ms Julie O'Neill/ Áine McEvoy
Established in 1992, taking its name from the
street where it was originally located–Greenlane in
Dingle town. Policy is to show contemporary Irish
paintings and sculpture by leading Irish artists.
Paintings by Liam O'Neill, Tomás Ó Ciobháin,
Patsy Farr and Michael Flaherty with sculpture by
Ana Duncan and Hans Blank.
Submission Policy Welcomes submissions from

arists via email.
Price range €30–€25,000
No of exhibitions annually 9

Hallward Gallery
65 Merrion Square, Dublin 2
T 01 6621482/3
F 01 6621700
E info@hallwardgallery.com
Opened in 1991 to show Irish contemporary fine
art and encourage emerging talents.

Hillsboro Fine Art
49 Parnell Square West, Dublin 1
E info@hillsborofineart.com
W www.hillsborofineart.com
Founded in 1995, the gallery has recently moved to
Parnell Square in the cultural and social heart of
Georgian Dublin. Deals in works by leading
twentieth- and twenty-first century artists from
Ireland, UK, Europe and the USA. Artists
represented include Alex Katz, John Hoyland,
Gillian Ayres, Michael Warren, Tjibbe
Hooghiemstra and John Noel Smith. Large
inventory of drawings, paintings and sculpture.
Price range €500–€250,000
No of exhibitions annually 10

Howth Harbour Gallery
6 Abbey Street, Howth Village, Howth, County
Dublin
T 01 8393366
E gjb97@dial.pipex.com
W www.gjb97.dial.pipex.com
Deals in contemporary and traditional paintings
and drawings, with an emphasis on Irish scenes.

James Joyce House of the Dead
15 Usher's Island, Dublin 8
T 01 6728008
F 085 7262855
E info@jamesjoycehouse.com
W www.jamesjoycehouse.com
Contact Connor Regan
Founded 2000, exhibiting contemporary Irish and
European art of all genres and media.
Submission Policy Email medium resolution
jpegs, maximum 15. Include brief CV, media and
prices.
No of exhibitions annually 12
Cost to hire or rent Price on application.

Joan Clancy Gallery (Danlann Joan Clancy)
Mullinahorna, Ring, County Waterford

T 058 46205
E info@joanclancygallery.com
W www.joanclancygallery.com
A small private purpose-built space established in
1999, specializing in new and emerging as well as
established artists. Situated in the scenic Irish-
speaking area of Ring, the gallery overlooks
Dungarvan Bay and the Comeragh and
Knockmealdown Mountains, and is known as
'County Waterford's Unique Gaeltacht Gallery'.
Submission Policy Favours wall-mounted works.
Submissions welcome from artists accompanied
by CV, artist statement, digital
images/slides/photos and sae.
Price range €200–€3,500
No of exhibitions annually 5

Jones Art Gallery
Harbour Mill, Davitt's Quay, Dungarvan, County
Waterford
T 058 45610
E cjones@thejonesartgallery.com
W www.thejonesartgallery.com
Founded in 2004, with the intention of bringing
the work of Irish artists to public attention in
Waterford. Artists include John Nolan, Molly
Poencet and many up-and-coming young artists.
Submission Policy All artists welcome to contact
gallery.
Price range From €100
No of exhibitions annually 12–14

Jorgensen Fine Art
29 Molesworth Street, Dublin 2
T 01 6619758 / 9
F 01 6619760
E info@jorgensenfineart.com
W www.jorgensenfineart.com
Contact Sile Connaughton Deeny or Kevin Gaines
Established in 1991, specializing in late-
nineteenth- and early-twentieth-century Irish,
British and European paintings, drawings,
watercolours and sculptures (of which the gallery
has three major exhibitions annually). Featured
artists include Roderic O'Conor, Paul Henry, Mary
Swanzy, George Campbell, Rose Barton, Evie Hone
and Mainie Jellett. Also hosts approx. six solo
exhibitions of contemporary Irish and
international artists such as Barbara Rae, Olivia
Musgrave, Alexey Krasnovsky, Joe Dunne, John
Long, Robert Wraith and Anna Kostenko.
Submission Policy Areas excluded: paintings and
sculpture pre-1850. Submissions from living
artists welcome.

Price range €300–€100,000
No of exhibitions annually 10

Keane on Ceramics
Francis Keane, Pier Road, Kinsale, County Cork
T 021 4774553
E keaneceramics@oceanfree.net
One of Ireland's leading ceramics galleries for
fifteen years, specializing in one-off ceramics.
Submission Policy Studio ceramics only.
Price range €20–€20,000
No of exhibitions annually 2

Kenmare Art Gallery
Bridge Street, Kenmare, County Kerry
T 064 42999
E martinaviscardi@eircom.net
W www.kenmareartgallery.com
Exhibits works by artists including Robin
Forrester, Tim Goulding, John Philip Murray,
Nealie Sullivan, Claudio Viscardi and Sarah
Walker. Many works influenced by the local Beara
area.

The Kenny Gallery
High Street/Middle Street, Galway
T 091 534760
F 091 568544
E art@kennys.ie
W www.kennys.ie
Contact Tom Kenny
Has been selling original works of art for over half
a century. Has hosted major exhibitions by George
Campbell, Sean Keating, Andy Warhol, Kenneth
Webb, Jack B. Yeats and Paul Henry. The
conversion of the bookshop to the largest
commercial art gallery in Ireland took place early
in 2006 and extends from street to street over
three floors. Exhibits national and international art
across variety of media. Ongoing collections of
artworks from almost two hundred artists.
Submission Policy Send a number of images of
work and a profile/CV of the artist.
Price range €100 to €100,000
No of exhibitions annually 15 solo exhibitions and 5
group exhibitions.

Kerlin Gallery
Anne's Lane, South Anne Street, Dublin 2
T 01 6709093
F 01 6709096
E gallery@kerlin.ie
W www.kerlingallery.com
Established in 1988, one of Ireland's most

important galleries with a programme of national
and international contemporary art. Offers 3,600
sq. ft of exhibition space on two floors.

Kevin Kavanagh Gallery
66 Great Strand Street, Dublin 1
T 01 874 0064.
E info@kevinkavanaghgallery.ie
W www.kevinkavanaghgallery.ie
Major contemporary art gallery, hosting mostly
solo, but some group, shows.

Kilcock Art Gallery
School Street, Kilcock, Kildare
T 01 6287619
F 01 6284293
E info@kilcockartgallery.ie
W www.kilcockartg
Founded in 1978, dealing in fine paintings,
sculpture and prints by major Irish artists. Works
with both individual and corporate clients.

Killarney Art Gallery
13 Main Street, Killarney
T 064 34628
E art@irishartcollector.com
W www.irishartcollector.com
Contact Declan and Brenda Mulvany
Founded 15 years ago to present leading Irish
artists, including Mark O'Neill, Ted Jones, James
English, James Brohan, Liam O'Neill and Paul
Kelly. Has worldwide exclusivity on Ted Jones's
work, including his signed limited edition prints.
Submission Policy Artists are encouraged to send
digital pictures of their work via email.
Price range €400–€20,000
No of exhibitions annually Two major exhibitions
each year, one in September and one in December.
Also has a featured artist mini-exhibition every
month.

Kinsale Art Gallery
Pier Head, Kinsale, Cork
T 021 477 3622
E b.andrews@kinsale-art-gallery.ie
W www.kinsale-art-gallery.ie/
Specializes in paintings (contemporary and
traditional) and drawings.

La Gallerie
32 Grand Parade, Cork
T 021 427 7376
Deals in paintings, drawings and prints. Artists
include James Flack, Maurice Henderson, Pat

Maher, Liz Morris and Victor Richardson. Framing service also offered.

Lavit Gallery

5 Father Mathew Street, Cork
T 021 4277749
F 021 4279123
E thelavitgallery@eircom.net
Shows paintings, prints and photography as well as sculpture and ceramics from established Irish artists.

Legge Gallery

9 Chelmsford la Ranelagh, Dublin 6
T 01 4962399
Specializes in contemporary paintings and offers comprehensive framing service.

Leinster Gallery

27 South Frederick Street, Dublin 2
T 01 6790834
E art@leinstergallery.com
W www.leinstergallery.com
Located in a restored Georgian town house, specializing in twentieth-century and contemporary Irish art. Shows several solo and seasonal mixed exhibitions a year. A constantly changing exhibition of pieces by gallery artists is also on display.
No of exhibitions annually 6

Lemon Street Gallery

24–26 City Quay, Dublin 2
T 01 6710244
F 01 6710240
E lea@lemonstreet.com
W www.lemonstreet.com
Shows contemporary graphic art by national and international artists.

Limerick Printmakers Studio and Gallery

4 Robert Street, Limerick
T 061 311806
E limprintmakers@eircom.net
W www.limerickprintmakers.com
Contact Melissa O'Brien
Founded in 1999, dedicated to supporting artists of all art forms and at all stages in their career. Work shown includes a wide variety of media such as printmaking, painting, photography, film, installation and performance art. Exhibiting artists include Martin Finnin, Jack Donovan, Brian Mac Mahon, Charlie Harper, Des Mac Mahon, Suzannah O'Reilly, Clare Gilmour, Gillian Kenny and Martin Shannon. 24-hour access is available and there are facilities for etching, lithography and silkscreen, woodcut, monoprint, photography and digital print. Annual group exhibitions are held for studio members as well as an open submission print show.
Submission Policy Open to artists in any media. Send a cover letter, CV, artist's statement and visuals of the work.
Price range €50–€10,000
No of exhibitions annually 10
Cost to hire or rent Artists are not charged for the use of the space but the cost of the exhibition opening is the responsibility of the artist/s. Limerick Printmakers provides some financial support and commission is kept to a low of 30%.

Magil Fine Art

13A Bachelors Walk, Dublin 1
T 01 8720618
F 01 8720618
E magil_art@hotmail.com
W www.magilfineart.com
Contact Bernadette Murphy
Founded in 1999, specializing in contemporary and twentieth-century Irish art. Recently branched into contemporary Russian art, travelling to St Petersburg and Moscow to source same. Framing and restoration work offered by qualified in-house fine art restorer. Valuations of paintings also offered.
Submission Policy Submissions welcome from artists.
Price range €500–€2,500
No of exhibitions annually 6

Mill Cove Gallery

Castletownbere, County Cork
T 027 70393
E millcove@iol.ie
W www.millcovegallery.com
Opened in 2000, showing contemporary fine art by established and emerging artists.

Molesworth Gallery

16 Molesworth Street, Dublin 2
T 01 679 1548
F 01 679 6667
E molesworth.gallery@indigo.ie
W www.molesworthgallery.com
Founded in 1999 to exhibit contemporary painting and sculpture by emerging and established artists. The gallery represents about twenty artists, hosting ten or so mainly solo exhbitions annually. A broad

sprectrum of artists are represented including young representational painters (Blaise Smith, Maeve McCarthy ARHA, John Hearne and Sheila Pomeroy), St Ives based abstract landscape painter Padraig MacMiadhachain, photorealist Patrick Redmond and sculptor Anna Linnane.
Submission Policy Do not send huge email attachments or unsolicited CDs. Will not necessarily reply to every submission.
Price range €500–€20,000
No of exhibitions annually 10

Mothers Tankstation
41–43 Watling Street, Ushers Island, Dublin 8
T 01 6717654
E gallery@motherstankstation.com
W www.motherstankstation.com
Contact Finola Jones
Takes an innovative approach to contemporary visual art, working with Irish and international artists at different career stages who demonstrate individuality and a distinct vision. Artists include Petri Ala-Maunus, Margrét H Blöndel, Ian Burns, Nina Canell, Atsushi Kaga, Ciaran Murphy, Alan Phelan, Garrett Phelan and David Sherry.
No of exhibitions annually 6

Mulvany Bros.
Kingswood Art Gallery, Kingswood Cross
Old Naas Road, Dublin 22
T 01 4594242
E gallery@mulvanybros.ie
W www.mulvanybros.ie
Established in 1885, specializing in original paintings, prints and engravings. Sells wide rang of art materials and offers framing and restoration services.

Narrow Space
14 Mitchel Street, Clonmel, County Tipperary
T 052 27838
E thenarrowspace@eircom.net
W wwww.thenarrowspace.com
Contact Aisling Kilroy
Opened in late 2003, committed to showcasing the work of both established and up-and-coming Irish and international artists. Artists shown include John Behan RHA, Mercè Cañadell, Eoin de Leastar, Lucy Doyle, Ana Duncan, Ella Kavanagh, James MacCarthy, Patrick Morrison, Eilis O'Toole and Robert Ryan. In addition to painting and sculpture, Aisling Kilroy has a keen interest in ceramics and regularly shows the work of both established and younger ceramicists including

Bernadette Doolan, Sara Flynn, Catherine Hunter, Bridget Lyons, Maura Smyth and Grainne Watts.
Submission Policy Submissions from artists are welcome. Interested artists should send covering letter, CV and CD, a minimum of six months in advance of hoped-for exhibition.
Price range €150–€12,000+
No of exhibitions annually Minimum of eight, including groups shows at summer and Christmas.

Norman Villa Gallery
86 Lower Salthill, Galway
T 091 521131
F 091 521131
E info@normanvillagallery.com
W www.normanvillagallery.com
Opened 2004, specializing in contemporary Irish art. Aims to support and build relationships with artists. Artists represented include Christopher Banahan, Brian Burke, Mary Donnelly, John Ffrench, Philip Lindey and Lisa Sweeney.
Submission Policy Letter of introduction required plus a CV and a CD of works along with any proposals. Artists welcome to visit the gallery.
Price range €300–€30,000
No of exhibitions annually 10
Cost to hire or rent Open to discussion

Oisin Art Gallery
44 Westland Row, Dublin 2
T 01 6611315
F 01 6610464
E info@oisingallery.com
W www.oisingallery.com
Established in 1978, showing Irish and international artists, both established and emerging. Specializes in original fine art paintings and also displays a small selection of sculpture. Exhibitions are held every four to six weeks and two annual group shows are held in July and November. Artists include Ronan Goti, Katy Simpson, Katherine Liddy, Alan Kenny, David Turner, Thomas Halloran and Tina Spratt. Represents over forty artists in all and also offers a consultancy service.
Submission Policy For submissions by post, send a portfolio of recent works (slides/hardcopy printed images/digital images on CD; clearly indicate details such as size, medium and framing) and include details of previous exhibitions, gallery representation (if any) and an approximate price guide if currently exhibiting. Submissions should be clearly marked with contact details and will only

be returned if accompanied with an sae. Mark for the attention of Antoinette L. Sinclair, Gallery Curator. If submitting by email, forward details of website or a selection of images (ensuring that file size per email is no larger than 1MB) to AntoinetteL@oisingallery.com.
Price range €900–€20,000
No of exhibitions annually 8

Oriel Gallery
17 Clare Street, Dublin 2
T 01 6763410
F 01 6763410
E oriel@eircom.net
W www.theoriel.com
Opened in 1968, specializing in Irish works from the eighteenth to the twenty-first centuries. The oldest independent gallery in Ireland.

Origin Gallery
83 Harcourt Street, Dublin 2
T 01 4785159
F 01 4785826
E origingallery@eircom.net
Contact Noelle Campbell-Sharp
Associated with the Cill Rialaig Artists Retreat. Focus on representing young, emerging talent.
Submission Policy 'Cutting Edge' contemporary art from young and mid-career artists – painting in particular.
Price range €600–€6,000
No of exhibitions annually 10 solo and 2 group shows

Original Print Gallery
4 Temple Bar, Dublin 2
T 01 6773657
E info@originalprint.ie
W www.originalprint.ie
In the Temple Bar area of Dublin, a contemporary, custom-built space, exhibiting framed and unframed original prints. The gallery has been in operation for over ten years. Showcases Irish and international printmakers including Mary Fitzgerald, Stephen Lawlor, Margaret McLoughlin, Richard Gorman, Maria Simonds-Gooding, Christian Bozon, Albert Irvin and Anthony Frost.
Submission Policy Artists should send a CD-Rom with images, CV and artist's statement, or email the same. Exclusively represents printmakers, predominently Irish, but also international.
Price range €30–€1,500 unframed.
No of exhibitions annually 6–8, as well as exhibitions of artists' work from the gallery's

portfolio of over 150 artists. Twice a year the Black Church Print Studio holds group exhibitions.

OSB Gallery Ltd
Church Hill, Enniskerry, County Wicklow
T 01 2862065
F 01 2862075
E info@osbgallery.com
W www.osbgallery.com
Exhibits contemporary Irish art, including sculpture and ceramics, from new and established artists.

Pallas Studios
17 Foley Street, Dublin 1
T 01 8561404
E info@pallasstudios.org
W www.pallasstudios.org
Founded in 1996 to facilitate artist-initiated projects/exhibitions in urban settings. Opened a dedicated gallery space in 2007 and has studio facilities for thirty artists in four buildings.
Submission Policy Only send proposals via email.
No of exhibitions annually 8

Paul Kane Gallery
6 Merrion Square, Dublin 2
W www.thepaulkanegallery.com
Opened in 1997, making its name by exhibiting dynamic, emerging, contemporary artists. Artists, many of whom are well established, include Marc Reilly, Megan Eustace, Colin Crotty and Leonard Sheil.

People's Art Hall
Unit 28b, Top Floor, Powerscourt Tower, Dublin 2
T 01 6725432
General gallery selling paintings and drawings.

People's Gallery
2 Shear Street, Cork
T 021 4223577
E thepeoplesgallery@eircom.net
W www.thepeoplesgallery.tripod.com
Deals in traditional and contemporary paintings, drawings, prints and sculpture from national and international artists.

Rowan Tree
Glanmore Lake, Lauragh, Killarney, County Kerry
T 064 83982
E healysmits@hotmail.com
W www.deborahhealy.com
Originally founded in 1996 at The Old Forge,

Ardea, Tuosist by Joop Smits and Deborah Healy, Rowan Tree is a collective of independent artists living and working in south-west Ireland. Artists exhibited include Matt Lamb, John Kingerlee, Lili le Cain, Thomas Kay, Dermot McCarthy, Con Kelleher, Christopher O'Connor, Joan Hodes, Joop Smits and Deborah Healy. Visitors welcome, by appointment.
Submission Policy Artists by invitation or personal contact.
Price range €100–€50,000
No of exhibitions annually 4 (and by appointment year round)

Rubicon Gallery
10 St. Stephens Green, Dublin 2
T 01 6708055
E info@rubicongallery.ie
W www.rubicongallery.ie
Contact Iseult Dunne (Director) and Cate Kelliher (Director)
Opened in 1995 with the core objective of enabling contemporary Irish and international artists to realize projects in all media through/in the gallery venue or elsewhere. Annually presents ten exhibitions in Dublin, mostly solo projects with some curated events. Produces 4–6 publications and participates in international art fairs, commissioning new works and introducing Irish artists in Europe and the rest of the world.
No of exhibitions annually 10 (mostly solo-projects and some curated events).

Sandford Gallery
Ranelagh, Dublin 6
T 01 4910320
F 087 2361132
E art@sandfordgallery.net
W www.sandfsordgallery.net
Shows contemporary Irish art.

Sarah Walker
The Pier, Castletownbere, County Cork
T 027 70387
F 027 70378
E sarahwalker@eircom.net
W www.sarahwalker.ie
Founded 2000, mostly showing the owner's paintings but with one exhibition in the Summer for various artists. Past exhibitors include Frieda Meaney, Monika Fabig, Margaret Fitzgibbon, Rachel Parry, Esther Balazs and Corban Walker.
Submission Policy Interested in artists submitting ideas for installation work.

Price range €400–€11,000
No of exhibitions annually 1 exhibition with opening, otherwise permanent display of Sarah Walker.
Cost to hire or rent Negotiable

Siopa Cill Rialaig Gallery
Ballinskelligs, County Kerry
T 066 9479277
F 066 9479324
E cillrialaigarts@esatclear.ie
Contact Mary O'Connor
Impressive round stone thatched building in much visited Ballinskelligs. Only work by previous Cill Rialaig Retreat residents exhibited.
Submission Policy Leading Irish and international artists represented in association with Cill Rialaig Artists Retreat.
Price range €200–€20,000
No of exhibitions annually 6

Solo Arte
Coolgower, Tramore Road, Waterford City
T 051 355758
F 051 355758
E info@soloarte.ie
W www.soloarte.ie
Gallery specializing in contemporary Irish and European art.

Solomon Gallery
Powerscourt Townhouse, South William Street Dublin 2
T 01 6794237
E info@solomongallery.com
W www.solomongallery.com
Contact Tara Murphy
Established in 1981, one of Ireland's leading contemporary art galleries and dealers in important Irish twentieth-century paintings and sculpture. Represents Irish and international artists working primarily in a figurative style. Solo exhibitions are mounted every three weeks and two annual group shows are held in August and December. In addition to hosting regular exhibitions, Solomon also deals in fine Irish period paintings and sculpture, including work by Jack B. Yeats, Louis le Brocquy HRHA, William Scott and F.E. McWilliam.
Submission Policy Welcomes artist applications. Send six slides/photographs, resume, statement and catalogues.
Price range €700–€250,000
No of exhibitions annually 14

Spiller Art

19 Sandymount Green, Dublin 4
E info@spillerart.com
W www.spillerart.com
Runs programmes of changing shows throughout the year. Also holds a permanent stock by artists such as Brian Ballard, George Campbell, George Russell, Graham Knuttel, James H. Craig, Kenneth Webb, Maurice C. Wilks, Norah McGuinness and Tony O'Malley.

Stone Gallery

70 Pearse Street, Dublin 2
T 01 6711020
F 01 6752166
E art@stonegallery.ie
W www.stonegallery.ie
Contact Cleo Fagan
Opened in 2005, aiming to provide a platform for the work of emerging, Irish and, to an important but lesser degree, international visual artists. Focus on exhibiting 2D media (with an emphasis on contemporary painting) but also includes work in a range of media in an innovative programme. Endeavours to support the exhibition programme with a series of publications and artist/curator talks and to bring the work of associated artists to an international audience.
Submission Policy Does not accept unsolicited submissions.
Price range €150–€10,000
No of exhibitions annually 9

Taylor Galleries

16 Kildare Street, Dublin 2
T 01 6766055
F 01 6766642
Gallery dealing in contemporary drawings, paintings and prints, as well as sculpture and ceramics. Featured artists include William Crozier, Louis Le Brocquy, Sean McSweeny, Patrick Scott and Charles Tyrrell.

Temple Bar Gallery and Studios

5–9 Temple Bar, Dublin 2
T 01 671 0073
F 01 677 7527
E info@templebargallery.com
W www.templebargallery.com
Centrally located in Dublin's Cultural Quarter, dedicated to the practice and promotion of contemporary visual art. Organization was established by artists in its present location in 1983 and has since developed into one of the largest gallery and studio complexes in Europe. There are 29 studios occupied by artists either as full studio members or on short-term projects.
Submission Policy Generally does not welcome submissions from artists for the gallery programme. Applications to studio spaces are invited on an annual basis usually advertised in March/April with the deadline in May.
No of exhibitions annually 8

Tigh Filí

MacCurtain Street, Cork
T 021 4509274
E admin@cwpc.ie
W www.tighfili.com
Split into a main exhibition space, Gallery 9, and a second alternative space, Shrine 9, which jointly host around 18 exhibitions per year. Main gallery can show large sculpture pieces while the alternative space is used particularly for new media and soundworks. Gallery exhibits both established and emerging artists from Ireland and throughout Europe.

Tuckmill Gallery

Dublin Road, Naas, County Kildare
T 045 879761
W www.kildare.ie/arts/housing/tuckmill-gallery.htm
Shows painting, sculpture, wood-turning and ceramics by local artists. Annual open exhibition held each mid-November, plus one solo exhibition a year.

Urban Retreat

South Block, HQ Building, Hanover Quay
Dublin 2
T 01 6337865
E urbanretreatgallery@gmail.com
Cill Rialaig Retreat's Gallery in Dublin. Only past Cill Rialaig residents art exhibited. Opened December 2006.
Price range €500–€25,000
No of exhibitions annually 8

Waldock Gallery

Blackrock Shopping Centre, County Dublin
T 01 2781861
F 01 2781861
E sales@irishpaintings.com
W www.irishpaintings.com
Over twenty years experience of selling professional contemporary Irish paintings.

Waterfront Gallery
Rosses Point, Sligo
T 071 9151688
E waterfrontart@eircom.net
W www.waterfrontart.com
Opened in 2004, showing an eclectic range of
work by local, national and international artists.

Western Light Art Gallery
The Sandybanks, Keel, Achill Island, County Mayo
T 098 43325
E cannonphoto@eircom.net
W www.art-gallery-ireland.com
Opened in 1989 and represents artists including
John Behan RHA, Rene Boell, Alexandra Van
Tuyll, Alex McKenna, Sean Cannon (photography)
and William Mulhall. Has become know for
landscape work from west Mayo.
Submission Policy Send CV, list of exhibitions and
images on CD.
Price range To €2,500
No of exhibitions annually Continuous group
exhibition from Easter to November.

William Frank Gallery
91 Monkstown Road, Monkstown Village
T 01 214 8547
E info@williamfrankgallery.com
W www.williamfrankgallery.com
Specializes in contemporary and traditional
paintings, drawing and sculpture.

Yello Gallery
35 Kildare Street, Dublin 2
T 01 6449459
F 01 6449459
E oliversears@yellogallery.net
W www.yellogallery.net
Opened in 1992, specializing in modern and
contemporary Irish and international art. Stocks
wide range of prints as well as paintings by both
emerging and established artists. Will also source
works on request.

What have art galleries ever done for me?

Niru Ratnam

What's the point of commercial representation for an artist? Well, try and think of any artists enjoying either critical or commercial success without gallery backing – in the UK there are a handful at most. Representation is, at its worst, a necessary, financial evil. However, things are usually much better than that – a good gallery can be a place of like-minded souls who offer you a group identity, promote your career through staging solo shows, take your work to international art fairs and introduce curators to your oeuvre. More practically, they can cover production costs, offer storage facilities and take on all that boring administrative work that grows exponentially as your career takes off.

In the past twenty years there have been some great instances of galleries and artists becoming intertwined – the Lisson Gallery and its stable of sculptors such as Tony Cragg, Anish Kapoor and Richard Deacon are a good example from the 1980s and, of course, White Cube and the so-called Young British Artists in the 1990s are another. Both examples were very much a case of the galleries developing in tandem with a group of artists who had a similar mindset. But in the 1980s and early 1990s there were relatively few galleries in the UK – now in the wake of a booming art market there are hundreds in London alone.

Get with the programme

No two galleries are exactly alike, but with the wealth of information and listings readily available on the internet there is no excuse for not knowing a gallery's programme and something about the kinds of artists they represent already. Do some preliminary research on the web, then visit the ones you like, get on their mailing lists and start going to their private views. The commercial gallery world is unlike many other fields in the creative industries because the social dimension plays such a key role in doing business. And yes, this 'social dimension' is often a pub next to a particular gallery that plays host to post private-view drinks. Now this might seem anachronistic in an age of hyper-professionalism, but it is still undoubtedly a large part of the way galleries work – the particular vibe each one has tends to come out in the social networks they create.

If in doubt, DIY

Although not the only way to get to know galleries, doing your homework is more effective than bunging your life's work onto a CD and sending it with a begging letter to a whole string of them. I can safely say that this, while being a common tactic, is one that has about as much chance of succeeding as a slush-pile manuscript sitting in a publisher's office has of winning the Booker Prize. And if there isn't a gallery doing exactly what you like, there's a good argument for doing it yourself. Artist-run spaces and shows have a vital role to play – not only can they showcase new work, but they can offer a non-commercial environment in which to exhibit. Our old space down the street that originally housed our gallery STORE is now an artist-driven space called Associates and I've recently been getting piqued because they seem to get more folk through the doors at their private views than us (and even more piqued at being 'persuaded' to help clear up the beer bottles afterwards). Financing for artist-run spaces and small commercial galleries can come from various sources whether from Arts Council funding, from rent gathered by sharing studio space or from private backers.

Extracurricular interactivity

What unites all of these approaches is an emphasis on shared social and creative spaces. In some ways the networks that galleries form are a grown-up version of what happens at art schools – they provide a group of like-minded individuals with whom you can talk about your work. This is why being an artist is not like being a critic (who tend to work in splendid isolation) or an arts administrator (who tend to

work in office line-managed structures).
Whether you want to be an artist showing with
a gallery or run an artists' space or indeed even
start up your own commercial gallery, you have
to be prepared to interact on a regular basis with
other members of the art world. And once you
are at a gallery, either as an artist or running it,
you'll realize that this process of
communication is a vital part of a gallery –
conversely, it is a bad sign for both an artist and
a gallerist if either party goes quiet.

A family environment

Gallery representation is often portrayed as an
unromantic, business-orientated deal. This
doesn't have to be, and often isn't, the case. A
good relationship with a commercial dealer
should result in your career accelerating and
create a forum for thinking about and
discussing your work with peers. As Dan
Holdsworth, one of STORE's artists says (he's
sitting next to me as I write this drinking the
gallery's endless supply of coffee), 'Erm, it's a
lifestyle thing. It's to do with a certain
optimism.' I think this might be a vote of
confidence.

Niru Ratnam is a curator, writer, art historian and
co-director of STORE, a gallery that opened in
Hoxton Street in East London in June 2003

02

Public museums and galleries

Culture clashes:
Are museums where artists
go to die?

Iwona Blazwick

*Museums: cemeteries! ... Identical, surely in
the sinister promiscuity of so many bodies
unknown to one another. Museums: public
dormitories where one lies forever beside hated
or unknown beings. Museums: absurd abattoirs
of painters and sculptors ferociously slaughtering
each other...(cemeteries of empty exertion.
Calvaries of crucified dreams, registries of aborted
beginnings!). ... Smash them...pitilessly.*
– F.T. Marinetti, Futurist Manifesto, *Le Figaro*,
20 February 1909

A hundred years on from the Futurists' demand
for their destruction, museums of art are more
ubiquitous and powerful than ever before.
Ranked as one of the most successful brands in
the world, Tate joins the Guggenheim in Bilbao,
the Centre Georges Pompidou in Paris and
MoMA in New York, as not only a repository of
art but also an urban spectacle, a destination for
mass entertainment and a source of cultural
capital. Museums are platforms for corporate
promotions and political ambitions. They not
only bestow value on art; they also generate
revenues from it. Why should artists have
anything to do with them?

Artists' love–hate relationship with the
institution stems as much from being left
out of the 'absurd abattoir' as being made
part of it. The modern museum collects art
and arranges it into a narrative sequence –
often chronological, sometimes thematic.
It also presents high-profile temporary
exhibitions, increasingly of living artists.
And so it makes history, as much by its
exclusions as its inclusions. Until the end
of the twentieth century, many artists who
happened to be female, of colour, living
outside the West, or just not making objects,
were absented from the 'cemeteries of empty

exertion' and consequently found themselves
also absent from art history and from the
art market.

But museums and public galleries haven't
stood still. Fired by the assaults of the avant-
garde they have grown ever more dynamic and
central to the life of art. So what makes them
important for artists?

Inspiration and influence

To enter the modern art museum is to
move across time and space, to revel in
aesthetic, phenomenological and even erotic
sensations that are encapsulated both in
individual works of art and the spaces between
them. A museum's collection also immerses
us in historical, political and mythic narratives.
These might generate intense stimulation
but also provocation, even revulsion. Critical
judgments, assessments of technique and
wrestling with meaning must all surely be
part of the work of the artist immeasurably
enhanced by an encounter with the
history of art.

Finding love

We rarely encounter works of art in isolation.
Rather, they are experienced in relation to each
other in a series of juxtapositions. These can
be very contentious – why is this work hung
next to that work and what do they say about
each other? The display of a collection or
the installation of a show is like arranging
words in a sentence: curators create meta-
narratives that may enhance – or distort –
the meaning of works of art. Often these
arrangements reveal completely unexpected
qualities in works of art by different
practitioners.

These juxtapositions also include the
architecture of the museum – its windows,
doorways, corridors and stairwells, each of
which impact on our experience of the work.
Finally, we see works of art in juxtaposition with
other people. Museums are great places to look
at each other, which is why they are popular

cruising destinations and great places to pick people up.

Being loved and understood

To have your work acquired by a museum is perhaps the most powerful endorsement of its value, not just in monetary but also in symbolic terms. Entering a collection marks entry into a grand narrative.

Museums are also scientific institutions, dedicated to the conservation and study of the objects of art. Conservators analyze the effects of environment, movement and time on the art object and will go to extraordinary lengths to guarantee its preservation for posterity and to restore it lovingly to perfection in the face of damage or old age.

To have a work in a museum collection is also to offer it to art-historical appraisal through indexes and catalogue entries. Curators are often scholars who use expert art-historical and technical knowledge to investigate the origin, technique and provenance of a work. Artists can describe their creative processes, motivations and intentions through exhibition guides and publications. Conversely, these interpretive tools offer invaluable research materials to artists investigating individuals, themes and movements across time.

Having room to breathe

Since the founding of what some would call the first museum of modern art, the Louvre, museum architecture has mutated from palace to pavilion, from architect's signature piece to factory conversion. Throughout the twentieth century there has also been a shift in art from offering a picture of the world to creating a world in its own right. Sculpture has expanded into environment, picture-making has mutated into projection. Just as works of art have become bigger, so have public museums and galleries. They are often the only kind of buildings that can physically accommodate works of art that defy domestic space.

It is as a platform for an encounter with the public that is the most vital aspect of the museum or public gallery. When a work of art makes its debut into the exhibition space, it begins a dynamic and ever-changing encounter with the viewer. Arguably the point where a work of art comes to life, it can communicate with an audience far wider than could ever be reached in a studio, private collection or commercial gallery.

Changing the world

The great works of art we can encounter in the museum can move us and inspire profound philosophical meditations on the nature of being and the world around us. Museums are also full of representations. However, the life experience and aesthetic sensibilities of entire sections of society may never surface in their parades of movements and masterpieces. The inclusion of art by those historically left out, by virtue of gender or geography, also offers a moment of recognition to those communities that feel disenfranchised. Not only may they encounter their own view of the world, but they might also find public recognition for an artist from their community.

Making money

A popular misconception about artists is that they don't need to eat. The media and the public are often outraged that an artist has exchanged a work of art for money, in a way that they seldom do in relation to sports, pop or film stars. Nonetheless, most artists struggle to survive through their art. Museums are beneficial in two ways: they both buy works of art and also provide employment.

The most skilled and sensitive handlers of art are artists themselves; most technical teams in museums and galleries are made up of artists. The growth of education departments has also seen artists become educators, working with a range of audiences – from schoolchildren to senior citizens – on interpreting art and using their experience of an exhibition to tap into their own creativity.

Artists also make the best curators. For many, curating, writing and promoting the work of other artists is a way of making art.

The operation of a museum or even a small municipal gallery involves many people; not just curators and education staff, but also registrars, technicians, guards, reception staff, accountants, press officers, fund-raisers, editors, designers, archivists and librarians. These positions offer opportunities for being involved in art and enjoying your job, while making a bit of money.

The downside

Even if you are lucky enough to have your work acquired by a museum, there is no guarantee that it might not just languish in its crate, unseen for decades. An artist's oeuvre might be reduced to representing a fleeting moment in the parade of movements – now past – or 'isms' – now unfashionable. Worse still, artists might find their work on display with art they despise. Some may shudder at the interpretations a curator imposes on their art through labels and catalogues, establishing misconceptions for posterity. Others may feel discomfort as they find the art they created to be part of the flux of people and places being suspended in the timeless, placeless vacuum of the white cube – or reduced to a trophy for a multinational marketing campaign. The worst of all is being 'de-accessioned' – the fancy euphemism for having your work sold by a museum.

Visitors, too, can experience the downside of museums: they might feel uncomfortable with the increasingly corporate style of museum architecture or overwhelmed by the throngs who might be just as happy in a shopping mall.

Hope on the horizon

None of this can detract from the fact that museums and public galleries are playing an ever more central role in providing a platform for art in society. In Britain, where museums are free, audiences are expanding exponentially every year. The media are increasingly recognizing that readers and viewers want engaged, knowledgeable criticism and guidance, and not just sensationalism. Politicians are waking up to the fact that there is a substantial economy generated by artists and art institutions, and that ordinary people derive enormous satisfaction from their encounters with contemporary as well as historical art.

Rather than being mausoleums, these spaces can be playgrounds, cruising destinations, laboratories, political platforms, temples of worship, black boxes or white cubes – it's up to you.

Iwona Blazwick is the Director of the Whitechapel Gallery and an independent curator and critic.

Public museums and galleries
East Anglia

Boxfield Gallery
Stevenage Arts and Leisure Centre, Lytton Way
Stevenage, SG1 1RZ
T 01438 242644
F 01438 242342 / 242679
E william.barnard@stevenage-leisure.co.uk
W www.stevenage-leisure/gordoncraig/
arts_crafts.htm
Part of the Gordon Craig Theatre situated within
the Stevenage Leisure Centre complex and opened
in 1975. Hosts ten exhibitions per year (suitable for
large-scale works and group shows). The smaller
Foxer Gallery puts on twelve exhibitions per year
(suitable for water-colourists, printmakers and
photographers).
Submission Policy Application by portfolio and
interview with the Visual Arts Officer. Will show
artists of national and local standing, and both
retrospective or topical shows.
Talks/Events/Education Outreach to all local
schools. Workshop and classes run in studio
facilities for all age and skill groups. Also
competitions.

Broughton House Gallery
98 King Street, Cambridge, CB1 1LN
T 01223 314960
E bhgallery@btconnect.com
W www.broughtonhousegallery.co.uk
Founded in 1987. Hosts six exhibitions (solo, duo,
theme) a year. Home of the Gwen Raverat Archive
of wood engravings (over four hundred for sale).
Submission Policy Applications with images and
CV, etc.

Bury St Edmunds Art Gallery
The Market Cross, Bury St Edmunds, IP33 1BT
T 01284 762081
E enquiries@burystedmundsartgallery.org
W www.burystedmundsartgallery.org
A contemporary art gallery in the centre of the
market town, situated in a Robert Adam building.
Showing changing exhibitions throughout the
year. The shop sells both regional and national
makers in jewellery, ceramics, textiles, artist prints
and handmade cards.
Talks/Events/Education The exhibition
programme is supported by events, talks and
workshops related to current exhibition.

Fitzwilliam Museum
Trumpington Street, Cambridge, CB2 1RB
T 01223 332900
F 01223 332923
E fitzmuseum-enquiries@lists.cam.ac.uk
W www.fitzmuseum.cam.ac.uk
Founded in 1816 by the bequest of the Seventh
Viscount Fitzwilliam to the University of
Cambridge. Houses collections of art and
antiquities spanning centuries and civilizations.
Highlights include antiquities from Egypt, the
Ancient Near East, Greece, Rome and Cyprus;
English and European pottery and glass; sculpture;
Oriental art; Korean ceramics; coins and medals;
masterpieces by Domenico Veneziano, Leonardo
da Vinci, Titian, Rembrandt, Rubens and Van
Dyck; outstanding works by British artists
including Gainsborough, Reynolds, Stubbs and
Constable; and a collection of twentieth-century
art. Runs programme of temporary exhibitions,
events, courses and activities for all ages.

Focal Point Gallery
Southend Central Library, Victoria Avenue
Southend-on-Sea, SS2 6EX
T 01702 534108
F 01702 469241
E focalpointgallery@southend.gov.uk
W www.focalpoint.org.uk
Established in 1991 and run by Southend-on-Sea
Borough Council, Focal Point Gallery specializes
in photography and media arts. Changing
exhibition programme of around six shows per
year accompanied by regular events.
Submission Policy Specializes in photography and
lens-based media. Guidelines on submitting a
proposal are available on the gallery website.
Talks/Events/Education Runs a regular programme
of events for adults, children and family groups to
accompany exhibitions. These include artists' talks
and workshops, film screenings and drop-in events.
Free exhibition tours can be arranged by gallery
staff for school, college and community groups who
book in advance.

Gainsborough's House
46 Gainsborough Street, Sudbury, CO10 2EU
T 01787 372958
F 01787 376991
E mail@gainsborough.org
W www.gainsborough.org
The museum and art gallery at the birthplace of
Thomas Gainsborough (1727–1788) with an
outstanding collection of his paintings, drawings

and prints. The House also offers visitors a varied programme of temporary exhibitions. The annual programme includes one or two contemporary exhibitions of work that relate to the collection, its location or the legacy of Gainsborough, as well as contemporary sculpture in the garden. The print workshop is available to members and runs a year-round programme of printmaking courses.
Talks/Events/Education Life classes, children's art workshops and art lectures are held throughout the year.

Kettle's Yard

Castle Street, Cambridge, CB3 0AQ
T 01223 352124
F 01223 324377
E mail@kettlesyard.cam.ac.uk
W www.kettlesyard.co.uk
Once the home of Jim Ede, a curator at the Tate Gallery. The house displays Ede's collection, including works by Ben and Winifred Nicholson, Alfred Wallis, Christopher Wood, David Jones, Joan Miro, Henri Gaudier-Brzeska, Constantin Brancusi, Henry Moore and Barbara Hepworth. Holds regular exhibitions of modern and contemporary art, including a biannual open exhibition of artists working in the Eastern region.
Submission Policy Include an outline of proposed project together with examples of work and an sae for return of material.
Talks/Events/Education There is a wide programme of events, open to all. Details on web site. Prices and times vary. Some events, including regular lunch time talks, are free.

King's Lynn Arts Centre

27–29 King Street, King's Lynn, PE30 1HA
T 01553 779095
F 01553 766834
E lfalconbridge@west-norfolk.gov.uk
W www.kingslynnarts.co.uk
Founded in the 1960s, including four main exhibition spaces covering film and video, sculpture, painting, drawing, photography, textiles, ceramics and crafts showcases. There are also workshops in association with the exhibitions, informal art lectures and a Saturday art club. Some annual highlights include the Eastern Open (a competition with cash prizes for artists in East Anglia), King's Lynn Festival and Christmas Crafts Fair.

Letchworth Museum and Art Gallery

Broadway, Letchworth Garden City, SG6 3PF
T 01462 685647

F 01462 481879
E letchworth.museum@north-herts.gov.uk
W www.north-herts.gov.uk
Founded in 1914 by the Letchworth Naturalists' Society. Main permanent displays are on archaeology, particularly Iron Age and Roman, and natural history. Has regular temporary displays of works from the museum's fine- and decorative-art collections, and its social history collection. Art collections include the largest holding of works by Camden Town artist William Ratcliffe. Also has a good collection of oils by Margaret Thomas. Decorative art includes glass and ceramics.
Submission Policy Exhibits work in all media except digital and film.

Minories Art Gallery

High Street, Colchester, CO1 1UE
T 01206 577067
F 01206 577161
Shows contemporary art and sculpture.

Norwich Castle Museum and Art Gallery

Shirehall, Market Avenue, Norwich
NR1 3JQ
T 01603 493625
F 01603 493623
E museums@norfolk.gov.uk
W www.museums.norfolk.gov.uk
One of the city's most famous landmarks, Norwich Castle was built by the Normans as a Royal Palace nine hundred years ago. The gallery houses an important collection of fine art.
Talks/Events/Education Holds regular talks and events connected to exhibitions, some of which are free.

Norwich Gallery

Norwich School of Art & Design, St George Street Norwich, NR3 1BB
T 01603 610561
E info@norwichgallery.co.uk
W www.norwichgallery.co.uk
Shows temporary exhibitions of contemporary art all year round. Forty national and international artists go to Norwich each year to show painting, sculpture, photography, video and new media.
Submission Policy Artists should send a CV, a maximum of ten slides or CD and a written proposal/supporting statement.
Talks/Events/Education Conferences are organized to support specific exhibitions (approximately eight per year). Open to artists and the public, free of charge.

Saffron Walden Museum

Museum Street, Saffron Walden, CB10 1JL
T 01799 510333
F 01799 510333
E museum@uttlesford.gov.uk
Founded in 1835. Collections include decorative arts (ceramics and glass), textiles, woodwork, prints, photos and drawings. Limited amount of fine art.
Submission Policy Small special exhibition space is programmed two to three years ahead. Art exhibitions tend to have local connections or relevance to collections.
Talks/Events/Education Events held but infrequently; some free (e.g. ceramics workshop).

Sainsbury Centre for Visual Arts

University of East Anglia, Norwich, NR4 7TJ
T 01603 593199
F 01603 591053
E scva@uea.ac.uk
W www.scva.ac.uk
Designed by Sir Norman Foster and opened in 1978, the building is home to three permanent collections of international importance and also affords space for special exhibitions and the delivery of a wide range of educational and public programmes. Some exhibitions are developed by the Sainsbury Centre, some in partnership with other galleries and others by external curators or institutions.
Talks/Events/Education Organizes over one hundred and twenty events a year (some free).

Sir Alfred Munnings Art Museum

Castle House, Castle Hill, Dedham, CO7 6AZ
T 01206 322127
F 01206 322127
W www.siralfredmunnings.co.uk
Sir Alfred Munnings KCVO PRA lived and worked at Castle House from 1919 until his death in 1959. The house has a comprehensive collection of Munnings's work, some of which is housed in his studio.

The Town Hall Galleries

Cornhill, Ipswich, IP1 1DH
T 01473 432863
E visualarts@ipswich.gov.uk
W www.townhallgalleries.org.uk
Consists of three galleries. Gallery 1: Visual Arts Ipswich has a changing programme of contemporary visual art featuring artists from the region and beyond. Also houses a resource area.

Gallery 2: Suffolk Craft Society programme showcasing contemporary designers and makers. Also includes an activity and art store. Gallery 3: Ipswich Museums Service has displays and activities linked to community heritage and the town's recent past. Includes a project space.

University of Essex Collection of Latin American Art (UECLAA)

Department of Art History and Theory, University of Essex, Wivenhoe Park, Colchester, CO4 3SQ
T 01206 873971
F 01206 873702
E gsalgaa@essex.ac.uk
W www.essex.ac.uk/ueclaa/ueclaaWelcome.htm
Founded in 1993, the only public collection in Europe dedicated exclusively to modern and contemporary Latin American art. The collection comprises over six hundred works by modern and contemporary artists including Carlos Cruz-Diez, Guillermo Kuitca, Roberto Matta, Cildo Meireles, Ana Maria Pacheco, Nadin Ospina, Fernando de Szyszlo, Rufino Tamayo and Mariana Yampolsky. UECLAA Online is a fully-searchable catalogue available to internet users worldwide.

University of Hertfordshire (UH) Galleries

College Lane, Hatfield, AL10 9AB
T 01707 285376
F 01707 285310
E colsmbs@herts.ac.uk
W perseus.herts.ac.uk/uhinfo/schools/art/uhgalleries/index.cfm
Founded in 1996, aiming to offer exhibition and publishing opportunities to artists, designers and makers in the early stages of their careers. Collection based on acquisitions from past programming.
Submission Policy Submissions from professional artists and groups welcome. Short text and some images sufficient in the first instance.
Talks/Events/Education Currently establishing an education programme.

Watford Museum

194 Lower High Street, Watford, WD17 2DT
T 01923 232297
F 01923 224772
E info@watfordmuseum.org.uk
W www.watfordmuseum.org.uk
Housed in the former Benskins Brewery Mansion and includes the Cassiobury Collection of fine art. A changing programme of exhibitions gives opportunities for local artists to display their work.

Submission Policy Opportunities are available for local artists to display and be employed to deliver art workshops and projects.
Talks/Events/Education Active programme includes workshops for children and adults, and talks on local art and history.

East Midlands

20-21 Visual Arts Centre
St John's Church, Church Square, Scunthorpe
DN15 6TB
T 01724 297070
F 01724 297080
E 20-21.epd@northlincs.gov.uk
W www.northlincs.gov.uk/20-21
Founded in 2001 and housed in a converted church. An exhibition centre focusing on contemporary fine art, crafts and design. Has six exhibition spaces including an outdoor sculpture courtyard. The centre also houses a contemporary art and craft shop and holds artist-led workshops for all age ranges.
Submission Policy Welcomes submissions from contemporary artists working in all media. An exhibition request form is available online or from 20-21.
Talks/Events/Education Continuous programme of events and courses (prices vary).

Alfred East Art Gallery
c/o Coach House, Sheep Street, Kettering, NN16 0AN
T 01536 534274
F 01536 534370
E museum@kettering.gov.uk
W www.kettering.gov.uk/gallery
Opened in 1913 with an initial donation of seventy works by Sir Alfred East. Has subsequently expanded its collections to nine hundred works including major collections of East and Thomas Cooper Gotch alongside other local artists, and contemporary art collected between the 1950s and 1980s. Temporary exhibitions by local artists and national touring groups are on display all year as well the permanent collection.
Submission Policy Programmes a year in advance. For terms and conditions, phone or see website.
Talks/Events/Education Monthly talks programme (£3 or £1.50 concessions in 2007) and occasional workshops.

Angel Row Gallery
Central Library Building, 3 Angel Row, Nottingham, NG1 6HP
T 0115 9152869
F 0115 9152860
E angelrow.info@nottinghamcity.gov.uk
W www.angelrowgallery.com
A leading venue for contemporary art. The scope of the programme is broad, reflecting the diversity of trends within contemporary visual-art practice.
Submission Policy Contact the gallery to check if it is accepting submissions.
Talks/Events/Education The gallery provides a programme of workshops, short courses, talks and live events.

Brewhouse Gallery
The Old Malthouse, Springfield Road, Grantham
NG31 7BG
T 01476 576703
F 01476 576703
E lmtbrady@aol.com
W www.grantham-online.co.uk/pp/business/detail.asp?id=20619
A public gallery of painting, sculpture, prints and furniture, as well as commissioned work. Runs art workshops, and community projects in schools, businesses and organizations. Participates in public art including mosaics, mapmaking, textiles, murals and temporary installations. Also offers framing, antique restoration and consultation services.

Burghley
Burghley House, Stamford, PE9 3JY
T 01780 752451
F 01780 480125
E burghley@burghley.co.uk
W www.burghley.co.uk
One of the grandest houses of the Elizabethan age. Includes imposing painted ceilings by Antonio Verrio, over four hundred paintings and an important collection of Japanese porcelain.
Submission Policy Burghley's sculpture garden features new exhibitions annually to showcase work from new artists. Burghley also hosts several exhibitions throughout the year for artists working in a variety of media.

Derby Museum and Art Gallery
The Strand, Derby, DE1 1BS
T 01332 716659
F 01332 716670
E exhibitions@derby.gov.uk
W www.visitderby.co.uk
Shows contemporary artists of international, national and regional importance. Work includes digital media, photography, sculpture, textiles,

decorative and applied art, contemporary and fine art, together with the museum's reserve collection. Main collections: Joseph Wright of Derby, Derby Porcelains, Military, Natural History, Archaeology, Social History, Egyptology.
Submission Policy Applications welcomed. Email or phone exhibitions team to receive an exhibition proposal form.
Talks/Events/Education Exhibitions are accompanied by talks and lectures for the public, other artists and students. Workshops and related activities for both children and adults. See website for details.

Djanogly Art Gallery
Lakeside Arts Centre, University Park
Nottingham, NG7 2RD
T 0115 9513192
F 0115 9513194
W www.lakesidearts.org.uk
The exhibition programme ranges from major historical shows to groundbreaking contemporary installations.

Future Factory
Nottingham Trent University, Dryden Street
Nottingham, NG1 4GG
T 0115 8486131
F 0115 8486132
E sam.rose@ntu.ac.uk
W www2.ntu.ac.uk/ntsad/bonington/
Houses the Bonington and 1851 art galleries, as well as the performance venue Powerhouse. The venues present work of multidisciplinary art forms, with emphasis on new media, performance, live art and installation work.
Talks/Events/Education Active education programme. Contact sam.rose@ntu.ac.uk or annette.foster@ntu.ac.uk.

Harley Gallery
Welbeck, Worksop, S80 3LW
T 01909 501700
F 01909 488747
E info@harley-welbeck.co.uk
W www.harleygallery.co.uk
Built in 1994 on the site of the original nineteenth-century gasworks for Welbeck Estate. Includes three gallery spaces, displaying a changing programme of contemporary art and craft, and a museum with select displays of objects from the Portland Collection.
Submission Policy Artists should apply in writing to Lisa Gee (Director).

Leicester City Art Gallery
90 Granby Street, Leicester, LE1 1DJ
W www.leicester.gov.uk/citygallery
Three exhibition spaces, including fine art and crafts. Changing exhibitions programme (twelve shows per year). Programme is balanced to include all art and craft disciplines and aims to show local, regional, national and international work.

Northampton Museum and Art Gallery
Guildhall Road, Northampton, NN1 1DP
T 01604 838111
F 01604 83872
E museums@northampton.gov.uk
W www.northampton.gov.uk/museums
Founded in 1865. Collections include fifteenth- and eighteenth-century Italian and British art, and Oriental and British ceramics.
Submission Policy Any application welcome (only criterion being the enrichment of visitors' experience) but currently oversubscribed.
Talks/Events/Education Talks and educational events frequently held and often free, although not specifically aimed at artists. Opportunities for artists and practitioners to lead and/or devise workshops, etc.

Picture House Centre for Photography
3rd Floor, International House, 125 Granby Street
Leicester, LE1 6FD
T 0116 2555282
F 0116 2555282
E photo@pichouse.demon.co.uk
W www.pichouse.org.uk
In its thirteenth year as a cooperative, focusing on the art of traditional and digital photography. Exhibitions, reference collection and coffee bar are open to all. Existing users range from newcomers to professionals, attracted by the extensive facilities. Subscription scheme offered for access to practical facilities.
Talks/Events/Education Various talks, workshops, courses and events are held throughout the year.

Q Arts Gallery
35–36 Queen Street, Derby, DE1 3DU
T 01332 295858
F 01332 295859
E create@q-arts.co.uk
W www.q-arts.co.uk
A contemporary visual arts organization working with moving image, photography and digital media. The gallery is committed to showing a wide range of in-house curated exhibitions and touring

exhibitions comprising local, regional, national and international artists. In 2006 QUAD, a dynamic, regional centre for contemporary visual arts and media, was created through a merger of Metro Cinema and Q Arts working in partnership with the City Council.

Submission Policy The curated programme is booked eighteen months to two years in advance. Artists wishing to submit for exhibition should send or bring in a proposal and samples of their work in any format. Do not bring in the work itself unless under prior arrangement.

Talks/Events/Education Each exhibition is accompanied by an artist talk ('Feedback') and a musical or performance response to the artwork ('Playback'). These events are free and open to all.

Rugby Art Gallery and Museum

Little Elborow Street, Rugby, CV21 3BZ
T 01788 533201
F 01788 533204
E rugbyartgalleryandmuseum@rugby.gov.uk
W www.rugbygalleryandmuseum.org.uk
Rugby Art Gallery and Museum hosts temporary exhibitions of contemporary visual art and craft, and work from the Rugby Collection of 20th century British Art, which includes pieces by Freud, Lowry, Spencer, Hepworth and Sutherland.

Usher Gallery

Lindum Road, Lincoln, LN2 1NN
T 01522 527980
F 01522 560165
E usher.gallery@lincolnshire.gov.uk
Founded in 1926 to house the collection of James Ward Usher and set in the grounds of the Temple Gardens. Includes paintings by J.M.W. Turner, Thomas Girtin, John Piper, L.S. Lowry and Duncan Grant, as well as works by Lincolnshire artists. Since 1999 the Usher Gallery has commissioned annual residencies.

London

Architectural Association

36 Bedford Square, London, WC1B 3ES
T 020 78874000
F 020 74140782
E press@aaschool.ac.uk
W www.aaschool.ac.uk
Annually hosts five main gallery exhibitions, ten smaller exhibitions in its other exhibition spaces, and an end-of-year show, 'Projects Review' in July. Exhibitions primarily focus on current debate

within the architectural and design world and themes relating to projects being undertaken at the school. All exhibitions are open to the public and there is no admission fee.

Submission Policy Artists should have an architectural direction or concern. Applications in writing only. Do not include original material.

Talks/Events/Education Each exhibition has related lectures and events, which are free to attend and publicized online.

Arts Gallery

University of the Arts London, 65 Davies Street London, W1K 5DA
T 020 7514 8083
F 020 7514 8179
E gallery@arts.ac.uk
W www.arts.ac.uk
Exists to promote the work of alumni of University of the Arts London. Primary emphasis on those who have been practising for at least two years since graduation. Aims to reflect the diversity of practice across the Colleges of the University and to remain at the cutting edge of art and design. Opened in 1993 and underwent major refurbishment in 2006.

Submission Policy To make an application to exhibit, contact the gallery for a proposal application form.

Talks/Events/Education Public talks by exhibitors are held to coincide with most exhibitions.

Austrian Cultural Forum London

28 Rutland Gate, London, SW7 1PQ
T 020 75848653
F 020 72250470
E culture@austria.org.uk
W www.austria.org.uk/culture
Founded in 1956, the Austrian Cultural Forum in London promotes cultural contacts between the UK and Austria by organizing events and supporting artists and projects in the fields of the visual arts, music, performing arts, literature and film. Also runs academic symposia and public discussions.

Talks/Events/Education If not stated otherwise, events at the Austrian Cultural Forum London are free.

Bankside Gallery

48 Hopton Street, London, SE1 9JH
T 020 79287521
F 020 79282820
E info@banksidegallery.com
W www.banksidegallery.com

The gallery of the Royal Watercolour Society and the Royal Society of Painter-Printmakers. Runs changing exhibitions featuring contemporary watercolours and prints by members of both societies, as well as work by invited guests in a variety of media, including video installation, photography and oil painting.
Submission Policy Elections for both Societies take place in February/March each year. Contact the gallery for further details. The Royal Watercolour Society organizes an annual open watercolour competition called 21st Century Watercolour in February. Successful entries of water-based paintings on paper will be shown at Bankside Gallery and successful applicants will be invited to apply for election to the Royal Watercolour Society.
Talks/Events/Education Holds workshops, talks, lectures and demonstrations, free to friends of the gallery. See website for details.

Barbican Art Gallery
Silk Street, London, EC2Y 8DS
T 0845 1216828
E artinfo@barbican.org.uk
W www.barbican.org.uk/gallery/index.htm
Europe's largest multi-arts and conference venue, with a regularly changing exhibitions programme backed by talks and workshops.
Talks/Events/Education There is a regular programme of Wednesday-evening talks. To book, call the box office on the number above.

Beaconsfield
22 Newport Street, Vauxhall, London, SE11 6AY
T 020 75826465
F 020 75826486
E mail@beaconsfield.ltd.uk
W www.beaconsfield.ltd.uk
Founded in 1994, an independent, commissioning organization and artist-led space for contemporary art.
Submission Policy Three galleries available for hire (but not for exhibitions). Contact Rachel Fleming-Mulford
Talks/Events/Education Provides talks and events and maintains links with higher education and schools. For further information or to book a visit contact Naomi Siderfin or Rachel Fleming-Mulford.

Bloomberg SPACE
50 Finsbury Square, London, EC2A 1HD
T 020 73307959
E gallery@bloomberg.net
W www.bloomberg.com
Founded in 2002. Not a conventional corporate art collection, but rather a dynamic space dedicated to commissioning and exhibiting contemporary art.
Submission Policy Programmed by three independent freelance curators. Does not accept open submissions.
Talks/Events/Education Every exhibition is accompanied by an events programme, free and open to all.

Bow Arts Trust and Nunnery Gallery
181–183 Bow Road, London, E3 2SJ
T 020 89807774
F 020 89807770
E info@bowarts.com
W www.bowarts.com
Founded in 1995 as an educational arts charity. The Nunnery Gallery is a contemporary project space that initiates and develops projects that reflect and address issues in contemporary art, and in doing so works with a range of artists, curators, writers and arts organizations. Holds approximately five exhibitions per year including a guest-curated in-house summer show. Previous curators include Mo Mowlam, David Dimbleby and Graham Norton. It is available for hire for a variety of functions.
Submission Policy Gallery proposals and applications are required eight to twelve months before the projected start date. Include images, biographies, a clear outline of show and a clear and realistic budget structure.
Talks/Events/Education Free educational events, seminars and talks usually accompany each show in the gallery. Occasional skills-sharing workshops for local artists.

British Museum
Great Russell Street, London, WC1H 8DG
T 020 73238000
E information@thebritishmuseum.ac.uk
W www.thebritishmuseum.ac.uk
Founded in 1753, the first national public museum in the world. From the outset its collection was made available to every citizen, to all 'studious and curious' people regardless of rank or status, free of charge. Its role is to display the world's great civilizations and cultures, and to tell the story of human achievement throughout its ages. Its collections include archaeological and ethnographic material, prints and drawings and coins and medals.
Submission Policy The museum does show and collect work by living artists through the

Department of Prints and Drawings and Africa, Oceania and the Americas. It does not welcome submissions direct from artists, however.
Talks/Events/Education Runs a full education programme that covers all aspects of its collections. Many events are free.

Brunei Gallery

School of Oriental and African Studies, Thornhaugh Street, London, WC1H 0XG
T 020 78984046
F 020 78984259
E gallery@soas.ac.uk
W www.soas.ac.uk/gallery
Founded in 1995 and run as a non-commercial gallery. As part of the School of Oriental and African Studies (University of London), Europe's leading centre for the study of Asia and Africa, the gallery is dedicated to showing work of and from Asia and Africa, of both a historical and contemporary nature, through a programme of changing exhibitions.

Cafe Gallery Projects London

Cafe Gallery – Centre of Southwark Park, London SE16 2UA
T 020 72371230
E cgp.mail@virgin.net
W www.cafegalleryprojects.org
Founded in 1984, a major south-east London artist-led exhibition space. It was rebuilt in 2000 with money from the National Lottery. Dilston Grove (south-west corner of Southwark Park) opened in 1999, a space for installation, site-specific and experimental art. Cafe Gallery Projects London are administered by the Bermondsey Artists' Group. All exhibitions and events are free.
Submission Policy Unsolicited applications are viewed at the end of September. There is an unselected open exhibition every November/December.
Talks/Events/Education Holds artists talks and has a varied education programme. Information available on the website.

Camden Arts Centre

Arkwright Road, London, NW3 6DG
T 020 74725500
F 020 74725501
E info@camdenartscentre.org
W www.camdenartscentre.org
A centre for contemporary visual arts and art education, comprising three gallery spaces and three studios, where visitors are invited to actively engage with art, artists and ideas through a frequently changing programme of exhibitions and education. The centre is housed in a grade II-listed building that began life in 1898 as a library and was converted into an arts centre in 1964.
Submission Policy Proposals from artists are welcome although majority of exhibitions and residencies arise from direct invitations to artists and curators.
Talks/Events/Education Full programme of courses, talks and events. For more information see website or contact by phone.

CHELSEA space

Chelsea College of Art & Design, 16 John Islip Street, Millbank, London, SW1T 4JU
T 020 75146000 ext.3710
E d.s.smith@chelsea.arts.ac.uk
W www.chelsea.arts.ac.uk
Opened in 2005 and set within Chelsea College of Art & Design's campus next to Tate Britain, CHELSEA Space is a research development centre for invited contemporary art and design professionals. Some shows draw specifically on Chelsea's special collections of artists' books, ephemera, multiples, etc. Experimental music and performance are often integral parts of exhibitions.
Submission Policy Does not accept submissions from artists.
Talks/Events/Education Regular public events including free talks, concerts and conferences are held.

Chisenhale Gallery

64 Chisenhale Road, London, E3 5QZ
T 020 89814518
F 020 89807169
E mail@chisenhale.org.uk
W www.chisenhale.org.uk
Founded in 1986. One of London's most important public spaces for contemporary art, in a converted factory offering 2,500 sq. ft of space with a dedicated education studio. A charitable organization whose mission is to encourage and promote innovation and experimentation in contemporary visual arts and art education. Organizes five solo exhibitions each year from British and international artists.
Submission Policy Unsolicited proposals are very rarely taken up as part of the Director's gallery programme.
Talks/Events/Education Organizes free talks, events and conferences alongside each exhibition and education project.

Courtauld Institute of Art Gallery
Somerset House, Strand, London, WC2R 0RN
T 020 78482526
F 020 78482589
E galleryinfo@courtauld.ac.uk
W www.courtauld.ac.uk
Among the most important small collections in
Britain, including world-famous Impressionist
and Post-Impressionist paintings, as well as Old
Master paintings, sculpture and decorative arts
from the fourteenth to twentieth centuries.
Founded in 1932 and housed at Somerset House,
one of the finest eighteenth-century buildings in
London. Resources include a book library and two
image libraries of national significance.
Submission Policy Does not show living artists'
work apart from well-known or successful
contemporary artists.
Talks/Events/Education Regular talks, lectures,
and activities are often free on purchasing an
admission ticket.

Croydon Museum Service
Clocktower, Katharine Street, Croydon, CR9 1ET
T 020 82531022
F 020 82531003
E museum@croydon.gov.uk
W www.croydon.gov.uk/clocktower
A multipurpose cultural centre with three
galleries, including the Riesco Gallery of Chinese
Pottery and Porcelain and a gallery for
programmed temporary exhibitions. Also
manages a programme of changing exhibitions by
local artists in the café-gallery.

Czech Centre London
13 Harley Street, London, W1G 9QG
T 020 73075180
F 020 73233709
E info@czechcentre.org.uk
W www.czechcentres.cz/london
Organizes frequent exhibitions of Czech art.

Design Museum
Shad Thames, London, SE1 2YD
T 0870 909 9009
F 0870 909 1909
E info@designmuseum.org
W www.designmuseum.org
Leading museum of design, fashion and
architecture. Constantly changing programme of
exhibitions, ranging from design history to
innovations in contemporary design.
Talks/Events/Education Hosts talks by some of the

world's leading designers and architects, from
Jonathan Ive to Zaha Hadid.

Dilston Grove
Clare College Mission Church, South-west corner
of Southwark Park, London, SE16 2UA
E cgp.mail@virgin.net
W www.cafegalleryprojects.com
Opened in 1999 and run by Café Gallery Projects.
Based in a former concrete-built church, one of
London's last remaining regularly programmed
'raw' exhibition space. Aims to provide a venue for
large-scale installations, experimental work,
performance and video events.

Dulwich Picture Gallery
Gallery Road, London, SE21 7AD
T 020 86935254
F 020 82998700
E info@dulwichpicturegallery.org.uk
W www.dulwichpicturegallery.org.uk
Founded in 1811. Houses a collection of seventeenth-
and eighteenth-century Old Masters, including
Rembrandt, Poussin, Claude, Rubens, Murillo, Van
Dyck, Watteau and Gainsborough, collected by the
King of Poland in the 1790s. When Poland was
partitioned, Dulwich Picture Gallery was designed
for the collection by the famed Regency architect Sir
John Soane. The gallery houses loan exhibitions as
well as the permanent collection.
Submission Policy Has occasional exhibitions of
living artists (Lucian Freud, Paula Rego, Howard
Hodgkin, Eileen Cooper RA, and Humphrey
Ocean RA for example). From time to time also
has an artist-in-residence, who reinterprets the
collection and teaches.
Talks/Events/Education The education
department runs many courses including
masterclasses.

Estorick Collection of Modern Italian Art
39a Canonbury Square, London, N1 2AN
T 020 77049522
F 020 77049531
E curator@estorickcollection.com
W www.estorickcollection.com
Formed by Eric and Salome Estorick during the
1950s and housed in a converted Georgian villa,
the collection has been open to the public since
1998. Known internationally for its core of Futurist
works, as well as figurative painting and sculpture
from 1895 to the 1950s. Artists include Balla,
Boccioni, Carra, Russolo, Severini, de Chirico,
Modigliani and Morandi. Also runs a programme

of temporary exhibitions, all connected to the permanent collection.

Submission Policy Does not accept applications from contemporary artists.

Fashion Space Gallery

20 John Princes Street, London, W1G 0BJ

T 020 75142998 / 75147701
F 020 75148388
E pr@fashion.arts.ac.uk
W www.fashion.arts.ac.uk

A contemporary exhibition space located in the heart of London's West End. Based within London College of Fashion, the gallery runs a programme of exhibitions by students, staff and visiting artists. Displays of fashion, photography and fine art can be visited for free all year round.

Submission Policy Artists' exhibition proposals are judged upon individual merit and should be submitted to the Events Office for consideration.

Fleming Collection

13 Berkeley Street, London, W1J 8DU

T 020 74095730
F 020 74095601
E flemingcollection@ffandp.com
W www.flemingcollection.co.uk

Opened to the public in 2002, consisting of works by Scottish artists from 1770 to the present day. Includes works by early nineteenth-century artists, the Glasgow Boys, the Scottish Colourists, the Edinburgh School and many contemporary Scottish names. Holds four exhibitions a year drawn from the collection as well as loans from public and private collections.

Talks/Events/Education Regular public lectures and events. There is also a Friends Association and Patrons Group.

Foundling Museum

40 Brunswick Square, London, WC1N 1AZ

T 020 78413600
F 020 78413601
E enquiries@foundlingmuseum.org.uk
W www.foundlingmuseum.org.uk

London's first public art gallery and the precursor to the Royal Academy, created by William Hogarth in Thomas Coram's Foundling Hospital in the eighteenth century. The collection contains works by Hogarth, Reynolds, Gainsborough, Wilson, Hayman, Highmore, Roubiliac and Rysbrack, displayed as they would have been seen by visitors to the hospital in the 1700s. Permanent social history exhibition and temporary exhibitions

include contemporary artists.

Submission Policy Submissions welcome which are relevant to Museum's history or collections (otherwise will not be considered). Café available for more general work.

Talks/Events/Education A variety of talks, workshops, concerts and other events, some of which are free. Details can be found in 'What's on' leaflet.

Geffrye Museum

136 Kingsland Road, Shoreditch, London, E2 8EA

T 020 77399893
F 020 77295647
E info@geffrye-museum.org.uk
W www.geffrye-museum.org.uk

Established in 1914, the museum's specialist area of research is middle-class domestic interiors and gardens. It presents the history of English interiors from 1600 to the present day through a chronological sequence of period rooms containing furniture, paintings and decorative arts. Also has a series of period gardens.

Gilbert Collection

Somerset House, Strand, London, WC2R 1LA

T 020 74209400
F 020 74209440
W www.gilbert-collection.org.uk

Opened in 2000. Comprises gifts given to the nation by the late Sir Arthur Gilbert, including fine examples of silver snuffboxes Italian mosaics. Also holds related temporary exhibitions.

Talks/Events/Education Gallery talks held each Thursday from 1.15 pm to 1.35 pm (free with admission). For information on other educational events, call 020 74209406 or email education@somerset-house.org.uk.

Goethe-Institut London

50 Princes Gate, Exhibition Road, London SW7 2PH

T 020 75964000
F 020 75940240
E arts@london.goethe.org
W www.goethe.de/london

The Goethe-Institut is the cultural institute of the Federal Republic of Germany with a global reach. Promotes knowledge of the German language abroad and fosters international cultural cooperation. The gallery at Hugo's Restaurant focuses on young German photography. Also displays films and video installations on the in-house cinema screen.

Submission Policy Focus on photographic works with a strong German element. A clear link to the institute's key themes is necessary.
Talks/Events/Education Frequently invites artists for panel discussions and artist talks. Admission is usually £3.

Guildhall Art Gallery

Guildhall Yard, London, EC2T 2EJ
T 020 73323700
F 020 73323342
E guildhall.artgallery@cityoflondon.gov.uk
W www.guildhall-art-gallery.org.uk
Originally founded in 1885 to house the City of London's art collection. A new gallery opened in 1999. Holds collections of Pre-Raphaelite works and images of London and its people from the sixteenth century to the present. Now specializes in London-related material.
Talks/Events/Education For education information phone 020 73321632.

Hayward Gallery

Belvedere Road, London, SE1 8XX
T 020 79605226
E hginfo@hayward.org.uk
W www.hayward.org.uk
Opened in 1968. An icon of 1960s brutalist architecture. Has a programme of four to five temporary exhibitions each year. The Waterloo Sunset was opened in 2004, designed by Dan Graham in association with Howarth Tompkins Architects, to provide the gallery with a new space.
Talks/Events/Education A creative programme of talks and events runs alongside each exhibition.

Hermitage Rooms at Somerset House

Somerset House, Strand, London, WC2R 1LA
T 020 78454600
F 020 78454637
W www.hermitagerooms.org.uk
Opened in 2000 and now administered by the Courtauld, the first exhibition space to be created in the West to show rotating exhibitions of works from the collections of the State Hermitage Museum in St Petersburg.
Talks/Events/Education Gallery talks each Friday from 1.15 pm to 1.35 pm (free with admission). For further information, call 020 74209406 or email education@somerset-house.org.uk.

Imperial War Museum

Lambeth Road, London, SE1 6HZ
T 020 7416 5320/1

F 020 7416 5409
E art@iwm.org.uk
W www.iwm.org.uk
The national museum of conflict involving Britain and the Commonwealth since 1914. Founded in 1917, the museum seeks to provide for, and to encourage, the study and understanding of the history of modern war. The collections include 120 million ft of cine film, 30,000 posters and some of the nation's best-known twentieth-century paintings.
Submission Policy The Artists Records Committee commissions work on specific projects.
Talks/Events/Education Hosts a varied programme of talks and events. For details visit website or call 020 74165320.

Institute of Contemporary Arts (ICA)

The Mall, London, SW1Y 5AH
T 020 79300493
E exhibit@ica.org.uk
W www.ica.org.uk
A London arts centre presenting contemporary film, exhibitions on contemporary art, new media, talks, club nights, music, dance and other events. The ICA is a membership organization and also provides opportunities for networking.
Talks/Events/Education Projects include an innovative PhD programme, programmes of talks, a short film festival called 'jumpcut', a club called 'uncut' for new film and video makers, and a creative entrepreneurs club (www.club2.org.uk)

Institute of International Visual Arts (inIVA)

6–8 Standard Place, Rivington Street, London EC2A 3BE
T 020 77299616
F 020 77299509
E institute@iniva.org
W www.iniva.org
Since it was established in 1994, inIVA has developed and produced a diverse portfolio of projects that have engaged audiences throughout the UK and worldwide in a creative dialogue with contemporary art. Creates exhibitions and publications, as well as multimedia, education and research projects designed to bring the work of artists from culturally diverse backgrounds to the attention of the widest possible public.
Submission Policy Proposals for education or research projects should be submitted to Indie Choudhury (Projects Curator) at indie@iniva.org. Proposals should include details of the nature of the proposed project (e.g.talk, learning activity, research) and a brief synopsis (no more than one

page). If applicable, also include a statement on artist's practice (no more than one page), potential or identified collaborators, participants and audience, biographical information (no more than one page) and any supporting material (text, image, audio and/or visual).

Iveagh Bequest
Kenwood House, Hampstead Lane, London
NW3 7JR
T 020 84381286
F 020 76540172
W www.english-heritage.org.uk
Founded in 1827. The gift of Arthur Cecil Guinness to the nation. The grade I-listed Adam building contains Guinness's collection of masters, including works by Rembrandt, Vermeer, Gainsborough, Turner, Constable, Van Dyck and Reynolds.

Jewish Museum
Raymond Burton House, 129–131 Albert Street
London, NW1 7NB
T 020 72841997
F 020 72679008
E admin@jmus.org.uk
W www.jewishmuseum.org.uk
Founded in 1932 and moved to Camden Town location in 1995. The art collection includes Jewish ceremonial art and a collection of paintings, prints and drawings.

Leighton House Museum
12 Holland Park Road, London, W14 8LZ
T 020 76023316
F 020 73712467
E museums@rbkc.gov.uk
W www.rbkc.gov.uk/leightonhousemuseum
Former home of the eminent Victorian artist and president of the Royal Academy, Frederic, Lord Leighton. House includes a substantial collection of Leighton's work as well as important examples by his contemporaries including G.F. Watts, Edward Burne-Jones and Waterhouse. A temporary exhibition gallery is used for a programme of exhibitions exploring Victorian painting, design and architecture and Leighton's interest in the art of the Middle East. Work by contemporary artists is also shown.
Submission Policy Work exhibited by living artists exploring themes of 'East meets West' or by artists from the Middle East.

London Jewish Cultural Centre
Ivy House, 94–96 North End Road

London, NW11 7HU
T 020 84575000
F 020 84575024
E admin@ljcc.org.uk
W www.ljcc.org.uk
Hosts exhibitions as part of cultural and educational programmes aimed at a broad audience of Jews and non-Jews, encouraging inter-faith and inter-cultural dialogue and activities.
Talks/Events/Education Holds events on most Tuesdays and Thursdays (usually cost £5). Also runs mid-week courses.

London Print Studio Gallery
425 Harrow Road, London, W10 4RE
T 020 89693247
E info@londonprintstudio.org.uk
W www.londonprintstudio.org.uk
Promotes the graphic arts in both traditional and innovative media. Presents programmes of projects and exhibitions that reflect the cultural diversity of London.

Museum of Installation
175 Deptford High Street, London, SE8
T 020 86928778
E moi@dircon.co.uk
Provides a venue for the making, appraisal and discussion of major installation works (usually of a site-specific, time-based nature). Around four to five exhibitions per year at main venue.

National Gallery
Trafalgar Square, London, WC2N 5DN
T 020 77472885
F 020 77472423
E information@ng-london.org.uk
W www.nationalgallery.org.uk
In April 1824 the House of Commons agreed to pay £57,000 for the picture collection of the banker John Julius Angerstein and in 1831 decided to build a permanent home for the gallery in Trafalgar Square. The permanent collection spans the period from about 1250 to 1900 and consists of western European paintings. The entire permanent collection and long-term loans are illustrated and described in the collection online. Also hosts many exhibitions.

National Maritime Museum
Park Row, Greenwich, London, SE10 9NF
T 020 83126565
F 020 83126632
W www.nmm.ac.uk

Opened in 1937. A museum celebrating Britain's seagoing history. Includes an extensive collection of maritime art works.

National Portrait Gallery
St Martin's Place, London, WC2H 0HE
T 020 73122463
F 020 73060056
E jrowbotham@npg.org.uk
W www.npg.org.uk
Founded in 1856. The primary collection consists of over 10,500 portraits and constitutes a record of the people who have shaped the history and culture of the UK. Admission to the gallery is free, although an entry fee is charged for some special exhibitions.
Talks/Events/Education Every month the gallery offers a wide variety of talks and events. Most activities are free with no need to book.

The Orangery and Ice House Galleries
Holland Park, London, W8 6LU
T 020 7603 1123
F 020 7371 2467
E sally.dobinson@rbkc.gov.uk
W www.rbkc.gov.uk/theorangery and www.rbkc.gov.uk/theicehouse
Available for hire for public exhibitions of the visual and applied arts. The galleries are situated in the grounds of Holland Park.
Submission Policy Artists should submit six slides of work with a CV and details of any previous exhibitions. The gallery welcomes works from every discipline. Artists' work is approved by a selection panel, which sits annually during November. The Orangery Gallery costs about £550 for thirteen days and the Ice House Gallery roughly £650 for twenty days. Artists set up and take down their own exhibitions.

Photofusion
17a Electric Lane, Brixton, London, SW9 8LA
T 020 77385774
E info@photofusion.org
W www.photofusion.org
Founded in 1981. Aims to encourage all members of the community to use and enjoy its photographic facilities and to raise the profile of the photographic arts in London and the UK. Provides access to a full range of facilities including a contemporary gallery space, studio, digital imaging training, picture library, agency, darkrooms, and an ongoing education programme for professional, student and amateur photographers.

Submission Policy The gallery accepts proposals from photographers. The programme promotes diversity within the photographic arts reflecting on current cultural and political issues that have widespread relevance.
Talks/Events/Education An ongoing education programme includes basic to advanced technical courses on darkroom and digital practices and a professional development programme.

The Photographers' Gallery
5 & 8 Great Newport Street, London, WC2H 7HY
T 020 78311772
F 020 78369704
E info@photonet.org.uk
W www.photonet.org.uk
Founded in 1971. The first independent gallery in Britain devoted to photography. Has developed a reputation as the UK's primary venue for contemporary photography and was first in the country to show key names in world photography such as André Kertész, Jacques-Henri Lartigue and Irving Penn. Runs an integrated programme of exhibitions and educational events as well as an internationally renowned bookshop and print sales. Has recently acquired 16–18 Ramillies Street in London's Soho for future expansion of the gallery.
Submission Policy For exhibition submissions, visit the gallery website to download an application form and receive further information.
Talks/Events/Education Presents an ongoing programme of talks and events that offers access to ideas about photography to non-specialist and specialist audiences. Some events are free and others charged for.

PM Gallery and House
Walpole Park, Mattock Lane, Ealing
London, W5 5EQ
T 020 85671227
E pmgalleryandhouse@ealing.gov.uk
Comprises Pitshanger Manor (owned and designed by Sir John Soane) and an extension to the house, built in 1940. The largest art gallery in west London, hosting exhibitions of professional contemporary art, in all media. Includes a large collection of ceramics by the Martin Brothers produced between 1873 and 1923.

Pump House Gallery
Battersea Park, London, SW11 4NJ
T 020 73500523
F 020 7228 9062

E pumphouse@wandsworth.gov.uk
W www.wandsworth.gov.uk/gallery
A public contemporary-art space located in a Victorian listed building in Battersea Park. Offers a diverse and innovative year-round exhibition programme in four gallery spaces.
Talks/Events/Education Holds a range of talks and workshops for both artists and the general public. Call gallery for current information.

The Queen's Gallery
Buckingham Palace, London, SW1A 1AA
T 020 77667301
F 020 79309625
E press@royalcollection.org.uk
W www.royal.gov.uk
Reopened in 2002 to celebrate the Queen's Golden Jubilee, the gallery hosts a series of changing exhibitions of works of art from the Royal Collection.
Talks/Events/Education Private evening tours available for pre-booked groups (admission charged).

Royal Academy of Arts
Burlington House, Piccadilly, London, W1J 0BD
T 020 73008000
W www.royalacademy.org.uk
Founded in 1768. An independent fine arts institution that supports contemporary artists and promotes interest in the arts through a comprehensive exhibition programme.
Talks/Events/Education Designs events to help stimulate understanding and provide a focus for the interests of artists and art-lovers.

Royal College of Art
Kensington Gore, London, SW7 2EU
T 020 75904444
F 020 75904500
E info@rca.ac.uk
W www.rca.ac.uk
The world's only wholly postgraduate university of art and design. Displays a changing programme of student exhibitions and hosts external events, such as art fairs and prizes.
Talks/Events/Education Regular series of talks, lectures and symposia, regularly featuring leading figures from the art and design world. Many events are free.

Royal Institute of British Architects (RIBA) Gallery
66 Portland Place, London, W1B 1AD
T 020 75805533
F 020 73073703
E gallery@inst.riba.org
W www.riba-gallery.com
Promotes excellence in architecture through a programme of exhibitions, lectures, debates and outreach activities. Houses the RIBA collections of drawings and manuscripts and collections of paintings, models and photographs.
Submission Policy Work must be related to architecture. Submissions in writing.
Talks/Events/Education Three seasons per year of talks by architects and conferences, etc. All open to members of the public.

Saatchi Gallery
Duke of York's HQ, King's Road, London
T 020 79288195
W www.saatchi-gallery.co.uk
Based around the collection of Charles Saatchi, one of the UK's leading arts patrons. Aims to provide a forum for contemporary art, presenting work by largely unseen young artists or by established international artists whose work has rarely or never been exhibited in the UK. Due to open at its new Chelsea location in Nov. 2007.

Serpentine Gallery
Kensington Gardens, London, W2 3XA
T 020 74026075
F 020 74024103
E information@serpentinegallery.org
W www.serpentinegallery.org
A publicly funded modern- and contemporary-art gallery located in Kensington Gardens, in the heart of central London. The gallery has gained an international reputation for its exhibition, architecture and education programmes, and showcases both established artists and artists in the early stages of their career. Free admission.
Submission Policy Accepts exhibition proposals from artists and curators. Programming is decided by the Gallery Director and Chief Curator.
Talks/Events/Education Education programme consists of free public gallery talks, events, seminars, artist residencies and workshops that welcome artist participation.

Sir John Soane's Museum
13 Lincoln's Inn Fields, London, WC2A 3BP
T 020 74052107
F 020 78313957
E jbrock@soane.org.uk
W www.soane.org
Sir John Soane's (1753–1837) house, which became

a museum after his death. The collection includes paintings by Hogarth, Canaletto, Turner and Reynolds, antique sculpture, plaster casts, architectural models, and the sarcophagus of Pharaoh Seti I.
Talks/Events/Education Regular talks and courses throughout the year.

South London Gallery
65 Peckham Road, London, SE5 8UH
T 020 77036120
F 020 72524730
E mail@southlondongallery.org
W www.southlondongallery.org
Shows the work of mid-career British artists, and emerging and established international artists, in an annual programme of contemporary art exhibitions, live art and off-site projects complemented by workshops, events, residencies, artists' talks and outreach projects.
Talks/Events/Education Educational events and community projects are open to artists and general public. Further details can be found on website.

Stanley Picker Gallery
Faculty of Art, Design & Architecture
Kingston University, Knights Park
Kingston upon Thames, KT12QJ
T 020 8547 8074
E picker@kingston.ac.uk
W www.kingston.ac.uk/picker
Established in 1997, working with artists, designers and musicians to facilitate and provide access to a broad programme of exhibitions, collaborative projects, events and education initiatives. Also available for hire.

Tate Britain
Millbank, London, SW1T 4RG
T 020 78878008
E information@tate.org.uk
W www.tate.org.uk
Tells the story of British art from 1500 to the present day, through the largest collection of it in the world. Includes masterpieces from the Pre-Raphaelites, Turner, Gainsborough, Blake, Constable, Bacon, Hepworth and Gormley. Also holds six temporary exhibitions annually, focusing on the work of well-known British artists or movements.
Talks/Events/Education A wide range of events, courses, seminars and workshops, many of which are free.

Tate Modern
Bankside, London, SE1 9TG
T 020 78878888
W www.tate.org.uk
National museum of modern art, opened in the restored Bankside power station in 2000.

University College London (UCL) Art Collections
Strang Print Room, University College London, Gower Street, London, WC1E 6BT
T 020 76792540
F 020 78132803
E college.art@ucl.ac.uk
W www.art.museum.ucl.ac.uk
Founded in 1847 with the gift of John Flaxman's sculpture models to UCL, the collection includes sixteenth- to eighteenth-century Old Master prints and drawings from northern Europe, English watercolours, Japanese Ukiyo-E Prints and the Slade Collection of student prize works, which illustrates the history of the Slade School of Fine Art and includes works by Augustus John, William Orpen, Gwen John, Stanley Spencer, David Bomberg, Dora Carrington and Paula Rego.
Submission Policy Work by living artists is limited to works by artists who attended the Slade School of Fine Art.
Talks/Events/Education Two to four gallery talks and workshops per term, all free. Open to all groups or individuals wishing to work from the collection. Appointments may be booked.

Victoria & Albert Museum
Cromwell Road, London, SW7 2RL
T 020 79422000
E vanda@vam.ac.uk
W www.vam.ac.uk
One of the world's leading museums of art and design, with collections of great scope and diversity covering three thousand years of civilization.
Talks/Events/Education A wide range of events and activities for families, adults, older learners, students, teachers and young professionals complement the exhibitions and collections.

Wallace Collection
Hertford House, Manchester Square, London W1U 3BN
T 020 75639500
F 020 72242155
W www.wallacecollection.org
A national museum based around one of the finest private collections of art ever assembled by one family. It was bequeathed to the nation by Lady

Wallace, widow of Sir Richard Wallace, in 1897 and opened to the public in 1900. Among its holdings are an important collection of French eighteenth-century pictures, porcelain and furniture, and an extensive range of seventeenth-century paintings. **Talks/Events/Education** Produces a quarterly publication, *What's On*, detailing lectures, seminars and other events.

Wapping Project
Wapping Hydraulic Power Station, Wapping Wall London, E1W 3ST
T 020 76802080
W www.thewappingproject.com
Opened in 2000, a centre for the arts in east London, located in the historic Wapping Hydraulic Power Station. A multipurpose exhibition and performance space, featuring newly commissioned works by visual artists, choreographers, composers, writers, poets, designers and film-makers.

Wellcome Trust
215 Euston Road, London, NW1 2BE
T 020 76118888
F 020 76118545
E contact@wellcome.ac.uk
W www.wellcome.ac.uk
Organizes exhibitions on science and art in a range of exhibition initiatives including shows at the Science Museum, British Museum and TwoTen Gallery. A suite of permanent and temporary exhibition spaces is a major feature of the trust's new public facility, scheduled to open in 2007.
Talks/Events/Education Has collaborated with the Institute of Contemporary Arts on a series of public debates on science and its applications in broad contexts.

Whitechapel Gallery
80–82 Whitechapel High Street, London, E1 7QX
T 020 75227888
F 020 75227887
E info@whitechapel.org
W www.whitechapel.org
In the heart of east London for over a century. Has provided a platform for many of Britain's most significant artists, from Gilbert & George to Lucian Freud, Peter Doig to Mark Wallinger, as well as premiering key international artists such as Pablo Picasso, Frida Kahlo, Jackson Pollock, Mark Rothko and Nan Goldin. In addition to exhibitions, the gallery provides a platform for leading art practitioners, commentators and thinkers through

talks, debates and events. Also offers an education programme to cultivate a deeper appreciation of the creative process and of the work of modern and contemporary artists. With every exhibition, catalogues are produced and artists donate limited editions; proceeds go towards supporting the programmes.
Submission Policy Runs a yearly submission exhibition called the East End Academy, showcasing new work from emerging artists living and working in east London.

North-east

Ad Hoc Gallery
Buddle Arts Centre, 258b Station Road Wallsend, NE28 8RG
T 0191 2007132
F 0191 2007142
E the.buddle@northtyneside.gov.uk
W www.northtynesidearts.org.uk
Located within the Buddle Arts Centre and managed by North Tyneside Arts. The gallery's key objective is to promote and maintain a balanced programme that is accessible to audiences, supportive of artists, and provides opportunities for schools, community groups and the voluntary arts sector to exhibit in a dedicated contemporary gallery space.
Submission Policy Approximately six to ten exhibitions per year. Proposals are welcome from artists, curators and artists' groups at any time.

BALTIC Centre for Contemporary Art
South Shore Road, Gateshead
NE8 3BA
T 0191 4781810
E info@balticmill.com
W www.balticmill.com
Opened in 2002. A major international centre for contemporary art. The landmark building is situated on the south bank of the River Tyne in Gateshead. With no permanent collection, it provides a programme that places a heavy emphasis on commissions, invitations to artists and the work of artists-in-residence.
Submission Policy Programmed two years in advance. The majority of exhibitions and residencies arise from direct invitations to artists and curators. Rarely able to accommodate unsolicited submissions for exhibitions.
Talks/Events/Education Runs education and public programmes, and artists' workshops, talks and seminars. Most are free.

Berwick Gymnasium Art Gallery

Berwick Barracks, Berwick-upon-Tweed
TD15 1DG
T 01289 304493
Opened in 1993, the gallery has established itself
as a leading venue for contemporary art and artists
in the region. Details of current exhibitions are
available from English Heritage.

Billingham Art Gallery

Queensway, Billingham Town Centre, Billingham
Stockton-on-Tees, TS23 2LN
T 01642 397590
F 01642 397594
E billinghamartgallery@stockton.gov.uk
W www.stockton.gov.uk/citizenservices/
leisureandents/artandculture/artscentres
Exhibits work by local artists.
Talks/Events/Education Runs art classes and
workshops for adults.

Bowes Museum

Barnard Castle, Barnard Castle, DL12 8NP
T 01833 690606
F 01833 637163
E info@bowesmuseum.org.uk
W www.bowesmuseum.org.uk
Based on an extensive collection of European fine
and decorative arts of the period between 1400 and
1875, originally collected by John and Josephine
Bowes in the nineteenth century.
Submission Policy A limited number of artists'
works are represented in the museum's exhibition
programme. Applications can be made by post.
Talks/Events/Education Some events are free.

Customs House

Mill Dam, South Shields, NE33 1ES
T 0191 4541234
F 0191 4565979
E mail@customshouse.co.uk
W www.customshouse.co.uk
Shows contemporary visual art by local, regional,
national and international artists working in a
variety of art forms and styles, and working from
differing theoretical backgrounds. Artists are at
varying stages of their careers.
Submission Policy Submission guidelines are
available on the website.
Talks/Events/Education Free lectures, talks,
activities and workshops relating to artist's
exhibitions and projects currently shown.
Events held in gallery and as part of outreach
programme.

Durham Light Infantry Museum and Durham Art Gallery

Aykley Heads, Durham, DH1 5TU
T 0191 3842214
F 0191 3861770
E dli@durham.gov.uk
W www.durham.gov.uk/dli
Founded in 1968, the museum features displays
covering the history of the County Regiment, the
Durham Light Infantry. The art gallery provides a
changing programme of exhibitions related to all
aspects of the visual arts, linked to an ongoing
series of workshops, concerts and other events.
Submission Policy Applications are welcomed
from all fields of artistic activity.
Talks/Events/Education Most activities are aimed
at general and family audiences. More specific
events may be held depending on the current
exhibition.

Green Dragon Museum and Focus Photography Gallery

Theatre Yard, Calverts Lane, Stockton-on-Tees
TS18 1JZ
T 01642 527982
E greendragon@stockton.gov.uk
W www.stockton.gov.uk/museums
Located in the historic Georgian area of Stockton,
the building houses a local history and archive
photography gallery on the upper floor and the
Focus Gallery on the ground floor. The Focus
Gallery has a varied programme of photographic
displays throughout the year.
Submission Policy Artists may submit
photography or digital-art exhibition proposals
at any time. Contact the Exhibitions Coordinator
for details.
Talks/Events/Education Occasional free
photography-based events or talks.

Hatton Gallery

The Quadrangle, Newcastle University
Newcastle-upon-Tyne, NE1 7RU
T 0191 2226059
F 0191 2223454
E hatton-gallery@ncl.ac.uk
W www.ncl.ac.uk/hatton
Presents a programme of historical and
contemporary exhibitions. Over recent years this
programme has included major historical
monographs, diverse partnership projects and new
commissions from leading contemporary artists.
On permanent display is Kurt Schwitters'
Merzbarn, considered one of the seminal artworks

of the twentieth century. The permanent collection comprises over 3,500 works, ranging from the Renaissance to the twentieth century, and includes works in painting, sculpture, printmaking and drawing. Also runs a learning programme and has an active Friends group.

Submission Policy Unsolicited exhibition proposals will be considered by the programming team. However, the gallery normally initiates projects.

Talks/Events/Education Regularly holds talks and educational events for individuals, community groups and schools. Contact the gallery for further details.

Laing Art Gallery

Blandford Square, Newcastle-upon-Tyne, NE1 4JA
W www.twmuseums.org.uk/laing/
Founded in 1901. Houses an extensive collection of British oil paintings, watercolours, ceramics, silver and glassware. There is also an active temporary exhibition programme.

mima – Middlesbrough Institute of Modern Art

c/o Museums and Galleries, Regeneration,
1st Floor, Civic Centre, Middlesbrough, TS1 2YB
T 01642 729288
E mima@middlesbrough.gov.uk
W www.middlesbrough.gov.uk
A major new modern and contemporary art gallery that opened in 2006. Hosts an internationally important programme of exhibitions, presenting the very best of art and craft from 1900 to the present day. Exhibited artists are to include Ben Nicholson, David Bomberg, L.S. Lowry, Stanley Spencer, Gwen John, David Hockney and Bridget Riley.

Myles Meehan Gallery

Darlington Arts Centre, Vane Terrace, Darlington
DL3 7AX
T 01325 348845
F 01325 365794
E wendy.scott@darlington.gov.uk
W www.darlingtonarts.co.uk
Founded in 1983, supporting new and emerging innovative artists. Provides visitors with a balanced programme of media including installation and film, sculpture, painting, textiles and photography.

Submission Policy Welcomes innovative and contemporary exhibition applications with a focus on collaboration and experimentation.

Newcastle Arts Centre

67 Westgate Road, Newcastle-upon-Tyne
NE1 1SG

E venue@newcastle-arts-centre.co.uk
W www.newcastle-arts-centre.co.uk
Opened in 1988, the centre is only 100m from Newcastle Central Station and Metro. Underwent an extensive upgrade in 2000 to include a full-time gallery and art materials store. The gallery holds frequent exhibitions.

Northern Gallery for Contemporary Art

City Library and Arts Centre, Fawcett Street
Sunderland, SR1 1RE
T 0191 5141235
F 0191 5148444
E ngca@sunderland.gov.uk
W www.ngca.co.uk
Opened in 1995 as part of the Sunderland City Library and Arts Centre. Presents changing exhibitions of new work by emerging and established artists from the UK and abroad.

Submission Policy Artists wishing to apply should send six images, CV and artist's statement addressed to the Programme Director.

Talks/Events/Education Gallery talks accompany major exhibitions.

Shipley Art Gallery

Prince Consort Road, Gateshead
NE8 4JB
T 0191 4771495
W www.twmuseums.org.uk/shipley
Permanent collection includes studio ceramics, glass, metalwork, jewellery, textiles and furniture. Collection of historical paintings has examples of Dutch and Flemish Old Masters. Temporary programme of mainly craft-based exhibitions.

Talks/Events/Education Hosts a wide range of regular events and activities.

South Shields Museum and Art Gallery

Ocean Road, South Shields, NE33 2JA
T 0191 4568740
F 0191 4567850
W www.twmuseums.org.uk/southshields
Includes extensive collection of fine and applied art.

Sunderland Museum and Winter Gardens

Burdon Road, Sunderland
SR1 1PP
T 0191 5532323
F 0191 5537828
W www.twmuseums.org.uk/sunderland
Gallery houses works by by L.S. Lowry alongside an important collection of Victorian masterpieces.

Northern Ireland

Ards Arts Centre
Ards Town Hall, Conway Square, Newtownards
BT23 4NP
T 028 91810803
F 028 91823131
Presents varied monthly programme of visual arts,
primarily in two galleries in the town arts centre.
Covers range of media and styles, by local, national
and international artists.

Armagh County Museum
The Mall East, Armagh, BT61 9BE
T 028 37523070
F 028 37522631
E acm.um@nics.gov.uk
W www.armaghcountymuseum.org.uk
Two exhibition spaces regularly display the
museum's collection. Featured artists include
James Black, Tom Carr, William Conor, James
Humbert Craig, T.P. Flanagan, Charles Lamb,
John Luke, J.B. Vallely and G.W. Russell.

Belfast Exposed Photography
The Exchange Place, 23 Donegall Street, Belfast
BT1 2FF
T 028 90230965
F 028 90314343
E info@belfastexposed.org
W www.belfastexposed.org
A photographic resource, archive and Northern
Ireland's only dedicated photography gallery.
Through its annual programme of exhibitions and
the commissioning of new work, it aims to raise
the profile of photography as an art form. Active in
project origination, production of publications and
generation of discussion through seminars and
talks around projects.
Submission Policy Only exhibits and supports
photographic projects. There is no formal
application process. Project proposals, artist's
statement, examples of work, CVs etc. should be
submitted to the Exhibition Manager in a MAC-
compatible format. Work is looked at once a year in
January and applicants should receive a response
after this.
Talks/Events/Education Hosts a number of
workshops for both indviduals and facilitators.
Contact for further details.

Catalyst Arts
5 College Court, Belfast, BT1 6BS

T 028 90313303
F 028 90312737
E info@catalystarts.org
W www.catalystarts.org
A non-commercial artist-run gallery and resource
centre based in Belfast, which celebrated its tenth
anniversary in 2003. Aims to maintain, to the
highest possible standard, a Northern Irish centre
for contemporary arts. The organization is run by a
volunteer committee of artists who work there for
a two-year period on a rolling committee basis.

Fenderesky Gallery
2–4 University Road, Belfast, BT7 1NH
T 028 90235245
Occupies three areas of the Crescent Arts Centre,
with exhibitions of contemporary Irish artists.
Shows last up to four weeks.

Golden Thread Gallery
Brookfield Mill, 333 Crumlin Road, Belfast
BT14 7EA
T 028 90352333
E info@gtgallery.fsnet.co.uk
W www.gtgallery.fsnet.co.uk
Reconstituted in 2001. Aims to contribute to the
visual arts provision in Northern Ireland by
creating an accessible, high quality programme of
exhibitions, touring products, commercial
opportunities for artists and complimentary
education/outreach activities. Over the coming
years the Gallery will be realizing a series of
exhibitions and publications titled 'Collective
Histories of Northern Irish Art' alongside its
continued commitment to creating major curated
solo and group exhibitions by local and
international contemporary artists.
Submission Policy Runs a curated program of
activities and does not encourage submissions.
Talks/Events/Education Artists talks, gallery talks
and tours are free. Contact gallery for details.

Island Arts Centre
Lisburn, BT27 4RL
T 028 92509250
F 028 92509288
E enquiries@lisburn.gov.uk
An arts centre that includes an artist-in-residence
studio, artists' studios and exhibition galleries.

Naughton Gallery at Queens
Lanyon Building, Queens University
Belfast, BT7 1NN
T 028 90273580

E art@qub.ac.uk
W www.naughtongallery.org
Founded in 2001, holding Queens's fine-art collection, compiled since the mid-nineteenth century. Includes an extensive selection of landscapes, genre paintings and portraits as well as sculpture and silver. Irish artists include Sir John Lavery, William Conor, James Humbert Craig, Louis le Brocquy, Paul Henry, John Luke and Frank McKelvey. Queen's has an active and wide-ranging acquisitions and commissioning policy. Also provides a platform for local, national and international artists through a programme of temporary exhibitions across whole range of artistic practice.
Submission Policy Artists should submit work to the Curator of Art for presentation to the Art Board. Annual open art competition linked to area of academic endeavour and an annual residency.
Talks/Events/Education Regular free talks, lectures and artist's workshops.

Old Museum Arts Centre
7 College Square North, Belfast, BT1 6AR
T 028 90235053
F 028 90233332
W www.oldmuseumartscentre.org
Established in 1990, with a visual arts programme committed to presenting new and emerging as well as established visual artists from the UK, Ireland and beyond. Work is exhibited in a small white-box gallery space and exhibitions change on a six-weekly basis.
Submission Policy Exhibition is by invitation only. Proposals are welcome from interested artists.

Ormeau Baths Gallery
18a Ormeau Avenue, Belfast, BT2 8HS
T 028 90321402
F 028 90312232
E admin@obgonline.net
W www.obgonline.net
Opened in 1995, showing major exhibitions of work by contemporary artists of national and international standing.

Safehouse
25 Lower Donegall Street, Belfast
BT1 2FF
T 028 90314499
F 028 90319950
E info@safehouseartsspace.org
W www.safehousearts.org
Has a varied programme of contemporary

paintings, traditional paintings, drawings, sculpture and ceramics.

Ulster Museum
Botanic Gardens, Belfast, BT9 5AB
T 028 90383000
W www.ulstermuseum.org.uk
Home to the most important public holdings of art in Northern Ireland, collected since the 1880s. Includes collections of continental Old Masters and icons, seventeenth-, eighteenth-, and nineteenth-century British masters, twentieth-century British, European and American paintings, and Irish painting from the seventeenth century to the present. Also has sculpture by the likes of Henry Moore, Barbara Hepworth, F.E. McWilliam, Kenneth Armitage, Anthony Caro, Philip King, Barry Flanagan and Isamo Noguchi.

Waterfront Hall
2 Lanyon Place, Belfast, BT1 3WH
T 028 90334400
F 028 90249862
W www.waterfront.co.uk
A major arts and entertainment centre, with a regularly changing programme of exhibitions.

North-west

Abbot Hall Art Gallery
Kendal, Kendal, LA9 5AL
T 01539 722464
F 01539 722494
E info@abbothall.org.uk
W www.abbothall.org.uk
A small independent gallery with a reputation for showing important exhibitions of British artists. The permanent collection includes eighteenth-century portraits by George Romney and watercolours by Turner and Ruskin. The modern collection includes works by Ben Nicholson, Kurt Schwitters, Lucian Freud, Bridget Riley and Paula Rego.
Submission Policy Main gallery shows British art and artists. All media considered. Coffee shop has a focus on printmaking. Exhibition proposals considered by a curatorial panel.
Talks/Events/Education Hosts lectures, 'meet the artist' events and walking tours associated with the exhibitions programme (ticketed; admission charge applies).

Astley Hall Museum and Art Gallery
Astley Park, off Hallgate, Chorley, PR71NP
T 01257 515555

E astley.hall@chorley.gov.uk
W www.chorley.gov.uk
A grade-I listed, refashioned Elizabethan mansion
with a Renassiance-style great hall. The art gallery
hosts four temporary exhibitions each year.
Submission Policy Exhibition proposals welcome
from established and up-and-coming artists.
Talks/Events/Education Talks and courses held
throughout the year and educational visits (all
levels) welcomed.

Beacon Harbour Gallery Whitehaven

West Strand, Whitehaven, CA28 7LY
T 01946 592302
F 01946 598150
E thebeacon@copelandbc.gov.uk
W www.thebeacon-whitehaven.co.uk
Founded in 1996 on Whitehaven's harbourside,
home to the town's museum collection and art
gallery. Regular exhibitions change every six
weeks, featuring local and national artists using a
variety of mediums. Admission is free.
Submission Policy Artists in any medium are
welcome to submit exhibition proposals for
consideration by exhibition panel each autumn.
Talks/Events/Education School activity sessions
available and young people's craft workshops held
every school holiday.

Blackwell Arts & Crafts House

Bowness-on-Windermere, LA23 3JT
T 015394 46139
F 015394 88486
E info@blackwell.org.uk
W www.blackwell.org.uk
An Arts and Crafts Movement house dating from
1900. Blackwell was restored by the Lakeland Arts
Trust and opened to the public in 2001 as a
showcase for important Arts and Crafts furniture
and objects, and a platform for contemporary craft.
The growing collection includes important
examples of the arts and crafts, twentieth-century
and contemporary applied arts.
Submission Policy Send a CV and details, including
images, to Harvey Wilkinson (Curator). Exhibitions
are planned at least a year ahead. The shop and
selling exhibitions concentrate on contemporary
craft (e.g. jewellery, ceramics, glass, textiles).
Talks/Events/Education Evening lectures and
occasional workshops, which artists are welcome
to attend. 2005 lecture prices: £5 for students and
Friends, patrons and benefactors of the Lakeland
Arts Trust; £7.50 for non-members. Prices of
courses may vary.

Bluecoat Display Centre

Bluecoat Chambers, College Lane, Liverpool
L1 3BX
T 0151 7094014
F 0151 7078106
E crafts@bluecoatdisplaycentre.com
W www.bluecoatdisplaycentre.com
Founded in 1959 as a not-for-profit organization to
exhibit and retail the finest contemporary applied
art, including jewellery, ceramics and glass.
Submission Policy Artists working in
contemporary craft media should apply to
Maureen Bampton (Director) with images, CV,
supporting statement and price guide to the work
illustrated. A selection committee meets regularly
to consider new work.
Talks/Events/Education Occasional events; details
via mailing list or website.

Bolton Museum, Art Gallery and Aquarium

Le Mans Crescent, Bolton, BL1 1SE
T 01204 332211
F 01204 332241
E museum.customerservices@bolton.gov.uk
W www.boltonmuseums.org.uk
Bolton Museum, founded in the nineteenth century,
has collections ranging from fine and decorative art
to Egyptian archaeology. The art collections include
seventeenth- to twenty-first century works of art and
the Mass Observation Archive.
Submission Policy Exhibits living artists with
connections to Bolton and the north-west.
Talks/Events/Education Holds a range of events
that are usually free of charge. Contact the
museum for more details.

Bury Art Gallery, Museum and Archives

Moss Street, Bury, BL9 0DR
T 0161 2535878
F 0161 2535857
E artgallery@bury.gov.uk
W www.bury.gov.uk/arts
Opened in 1901, the art gallery houses an
internationally important collection of Victorian
paintings, including works by Turner, Constable and
Landseer. These pictures are hung alongside
twentieth-century works in a display called
'Contrasts'. The temporary exhibition programme is
driven by contemporary-art shows, showcasing both
international and up-and-coming artists. Recent
commissions include a neon installation in the Ring
Balcony by Maurizio Nannucci. The museum has
recently been transformed into a light, contemporary
exhibition space in a minimalist design.

Submission Policy Artists' applications for exhibitions should be addressed to the curator. Calls for submissions to themed exhibitions are advertised through a-n.

Talks/Events/Education Hosts talks, events, workshops, and family-friendly and adult learning activities relating to the building, exhibitions and collections.

Castlefield Gallery

2 Hewitt Street, Manchester, M15 4GB
T 0161 8328034
F 0161 8192295
E info@castlefieldgallery.co.uk
W www.castlefieldgallery.co.uk
Founded by Manchester's Artists Studio Association in 1984. The gallery presents six main exhibitions per year, focusing on new and commissioned work. Supports emergent practice through 'Project Space' residency, and artists' film and video through 'Purescreen' events consisting of an annual 'open call'-curated screening programme.

Submission Policy Welcomes exhibition proposals in any art form by artists and curators. Deadline is the last day of February each year, for programming twelve months in advance.

Talks/Events/Education Presents interpretive exhibition and professional-development talks and events. All events are free unless otherwise stated and require booking.

Chinese Arts Centre

Market Buildings, 7 Thomas Street, Manchester M4 1EU
T 0161 8327271
F 0161 8327513
E info@chinese-arts-centre.org
W www.chinese-arts-centre.org
Founded in 1986, the centre is the UK flagship for the promotion and interpretation of Chinese arts and culture. Initiatives include exhibitions of contemporary art by artists of Chinese descent, an education programme, an artist-in-residence scheme and surgeries offering advice on subjects ranging from 'How to write an exhibition proposal' to 'How to apply for funding'. The building houses a large main gallery, the smaller Breathe Gallery and a fully equipped education and conference suite.

Submission Policy To submit work for consideration for future exhibitions or residencies, contact the Exhibitions Co-ordinator or Curator for details and an application. Artists specializing in traditional Chinese arts who would like to be involved in the education programme should

contact the Participation Programme Manager.

Talks/Events/Education Regularly programmes artist-led exhibition events, family-friendly events, workshops and seminars. Browse the website or contact directly for further information about current activities and to book tickets

Cornerhouse

70 Oxford Street, Manchester, M1 5NH
T 0161 200 1500
E exhibitions@cornerhouse.org
W www.cornerhouse.org
Opened in 1985 as Manchester's centre for international contemporary art and film. Exhibitions and events bring together artists, critics, curators, filmmakers, educators and audiences to discuss contemporary culture. The programme of visual art, film and moving image aims to question currently accepted art and cultural practice.

Submission Policy Submissions from north-west based artists are considered for projects in the café and bar areas. Applicants should sent a proposal, CV and images (slide/CD-ROM).

Talks/Events/Education Runs a programme of events examining relevant issues within contemporary art including curators' talks, Q&As, discussions and live perfomances. Specifically curated events for artists, students and the public are regular and often free.

Dock Museum

North Road, Barrow-in-Furness, LA14 2PW
T 01229 894444
E dockmuseum@barrowbc.gov.uk
W www.dockmuseum.org.uk
Has a small fine-art gallery displaying a selection of works collected over the past hundred years. The gallery includes work by local artists William McDowell, Edward Beckett and John Duffin.

Folly

26 Castle Park, Lancaster, LA1 1YQ
T 01524 388550
F 01524 388550
E director@folly.co.uk
W www.folly.co.uk
Founded in 1982. A non-profit media arts organization that promotes photographic, video and new-media work. There is an annual members' exhibition.

Talks/Events/Education Events include summer courses, webstreaming, live events, video, audio and purescreen showings.

Foundation for Art and Creative Technology (FACT)

88 Wood Street, Liverpool, L1 4DQ
T 0151 7074450
F 0151 7074445
E info@fact.co.uk
W www.fact.co.uk
Opened in 2003 and dedicated to inspiring and promoting creativity through film, video and new and emerging media forms. It was the first cultural building to be purpose-built in Liverpool for sixty years. Combines state-of-the-art cinemas, galleries and flexible exhibition spaces.
Submission Policy Presents exisiting work and commissions new pieces from artists working in the field of new media. The exhibitions are programmed by the Exhibitions Department, which can be contacted on 0151 7074444.
Talks/Events/Education Regular talks and events open to the public linked to exhibitions and films at FACT.

Gallery Oldham

Oldham Cultural Quarter, Greaves Street, Oldham OL1 1AL
T 0161 770 4653
F 0161 770 4669
E galleryoldham@oldham.gov.uk
W www.galleryoldham.org.uk
The new building opened in 2002 and forms the first phase of Oldham's Cultural Quarter development. A changing exhibition programme incorporates extensive Art, Social History and Natural History collections alongside touring work, newly commissioned and contemporary art, international art and work produced with local communities.
Submission Policy Exhibition proposals should be sent to the Senior Exhibition and Collection Co-ordinator for consideration.
Talks/Events/Education Regular events include gallery talks, family activities and live music.

Grizedale Sculpture Park

Grizedale, Ambleside, LA22 0QJ
T 01229 860291
F 01229 860050
W www.grizedale.org
A major sculpture park, set in a dramatic Cumbrian setting.

Grosvenor Museum

27 Grosvenor Street, Chester, CH1 2DD
T 01244 402024
F 01244 347587
E p.boughton@chester.gov.uk
W www.grosvenormuseum.co.uk
Opened in 1886, with collections of archaeology, fine and decorative arts (including Chester silver), natural history and social history. Art shown is related to Cheshire or North Wales, illuminating artistic practice and patronage in the region since the sixteenth century. Also has a growing contemporary collection and a multidisciplinary exhibition programme.
Submission Policy Hosts a biennial open art exhibition. There are also a small number of solo and group shows each year by artists from Cheshire and North Wales.
Talks/Events/Education A full programme of public events including lectures, gallery tours, and art and craft workshops for children and adults. Some are free.

Harris Museum and Art Gallery

Market Square, Preston, PR1 2PP
T 01772 258248
F 01772 886764
E harris.museum@preston.gov.uk
W www.harrismuseum.org.uk
A grade I-listed building and an outstanding example of Greek Revival architecture. Opened in 1893, it houses a major collection of historical and contemporary painting and sculpture, including work by L.S. Lowry, Lucian Freud, Stanley Spencer, Walter Sickert, Jacob Epstein and J.W. Waterhouse. Decorative art includes ceramics, costume and glass. Also runs programme of temporary exhibitions including international contemporary art, historical art and local history.
Submission Policy Opportunities for a small number of professional artists to exhibit as part of the stairway exhibitions programme. Contact Exhibitions Assistant.
Talks/Events/Education A full programme of public events including lectures, gallery tours, and art and craft workshops for children and adults. Some are free.

Lady Lever Art Gallery

Port Sunlight Village, Wirral, CH62 5EQ
T 0151 4784136
E ladylever@liverpoolmuseums.org.uk
W www.ladyleverartgallery.org.uk
Home to the extensive personal collection of William Hesketh Lever, first Lord Leverhulme, an entrepreneur who made his fortune as founder of Lever Brothers. Holds a large collection of British

eighteenth- and nineteenth-century art, including Victorian and Pre-Raphaelite paintings by artists such as Leighton and Rossetti. Also exhibits a collection of the 'Sunlight Soap' paintings.
Talks/Events/Education Free talks and tours.

The Lowry
Pier 8, Salford Quays, Salford, M50 3AZ
T 0870 111 2020
F 0161 8762021
E info@thelowry.com
W www.thelowry.com
Centred around the L.S. Lowry Collection, with regularly changing displays encouraging visitors to take a fresh look at the artist. Other exhibitions place emphasis on the work of contemporary artists and photographers, and particularly on the locality and context of The Lowry. These shows often complement the Lowry Collection.
Submission Policy Welcomes applications. Submit proposals to the Exhibitions Programmer.

Manchester Art Gallery
Mosley Street, Manchester, M2 3JL
T 0161 2358888
F 0161 2358899
E t.wilcox@manchester.gov.uk
W www.manchestergalleries.org
Houses an extensive art collection with a varied programme of special exhibitions and events. Particularly strong collection of nineteenth- and twentieth-century British paintings in both oil and watercolour. Featured artists include Henry Moore, Paul Nash, Ben Nicholson, Francis Bacon, Lucien Freud and David Hockney. Also important collections of Impressionist and seventeenth-century Dutch paintings, and decorative art, craft and design.

Ruskin Gallery
Ruskin Museum, Coniston, LA21 8DU
T 015394 41164
W www.ruskinmuseum.com
Gallery contains works by John Ruskin, J.M.W. Turner and W.G. Collingwood.

Saddleworth Museum
High Street, Uppermill, Oldham, OL3 6HS
T 01457 874093
F 01457 870336
E curator@saddleworthmuseum.co.uk
W www.saddleworthmuseum.co.uk
Opened in 1962 and housed in a Victorian Mill. Exhibitions change every six weeks and showcase

the best local and regional contemporary art. Email for gallery information pack.

Salford Museum and Art Gallery
Peel Park, Crescent, Salford, M5 4WU
T 0161 7362649
F 0161 7459490
E salford.museum@salford.gov.uk
W www.salford.gov.uk
Houses an extensive collection of paintings, pottery and fine art.

Sudley House
Mossley Hill Road, Liverpool, L18 8BX
T 0151 7243245
E sudleyhouse@liverpoolmuseums.org.uk
W www.sudleyhouse.org.uk
Situated in Mossley Hill, the house belonged to Victorian ship-owner George Holt, whose extensive art collection is exhibited. Highlights include works by Landseer, Turner, Millais, Romney, Reynolds, Gainsborough, Benjamin Spence and Conrad Dressler. Was scheduled to re-open in 2007 following a refurbishment.

Tate Liverpool
Albert Dock, Liverpool, L3 4BB
T 0151 7027400
F 0151 7027401
E liverpoolinfo@tate.org.uk
W www.tate.org.uk/liverpool
Opened in 1988, displaying modern and contemporary art from 1900 to the present day.
Submission Policy Send a covering letter, CV and visuals to the Exhibitions Department at Tate Liverpool.
Talks/Events/Education A programme of free introductory tours, exhibition talks and lectures. Also special events around exhibitions and displays.

Tullie House Museum and Art Gallery
Castle Street, Carlisle, CA3 8TP
T 01228 534781 ext.246
F 01228 810249
E enquiries@tulliehouse.co.uk
W www.tulliehouse.co.uk
Established since 1893, owned and managed by Carlisle City Council. Significant collections of fine and decorative arts, human history and natural sciences. Underwent redevelopment in 1990, which included building the Border Galleries and a purpose-built art gallery. The latter hosts a changing programme of primarily contemporary-art exhibitions of regional, national and

international significance.
Submission Policy Artists' proposals should be submitted in the form of an exhibition outline, CV(s) and a selection of good-quality images.
Talks/Events/Education Presents a wide range of events and activities, from free drop-ins to workshops and illustrated talks.

Turnpike Gallery
Civic Square, Market St, Leigh, WN7 1EB
T 01942 404469
F 01942 404447
E turnpikegallery@wlct.org
W www.wlct.org/turnpike
Built in 1971. The only purpose-built public gallery in the borough of Wigan. Presents around six to eight exhibitions per year, including new commissions, solo, group, community and touring shows, reflecting contemporary visual arts practice by artists with a local, regional or national profile. The gallery has a commitment to developing learning and outreach opportunities for the local community.
Submission Policy Artists are welcome to submit exhibition proposals to the gallery, but only a very few such proposals will make up part of the programme.
Talks/Events/Education Talks associated with exhibitions and other educational/training events for artists are usually free, and arranged on an occasional basis.

University of Liverpool Art Gallery
3 Abercromby Square, Liverpool, L69 7WY
T 0151 7942348
F 0151 7942343
E artgall@liv.ac.uk
W www.liv.ac.uk/artgall/
Fine and decorative art from the university collections, displayed in an elegant Georgian house. Includes works by Turner, Wright of Derby, Burne-Jones, Augustus John, Epstein, Freud and Frink.
Submission Policy Apply in writing to the Curator.
Talks/Events/Education Talks and events advertised on website. Free of charge.

Viewpoint Photography Gallery
The Old Fire Station, The Crescent, Salford, M6
T 0161 7371040
Has a programme of regularly changing photography exhibitions.

Walker Art Gallery
William Brown Street, Liverpool, L3 8EL

T 0151 4784199
E stephen.guy@liverpoolmuseums.org.uk
W www.thewalker.org.uk
Founded in 1877 and popularly regarded as the National Gallery of the north. Exhibits an internationally important collection of art from the fourteenth- to the twenty-first centuries. Especially rich in European Old Masters, Victorian and Pre-Raphaelite pictures and modern British works.
Talks/Events/Education Extensive free talks and educational events open to all. Often themed on exhibitions or particular art works.

Whitworth Art Gallery
University of Manchester, Oxford Road Manchester, M15 6ER
T 0161 2757450
F 0161 2757451
E whitworth@manchester.ac.uk
W www.manchester.ac.uk/whitworth
Founded in 1889, the gallery has been part of the university since 1958. Houses important collections of watercolours, prints, drawings, modern art and sculpture, as well as the largest collections of textiles and wallpapers outside London.
Submission Policy Gallery exhibition policy available on website.
Talks/Events/Education Education Department organizes a full programme of activities for formal and informal learning. Special events and talks are available from time to time.

Wordsworth Trust
Dove Cottage, Grasmere, Cumbria, LA22 9SH
T 01539435544
F 01539435748
E enquiries@wordsworth.org.uk
W www.wordsworth.org.uk
Established in 1891, the Wordsworth Trust cares for the only designated (of international and national significance) collection in Cumbria. Exhibitions are held year round in both the Wordsworth Museum and the contemporary art gallery. Also runs a prestigious residencies programme. Past residents include Conrad Atkinson, Judith Dean, Kate Davis and Daniel Sturgis. The manuscripts and books collection is regarded as the greatest poetry library of the Romantic period in Britain. The fine-art collection includes paintings by John Constable, David Cox, J.M.W. Turner, Joseph Wright of Derby, James Gillray, Sir Joshua Reynolds and an extensive collection of landscape drawings.
Submission Policy Write to the Arts Officer with

covering letter, CV and samples of work.
Talks/Events/Education There is a yearly
programme of events that can be checked on
www.wordsworth.org.uk.

Scotland

Aberdeen Art Gallery
Schoolhill, Aberdeen, AB10 1FQ
T 01224 523700
F 01224 632133
E info@aagm.co.uk
W www.aberdeencity.gov.uk
Houses an important fine-art collection with
particularly good examples of nineteenth-,
twentieth- and twenty-first century works and a
diverse applied art collection. Hosts a programme
of special exhibitions.
Submission Policy Submissions should be sent to
Jason Williamson (Exhibitions Officer) at the above
address. To discuss proposals prior to submisson,
phone 01224 523713.

An Tuireann Arts Centre
Ross Memorial Building, Struan Road, Portree
Isle of Skye, IV51 9EG
T 01478 613306
F 01479 613156
E info@antuireann.org.uk
W www.antuireann.org.uk
Established since 1989. A public space with two
galleries. An Tuireann is an arts development
organization and a creative hub. It provides a high
quality venue and outreach opportunities for
artists, audiences, and participants to increase
public understanding of contemporary visual arts
practise of international, national, and local
significance.
Submission Policy Welcomes applications from all
disciplines. Supply high-quality images on CD,
transparency or photo with CV and statement. No
deadline.
Talks/Events/Education Many artist-led courses
are available. 1–2 day courses vary in price from
free to £100. Check website for details.

Burrell Collection
Pollok Country Park, 2060 Pollokshaws Road
Glasgow, G43 1AT
T 0141 2872550
F 0141 2872597
E museums@cls.glasgow.gov.uk
W www.glasgowmuseums.com
Major collections include medieval art, tapestries,

alabasters, stained glass, English oak furniture,
European paintings by Degas and Cézanne,
Islamic art, and modern sculpture by Epstein and
Rodin. Also has collection of works from ancient
China, Egypt, Greece and Rome.
Submission Policy Exhibition proposals
considered at monthly meetings of Exhibitions
Committee. Email museums@cls.glasgow.gov.uk
in the first instance.
Talks/Events/Education Ongoing events
programme, mostly free.

Centre for Contemporary Arts (CCA)
350 Sauchiehall Street, Glasgow, G2 3JD
T 0141 3524900
F 0141 3323226
E gen@cca-glasgow.com
W www.cca-glasgow.com
Six flexible arts spaces presenting the best in
contemporary visual art, film, music,
performance, etc.
Talks/Events/Education 'CCA:Participate' includes
events for adults and children as well as special
seminars for artists and practitioners, providing a
platform for discussion, learning and sharing
experience of the contemporary arts.

The Changing Room
35 The Arcade, King Street, Stirling, FK8 1AX
T 01786 479361
F 01786 479361
E info@changingroom.sol.co.uk
W www.stirling.gov.uk/changingroom
Established in 1997 to support the development of
contemporary visual art in Scotland. Hosts a year-
round programme of exhibitions, events and
projects.
Submission Policy Takes exhibition proposals at an
annual deadline. Artists can submit material for
the artist directory at any time.
Talks/Events/Education Regular talks with artists,
ranging from recent graduates to the well-known,
local to international. Holds an annual
professional-development and networking event,
as well as events and classes open to anyone.

City Art Centre (CAC)
2 Market Street, Edinburgh, EH1 1DE
T 0131 5293993
F 0131 5293977
E enquiries@city-art-centre.demon.uk
W www.cac.org.uk
Founded in 1980, the CAC is home to a large
range of Edinburgh's fine-art collections.

Temporary exhibits in the past have ranged from Star Wars to the Glasgow Boys, the Titanic to Cecil Beaton.
Submission Policy Submissions from artists welcome.
Talks/Events/Education Occasional events (prices vary).

Collective Gallery

22–28 Cockburn Street, Edinburgh, EH1 1NY
T 0131 2201260
E mail@collectivegallery.net
W www.collectivegallery.net
Originally established as an artist-run space in 1984, the Collective has developed into an independent, publicly funded exhibition, commissioning and development agency. Aims to support emergent Scottish contemporary art and artists within the context of an international programme.
Submission Policy There are two deadlines a year for submitting applications – contact the gallery for details.
Talks/Events/Education Organizes regular talks and events for all exhibitions.

Crawford Arts Centre

93 North Street, St Andrews, KY16 9AD
T 01334 474610
F 01334 479880
W www.crawfordarts.free-online.co.uk
Founded in 1977 and run by a charitable company since 1988. A programme of mostly contemporary visual art and craft is shown throughout the year.
Submission Policy Professional artists should send visuals, CV and info. (NB: the centre's structure changed in 2006 and is affecting programming in the short term.)
Talks/Events/Education Talks and exhibition tours held several times per year (mostly free); open to all. Art classes (e.g. life drawing) held in autumn and winter (not free).

Dean Gallery

73 Belford Road, Edinburgh, EH4 3DS
T 0131 6246200
F 0131 3432802
E deaninfo@nationalgalleries.org
W www.nationalgalleries.org
An art centre situated in parkland opposite the Scottish National Gallery of Modern Art. Opened in 1999, it provides a home for the Eduardo Paolozzi gift of sculpture and graphic art, including a reconstruction of Paolozzi's studio. Also houses the Scottish National Gallery of Modern Art's renowned Dada and Surrealist collections, one of the best collections of Surrealist art in the world. Contains a library and archive, and a gallery fitted out as a library for the display of artists' books. Shows temporary exhibitions on a regular basis. In the grounds are sculptures by Bourdelle, Rickey, Hamilton Finlay, Paolozzi and Turnbull.
Talks/Events/Education Various talks, events and lectures throughout the year. Contact the gallery for further information.

Dick Institute

Dean Castle Country Park, Dean Road
Kilmarnock, KA3 1XB
T 01563 522702
F 01563 573333
W www.east-ayrshire.gov.uk/comser/ arts_museums/joint_di_page.asp
Opened in 1901. Two art galleries and three museum galleries house permanent and temporary displays of fine and contemporary art and craft.

Duff House Country House Gallery

Banff, AB45 3SX
T 01261 818181
F 01261 818900
E duff.house@aberdeenshire.gov.uk
W www.duffhouse.com
Duff House was designed by William Adam and built between 1735 and 1740 for the Earls Fife. It now houses a permanent collection, including furniture, tapestries, and Old Masters by artists such as Sir Henry Raeburn, El Greco and François Boucher. Regular visiting exhibitions are held.

Dundee Contemporary Arts

152 Nethergate, Dundee, DD1 4DY
T 01382 909900
F 01382 909221
E dca@dca.org.uk
W www.dca.org.uk
An internationally renowned centre for the arts, opened in 1999. Houses five floors of cinemas, galleries, artists' facilities, education resources and the University of Dundee Visual Research Centre.

Fruitmarket Gallery

45 Market Street, Edinburgh, EH1 1DF
T 0131 2252383
F 0131 2203130
E info@fruitmarket.co.uk
W www.fruitmarket.co.uk

Established in 1984 as an independent public gallery. Committed to exhibiting contemporary art made by established and emerging international and Scottish artists. Major recent exhibitions include Ellen Gallagher, Fred Tomaselli and Louise Bourgeois in 2004, Hiroshi Sugimoto in 2002 and Shirin Neshat in 2000. Exhibitions emphasize new work as part of a consistent and developing artistic practice, and seek to engage new and existing audiences through an integrated education, interpretation and publishing programme.
Submission Policy Submissions made directly to the Gallery Director. The gallery programme is subject to fourteen months' lead time.
Talks/Events/Education Free gallery tours and artist's talk for each exhibition. Workshops for adults, young people and small children for a small fee.

Gallery of Modern Art
Royal Exchange Square, Glasgow, G1 3AH
T 0141 2291996
F 0141 2045316
E museums@cls.glasgow.gov.uk
W www.glasgowmuseums.com
Opened in 1996. Housed in an elegant Neoclassical building in the heart of Glasgow city centre. Refurbished to hold the city's contemporary-art collection, the building is an appealing combination of old and new architecture, incorporating a number of artists' commissions. Displays work by local and international artists as well as addressing contemporary social issues through major bi-annual projects.
Submission Policy Exhibition proposals are considered at monthly meetings of Exhibitions Committee. Email museums@cls.glasgow.gov.uk in the first instance.
Talks/Events/Education Ongoing events programme, mostly free.

Hunterian Art Gallery
82 Hillhead Street, University of Glasgow
Glasgow, G12 8QQ
T 0141 3305431
F 0141 3303618
E hunter@museum.gla.ac.uk
W www.hunterian.gla.ac.uk
In 1783 William Hunter bequeathed his substantial and varied collections to the University of Glasgow and the museum was opened to the public in 1807. In 1870 the Hunterian collections were transferred to the university's present site. The art collection is now housed separately. There are five collections:

Mackintosh House, Glasgow Boys, Mackintosh Collection, Scottish Colourists and the Whistler Collection.

Inverleith House
The Royal Botanic Garden, Edinburgh, EH3 5LR
T 0131 2482983
F 0131 2482901
E ihouse@rbge.org.uk
W www.rbge.org.uk
A Georgian mansion set within the 73-acre landscaped grounds of the Royal Botanic Garden Edinburgh. Runs a programme of solo exhibitions (by invitation only) on three floors of naturally-lit rooms. Internationally-based artists have included Carl Andre, Roni Horn, Agnes Martin, Ed Ruscha, Robert Ryman, Cy Twombly, Lawrence Weiner and Franz West. Scottish artists include Ian Hamilton Finlay, Douglas Gordon, Jim Lambie, Lucy McKenzie and Richard Wright. A purpose-built room runs a programme of exhibitions resulting from education projects with children and adults who might otherwise be denied normal access to the visual arts, including those with visual impairments.
Talks/Events/Education Talks and workshops accompany most exhibitions.

Kelvingrove Art Gallery and Museum
Argyle Street, Glasgow, G3 8AG
T 0141 2769599
W www.glasgowmuseums.com
Opened in 1901 and reopened in summer 2006 after a three-year restoration project. Large fine- and applied-art collections, including several major European works as well as natural history, ethnography, and arms and armour.
Submission Policy All exhibition proposals are considered by an exhibition committee that meets monthly. In the first instance email museums@cls.glasgow.gov.uk.

Kirkcaldy Museum and Art Gallery
War Memorial Gardens, Kirkcaldy
KY1 1YG
T 01592 412860
F 01592 412870
E Kirkcaldy.museum@fife.gov.uk
W www.fifedirect.org.uk/museums
Founded in 1925, housing a collection of fine and decorative arts of local and national importance. Holds an outstanding collection of eighteenth- to twentieth-century Scottish paintings, including large bodies of work by William McTaggart and Scottish Colourist S.J. Peploe. Also has three

galleries showing a changing programme of temporary exhibitions.

Submission Policy Applications should be in writing to the Exhibitions Officer.

Talks/Events/Education Occasional talks and workshops, advertised in the local press.

The Lighthouse

Scotland's Centre for Architecture, Design and the City, 11 Mitchell Lane, Glasgow, G1 3NU

T 0141 2216362
F 0141 2216395
E enquiries@thelighthouse.co.uk

The building comprises 1,400m2 of exhibition space. Shows fifteen to twenty exhibitions per year, many of international calibre. Also contains a Charles Rennie Mackintosh interpretation centre and a dedicated education floor, including workshop, computer laboratory, gallery space and an innovative project called the Urban Learning Space.

McLellan Galleries

270 Sauchiehall Street, Glasgow, G2 3EH

T 0141 5654137
F 0141 5654111
E museums@cls.glasgow.gov.uk
W www.glasgowmuseums.com

Built in 1856. The galleries were ravaged by fire in the 1980s but reopened in 1990 following a £3m restoration, when it was the largest high-quality, air-conditioned, temporary exhibition space outside of London. NB: The gallery is currently closed. See website for further information.

Mount Stuart

Isle of Bute, PA20 9LR

T 01700 503877
F 01700 505313
E contactus@mountstuart.com
W www.mountstuart.com

Opened to the public in 1995. Aims to promote public interest in contemporary visual arts by bringing exhibitions of an international standard to Bute and Argyll.

Talks/Events/Education The programme for each exhibition includes artists' talks and school and adult workshops. Free of charge.

Museum of Scotland

Chambers Street, Edinburgh, EH1 1JF

T 0131 2474422
F 0131 2204819
E info@nms.ac.uk
W www.nms.ac.uk/scotland

The museum presents the history of Scotland through collections ranging from everyday objects to some of Scotland's most precious treasures.

Talks/Events/Education Regular educational events for families.

National Gallery Of Scotland

The Mound, Edinburgh, EH2 2EL

T 0131 624 6200
F 0131 220 0917
E nginfo@nationalgalleries.org
W www.nationalgalleries.org

Home to Scotland's greatest collection of European paintings and sculpture from the Renaissance to Post-Impressionism. The collection of watercolours, prints and drawings features some twenty thousand items and is particularly rich in Italian and Netherlandish drawings. Also has a comprehensive collection of Scottish art, representing all the major names including Ramsay, Raeburn, McTaggart and Wilkie. The Playfair Project recently extended and upgraded the gallery's site on the Mound to incorporate the newly refurbished Royal Scottish Academy Building, which hosts a series of exhibitions all year round, and the Weston Link, which is connected by means of a modern underground visitor facility including a state-of-the-art education centre and lecture theatre.

Talks/Events/Education Various talks, events and lectures throughout the year. Contact the gallery for further information.

National War Museum

Edinburgh Castle, Edinburgh, EH1 2NG

T 0131 2474413
F 0131 2253848
E info@nms.ac.uk
W www.nms@ac.uk/war

Collections of paintings, prints, ceramics and glass illustrating everything from world-changing events to the everyday lives of Scottish servicemen.

Peacock Visual Arts

21 Castle Street, off the Castlegate, Aberdeen AB11 5BQ

T 01224 639539
F 01224 627094
E info@peacockvisualarts.co.uk
W www.peacockvisualarts.co.uk

A contemporary visual arts organization supported by Aberdeen City Council and the Scottish Arts Council. Established in 1974 as a printmaking workshop, the facility has developed into a centre

for the promotion of art and visual media.
Submission Policy All submissions for projects
and proposals welcome. Contact Monika Vykonkal
(Curator) in the first instance at
monika@peacockvisualarts.co.uk.
Talks/Events/Education Frequent talks,
educational events and courses throughout the
year. Admission is free.

The Queen's Gallery, Palace of Holyroodhouse
The Palace of Holyroodhouse, Edinburgh
EH8 8DX
T 0131 5565100
F 020 79309625
E press@royalcollection.org.uk
W www.royal.gov.uk
Opened in 2002 to celebrate the Queen's Golden
Jubilee, the gallery hosts a series of changing
exhibitions of works of art (predominantly works
on paper) from the Royal Collection.
Talks/Events/Education Private evening tours
available for pre-booked groups (admission
charged).

Royal Museum
Chambers Street, Edinburgh
EH1 1JF
T 0131 2474422
F 0131 2204819
E info@nms.ac.uk
W www.nms.ac.uk/royal
Covers life, the universe and beyond with
international collections of decorative arts,
science and industry, archeology and the natural
world.
Talks/Events/Education Regular educational
events for adults and families, plus a series of
evening lectures and concerts.

Royal Scottish Academy Building
The Mound, Edinburgh, EH2 2EL
T 0131 6246200
F 0131 6237126
E enquiries@nationalgalleries.org
W www.nationalgalleries.org
Designed by architect William Henry Playfair at
the junction of Princes Street and the Mound. Has
undergone refurbishment by the National
Galleries of Scotland and offers nearly 1,500m2 of
international exhibition space, housed in eleven
galleries.
Talks/Events/Education A range of free public
events is created to appeal to as many people as
possible.

Scottish National Gallery of Modern Art
75 Belford Road, Edinburgh, EH4 3DR
T 0131 6246200
F 0131 6237126
E enquiries@nationalgalleries.org
W www.nationalgalleries.org
Opened in 1960, with a small number of twentieth-
century works from the National Gallery of
Scotland. Now comprises more than five thousand
items, ranging from the late nineteenth century to
the present and encompassing a wide variety of
media, from paintings, bronzes and works on
paper, to kinetic sculpture and video installations.
Talks/Events/Education A range of free public
events.

Scottish National Portrait Gallery
1 Queen Street, Edinburgh, EH2 1JD
T 0131 6246200
F 0131 5583691
E pginfo@nationalgalleries.org
W www.nationalgalleries.org
Situated in the heart of the New Town on Queen
Street. Provides a unique visual history of
Scotland, told through portraits of the figures who
shaped it. Includes work not only by Scottish
artists but by great English, European and
American masters such as Van Dyck,
Gainsborough, Rodin and Kokoschka. Also
displays sculptures, miniatures, coins, medallions,
drawings and watercolours. The Scottish National
Photography Collection is also based at the gallery.
Talks/Events/Education Various talks, events and
lectures held throughout the year.

St Mungo Museum of Religious Life and Art
2 Castle Street, Glasgow, G4 0RH
T 0141 5532557
F 0141 5524744
E museums@cls.glasgow.gov.uk
W www.glasgowmuseums.com
Opened in April 1993. The aim of the museum is
to promote understanding and respect between
people of different faiths and none. Displays
occupy three floors and are divided into four
exhibition areas: the Gallery of Religious Art, the
Gallery of Religious Life, the Scottish Gallery and a
temporary exhibition space.
Submission Policy All exhibition proposals are
considered by an exhibition committee that meets
monthly. In the first instance email
museums@cls.glasgow.gov.uk.
Talks/Events/Education Ongoing events
programme, mostly free.

Talbot Rice Gallery
University of Edinburgh, Old College
South Bridge, Edinburgh, EH8 9YL
T 0131 6502211
F 0131 6502213
E info.talbotrice@ed.ac.uk
W www.trg.ed.ac.uk
Established in 1975, the public gallery of the
University of Edinburgh. Presenting major
contemporary exhibitions in the White Gallery,
showing a variety of painting, sculpture, drawing
and installation along with the round room
programme, a unique architectural space showing
small installations and experimental projects. The
University's fine-art collections are on display in
the Georgian Gallery. Admission to all galleries
and events is free.
Talks/Events/Education Has a broad educational
remit, offering a programme of regular tours,
lectures, seminars and artists' talks accompanying
each exhibition (free to the public).

Timespan
Dunrobin Street, Helmsdale, Sutherland, KW8 6JX
T 01431 821327
F 01431 821058
E enquiries@timespan.org.uk
W www.timespan.org.uk
A museum and gallery with changing exhibitions
of contemporary art.

Transmission
45 King Street, Glasgow, G1 5QP
T 0141 5527141
F 0141 5521577
E info@transmissiongallery.org
W www.transmissiongallery.org
An artist-run space set up in 1983 by graduates
from Glasgow School of Art who were dissatisfied
with the lack of exhibition spaces and opportunities
for young artists in Glasgow. Through support from
the Scottish Arts Council, they manage and
maintain a space in which to exhibit their work and
that of local artists and invited artists working
nationally and internationally.
Talks/Events/Education Maintains an image bank
of slides, which are made available to visiting
curators and artists.

Verdant Works
West Henderson's Wynd, Dundee, DD1 5BT
T 01382 225282
F 01382 221612
E admin@dundeeheritage.co.uk

W www.verdantworks.com
A museum of Dundee's textile industries
(primarily focused on jute), opened in 1996 and
housed in a nineteenth-century mill building.
Submission Policy The Exhibitions Director
assesses all potential exhibitions for quality and
suitability. Two- and three-dimensional material
can be shown. Booked up a year in advance.

South-east

ArtSway
Station Road, Sway, SO41 6BA
T 01590 682260
F 01590 681989
E mail@artsway.org.uk
W www.artsway.org.uk
Established in 1997, ArtSway is a contemporary
visual arts venue deep in the New Forest. In
addition to a programme of high-quality
contemporary art exhibitions of international
significance, the gallery also hosts artists-in-
residence and offers professional development and
production facilities for artists. The white cube
galleries were designed by architect Tony Fretton.
Submission Policy See website for information
on residency opportunities and deadlines
for the ArtSway open exhibition held annually
in December and January. Submission by
proposal are welcomed but opportunities are
very limited.
Talks/Events/Education Offers free gallery talks
throughout the year by artists and staff.
A comprehensive range of workshops and
short-courses are offered throughout the
year including regular life-drawing sessions
and holiday workshops. ArtSway also develops
specific workshops and courses for various
groups including children, young people and those
who are normally excluded from engaging in
creativity.

Ashmolean Museum
Beaumont Street, Oxford, OX1 2PH
T 01865 278000
F 01865 278018
W www.ashmol.ox.ac.uk
Founded in 1683, the Ashmolean is one of the
oldest museums in the world. The collection
includes everything from Chinese watercolours to
Renaissance drawings and Picasso paintings.
Submission Policy For artist submissions, send
information to Dr Christopher Brown (Director
of the Ashmolean).

Talks/Events/Education Presents study days, lectures and talks. All groups must book. Telephone 01865 278015 for further information.

Aspex Gallery
27 Brougham Road, Southsea, Portsmouth
PO5 4PA
T 023 92812121
F 023 92812121
E info@aspex.org.uk
W www.aspex.org.uk
Exists to provide the people of Portsmouth and the locality plus visitors with some of the most innovative contemporary visual arts locally, nationally, and internationally. The exhibitions policy is to show work of high quality that reveals the full potential of the artist or artists chosen. In the main it has concentrated on younger artists who are in the possession of a body of work that has not been seen in public (or in the region). Access Aspex, a small exhibition and project space, focuses on the work of artists based in Portsmouth and the south-east region. This space is suited to small-scale work or that of an experimental nature.
Submission Policy Proposals from artists and curators are welcomed. See the background section on the website.
Talks/Events/Education Programme of free artist's talks alongside each exhibition. Aspex Artists' Resource Centre (ARC) provides information, guidance and support for artists.

Brighton Museum and Art Gallery
Royal Pavilion Gardens, Brighton, BN1 1EE
T 01273 290900
F 01273 292871
E museums@brighton-hove.gov.uk
W www.virtualmuseum.info
Following a £10m redevelopment in 2002, the gallery has become one of the most visited museums in the south-east. Includes nationally important collections of twentieth-century art and design, fashion, paintings, ceramics and world art.
Talks/Events/Education Runs programme of special events, talks and courses.

Buckinghamshire Art Gallery
Buckinghamshire County Museum, Church Street, Aylesbury, HP20 2QP
T 01296 331441
F 01296 334884
E museumwebsiteenquiries@buckscc.gov.uk
W www.buckscc.gov.uk/museum/index.stm
Housed in a fifteenth-century building refurbished

in 1995, the gallery has a permanent collection. Up to five exhibitions, ranging across a variety of art forms and subjects, are held annually.
Talks/Events/Education Hosts various events, activities and gallery talks.

Cass Sculpture Foundation
Sculpture Park, Goodwood, Chichester, PO18 0QP
T 01243 538449
F 01243 531853
E info@sculpture.org.uk
W www.sculpture.org.uk
Focusing on twenty-first century British sculpture, the park consists of twenty-six acres of woodland in an area of outstanding natural beauty, containing over sixty large-scale sculptures by Britain's leading artists. The foundation was established in 1994 as a charity and aims to empower sculptors (both young and established) to take their careers to a new level.

Charleston Farmhouse and Gallery
The Charleston Trust, Firle, Lewes, BN8 6LL
T 01323 811626
F 01323 811628
E info@charleston.org.uk
W www.charleston.org.uk
Founded in 1981 to conserve Charleston Farmhouse, a unique example of the decorative art and bohemian ideals of the Bloomsbury artists Vanessa Bell and Duncan Grant. Open to visitors and stages workshops and events.
Submission Policy The gallery is open to established artists in all media (applications close 30 September for the following season; contact c.baron@charleston.org.uk). Free to exhibit. Twenty per cent commission taken.
Talks/Events/Education Welcomes applications by artists to lead workshops for children and young people. Work should use Charleston as the inspiration. In addition, there is a full annual programme of special events, lectures and creative workshops open to all.

Christ Church Picture Gallery
Christ Church, St Aldates, Oxford, OX1 1DP
T 01865 276172
F 01865 202429
E picturegallery@chch.ox.ac.uk
W www.christ-church.ox.ac.uk
Houses an internationally important collection of Old Master paintings, drawings and prints in a listed modern building. Especially known for its holdings of Italian art, dating from the early

Renaissance to the eighteenth century. Among its highlights are paintings by Filipino Lippi, Veronese, Tintoretto, Annibale Carracci and Salvator Rosa, together with drawings by Leonardo, Michelangelo and Raphael. Also possesses a small number of works by renowned northern European artists, including Van Dyck, Rubens, Frans Hals and Hugo Van der Goes. The gallery holds regular exhibitions of its Old Master drawings and shows by local living artists.
Submission Policy Artists should consider what will fit into the gallery and exhibition programme. Send illustrative material, CV and covering letter. No hire charge. Twenty-five per cent commission.
Talks/Events/Education Free guided tours every Thursday at 2.15 p.m. Special talks relating to current exhibitions or the collection held from time to time.

Crafts Study Centre
University College for the Creative Arts at Farnham, Falkner Road, Farnham, GU9 7DS
T 01252 891450
F 01252 891451
E craftscentre@ucreative.ac.uk
W www.csc.ucreative.ac.uk
Established in 1970. Located at the front of the Farnham campus of the University College for the Creative Arts in Surrey, it is the first purpose-built museum and research facility for modern and contemporary crafts. Two galleries feature free exhibitions and a research room/library is available for booking by individual researchers and groups by appointment. Annual exhibitions in the ground floor Tanner Gallery show items from the Centre's collections and archives including ceramics, textiles, calligraphy, wood and metalwork. Today's makers feature in new exhibitions held every three months in the first floor gallery.
Submission Policy Programme is selected up to two years in advance. Proposals from contemporary craft practitioners should be made in writing to the Director.
Talks/Events/Education Gallery Talks featuring contemporary artist-makers and curator's are held to accompany most exhibitons. For details visit the 'Events' page on the website.

De La Warr Pavilion
Marina, Bexhill on Sea, TN40 1DP
T 01424 787949
F 01424 787940
E sally.ann.lycett@dlwp.com
W www.dlwp.com

Built in 1935, this grade I-listed Modernist building is a leading centre for contemporary art, architecture and live performance.
Submission Policy Contact Celia Davies (Head of Exhibitions) at celia.davies@dlwp.com.
Talks/Events/Education Talks are a major part of the programme.

Ditchling Museum
Church Lane, Ditchling, BN6 8TB
T 01273 844744
E info@ditchling-museum.com
W www.ditchling-museum.com
Home to the artists Eric Gill, Edward Johnston and Frank Brangwyn in the twentieth century. Gill founded the artists' community of St Joseph and St Dominic, which included artists, letterers, weavers and silversmiths. Much of their work and that of other artists drawn to the area is represented in the collection. The museum has a temporary exhibition space and holds three or four exhibitions per year.
Submission Policy Open to written submissions only. The museum cannot return images, etc. and will only be able to respond to artists that it feels may be suitable to exhibit.
Talks/Events/Education Talks and events throughout the year.

Eastleigh Museum
25 High Street, Eastleigh, SO50 5LF
T 023 80643026
F 023 80653582
E gill.budden@hants.gov.uk
W www.hants.gov.uk/museum/eastlmus
Holds regularly changing special exhibitions, which include art, crafts, photography, local and natural history. National and regional touring exhibitions shown, as well as the work of local artists, societies and collectors.
Talks/Events/Education Talks accompany some exhibitions. Admission is free.

Foyer Gallery and James Hockey Gallery
University College for the Creative Arts, Falkner Road, Farnham, GU9 7DS
T 01252 892646 / 892668
F 01252 892667
W www.ucreative.ac.uk
Established in 1998 and 1969 respectively, the Foyer Gallery and James Hockey Gallery are public exhibition spaces showing a wide range of work, including art, craft, design and lens-based media. They aim to present work of lasting and

educational importance. Respect for professional practice remains vital.

Submission Policy The exhibitions programme focuses on contemporary work. Application procedures are available from the Galleries Office.

Talks/Events/Education Workshops and public events are associated with most exhibitions and open to an inclusive audience of professionals, amateurs and general visitors.

Gardner Arts Centre

University of Sussex Campus, Falmer, Brighton BN1 9RA
T 01273 685447
F 01273 678551
E info@gardnerarts.co.uk
W www.gardnerarts.co.uk

Based on the campus of the University of Sussex and housed in an eccentric grade II-listed building designed by Sir Basil Spence, the Gardner Arts Centre was opened in 1969 as the first university campus arts centre. It has a 480-seat purpose-built theatre, a visual-art gallery and studio space, and runs a programme of exhibitions of modern art.

Talks/Events/Education An extensive range of art classes and workshops is offered. To request an education resource guide, contact Gardner Education on 01273 685447 or go to the website.

Guildford House Gallery

155 High Street, Guildford, GU1 3AJ
T 01483 444742
F 01483 444742
E guildfordhouse@guildford.gov.uk
W www.guildfordhouse.co.uk

Home of Guildford Borough's art collection since 1959. Has a varied programme of temporary exhibitions including local groups, touring exhibitions and the Guildford Borough's own art collection.

Submission Policy Artists must be connected to Guildford or Surrey. The waiting list is approximately two years.

Talks/Events/Education A programme of free talks, workshops and tours accompanies the exhibition programme.

Herbert Read Gallery

University College for the Creative Arts, New Dover Road, Canterbury, CT1 3AN
T 01227 817364
E bferrell@ucreative.ac.uk
W www.ucreative.ac.uk

Featuring the work of international artists and designers, programmed to compliment the work of students and teaching staff. Fully open to the public.

HMAG (Hastings Museum and Art Gallery)

Johns Place, Bohemia Road, Hastings, TN34 1ET
T 0845 2741052
F 01424 451165
E museum@hastings.gov.uk
W www.hmag.org.uk

Houses historical and cultural displays, a local studies room and an art gallery, with collections of fine and applied art. The gallery focuses on contemporary visual art, with occasional art history exhibitions. There are 4–5 exhibitions in each year's programme.

Submission Policy Artists should submit exhibition proposals in writing (with illustrations of their work) to the Exhibitions Officer.

Talks/Events/Education Workshops and talks are arranged with each exhibition. These are usually free but on occasion may have a nominal fee.

Hove Museum and Art Gallery

19 New Church Road, Hove, BN3 4AB
T 01273 290200
E museums@brighton-hove.gov.uk
W www.virtualmuseum.info

Houses permanent collections of toys, film, local history, paintings and contemporary craft. Underwent major redevelopment in 2003. Hosts temporary exhibitions of varying forms of art (paintings, photography, craft, etc.).

Submission Policy Contact the Exhibitions Office for more details on 01273 292852.

Talks/Events/Education Runs a programme of events, talks and courses.

Jelly Leg'd Chicken

The Town Hall, Blagrave Street, Reading, RG1 1QH
T 0118 9507926
F 0118 9507936
E babes@jelly.org.uk
W www.jelly.org.uk

Opened in Reading Town Hall in 2004 after five years in Reading's Oracle Shopping Centre. Set up in 1993 to exhibit quirky, innovative and enduring art. Has worked across many art forms including drawing, sculpture, mosaic, painting, jewellery, ceramics, textiles, architectural drawing, mixed media, printmaking, masks and digital animation.

Submission Policy Artists are welcome to apply by email to curator@jelly.org.uk.

Talks/Events/Education Offers workshops, gallery

visits, a database of tutors, training, consultancy and a mentoring scheme. For details contact Morag Scally or Marje Doyle on 0118 9507926, or by email at education@jelly.org.uk.

John Hansard Gallery
University of Southampton, Highfield
Southampton, SO17 1BJ
T 023 80592158
F 023 80594192
E info@hansardgallery.org.uk
W www.hansardgallery.org.uk
Submission Policy The gallery does not represent artists. The selection process is made at the discretion of the Director and Exhibitions Officer.
Talks/Events/Education Presents a wide programme of talks, symposia and conferences, tours and workshops. Talks are free and normally accompany each new show. For symposia and conferences, a fee is charged.

Manor House Gallery
Chipping Norton, OX7 5LH
T 01608 642620
E luigi@manorhousegallery.co.uk
W www.manorhousegallery.co.uk
Shows oils and watercolours by contemporary British painters.

Metropole Galleries
The Leas, Folkestone, CT20 2LS
T 01303 244706
F 01303 851353
E info@metropole.org.uk
W www.metropole.org.uk
Founded in 1960. Has hosted a broad range of exhibitions over the years. Current priorities are to present contemporary art with meaning and resonance for the locale and physical space. In most cases the galleries work with artists to devise exhibitions. Has a strong education and audience development programme.
Submission Policy Artists should send details about themselves, their work and what they would like to produce for the Metropole. Applicants are advised to visit the gallery in advance as the space is rather unusual.
Talks/Events/Education Hosts occasional talks, discussions, etc.

Millais Gallery
Southampton Solent University, East Park Terrace,
Southampton, SO14 0YN
T 023 80319916
F 023 80334161
E millais.gallery@solent.ac.uk
W www.millais.solent.ac.uk
A city-centre public art gallery committed to the exhibition of mainly contemporary visual arts that address issues of relevance to culturally diverse communities locally, regionally and nationally. The programme of exhibitions and events complements the work of staff and students in art, design and media.
Submission Policy Artists may submit proposals to the Curator.
Talks/Events/Education Public talks during each exhibition. All are welcome and admission is free.

Milton Keynes Gallery
900 Midsummer Boulevard
Central Milton Keynes, MK9 3QA
T 01908 676900
F 01908 558308
E info@mk-g.org
W www.mk-g.org
Opened in 1999, Milton Keynes Gallery presents around six free exhibitions of contemporary art per year from around the world. Aims to stimulate participation and debate, building relationships between artists and audiences. It has three inter-connected strands: gallery exhibitions, off-site projects in and around the city, and education events aimed at interpreting and generating critical debate about the practice of contemporary artists and their relationship with their audience.
Talks/Events/Education Series of 'In Conversation' events with artists and critics and free lectures on related programme.

Modern Art Oxford
30 Pembroke Street, Oxford, OX1 1BP
T 01865 722733
F 01865 722573
E info@modernartoxford.org.uk
W www.modernartoxford.org.uk
Established in 1965, a leading public gallery. Working with artists from around the world to enable audiences and communities to participate in and engage with contemporary art. Admission to the gallery and all exhibitions is free.
Talks/Events/Education During exhibitions, gallery runs workshops for families, students, teachers and schools. Artist talks and free exhibition tours are open to all. Booking is essential for workshops, courses and artist talks and entry is subject to availability. Some events are subject to ticket prices, for which concessions are often available.

Open Hand Open Space
571 Oxford Road, Reading, RG30 1HL
T 0118 9597752
E info@ohos.org.uk
W www.ohos.org.uk
Artist-run studios and public gallery, established over twenty-four years ago by former Reading University MA students to provide arts and artists' provisions for the local area (while showing international shows). Previous members include Cornelia Parker and Paul Bonaventura.
Submission Policy Members' applications should include a CV and slides. The gallery welcomes detailed proposals for shows by artists, which are then presented to a programming committee that declares whether suitable by group vote.
Talks/Events/Education All events are free. Hosts numerous artists' talks, seminars and visiting artists throughout the year, usually corresponding to the current exhibit.

Pallant House Gallery
9 North Pallant, Chichester, PO19 1TJ
T 01243 774557
F 01243 536038
E info@pallant.org.uk
W www.pallant.org.uk
The Gallery of Modern Art in the South, located in a Queen Anne townhouse and a contemporary building holding a major collection of twentieth-century British art. Extensive exhibition programme includes international touring exhibitions and print room shows. The collection includes important works by, among others, Auerbach, Blake, Bomberg, Caulfield, Freud, Goldsworthy, Hamilton, Hodgkin, Langlands and Bell, Moore, Nicholson, Paolozzi, Piper, Sickert and Sutherland.
Talks/Events/Education Talks and educational events throughout the year.

Parham House
Parham Park, Storrington, Pulborough, RH20 4HS
T 01903 742021
F 01903 746557
E enquiries@parhaminsussex.co.uk
W www.parhaminsussex.co.uk
Opened to visitors in 1948. An important collection of paintings by artists such as Gainsborough, Lely, Barlow, Stubbs, Badmin, Muncaster, Devis, Castro, Lutterhuys, Peake, Wootton and Zoffany. Shown in light panelled rooms of Elizabethan house. Open from Easter to September on Wednesdays, Thursdays, Sundays and Bank Holiday Mondays, as well as Tuesdays and Fridays in August.
Submission Policy Does not show any living artists.

Pitt Rivers Museum
South Parks Road, Oxford, OX1 3PP
T 01865 270927
F 01865 270943
E prm@prm.ox.ac.uk
W www.prm.ox.ac.uk
Founded in 1884 when General Pitt Rivers gave 18,000 objects to the university, the museum now houses over 500,000 objects from around the world and across time. Collections include textiles and looms, Benin brasses and ivories, masks, sculpture, jewellery and ceramics.
Submission Policy Welcomes submissions by 1 October each year for its occasional programme of exhibitions and installations relating to the collections (and developed in collaboration with curatorial staff).
Talks/Events/Education A changing programme of activities and events are listed on the website.

Portsmouth City Museum and Records Office
Museum Road, Portsmouth, PO1 2LJ
T 023 9282 7261
F 023 9287 5276
E Christopher.Spendlove@portsmouthcc.gov.uk
W www.portsmouthmuseums.co.uk
The museum's main display is 'The Story of Portsmouth'. It also features a fine- and decorative-art gallery, and a temporary exhibition gallery with regular changing exhibitions. Among the most important exhibits are collections of seventeenth-century furniture, Art Deco furniture, Frank Dobson sculptures, Ceri Richards relief work and paintings by Turner and Ronald Ossory Dunlop.

Quay Arts
Ser Street, Newport Harbour, Newport, PO30 5BD
T 01983 822490
F 01983 526606
E info@quayarts.org
W www.quayarts.org
Founded in 1979. Has three gallery spaces showing work by international, national and local artists. Also has seven artists' studios for hire.
Submission Policy Submit images of work to Jo Johnson (Exhibitions Organizer) at j.johnson@quayarts.org.
Talks/Events/Education Has a full programme of talks and courses for artists of all levels. Some are

free. In July and August there is a summer school for artists.

Rochester Art Gallery
95 High Street, Rochester, ME1 1LX
T 01634 338319
E arts@medway.gov.uk
Holds regularly changing exhibitions of fine art and photography.

Russell-Cotes Art Gallery and Museum
East Cliff, Bournemouth, BH1 3AA
T 01202 451858
F 01202 451851
E russell-cotes@bournemouth.gov.uk
Home to three permanent collections: art, Japan and sculpture.

Sidney Cooper Gallery
St Peter's Street, Canterbury, CT1 2B Q
T 01227 453267
E gallery@canterbury.ac.uk
W www.canterbury.ac.uk
Founded in 2004 by Canterbury Christ Church University College, the gallery shows contemporary work by local, national and international artists. Aims to show the process of making art, supported by lectures and a public programme.
Submission Policy Welcomes portfolio-backed submissions from artists in all media. Yearly programme decided by November. Exclusive university use from mid-June to mid-September.
Talks/Events/Education Each exhibition is supported by free lectures, workshops and sometimes concerts.

Southampton City Art Gallery
Civic Centre, Commercial Road, Southampton SO14 7LP
T 023 80832277
F 023 80832153
E art.gallery@southampton.gov.uk
W www.southampton.gov.uk/leisure/arts/art%2Dgallery
Collection comprises 3,500 works, with the earliest being Allegretto Nuzzi's fourteenth-century altarpiece. Also includes seventeenth-century Dutch landscapes and French Impressionist paintings. The modern-art holdings include works by Sir Stanley Spencer, Philip Wilson Steer, Tony Cragg, Richard Long, Shirazeh Houshiary, Antony Gormley, Michael Craig-Martin and Chris Ofili.
Talks/Events/Education Workshops for children and adults and also gallery talks.

St Barbe Museum and Art Gallery
New Street, Lymington, SO41 9BH
T 01590 676969
F 01590 679997
E office@stbarbe-museum.org.uk
W www.stbarbe-museum.org.uk
Opened in 1999, with art works related to the local area.

Stanley Spencer Gallery
The Kings Hall, High Street, Cookham SL6 9SJ
T 01628 471885
E info@stanleyspencer.org.uk
W www.stanleyspencer.org.uk
Opened in 1962, devoted exclusively to Spencer's work and life. The gallery has recently undergone extensive refurbishment.

Towner Art Gallery
High Street, Old Town, Eastbourne BN20 8BB
T 01323 417961
F 01323 648182
E townergallery@eastbourne.gov.uk
W www.eastbourne.gov.uk
A local-authority art gallery founded in 1923. The permanent fine-art collection holds in excess of four thousand works by artists including Eric Ravilious, Christopher Wood and Alfred Wallis. Has a lively temporary (contemporary) exhibitions programme. Relocated to a new purpose-built facility.
Submission Policy Welcomes exhibition proposals from living artists, addressed for the attention of the Curator.
Talks/Events/Education Talks accompany some temporary exhibitions, changing approximately every six to eight weeks (some are free). Often held on Thursday evenings or Saturday afternoons.

Trinity Gallery
Trinity Theatre, Church Road, Tunbridge Wells, TN1 7JP
T 01892 678670
F 01892 678680
E info@trinitytheatre.net
W www.trinitytheatre.net
Founded in 1977, the gallery runs a programme aimed at showing diverse contemporary art.
Submission Policy Contact the gallery for an application form. Can only accommodate work that can hang on the wall. Exhibitions are generally monthly.

Tunbridge Wells Museum and Art Gallery

Civic Centre, Mount Pleasant, Tunbridge Wells
TN1 1JN
T 01892 554171
F 01892 554131
E museum@tunbridgewells.gov.uk
W www.tunbridgewellsmuseum.org
Gallery space is used for six exhibitions a year,
ranging from the work of local artists and
craftspeople to selections from the Museum's
collection, and from exhibitions created by artists
working in residence with local community groups
to national touring exhibitions. Major art
collections held by the Museum include the
Ashton Bequest of Victorian Oil paintings, early
photographs by Henry Peach Robinson and work
by Charles Tattershall Dodd.
Submission Policy Artists are selected for the
following year by a bi-annual exhibitions panel.
Talks/Events/Education Various educational
workshops and events are held with specific
exhibitions. There is usually something every two
months. Anyone is welcome to attend and the
events are free.

University of Brighton Gallery

Grand Parade, Brighton, BN2 0JY
T 01273 643010
F 01273 643038
E g.wilson@brighton.ac.uk
W www.brighton.ac.uk/gallery-theatre/
Housed within the university's Faculty of Arts and
Architecture and curated by the Centre for
Contemporary Visual Arts. Holds between eight
to twelve exhibitions per year, including the
university's own student shows, touring
exhibitions, shows by leading contemporary artists
and installations.
Submission Policy Only exhibits contemporary
collections. Proposals are welcomed from
interested artists or groups.
Talks/Events/Education The university has a
number of full- and part-time courses, plus talks
and lectures open to the public.

Waddesdon Manor

Waddesdon, nr Aylesbury, HP18 0JH
T 01296 653211/226
E vicky.darby@nationaltrust.org.uk
W www.waddesdon.org.uk
Waddesdon Manor was built between 1874 and
1889 by Baron Ferdinand de Rothschild to display
his collection of art treasures and entertain the
fashionable world. Contains textiles and decorative

arts from the eighteenth century, important
examples of English portraiture, several Dutch Old
Masters and a fine collection of Sevres porcelain.
Talks/Events/Education Many public events are
organized each season, details of which are
available on the website or in a diary of events. The
events focus on the exhibitions of the year or on
items in the collection that are of particular note
like the Sevres or furniture.

Winchester Gallery

Winchester School of Art, Park Avenue,
Winchester, SO23 8DL
T 01962 852500
E WING@soton.ac.uk
W WING.org.UK and fotonet.org.UK
Offers a programme of contemporary visual art,
craft, photography and new media along with
Winchester School of Art Degree Exhibitions. Also
holds off-site exhibitions in venues up and down
the country which don't usually have exhibitions.
Runs strong educational programme involving
contemporary artists. The Gallery is amalgamated
with Fotonet, a photography and new media
website offering on line exhibitions, international
symposia and portfolio days.

Windsor & Royal Borough Museum (W&RBM)

Windsor Library, Bachelors Acre, Windsor
SL4 1ER
T 01628 796829
F 01628 796121
E museum.collections@rbwm.gov.uk
W www.rbwm.gov.uk/web/museum_index.htm
Small local history collection which achieved
registered museum status in 2002. Aims to make
the history of the borough accessible to residents
and visitors. The collection includes 6,000 objects
including prehistoric tools, Roman and Saxon
artefacts, maps, textiles, paintings, objects and
ephemera from before Victorian times to the
1950s. Currently without a dedicated exhibition
space, small displays are housed in Windsor
Library and other borough venues. Museum Store
open by appointment. Loans boxes of artefacts for
use in schools are administered from Reading
Museum Service (T 0118 9399800).
Submission Policy No space to show living artists.
Talks/Events/Education Friends of W&RBM have
an annual calendar of historical talks and visits.
Talks cost approximately £2 each. (T 01753 774642)

Worthing Museum and Art Gallery

Chapel Road, Worthing, BN11 1HP

T 01903 221150
F 01903 236277
E museum@worthing.gov.uk
W www.worthing.gov.uk/Leisure/
MuseumArtGallery
Collections include British works (by artists
including Hitchens, Pissarro and Hunt), European
works (by artists including Roerich, Hobbema and
Wynants) and a piece from the School of Bassano.
Works by local artists are also represented. There is
a small sculpture collection and decorative arts and
textiles. The Studio was opened in the early 1990s
as a temporary exhibition space for the museum's
collections as well as invited artists and groups.

South-west

Arnolfini
16 Narrow Quay, Bristol, BS1 4QA
T 0117 9172300
F 0117 9172303
E info@arnolfini.org.uk
W www.arnolfini.org.uk
Created in 1961. An internationally renowned
contemporary arts centre situated in Bristol's
vibrant harbourside, presenting new, innovative
work in visual arts, performance, dance, film,
literature and music. Closed for a major
refurbishment in autumn 2003 and reopened in
summer 2005 with upgraded and extended
facilities. Open seven days a week, with free
admission to the building, exhibitions and café-bar.
Submission Policy For further information,
contact the Exhibitions Department.
Talks/Events/Education Education programme
includes talks, tours, workshops and events.

The Art Gym
Petherton Road, Hengrove, Bristol
BS14 9BU
T 0117 3772800 ext.268
F 0117 3772807
E rfitzger@hengrove.bristol.sch.uk
W www.theartgym.co.uk
Purpose-built in 2002, a non-commercial gallery
space hosting exhibitions from contemporary
artists working in all media. Ongoing exhibition
programme shows established, international
artists, emerging contemporary artists, and
individual curatorial projects. Based in the
grounds of Hengrove Community Arts College.
Submission Policy The gallery accepts proposals
from artists and curators. Contact the Art College
Manager for a submission pack. Artists and

curators are advised to consider the context of the
space when developing a proposal.
Talks/Events/Education Ongoing programme of
educational activities and workshops. For full
details contact the Gallery Manager on 0117
3772800 ext.268.

Barbara Hepworth Museum and Sculpture Garden
Barnoon Hill, St Ives, TR26 1AD
T 01736 796226
W www.tate.org.uk/stives/hepworth.htm
Run by the Tate since 1980 and now an integral
part of Tate St Ives. Hepworth, who died in 1975,
asked in her will that Trewyn Studios and the
adjacent garden, with a group of her sculptures
placed as she wished, be permanently open to the
public.

Bristol's City Museum and Art Gallery
Queens Road, Bristol, BS8 1RL
T 0117 9223571
F 0117 9222047
E general_museum@bristol-city.gov.uk
W www.bristol-city.gov.uk/museums
Contains several galleries of fine and applied art,
including works from the Bristol School, Old
Masters, and British works from the seventeenth
to the twentieth centuries. Houses important
collections of Eastern art, largely Chinese and
Japanese, and has an ever-changing programme
of temporary exhibitions and a public events
programme.
Talks/Events/Education Programme of events
includes talks which are free and open to anyone.

Burton Art Gallery and Museum
Kingsley Road, Bideford
EX39 2QQ
T 01237 471455
F 01237 473813
E burtonartgallery@torridge.gov.uk
W www.burtonartgallery.co.uk
Founded in 1951 with a core collection of English
watercolours and ceramics. Rebuilt in 1993 and
extended to three gallery spaces, a craft gallery and
a local museum. Shows about twenty visiting
exhibitions a year, ranging from national touring
shows to mixed exhibitions and the work of
individual artists.
Submission Policy Interested in all kinds of art and
craft, with a leaning towards accessible art.
Talks/Events/Education Hosts artists' talks and
workshops.

Cheltenham Art Gallery & Museum

Clarence Street, Cheltenham, GL50 3JT
T 01242 237431
F 01242 262334
E ArtGallery@cheltenham.gov.uk
W www.cheltenham.artgallery.museum
Houses a major collection relating to the Arts
and Crafts Movement including furniture and
metalwork made by Cotswold craftsmen, inspired
by William Morris. Additional collections include
rare Chinese and English pottery, four hundred
years of painting by Dutch and British artists, and
the story of Edward Wilson, Cheltenham's
Antarctic explorer. Special exhibitions are held
throughout the year and the museum also has a
shop and café
Submission Policy Artists should write in with a
CV and photos or slides of their work. Artists
should have some connection with Cheltenham,
the Cotswolds or Gloucestershire.
Talks/Events/Education Workshops, talks and
events held at various times throughout the year.

Design Collection Museum

Arts Institute at Bournemouth, Fern Barrow,
Wallisdown, Poole, BH12 5HH
T 01202 533011
F 01202 537729
E designcollection@aic.ac.uk
W www.aic.ac.uk
Founded in 1988. Became a registered museum in
2001. A study and research resource that facilitates
an understanding and appreciation of
international mass-produced popular design and
culture of the twentieth- and twenty-first centuries.
Diverse yet cohesive collections consist of
approximately 7,500 items which relate directly to
the academic courses and specialist areas of study
offered at the Institute. Organized into key
collection categories that identify specific object
types (e.g. electrical, product design, fashion,
printed ephemera, plastics, packaging, etc.).
Submission Policy The collection comprises
examples of mass-produced twentieth- and twenty-
first-century design only.

Dorset County Museum

High West Street, Dorchester, DT1 1XA
T 01305 262735
F 01305 257180
E dorsetcountymuseum@dor-mus.demon.co.uk
W www.dorsetcountymuseum.org
Founded in 1846. Has a diverse art collection,
including works by Gainsborough, Sir James

Thornhill, Alfred Wallis, Christopher Wood and
several thousand watercolours by Henry Joseph
Moule, a prolific nineteenth-century Dorset
watercolourist. Only a small proportion of the
museum's several thousand engravings, oil
paintings and watercolours are on show. However,
the museum has a policy to show this work as part
of its temporary exhibition programme and it is
possible to make an appointment to see items that
are not on display.
Submission Policy All media accepted for the
regular temporary exhibitions programme.
Proposals submitted to a selection committee,
which meets five times a year. Thirty per cent
commission.

Fox Talbot Museum

High Street, Lacock, nr Chippenham
SN15 2LG
T 01249 730176
W www.nationaltrust.org.uk
Commemorates the life and work of William
Henry Fox Talbot (1800–1877), who in 1835
discovered the negative-positive photographic
process. The museum is located inside a medieval
barn at the entrance to Lacock Abbey, with the
upper gallery hosting two to three annual
exhibitions showing work by contemporary and
nineteenth-century photographers.

The Gallery

Lighthouse, Poole's Centre for the Arts, Kingland
Road, Poole, BH15 1UG
T 08700 668701
F 08700 668076
E oliviah@lighthousepoole.co.uk
W www.lighthousepoole.co.uk
Reopened in 2002 following major refurbishment.
Part of the largest arts centre outside London, the
gallery is programmed in partnership with The
Study Gallery of Modern Art in Poole. Enquiries
regarding exhibition opportunities should be made
direct to The Study Gallery.
Submission Policy Bi-annual open exhibition
(details on website) open to residents of the BH
and DT postcode areas.

Gloucester City Museum and Art Gallery

Brunswick Road, Gloucester
GL1 1HP
T 01452 396131
F 01452 410898
Opened in 1860, with important collection of fine
and applied art.

Holburne Museum of Art

Great Pulteney Street, Bath
BA2 4DB
T 01225 466669
F 01225 333121
E holburne@bath.ac.uk
W www.bath.ac.uk/Holburne
Located in the former Georgian Sydney Hotel,
housing a display of fine and decorative arts
collected by Sir William Holburne, including
English and continental silver, porcelain, maiolica,
glass and Renaissance bronzes. The picture gallery
contains works by Turner, Guardi, Stubbs plus
notable portraits of Bath society by Gainsborough.
There are also several temporary exhibitions
during the year.
Talks/Events/Education The Holburne hosts
lunchtime and evening lectures as well as day
courses which may be suitable for artists to attend.
Fee applicable.

Kelmscott Manor

Kelmscott, Lechlade, GL7 3HJ
T 01367 253348
F 01367 253754
E admin@kelmscottmanor.co.uk
W www.kelmscottmanor.co.uk
The country home of William Morris (poet,
craftsman, artist and socialist) from 1871 until his
death in 1896. The house contains a collection of
the possessions and works of Morris and his
associates, including furniture, textiles, ceramics
and paintings.

Museum of East Asian Art

12 Bennett Street, Bath, BA1 2QJ
T 01225 464640
F 01225 461718
E museum@east-asian-art.freeserve.co.uk
W www.meaa.org.uk
Situated in a restored Georgian house, housing a
fine collection of ceramics, jades, bronzes and
more from China, Japan, Korea and South-east
Asia. Since opening to the public in 1993, the
museum has become one of the most extensive
collections of East Asian art outside London, with
almost 2,000 objects dating from c. 5000 BC to
the present day.
Submission Policy Apply directly by post, phone or
email. Art work should be relevant to East Asia.
Talks/Events/Education Holds creative adult
workshops, talks, tours and children's workshops.
Price ranges from free events to some workshops
costing £15.

National Monuments Record Centre

Kemble Drive, Churchward, Swindon, SN2 2GZ
T 01793 414600
W www.english-heritage.org.uk
The centre is home to the archive of England's
heritage. Holds a stock of over ten million
photographs, drawings and other documents
recording the archaeology and architecture of
England.

Nature In Art

Wallsworth Hall, Twigworth, Gloucester, GL2 9PA
T 01452 731422
F 01452 730937
E ninart@globlnet.co.uk
W www.nature-in-art.org.uk
The world's first museum dedicated exclusively to
art inspired by nature.

New Art Centre

Roche Court, East Winterslow, Salisbury, SP5 1BG
T 01980 862244
F 01980 862447
E nac@sculpture.uk.com
W www.sculpture.uk.com
Founded in 1958, specializing in British and
international sculpture from 1950 onwards, in
parkland, a gallery and an Artists' House.
Exhibition programme of 5–6 shows a year. Sole
representative of the Estate of Barbara Hepworth
(1903–1975). Other featured artists include Antony
Gormley, Richard Long, Alison Wilding, Richard
Deacon, Henry Moore, Anthony Caro, Kenneth
Armitage, Anya Gallaccio, Barry Flanagan and
Gavin Turk.
Talks/Events/Education Contact the Roche Court
Educational Trust at edu@sculpture.uk.com

Newlyn Art Gallery

24 New Road, Newlyn, Penzance, TR18 5PZ
T 01736 363715
F 01736 331578
E mail@Newlynartgallery.co.uk
W www.Newlynartgallery.co.uk
Opened in 1895, having been built with money
from the well-known philanthropist John
Passmore Edwards on land given for the purpose
by the LeGrice family. Aims to allow the widest
possible accessibility to contemporary art of the
highest quality.

P.J. Crook Foundation

39 Priory Lane, Bishop's Cleeve, Cheltenham
GL52 8JL

T 01242 675963
E museum@pjcrook.com
W www.pjcrook.com/museum.html
Established in 2004 with the aim of opening and maintaining Crook's studios and house as an educational resource and for the benefit of the public. Exhibits significant paintings from throughout Crook's career, as well as works by artists who taught her, are from the region or have relevance to the main collection (particularly women artists and Surrealism, and prints and works on paper).
Submission Policy Hopes to curate shows by living artists in future years but is not seeking applications at present.

Penlee House Gallery and Museum
Morrab Road, Penzance, TR18 4HE
T 01736 363625
F 01736 361312
E info@penleehouse.org.uk
W www.penleehouse.org.uk
Founded in 1839, the district museum and art gallery for Penzance and Penwith. A programme of changing art exhibitions exclusively focuses on the historic art of west Cornwall, often featuring the Newlyn and Lamorna artists' colonies (1880–1940). Note that Penlee House does not have a contemporary art remit and opportunities for artists are therefore limited to workshops and/or partnership activities with other exhibition venues.
Submission Policy Does not handle or show any living artists and therefore does not welcome submissions.
Talks/Events/Education Holds regular talks, educational events and occasional artist-led workshops.

Penwith Galleries and Penwith Society of Arts
Back Road West, St Ives, TR26 1NL
T 01736 795579
Founded in 1949. Aims to encourage practising artists and craftworkers in Cornwall and to promote public interest in the arts. The organization includes public galleries, artists' studios and a bookshop and a print workshop. Holds continuous exhibitions of paintings, ceramics and sculpture.

Plymouth City Museums and Art Gallery
Drake Circus, Plymouth, PL4 8AJ
T 01752 304774
F 01752 304775
E plymouth.museum@plymouth.gov.uk
W www.plymouthmuseum.gov.uk,

www.cottoniancollection.org.uk
The current museum opened in 1910 and houses the designated Cottonian Collection featuring paintings by Plymouth-born Joshua Reynolds. The collection includes maritime pictures, oil paintings, watercolours, prints, drawings and ceramics. Good examples of works from the Newlyn School and by other important local painters. Free, regularly changing exhibitions.
Submission Policy Annual exhibitions open to non-members by Plymouth Society of Artists and Plymouth Arts Club. Phone for details.
Talks/Events/Education Free Tuesday-lunchtime talks, regular family and children's activities and other events.

Prema
South Street, Uley, nr Dursley, GL11 5SS
T 01453 860703
E info@prema.demon.co.uk
W www.prema.demon.co.uk
Founded almost thirty years ago, this small, independent rural arts centre has a year-round programme of arts activities (performances, classes, workshops, exhibitions, installations, etc.). The main exhibition space is multifunctional; a smaller space is available, though less often used. Exhibitions last five to six weeks.
Submission Policy First contact by phone or email, then send in a CV and images (as attachments, on CD or as hard copies), and then discuss with the Director.
Talks/Events/Education Regular classes and workshops, all artist-led. Occasionally artists' talks.

R O O M
4 Alfred Place, Redcliffe, Bristol, BS1 6ST
T 0117 9273778
F 0117 9273788
E sandie.macrae@netgates.co.uk
W www.roomartspace.co.uk
Founded in 2003. An artist-led space in a new building made specially for the purpose. Shows have been mainly film, video and photography, with a strong critical and theoretical grounding.
Submission Policy Interested in innovative work showing different approaches, with a particular focus on lens-based works including photography, film and video. Also shows performance, and there is potential for installation, taking account of the space, which can be extended into the courtyard.
Talks/Events/Education Hosts artists' talks and single-evening events called 'VIEWINGROOMS', which are about artists' methodologies.

Red House Museum and Art Gallery
Quay Road, Christchurch, BH23 1BU
T 01202 482860
F 01202 481924
W www.hants.gov.uk/museum/redhouse
Built as a workhouse in 1764, the building now
houses several locally relevant collections,
including an extensive range of Arts and Crafts
pieces. Also hosts temporary exhibitions.

Royal Cornwall Museum
River Street, Truro, TR1 2SJ
T 01872 272205
F 01872 240514
E enquiries@royalcornwallmuseum.org.uk
W www.royalcornwallmuseum.org.uk
Founded in 1818. Owned and managed by the
Royal Institution of Cornwall, which was created to
provide lectures, facilities for study and a museum.
Offers a varied programme for both children and
adults.

Royal West of England Academy (RWA)
Queen's Road, Clifton, Bristol, BS8 1PX
T 0117 9735129
F 0117 9237874
E info@rwa.org.uk
W www.rwa.org.uk
Founded in 1944 as Bristol's first art gallery.
Houses five naturally-lit galleries. Stages major
solo, mixed and open exhibitions all year round,
and has a collection of works spanning the
nineteenth, twentieth and twenty-first centuries.
Submission Policy Annual Autumn Exhibition is
an open exhibition of painting, printmaking,
sculpture and architecture. Entry regulations
available from August from www.rwa.org.uk.
Talks/Events/Education A programme of
educational activities accompanies each exhibition.
These include lectures, gallery tours,
demonstrations and workshops. Charges may apply.

SPACEX
45 Preston Street, Exeter, EX1 1DF
T 01392 431786
F 01392 213786
E mail@spacex.org.uk
W www.spacex.org.uk
Established in 1974 by an Exeter-based artists'
cooperative, extending the SPACE philosophy of
artist-led studios and exhibition initiatives beyond
London. A publicly-funded contemporary art space
and registered educational charity. Encourages
public engagement with the latest developments in
contemporary art through commissioned projects,
exhibitions, events and activities for all ages.
Talks/Events/Education A regular programme of
talks, symposia and workshops, as well as
participatory projects out of the gallery. Also
weekly after-school and Saturday Art Club
activities for children and young people.

St Ives Society of Artists Gallery
Norway Square, St Ives, TR26 2SX
T 01736 795582
E gallery@stisa.co.uk
W www.stivessocietyofartists.com and also
www.stisa.co.uk
The society first organized exhibitions of
members' work in 1927. There are two galleries,
with the main gallery housing several exhibitions
during the year of contemporary work including
traditional as well as semi-abstract. Some
exhibitions feature work from artists and
organizations outside the membership. The
Mariners' Gallery is available for hire by artists or
artist groups.
Submission Policy Welcomes applications for
membership by artists from Cornwall. Work must
be of a high standard.
Talks/Events/Education Hopes to hold educational
courses within the gallery. Details will appear on
the website.

Study Gallery
North Road, Parkstone, Poole, BH14 0LS
T 01202 205200
F 01202 205240
E info@thestudygallery.org
W www.thestudygallery.org
Opened in 2000. Runs feature exhibitions
presenting work in different forms on changing
themes and of high professional status. Also has a
programme of project exhibitions, displaying the
results of projects that the gallery initiates or is
involved in through partnerships. Home to
Bournemouth and Poole College's mid-twentieth-
century art collection, including work by Henry
Moore, Barbara Hepworth, Ivon Hitchens and
Bridget Riley.

Swindon Community Heritage Museum and Art Gallery
Bath Road, Swindon, SN1 4BA
T 01793 466556
W www.steam-museum.org.uk
A museum and art gallery telling the story of local
history.

Tate St Ives
Porthmeor Beach, St Ives, TR26 1TG
T 01736 796226
F 01736 793794
E tatestivesinfo@tate.org.uk
W www.tate.org.uk/stives
Open since 1993. Aims, through its varied
international exhibition programme and education
programmes, to encourage a greater
understanding and enjoyment of modern and
contemporary art in the cultural context of St Ives.
A selection of works from the St Ives School of
Artists is always on display. Three seasons of
exhibitions each year show major figures in British
contemporary art.
Talks/Events/Education An extensive programme
of talks, events and study days (some free and
some chargeable).

text + work – the gallery
Arts Institute at Bournemouth, Wallisdown, Poole
BH12 5HH
T 01202 363351
F 01202 537729
E vmcclean@aib.ac.uk
W www.textandwork.org.uk
The concept of text + work underpins the
exhibition programme in the gallery, promoting
dialogue between innovative contemporary art and
design practice and its theoretical context. It
provides a platform for practitioners, writers and
curators who wish to examine and extend the
boundaries between contemporary practice and
critical discourse. There are gallery events, critical
texts, touring exhibtions, shared and networked
exhibitions, and a website. A text (essay) is
published to accompany each exhibition. The
programme includes collections on loan from
galleries and museums, as well as initiated and
curated exhibitions by some of today's leading
artists and critical writers including Ian McKeever
and David Miller (poet), Susan Stockwell and
Rosemary Miles (Curator, Victoria & Albert
Museum). The gallery also functions as a learning
resource and is integrated into the teaching,
learning and research practice undertaken at the
Institute. Student work is displayed in the
Summer Show exhibitions and students have the
opportunity to propose or curate shows as part of
the gallery programme.
Submission Policy Refer to the website for an
application pack and additional information.
Talks/Events/Education All exhibitions are
supported by a text+work talk/event. For further

information on touring exhibtions, publications and
events, contact Violet McClean (Gallery Officer).

Victoria Art Gallery
Bridge Street, Bath, BA2 4AT
T 01225 477232
F 01225 477231
E victoria_enquiries@bathnes.gov.uk
W www.victoriagal.org.uk
The permanent collection occupies two rooms on
the first floor, while the ground floor is given over
to two temporary exhibition spaces, which change
every two months. Permanent collections range
from the fifteenth century to the present day and
were formed mainly by gift and bequest since the
building first opened in 1900. Highlights include
eighteenth-century portraits, views of Bath,
Victorian paintings, English Delftware and
Staffordshire ceramic dogs. Modern artists include
John Nash, Walter Sickert, William Roberts and
Kenneth Armitage.

Watershed
1 Canon's Road, Harbourside, Bristol, BS15TX
T 0117 9276444
E info@watershed.co.uk
W www.watershed.co.uk
A media centre for the digital age, with a
programme of feature films, video, digital media,
courses and events presented in three cinemas,
three event suites and online.
Talks/Events/Education Runs an extensive education
programme and a programme of digital courses.
Other events include talks such as the 'Alternative
Series', run by the Centre for Critical Theory at
Bristol UWE in conjunction with Watershed.

Wales

Aberystwyth Arts Centre
Penglais Hill, Aberystwyth, SY23 3DE
T 01970 621634
F 01970 622883
E s2s@aber.ac.uk
W www.aber.ac.uk/artscentre
Houses a concert-hall theatre, gallery spaces
specializing in large-scale contemporary-art shows
and photography exhibitions, studio-theatre
workshop spaces, two cafés, a cinema, craft design
shop, bookshop and bars. Hosts one of Britain's
most important collections of studio ceramics.
Submission Policy Apply in writing with visuals to
Eve Ropek. Applications are put before a
programming committee.

Talks/Events/Education Courses, workshops and talks are held on a weekly basis. Other specialized events covering all art forms are held annually.

Andrew Logan Museum of Sculpture

Berriew, nr Welshpool, SY22 8AH
T 01686 640689
E info@andrewlogan.com
W www.andrewlogan.com
A collection of works by sculptor Andrew Logan.

The Bleddfa Centre

Bleddfa, Knighton, LD7 1PA
T 01547 550377
F 01547 550370
E enquiries@bleddfacentre.com
W www.bleddfacentre.com
The Old School Gallery hosts exhibitions of paintings, sculpture and crafts, while the Hall Barn hosts meetings, talks and workshops, all with a spiritual content.
Submission Policy Artists must exhibit work which shows a link between creativity and spirituality.

Chapter Gallery

Chapter Arts Centre, Market Road, Canton
Cardiff, CF5 1QE
T 029 2031 1055
F 029 2031 1059
E visual.arts@chapter.org
W www.chapter.org
Established more than thirty years ago, Chapter Arts Centre comprises a gallery with two residency studios, a theatre, two cinema screens, a bar-restaurant and fifty additional artists' studios. Operates an international programme of contemporary visual arts activity. This is achieved through commissioning new work, touring exhibitions, a programme of international residencies and exhibitions, publishing, and creating forums for critical reflection via commissioned essays and a programme of talks and events. Recent commissions and exhibitions have included Ansuman Biswas, Harold Offeh, Erika Tan, Nadia Hebson, Zoë Mendleson, Joel Tomlin, Salla Tykkä, Simon Pope, Julian Rosefeldt and Chris Evans. Also established May You Live In Interesting Times, Cardiff's biannual city-wide Festival of Creative Technology (mayyouliveininterestingtimes.org).
Submission Policy Exhibition is generally by invitation only.
Talks/Events/Education Hosts a wide programme of talks and events. See website for details. Also has a

Gallery Shop that includes magazines, books and a wide selection of art-related products and gifts.

Ffotogallery

c/o Chapter, Market Road, Cardiff, CF5 1QE
T 029 20341667
F 029 20341672
E info@ffotogallery.org
W www.ffotogallery.org
The national development agency for photography in Wales. Initiates exhibitions that explore mainstream documentary photography as well as more expansive uses of the medium, which may involve the use of projection and other forms of extended and digital media. The gallery's exhibition programme is run from the grade II-listed Turner House Gallery in Penarth, a ten-minute drive from Cardiff. Hosts touring exhibitions, collaborates with other organizations and runs education and outreach programmes.
Submission Policy All work by artists working with any form of lens-based art considered.
Talks/Events/Education Runs a regular programme of gallery talks and an extensive programme of photography and digital courses and classes. The talks programme is free.

Glynn Vivian Art Gallery

Alexandra Road, Swansea, SA1 5DZ
T 01792 516900
F 01792 516903
E glynn.vivian.gallery@swansea.gov.uk
W www.glynnviviangallery.org
Founded in 1911. An Edwardian gallery offering a broad range of visual arts from the original bequest of Richard Glynn Vivian (1835–1910) to art of the twentieth century. The latter is well represented with painting and sculpture by Hepworth, Nicholson and Nash alongside Welsh artists such as Ceri Richards, Gwen John and Augustus John. The exhibitions programme in the modern wing gives a contemporary overview of the arts in local, national and international contexts.
Submission Policy Applications are considered throughout the year, and should include a CV, examples of the work (on slides, CD, video, DVD, etc.), plus publications and support material.
Talks/Events/Education An education service for schools and a programme of artists' talks and events, plus lectures organized by Friends of the gallery.

Howard Gardens Gallery

Cardiff School of Art and Design, UWK Howard

Gardens, Cardiff, CF24 0SP
T 029 20418608
F 029 20416944
E rcox@uwk.ac.uk
Situated at the centre of Cardiff School of Art and
Design, the programme presents a combination of
contemporary fine-art and craft exhibitions from
local, national and international sources. Also
holds annual BA degree and MA postgraduate
exhibitions in the summer and autumn terms.
Submission Policy Contemporary visual artists and
craftspeople may apply during the academic year
(September to June) with a CV, ten slides and sae.
Talks/Events/Education Occasional seminars and
conferences associated with specific exhibitions.

National Museum and Gallery, Cardiff
Cathays Park, Cardiff, CF10 3NP
T 029 20397951
E art@nmgw.ac.uk
W www.nmgw.ac.uk/www.php/art/
Collections include the Williams-Wynn Collection,
the De Winton Collection of European porcelain,
the Morton Nance Collection of Welsh ceramics,
the Davies Sisters' Collection, historical paintings,
works on paper and contemporary craft. The
Davies Collection is one of the great British art
collections of the twentieth century and was
donated to the museum in the 1950s. Historical
paintings includes sixteenth-century Welsh
portraits, a collection of miniatures and works
from across Europe.

Oriel Davies Gallery
The Park, Newtown, SY16 2NZ
T 01686 625041
F 01686 623633
E enquiries@orieldavies.org
W www.orieldavies.org
Formerly Oriel 31, Oriel Davies Gallery was started
in Newtown in 1985 as a contemporary-art gallery
in Mid-Wales. Following an extensive three-year
refurbishment beginning in 2002, it now boasts
two new galleries that cater specifically to
displaying temporary exhibitions of modern and
contemporary art.
Submission Policy Welcomes applications from
contemporary artists to exhibit but does not
represent artists.

Oriel Mostyn Gallery
12 Vaughan Street, Llandudno, LL30 1AB
T 01492 879201
F 01492 878869

E info@mostyn.org
W www.mostyn.org
Founded in 1978 as a gallery for contemporary
arts. Shows five or six changing exhibitions of all
contemporary art forms per year.
Submission Policy The gallery references and
curates its own shows and collaborates with other
galleries, but submissions from artists are
considered. There is an annual open exhibition
with a £6,000 prize, where entries are solicited
from artists without conditions of age, theme or
any other restriction.
Talks/Events/Education Free 'Artists Talking' series,
where exhibiting artists discuss their work. Other
events are also organized, some of which are free.

Riverfront
Bristol Packet Wharf, Newport, NP20 1HG
E riverfront@newport.gov.uk
W www.newport.gov.uk/_dc/
index.cfm?fuseaction=riverfront.homepage
In 1999 Newport received funding for a new arts
centre, which includes a small gallery displaying
exhibitions of art, design and photography. Rooms
are available for hire.

Royal Cambrian Academy of Art
Crown Lane, Conwy, LL32 8AN
T 01492 593413
E rca@rcaconwy.org
W www.rcaconwy.org
Founded in 1881. Home to a significant collection
of Welsh art.

School of Art Gallery and Museum
The University of Wales, Aberystwyth
Buarth Mawr, Aberystwyth
SY23 1NG
T 01970 622460
F 01970 622461
E neh@aber.ac.uk
W www.aber.ac.uk/museum
Has changing exhibitions from the permanent
collection and touring shows. The collection
includes graphic art from the fifteenth century to
the present, art in Wales since 1945, contemporary
Welsh and post-war Italian photography, early
twentieth-century pioneer and contemporary
British studio pottery, eighteenth- and nineteenth-
century slipware, Swansea and Nantgarw
porcelain, art pottery and Oriental ceramics
(Ceramics Collection is housed in Aberystwyth
Arts Centre). Studies of the collection by
appointment.

Tabernacle – MOMA Wales

Heol Penrallt, Machynlleth, SY20 8AJ
T 01654 703355
F 01654 702160
W www.momawales.org.uk
MOMA Wales has grown up alongside the
Tabernacle, a former Wesleyan chapel, which in
1986 reopened as a centre for the performing arts.
It has six exhibition spaces, which house,
throughout the year, the Tabernacle Collection
and modern Welsh art. Individual artists are
spotlighted in temporary exhibitions.
Talks/Events/Education Workshops for adults and
children in July. Tabernacle Art Competition in
August, with winners chosen by expert judges and
the public. Many works in MOMA Wales for sale.

Tenby Museum and Gallery

Castle Hill, Tenby, SA70 7BP
T 01834 842809
E tenbymuseum@hotmail.com
W www.tenbymuseum.free-online.co.uk
The permanent collection includes works by
Augustus John, Gwen John, Nina Hamnet, E.J.
Head, Julius Caesar Ibbetson, John Piper and
David Jones.

Wrexham Arts Centre

Rhosddu Road, Wrexham, LL11 1AU
T 01978 292093
F 01978 292611
E arts.centre@wrexham.gov.uk
W www.wrexham.gov.uk/arts
Established in 1973, the centre is funded by the
Arts Council of Wales and local-authority
administered. Exhibits contemporary, temporary
visual and applied art exhibitions highlighting a
variety of artists and media. Works in collaboration
with many partners. Hosts and tours exhibitions.
Submission Policy Artists can send in exhibition
proposal, including images, CV and vision of
proposed exhibition.
Talks/Events/Education An education programme
supports every exhibition and can include talks
and workshops.

West Midlands

Barber Institute of Fine Arts

University of Birmingham, Edgbaston,
Birmingham, B15 2TS
T 0121 4147333
F 0121 4143370
E info@barber.org.uk

W www.barber.org.uk
Comprises works from the thirteenth to the
twentieth centuries, with particularly important
Old Master and Impressionist collections. The
gallery includes work by Baschenis, Bellini,
Botticelli, Degas, Delacroix, Gainsborough,
Gauguin, Holbein, Ingres, Magritte, Manet,
Matisse, Monet, Picasso, Poussin, Rembrandt,
Rodin, Rossetti, Rubens, Schiele, Stom, Turner,
Van Dyck, van Gogh, Veronese and Whistler.

Birmingham Museum and Art Gallery

Chamberlain Square, Birmingham, B3 3DH
T 0121 3032834 / 3031966
F 0121 3031394
E bmag_enquiries@birmingham.gov.uk
W www.bmag.org.uk/museum_and_art_gallery/
Founded in 1885. The collections cover fine and
applied arts, archaeology and ethnography, and
local and industrial history. The fine- and applied-
art collections include paintings and drawings,
British watercolours and arts and crafts. There is
an ever-changing programme of temporary
exhibitions and the permanent collection includes
the Pre-Raphaelites. Major shows are housed in
the restored gas hall. Entrance to the museum and
art gallery is free.

Compton Verney

Compton Verney, CV35 9HZ
T 01926 645500
F 01926 645501
E info@comptonverney.org.uk
W www.comptonverney.org.uk
Launched in 2004. Collections include Naples
(1600 to 1800), German (1450 to 1650), Chinese
bronzes, British portraits, British folk art and the
Marx-Lambert Collection of popular art. Also runs
a major temporary exhibitions programme.
Talks/Events/Education An extensive events
programme accompanies each exhibition. Events
are charged for.

Herbert Museum and Art Gallery

Jordan Well, Coventry, CV1 5QP
T 024 76832381
F 024 76832410
E artsandheritage@coventry.gov.uk
W www.coventrymuseum.org.uk
The visual arts collection features mainly British
twentieth-century art (particularly of the 1950s and
1960s). Other main areas collected include British
watercolours and prints, pre-1900 British
paintings, British figure drawings from 1800,

images of Lady Godiva, works by local nineteenth-century artist David Gee, Far Eastern ceramics, Western seventeenth-century art, world art, and topographical views of Coventry and Warwickshire.

Hereford Museum and Art Gallery

Broad Street, Hereford, HR4 9AU
T 01432 260692
F 01432 342492
E herefordmuseums@herefordshire.gov.uk
W www.herefordshire.gov.uk (click on Leisure and Museums)
The museum was founded in 1874 and the gallery added as an extension in the 1920s. Houses changing exhibitions of a wide variety of media and styles. Has an extensive collection of fine art, costume and social history, as well as natural history and archaeology.
Submission Policy All submissions welcome, but especially interested in applications from artists who have considered accessibility for the visually impaired.
Talks/Events/Education Exhibitions are often accompanied by talks (a small fee is usually charged). Workshops are usually aimed at non-professionals.

Ikon Gallery

1 Oozells Square, Brindleyplace, Birmingham B1 2HS
T 0121 2480708
F 0121 2480709
E programming@ikon-gallery.co.uk
W www.ikon-gallery.co.uk
Founded about forty years ago and originally a small kiosk in the Bull Ring. It is now housed in the neo-Gothic Oozells Street School. Holds temporary exhibitions in a variety of media and organizes programmes outside the gallery.
Talks/Events/Education A variety of talks, tours, workshops and seminars are held. For education enquiries, email education@ikon-gallery.co.uk. In addition, a limited number of placements are offered to third-year art students; for details contact Andrew Tims at a.tims@ikon-gallery.co.uk or telephone the number above.

Leamington Spa Art Gallery and Museum

The Royal Pump Rooms, The Parade
Leamington Spa, CV32 4AA
T 01926 742700
F 01926 742705
E prooms@warwickdc.gov.uk

W www.royal-pump-rooms.co.uk
Opened at the Royal Pump Rooms in 1999. Facilities include an art gallery, a museum with a historic hammam room, a temporary exhibition space, an interactive learning gallery and an education room. The permanent exhibition of art works from the collection changes every eighteen months. A new collection of contemporary works explores links between art and medical science. Shows exhibitions of contemporary art, historical art and social history for an average of six to eight weeks at a time.
Submission Policy Exhibition proposals from individuals or groups should be addressed to the Art Gallery Curator at the postal address above.
Talks/Events/Education Details of events given in the quarterly Exhibition & Events publication.

Mead Gallery

Warwick Arts Centre, University of Warwick
Coventry, CV4 7AL
T 024 76522589
F 024 76572664
E meadgallery@warwick.ac.uk
W www.warwickartscentre.co.uk
Hosts curated exhibitions of international contemporary art and runs an access programme utilizing expertise within the university. The university art collection was founded in 1966 and includes over eight hundred works of modern and contemporary art on open display across campus, including paintings, prints, sculptures, photographs and ceramics.
Submission Policy Welcomes submissions with previous permission from the Senior Curator, although the programme is booked up well in advance.
Talks/Events/Education Open during term time only and holds talks and events relating to each exhibition.

Meadow Gallery

Cumberley, Knowbury, Ludlow, SY8 3LJ
T 01584 891659
E info@meadowgallery.co.uk
W www.meadowgallery.co.uk
A West Midlands-based contemporary arts organization which produces site-specific exhibitions in outdoor locations, and commissions new work. It operates as a 'roving' gallery working alongside venues with similar or compatible aims (garden, landscape or historic house open to the public) to present contemporary art in an outdoor context.

New Art Gallery, Walsall

Gallery Square, Walsall, WS2 8LG
T 01922 654400
F 01922 654401
E info@artatwalsall.org.uk
W www.artatwalsall.org.uk
Has collections of European art, including major paintings by Rembrandt, Goya, Constable, Manet, Degas and Freud. The Garman Ryan Collection galleries chart the career of Jacob Epstein. There is also an interactive children's gallery, library and changing exhibitions programme.
Talks/Events/Education Holds events and activities, family workshops, artists' talks about exhibitions, and introductory talks about the Garman Ryan Collection.

Potteries Museum and Art Gallery

Bethesda Street, City Centre, Stoke-on-Trent
ST1 3DW
T 01782 232323
F 01782 232500
E museums@stoke.gov.uk
W www.stoke.gov.uk/museums
Opened in 1981, the museum houses the world's greatest collection of Staffordshire ceramics, plus displays of art and local history. There is also a lively programme of exhibitions and events, with the emphasis on contemporary art and craft.
Submission Policy Shows work by artists either based in the region or with a national or international reputation.
Talks/Events/Education Organizes talks and events for specific exhibitions on a regular basis. There is a charge for each event.

Shire Hall Gallery

Market Square, Stafford, ST16 2LD
T 01785 278345
E shirehallgallery@staffordshire.gov.uk
Dedicated to promoting the visual arts and crafts across a range of subjects and styles. Comprises seven hundred prints, drawings, watercolours, maps and oil paintings.

Shrewsbury Museum and Art Gallery

Rowley's House, Barker Street, Shrewsbury
SY1 1QH
T 01743 361196
F 01743 358411
E museums@shrewsbury.gov.uk
W www.shrewsburymuseums.com
www.darwincountry.org

The museum is to be closed to the public for an extended period, pending a major redevelopment at a new venue. Rowley's House will be open for some special exhibitions, including the Open Art Exhibition in 2007 and 2009.
Submission Policy Annual open art competition and exhibition (May closing date), linked to Darwin Festival & Symposium (www.darwinshrewsbury.org). See also www.mediamaker.tv for details of media arts partnership programme.
Talks/Events/Education Occasional exhibition-related events, on a one-off basis. Support for young and emerging artists through media*maker* and Young Curators project.

Wolverhampton Art Gallery

Lichfield Street, Wolverhampton, WV1 1DU
T 01902 552055
F 01902 552053
E info@wolverhamptonart.org.uk
W www.wolverhamptonart.org.uk
Built in 1884 and situated in the heart of the town centre. The gallery's collections include contemporary Pop Art, displays of Victorian and Georgian paintings and video and digital media. 2007 saw the completion of a new extension which increased exhibition space, allowing the gallery to provide a dedicated space for its contemporary art and Pop Art collections. The gallery also manages The Makers Dozen Studios, artist studios situated within the art gallery complex, purpose-designed for artists and makers.

Yorkshire and Humberside

Cartwright Hall Art Gallery

Lister Park, Bradford, BD9 4NS
T 01274 431212
F 01274 481045
E cartwright.hall@bradford.gov.uk
W www.city-of-bradford.com/cartwright-hall.html
Built in 1904 in Baroque style as an art gallery. Houses permanent collections of nineteenth- and twentieth-century British art (particularly strong in Victorian art), arts from the Indian subcontinent and contemporary South Asian art. Also shows temporary exhibitions.

Cooper Gallery

Church Street, Barnsley
S70 2AH
T 01226 242905
F 01226 297283

W www.barnsley.gov.uk/tourism/coopergallery/index.asp
Founded in 1912 to house the collection of Samuel Joshua Cooper. The permanent collection holds paintings, watercolours and drawings from the seventeenth to the twentieth centuries. Also hosts visiting contemporary exhibitions, such as the South Yorkshire Open Art Exhibition.
Talks/Events/Education Full year-round programme of artists' talks, workshops and schools activities.

Dean Clough Galleries
Halifax, HX3 5AX
T 01422 250250
F 01422 255250
E dean.clough.ltd@deanclough.com
W www.deanclough.com
An arts, business and design complex created on the derelict site of what was once the world's largest carpet mill. Eight galleries host a range of exhibitions spanning the arts. The Dean Clough Studios, based in Mill House, the Stable Yard and the Band Room, house twenty-four fine artists, designers and craftworkers working in a variety of media.

Ferens Art Gallery
Queen Victoria Square, Hull, HU1 3RA
T 01482 613902
F 01482 613710
E museums@hullcc.gov.uk
W www.hullcc.gov.uk/museums
Opened in 1927, the gallery combines an internationally renowned permanent collection and a programme of temporary exhibitions. Particular strengths of the collection include European Old Masters (notably Dutch and Flemish), portraiture, marine paintings, and modern and contemporary British art.
Submission Policy Welcomes written proposals from artists involved in fine art. For the temporary exhibitions programme include a CV, statement and good-quality visuals.
Talks/Events/Education Frequently holds talks and education events, most of which are free.

Graves Art Gallery
Surrey Street, Sheffield, S1 1XZ
T 0114 2782600
F 0114 2782604
W www.shef.ac.uk/city/artgals/graves.html
Founded in 1934, the gallery covers all periods of British art from the sixteenth century to the present. Other collections include French, Italian, Spanish and Dutch paintings of all major periods, watercolours, drawings and prints, and a collection of decorative art from diverse cultures (including the Grice Collection of Chinese ivories). Also hosts temporary exhibitions.

Harewood House
Harewood, Leeds, LS17 9LG
T 0113 2181010
F 0113 2181002
E info@harewood.org
W www.harewood.org
The home of the Lascelles family, built in 1759–71 by John Carr in the Palladian style with interiors by Robert Adam. The house was altered and heightened in 1843 by Sir Charles Barry in an Italianate style. Has rich and diverse fine and decorative art collections range from Chippendale furniture to Renaissance masterpieces and works from the sixteenth to twentieth centuries. British artists are represented by works of Romney, Reynolds, Cotman and Turner. Decorative collections include a collection of Sèvres porcelain with a tea service made for Queen Marie-Antoinettte and clocks made by the royal clockmaker Benjamin Vulliamy. There are approximately 7,000 objects, 10,000 photographs and approximately 100,000 archival items in the collections. In addition to displaying the collections of the house, there is a programme of temporary exhibitions of historical and contemporary art.
Talks/Events/Education There is a programme of lectures, demonstrations and workshops given by experts and artists, which runs all year.

Henry Moore Institute
74 The Headrow, Leeds, LS1 3AH
T 0113 2467467
F 0113 2461481
E info@henry-moore.ac.uk
W www.henry-moore-fdn.co.uk
A centre for the study of sculpture, with exhibition galleries and an active research programme. Originally set up in partnership between the Henry Moore Foundation and Leeds City Council in the city where Moore began his training as a sculptor, it is now concerned with a wide variety of sculpture, both historical and contemporary. The institute, an award-winning, architecturally designed building, opened in 1993 and comprises a suite of galleries on the ground floor, the library and archive on the first floor, and a seminar room in the basement.

Submission Policy Welcomes applications for research fellowships from artists and academics. Deadline for applications each year is usually end of first week in January.
Talks/Events/Education Runs a series of complementary Wednesday-evening talks for each of its main exhibitions, as well as seminars and conferences. Events are usually free.

Huddersfield Art Gallery
Princess Alexandra Walk, Huddersfield, HD1 2SU
T 01484 221962
F 01484 221952
E robert.hall@kirklees.gov.uk
W www.kirklees.gov.uk/art
In current building (along with library) since 1945. The collection consists mainly of twentieth-century British art in all media. Exhibitions throughout the year include one-person and group shows, and touring shows (Arts Council, Crafts Council, etc.). Current interests particularly in post-war British art, especially sculpture and Constructivism.
Submission Policy Written or emailed submissions with slides or CD are accepted. Unlikely to exhibit without local or regional link.
Talks/Events/Education Contact the Education and Outreach Officer for further details.

Hull Maritime Museum
Queen Victoria Square, Hull, HU1 3DX
T 01482 613902
F 01482 613710
E Arthur.Credland@hullcc.gov.uk
W www.hullcc.gov.uk/museums
Maritime collections go back to 1822. Includes marine paintings (chiefly by local artists), decorative arts of the sea and an outstanding collection of scrimshaw work (carved whale bone and ivory). Recent exhibitions have shown the work of David Bell and Colin Verity.
Submission Policy Interested in work incorporating maritime themes, decorative art with sea connections, or marine painting in the traditional sense.

Impressions Gallery
33 Manor Row, Bradford, BD1 4PS
T 08450 515882
F 01274 734635
E enquiries@impressions-gallery.com
W www.impressions-gallery.com
Leading gallery of contemporary art, specializing in photography. Re-opened in a new Bradford gallery space in 2007 with enhanced facilities.

Submission Policy Does not generally solicit exhibition proposals. However, artists may contact the gallery for details of how to submit an unsolicited proposal.
Talks/Events/Education Offers range of events including talks by exhibiting artists, film screenings, gallery tours and workshops. Many events are free.

Leeds City Art Gallery
The Headrow, Leeds, LS1 3AA
W www.leeds.gov.uk/artgallery
Emphasis is on significant and interesting new developments in contemporary art and exhibitions that explore the history of nineteenth- and twentieth-century art. Works on paper include pieces by Turner, Rembrandt, Cotman, Cozens, Girtin, Derain, Sisley, Rose Garrard and Atkinson Grimshaw. Recent contemporary-art acquisitions include works by Bill Woodrow, Paula Rego, Mark Wallinger, Stephen Willats, Alison Wilding and Bridget Riley. With support from the Henry Moore Foundation, the modern sculpture collection is second only to that of the Tate.
Submission Policy The exhibitions programme is put together twelve to eighteen months in advance, and larger-scale exhibitions at least two years in advance. Welcomes applications from artists. Send a proposal outlining the exhibition, supporting visual material (preferably transparencies or slides; five or six and not more than fifteen), which will be returned, a CV and an outline of what makes the proposal distinctive and how it might be of interest to the gallery's audiences. Send to Nigel Walsh (Exhibitions Curator).

Leeds Met Gallery and Studio Theatre
Leeds Metropolitan University, Civic Quarter Leeds, LS1 3HE
T 0113 2833140
F 0113 283 5999
E gallerytheatre@leedsmet.ac.uk
W www.leedsmet.ac.uk/arts
Founded in 1990. Six exhibitions held each year, including shows based on artists' proposals, initiated projects and occasional hired-in exhibitions.
Submission Policy Submissions should contain good-quality visuals in a format that best represents the work (e.g.slides, video, DVD, CD; digital images should be PC-compatible). Also include a statement about the content of the work, a CV and supporting website links. Do not send full proposals by email. Proposals will be

considered by the curator in consultation with education and technical staff at fixed points in the year (mid-November, mid-March and mid-June).
Talks/Events/Education Most exhibitions include an education strand, such as talks and critical feedback. These events are generally free of charge.

Mercer Art Gallery
Swan Road, Harrogate, HG1 2SA
T 01423 556188
F 01423 556130
E museums@harrogate.gov.uk
W www.harrogate.gov.uk/museums
Founded in 1991 in the Promenade Rooms to house the Harrogate Fine Art Collection. The permanent collection is shown in changing themed displays as part of annnual programme of exhibitions of both historic and contemporary art.
Submission Policy Submissions welcome from living artists. Written proposals by post only. Artists with regional connections favoured.
Talks/Events/Education Wide ranging programmes of events, talks and courses for a broad audience. Some charging, some free.

Millennium Galleries
Arundel Gate, Sheffield, S1 2PP
T 0114 2782600
W www.sheffieldgalleries.org.uk/coresite/html/millennium.asp
Displays visual arts, craft and design. Incorporates a special exhibition gallery, a craft and design gallery, a metalwork gallery and the Ruskin Gallery, containing a collection compiled by John Ruskin over many years.
Talks/Events/Education The learning centre organizes talks, events and practical workshops.

National Media Museum
Pictureville, Bradford, BD1 1NQ
T 0870 7010200
F 01274 723155
E talk.nmpft@nmsi.ac.uk
W www.nmpft.org.uk
Founded in 1983, with collections covering the past, present and future of the three media. Includes the Royal Photographic Society Collection, the National Collection, the Daily Herald Archive and the National Cinematography Collection. Formerly called the National Museum of Photography, Film & Television.
Submission Policy All three of the museum's subject media, taking account of new technologies (such as digital imaging), are covered. The

submission of exhibition proposals is encouraged. New work is regularly commissioned. For more details, telephone 01274 203325.
Talks/Events/Education The frequency of events changes depending on subject matter and time of year. Some are subject to charges.

Newby Hall and Gardens
The Estate Office, Newby Hall, Ripon, HG4 5AE
T 01423 322583
F 01423 324452
W www.newbyhall.com
Now in its seventh year, the Sculpture Park (which opens 1 June) at Newby Hall is set among 25 acres of award-winning gardens, park and woodland surrounding one of Robert Adam's finest houses. A number of art exhibitions are held in the Grantham Room each season.
Submission Policy The Sculpture Park includes high quality work across a range of style, media and price by both established and emerging artists.

North Light Gallery
Armitage Bridge, Huddersfield, HD4 7NR
T 01484 340003
F 01484 340001
W www.northlightgallery.org.uk
Opened in 2000 to show contemporary British art. A charity, the gallery was created out of a nineteenth-century wool textile mill and is available to hire by artists or groups of artists or other museums. Houses a collection of Yorkshire artists in 15,000 sq. ft of airy industrial space.
Submission Policy To show, the artist must finance the costs of transport, catalogue, insurance, invitation cards and printing.
Talks/Events/Education Artists must be prepared to give one talk as part of exhibition.

S10 Gallery
Ashgate House, Ashgate Road, Sheffield, S10 3BZ
T 0114 2678883
F 0114 2678894
E s10gallery@aol.com
W www.s10gallery.com
Holds monthly exhibitions covering a cross-section of the arts. Run by the charity For A Better Life with Epilepsy (FABLE).

Salts Mill
Shipley, Saltaire, BD18 3LB
T 01274 531185
F 01274 531184
E post@saltsmill.demon.co.uk

W www.saltsmill.org.uk
Includes an extensive collection of works by David Hockney, housed in the 1853 Gallery.

Scarborough Art Gallery

The Crescent, Scarborough, YO11 2HG
T 01723 374753
F 01723 376941
E museuminfo@scarborough.gov.uk
W www.scarboroughmuseums.org.uk
Housed in an Italianate villa built in the 1840s, the permanent collection includes works by Grimshaw, H.B. Carter, Lord Leighton, Ivon Hitchens, Matthew Smith, Edward Bawden and Eric Ravilious. Also runs a temporary exhibition programme.

Site Gallery

1 Brown Street, Sheffield, S1 2BS
T 0114 2812077
F 0114 2812078
E info@sitegallery.org
W www.sitegallery.org
Founded as Untitled Gallery in 1978 by a group of photographers who set up a darkroom and gallery in a small shop. Site Gallery launched in 1995, giving a new direction to the gallery's programming of exhibitions and events by incorporating the new and experimental, digital and multimedia alongside traditional forms of image production. Also runs commissioning and residency programme.
Talks/Events/Education Education and training activities and open-access production facilities.

Towneley Hall Art Gallery & Museum

Towneley Park, Burnley, BB11 3RP
T 01282 424213
F 01282 436138
E towneley@burnley.gov.uk
W www.towneleyhall.org.uk
A country house opened as Burnley's art gallery in 1902. Houses permanent collection of eighteenth–twentieth century oils and watercolours and hosts regular contemporary exhibitions. Various rooms available for small and medium sized exhibitions.
Submission Policy CV and image of work with details of medium, sizes etc. to the curator.
Talks/Events/Education Occasional artists demonstrations, usually held on Sundays.

Wakefield Art Gallery

Wentworth Terrace, Wakefield, WF1 3QW
T 01924 305796
F 01924 305770

E museumsandarts@wakefield.gov.uk
W www.wakefield.gov.uk
Houses a distinguished collection of modern British art, including internationally significant works by locally born sculptors Barbara Hepworth and Henry Moore. The Gott Collection contains over a thousand works on paper relating to the topography and architecture of Yorkshire from the 1700s. Also has notable Edwardian and Victorian paintings, British portraiture and seventeenth-century Italian and northern European paintings and drawings. The decorative-art collection contains a range of eighteenth-century British and European wares and a small collection of studio pottery and contemporary craft. In 2008 the museum will be supeceded by The Hepworth, a major new gallery being built on Wakefield's waterfront.
Submission Policy Exhibition proposals accepted from regional and national artists. Art and design relevant to the region or permanent collection particularly welcome.
Talks/Events/Education A regular programme of events and activities for children and adults.

West Yorkshire Print Workshop

75a Huddersfield Road, Mirfield, WF14 8AT
T 01924 497646
F 01924 497646
E print.workshop@btconnect.com
W westyorkshireprintworkshop.co.uk
Founded in 1981, running printmaking workshops for adults. Also has open access facilities available for members and a number of artists's studios. Curates exhibitions for members at various venues including Dean Clough Gallerie, Halifax.
Submission Policy Only sells work from members.
Talks/Events/Education Runs specialist printmaking courses one weekend a month.

York City Art Gallery

Exhibition Square, York, YO1 7EW
T 01904 687687
E art.gallery@ymt.org.uk
W www.york.art.museum
Founded in 1879 and houses notable collections of continental Old Masters from the fourteenth to the eighteenth centuries, British paintings from the seventeenth to the twentieth centuries, and twentieth-century studio ceramics. The galleries were rehung in 2005 in thematic displays.

Yorkshire Sculpture Park

West Bretton, Wakefield, WF4 4LG
T 01924 832631

F 01924 832600
E info@ysp.co.uk
W www.ysp.co.uk
Founded in 1977, an international, outdoor centre for modern and contemporary sculpture. Changing exhibitions and projects are sited in five hundred acres of historical gardens and parkland, four indoor galleries and an award-winning visitor centre. Outdoor sculpture includes work by Barbara Hepworth, Anthony Caro, Antony Gormley, Elisabeth Frink and Sol LeWitt as well as one of the world's largest open air displays of bronzes by Henry Moore.
Talks/Events/Education Educational events are held throughout the year and include workshops, sculpture courses, lectures, study days talks and tours.

Ireland

The Ark
11a Eustace Street, Dublin 2
T 01 6707788
F 01 6707758
E boxoffice@ark.ie
W www.ark.ie
Opened in 1995, Europe's first custom-designed cultural centre devoted exclusively to innovative arts programming for children. Houses an indoor theatre, an outdoor amphitheatre, gallery spaces and a workshop. The centre provides entertaining and stimulating programmes across the arts for children aged between 4 and 14 years and their families. The programme changes regularly and features plays, exhibitions, workshops, festivals, concerts, readings, opera, dance and multimedia.
Talks/Events/Education The Ark offers interactive programmes for primary schools during school time and for individual children and family groups at other times.

Bank of Ireland Arts Centre
Foster Place, Temple Bar, Dublin 2
T 01 671 2261
E boi.arts@boimail.com
W www.boi.ie/artscentre
A part of the Bank's ongoing support programme of cultural and artistic events, which includes 'Stagewise' performing arts and exhibitions. Most events are free of charge. In addition to its other facilities, the Arts Centre offers an exhibition space, showcasing a diverse selection of established and emerging Irish artists. Also available for charitable organizations and

travelling exhibitions. Displays usually run for two to three weeks each throughout the year, with minimum commission for the artists.

Beit Art Collection
Russborough House, Blessington, County Wicklow
T 045 865239
F 045 865054
E russborough@eircom.net
Includes paintings by Vernet, Guardi, Bellotto, Gainsborough, Rubens and Reynolds.

Belltable Arts Centre
69 O'Connell Street, Limerick
T 061 319866
F 061 418552
E info@belltable.ie
W www.belltable.ie
Belltable provides access to all forms of performance and visual arts, as well as developing outreach and education programmes. It is among the major venues hosting 'v + a, the exhibition of visual+art', an annual exhibition of contemporary art, now in its thirtieth year.

Bourn Vincent Gallery
Foundation Building, University, Limerick
T 061 213052
Offers gallery facilities for professional artists from around Ireland to show and sell their work. No commission taken.

Butler Gallery
The Castle, Kilkenny
T 056 7761106
F 056 7770031
E info@butlergallery.com
W www.butlergallery.com
Established in 1942, a major contemporary art space hosting established international artists as well as local emerging artists.

Carlow Public Art Collection
County Library, Dublin Street, Carlow
T 059 9131126
Exhibits local crafts and paintings.

Chester Beatty Library
Dublin Castle, Dublin 2
T 01 4070750
F 01 4070760
E info@cbl.ie
W www.cbl.ie

One of Ireland's National Cultural Institutions, the library was established in Dublin in 1950 by Sir Alfred Chester Beatty and moved to its present location at Dublin Castle in 2000. The Library is both an art museum and library, housing a collection of Islamic manuscripts, Chinese, Japanese, Indian and other Oriental art; early papyri; and early Christian manuscripts, western prints and printed books. Admission is free. The CBL Reference Library contains 8,000 volumes relating to the collection.
Talks/Events/Education Hosts talks, demonstrations in techniques (such as calligraphy, painting, printing) and public tours and films. All free of charge.

Clonmel Gallery
Clonmel, South Tipperary
Gallery of paintings by range of notable Irish artists of the twentieth century.

Courthouse Arts Centre
Tinahely, County Wicklow
T 0402 38529
E tinahely@iol.ie
W www.tinahely-courthouse.ie
The courthouse in Tinahely was built in 1843 and reopened in 1996 as a centre for arts, culture and heritage. Presents a varied programme of events including visual arts exhibitions and installations, musical and theatre performances, and arthouse and foreign cinema. The visual arts programme aims to provide a space for art in virtually all media, by both emerging and established artists from Ireland and abroad.
Submission Policy Artists wishing to be considered for an exhibition are encouraged to contact the Centre. Annual selection process takes place in June. Send a CV and up to twelve slides (and sae), a CD or other photographic documentation of your work to Shelley Hayes.

Crawford Municipal Art Gallery
Emmet Place, Cork
T 021 4907855
F 021 4805043
E crawfordinfo@eircom.net
W www.crawfordartgallery.com
The city art museum for Cork has a permanent collection comprising over 2,000 works, ranging from eighteenth-century Irish and European painting and sculpture through to contemporary video installations. At its heart is a collection of Greek and Roman sculpture casts. It is also

particularly strong in Irish art of the nineteenth and early-twentieth centuries. Admission is free.
Submission Policy Artists can submit work for the annual 'Crawford Open' exhibition of contemporary art. Contact Anne Boddaert (021 4907857) for information.

Douglas Hyde Gallery
Trinity College, Dublin 2
T 01 6081116
F 01 6708330
E dhgallery@tcd.ie
W www.douglashydegallery.com
Opened in 1978 and forms part of Trinity College's Arts block. Particular focus on installations, photography/video, conceptual work and painting. Has held exhibitions in recent years by celebrated older modern and contemporary artists such as Gerhard Richter, Bruce Nauman and Louise Bourgeois. More typically works with the younger generation though (Marlene Dumas, Peter Doig, Felix Gonzalez-Torres, Gabriel Orozco and Luc Tuymans all held their first one-person Irish exhibitions here). Many Irish artists have held major exhibitions at the gallery, including Gerard Byrne and Michael Craig-Martin.
Talks/Events/Education Staff, student guides, artists and other guest speakers give regular talks during the shows.

Draíocht Arts Centre
The Blanchardstown Centre, Blanchardstown, Dublin 15
T 01 885 2622
F 01 824 3434
E marketing@draiocht.ie
W www.draiocht.ie
Ireland's largest purpose built arts centre, opened in 2001. Aims to provide stimulating and accessible arts programming to visitors from Dublin 15 and its environs. Children, young people and families form a major part of the audience base. The multi-purpose venue is used for a broad range of activities, including contemporary visual arts and crafts, multi-media arts activities, music, drama and dance. The centre has two gallery spaces, a self-contained artist's studio and other spaces available for hire. Also offers artists-in-residence schemes, community outreach and education projects and conference facilities.
Submission Policy Applications accepted all year round. Contact Carissa Farrell (T 01 8098026 or email carissa@draiocht.ie) for further information.

Talks/Events/Education Regular evening courses for adults, teaching basic skills in painting, pottery techniques and art appreciation.

The Dublin City Gallery, Hugh Lane
Charlemont House, Parnell Square North
Dublin 1
T 01 2225550
F 01 8741132
E info.hughlane@dublincity.ie
W www.hughlane.ie
Houses one of Ireland's foremost collections of modern and contemporary art. The original collection, donated by the Gallery's founder Sir Hugh Lane, has grown to almost 2,000 artworks and includes paintings, sculpture, works on paper and stained glass. The collection ranges from the Impressionist masterpieces of Manet, Monet, Renoir and Degas to works by leading national and international contemporary artists. Also has a temporary exhibitions programme and stages historical and retrospective exhibitions, particularly of Irish art. A recent €13 million expansion added a contemporary wing and thirteen new galleries to complement the existing thirteen galleries in Charlemont House, the gallery's home since 1933.
Talks/Events/Education Adult education courses and weekend lecture series. For further information contact Katy Fitzpatrick, Education Curator (T 01 2225553).

Dublin Writers' Museum
18 Parnell Square, Dublin 1
T 01 8722077
F 01 8722231
W www.writersmuseum.com
Includes protraits of many of Ireland's most famous writers.

Dunamaise Arts Centre
Church Street, Portlaoise
T 057 866 3356
F 057 866 3357
E info@dunamaise.ie
W www.dunamaise.ie
Aims to provide the people of Laois and the surrounding counties with access to the best in contemporary arts practice, both professional and community, in the performing and visual arts. Funded by the Arts Council and Laois County Council, the centre presents work by leading local, national and international performance and visual artists.

Submission Policy Submit a CV and portfolio of work to the Director, Louise Donlon. Closing dates for applications on website.

Gallery of Photography
Meeting House Square, Temple Bar, Dublin 2
T 01 6714654
F 01 6709293
E gallery@irish-photography.com
W www.irish-photography.com
Founded in 1978, a leading non-profit gallery for photography, exhibiting many major names. Moved to current location (complete with well-equipped darkrooms) in 1995.
Talks/Events/Education The gallery runs a wide range of courses and talks all year to facilitate both the analogue and digital photographer.

Galway Arts Centre
47 Dominick Street, Galway
T 091 565886
F 091 568642
E info@galwayartscentre.ie
W www.galwayartscentre.ie
Operates from two buildings, both located in Galway city centre. First established in 1982 at 23 Nun's Island, in 1988 the centre took over its second premises at 47 Dominick Street, which houses its art galleries, workshop/studios and administrative offices. Aims to nurture all forms of artistic activity, to facilitate emerging artists and arts groups, to heighten awareness of the arts via its education programme and to provide access to its facilities for all sectors of the community. Exhibits work in a range of media including painting, print sculpture and new media
Submission Policy Artists are welcome to submit work throughout the year, on CD/DVD/slides. Submissions to be made to Maeve Mulreann (Visual Arts Officer).
Talks/Events/Education Classes in lifedrawing, still life drawing and painting, photography and history of art. Courses run for 10 weeks. Contact Victoria Mc Cormack (T: 091 565886 or email victoria@galwayartscentre.ie).

Garter Lane Arts Centre
5 O'Connell Street, Waterford
T 051 877153
E antonia@garterlane.ie
W www.garterlane.ie
Gallery opened in 1984 in a late-eighteenth century town house which was used as the Waterford Municipal Library until 1983. The

building also houses a children's art room, artists' studios and a dance room. Shows current visual art practice of local, national and international standing. Also exhibits the work of recent graduates/new artists.

Submission Policy Propoosals should include a current CV, brief artist statement and images of current work in slide, photographic or digital format. The Gallery takes 25% on all work sold. Calls for submission are advertised through the Visual Arts Bulletin etc.

Talks/Events/Education Artists are invited to give talks about their work. Various children's and adult classes are held through the year.

Glebe House and Gallery

Churchill, Letterkenny, County Donegal
T 074 9137071
F 074 9137521
E info@heritageireland.ie
W www.heritageireland.ie
Home to the Derek Hill Permanent Collection, which includes 300 works by leading twentieth century artists, both Irish and international. The house itself has fine collection of William Morris designs and examples of Islamic and Japanese art.

Helen Hooker O'Malley Roelofs Sculpture Collection

Castletroy, Limerick
T 061 333644
Permanent collection of around forty sculptures by Helen Hooker O' Malley Roelofs (1906–1993) held at the University of Limerick. Subjects include Eamon De Valera, Seamus Heaney, Samuel Beckett and James Galway, cast during 1992–93 at the Dublin Art Foundry.

Hunt Museum

Rutland Street, Limerick
T 061 312833
F 061 312834
E info@huntmuseum.com
W www.huntmuseum.com
One of Ireland's most important private art collections of art, spanning the centuries and including works from Picasso, Renoir and Yeats.

Irish Museum of Modern Art

Royal Hospital, Military Road, Kilmainham
Dublin 8
T 01 6129900
F 01 6129999
E info@imma.ie
W www.imma.ie
Ireland's leading national institution for the collection and presentation of modern and contemporary art. Presents a wide variety of art in a programme of exhibitions, which regularly includes bodies of work from its own Collection and its award-winning Education and Community Department. It also creates access to art and artists through its Studio and National programmes. The museum is housed in the seventeenth-century Royal Hospital building, whose grounds include a formal garden, meadow and medieval burial grounds.

Submission Policy Artists should send in a CV with an example of three slides of their work.

Talks/Events/Education Has a regular series of talks, lectures and events to allow the general public and targeted audiences an opportunity to interact with a cross section of artists, curators and specialists. All talks and lectures are free and open to the public.

Leitrim Sculpture Centre

Manorhamilton, County Leitrim
T 072 56098 / 071 985098
Provides training and workshops facilities for sculptors and more general support for local visual artists working in a variety of media. The Centre was founded by the Manorhamilton Arts Group whose members include a number of locally-based full-time artists of national and international repute in stone, wood and bronze.

Letterkenny Arts Centre

Central Library, Oliver Plunkett Road, Letterkenny
T 074 9129186
F 074 9123276
E lkarts@eircom.net
W www.donegalculture.com
Specializes in visual arts, community arts, music, literature and film and hosts a programme of exhibitions, performances, festivals and workshops in the Centre and other spaces across Donegal. Admission to all exhibitions is free. A New Regional Cultural Centre was scheduled to be completed by the end of 2006, costing €4.5 million. The 1,700 m2 building includes a dedicated digital media space, two exhibition galleries and three multi-purpose workshops.

Lewis Glucksman Gallery

University College Cork, Western Road, Cork
T 021 4901844
F 021 4901823

E info@glucksman.org
W www.glucksman.org
Opened in 2004 as a cultural and educational institution to promote the research, creation and exploration of the visual arts. Located in a landmark building that includes display spaces, lecture facilities, a riverside restaurant and specialist art bookshop. The shop stocks a wide range of art, architecture, design and culture books, alongside exhibition catalogues and the largest selection of art magazines in Ireland. A book ordering service is available and there are monthly promotions. Exhibitions programme places particular emphasis on the role of visual media in communicating knowledge. Central to this is the creation of discursive relationships between academic disciplines and art practice, reflected in exhibitions that span various media and historical periods.
Submission Policy Does not accept unsolicited proposals for its artistic programme.
Talks/Events/Education Offers a wide range of art workshops, film screenings, seminars, lecture series and artists' talks, many of which are available free of charge.

Limerick City Gallery of Art

Carnegie Building, Pery Square, Limerick
T 061 310633
F 061 310228
E lcgartzz@iol.ie
W www.limerickcorp.ie
Founded in 1948 as a purpose-built gallery addition to the Carnegie Free Library and Museum. Now all the building is used as exhibition space and recently a new South Wing Gallery was added. LCGA houses a permanent collection of paintings, sculptures and drawings by early eighteenth-, nineteenth- and twentieth-century Irish artists. The gallery is the home of the Irish National Collection of Contemporary Drawing, the Michael O'Connor Poster Collection and also hosts exhibitions by contemporary Irish and International artists including the annual EV+A (Exhibition of Visual Art). There are 40–45 temporary exhibitions per annum and admission is free.
Submission Policy Submissions for exhibition are welcome. Contact the gallery for any relevant information.

Linenhall Arts Centre

Linenhall Street, Castlebar, County Mayo
T 094 9023733

F 094 9026162
E linenhall@anu.ie
W www.thelinenhall.com
Established in 1990, the Linenhall exhibits a range of contemporary art in all disciplines with work ranging from that of young emerging artists to those of international reputation, both Irish and non-Irish. Produces an invitation/catalogue to accompany each exhibition and is responsible for promoting the exhibition. Also organizes associated gallery talks and an extensive schools programme of workshops. Offers support to visual artists and acts as a contact point for arts-oriented inquiries.
Submission Policy Invites submissions for specific visual arts-based projects and events both in-house and externally. Submissions judged by a panel. Send 8–10 images on 35mm slide or CD, plus CV and statement of intent.
Talks/Events/Education Talks take place regularly and are generally free.

The Market House

Market Street, Monaghan Town
T 047 38162
F 047 71113
E themarkethouse@eircom.net
W www.themarkethouse.ie
Showing work by artists from Ireland and overseas. 12–15 shows annually. Owned and run by Monaghan County Council.
Talks/Events/Education Every exhibition involves the artist holding a talk and workshop.

Maynooth Exhibition Centre

St. Patrick's College, Maynooth, County Kildare
T 01 6285222
F 01 7083954
W kildare.ie/arts/housing/maynooth-exhibition-centre.htm
Opened in 1992, an exhibition space in the foyer of the Arts Block shows local, national and international works.

Model Arts and Niland Gallery

The Mall, Sligo
T 071 9141405
F 071 9143694
E info@modelart.ie
W www.modelart.ie
A vibrant centre for the arts in Sligo, with an extensive visual and performing arts programme. Built in 1862 as a Model School, the present building was completely refurbished, extended

and reopened in 2000. Home to the Niland Art Collection, which has over 260 paintings, drawings and prints by leading Irish artists including works by John and Jack B. Yeats, Estella Solomons, Paul Henry, Sean Keating and Louis Le Broquy. The contemporary exhibition programme features nine solo or group exhibitions annually drawn from local, national and international artists. Previous artists have included Vivienne Roche, John Shinnors, Camille Souter and Barrie Cooke. Admission is free.
Talks/Events/Education Painting, life drawing, printing and creativity workshops.

Monaghan County Museum
1–2 Hill Street, Monaghan
T 047 82928
F 047 71189
E comuseum@monaghancoco.ie
W www.monaghan.ie/museum
Opened in 1974, becoming the first local authority-funded museum in the Republic of Ireland. Displays Monaghan's rich culture and heritage in its permanent exhibition galleries. Its collection consists of over 7,000 objects spanning some 9,000 years. There is a reference library with an extensive collection of periodicals and journals, particularly useful for archaeology and the arts. Admission to the museum is free.
Talks/Events/Education Occasionally holds lecture series inspired by the collection.

National Gallery of Ireland
Merrion Square West and Clare Street, Dublin 2
T 01 6615133
F 01 6615372
E info@ngi.ie
W www.nationalgallery.ie
Founded in 1854 and opened to the public in 1864, the National Gallery of Ireland today houses over 13,000 items, including European Old Master paintings (fourteenth to twentieth centuries), Irish paintings (seventeenth century to present) and a collection of European and Irish prints, drawings, miniatures and sculpture. Among the major artists represented are Fra Angelico, Rembrandt, Poussin, Vermeer, Caravaggio, Goya, Joshua Reynolds, Thomas Gainsborough, James Barry, O'Conor, William Orpen and John Lavery. The Gallery also offers extensive research services, a fine art library, print room, the centre for the study of Irish art and the Yeats Archive. There is also a picture library service. The gallery runs a varied exhibitions programme; education and outreach

activities, a publishing arm and a bookshop. Admission to the permanent collection is free.
Talks/Events/Education There is a regular programme of activities, including talks, tours, and workshops for both adults and young people, teachers and school groups. Nearly all events are free

National Photographic Archive
Meeting House Square, Temple Bar, Dublin 2
T 01 6030374
F 01 6777451
E photoarchive@nli.ie
W www.nli.ie/a_intro.htm
Comprises approximately 600,000 photographs, the vast majority of which are Irish. While most of the collections are historical there are also some contemporary collections. Subject matter ranges from topographical views to studio portraits, and from political events to early tourist photographs. The collections also include prints, manuscripts, music, books and periodicals. The Library maintains an active collecting policy and additional material is constantly added to the collections. There is a Reading Room, an exhibition area and a small shop. An online catalogue is accessible via the website or in the Reading Room.

National Print Museum of Ireland
Garrison Chapel, Beggars Bush, Dublin 4
T 01 6603770
F 01 6673545
E npmuseum@iol.ie
W www.iol.ie/~npmuseum/
Documents, preserves, exhibits and encourages the future development of the printing craft in Ireland. Provides an archive and study facilities for students researching printing in Ireland.
Talks/Events/Education One- or two-day workshops for adults are held teaching skills such as print-making, calligraphy and paper-making.

National Self-Portrait Collection of Ireland
Castletroy, Limerick
T 061 333644
Shows over 375 mixed media pieces by artists including Derek Hill, Andrew Kearney, Sean Keating, Alice Maher and Sarah Purser. New additions exhibition held each June.

Office of Public Works
Art Management Office, 51 St Stephen's Green, Dublin 2
T 01 6476000

F 01 6610747
E info@opw.ie
W www.opw.ie
The OPW manages the State art collection, which includes nearly 6,000 pieces by over 1,250 artists, located in State buildings throughout Ireland. OPW's funding for art in State buildings comes from a scheme which involves setting aside a basic 1% of all construction budgets for artistic features.

Old Market House Arts Centre
Lower Main Street, Dungarvan
T 058 48944
F 058 42911
E artscentre@waterfordcoco.ie
W www.waterfordcoco.ie
Opened in 2000 as an arts centre for County Waterford. Displays work in a variety of media including photographs, paintings and installations. Admission is free.
Submission Policy Applications to exhibit reviewed on regular basis. Send a one-page written statement of work, 6–12 slides or colour photographs of work, CV, indication of availability and selling price of work.

Project Arts Centre
39 East Essex Street, Temple Bar, Dublin 2
T 01 8819613/4
F 01 0792310
E info@project.ie
W www.project.ie
The Arts Centre shows temporary exhibitions of contemporary art.
Submission Policy All work is selected by the Curator.
Talks/Events/Education There is a free talk with every show.

Riverbank Arts Centre
Main Street, Newbridge, County Kildare
T 045 448333
F 045 432490
E artscentre@riverbank.ie
W www.riverbank.ie
Provides a high-profile, regionally and nationally significant visual arts venue. Gallery facilities include a foyer exhibition area and a designiated exhibition (white box) space.
Submission Policy Send a letter of proposal outlining the kind of exhibition envisaged, biographical information, visual documentation and copies of press releases (if any).

Sculpture in Woodland
c/o Coillte, Newtownmountkennedy, County Wicklow.
T 01 2011132
F 01 2011199
E sculpinfo@coillte.ie
W www.sculptureinwoodland.ie
A public art collection which aims to provide artists with the resources to create works of artistic excellence in a natural environment. Supports emerging and established artists from Ireland and abroad. Also seeks to increase public awareness of wood as an artistic medium.
Talks/Events/Education Runs educational and outreach programmes primarily for Wicklow-based schools and groups, and participates in National Tree Week, Heritage Week and other national events.

Sirius Arts Centre
Cobh, County Cork
T 021 4813790
F 021 4813790
E cobharts@iol.ie
W www.iol.ie/~cobharts
A multidisciplinary non-profit centre for the arts in the East Cork area, established in 1988. Annual programme focuses on raising artistic awareness, providing opportunities for participation in and enjoyment of the arts. Also runs a prestigious artists-in-residence programme.

Sligo Art Gallery
Yeats Memorial Building, Hyde Bridge, Sligo
T 071 45847
F 071 47426
E sagal@iol.ie
W www.sligoartgallery.com
Founded in 1977 under the auspices of the Yeats Society to provide exhibition facilities for all art forms, with a particular emphasis on contemporary art. Mounts 15–20 major exhibitions annually. There are also a number of showings outside the Gallery and projects which involve active public participation. Artists whose work has been individually exhibited include Patrick Collins, Antoni Tapies, Mary Swanzy and Patrick Heron. Solo show opportunities are given to emerging artists each year. Organizes the annual Iontas National Small Works Art Competition and Exhibition to provide a forum for contemporary Irish artists working in small format in any medium.
Submission Policy The Iontas National Small

Works Art Competition requests entries in any medium (maximum size of 600mm/60cm in their greatest dimension including frame or plinth).

South Tipperary Arts Centre
Nelson Street, Clonmel
T 052 27877
F 052 27866
E stac@eircom.net
W www.southtipparts.com
Founded 1996. Holds twelve exhibitions per year from Irish and international artists. The Centre welcomes innovative and challenging proposals from established artists and from artists who wish to present a debut exhibition.
Submission Policy Submissions should have strong visual support with a minimum of six slides or CD with six images, a proposal and CV.
Talks/Events/Education Hosts gallery talks by exhibiting artists, art appreciation classes and ongoing workshops in the Centre and around the region.

Toradh Gallery
Meath County Council Offices, Duleek
T 041 9880733
F 041 9880139
E toradhgallery@meathcoco.ie
W www.meath.ie/art_collection
Places particular emphasis on the work of emerging artists from Meath. In recent years Meath County Council has introduced a policy of purchasing at least one piece of work from each exhibiting artist at the Gallery. Collection consists of paintings, prints and sculpture representing over a century of art in Ireland, through a wide variety of styles. Artists featured in the collection include Maurice MacGonigal, Charles Lamb, Norah McGuinness and George Campbell. A selection of works can be viewed via an online catalogue (see website).

Triskel Arts Centre
Tobin Street, Cork
T 021 4272022
F 021 4272592
E info@triskelartscentre.com
W www.triskelart.com
An art space hosting public art, exhibitions, performances, residencies, film, literature events and festivals. Has a building, 'Triskel', and uses a variety of temporary spaces across the city.

Tyrone Guthrie Centre
Newbliss, County Monaghan
T 047 54003
F 047 54380
E info@tyroneguthrie.ie
W www.tyroneguthrie.ie
Offers artists's residencies in the house of the former actor and theatre director.

Watercolour Society of Ireland's Permanent Collection
Castletroy, Limerick
T 061 333644
A permanent collection of over 150 watercolours, added to annually by the Society. Includes works by artists such as Pheobe Donovan, Arthur Gibney, Jo Kinney and Muiris McGonagle. Free to the public during office hours and concert performances.

West Cork Arts Centre
North Street, Skibbereen, County Cork
T 028 22090
F 028 23237
E info@westcorkartscentre.com
W www.westcorkartscentre.com
Established in 1985 in Skibbereen, County Cork. It is a publicly funded arts facility that creates opportunities for the people of West Cork to have access to local and global arts practice of excellence. It supports a multi-disciplinary arts program with a focus on modern and contemporary visual art and a range of education and community programmes.

Wexford Arts Centre
Cornmarket, Wexford, County Wexford
T 053 23764
F 053 24544
E wexfordartscentre@eircom.net
W www.wexfordartscentre.ie
Runs programme of regular visual arts shows.

03

The Internet

The internet, Your Gallery and you

Rebecca Wilson

In December 2006 *TIME* announced its Person of the Year as 'You', arguing that no individual has had the same impact in 2006 as the billions of people who use the internet. For the first time in its history, the magazine gave its annual award not to one person, but to all the people who together have created what it termed 'a new digital democracy'. Online sites such as MySpace and YouTube have enabled millions of people all over the world to make global connections, to find audiences for their work – and all without the approval or aid of experts and professionals. As *TIME* put it, 'It's a story about community and collaboration on a scale never seen before.'

The collector Charles Saatchi, an influential force in the art world over the past 20 years, saw the huge potential for a site similar to MySpace, but dedicated to artists and the art world. In April 2006 the Saatchi Gallery launched Your Gallery (saatchigallery.com/yourgallery), a site designed to provide a global platform for artists all over the world to exhibit their work and to connect with other artists, dealers, collectors and exhibition curators. As Saatchi commented at the time, 'Many artists find it very hard to break into the gallery world. If they don't have the connections or aren't skilled at selling themselves, even good artists can struggle. We think that artists and collectors will benefit from working together without the dealer commission, and dealers have seemed to welcome the chance to view a lot of artists both domestically and internationally in their own time without commitment.'

Your Gallery is a non-profit site, now used by over 20,000 artists, each of whom have their own homepages on the site. Artists can upload images, information about themselves and their work, and contact details. No fee is charged for this service and the Saatchi Gallery takes no commission when artists sell their work via the site.

Your Gallery also publishes an online daily art magazine covering the international art world, publishing previews and reviews of exhibitions, tips on art to buy and emerging artists to watch out for, interviews with artists, book reviews, essays on topical issues and a weekly round-up of art news. Readers can also air their views on Your Gallery's public blog, take part in discussions on its forum and artists registered on the site can chat live to other Your Gallery artists and receive feedback on their work, expanding their circle of contacts and friends around the world. They can swap notes on their work and interests, find out about trends in different countries, learn about new techniques from other artists, and feel part of a huge community of like-minded, creative people.

Within six weeks Your Gallery had attracted over 1.7 million visitors from all over the world (the split for both artists and visitors to the site is one third from the UK, one third from the US and one third from the rest of the world) with thousands of artists exhibiting their work for the first time. Most registered artists don't have gallery representation, but many do and Your Gallery gives them access to far more people than an exhibition at a commercial gallery. As a result of posting images on the site, artists have sold their work, participated in exhibitions and have been taken on by galleries who might never have seen their art.

In November 2006 the Saatchi Gallery introduced another element to its Your Gallery site. Stuart, short for 'student art' (www.saatchi-gallery.co.uk/stuart/), functions in the same way as Your Gallery, but is exclusively designed for art students. This initiative not only tapped into collectors' and dealers' hunger to snap up work before art school degree shows, but also appealed to young people who have grown up using the internet and are its most frequent users.

Whether it is used to exhibit art or to convey information about the art world on a daily basis, the internet is perceived by some critics, dealers

and publishers of print magazines as a potential
threat – the *Guardian*'s critic Jonathan Jones
went so far as to suggest that showing art on
sites such as Your Gallery 'may undermine the
entire system of dealers, magazines and art
fairs that calls itself the "art world".' Even if
Jones's prediction proves not to be the case,
sites such as Your Gallery and Stuart have
provided an alternative platform for artists to
exhibit their work and make contacts, and for
the international art community to encounter
art being made beyond the so-called capitals of
the art world. Your Gallery has enabled
traditional hierarchies within the art world to be
circumvented – no longer is it necessary for
critics to give their approval before an artist's
work is noticed and bought, no longer does an
artist have to be on the books of a prestigious
gallery in order to attract collectors to their
work.

Rebecca Wilson, formerly deputy editor of *Modern
Painters* and editor of *ArtReview*, is the editor of
the online magazine *Your Gallery*

The Internet

Online Art News, Magazines and Listings

24 Hour Museum
E info@www.24hourmuseum.org.uk
W www.24hourmuseum.org.uk
The UK's national virtual museum, offering content including daily arts and museum news, exhibition reviews and in-depth online trails. Promotes publicly funded UK museums, galleries and heritage attractions and seeks to develop new audiences for UK culture. Venue and listings information is driven by a searchable database of over three thousand museum, gallery and heritage sites.
Submission Policy Welcomes press releases from not-for-profit galleries and museums.

a-n The Artists Information Company / a-n Magazine
E info@a-n.co.uk
W www.a-n.co.uk
National organization with a mission to stimulate and support contemporary visual arts practice. Resources on www.a-n.co.uk include daily updated artists' jobs and opportunities, publications on making a living, establishing a charge rate and other professional practice issues, past and current issues of a-n Magazine (monthly magazine for professional artists and their collaborators), news and reviews, professional development toolkits, What's On and artists' directory listings, networking information and more. Some free resources but full access is reserved for a-n subscribers. An annual subscription starts from £28 available at www.a-n.co.uk/subscribe

Art Guide
E artguide@cogapp.com
W www.artguide.org
Founded in the late 1990s. A free online database of museums and galleries across the UK and Ireland. Visitors can search the site by artist and by special interest. Also a comprehensive, up-to-date exhibitions guide.

Art MoCo
E sabine@mocoloco.com
W www.mocoloco.com/art
A web magazine featuring contemporary art news and views.

Art News Blog
W www.artnewsblog.com
A selection of visual art news, art reviews and art related stories taken from the web.

art-online – The Fine Art Directory
W www.art-online.com
Contains links to editor-reviewed websites organized into the subject categories of art history, the art market, art venues, artists, education, employment, events, galleries, governments, legal, museums, professionals, resources, rewards and shopping.

art-shopper
E mail@art-shopper.co.uk
W www.art-shopper.com
Guide to commercial galleries throughout the UK.

artcourses.co.uk
E thah@artcourses.co.uk
W www.artcourses.co.uk
Contact:Jonathan Wickens
An online directory of art classes, craft workshops, painting holidays, etc. Europe-wide coverage of all media and all levels. Course providers with or without their own website can apply for an entry via the website. Offers a starter webpage service for artists without websites.

artdaily.com
E ignacio@artdaily.com
W www.artdaily.com
Contact:Ignacio Villarreal (Editor and Publisher)
Founded in 1996. The 'first art newspaper on the net'.

artefact
W www.artefact.co.uk
Online editions of *Galleries* and *The Collector* magazines, with searchable databases.

ArtInLiverpool.com
W www.artinliverpool.com
Includes gallery listings, blogs, artist profiles, a forum and art news for Liverpool.

artist-info: Contemporary Art Database
E mail@artist-info.com
W www.artist-info.com
An international contemporary art database. Includes artists, galleries and museums search function as well as extensive classifieds and offers from galleries.

Artlistings.com

W www.artlistings.com
An extensive art-related directory, encompassing galleries, schools, assorted media and profiles of famous artists.

Arts Culture Media Jobs

W www.artsculturemediajobs.com
Online database of jobs for people in the creative industries.

Arts Hub

E info@artshub.co.uk
W www.artshub.co.uk
A resource for UK arts workers, containing news and information on jobs and events.

Arts Journal

E mclennan@artsjournal.com
W www.artsjournal.com
A weekday digest of some of the best arts and cultural journalism in the English-speaking world. Combs more than two hundred English-language newspapers, magazines and publications every day.

Arts Professional Online

E editors@artsprofessional.co.uk
W www.artsprofessional.co.uk
The web edition of the leading arts management magazine.

ArtSouthEast

E editor@artsoutheast.co.uk
W www.artsoutheast.co.uk
An online gateway to arts events and information in the south-east of England.

Artupdate.com

E info@artupdate.com
W www.artupdate.com
A contemporary art exhibitions information service in print and online for a worldwide audience. Publishes bimonthly gallery maps for cities including London, Paris and New York, as well as an updated international online gallery directory.

Conservation Register

E info@conservationregister.com
W www.conservationregister.com
Online information on conservator-restorers throughout the UK and Ireland. Also offers guidance on caring for art, antiques and decorative features of buildings.

Submission Policy The criteria for inclusion in the Conservation Register, which include professional accreditation, can be viewed on the website.

Designspotter

W www.designspotter.com
A design web magazine dedicated to everything related to contemporary design. Offers young designers a platform to upload an image of their work, a short description and a weblink.

Digital Consciousness

W www.digitalconsciousness.com
A public database of contemporary art, with art and biographies of emerging and established artists exhibited through galleries and artists' pages.

The Gallery Channel

E support@thegallerychannel.com
W www.thegallerychannel.com
An online illustrated and searchable database of galleries, venues, artists and exhibitions worldwide. Since 1998 the database has grown to include more than 12,000 venues, 28,000 exhibitions and 27,000 artists. Add listings free of charge.
Submission Policy Open submission policy.

Global Art Jobs

W www.globalartjobs.com
A website with details of international visual arts vacancies.

KultureFlash

E events@kultureflash.net
W www.kultureflash.net
A free, weekly newsletter covering contemporary culture in and around London. Does not receive any payment from venues, artists, managers or promoters.

National Disability Arts Forum (NDAF)

E silvie@ndaf.org
W www.ndaf.org
Contact Silvie Fisch
NDAF's ArtsAccessUK is an online database of disabled access provided by art venues throughout the UK. Also displays the work of disabled artists on its website, and publishes a free weekly enewsletter.

New Exhibitions of Contemporary Art

E listings@newexhibitions.com
W www.newexhibitions.com
Founded in 1978. A bi-monthly, contemporary art

listings brochure free of charge at all galleries listed and web site version with linked gallery locations.

NewsGrist
newsgrist.typepad.com/underbelly
With extensive comment on art issues. Describes itself as 'where spin is art.'

Online Arts Consultants and Trainers Register
E arts@dimensions.co.uk
W www.arts-consultants.org.uk
Online register for organizations looking for consultants or trainers, or for consultants and trainers seeking to increase their public presence.

re-title.com
E info@re-title.com
W www.re-title.com
A dynamic resource and networking tool for the active international contemporary art community. Encourages dialogue and exchange of creativity between members and their audience. Includes searchable directories of artists and galleries. Artist members recieve self-editing porfolio pages, regular international 'artist opportunities' newsletters and the opportunity to post their exhibitions in the exhibitions directory.
Submission Policy Applications are encouraged from all active emerging contemporary artists, curators and galleries.

theSeer.info
E creativedevelopment@brent.gov.uk
W www.theSeer.info
Contact Abi Palmer
An arts directory and information website piloted by the London Borough of Brent and Royal Borough of Kensington and Chelsea in partnership with Arts Council England in London. The longer-term aspiration for the site is to be a free resource for all thirty-three of London's boroughs.

The UK Sponsorship Database
E info@uksponsorship.com
W www.uksponsorship.com
Contact Richard Fox
Founded in 2000. Offers those seeking sponsorship a means of displaying their sponsorship offering and requirements to sponsors via a categorized, online database. A range of formats and prices for listings is available. Low cost listings start at a one-off cost of £15.00.

WorldwideReview.com
W www.worldwidereview.com
Website for art and culture reviews, with a mix of open submissions and regular reviewers. No restriction on subject though focus is on contemporary art.

Online Art Networks and Communities

AHDS Visual Arts
E info@visualarts.ahds.ac.uk
W visualarts.ahds.ac.uk
Based at the University College for the Creative Arts at Canterbury, Epsom, Farnham, Maidstone and Rochester. Aim is to support the research and learning and teaching communities by providing high-quality digital resources for the visual arts, delivered through robust systems for internet access and the long-term preservation of educational resources.

APD
E apd@a-n.co.uk
W www.apd-network.info
The Artists' Professional Development (APD) network, initiated by a-n in 2001, is a UK-wide intelligence and exchange forum for organizations that are proactively developing information, advice, training and professional-development services for visual and applied artists.
Submission Policy Organisations for whom professional development provision is a core function are invited to visit www.apd-network.info to download an information pack on joining the network.

Art History Today
W arthistorytoday.blogspot.com
'David Packwood's art news blog and general musings on art history.'

Art in Context
E editor@artincontext.org
W www.artincontext.org
Established in 1995, offering free public access to information added by curators, dealers, artists, writers and others from around the world.

Art on the Net
E webmasters@art.net
W www.art.net

An international collective of artists sharing their works on the Internet. Currently represents over one hundred artists.

ArtForums.co.uk

W www.artforums.co.uk
Includes forums for artists, art-lovers and those looking to buy.

ArtNews.info

E info@artnews.info
W www.artnews.info
A non-profit online network where art professionals can explore, publish and exchange information on contemporary art. Includes free exhibition calendar and online catalogues for artists, galleries, curators and collectors.

artquest

E info@artquest.org.uk
W www.artquest.org.uk
Contact Stephen Beddoe (Programme Manager). Provides advice, information and support to visual artists and craftspeople living in London.

ArtRabbit

W www.artrabbit.com
Aims to accommodate the needs and desires of today's art world and art enthusiasts. Includes a forum, extensive listings and opinion pieces.

Asian Arts Access

E kalwant.ajimal@which.net
W www.asianartsaccess.org
The website for Asian Arts Access, an arts development agency, research and development organization and production house.

Backspace

E info@backspace.org
W www.bak.spc.org
An 'open environment for exploration and expression on the Internet and the focal point for related events, audio, visual and otherwise, with particular bias toward the diverse talents of its subscribers'

Creative Futures

W www.creativefutures.cadise.ac.uk
Contact Helen Day (Project Administrator)
A specialist careers resource for creative and performing arts, design and communications students to connect with arts and creative industry employers.

CreativePeople

E info@creativepeople.org.uk
W www.creativepeople.org.uk
Contact Barbara Brunsdon
A UK network of organizations, individually supplying training and professional-development information, advice and guidance services to current and aspiring arts and crafts practitioners. Details of and links to the member organizations are provided on the website. CreativePeople is supported by Arts Council England and as well as signposting arts practitioners to resources, the network provides a peer community for anyone supplying professional development services in the sector.
Submission Policy Address for postal applications: PO Box 2677, Caterham, CR3 6WJ
T 01883 371112

Cybersalon

E lewis@cybersalon.org
W www.cybersalon.org
Contact Lewis Sykes
Aims to be a forum for debate and discussion on digital-media issues, a showcase for new work and a meeting place for people to exchange ideas and make new contacts.

digital art source

E contact@digitalartsource.com
W www.digitalartsource.com
An online resource for digital art and culture information.

The Digital Artist

E carol@thedigitalartist.com
W www.thedigitalartist.com
Contact Carol Pentleton
An exhibition site for artists, designers and artisans. Free exhibits include name, contact information, biography, artist's statement, webpage link and one image. Exhibitors are from around the world, from students to established professionals. Offers free monthly newsletters and e-books, classifieds, forums and articles.
Submission Policy Artists, designers and artisans in all media welcome.

electronic flux corporation (e-flux)

W www.e-flux.com
A New York-based information bureau dedicated to worldwide distribution of intelligence via the internet for contemporary visual arts institutions.

Foundation for Art and Creative Technology (FACT)

E info@fact.co.uk
W www.fact.co.uk
Commissions, exhibits, promotes and supports artists' work and innovation in the fields of film, video and creative technology. Founded in 1988 as Moviola, FACT has commissioned and presented over 100 digital media artworks with artists including Mark Wallinger, Barbara Kruger, Tony Oursler and Isaac Julien.

Furtherfield

E info@furtherfield.org
W www.furtherfield.org
Contact Marc Garrett
Creates 'imaginative strategies that actively communicate ideas and issues in a range of digital and terrestrial media contexts'. Features works online and organizes global, contributory projects on the internet, the streets and at public venues simultaneously.

Hidden Art

E info@hiddenart.co.uk
W www.hiddenart.com
A membership organization that supports and promotes designer-makers, while offering companies and members of the public access to original design. Focuses on works or products with a predominantly functional use, covering a broad range of disciplines including textiles, furniture, lighting, interior products, ceramics, glass design, fashion accessories and jewellery.
Submission Policy Can only support designer-makers, not visual or fine artists. There is no selection procedure for membership – selection procedures are only required for certain projects.

irational

E irational@irational.org
W www.irational.org
An 'international system for deploying "irational" information, services and products for the displaced and roaming'. Supports independent artists and organizations creating work that pushes the boundaries between the corporate realms of business, art and engineering.

Intute Arts and Humanities

E artsandhumanities@intute.ac.uk
W www.intute.ac.uk/artsandhumanities
Contact Jayne Burgess
Formerly known as Artifact, this is a free, searchable guide to the best of the web for the arts and creative industries' teaching, learning and research community. Part of Intute, aimed at internet users in UK further and higher education but freely available to all.

MadforArts

W www.madforarts.org
A web and television project that aims to encourage people with mental health issues to talk about public art that inspires them.

metamute

E mute@metamute.org
W www.metamute.org
A web platform for debates on culture, politics and globalization.

nettime

W www.nettime.org
A mailing list and 'an effort to formulate an international, networked discourse that neither promotes a dominant euphoria (to sell products) nor continues the cynical pessimism, spread by journalists and intellectuals in the "old" media who generalize about "new" media with no clear understanding of their communication aspects.'

No Knock Room

E info@noknockroom.com
W www.noknockroom.com/indexmain.php
A contemporary art portal which opened in 2006 with the aim of supporting emerging artists and showcasing trends in contemporary art.

Rhizome.org

E webmaster@rhizome.org
W www.rhizome.org
A non-profit organization founded in 1996 to provide an online platform for the global new-media art community.

stot

E stot@stot.org
W www.stot.org
Contact Jonathan Rust
A not-for-profit contemporary art platform that, in addition to producing artist projects, facilitates a comprehensive online resource of thousands of links to international galleries, festivals, fairs, biennials, publications and residencies. Also includes an extensive section devoted to new media, and user forums providing an outlet for news and opportunities in related arts.

Trans Artists
E info@transartists.nl
W www.transartists.nl
Offers independent information to artists, artist-run initiatives and cultural institutions about cultural exchanges, residency programmes and work opportunities in the Netherlands and abroad.

Universes in Universe – Worlds of Art
E info@universes-in-universe.de
W www.universes-in-universe.de
A non-commercial online information system focusing on the visual arts of Africa, Latin America and Asia within the context of international art processes.

Online Galleries

absolutearts.com and World Wide Arts Resources Corp.
E help@absolutearts.com
W www.absolutearts.com and wwar.com
Contact Janet Thomas
One of the largest art sites on the internet, wwar.com (founded in 1995) expanded in 1999 to include absolutearts.com, which began as a daily arts news outlet and is now a comprehensive contemporary art online portfolio and art sales programme, with artists selecting a level of online portfolio from free to premiere. Also offers artblogs written by artists, curators and collectors from around the world.
Submission Policy Arts news submissions should be complete press releases in English and must be received two weeks before exhibition opening. The venue, exhibition or artists must have a website.

apob Original Art Galleries
E info@apob.co.uk
W www.apob.co.uk
Showcase of work by UK artists, all for sale. Currently over 300 artists showing over 2,000 works across genres.

Art in the City
E admin@artinthecity.co.uk
W www.ArtintheCity.co.uk
Founded in 2003, now with over fifty professional or semi-professional artists. Each artist page has room for sixteen pictures, with artist maintaining total control over editorial and picture content via access to a secure database. Includes personal email and message system. Artists able to show work at two quality sites in Manchester City Centre. (Small extra charges for these exhibitions). No commission on sales from the site organized by artist.
Submission Policy Artists need to complete internet application and submit work. Small annual charge on acceptance. Maximum of 16 pictures on own page.

Art Industri
W www.artindustri.com
Promotes the work of students, amateur and professional artists, and art galleries via a network of sites offering promotional tools, reference information and resource services to the art community.

artart.co.uk
E curator@artart.co.uk
W www.artart.co.uk
Contact Lawrie Simonson
Founded in 2000, offering a platform to professional artists to exhibit and offer for sale works of art. Has a varied stable of professional artists and welcomes recent arts graduates onto the site. Tends to show predominantly modern painting and sculpture but also a good selection of other specialized media including ceramics and photography.
Submission Policy Requires 8–12 images/jpegs of good quality, CV and statement.

Artistri
W www.artistri.co.uk
Online gallery showcasing original modern art by graduates and exceptional undergraduates from Scottish Art Schools.

artrat
E enquiries@artrat.co.uk
W www.artrat.co.uk
Contact Thomas Fazzini
Founded in 2003. A platform for new and established artists to exhibit and sell their work. Free to exhibit. Commission applies if sold through the site. Also features regularly updated interviews with cutting-edge artists, musicians and actors as well as current views and reviews.

artroof.com
E info@artroof.com
W www.artroof.com
Helps artists to establish an online art gallery in a few minutes.

ArtsCurator Ltd
E info@artsCurator.co.uk
W www.artscurator.co.uk
Contact Simon Clark
Formed in 2004 to provide a fully supported service for artists who wish to promote their work via the internet. Each artist gets their own content-managed website, which takes no technical expertise to update.

Artshole.co.uk
E tony@artshole.co.uk
W www.artshole.co.uk
Founded in 2002, providing professional, emerging and student artists with a free platform to showcase and sell their art work. Currently shows over two thousand artists. Free listings section and many online links and resourses.

axis
E info@axisweb.org
W www.axisartists.org.uk
An online guide to practising artists in the UK. For each artist there is detailed information, examples of art works, projects and links to further information.

britart.com
W www.britart.com
An online forum for buying and selling UK art works.

Clikpic
E support@clikpic.com
W www.clikpic.com
Offers websites for artists for a small annual subscription. With an easy-to-use template system and a range of design schemes created especially for artists and photographers, artists can create a professional-looking website within hours, which can be edited at will. Works sold online via PayPal. Free seven-day trial for interested artists.

Counter-
E info@countereditions.com
W www.countereditions.com
A website of prints and multiples by contemporary artists.

DegreeArt.com
E info@DegreeArt.com
W www.DegreeArt.com
Contact Elinor Olisa or Isobel Beauchamp
Established in 2003, inviting clients to buy, rent or commission contemporary artwork created by students and recent graduates from the UK's leading art establishments. Artists showcased through the web, in exhibitions and at art fairs. Represents all genres including painting, photography, sculpture, print, design, installation, video and drawing and can offer support and advice on marketing to our artists.
Submission Policy Accepts applications from current students and artists who graduated within three years. Application details on website.

eyestorm
E emma.poole@eyestorm.com
W www.eyestorm.com
Contact Angie Davey
Founded in 1999. An online company offering exclusive signed limited-edition prints by many leading contemporary artists, including Damien Hirst, Jeff Koons, Peter Blake and Helmut Newton.

Fine Art Surrey
E leon@fineartsurrey.com
W www.fineartsurrey.com
Contact Leon Deith
An international online gallery selling oil paintings, watercolours, sculpture and prints by British contemporary and traditional artists including members of the Federation of British Artists and other leading art societies. Spearheading sales into China, Russia and the Middle East, with future exhibitions planned. Price range from £95–£150,000.
Submission Policy Always looking for new artists. In first instance visit the website and submit via artists' registration.

Fine Artz Virtual Gallery
E enquiries@fineartz.com
W www.fineartz.com
A virtual art gallery displaying work from new and emerging fine artists from the UK and beyond.

folk archive
E folk@folkarchive.co.uk
W www.folkarchive.co.uk
Ongoing project to show contemporary folk art from all parts of Britain and Ireland. Organizes touring exhibitions of some material. Check with British Council for more information.
Submission Policy Not actively seeking submissions.

Fotonet

E office@fotonet.org.uk
W www.fotonet.org.uk
Contact Susie Medley (Director)
A website showing curated online exhibitions and a source of information for photographers. Run by Fotonet (founded in 1999), a photography development organization based at the Winchester Gallery, Winchester School of Art.

InsideSpace

E enquiries@insidespace.com
W www.insidespace.com
Founded in 2000, operating from a gallery in the West End and from Selfridges on Oxford Street. Specializes in affordable, striking, often humorous art for the design-conscious buyer. Particular focus on photography but does exhibit paintings, drawings, original prints and multiples. Also operates a corporate art consultancy service and is active in the office, healthcare, hotel and leisure markets.
Submission Policy Email jpegs of work. The gallery does not exhibit installations or video work.

Irving Sandler Artists File

E artfile@artistsspace.org
W afonline.artistsspace.org
A digitized image database and slide registry open to the public free-of-charge. Regularly used by curators, artists, gallery owners, collectors, consultants, and students. Artists can include 12 images, statement and resume in their online portfolio. No fee to join or view the Artists File, and users contact the artists directly.

JoeDaisy Studio

E studio@joedaisy.co.uk
W www.joedaisy.co.uk
Contact Caroline Hulse (Senior Partner)
Leading corporate art suppliers, located in a Grade-II listed building in the conservation area of Mapledurham. Offers a number of artists' resources, including studio space, painting days and weekends, giclee printing and assistance to artists. Extensive online gallery.
Submission Policy Relocated to the new studio space in August 2005 and now able to show artists' work and offer studio space and painting tuition.

Londonart.co.uk

E paul@londonart.co.uk
W www.londonart.co.uk
Contact Paul Wynter

Set up in 1997 to provide artists with an opportunity to show their work online, and buyers with a wide choice of original contemporary art. The site now offers 15,000 works for sale from over 900 artists, with prices ranging from £50 to over £40,000. There are five painting categories (figurative, landscape, abstract, still life and drawing) and four other categories (digital, sculpture, photography and other).
Submission Policy Welcomes applications from visual artists making original contemporary art. All applications will be carefully considered.

Mini Gallery

E enquiries@minigalleryworld.com
W www.minigalleryworld.com
Contact Hazel Semple or Chris Storey
Established in 2002, showcasing art by self-representing contemporary artists. Each member artist has own mini-website, including online gallery space to display and sell art commission-free, and is provided with all the tools necessary to manage their online profile.
Submission Policy Applications are welcome at any time via the online application form.

On-lineGallery

E info@on-linegallery.co.uk
W www.on-linegallery.co.uk
Contact Laureen Bromley
Founded in 2005, selling hundreds of original art pieces and art prints from a number of artists. Works range from watercolour landscapes to abstract oils and photography, all available to buy online. Different membership options offered depending on the needs of the artist, starting with free membership with a 37.5% commission on sales and rising to a £30 monthly membership fee with 5% commission on sales.
Submission Policy Before acceptance, an artist must submit at least 3 images for approval.

Paintings and Prints 2 – Artists of the World

W www.paintingsandprints2.com
Contact John and Susan Wood
Founded in 1999. An artists' directory including paintings and prints by various amateur and semi-professional artists.

Paprika Gallery

E info@paprikagallery.co.uk
W www.paprikagallery.co.uk
Contact Julia Phillips
Internet-based gallery and shop, offering artists a

cost-effective way of presenting their work to a large audience.

Submission Policy Inclusion is by application and artists are carefully selected to maintain a high standard. All artists are offered a free internet presence, with the gallery operating on a commission-only basis. Artists are under no obligation to sell their work solely through the Gallery and are encouraged to actively market their work elsewhere. Applications are welcomed from all disciplines.

scotlandart.com
E enquiries@scotlandart.com
W www.scotlandart.com
The largest original art website in Scotland.

shopforprints.com
E shopforprints@shopforprints.com
W www.shopforprints.com
Contact Peter Learoyd
The online shop for art prints, photographic prints and posters. Allows artists, cartographers and photographers to feature images of their work in online galleries and sell fine-art giclée reproduction prints easily and with minimum involvement. Offers worldwide customers constant access to buy prints online at a variety of sizes and on a range of different materials. Pays a monthly royalty of 50% of the selling price to the artist for every print sold.

Stuart
W www.saatchi-gallery.co.uk/stuart/
Supported by the Saatchi Gallery, an online resource where art students can showcase their work by uploading photos, profiles, videos and images.

Studioworx Contemporary Art Ltd
E help@studioworx.co.uk
W www.studioworx.co.uk
Contact Mark Withers
Founded in 2004, an online art store which has sold over 800 works. Specializes in abstract, pop art, naturalistic, surreal and futuristic works. Prices start at £25. Artists include Mark Withers, Tom Reed, Rachel Stewart and Joh Jackson.

Your Gallery
W www.saatchi-gallery.co.uk/yourgallery
Free resource offering online space to artists. Supported by the Saatchi Gallery. The order that artists appear on the website is random and changes regularly.

Online Reference

Art & Architecture Thesaurus Online
E AAT@getty.edu
W www.getty.edu/research/conducting_research/vocabularies/aat
A structured vocabulary of 133,000 terms, descriptions, bibliographic citations and other information relating to fine art, architecture, decorative arts, archival materials and material culture.

Art Movements
W www.artmovements.co.uk
A concise reference guide to the major art movements and periods.

Artcyclopedia
E jmalyon@artcyclopedia.com
W www.artcyclopedia.com
Aims to be 'the definitive guide to museum-quality fine art on the Internet'

ArtInfo
E newseditors@artinfo.com
W www.artinfo.com
Run by LTB Media, features include news, an artprice database, a calendar of international events, a directory of artists and art institutions, cultural travel guides, job listings, analysis of market trends and education information.

Artlex Art Dictionary
W www.artlex.com
Offers over 3,500 definitions of terms relevant to art and visual culture. Includes images, pronunciation notes, quotations and cross-references.

artnet
E jlaplaca@artnet.com
W www.artnet.com
A site for buying, selling and researching fine art online. Serves dealers and buyers alike by providing a survey of the market and its pricing trends. A price database represents auction results from over 500 international auction houses since 1985, covering more than 2.6 million art works by over 180,000 artists.

artprice.com
W www.artprice.com
Leading information source on the art market. Hosts a database of over 20 million auction prices

and indices, auction results and over 300,000 artists.

British Arts
E arts@britisharts.co.uk
W www.britisharts.co.uk
Wideranging guide to the British art scene, including online resources, a shop, printing information and guides to different artists and styles.

Creative Space Agency
E info@creativespaceagency.org.uk
W www.creativespaceagency.org.uk
Offers help to the creative sector on how to make use of temporarily vacant space and buildings in London.

culturebase.net
E info@culturebase.net.
W www.culturebase.net
An online information source on contemporary international artists from all fields.

culture.info
W uk.culture.info
Provides links to key UK cultural information and resource websites including associations and networks; funding and development bodies; support and resource agencies; and portals and information sources.

FindArtInfo.com
E contact@findartinfo.com
W www.findartinfo.com
Contains price information for fine art across genres, styles and eras.

Grove Art Online
W www.groveart.com

A subscription website offering online content of the Grove Dictionary of Art. Contains over 45,000 articles on fine arts, decorative arts, and architecture and 130,000 art images, with links to museums and galleries around the world. Fully explorable.

Own Art
W www.artscouncil.org.uk/ownart
An online guide to Arts Council England's interest-free loan scheme for purchasing art.

Own It
E info@own-it.org
W www.own-it.org
Offers free advice, resources and events on the protection, management and exploitation of intellectual property for creative businesses, including information on copyright, design rights, trademarks, licensing, royalties and contracts. Membership is free and members can: attend events; download event podcasts, sample legal contracts and legal factsheets; access free IP legal advice and attend IP clinics (free 45-minute one-to-ones with lawyers).

the-artists.org
W www.the-artists.org
A database of biographical information on leading twentieth-century and contemporary visual artists.

Visual Collections
E carto@luna-img.com
W www.davidrumsey.com/collections
A searchable archive of over 300,000 images of fine art works, photographs, maps and other items from thirty-five major international museum, academic and private collections. Administered by Cartography Associates.

A different kind of enthusiast

Jeremy Deller

Jeremy Deller occupies a radically different position to most artists in the UK. Perhaps as a result of not progressing through an art school system, his work has never conformed to any one mode of production and consists of anything from performance, photography and film to public art or even music. Indeed, many of his works are collaborations with other artists, musicians, scientists or ordinary members of the public. In 1995 Deller conceived 'Acid Brass', a series of concerts in which compositions taken from acid-house music were reinterpreted by the Williams Fairey Brass Band at prominent events such as the opening of Tate Modern. Famously in 2001, he staged a re-enactment of a 1984 pitched battle between police and striking Yorkshire miners – many of whom were embroiled in the original fighting – all of which was filmed by film director Mike Figgis and televized as 'The Battle of Orgreave'. Deller has, at varying times, organized other participatory art marches and street parades that highlight a whole range of historical, contemporary, political and social concerns. Often he turns curator: the 'Folk Archive' (www.folkarchive.co.uk), which he initiated with fellow artist Alan Kane, is an ongoing investigation into the state of contemporary folk art in Britain. Despite Deller's contrary and complex role as an artist, he was awarded the ultimate industry accolade – the Turner Prize – in 2004 and has exhibited and sold work internationally. His open-ended artistic practice is one of the many diverse ways that exist to pursue a career as an artist. Here he discusses how to be, or perhaps how not to be, an alternative artist.

Do you see yourself as an alternative artist, or would you characterize your work as conceptual art?
I'm an artist.

Did you study art with a view to a professional career?
No, in fact I did art history at university.

How did your background in art history influence your work?
I studied 17th-century Baroque art, which was a movement that actively sought an audience, in that the work often tried to involve the spectator through a variety of devices such as eye contact, lighting or a realistic depiction of the body. The Catholic church at that time was going through the Counter Reformation, a back-to-basics approach to the religion that stripped it to its essentials, meaning that the faithful were put at the centre of the action, most literally in the art works. I'm interested in the relationship between audience, artist, spectator and how these distinctions can be melted.

What kind of work did you begin making as an artist?
Small works on paper and small interventions; cheap work basically, as I had very little money.

How did you get your first break in the art world?
There isn't such a thing, or there wasn't for me. It was about a series of breaks, maybe five to ten different ones, but you make your own breaks; they don't fall into your lap.

Why are collaborations so important to you?
They're fun and you never know where you'll end up. Making art can be a lonely business so it's good to work with someone on projects.

How do you include members of the public?
I approach them; it's as simple as that.

How might you explain your practice to the layman?
I work with what's around me, I make small films, I work with people who are often experts in their field – which can mean musicians or scientists – and I organize exhibitions of other people's work.

Would you encourage artists to experiment beyond traditional categories of art-making – paintings, sculpture, photography, etc?
Yes, of course, but only if it's something you would want to do. There's no point forcing something.

Does winning the Turner Prize somehow validate your practice, or change the audience for your work?
It validates it for other people and it's a good calling card in that people know what I do, which can make things easier.

What about material costs? Are yours lower than the average painter or sculptor?
I don't know what an average artist spends, but I travel a lot and that can be expensive, especially in the UK.

Do you need a studio to produce your kind of work? If so, what's in it?
It's more of an office with a phone and a computer. Some of my archive is here as well. It's a small room 10 x 12 feet but it's OK; there's not much space to stretch out.

Is it harder to get gallery support for your kind of work?
No, I think galleries are always keen to work with a variety of artists. A good dealer will see commercial potential where others don't.

Have you approached funding in other ways? Perhaps government or Arts Council, private or commercial sponsorship?
I have a phobia of filling in forms so I try to do this as little as possible. Much of my work is sponsored but luckily that part of the equation is something I have little to do with.

Often your work doesn't have any tangible product. Do you consciously make art that's not commercially viable?
Sometimes it just happens like that, especially if the end result is something that I haven't made myself or is a large collaboration. On the other hand I do make work that has a definite product that can be sold. It really boils down to what is suitable for each project.

Does this signify a political intent in the work?
If anything it's a way of trying to limit the amount of stuff in the world. You only have to go to an art fair to see how much unnecessary art there is in the world.

What can you sell to support a conceptual or alternative art career – films or photographic documentation, for example?
Yes, those two are the main ways, also ephemera, drawings (not that I draw); it can be anything really and is again dependent on the skill of the dealer to imagine how something can be represented.

How did you finance a big production like the Battle of Orgreave? Did you have to pay for extras, cameras and everything?
Channel 4 mainly paid for that. I had nothing to do with the financial aspect, but the majority of the money went to the extras. There were 1,000 of them and they each got paid for two days' work. It was really good to pay them as so often everyone has to work for free on art projects – the artist especially – it's so boring.

What other kind of support do you need for a big work like this – assistants, production teams?
There were two production companies working on that piece: Artangel and the TV production company chosen by Channel 4. It would have been impossible otherwise and would have sent me to an early grave. There were literally hundreds of people working on it towards the end.

How does your work develop – on paper, in your head, over the phone or email?
Some would argue it doesn't develop; in a variety of ways, often from a written idea or just thinking about things. The moment just before I fall asleep can be quite good.

How many of your ideas never get produced and why?

Like anyone I have more ideas than art work. Thank God some of my ideas never make it because they're so bad. A few things regretfully can't be made because they are more or less impossible, given budget and time constraints.

How important is travel to your work and why? How much time do you spend in London currently?

I go where I'm asked to go, i.e. where the work is. At the moment the USA seems to be a place where I am in demand. It broadens the bank balance as well as my horizons. It's good to get out of London and not to be too reliant on the London art scene and I don't have a gallery here, which is a bit odd now that I come to think about it. On average I am away a week to ten days a month.

Have you ever thought about turning to painting or photography or more traditional ways of art-making?

I can't paint, although I'd like to, as it seems so settled and cosy. If it's going well, I actually think I'm quite traditional. Most of the general public by now has a pretty good handle on conceptual art. I think the Tate and the Turner Prize especially have helped with that.

The 'Folk Archive' is an interesting concept. Can you explain the idea behind it a little?

It's an ongoing accumulation of material that looks at UK folk and popular art as it is today, I do it with a friend, Alan Kane. It deals with the creative life of the UK and is really things that visually and conceptually excite us made by people all around the country.

You are essentially building up a collection of work by other people, so what is your role in this activity – collector, curator or artist?

Most of the stuff we don't actually own and we don't have the space to store it all, so we have to borrow the works when we put on the shows. We are essentially enthusiasts who have a bit of clout in the art world.

Is there a right or wrong way to be an artist?

Hopefully wrong – as that's when it's good.

04

Suppliers and services

Construct your ambition: Making grand ideas become realities

Mike Smith

The range of materials, techniques and services available to artists is becoming more astonishing every day. As you might expect, any choice of materials derives naturally from the sorts of references and influences required of the work. For example, you may want the traditional associations of bronze-casting and marble sculpture, the highly finished industrial aesthetic, or even something in between made from plaster or wood. The crucial factor in these artistic choices is to know what you want and why you want it, in which case many of your problems will solve themselves.

An artist needs to be interested in the process of making their own work, but if they do not have access to the facilities, space or skills to make the work they have envisioned, there are others who can help. Art fabricators such as myself can work with artists in lots of different ways – we can advise or consult on a project, aid the design of an object, make a part of something or make the whole work from start to finish, including transportation and installation.

I started out as a studio assistant while at Camberwell College in the 1980s, working for painters such as Ian McKeever and Christopher Le Brun, stretching, preparing and priming canvases. It is vital to learn these skills because even if you get to a position where you can employ someone else to help out, then at least you can explain whether you like the painting surface to be loose or as tight as a drum.

My knowledge grew as I began to experiment in different materials such as wax, steel and formica, while assisting the sculptor Edward Allington as well as hanging shows and making pieces of furniture for galleries in my spare time and at weekends.

As soon as I finished college in 1989, I set up as a business and went into production full-time. Eventually in 1994 I stopped my own art practice because the prospect of making work with others was more exciting and offered more possibilities. Initially I worked with a relatively small number of artists and galleries. It was during this period that I constructed a number of works for Damien Hirst's first major London show, 'Internal Affairs', at the Institute of Contemporary Arts in 1991, developing a method of manufacturing his trademark vitrines of glass and steel. More recently the studio produced a large-scale, site-specific house by Michael Landy called *Semi-Detached* for Tate Britain in 2004 that weighed around thirteen tonnes and consisted of ten truckloads of panels and components, which was later demolished.

Although you can get emotionally attached to a work of art, what I really enjoy is the collaboration, the whole discursive process of bringing something new into the world; from the initial exchange of information via conversations and sketches through to the finished three-dimensional object. Of course, the big projects are more risky, challenging and ultimately more rewarding, but even if you are not working on a grand scale, there are some points to bear in mind before attempting to realize your project.

Sourcing materials

The Internet has made it much easier to find materials, specialist equipment or companies that can supply and cut material to order. Advances in technology have produced the means to create very particular objects. One particular technique is known as rapid prototyping; this involves constructing a computer model that is then rendered in plastic by a machine, so avoiding the costs and trouble of making a mould and then casting a maquette, although it also has limitations because of the cost and the size of objects that can be produced.

A problem you may face is finding companies that are sympathetic and prepared to engage in what you are doing. They needn't know the philosophical reasoning behind your work, but the more artists have thought about their work and developed the structure of a piece themselves, the better informed an engineering firm or a cabinetmaker will be in achieving the desired specification. Once you have invested a little time and effort into research and development (especially in the details of a project), try to go with an open mind – avoid being too vague or getting overly defensive – as this will allow the technical or material dialogue with a third party to be far more productive.

Fabrication

There has been a steady demise in artists' ability to handle materials, partly because there are so many health and safety conditions at colleges that students can no longer use machinery anymore owing to the institutions' fear of being sued. Much of a work's fabrication – whether it is in plastic or resin, made from copper, stainless steel, brass or aluminium, painted, carved, handmade or machined – is down to your curiosity about how things are made and how you can manipulate a material to suit your aims and ideas.

A lot of people think that if they can imagine a work of art, then it can be made, but often the creation of an object is subject to all sorts of negotiation and compromise. Again, if you know what you want and have a sense of why you want it to look a certain way, then your aesthetic concerns are more likely to prevail.

Budget

There are many things to bear in mind when drawing up an initial budget for a work of art, including its making, delivering, installing and the all-important VAT. Artists often waive the idea that they are actually going to make any money from it themselves, but you should nonetheless value your own time – especially if

you are not yet making a living from your art – and only consider doing something for an insignificant financial return if it is potentially an investment in your future. Depending on where you are in your career and your position in the art market, there is no reason to invest everything you have in making one piece. Someone once asked me to make a two-metre-deep water tank for a performance that had to be big enough for someone to swim in but also had to be built in a tiny venue in half a day. Apart from the fact that it would have buckled the hollow gallery floor, the £2,500 budget would only have bought a few square metres of glass. So, make sure that absolutely everything is accounted for in your budgets, and factor in all logistics such as manoeuvrability, specialist equipment, planning permission, and health and safety requirements.

Planning and safety

Many artists involved in commissioned, semi-permanent or public art for the first time make assumptions about what they can do in a public space, without proper regard for the complicated issues of planning permission or health and safety. Much of it is common sense – knowing that if you mix bleach and chlorine you get a deadly gas, for instance – so always read the labels and take your work seriously.

If you are not well prepared on these topics, you can waste a lot of time putting forward a proposal that will fall foul of the rules and regulations in the final reckoning. We have had a lot of experience with these issues and found ways to circumvent or incorporate them without prohibitive compromise. Before we went to install Rachel Whiteread's *Monument* on the empty plinth in Trafalgar Square, we discovered that it was not possible to drive vehicles onto the square and we were not permitted to drill holes in the plinth. Not only did we have to get the eleven-tonne resin piece there by closing major roads and avoiding low bridges, but we then had to crane it into position between two and five o'clock in the morning, when the centre of London was full of drunks, and figure out a way to secure it that wasn't mechanical or architecturally invasive.

Crating and conservation

Although custom-made crates may seem excessive and expensive, they can protect and greatly prolong the life of a sculpture or installation, or even keep a painting clean almost indefinitely. There is always a chance that a work might get damaged because you cannot be there every time it is handled or moved, but if it is in a box it will hopefully arrive at its destination in one piece. If your work is in multiple parts already, then these should definitely be crated and kept together.

Conservation and cost are intrinsically linked, so if an art work is not worth a huge amount of money then people will not be up in arms about conserving it. However, all artists, whatever their age or status, should think in the long term. We manufacture a variety of painting supports including aluminium panels for artists such as Gary Hume, Jason Martin and Ian Davenport. Apart from its rigidity, the aluminium substrate is profoundly stable; museum conservators know that if you put household paint on aluminium it will last a long time, but if you apply it to canvas it will rot and fall off, even if the surface is properly primed. Also, it is wise to keep some sort of record of a work's manufacture. Take note of what colours, materials and adhesives you used, and hold on to early sketches, computer drawings and invoices, in case something needs to be repaired, restored or even refabricated.

Mike Smith provides technical and intellectual engineering solutions for artists and has been designing and fabricating works of art for many prominent British artists for over fifteen years (www.mikesmithstudio.com).

Art materials retailers

East Anglia

Art Centre and Gallery
7 Howard Street, Bedford, MK40 3HS
T 01234 344784
F 01234360237
E info@artcentre.biz
Founded in 1923. A large store specializing in art
and craft materials and offering a complete
picture-framing service from own stocks. The
gallery holds regular exhibitions displaying works
by established artists. Gallery available for private
exhibitions. Phone for more information.

Berkhamsted Arts & Crafts
29–31 Lower Kings Road, Berkhamsted, HP4 2AB
T 01442 866632
E info@art4crafts.co.uk
W www.art4crafts.co.uk
Contact Paula Daddow
Established in 1972, stocking an extensive range of
art and craft materials. Small classes held on site.

Boons
48 The Howard Centre, Howardsgate
Welwyn Garden City, AL8 6HA
T 01707 325875
F 01707 325875
E sales@tuppers.co.uk
Contact Sandy Weller or Muriel Montgomery
A long-established retailer of art, craft and graphic
materials. Bespoke picture-framing service.
Limited-edition prints and framed art in gallery.

David Potter Ltd
The Old Forge, Rockland St Mary
Norwich, NR14 7AH
T 01508 538570
F 01508 538636
E info@davidpotter.co.uk
W www.davidpotter.co.uk
A manufacturer of a range of high-quality artists'
easels, studio furniture and accessories.

Heffers Art & Graphics
15–21 King Street, Cambridge, CB1 1LH
T 01223 568495
F 01223 568411
E michelet@heffers.co.uk
Suppliers of art materials to Cambridge artists and
students for the past thirty years. Orders by post,
email, telephone and fax welcome.

Hertfordshire Graphics Ltd
6 St Andrew Street, Hertford, SG14 1JE
T 01992 503636
F 01992 503244
E sales@hertfordshiregraphics.co.uk
W www.hertfordshiregraphics.co.uk
Contact Rod Lewis
Founded in 1983, originally supplying solely to
Hertfordshire graphic designers but now
including an art shop and gallery. A sponsor of
many local art events.

Hobbycraft – The Arts & Crafts Superstore
Westgate Park, Fodderwick, Basildon, SS14 1WP
T 0126 82240100
W www.hobbycraft.co.uk
Suppliers of arts and crafts materials with
branches nationwide.

Hussey and Greades Ltd
94 Hutton Road, Shenfield, CM15 8ND
T 01277 226262
F 01277 261289
E shen@husseyandgreades.co.uk
W www.husseyandgreades.co.uk
Contact Dan Culliton
Founded in 1955. Suppliers of art materials from
leading manufacturers. **Branches** 52 Moulsham
Street, Chelmsford CM2 0JA **T** 01245 268601

Jarrold's
1 London Street, Norwich, NR2 1JF
T 01603 660661
F 01603 611295
E info@jarroldthestore.co.uk
W www.jarroldthestore.co.uk
Contact Patrick Clarke (Art and Craft Head Buyer)
Founded in 1823. Respected retailer of leading-
brand art and craft materials.

KRC Brushes
110 Tolmers Road, Cuffley, EN6 4JR
T 07749270255
E krcbrushes@hotmail.com
W www.freewebs.com/krcbrushes
Contact Karen Rice
Established in 2004. Suppliers of discount, quality
artists' brushes to artists and students.

Laurence Mathews Art & Craft Store
1 Queens Road, Southend-on-Sea, SS1 1LT
T 01702 435196
F 01702 435377
E laurence.mathews@madasafish.com

An art and graphics materials supplier in business since 1948. Also offers a bespoke picture-framing service.

Tim's Art Supplies
85 Tilehouse Street, Hitchin, SG5 2DY
T 01462 455376
F 01462 421898
E info@timsartsupplies.co.uk
W www.timsartsupplies.co.uk
Contact Tim Farr
Founded in 1976, specializing in fine art, craft, graphic and office supplies for the artist and amateur, and offering a picture-framing service. Holds regular classes covering a range of subjects, for both adults and children. Mail order available.

Tina's
38 The Causeway, Burwell, Cambridge, CB5 0DU
T 01638 742785
Retailer of general art supplies.

Tindalls the Stationers Ltd
50–52 High Street, Newmarket, CB8 8LE
T 01638 668855
F 01638 663633
E sales@tindalls.co.uk
W www.tindalls.co.uk
Contact Jamie Gaskin
Branches 8 Bridge Street, St Ives PE27 5EG **T** 01480 493765 **F** 01480 493766; 4 Market Place, Ely CB7 4NP **T** 01353 669498 **F** 01353 669382

Windsor Gallery
167 London Road South, Lowestoft, NR33 0BL
T 01502 512278
E products@windsorgallery.fsnet.co.uk
W www.windsorgallery.fsnet.co.uk
Contact Ray Glanfield
Established in 1981. Stocks art and craft materials from a wide range of manufacturers. Also offers a bespoke framing service.

Wrights
15–16 Stanley Road, Great Yarmouth
NR30 1QJ
T 01493 844618
E wrights.norfolk@btopenworld.com
W www.wrightsofnorfolk.co.uk
A family business, started in 1957. Stocks a comprehensive range of all artist materials. Offers a full framing service, from supplying mouldings to framing finished articles.

East Midlands

Art & Craft Centre
86–88 Chilwell Road, Beeston, Nottingham
NG9 1ES
T 0115 9223743
Stocks wide range of arts and crafts materials.

Art Essentials
26 Main Street, Kimberley, Nottingham
NG16 2LL
T 0115 9385551
General art materials retailer.

The Art Shop
45a High Street, Oakham, Rutland, LE15 6AJ
T 01572 723943
F 01572 770068
E hopsdavis@aol.com
W www.artshop.co.uk
Contact Christine Davis
Founded in 1985. An independent retailer specializing in art and craft materials. Knowledgeable staff always available to give directions. Mail order and student discounts offered.

Boston Artstore
13a Pen Street, Boston, PE21 0BE
T 01205 353349
F 01205 353349
Contact Stephen Eede
Founded in 1985, providing a comprehensive range of art supplies for amateur and professional artists. Also offers classes for all ages in most media and can put on one-person or group exhibitions in gallery space.

Colemans of Stamford
39 High Street, Stamford, P69 2BE
T 01780 480635
F 01780 766424
E Stamford@colemangroup.co.uk
W www.colemans-online.co.uk
Contact Joan Dale
Established in 1969, stocking a wide range of materials and now operating twelve branches across Northants, Cambridgeshire, Bedfordshire and Herefordshire.

Dominoes of Leicester Ltd
66 High Street, Leicester, LE1 5YP
T 0116 2533363

F 0116 2628066
E ann.land@dominoestoys.co.uk
W www.dominoestoys.co.uk
Contact Tony Wilmot or Darroll Cramp
A large, independent retailer of arts and crafts, toys and models. Two artists staff the art room. Also has a comprehensive craft room covering most popular crafts.

Gadsby's

22 Market Place, Leicester, LE1 5GH
T 0116 2517792
F 0116 2517792
E info@gadsbys.co.uk
W www.gadsbys.co.uk, www.artshopper.co.uk
An art materials retailer. **Branches** 260 High Street, Lincoln LN2 1LH **T** 01522 527485; 347 High Street, Lincoln LN5 7DQ **T** 01522 527487; Unit 5 Quenn Street, Walsall WS2 9NX **T** 01922 623104; 33 New Briggate, Leeds LS3 8JD **T** 0113 2455326; 15 Darlington Street, Wolverhampton WV1 4HW **T** 01902 424029.

Hills of Newark Ltd

34–38 Barnbygate, Newark, NG24 1PZ
T 01636 702240
F 01636 612627
E sales@hillsofnewark.co.uk
W www.hillsofnewark.co.uk
Contact Nick Hill
Established in 1977. A family-run artists' materials shop with picture-framing service on the premises.

J. Ruddock Ltd

287 High Street, Lincoln
LN2 1AW
T 01522 528285
F 01522 532162
E shop@ruddocksoflincoln.co.uk
W www.ruddocksoflincoln.co.uk
Has supplied art materials for over a hundred years and runs courses in its own studios, including watercolour and life drawing.
Price range: £25 per day for main studios (e.g. for teaching or workshops).

John E Wright & Co. Ltd

Blue Print House, 115 Huntingdon Street, Nottingham, NG1 3NF
T 0115 950 6633
F 0115 958 5067
E sales@johnewright.com
W www.johnewright.com
Established 1900 as a plan printers. Suppliers of

fine art and graphic art materials and one of the leading suppliers of digital printing services in the East Midlands. Offices also in Derby and Leicester.

Pete Spowage

Estate House, 2 Byard Lane, Nottingham
NG1 2GJ
T 0115 9523683
F 0115 9523683
W www.pspowageartstudio.co.uk
Contact Pete Spowage
Established in 1998. Sells wide range of art supplies. Includes gallery of contemporary, original art.

SAA Home Shop

PO Box 50, Newark, NG23 5GY
T 0800 9801123
F 01949 844051
E info@saa.co.uk
W www.saa.co.uk
Catalogue with over 10,000 art material products, catering for all mediums, subjects and levels of artist. Includes instructional books and art tuition on DVD. Orders taken by phone, fax, post or via secure online ordering system.

Shawe's the Art Shop

68–70 Mansfield Road, Nottingham
NG1 3GY
T 0115 9418646
Stocks art and craft materials from leading suppliers.

London

A.P. Fitzpatrick

142 Cambridge Heath Road, Bethnal Green
London, E1 5QJ
T 020 77900884
A leading stockist of artists' pigments.

A.S. Handover Ltd

Unit 8, Leeds Place, Tollington Park
London, N4 3RF
T 020 72729624
F 020 72638670
E m_venus@handover.co.uk
W www.handover.co.uk
Contact Michael Venus
Founded in 1949, manufacturing artists' brushes in London. Will make small orders to customers' specifications. Also supplies tools, paints and sundries for artists and craftsmen.

Alustretch UK Limited
Unit 261, Grosvenor Terrace, London, SE5 0NP
T 07968 719361
F 0870 0512302
E stinson@alustretch.com
W www.alustretch.co.uk
Contact Bruce Stinson
Sells aluminium stretcher frames (warp and
distortion free, lightweight and easy to handle). In
a variety of profile depths or cut to size. Available
pre-assembled, stretched on site, or in kit form.
Can be stretched with a range of quality linens or
cottons. Price list available on request.

The Art Shop
117c High Street, Wanstead, London
E11 2RL
T 020 89890154
F 020 85188110
Contact Dill
Established in 1955 to serve local artists with all
products needed. Runs a service whereby specialist
materials can be ordered on a weekly basis. Also
sells a large range of craft materials for adults and
children.

Atlantis Art
7–9 Plumber's Row, London
E1 1EQ
T 020 73778855
F 020 73778850
W www.atlantisart.co.uk
One of London's leading suppliers of arts and
crafts materials. Mail order available.

Bird & Davis Ltd – The Artist's Manufactory
45 Holmes Road, Kentish Town, London
NW5 3AN
T 020 74853797
F 020 72840509
E birdltd@aol.com
W www.birdanddavis.co.uk
Contact Rob or Jayne
Established in 1928. One of the UK's oldest and
leading stretcher frame manufacturers for both
trade and retail. Bespoke canvases made to
exacting standards in various linens and cottons,
primed and unprimed. Also stocks a
comprehensive range of art materials and easels,
with student discounts offered. Mail order
available. Also offers easel hire. **Branches** The
Royal Academy, Schools Shop – Schools Entrance,
Burlington Gardens London W1 (open
Monday–Friday 10.00–11.30).

Booer & Sons Ltd
216–218 Eltham High Street, Eltham, London
SE9 1BA
T 020 88502503
F 020 88506323
Contact Brenda Jackson
Established for nearly ninety years. Wide range of
artists' materials and also a stationery department.

Canonbury Arts
266 Upper Street, Islington, London, N1 2UQ
T 020 72264652
F 020 77041781
E sc@canonburyarts.co.uk
W www.canonburyarts.co.uk
Contact Shaun, Lucy or Emelie
Established in 1949. A specialist art and sculpting
materials supplier, moulder and caster. Also offers
a picture-framing service.

Cass Art
66–67 Colebrooke Row, Islington, London
N1 8AB
T 020 79309940
E info@cassart.co.uk
W www.cassart.co.uk
Established for over 25 years. Wide range of
professional art materials, including brushes,
canvases, paints, pastels, portfolios, easels,
drawing pads and a large variety of papers
plus leading paint brands. 7,500 sq. ft
Islington flagship store now open.
Branches 13 Charing Cross Road, WC2; 220
Kensington High Street;
24 Berwick Street, W1. All open 7 days
a week.

Chromacolour International
Unit 5 Pilton Estate, Pitlake, Croydon
Surrey, CR0 3RA
T 020 8688 1991
F 020 8688 1441
E sales@chromacolour.co.uk
W www.chromacolour.co.uk
Contact Mrs Joanne Sullivan
Established over twenty-five years ago as
animation suppliers and still a market-leader in
this field. Manufacturers and suppliers of unique
artist paints in eighty vibrant colours, which can be
used as watercolour, acrylic, gouache, ink, wash or
as an impasto, all from the same tube or pot. Also
offers a full range of artist products including
custom made brushes, artists' paper and canvases.
Call 0800 592235

Colart Fine Art & Graphics Ltd

Whitefriars Avenue, Harrow, HA3 5RH
T 020 84243200
F 020 84243328
E n.montrose@colart.co.uk
W www.winsornewton.com
Contact Natasha Montrose
Among the world's largest suppliers and manufacturers of fine-art materials. Main brands include Windsor & Newton, Liquitex and Conte A Paris. Also distributes Artcare, Copic, Canson and Slater Harrison in the UK.

Cowling & Wilcox Ltd

26–28 Broadwick Street, London, W1V 1FG
T 020 77349557
F 020 74344513
E art@cowlingandwilcox.com
W www.cowlingandwilcox.com
Stocks a wide selection of portfolios, carrying cases and presentation books. Also fine-art, craft and graphic materials. Mail order service offered.

D & J Simons & Sons Ltd and SimonArt

SimonArt House, 122–150 Hackney Road
London, E2 7QS
T 020 77393744
F 020 77394452
E dsimons@djsimons.co.uk
W www.djsimons.co.uk
Company founded in 1900. Major stockists of Ferrario paints from Italy. Wide range of paints, artists' brushes, canvas products, pallets, painting mediums and accessories. Catalogue available on request.

Daler-Rowney Percy Street/Arch One Picture Framing

12 Percy Street, London, W1T 1DW
T 020 76368241
E dr@artmat.co.uk
W www.dalerrowney.co.uk or www.archonestudio.com
Situated on the site of the original 1952 George Rowney 'showroom', this is still the only shop to stock the entire range of Daler-Rowney art materials. Also offers a complete framing service including gilded and hand-finished frames and mount cutting.

Darcy Turner

175 Leytonstone Road, Stratford, London, E15 1LH
T 020 89818307
F 020 89818307
E darcyturner180@hotmail.com
W www.darcyturner.com
Practising artists who has devised the 'Stixx Newspaper Technology Construction System', an inexpensive and simple-to-use 3-D modelling medium. Has been widely used in national curriculum design technology projects.

Falkiner Fine Papers

76 Southampton Row, Bloomsbury, London
WC1B 4AR
T 020 78311151
F 020 74301248
E sales@falkiners.com
W www.falkiners.com
Owned by the Shepherds, Sangorski and Sutcliffe Group, Falkiners was founded in 1973, specializing in selling a large range of papers for all art, craft and conservation purposes. Artists are able to experiment with unusual papers sourced throughout the world including a range of Japanese papers and handmade sheets and can buy in volumes as low as a single sheet. Experienced staff are happy to guide the novice through the finer points of paper. Also has a wide selection of bookbinding supplies and materials in addition to providing a bespoke thesis and fine binding service. Customers include art students, bookbinders, printmakers, calligraphers, architects, film prop buyers and the arts and crafts enthusiasts.

Fielders

54 Wimbledon Hill Road, London, SW19 7PA
T 020 89465044
F 020 89441320
E shop@fielders.co.uk
W www.fielders.co.uk
Founded in 1928, specializing in art and craft materials, framing, copying/design services and art-related books. **Branches** 8 High Street, Kingston-upon-Thames KT1 1EY **T** 020 85471304
F 020 85472066

Gallery Gifts Ltd

157–159 High Street, Sutton, Surrey, SM1 1JH
T 020 86432945
F 020 86420990
E gallerygifts@hotmail.com
Contact Judith Palmer
Trading in art materials since 2001 and stocking major brands.

Green and Stone of Chelsea

259 Kings Road, London, SW3 5EL

T 020 73520837
F 020 73511098
E sales@greenandstone.com
W www.greenandstone.com
Established in 1927. One of the most highly
respected artists' material shops in Europe. Stock
includes painting and display easels in oak, beech
and mahogany, and oil paints by leading
manufacturers, including Mike Harding and
Jacques Blockx. Linen and cotton canvases are pre-
made or made to order. Also available are balanced
palettes, and handmade and antique papers.
Handmade picture frames are designed and made
to order (by appointment only). A mail order
service is available.

Harris Fine Art Ltd

712 High Road, North Finchley, London, N12 9QD
T 020 84452804
E sales@harrisfineart.co.uk
W www.harrisfineart.co.uk
Contact Mr C. Harris
Established in 1971, stocking a wide range of art
and craft materials from leading manufacturers.
Also offers a picture-framing service and a large
modern gallery space. Website gives secure online
ordering and guaranteed delivery.

Holloway Art & Stationers

222 Holloway Road, Islington, London, N7 8DA
T 020 76074738
F 020 77004943
E hollowayartandstationers@ouvip.com
A family business since 1874, stocking leading
brands of art, graphic and drafting materials
including airbrushes and compressors. **Branches**
Perrys, 777 Fulham Road SW6 5HA **T** 020
77367225 **F** 020 77366893. Perrys, 109 East
Street, Southampton SO14 3HD **T** 023 80339444
F 023 80231644

Intaglio Printmaker

9 Playhouse Court, 62 Southwark Bridge Road,
London, SE1 0AT
T 020 79282633
F 020 79282711
E info@intaglioprintmaker.com
W www.intaglioprintmaker.com
Opened in London in 1981, supplying extensive
range of printmaking materials sourced
worldwide. Also offers a reliable mail order service
to artists, studios and colleges. Initiated an artist-
in-residency scheme in the 1990s to provide
professional development opportunities for

graduate printmakers in the early stages of their
career. Also offers weekend workshops in
numerous specialist areas of printmaking.

Jackson's Art Supplies

1 Farleigh Place, Farleigh Road, London, N16 7SX
T 020 72540077
F 020 72540088
E sales@jacksonsart.co.uk
W www.jacksonsart.co.uk
A mail order supplier of quality art materials, with
over 50,000 customers worldwide.

John Jones Ltd

4 Morris Place, Stroud Green Road, London
N4 3JG
T 020 72815439
F 020 72815956
E info@johnjones.co.uk
W www.johnjones.co.uk
A family business offering bespoke museum
standard picture-framing and artist surfaces.
Specializes in artists' surfaces; bespoke stretchers
can be ordered to any format and size and are
produced in wood or aluminium. Also produces
panel surfaces in aluminium or paper. Extensive
contemporary framing service. Works for leading
galleries, collectors and artists. Also offers a fine
art photography and limited edition artist printing
service.

John Purcell Paper

15 Rumsey Road, London, SW9 0TR
T 020 77375199
F 020 77376765
E jpp@johnpurcell.net
W www.johnpurcell.net
A wholesale paper merchant based in south
London, supplying an extensive range of papers
and boards from stock suitable for many
applications including printmaking, drawing and
watercolour, inkjet printing, picture-framing,
bookbinding and commercial printing.
Comprehensive price list available on request.

L. Cornelissen & Son

105 Great Russell Street, London, WC1B 3RY
T 020 76361045
F 020 76363655
E info@cornelissen.com
W www.cornelissen.com
Established in 1855. Specialists in pigments,
gilding and printmaking as well as more widely
available materials. Provides a canvas-stretching

service and offers easel-hire/delivery for short periods. Fast worldwide mail order service. Two minutes' walk from either the British Museum or Tottenham Court Road tube station (exit 3).

London Art Ltd
132 Finchley Road, Hampstead, London, NW3 5HS
T 020 74331571/ 74356830
F 020 74331747
E email@londonart-shop.co.uk
W www.londonart-shop.co.uk
Specialists in art and craft materials with over fifteen years of experience. Also runs an online shop.

London Graphic Centre
16–18 Shelton Street, Covent Garden, London WC2H 9JL
T 020 77594500
F 020 77594585
E info@londongraphics.co.uk
W www.londongraphics.co.uk
Contact Andrew Parsonage
Established for over thirty years. One of Europe's largest independent dealers in art and graphic supplies. Over twenty thousand products available to order over the phone or by visiting flagship retail store in Covent Garden. As well as traditional artists' materials, also offers wide range of specialist papers and portfolios.

Lyndons Art & Graphics
197 Portobello Road, London, W11 2ED
T 020 77274357
F 020 77929429
Contact Peter Kalyan
Established in 1904. Supplies art and graphics materials. **Branches** 164 Portobello Road, London W11 2EB.

Michael Harding's Artists Oil Colours
88 Mile End Road, Whitechapel, London, E1 4UN
T 020 77028338
F 020 77910060
E oilpaint@michaelharding.freeserve.co.uk
W www.michaelharding.co.uk
Contact Michael Harding
Wholesale only (not open to the public). Founded in 1980, manufacturing the finest-quality oil paint available using recipes that date prior to the Industrial Revolution. Involved in restoration for, among others, the National Trust, English Heritage and the Tate. Seventy-four colours available, soon extending to over one hundred.

Available throughout the UK and through some major suppliers worldwide.

Owen Clark & Co. Ltd
129–133 Cranbrook Road, Ilford, Essex, IG1 4QB
T 020 84788478
F 020 84783983
E sales@owen-clark.fsnet.co.uk
W www.owenclark.com
Contact Tony Clark
A retail art and stationery store established in 1928. Specializes in educational supplies, serving hundreds of local secondary schools and colleges with art materials, technical drawing equipment and educational stationery. Also caters for needs of amateur and professional artists and offers a mail order service with generous discounts.

Paintworks Ltd
99–101 Kingsland Road, London, E2 8AG
T 020 77297451
F 020 77390439
E shop@paintworks.biz
W www.paintworks.biz
Contact Dorothy Wood
An artist-run shop and mail order service founded in 1985. A major national stockist of fine-art paints, canvas and papers, supplying the education sector. Offers a product and technical information resource and a conservation-framing service for contemporary art works in all media. Specialist advice available.

Paperchase Products Ltd
213–215 Tottenham Court Road, London, W1T 7PS
T 020 74676200
E write@paperchase.co.uk
W www.paperchase.co.uk
A flagship London store for innovative papers and stationery for over thirty years. Specializes in imported and effect papers, with a full selection of media and artists' requisites. The North of England flagship store is situated at St Marys Gate, Manchester.

Perrys Art & Office
777 Fulham Road, London, SW6 5HA
T 020 77367225
F 020 77366893
E info@perrysartoffice.com
Contact Nish Chande
Established in 1986. Stockists of a comprehensive range of art and craft materials including all leading brands.

R.K. Burt & Co. Ltd
57 Union Street, London, SE1 1SG
T 020 74076474
F 020 74033672
E sales@rkburt.co.uk
W www.rkburt.co.uk
Established in 1892. One of the largest wholesale paper merchants in the UK, specializing in high-quality paper for every type of artist use. The first wholesale distributor in the UK for many leading mills, with a reputation for commissioning paper produced to its own specifications as required.

Rembrandt Art & Crafts
P.O. Box 252, Twickenham, TW1 1XU
T 020 88980973
W www.craftwithus@aol.com
Contact Russell
Offers a bespoke canvas-making service. Stretching and framing services also available.

Russell & Chapple
68 Drury Lane, London, WC2B 5SP
T 020 78367521
F 020 74970554
E info@randc.net
W www.randc.net
Contact Andrew Milne
Founded in 1770. One of the UK's leading specialist suppliers of artists' canvas, selling a wide range of cottons, linens and canvases, both primed and unprimed. Products include canvases for digital printing, artists' stretcher bars and professional-quality artists' paints. Also offers a bespoke stretching service and can restretch original art work and inkjet prints to order.

Selwyn-Smith Studio
148 High Street, Teddington, TW11 8HZ
T 020 89730771
F 020 89730772
Contact Jo Selwyn-Smith
Founded in 2001. A traditional supplier of art materials specializing in the provision of drawing and painting equipment. The shop is always well stocked with both student- and artist-quality paint, a selection of stretched canvases, watercolour papers, easels and brushes.

Unik Art & Craft
4 Astoria Parade, Streatham High Road, London
SW16 1PR
T 020 87690422
F 020 86773737

E nwacke@btinternet.com
Founded in 2000, specializing in the supply of professional-artist materials and a wide range of craft materials.

Vandy's Art and Graphic Centre
621 Forest Road, Walthamstow, London, E17 4NE
T 020 85273492
Contact Zahir Mawani (Proprietor)
Stockists of fine-art and graphic materials. All major brands stocked.

Wheatsheaf Art Shop
56 Baker Street, London, W1U 7BU
T 020 7935 5510
F 020 7935 3794
E sales@wheatsheaf-art.co.uk
W www.wheatsheaf-art.co.uk
Contact Tony Berrington
Stockists of fine art and craft materials from leading manufacturers. Online shop. Mail order service available and experienced team on hand to answer questions. Founded in 1946.

North-east

The Art Shop
11–12 Bondgate, Darlington, DL3 7JE
T 01325 465484
E info@theartshop.co.uk
W www.theartshop.co.uk
Retails wide selection of arts and crafts materials.

The Art Shop
15 Station Road, Whitley Bay, NE26 2QY
T 0191 2511726
Stock range of artists' supplies from leading manufacturers.

The Art Shop and Kemble Gallery
62 Saddler Street, Durham
DH1 3NU
T 0191 3864034
Sells supplies to suit all artists and craftsmen. Also has a gallery space.

City Art
76 North Road, Durham, DH1 4SQ
T 0191 3831919
Comprehensive range of art materials.

City Art Store
23 Vine Place, Sunderland
SR1 3NA

T 0191 5659254
Stocks broad range of art and craft materials.

Details
67 Westgate Road, Newcastle-upon-Tyne
NE1 1SG
T 0191 2615999
W www.details.co.uk
Contact www.details.co.uk
Wide range of artists' supplies available.

Jarred's Arts & Craft
59 Borough Road, Middlesbrough, TS1 3AA
T 01642 222531
Art materials retailer.

Newcastle Arts Centre Ltd
67 Westgate Road, Newcastle-upon-Tyne
NE1 1SG
T 0191 2615618
F 0191 2322410
E venue@newcastle-arts-centre.co.uk
W www.newcastle-arts-centre.co.uk
Contact Helen Byrnes
Founded in 1981 as an arts development company,
operating a gallery, craft shop, art and design
materials store, bar, cafe, studio theatre and
studios.

R.R. Bailey
12 Grange Road, Newcastle-upon-Tyne
NE4 9LD
T 0191 2746126
Stocks broad range of major-name art and craft
materials.

Stratford & York Ltd
Whickham Industrial Estate, Swalwell
Newcastle-upon-Tyne, NE16 3BY
T 0191 4960111
F 0191 4960211
E andrew.eccles@delbanco.com
Contact Andrew Eccles (Sales Manager)
Manufacturers of fine-art brushes in the UK since
1939. Seeks to serve both professional artists and
accomplished amateurs. Each brush is made by
hand.

Team Valley Brush Co.
Whickham Industrial Estate, Swalwell
Newcastle-upon-Tyne,
NE16 3BY
T 0191 4960111
Specialist manufacturers of fine art brushes.

Ward's Arts & Crafts
Halifax Road, Dunston Industrial Estate
Gateshead, NE11 9HW
T 0191 4605915
F 0191 4608540
E info@doart.co.uk
W www.doart.co.uk
Established for over 150 years. One of the north's
leading retailers of arts and crafts supplies and
materials. Also offers a professional photographic
and repro lab providing high quality giclée
printing to artists.

Northern Ireland

Artquip
31a Upper Dunmurry Lane, Dunmurry
Belfast, BT17 0AA
T 028 90605552
Stocks broad range of art and craft supplies.

Bradbury Graphics
3 Lyndon Court, Queen Street, Belfast
BT1 6BT
T 028 90233535
F 028 90572065
E art@bradbury-graphics.co.uk
W www.bradburygraphics.co.uk
Contact Richard or Una
A city-centre store stocking a wide range of
branded art materials, stationery items and
presentation goods. Caters for all, from children to
established career artists and those associated with
creative industries such as technical drawing,
design and communication.

EDCO
47–49 Queen Street, Belfast
BT1 6HP
T 028 90324687
E theshop@edco.co.uk
W www.edco.co.uk
Major educational supplier with wide range of art
materials.

Milliken Bros
11 May Street, Greyabbey, Newtownards
County Down, BT22 2NE
T 028 42788005
F 028 42788293
E info@millikenbros.com
W www.millikenbros.com
Suppliers of fine art materials and makers of
stretched canvases.

Proctor & Co. Ltd
201–213 Castlereagh Road, Belfast, BT5 5FH
T 028 90456582
F 028 90732500
E proctors@btclick.com
W www.proctors.uk.com
Contact Carol McNaughton
Established for forty years, offering an extensive range of art, craft and stationery supplies. Printing service also available.

Scarva Pottery Supplies
Unit 20, Scarva Road Industrial Estate
Scarva Road, Banbridge, BT32 3QD
T 028 40669699
F 028 40669700
E david@scarvapottery.com
W www.scarvapottery.com
Contact David Maybin
In business for over twenty years. Stocks quality products for the professional potter, from raw materials to tools and equipment. Competitive pricing structure and delivery charges.

Vision Applied Arts & Crafts
42 Waring Street, Belfast, BT1 2ED
T 028 90246665
E geri@primavera.fsnet.co.uk
Comprehensive range of art and craft materials.

North-west

The Art House
The Triangle, Hanging Ditch, Manchester, M4 3TR
T 0161 8345545
General art materials supplier.

Artisan
115 Penny Lane, Allerton, Liverpool, L18 1DF
T 0151 7350707
Specialists in paper and textile art.

Artstat
Creative House, Tilson Road, Roundhouse Industrial Estate, Manchester
M23 9WR
T 0161 9023800
F 0161 9023801
Contact Patrick Swindell
Established in 1978. Wholesale distributors of artists' materials, craft and stationery products. Over eleven thousand items held in stock at the Manchester warehouse and showroom. Cash-and-carry facility or delivery by carrier.

Blots Pen & Ink Supplies
14 Lyndhurst Avenue, Prestwich
Manchester, M25 0GF
T 0161 7206916
F 0161 7206916
E sales@blotspens.co.uk
W www.blotspens.co.uk
Contact John Winstanley
Trading since 1993, specializing in the mail order of calligraphy pens, inks and sundries. Manufacturers of Iron Gall Ink, a medieval ink suitable for fine sketching and line and wash. Orders accepted online or via a paper catalogue.

Bluecoat Books & Art Ltd
Gostin's Building, 32–36 Hanover Street
Liverpool, L1 4LN
T 0151 7095449
F 0151 7087131
E paul.mccue@btconnect.com
W www.bluecoatbooks.com
Contact Paul McCue
Founded in 1988 at Bluecoat Arts Centre, a retail business selling art materials and specialist art books. Over 6,000 lines stocked at discounted prices.

Blyth's Artshop & Gallery
Amazon House, Brazil Street, Manchester, M1 3PJ
T 0161 236 1302
F 0161 228 0633
E sales@artmanchester.com
W www.artmanchester.com
A major supplier of fine art and graphics materials and accessories, with a gallery specializing in contemporary art and sculpture.

Chapter 1
35 Derby Street, Leek, ST13 6HU
T 01538 399885
F 01538 399885
E chapter.1@btconnect.com
Contact Ann Vaughan
Founded in 1990. A retailer of art materials, stationery and books.

Colours and Crafts
61 London Road, Alderley Edge, SK9 7DY
T 01625 586100
F 01625 586100
E seahorse6259@aol.com
Contact Stella Batchelor
Founded in 2003. An art and craft retail outlet on two sites (Alderley Edge and Victoria Mill, Foundry

Bank, Congleton, Cheshire). Workshops in all art and craft media available, lasting from half an hour to a full day.

Creative Shop Ltd
79 Strand Street, Douglas, Isle of Man, IM1 2EN
T 01624 628618
Founded in 1991, stocking artists' materials and craft supplies. Also sells fine-art prints and offers a framing service (bespoke and ready-made).

Daisy Designs (Crafts) Ltd
Hutpine House, 21 Sandown Lane,
Liverpool, L15 8HY
T 0151 7341385
E daisydesigns@yahoo.com
W www.daisy-designs.co.uk
Founded in 1993. Specialists in textile-based crafts.

Edwin Allen Arts & Crafts
14–16 Buttermarket Street, Warrington, WA1 2LR
T 01925 630264
F 01925 444620
E mike@edwinallen.co.uk
W www.edwin-allen.u-net.com
Contact Michael Allen
Founded in 1894 and still a family-run business. Specializes in the supply of fine-art materials, craft products, picture-framing and mount-cutting services.

Fred Aldous Ltd
37 Lever Street, Manchester, M1 1LW
T 0161 236 2477
F 0161 236 6075
E sales@fredaldous.net
W www.fredaldous.co.uk
Stocks wide supply of art and craft materials from array of major manufacturers.

Galleria Fine Arts
6 Green Street, Sanbach, CW11 1GX
T 01270 753233
F 01270 753233
Contact Peter Brown
Established in 1995, supplying a full range of artists' materials. Bespoke framing a speciality.

Granthams Art Discount
Graphics House, Charnley Road, Blackpool, FY1 4PE
T 01253 624402
F 01253 295743
E info@artdiscount.co.uk
W www.artdiscount.co.uk

Contact John Thompson
Founded in 1890, originally as a signwriting business. Moved into art materials supplies in the late 1960s and today operates out of two major sites. Orders can be made via website.

Heaton Cooper Studio Ltd
Grasmere, Ambleside, LA22 9SX
T 015394 35280
F 015394 35797
E info@heatoncooper.co.uk
W www.heatoncooper.co.uk
Contact John Heaton Cooper
Suppliers of high-quality art materials with worldwide mailing service available online or by phone. Stocks artists' accessories of all kinds, including a large range of brand-name and handmade papers. The retail shop is attached to the Heaton Cooper studio, selling originals and prints of works by the Heaton Cooper family.

Icthus Arts & Graphics
Graphic House, 106–110 School Lane, Didsbury, Manchester, M20 6HR
T 0161 4342560
Wide-ranging stock of art and craft materials.

Ken Bromley Art Supplies
Curzon House, Curzon Road, Bolton, BL1 4RW
T 0845 3303234
F 01204 381123
E sales@artsupplies.co.uk
W www.artsupplies.co.uk
Contact Laureen Bromley
Suppliers of art materials at discount prices. The company originated from the success of the Ken Bromley Perfect Paper Stretcher (invented during World War II). Since 1994, the shop has increased its range of paints, paper, canvas, brushes and accessories. Most business is carried out by mail order and via the online shopping site. Artists and tutors can also have a free link to their own website.

The Potters' Barn
Roughwood Lane, Hassall Green, Sandbach
CW11 4XX
T 01270 884080
E info@thepottersbarn.co.uk
W www.thepottersbarn.co.uk
Contact Andrew Pollard, Steve Marr
Founded in 1979. Suppliers of discus potter's wheels. Producers of handthrown reduction-fired stoneware, raku and pit-fired ware. Regular classes for adults and children in pottery. Courses in other

crafts run throughout the year. Group visits, parties, corporate events/team days and personal tuition also available.

Printing House
102 Main Street, Cockermouth, CA13 GLX
T 01900 824984
F 01900 823124
E info@printinghouse.co.uk
Contact Jenny Holliday
Founded in 1968, supplying materials for artists (ordering service available) and secondhand books. Occasional artists' workshops and advice on printing given. Working museum of printing.

R. Jackson & Sons
20 Slater Street, Liverpool, L1 4BS
T 0151 7092647
Wide range of artists materials. Also offers canvas stretching and picture framing services. Student discount available.

Rennies Arts & Crafts Ltd
61–63 Bold Street, Liverpool, L1 4EZ
T 0151 7080599
F 0151 7072362
Contact Duncan Rennie
Founded in 1975, offering a wide range of art and craft materials. Also specializes in limited-edition prints and a complete framing service.
Branches 34 Bridge Street, St Helens WA10 1NW; 3 Hill Street, Southport PR9 0PE; 30 Burscough Street, Ormskirk L39 2ES

Shinglers
Compston Road, Ambleside, LA22 9DR
T 015394 33433
F 015394 34634
W www.shinglers-ambleside.co.uk
Contact Elsie Dugdale
Suppliers of a broad range of art materials.

Studio Arts – Dodgson Fine Arts Ltd
50 North Road, Lancaster, LA1 1LT
T 01524 271810
F 01524 68013
E tonyd@studioarts.co.uk
W www.studioarts.co.uk
Contact Graeme Atkinson
Founded in 1972. Sells arts, graphics, crafts a nd cardmaking materials from major suppliers, with an online ecommerce website (www.studioartshop.com).

Turners Graphic Art & Drawing Office Supplies
91 Wellington Road South, Stockport, SK1 3SL
T 0161 4804713
F 0161 4764744
E jill@turnersart.co.uk
W www.turnersart.co.uk
Contact Jill Limmack
Founded over one hundred years ago and counts famous artists past and present among its customers. Specializes in all art materials for beginners to the experienced artist, students to drawing offices.

Ziggy Art Ltd
40 Dover Road, Birkdale, Southport, PR8 4TD
T 01704 551322
F 01704 565155
E sales@ziggyart.co.uk
W www.ziggyart.co.uk
Specializes in the online supply of all art and graphic materials, operating a next-day delivery service from a large stockholding.

Scotland

Alexander's Art Shop
58 South Clerk Street, Edinburgh, EH8 9PS
T 0131 6675257
Stocks arts and crafts supllies from range of major manufacturers.

Art Mediums Ltd
Block E, Unit 7 Glenwood Business Park, 50 Glenwood Place, Glasgow, G45 9UH
T 0141 6309339
E sales@artmediums.co.uk
W www.artmediums.co.uk
Supplier of specialized art and craft materials to educational outlets.

Artopia Ltd
37 High Street, Johnstone, PA5 8AJ
T 01505 321133
F 01505 321133
E info@artopia.uk.com
W www.artopia.uk.com
Contact Drew Stuart
Opened in 2004, retailing artists' materials from major manufacturers. Internet commerce also available.

Artstore at the Artschool Ltd
11 Dalhousie Street, Glasgow, G3 6RQ
T 0141 3311277

F 0141 3324470
General art supplies stockist.

Artwrap Ltd
4–5 West Park Place, Edinburgh, EH11 2DP
T 0131 3467878
Sells broad spectrum of arts and crafts materials.

Broadford Books and Gallery
Broadford, Isle of Skye, IV49 9AB
T 01471 822748
E broadfordbooks@lineone.net
W www.broadfordbooks.co.uk
Contact Ian and Rosemary Chard
In business since 1987, supplying a wide range of artists' materials and books. Also has a picture gallery and offers a full framing service using conservation-quality materials.

Burns & Harris (Retail) Ltd
97–99 Commercial Street, Dundee, DD1 2AF
T 01382 322591
F 01382 226979
E shop@burns-harris.co.uk
W www.burns-harris.co.uk
Contact Pauline Barker
Established in 1886, stocking art and craft supplies from leading manufacturers. Staff are happy to offer advice to beginners. **Branches** 11 The Postings, Kirkcaldy KY1 1HN **T** 01592 644004 **F** 01592 644004

Get Creative
1 Portobello High Street, Edinburgh, EH15 1DW
T 0131 6695214
Retails supplies for all arts and crafts.

Greyfriars Art Shop
20 Dundas Street, Edinburgh, EH3 6HZ
T 0131 5566565
E info@greyfriarsart.co.uk
W www.greyfriarsart.co.uk
Established 1840. Listed in 'The Times' among the top five art shops in the country. Large range of stock for painters and a knowledgeable staff. Closed Sundays.

Healthcraft
12 Commercial Road, Lerwick
Shetland, ZE1 0LX
T 01595 692924
W www.mysite.freeserve.com/healthcraft
Contact Lena Miller
Founded in 1990, selling a wide range of artists'

materials. Has a small gallery selling original paintings by local artists, as well as prints.

Henderson Art Shop
28a Raeburn Place, Edinburgh, EH4 1HN
T 0131 3327800
Retails broad selection of artists' materials.

InkSpot
Castle Street, Hamilton, ML3 6BU
T 01698 286401
F 01698 201300
E shop@inkspot.uk.com
W www.inkspot.uk.com
Contact Craig Moore
Specializes in art materials, stocking a full range of watercolours, oils, acrylics, gouache, pastels, etc. for the artist and hobbyist alike. Also provides classes, workshops and demonstrations for the not-so-experienced.

Just-Art
81 Morningside Road, Edinburgh, EH10 4AY
T 0131 4471671
E enquiries@just-art-online.co.uk
W www.just-art-online.co.uk
Contact Ritchie Collins
Founded in 1988 by Justine Marjoribanks, a working artist. Stock a wide range of artists' materials and also has a gallery. Specializes in providing advice from professional artists.

Kirkintilloch Fine Arts
110 Townhead, Kirkintilloch, Glasgow, G66 1NZ
Sells range of art materials and has gallery space.

Lemon Tree
15, Howard Court, Nerston Industrial Estate
East Kilbride, Glasgow, G74 4QZ
T 01355 570577
Offers range of art and craft supplies.

Millers City Art Shop
28 Stockwell Street, Glasgow, G1 4RT
T 0141 5531660
F 0141 553 1583
E info@millers-art.co.uk
W www.millers-art.co.uk
Contact Paul Miller
Suppliers to artists and crafters since 1824. Stocks many major manufacturers. Orders taken online.

Moray Office Supplies
Edgar Road, Elgin, IV30 6YQ

T 01343 549869
F 01343 549300
E sales@moray-office.co.uk
W www.morayoffice.co.uk
Contact Aileen Neil
Wide selection of art materials.

Mulberry Bush
77 Morningside Road, Edinburgh, EH10 4AY
T 0131 4475145
Wide range of art and craft supplies.

Penny's the Art Shop
91 High Street, Selkirk, TD7 4BZ
T 01750 720521
Founded in 1999 to supply artists' materials for
the many border artists and visitors. Selection of
large canvases.

South-east

Alec Tiranti Ltd
3 Pipers Court, Berkshire Drive (Off Enterprize
Way), Thatcham, RG19 4ER
T 0845 123 2100
F 0845 123 2101
E enquiries@tiranti.co.uk
W www.tiranti.co.uk
Founded 1895. Supplies a complete range of
sculptor's tools, materials and studio equipment.
Also has complete range of tools and materials for
the mould and model maker and a range of tools
and materials for the potter and ceramacist,
woodworker, restorer and stonecarver. **Branches** 27
Warren Street, London, W1T 5NB T 020 7636 8565.

Annetts (Horsham) Ltd
7B The Carfax, Horsham, RH12 1DW
T 01403 265878
F 01403 265878
Founded in 1964. An independent family-run art
store retailing artists' and craft supplies from most
major stockists.

Art for All
230 High Street, Bromley, BR1 1PQ
T 020 83139368
Founded in 1990. Supplies a range of art materials
to suit all levels in all media. Also runs art classes
and courses. Other services include framing.

Art-Write (Hythe) Ltd
90a High Street, Hythe, CT21 5AJ
T 01303 261925

F 01303 237933
E artwritehythe@hotmail.com
W www.artwritehythe.co.uk
Contact Clive Brown, Helen Brown or Louise
Moore
A family-run art supplier. Stocks a comprehensive
ranges of artists' materials and textbooks. A diary
detailing daily classes, courses and demonstrations
in the attached studio is available on request.

Artworker
Unit 1–3, 1–6 Grand Parade, Brighton, BN2 9QB
T 01273 689822
E sales@artworker.co.uk
W www.artworker.co.uk
Specialists in supplying products to the
graphics and publishing industries since 1972.
Branches 153/155 Ewell Road, Surbiton,
Surrey KT6 6AW T 020 8390 4661

Bovilles Art Shop
127–128, High Street, Uxbridge
UB8 1DJ
T 01895 450300
F 01895 450323
E sales@bovilles.co.uk
W www.bovilles.co.uk
Famous for art materials since 1904. Other
branches at Maidenhead, Amersham and Gerrards
Cross (see website for details).

Brackendale Arts
1 Sparvell Way, Camberley, GU15 3SF
T 01276 681344
F 01276 681344
W www.brackendalearts.co.uk
A family-owned company established for over
twenty years. Keeps a well-stocked and
comprehensive range of art and craft supplies.

Broad Canvas
20 Broad Street, Oxford, OX1 3AS
T 01865 244025
Art and craft supplies, including materials for
screen printers and framers. Small attached gallery.

Chromos (Tunbridge Wells) Ltd
58 High Street, Tunbridge Wells, TN1 1XF
T 01892 518854
F 01892 528967
Contact Suna Lambert
Established in 1996, stocking a comprehensive
range of fine art and craft materials from many
leading manufacturers. Also offers a canvas-

stretching service (all sizes) and is home to in-store fine art gallery and showroom.

Country Love Ceramics
37d Milton Park, Abingdon, OX14 4RT
T 01235 861700
F 01235 861900
E sales@countryloveceramics.co.uk
W www.countryloveceramics.com
Wholesale suppliers to the paint-your-own pottery market. Bisque, kilns, glazes, brushes and accessories all available. Full training and support given to business start-ups.

Creative Crafts
11 The Square, Winchester, SO23 9ES
T 01962 856266
E sales@creativecrafts.co.uk
W www.creativecrafts.co.uk
Contact Lyn Symonds
A retailer of fine-art supplies, founded in 1972. Also stocks a large range of craft materials.

Creative World
The Bishop Centre, Bath Road, Maidenhead SL6 0NX
T 01628 665422
F 01628 665424
E create@creativeworld.co.uk
W www.creativeworld.co.uk
Contact Sue Gowers
An art, craft and gift superstore founded in 1996. Aims to provide a comprehensive, carefully selected range and stocks over seventeen thousand products.

Daler-Rowney Ltd
P.O.Box 10, Bracknell, RG12 8ST
T 01344 461000
F 01344 486511
E customer.service@daler-rowney.com
W www.daler-rowney.com
Founded over two hundred years ago. Manufactures and distributes fine-art materials in more than 150 countries worldwide. A range of quality art materials encompasses more than 7,500 products.

Economy of Brighton
82 St Georges Road, Kemptown, Brighton BN2 1EF
T 01273 682831
F 01273 624466
E sales@economyofbrighton.co.uk

W www.economyofbrighton.co.uk
Over thirty years experience supplying broad range of art and craft supplies.

EKA Services Ltd
11–12 Hampton Court Parade, East Molesey KT8 9HB
T 020 89793466
E ekaservices@btclick.com
W www.ekaservices.co.uk
Contact Anup Patel
Established for over fifty years, stocking all major manufacturers of art and graphic materials.

Expressions
49 Kings Road, St Leonards-on-Sea, TN37 6DY
T 01424 446260
F 01424 442652
Contact Mr or Mrs King
Retails wide range of art and craft supplies and canvases. Friendly and knowledgable staff.

Forget Me Not
69–70 St James Street, Newport (Isle of Wight) PO30 1LQ
T 01983 522291
F 01983 522291
Contact Anne Toogood
Founded in 1984, supplying artists' materials, stationery, etc.

Godalming Art Shop
45 Bridge Street, Godalming, GU7 1HL
T 01483 423432
F 01483 423432
Contact Charlotte Albrecht or Alan Watson
Stocks a wide range of artists' materials from leading manufacturers, technical equipment and ancillary and craft materials.

Great Art (Gerstaecker UK Ltd)
Normandy House, 1 Nether Street, Alton GU34 1EA
T 0845 601 5772
F 01420 593333
E welcome@greatart.co.uk
W www.greatart.co.uk
Major supplier of quality artist's supplies and materials, including leading brands and hard-to-find specialist items. Over 35,000 products available at competitive prices, ranging from painting and drawing equipment to printing press and sculpture supply. Free delivery on all orders over £50. Stock most major brands.

Hearn & Scott

10 Bridge Street, Andover, SP10 1BH
T 01264 400200
F 01264 400205
E sales@hearnscott.co.uk
Contact Maureen Mallett
Established in 1973. A stationer, printer, digital copy shop and art shop. Also has a gallery where local artists exhibit their work.

Hockles

166 Kennington Road, Kennington, Oxford
OX1 5PG
T 01865 736611
E sales@hockles.com
W www.hockles.com
Opened in 2004, carrying a stock of 6,000 products.

Lunns of Ringwood

13 Christchurch Road, Ringwood, BH24 1DG
T 01425 480347/473335
F 01425 480347
E lunnsofringwood@btconnect.com
Contact Heidi Killen
A family-run business for nearly forty years. Stocks leading brands of art materials. Discounts on bulk orders and mail order available. New craft department opened in 2006.

On-linepaper.co.uk

Unit 19 Bassetts Manor, Butcherfield Lane,
Hartfield, TN7 4LA
T 01892 771245
F 01892 771241
E on-linep@per.co.uk
W www.on-linepaper.co.uk
Web-based seller of paper for art and design.

Oxford Craft Studio

443 Banbury Road, Oxford, OX2 8ED
T 01865 513909
Specialist manufacturers of ceramics and stockists of ceramic and craft materials.

Pure South

6 Meeting House Lane, Brighton, BN1 1HB
T 01273 321718
Stocks art, craft and interior design supplies.

Rural Art Company

Milton Ernest Garden Centre, Radwell Road,
Milton Ernest, MK44 1SH
T 01234 823592
F 01234 823562
Contact Pauline Hurst
An art materials shop and on-site framer. Also sells original paintings and prints, displayed on walls and in the garden-centre coffee shop. No charge for display but thirty per cent commission plus VAT taken on anything sold.

Sevenoaks Art Shop

45 London Road, Sevenoaks, TN13 1AR
T 01732 452551
E sevenoaksartshop@hotmail.com
Established in 1927, supplying fine-art materials and offering a picture-framing service.

Smitcraft

Unit 1, Eastern Road, Aldershot, GU12 4TE
T 01252 342626
F 01252 311700
E info@smitcraft.com
W www.smitcraft.com
Founded in 1938, a mail order supplier predominantly serving the institutional market e.g. hospitals, prisons, schools. Supplies over fifteen thousand art and craft items.

T.N. Lawrence & Son Ltd

208 Portland Road, Hove, BN3 5QT
T 01273 260260
F 01273 260270
E artbox@lawrence.co.uk
W www.lawrence.co.uk
Founded in 1859, specializing in the supply of printmaking and painting materials. Importing top quality brands from around the world. Fast, efficient mail order service.

T.S. Two

41 Queensway, Bletchley, Milton Keynes, MK2 2DR
T 01908 646521
F 01908 646526
E sales@tuppers.co.uk
Contact Olga Prentice or Jeff Wyatt
Retails art, craft and graphic materials and offers a bespoke framing service.

Terry Harrison Arts Limited

28 Cove Road, Cove, Farnborough, GU14 0EN
T 01252 545012
F 01252 545012
E harrisonarts@aol.com
W www.terryharrison.com
Contact Terry Harrison or Derek Whitcher
Books, videos, DVDs, brushes and art materials

are available via website. Terry Harrison himself is available to give demonstrations to art societies and other groups and holds workshops all over the UK.

ToolPost

35 Brunstock Beck, Didcot, OX11 7YG
T 01235 810658
F 01235 810905
E peter@toolpost.co.uk
W www.toolpost.co.uk
Contact Peter Hemsley
An online vendor of tools and materials, specializing in quality tools for woodturning, woodcarving and handcrafted woodworking. Other materials available include timber (hardwoods), finishes, adhesives, polishing systems, lathes and copy-carving machines. Delivers worldwide.

Tuppers

696 North Row, Lloyds Court
Central Milton Keynes, MK9 3AP
T 01908 678033
F 01908 663695
E sales@tuppers.co.uk
W www.tuppers.co.uk
Contact Nick Lambert
Retails art and graphic materials and provides bespoke framing service.

South-west

Alms House

20 Silver Street, Trowbridge
BA14 8AE
T 01225 776329
F 01225 774740
E mjcreek@almshouse.net
W www.almshouse.net
Contact Jim Creek
Founded in 1987, stocking a wide range of materials and offering art classes. Mail order available via website. Studio space occasionally available; rates on application.

Art at Bristol

44 Gloucester Road, Bishopston, Bristol
BS7 8AR
T 0117 9232259
F 0117 9232259
E enquires@artatbristol.co.uk
W www.artatbristol.co.uk
Extensive range of supplies for all artists, from the amateur to the professional.

Art Centre

135 High Street, nr Playhouse Theatre
Weston-super-Mare, BS23 1HN
T 01934 644102
E mikekbeaumont@aol.com
W www.artysus.co.uk
Contact Mike Beaumont
Established since 1992, with a large range of artists' materials including grounds, easels, brushes, paints and mounting boards. A comprehensive range of acrylics and pastels are held in stock. Silk, glass painting and other specialist materials are also available.

Art Centre and Tamar Valley Gallery

Block A, Florence Road Business Park, Kelly Bray
PL17 8EX
T 01579 383523
F 01579 384043
E artcentre@fsmail.net
Contact Darren Gardiner
Discount art and craft materials retailer. Also offers commercial framing service, art and craft classes and workshops, and an art gallery. Studios, classrooms and gallery space for hire.
Price range £10 – £50 per week.

The Art Shop

54 Castle Street, Trowbridge
BA14 8AU
T 01225 765139
Wide range of art and craft supplies.

Art@Bristol

44 Gloucester Road, Bishopston, Bristol, BS7 8AR
T 0117 9232259
E enquiries@artatbristol.co.uk
W www.artatbristol.co.uk
Contact Peter Probyn
Materials for professional and amateur artists, model-makers and animators. A wide variety of well-known and lesser-known products.

Artboxdirect

23–25 The Pollet, St Peter Port, Guernsey, GY2 4GB
T 01481 701351
F 01481 710383
E info@artboxdirect.co.uk
W www.artboxdirect.co.uk
Contact Julie Queripel
A premier art store for over twenty-five years. The internet selling arm of the Lexicon, with sales primarily to the UK and Europe. Four thousand products online from major manufacturers.

Artrageous
21 Sevier Street, Bristol, BS2 9LB
T 0117 9143025
F 0117 9085645
E artrageous@childrensscrapstore.co.uk
An arts, crafts and gift shop which is part of
Children's Scrapstore Charity. All profits are gift
aided to the charity.

Arts & Interiors Ltd
48 Princes Street, Yeovil, BA20 1EQ
T 01935 477790
F 01935 434183
E brenda.phil@ramlands.freeserve.co.uk
Contact Brenda Drayton

Axworthys' Group
4 Palace Avenue, Paignton, TQ3 3HA
T 01803 663320
F 01803 558869
E steveperry@axworthys.co.uk
W www.axworthys.co.uk
Contact Maureen Turpin
Established in 1868, stocking a full range of
products to suit the beginner up to the expert.

Blue Gallery
16 Joy Street, Barnstaple, EX31 1BS
T 01271 343536
F 01271 321896
E sales@bluegallery.co.uk
W www.bluegallery.co.uk
Contact Roy Smith
Specialist retailers of art and craft materials for
over forty years. Most leading suppliers stocked.
Online shopping.

Bristol Fine Art
72–74 Park Row, Bristol, BS1 5LE
T 0117 9260344
Offers all manner of artists' materials. Experienced
staff on hand to give advice.

Ceres Crafts Ltd
Lansdown Road, Bude, EX23 8BH
T 01288 354070
Contact Mr T.A. Miell
Established in 1981, selling a complete range of
artist materials and a comprehensive range of craft
materials and kits.

Cherry Art Centre
18–20 Ellacombe Road, Longwell Green
Bristol, BS30 9BA

T 0117 9048287
E mail@cherryartcentre.co.uk
Contact Lynne and Martyn Holehouse
Offers a range of services to artists, including
bespoke and ready-made picture frames, art and
craft materials, children's and adults' art classes
and 'Arty Parties'. As well as seasonal open art
exhibitions, the Centre offers luxury painting
holidays in Cornwall with tuition.

Compleat Artist
102 Crane Street, Salisbury, SP1 2QD
T 01722 335928
E martyn.kennard@tesco.net
W www.artmail.co.uk
Contact Martyn Kennard
Founded in 1952 by Edna Trott and now run by
Martyn Kennard. Caters for the student,
intermediate and professional artist. The bow-
fronted shop is situated on the bridge over the
River Avon on the North side. Mail order service
can be accessed via website or by phone.

Creativity
7–9 Worrall Road, Bristol, BS8 2UF
T 0117 9731710
E createbs8@aol.com
W www.creativitycraftsuppliers.co.uk
Family-run art and craft supplies shop with over
twenty-five years of experience.

F.J. Harris & Son
13 Green Street, Bath, BA1 2JZ
T 01225 462116
F 01225 338442
Contact Jackie Gluschke
Founded in 1821. A retail outlet for all art materials
for artists and students. A wide range of stretched
canvases.

Finelife
Foxcombe, Exford, Minehead, TA24 7NY
T 01643 831336
W www.artnetdirectory.co.uk/artistsmaterials/
pochade
Contact Peter Waymouth
Pochade (French for 'sketch') oil painter's field box
reintroduced in 2004. Takes three wet canvas
boards (8"x6" or 10"x8"), in-built palette, space for
tubes, brushes, etc.

Fred Keetch Gallery
46 The Strand, Exmouth, EX8 1AL
T 01395 227226

An art materials stockist, framer and gallery, exhibiting local artists' work.

Harberton Art Workshop
27 High Street, Totnes, TQ9 5NP
T 01803 862390
F 01803 867881
Founded in 1970, selling a comprehensive range of artists' materials from all the main suppliers.

Hardings
59–61 High Street, Shaftesbury, SP7 8JE
T 01747 852156
F 01747 851587
E hardshaf@freenetname.co.uk
Contact Tracey
Retail shop founded in the late nineteenth century.

Inside Art
18 Colliers Walk, Nailsea, Bristol, BS48 1RG
T 01275 859990
Wide range of general art materials for sale.

Jim's Mail Order
56 Fore Street, Redruth, TR15 2AQ
T 01209 211903
F 01209 313994
E enquiries@jims.org.uk
W www.jims-mail order.co.uk
Founded in 1984, supplying a range of art and craft materials.

Lexicon
23–25 The Pollet, St Peter Port, Guernsey, GY2 4GB
T 01481 721120
F 01481 710383
E sales@thelexicon.co.uk
W www.thelexicon.co.uk
Contact Julie Queripel
Operating as an art materials retailer for over twenty-five years.

Litchfield Artists' Centre
6 Southampton Road, Lymington, SO41 9GG
T 01590 672503
E artistsmaterials@yahoo.co.uk
W www.litchfieldartistscentre.co.uk
Contact P.D. Merrick
Founded in 1974 and still under the same owner/managers, Litchfield Artists Centre has grown to be the largest suppliers of artists materials in the New Forest. Stocks all major brands and many larger sized products that ordinary suppliers don't keep.

Minerva Graphics
12a Trim Street, Bath, BA1 1HB
T 01225 464054
Wide range of art and craft materials available.

Riverbank Centre
1a Pool Road, Kingswood, Bristol
BS15 1XL
T 0117 9674804
E riverbank.centre@tiscali.co.uk
Contact Gill Punter
Started in 2001. Sells art materials. Has teaching studio for up to fourteen people (covering range of media and age groups). Holds stock of original works. One exhibition per year (for charity).

Sanders
22 Grants Walk, St Austell
PL25 5AA
T 01726 73814
F 01726 69044
E enquiries@sandersartsupplies.co.uk
W www.sandersartsupplies.co.uk
Contact Ellie Atkinson
Started in 2001, stocking supplies from major manufacturers to suit all, from the beginner to the accomplished artist. Also an upstairs gallery.

Stationery/Art Ltd
104–105 High Street, Tewkesbury, GL20 5JZ
T 01684 273100
F 01684 273300
Contact Gordon Bird or Lynne Horsbrugh
Established on current site for over twenty years, carrying a wide range of artists' materials and craft and hobby materials.

T. N. Lawrence & Son Ltd
38 Barncoose Industrial Estate, Pool
Redruth, TR15 3RQ
T 01209 313181
F 01209 315353
E artbox@lawrence.co.uk
W www.lawrence.co.uk
Painting and printmaking supplies specialist, established 1859. Mail order and retail sales available, alongside an online shop.

Thornbury Arts
3a High Street, Thornbury, Bristol
BS35 2AE
T 01454 413722
Stocks art materials and also regularly shows printings, sculptures and ceramics.

Wales

The Art Shop
8 Cross Street, Abergavenny, NP7 5EH
T 01873 852690
F 01873 853516
E info@artshopandgallery.co.uk
W www.artshopandgallery.co.uk
Contact Pauline Griffiths
Founded in 2001. Housed in a renovated
sixteenth-century building, the ground floor stocks
a comprehensive range of artist's materials,
papers, specialist art and illustrated children's
books and Dover publications. First floor and
basement galleries show a regularly changing
programme of exhibitions of fine and applied arts.
Framing service offered. Collectorplan from Arts
Council of Wales available.

Artbox
7 De La Beche Street, Swansea, SA1 3EZ
T 01792 455433
F 01792 455433
E brian.harris@artbox-swansea.com
W www.artbox-swansea.com
Contact Brian Harris
Founded in 1997 and run by a qualified artist with
over twenty years' experience of art materials and
techniques. Complete picture-framing service also
available, along with colour-copying, laminating
service and comb-binding.

B Creative
1 Temperance Lane, Ystradgynlais, Swansea
SA9 1JP
T 01639 845091
Stockists of general art supplies.

Blades the Art Works
2 Cornwall Place, Mumbles, Swansea, SA3 4DP
T 01792 366673
Sells art and craft materials. Also has range of
photography, paintings and sculpture.

Browsers Bookshop
73 High Street, Porthmadog, Gwynedd
LL49 9EU
T 01766 512066
F 01766 512066
Contact Anne Davies or Sian Cowper
Founded in 1976. Retails artist and craft materials,
books and maps. Daily/weekly ordering for non-
stocked and unusual book/art items

Major Brushes Ltd
Units C2 and C3, Capital Point, Capital Business
Park, Parkway, Cardiff, CF3 2PY
T 029 20770835
E artproducts@majorbrushes.co.uk
W www.majorbrushes.co.uk
Contact Mr. Balazs Altordai
Founded in the early 1990s and now supplies over
80% of the brushes sold in the UK educational
market. Also offers broad variety of art and craft
materials, painting palettes, pots, stencils, clay
tools and specialist brushes.

Makit
21 Rectory Road, Cardiff, CF5 1QL
T 029 20343609
E janfarr@makit.co.uk
W www.makit.co.uk
Stocks good range of craft materials.

Mumbles Art & Craft Centre
Treasure, 29–33 Newton Road, Mumbles
Swansea, SA3 4AS
T 01792 410717
E info@mumblescraft.co.uk
W www.mumblescraft.co.uk
Opened in 1997 as a co-operative shop, run by the
members who sell materials and work which they
have designed and produced themselves. All the
members share in the running of the enterprise.
Selected guests are also invited to show their work
for set periods.

Pen and Paper Stationery Co.
13–17 Royal Arcade, Cardiff, CF10 1AE
T 029 20373738
F 029 20373038
E sales@penandpaper.co.uk
W www.penandpaper.co.uk
Contact Wendy
Stationery and art-materials store selling quality
pens and materials for the general artist. Also
holds a wide-ranging stock of papers for art and
craft.

West Midlands

Cromartie Hobbycraft Ltd
Park Hall Road, Longton, Stoke-on-Trent
ST3 5AY
T 01782 313947
F 01782 599723
E enquiries@cromartie.co.uk
W www.cromartie.co.uk

Over fifty years' experience of making kilns in Britain and one of the UK's leading distributors of colours and glazes.

Everyman Artist's Supply Co.
36–38 Islington Row, Edgbaston, Birmingham B15 1LD
T 0121 455 0099
F 0121 456 5983
E everymans@tiscali.co.uk
Contact D. Argall
All artist's materials supplied. Old Holland Oil stockist. Graphics Supplies. Canvas by the metre off the roll. **Branches** 169 Warwick Road, Olton, Solihull B92 7AR. **T** 0121 707 2323.

Fearnside's Art Ltd
34 Belle Vue Terrace, Malvern, WR14 4PZ
T 01684 573221
E fearnsides_arts@tiscali.co.uk
Contact John Edwards
A long-established business selling a wide range of art materials from all major suppliers. Signed prints also available and art tutoring classes held.

Fly Art & Crafts Company
Unit E5, The Pallasades, Birmingham, B2 4XA
T 0121 6436388
General supplier of materials for the arts and craft markets.

Harris-Moore Canvases Ltd
Unit 108 Jubilee Trades Centre, 130 Pershore Street, Birmingham, B5 6ND
T 0121 2480030
E sales@stretchershop.co.uk
W www.stretchershop.co.uk
Contact Louise Moore
A maker of bespoke artists' stretched canvases and linens. Specializes in deep-sided and gallery-wrapped canvases with a wide choice of fabrics and finishes. Any size made to order. National delivery from £6. Online shop on website.

Oasis Art & Graphics
68 East Meadway, Birmingham, B33 0AP
T 0121 7862988
W www.oasisag.co.uk
Wide range of art materials. Also undertakes comercial printing.

Paper House
19a Greengate Street, Stafford, ST16 2HS
T 01785 212953

F 01785 606611
Contact Martin Dalgarno
Founded in 1984. A retailer of fine-art materials operating from a large store in the centre of Stafford.

Spectrum Fine Art & Graphic Materials
5 Fletchers Walk, Paradise Place, Birmingham B3 3HJ
T 0121 2331780
F 0121 2331780
E info@spectrumfinearts.co.uk
W www.spectrumfinearts.co.uk
Stocks complete range of art materials plus instructional materials.

Tales Press
7 Dam Street, Lichfield, WS13 6AE
T 01543 256777
Contact Peter Mott
Established in 1970, selling artists' materials and needlework.

Vesey Art and Crafts
48–50 Chester Road, New Oscott, Sutton Coldfield B73 5DA
T 0121 3546350
F 0121 3550220
E sales@bigink.co.uk
W www.bigink.co.uk
Contact David Prestridge
Under new management from 2006. Specializes in selling artist and craft supplies, stocking all major manufacturers. Offers a bespoke picture-framing service with workshop on-site.

Yorkshire and Humberside

Art Centre
6 Albion Street, Halifax, HX1 1DU
T 01422 366936
E theartcentre@aol.com
Stocks a wide range of materials for arts and crafts from leading manufacturers.

Art Express
Design House, Sizers Court, Yeadon, Leeds LS19 7DP
T 0113 2500077
General art materials retailer.

The Art Shop
27 Shambles, York, YO1 7LX
T 01904 623898

Contact Mr or Mrs Fletcher
Situated in York's famous medieval street, stocking a comprehensive range of art, craft and graphics materials.

Artcraft
Stephen H. Smith's Garden & Leisure, Pool Road, Otley, LS21 1DY
T 01943 462195
F 01943 850074
E wharfe@artcraft.co.uk
W www.artcraft.co.uk
Established in 1966, stocking thousands of artists' and craft materials items.

Bar Street Arts Ltd
14 Bar Street, Scarborough, YO11 2HT
T 01723 507622
F 01723 507622
Contact Dave Colley
Founded in 1996. A specialist supplier of fine-art materials and papers, stocking many of the leading brands.

Biskit Tin
6 Regent Buildings, York Road, York, YO26 4LT
T 01904 787799
Well-established craft supply business.

Bottomleys Ltd
The Wheatsheaf Centre, Yorkshire Street, Rochdale, OL16 1JZ
T 01706 653211
F 01706 653229
E janice@bottomleys.com
W www.bottomleys.com
Contact Janice Bottomley
An art and craft retailer situated in the centre of Rochdale, stocking all manner of artists' supplies. Operates a mail order service and an online shop. Does not charge for delivery within UK. Regularly holds product demonstrations in the shop.

Calder Graphics
5 Byram Arcade, Westgate, Huddersfield, HD1 1ND
T 01484 422991
F 01484 421191
E calderg@brighousecomputers.co.uk
Founded in 1979, retailing a wide range of fine-art and craft products from most of the major manufacturers.

Centagraph
18 Station Parade, Harrogate, HG1 1UE
T 01423 566327
F 01423 505486
E info@centagraph.co.uk
W www.centagraph.co.uk
Large retail art and craft shop, offering a full range of fine art materials from all the leading manufacturers. Efficient and reliable mail order sevice available.

Discount Art
18 Wood Street, Wakefield, WF1 2ED
T 01924 201772
F 01924 369171
E info@discountart.co.uk
W www.discountart.co.uk
Contact Robert Burgess
Offers a large selection of art materials at discounted prices. A total studio service in art supplies with bulk prices on canvas and colour.

Mulberry Bush
Barkers Tower, Lendal Bridge, York, YO1 7DP
General art materials supplies.

Rainbow Arts & Crafts Of Easingworld
Chapel Street, Easingwold, York, YO61 3AE
T 01347 823962
Well-stocked arts and crafts shop.

S & A Frames and Art Centre
The Old Post Office, Yarra Road, Cleethorpes DN35 8LS
T 01472 697772
E saframes@aol.com
W www.artmaterial.co.uk
Contact Rolf Sperr
A large arts and crafts materials centre with regular art classes for adults and children.

Samuel Taylors
10 Central Road, Leeds
LS1 6DE
T 0113 2459737
Stocks extensive range of craft materials.

York Art & Framing
7 Castlegate, York
YO1 9RN
T 01904 637619
E framing@totalserve.co.uk
W www.yorkartandframing.co.uk
Supplies quality art materials to art enthusiasts and professionals. Also offers framing service.

Ireland

Abcon
63A Heather Road, Sandyford Industrial Estate, Dublin 18
T 01 2952444
Sells extensive range of art materials from major manufacturers.

Art & Craft Company
Merchants Square, Ennis, County Clare
T 065 6821559
E info@artandcraft.ie
W www.artandcraft.ie
Supplies wide range of arts and crafts materials.

Art & Craft Emporium / Silkes One Stop Stationery
64 Catherine Street, Limerick
T 061 417997
F 061 409958
E owensilke@iolfree.ie
Founded in the early 1990s, one of the largest art and craft suppliers in the south-west of Ireland, stocking many major manufacturers as well as craft supplies and ready made frames.

Art Choice Supplies
Unit 8, Ryebrook Industrial Estate, Maynooth Road, Leixlip
T 01 6247594
F 01 6247305
Retailer of wide range of art supplies and materials.

Art Materials Company
Terenure Enterprise Centre, 17 Rathfarnham Road, Terenure, Dublin 6W
T 01 4992248
F 01 4938399
E info@artmaterialsco.com
W www.artmaterialsco.com
Range of materials from leading manufacturers.

Art Upstairs
43 High Street, Sligo, County Sligo
T 071 9143158
Sells wide range of artists' supplies.

Artists (Quality Art Paints)
Brittas, Mountmellick, County Laois
T 0502 44204
F 0502 44437
E info@artiste-artpaints.com
W www.artiste-artpaints.com
Specialist paint manufacturers (available through wholesalers and school suppliers).

Blackrock Art & Hobby Shop
Unit 23–24, Blackrock Shopping Centre Blackrock, County Dublin
T 01 2832394
F 01 2832394
E info@artnhobby.ie
W www.artnhobby.ie
Retails wide range of art materials and craft supplies. 19 stores operate throughout Ireland.

Callan Art Supplies
107 Cois Cairn, Old Conna Avenue, Bray, County Wicklow
T 087 9391924
E sylvia@callanartsupplies.com
W www.callanartsupplies.com
Supplies art materials to artists, students, art groups and children's classes.

Carlow Art and Framing Shop
3 Lismard House, Tullow Street Carlow
T 059 9139100
F 059 9139100
E carlowartandframing@oceanfree.net
W www.carlowartandframing.com
Opened in 2002, run by self-taught artists specializing in oil, watercolour, acrylic and pastels. Also specialize in hand-finished frames. Retails art materials from major brand names and offers wide choice in readymade frames.

Cork Art Supplies Ltd
26–28 Princes Street, Cork
T 021 4277488
F 021 4277856
W www.corkartsupplies.com
Over twenty years of experience in retailing artists' supplies and materials. Also operates an online store, Ireland's first art and craft webstore.

Cregal Art
Monivea Road, Galway
T 091 751864
F 091 752449
E info@crgal.com
Opened in 1964, offering wide range of art, craft and framing products.
Branches 30 William Street, Limerick **T** 061 417910.

Daintree Paper
61 Camden Street, Dublin 2
T 01 4757500
E paper@daintree.ie
W www.daintreepaper.com
Suppliers of handmade and fine quality papers and accessories.

G.E. Kee
17 Bridge Street, Coleraine, BT52 1DR
T 028 70343525
E shop@kee-arts.demon.co.uk
W www.kee-arts.demon.co.uk
Opened in 1948. An arts and crafts retailer, gallery and framing service.

Kennedy Gallery
M. Kennedy & Sons Ltd, 12 Harcourt Street, Dublin 2
T 01 4751749
F 01 4753851
E gallery@kennedyart.com
W www.kennedyart.com
One of Ireland's oldest artists' materials shops, dating back to 1887. Family-run, selling wide range of supplies from leading manufacturers.

Leapfrog
Rock Street, Kenmare, Kerry
T 064 40994
E info@leapfrog.ie
W www.leapfrog.ie
Stocks wide array of artist supplies.

Mandel's Art Shop
Main Street, Castlebar, County Mayo
T 094 9022263
F 094 9022263
E info@artshop.ie
W www.artshop.ie
Stocks wide range of artists' supplies.

O'Sullivans
23–25 Grantham Street, Dublin 8
T 01 4700890
F 01 4700880
W www.dosgs.ie
Founded in 1935, a family-run fine art, craft and graphic materials superstore.

Paint Box
Terryland Retail Park Studio, County Galway
T 091 569579
Sells range of art materials. Framing service also offered.

Premier Arts & Craft Store
36 Florence Road, Bray, County Wicklow
T 01 2862130
F 01 2861188
E dpsstationers@eircom.net
Full range of artists' materials stocked. Under new ownership.

Art photography suppliers, developers and printers

AJ's Studio and Camera Supplies
T 01749 813044
E enquiries@aj-s.co.uk
W www.aj-s.co.uk
Established in 1994, specializing in new and used professional photographic equipment.

artistsprinting
Southgate Studios, 2–4 Southgate Road, London N1 3JJ
T 01608 641070
F 08700 549825
E mail@artistsprinting.com
W www.artistsprinting.co.uk
Contact Stephan
Offers large-format digital printing and unique installation and mounting techniques (specializing in one-off billboard format digital photography). Hosts workshops for artists in, among other subjects, file-processing for digital printing and mounting and display applications for digital prints. Collaborates with individual artists and groups working on digital printing or web-based projects.

Bob Rigby Photographic Limited
Store Street, Bollington, SK10 5PN
T 01625 575591
F 01625 574954
E info@bobrigby.com
W www.bobrigby.com
Family-owned business with over 20 years experience of supplying photographic equipment.

BPD Photech Ltd
Unit 20, Aston Court, Kingsland Grange, Warrington, WA1 4SG
T 01925 821281
F 01925 813375
E info@bpdphotech.com
W www.bpdphotech.com
Photographic printers since 1989, offering a

comprehensive range of professional colour processing services, specialising in CIBA or CIBACHROME prints from transparencies.

Calumet Photographic UK
Promandis House, Bradbourne Drive, Tilbrook
Milton Keynes, MK7 8AJ
T 01908 366344
F 01908 366322
E website@calumetphoto.co.uk
W www.calumetphoto.co.uk
A leading supplier of high-quality imaging products since 1939

Camden Camera Centre
28 Parkway, Camden Town, London, NW1 7AH
T 020 74857247
F 020 79160841
W www.camdencameracentre.co.uk
A photographic retailer established in 1989

Camera Centre
High Street, Hailsham, BN27 1AR
T 01323 840559
F 01323 442295
E robert@camcentre.co.uk
W www.camcentre.co.uk
Long-established retailer of new and old photographic equipment.

Cameraking.co.uk
Unit-20, Oliver Business Park, Oliver Road, Park Royal, London, NW10 7JB
T 0845 6443155
F 0845 6443115
E info@cameraking.co.uk
W www.cameraking.co.uk
Supplies extensive range of general photographic supplies and materials.

CameraWorld
14 Wells Street, London, W1T 3PB
T 020 76365005
F 020 76365006
E sales@cameraworld.co.uk
W www.cameraworld.co.uk
Photographic retailer established for over thirty-five years. Branches: 7 Exchange Way, High Chelmer Shopping Centre, Chelmsford, Essex CM1 1XB T 01245 255510 E Chelmer@cameraworld.co.uk

Chaudigital
19 Rosebery Avenue, London, EC1R 4SP

T 020 78333938
F 020 78379130
E sales@chaudigital.com
Founded in 1983, specializing in digital imaging services.

Colorama Digital Pro Lab & Studio
178 Wardour Street, London, W1F 8ZZ
T 020 74340649
E prolab1@colorama.co.uk
W www.coloramaprolab.co.uk
Offers extensive range of photographic products and services for all levels of photographer. Has two studios for hire, a makeover room and changing facilities, and a fully-equipped viewing room.

Cyclops Imaging Limited
Studio 1–4, 10–11 Archer Street, Soho, London
W1D 7AZ
T 020 77343300
F 020 77340101
E info@cyclopsimaging.net
W www.cyclopsimaging.net
Boutique-style Prolab and digital services company based in Soho, London. Specialists in art colour printing to 50x70 inches by award-winning printers.

Dale Photographic
60–62 The Balcony, The Merrion Centre, Leeds
LS2 8NG
T 0113 2454256
F 0113 2343869
E info@dalephotographic.co.uk
W www.dalephotographic.co.uk
Sells new and used photographic equipment.

The Darkroom UK Ltd
15 Berkeley Mews, High Street, Cheltenham
GL50 1DY
T 01242 239031
E info@the-darkroom.co.uk
W www.the-darkroom.co.uk
Offers wide range of printing and processing services to photographers and imaging businesses.

Direct Lighting
North London Freight Depot, York Way, London
N1 0UZ
T 0870 2046000
F 0870 2046001
E mail@directlighting.co.uk
W www.directlighting.co.uk
A still image, film and television production rental

company offering a wide range of photographic lighting, camera equipment and consumables to its clients.

Downtown Darkroom
12 Valentine Place, London, SE1 8QH
T 020 76200911
F 020 76200129
E darkroom@silverprint.co.uk
W www.silverprint.co.uk
Operating for around eighteen years, the lab recently underwent full refurbishment.

DTEK Systems
Parkside, Basingstoke Road, Reading, RG7 1AE
T 0870 4287008
F 0870 4287011
E sales@dteksys.co.uk
W www.dtek.co.uk
Suppliers of high-end imaging equipment.

Dunn's Imaging Group Plc
Chester Road, Cradley Heath, B64 6AA
T 01384 564770
F 01384 637165
E enquiries@dunns.co.uk
W www.dunns.co.uk
Offers wide range of photographic, printing and processing services.

Eden Imaging
Unit 6a, 9 Park Hill, Clapham
London, SW4 9NS
T 020 76278222
F 020 76274666
W info@edenimaging.co.uk
Offers processing services and studio hire.

F.E. Wrightson & Associates
47 West End, Kirkbymoorside
York, YO62 6AD
E info@fewrightson.co.uk
W www.fewrightson.co.uk
Family-run photographic laboratory.

Farnell Photographic Laboratory
Unit 26 Lakes, Enterprise Park, Caton Road,
Lancaster, LA1 3NX
T 01524 847647
F 01524 382403
E lab@farnells.plus.com
W www.farnellphotographiclab.co.uk
Professional photographic lab, offering array of printing, processing and finishing services.

Ffordes Photographic Ltd
The Kirk, Wester Balblair, By Beauly, IV4 7BQ
T 01463 783850
F 01463 782072
E info@ffordes.com
W www.ffordes.com
Stocks wide range of new and used photographic materials.

Films Ltd
1–5 Poland Street, London, W1F 8QB
T 020 74944508
Stock includes film, paper, boards, and processing and contact sheets.

Fixation
Suite 508, 71 Bondway, London, SW8 1SQ
T 020 75823294
F 020 75829050
E Sales@FixationUK.com
W www.fixationUK.com
Photographic suppliers, also offering rental and repair services.

Flash Centre
54 Brunswick Centre, London, WC1N 1AE
T 020 78376163
Stocks cameras and films, and distributes flash equipment to photographic studios.
Branches 2nd Floor, Mill 1, Mabgate Mills, Mabgate, Leeds LS9 7DZ **T** 0113 2470937; 2 Mount Street Business Centre, Mount Street, Birmingham, B7 5RD **T** 0121 3279220.

fotoLibra
Murmur Y Don, Harlech, LL46 2RA
T 020 83481234
E artists@fotoLibra.com
W www.fotoLibra.com
Contact Yvonne Seeley
Founded in 2005 as the first open access stock agency. Sells digital image rights for photographs, paintings and other artwork to professional picture buyers.

Four Corners
121 Roman Road, Bethnal Green, London
E2 0QN
T 020 89816111
F 020 89837866
E info@fourcornersfilm.co.uk
W www.fourcornersfilm.co.uk
Professional-standard film, video and darkroom facilities for film-makers, photographers and

artists working at all levels. Training offered in film specialisms and photographic techniques. Gallery run with digital projection facilities. Screenings, discussion and networking events organized.

Genie Imaging
Unit D4, Jaggard Way, Wandsworth, London
SW12 8SG
T 020 87721700
F 020 87721710
E info@genieimaging.co.uk
Established in 1987. A London-based photographic and digital-imaging laboratory.

Goldenshot Photos
Unit 26–27/37 Cremer Business Centre
37 Cremer Street, London, E2 8HD
T 020 7729 8724
E chriscooke@mac.com
W www.goldenshotphotos.co.uk
Contact Chris Cooke
Fine art photographic printing lab.

Grand Union
49/50 Eagle Wharf Road, London, N1
T 020 72530251
E davidgrandunion@aol.com
W www.grandunionweb.com
Established in Holborn Studios since 1990, offering range of printing and processing services.

Ian Stewart
4 Wood Walk, Wombwell, Barnsley, S73 ONG
T 07944 384418
E ijstew@bushinternet.com
Quality black and white hand processing and printing of traditional photographic film. Film from 35mm to 6 x 7cm roll accepted.

Intro 2020
Priors Way, Maidenhead, SL6 2HP
T 01628 674411
E service@intro2020.co.uk
W www.intro2020.co.uk
Importers and distributors of photographic products from a range of suppliers.

Jessops
Jessop House, Scudamore Road, Leicester
LE3 1TZ
T 0116 2326000
W www.jessops.com
Founded in 1935. A photographic retailer with over two hundred and seventy stores nationwide.

John Jones artSauce
4 Morris Place, Stroud Green Road, London, N4 3JG
T 020 72815439
E photo@johnjones.co.uk
W www.johnjones.co.uk
Contact Rod Taite
Provides a range of conservation framing, photographic and Giclée printing services for artists, photographers, collectors and businesses.

JP Distributrion
Hempstalls Lane, Newcastle-under-Lyme, ST5 OSW
T 01782 753300
F 01782 753399
E info@johnsons-photopia.co.uk
W www.johnsons-photopia.co.uk
The distribution division of Johnsons-photopia Ltd, which dates back to 1743. Exclusively distributing professional photographic brands including Namiya, Sekonic, Peli, Lastolite, Billingham, Gepe, Giottos and Schneider.

Kentmere Photographic Ltd
Staveley, Kendal, LA8 9PB
T 01539 821365
F 01539 821399
E sales@kentmere.co.uk
W www.kentmere.co.uk
Specialists in photographic paper, especially black and white.

Kingsley Photographic
90 Tottenham Court Road, London
W1T 4HL
E sales@kingsleyphoto.co.uk
W www.kingsleyphoto.co.uk
Family-run business with over 40 years experience of selling new and used camera and darkroom equipment.

KP Professional Sales Ltd
32 & 39 Clifton Road, Cambridge, CB1 7EB
T 01223 214514
F 01223 411904
E sales@kpprof.com
W www.kpprof.com
Established in 1968 to serve the needs of professional photographers in the Cambridge area, and now one of the biggest retailers outside of London.

Lab35
16 Blenheim Terrace, St John's Wood
London, NW8 OEB

T 020 7624 2244
W www.lab35.com
Founded in 1981 as a specialist laboratory for the
35mm photographer but fully embraces new
imaging technologies.

Linhof & Studio Ltd
Image House, 204 Leigh Road, Leigh-on-Sea
SS9 1BS
T 01702 716116
F 01702 716662
E info@linhofstudio.com
W www.linhofstudio.com
Stocks wide range of cameras and photographic
equipment.

London Camera Exchange Group
98 Strand, London, WC2R 0EW
T 020 73790200
E strand@lcegroup.co.uk
W www.lcegroup.co.uk
Offers new, used and digital cameras and parts.
Runs a mail order service. Branches nationwide.

M Billingham and Co.
Little Cottage Street, Brierley Hill
DY5 1RG
T 01384 482828
F 01384 482399
E admin@billingham.co.uk
W www.billingham.co.uk
Established in 1978, specialist retailers of camera
bags.

Metro Imaging Ltd
76 Clerkenwell Road, London, EC1M 5TN
T 020 78650000
F 020 78650001
W www.metroimaging.co.uk
Specialists in photographic and digital services.

Michael Dyer Associates Ltd
81a Endell Street, Covent Garden, London
WC2H 9DX
T 020 78368354 / 72400165
F 020 78362858
E photo@michaeldyer.co.uk
W www.michaeldyer.co.uk/
Founded over thirty-five years ago, offering high-
quality professional photographic services,
including studio and location photography, and a
full range of laboratory services. Clients comprise
mainly of artists, designers, publishers, and
architects. Offers discount for students.

Mifsuds Photographic
27 Bolton Street, Brixham, TQ5 9BZ
T 01803 852400
F 01803 855907
E info@mifsuds.com
W www.mifsuds.com
Major photographic supplier for over fifty years.

Monolab
1b St James's Street, Brighton, BN2 1RE
T 01273 686726
E info@monolab.biz
W www.monolab.biz
A professional black and white photographic
printers with long experience of photography,
printing and image manipulation.

Monoprint
Applegarth House, Tumbledown Hill, Cumnor,
Oxford, OX2 9QE
T 07989 777359
E enquiry@monoprint.co.uk
W www.monoprint.co.uk
Contact Lesley Annetts
Providing specialist black and white processing
and handprinting services for the professional and
amateur photographer since 1990. Each individual
print is assessed before being dispatched to ensure
customer satisfaction.

Morco
20 Oak Tree Business Park, Oak Tree Lane,
Mansfield, NG18 3HQ
T 01623 422828
F 01623 422818
E sales@morco.uk.com
W www.morco.uk.com
Stocks wide range of photographic materials.

Morris Photographic
102 High Street, Oxford, OX1 4BW
T 0845 430 2030
F 01865 793113
E sales@morrisphoto.co.uk
W www.morrisphoto.co.uk
Suppliers of broad range of photography
equipment, projectors and digital imaging
equipment.

MPS Photographic
Image House, 17 Carliol Square, Newcastle-upon-
Tyne, NE1 6UQ
T 0191 2323558
F 0191 2610990

E mps@mps-photographic.co.uk
W www.mps-photographic.co.uk
Specializes in range of printing, processing and imaging services.

MXV Photographic
Hempstead Rise, Uckfield, TN22 1QX
T 01825 761940
F 01825 761950
E sales@mxvphotographic.com
W www.mxvphotographic.com
Dealer in high-quality second-hand cameras and photography supplies.

OldTimerCameras.com
24 Market Place, Hatfield, AL10 0LN
T 01707 273773
E sales@otcworld.co.uk
W www.otcworld.co.uk
Established with aim of supplying manuals/instructions for every camera and accessory ever made.

Outback Printworks
Unit 27, Cremer Business Centre, Cremer Street, London, E2 8HD
T 020 77291144
F 020 77296555
W www.outbackprintworks.com
Photographic printworks.

Palm Laboratory
69 Rea Street, Birmingham, B5 6BB
T 0121 622 5504
E palmlabs@btconnect.com
W www.palmlabs.co.uk
A photographic processing specialist, established for over twenty-two years.

Park Cameras Ltd
115 Lower Church Road, Burgess Hill, RH15 9AA
T 01444 245318
F 01444 245319
E sales@parkcameras.com
W www.parkcameras.com
Established over thirty-five years ago, supplying general photographic equipment. **Branch** 16 The Broadway, Haywards Heath, West Sussex RH16 3AL T 01444 412181 F 01444 450200.

Paterson Photographic Ltd (UK)
4 Malthouse Road, Tipton, DY4 9AE
T 0121 5204830
F 0121 5204831

E sales@patersonphoto.co.uk
W www.patersonphoto.co.uk
Retails wide range of studio and darkroom equipment.

Photo Plus
14 High Street, Tibshelf, Alfreton, DE55 5NY
T 01773 875627
E photoplus@photoplus-uk.co.uk
W www.photoplus-uk.co.uk
Online suppliers of photographic and imaging equipment.

PhotoArtistry Ltd
Unit 5, 2 Pennard Close, Brackmills Industrial Estate, Northampton, NN4 7BE
T 01604 700608
F 01604 763834
E info@photoartistry.co.uk
W www.photoartistry.co.uk
Provides an online digital printing service to artists and photographers using novelty printing techniques.

Positive Images (UK Ltd)
3 Dee Road, Richmond, TW9 2JN
T 020 89409344
F 020 83321932
E info@positive-images.co.uk
W www.positive-images.co.uk
Photographic studio and processing laboratory

Potosi Ltd
Unit 23, Cremer Business Centre, 37 Cremer Street, London, E2 8HD
T 020 77295353
A photographic printworks, specializing in black and white.

Primary Colour
80 Kingsland Road, London, E2 8DP
T 020 77297140
E sales@primary-colour.com
W www.primary-colour.com
Established as a photographic lab but now an important supplier of photographic film processing, printing, digital imaging and display graphic services.

The Print Room
194 Brick Lane, London, E1 6SA
T 020 77399923
E info@theprintrooms.co.uk
W www.theprintrooms.com

Process Supplies (London) Ltd

13–25 Mount Pleasant, London, WC1X OAR
T 020 7837 2179
F 020 7837 8551
E sales@process-supplies.co.uk
W www.process-supplies.co.uk
Contact Neil Willes or Paul Willes
Established in 1928. Family-run business, offering a specialized supply service for all conventional and digital photographic materials, including films, papers, chemicals, archival storage pockets, leather portfolios, CDs and DVDs etc.

Professional Film Co. Ltd

65 Great Portland Street, London
W1W 7LW
T 020 75800700
F 020 75800701
Stocks films and photographic accessories. Also offers processing and printing services.

Rapid Eye

79 Leonard Street, London, EC2A 4QS
T 0871 8731257
E hire@rapideye.uk.com
W www.rapideye.uk.com
Opened in 1996 as an affordable colour print darkroom, where photographers could experiment with ideas and techniques. Services offered now include bespoke hand printing, film processing and proofing, a mini lab service providing film-to-digital and digital-to-print solutions, high-end film and print scanning, retouching services and inkjet printing. Also rents out an Imacon 848 film scanner by the hour.

Resolution Creative

204 Latimer Road, London, W10 6QY
T 020 89697333
F 020 89697444
E info@resolveandcreate.co.uk
W www.resolveandcreate.co.uk
Offers extensive range of photographic and digital supplies and services.

Retro Photographic

Wanstead, Alchester Road, Chesterton
OX26 1UN
T 01869 240345
F 07970 737013
E info@retrophotographic.com
W www.retrophotographic.com
Specialists in black and white photographic supplies.

Richards of Hull

Unit 1, Acorn Estate, Bontoft Avenue, Hull
HU5 4HF
T 01482 442422
F 01482 442362
E sales@richards.uk.com
W www.richards.uk.com
Manufacturers of darkroom and processing equipment.

Robert White

Unit 4, Alder Hills Industrial Estate, 16 Alder Hills, Poole, BH12 4AR
T 01202 723046
F 01202 737428
E sales@robertwhite.co.uk
W www.robertwhite.co.uk
Sells and distribute extensive selection of photographic equipment.

SamedaySnaps – Mitcham Arts

256 London Road, Mitcham, CR4 3HD
T 020 86850010
F 020 86408666
E samedaysnaps@mitchamarts.fsnet.co.uk
Contact Vijay
Specializes in digital imaging, printing on a variety of media, from photographic paper to canvas, from miniature to poster size. In-house picture-framing and stretching of canvas provided.

Scott Images

5 Church Road, Lawrence Hill, Bristol, BS5 9JJ
T 0117 9555527
E info@scottimages.co.uk
W www.scottimages.co.uk
Contact Scott
Founded 2004, specializing in digital photography/imaging. Can create stock images and photograph work for archive. Opened a studio and gallery space called Odigi in 2005, for emerging and established artists/curators who embrace new media. Gallery programme includes workshops, talks, clubs and opportunities for artists to sell their work in a weekly mini arts fair. Studio is availble for rent on an hourly basis for photography projects, exhibitions and more. Can supply materials for digital artists and film for photographers.
Price range £15 per hour

Second Hand Darkroom Supplies

The Old Manse, The Ridings, Leafield
OX29 9NN

T 01993 878323
F 01993 878111
E sales@secondhanddarkroom.co.uk
W www.secondhanddarkroom.co.uk
Offers good value darkroom equipment and
supplies.

Sigma Imaging (UK) Ltd
13 Little Mundells, Welwyn Garden City
AL7 1EW
E sales@sigma-imaging-uk.com
W www.sigma-imaging-uk.com
Family-owned business, distributing high-quality
lenses and cameras.

Sky Photographic Services Ltd
Ramillies Street, London, W1F 7AZ
T 020 74342266
Photo processing and printing chain.
Branches 64a Cannon Street, London EC4N **T** 020
72361019; 17–23 Southampton Row, London
WC1B **T** 020 72422504; 16 Andrews Road, London
E8 **T** 020 72544313

Tapestry. MM Ltd
51–52 Frith Street, London, W1D 4SH
T 020 78963100
F 020 78963109
E info@tapestrymm.com
W www.tapestrymm.com
Established in 1972. An independent creative
services company with wide experience of
photographic services.

Theatro Technis
26 Crowndale Road, London, NW1
T 020 73876617
F 020 73832545
E info@theatrotechnis.com
W www.theatrotechnis.com
Offers photographic darkroom facilities for
manual black and white and colour print and film
developing. Black and white chemicals are
provided but not colour.

Transpacolor Ltd
90 Commercial Square
Freemans Common, Leicester
LE2 7SR
T 0116 2550726
W www.transpacolor.com
Founded over twenty-six years ago, aiming to
provide a one-stop solution for photographic and
digital imaging needs.

The Vault
1 Dorset Place, Brighton
BN2 1ST
T 01273 670667
F 01273 688733
E info@thevaultimaging.co.uk
W www.thevaultimaging.co.uk
Offers professional-standard photographic digital
imaging services.

Warehouse Express
PO Box 659, Norwich, NR3 2WN
T 01603 258012
F 01603 258950
E Sales@warehouseexpress.com
W www.warehouseexpress.com
Retails extensive range of photographic
equipment.

Wey Cameras
76 Church Street, Weybridge, KT13 8DL
E webmaster@weycameras.co.uk
W www.weycameras.co.uk
Sells wide range of camera equipment from
leading manufacturers.

Zoom In Photography
Clapham Leisure Centre, Clapham Manor Street,
London, SW4 6DB
T 020 720 2891
E info@zoom-in.org
W www.zoom-in.org
Offers courses on using your camera.
Also has a gallery space.

Art book publishers

A&C Black Publishing
37 Soho Square, London, W1D 3QZ
T 020 77580200
W www.acblack.com
Founded in 1807. Subject areas include visual arts,
glass, ceramics and printmaking.

Antique Collectors' Club
Sandy Lane, Old Martlesham, Woodbridge
IP12 4SD
T 01394 389950
F 01394 389999
E sales@antique-acc.com
W www.antiquecollectorsclub.com
Publishes and distributes specialist books on
antiques, the decorative arts, gardens and
architecture.

Art Data

12 Bell Industrial Estate, 50 Cunnington Street
London, W4 5HB
T 020 87471061
F 020 87422319
E orders@artdata.co.uk
W www.artdata.co.uk
Contact Tim Borton
Established in 1978, primarily to distribute books
and catalogues of contemporary visual arts (fine
art, sculpture, architecture, photography, design,
illustration and fashion). Handles over five
thousand titles and sells throughout the world.
Also produces about six titles of its own a year.

Art Sales Index Ltd

1st Floor, 54 Station Road, Egham, TW20 9LF
T 01784 473136
F 01784 435207
E info@art-sales-index.com
W www.art-sales-index.com
Founded in 1968 to record the price and details of
works of fine art sold at auction to help collectors
and dealers to value art. The database has over 3.3
million entries and is available in book form, on
CD-ROM and on the web.

Ashgate Publishing Ltd

Gower House, Croft Road, Aldershot
GU11 3HR
T 01252 331551
F 01252 344405
W www.ashgate.com
Scholarly monographs in visual studies.

Ashmolean Museum Publications

Ashmolean Museum, Beaumont Street
Oxford, OX1 2PH
T 01865 278010
F 01865 278016
W www.ashmolean.org
Publishes widely on fine and applied arts.

Bardon Enterprises

6 Winter Road, Southsea, PO4 9BT
T 07752 873831
F 023 92874900
Specializes in books about art and music.

Black Dog Publishing

Unit 4.4 Tea Building, Shoreditch High Street,
London, E1 6JJ
T 020 76131922
F 020 76131944

E info@bdp.demon.co.uk
W www.bdpworld.com
Specializes in books on contemporary art,
architecture, design and photography.

Blackwell Publishing

9600 Garsington Road, Oxford, London
OX4 2DQ
T 01865 778315
F 01865 471775
E
customerservices@oxon.blackwellpublishing.com
W www.blackwellpublishing.com
A humanities and social sciences publisher with
an art and theory list. Longstanding relationships
with the journals *Art History* and *The Art Book*.

Book Works Publishing

19 Holywell Row, London, EC2A 4JB
T 020 72472203
F 020 72472540
E mail@bookworks.org.uk
W www.bookworks.org.uk
A publicly-funded contemporary visual arts
publisher, dedicated to distributing significant and
cutting-edge work to a wide audience.

Brepols Publishers

1 Jane Street, Saltaire, Shipley
BD18 3HA
The UK office of a Belgian academic publisher of
monographs and collections across the
humanities. Its imprint, Harvey Miller Publishers,
specializes in academic studies of medieval and
Renaissance art history.

British Museum Press

38 Russell Square, London, WC1B 3QQ
T 020 7323 1234
F 020 7436 7315
W www.britishmuseum.co.uk
Founded in 1973. Publishes around sixty books
each year.

BT Batsford

The Chrysalis Building, Bramley Road, London
W10 6SP
T 020 7314 1400
F 020 7314 1594
E saul.rice@chrysalisbooks.co.uk
W www.chrysalisbooks.co.uk
Contact Saul Rice
A Chrysalis Books Group imprint. Produces a
range of practical books for artists.

Cambridge University Press

The Edinburgh Building, Shaftesbury Road
Cambridge, CB2 2RU
T 01223 312393
F 01223 315052
W www.cambridge.org/uk
The oldest printing and publishing house in the
world, with an extensive art and architecture
backlist.

Collins and Brown

The Chrysalis Building, Bramley Road, London
W10 6SP
T 020 73141400
F 020 73141594
E sales@chrysalisbooks.co.uk
W www.chrysalisbooks.co.uk
Contact Laura Brudenell
A Chrysalis Books Group imprint. Publishes high-
quality practical art books for those keen to
improve their techniques or broaden their
specialities. Authors include John Raynes and
Albany Wiseman.

Constable & Robinson Ltd

3 The Lanchesters, 162 Fulham Palace Road
London, W6 9ER
T 020 87413663
F 020 87487562
E enquiries@constablerobinson.com
W www.constablerobinson.com
Contact Max Burnell
A general trade publisher with several landscape
photography titles.

David & Charles

Brunel House, Forde Close, Newton Abbot
TQ12 4PU
T 01626 323200
F 01626 323319
E postmaster@davidandcharles.co.uk
W www.davidandcharles.co.uk
An international publisher of illustrated non-
fiction books, including practical instruction books
on art techniques. Also the distributor in UK and
Europe of North Light art instruction books, and of
Dover Publications, including their range of books
of copyright-free range images.

Dorling Kindersley Ltd

The Penguin Group (UK), 80 Strand, London
WC2R ORL
T 020 70103000
F 020 70106060
W www.dk.com
An international publisher of highly illustrated
books, with a specialist arts and culture list.

Enitharmon Editions Ltd

26b Caversham Road, London, NW5 2DU
T 020 74825967
F 020 72841787
E books@enitharmon.co.uk
W www.enitharmon.co.uk
Contact Stephen Stuart-Smith
Established in 2001 as an associated company of
Enitharmon Press (founded in 1967). Specialist
publisher of artists' books, commissioning
collaborations between artists and writers, which
take the form of deluxe books incorporating
original art works.

Focal Press (an imprint of Elsevier)

Linacre House, Jordan Hill, Oxford, OX2 8DP
T 01865 314554
F 01865 314572
E St.Barrett@Elsevier.com
W www.focalpress.com
Contact Stephanie Barrett (Associate Editor)
Has enjoyed a reputation since being founded in
1938 as a leading publisher for quality technical
information and practical instruction in media
technology, with many titles becoming standard
texts for students and professionals. Subject areas
include: photography, digital imaging, graphics,
animation, gaming, film, television, video, digital
media, broadcast technology, communications,
journalism, new media, audio, theatre and live
performance.

Four Courts Press

7 Malpas Street, Dublin 8
T 01 4534668
F 01 4534672
E info@four-courts-press.ie
W www.four-courts-press.ie
Leading academic publisher founded in 1970.
Publishes around seventy titles per year, with an
important arts list.

Frances Lincoln Ltd

4 Torriano Mews, Torriano Avenue, London
NW5 2RZ
T 020 72844009
F 020 72675249
W www.franceslincoln.com
Publishes highly illustrated non-fiction, including
art and design.

Garnet Publishing

8 Southern Court, South Street, Reading
RG1 4QS
T 0118 9597847
F 0118 9597356
E info@garnetpublishing.co.uk
W www.garnetpublishing.co.uk
Contact Emma G. Hawker
Independent publishers, producing some art and architecture titles.

Giles de la Mare Publishers Ltd

P.O. Box 25351, London, NW5 1ZT
T 020 74852533
F 020 74852534
E gilesdelamare@dial.pipex.com
W www.gilesdelamare.co.uk
Began publishing in 1995. Publishes mainly non-fiction, especially art and architecture, biography, music, travel and current affairs.

Golden Cockerel Press Ltd

16 Barter Street, London, WC1A 2AH
T 020 74057979
F 020 74043598
E aup.uk@btinternet.com
An academic publisher with list of art titles.

Guild of Master Craftsman Publications Ltd

166 High Street, Lewes, BN7 1XU
T 01273 488005
F 01273 402866
E pubs@thegmcgroup.com
W www.thegmcgroup.com
Contact Liz Clarke
A publisher and distributor of over 1,000 craft books and magazines.

Halsgrove Publishing

Halsgrove House, Lower Moor Way, Tiverton
TQ13 9UY
T 01884 243242
F 01884 243325
E sales@halsgrove.com
W www.halsgrove.com
Contact Simon Butler
A publisher of books about art and artists, specializing in illustrated studies of individual artists and on books with a regional content. Often works with galleries and their artists to create publications to coincide with exhibitions.

Harvard University Press

Fitzroy House, 11 Chenies Street
London, WC1E 7EY
T 020 73060603
F 020 73060604
E info@HUP-MITpress.co.uk
W www.hup.harvard.edu
Produces scholarly books and serious works of general interest.

Hilmarton Manor Press

(Who's Who in Art), Hilmarton Manor, Calne
SN11 8SB
T 01249 760208
F 01249 760379
E whoswhoinart@tiscali.co.uk
W www.hilmartonpress.co.uk
Contact Charles Baile de Laperriere
The first edition of *Who's Who in Art* was published in 1927 and every two years thereafter. Hilmarton Manor Press, founded in 1969, specializes in the publishing and distribution of fine art and art reference books.

I.B. Tauris & Co. Ltd

6 Salem Road, London, W2 4BU
T 020 72431225
F 020 72431226
W www.ibtauris.com
An independent publishing house, producing both general and academic titles. Operates strong lists in art, architecture and visual culture.

Irish Academic Press

44 Northumberland Road, Dublin 4
T 020 89529526
F 020 89529242
E info@iap.ie
W www.iap.ie
Long-established Dublin-based publisher of high quality books of Irish interest. Publishing programme includes history, literature, arts and the media, and women's studies.

Koenig Books London

The Serpentine Gallery, Kensington Gardens,
London, W2 3XA
T 020 77064907
F 020 77064911
E info@koenigbooks.co.uk
W www.koenigbooks.co.uk
The UK art-book imprint of Buchhandlung Walther Koenig in Cologne.

Laurence King Publishing Ltd

4th Floor, 361–373 City Road, London, EC1V 1LR

T 020 7841 6900
F 020 7841 6910
E info@laurenceking.co.uk
W www.laurenceking.co.uk
Publisher of illustrated books. Specialist in graphic design, contemporary architecture, fashion, illustration, interiors, photography and art history for the student, professional and general reader.

The Lilliput Press
62–63 Sitric Road, Arbour Hill, Dublin 7
T 01 6711647
F 01 6711233
E info@lilliputpress.ie
W www.lilliputpress.ie
Founded in 1984 and has published around 150 titles, with a strong art and architecture list.

Liverpool University Press
4 Cambridge Street, Liverpool, L69 7ZU
T 0151 7942233
F 0151 7942235
E J.M.Smith@liv.ac.uk
W www.liverpool-unipress.co.uk
Publishes academic books and journals on a range of subjects including art and architecture.

Lund Humphries
Sardinia House, 51–52 Lincoln's Inn Fields
London, WC2A 3LZ
T 020 7440 7530
F 020 7440 7545
E info@lundhumphries.com
W www.lundhumphries.com
Contact Lucy Clark (Commissioning Editor) at lclark@lundhumphries.com
Illustrated artist monographs and exhibition catalogues.

Mainstream Publishing
7 Albany Street, Edinburgh, EH1 3UG
T 0131 5572959
F 0131 5568720
E enquiries@mainstreampublishing.com
W www.mainstreampublishing.com
Contact Bill Campbell
Founded in 1978. A publisher of a wide-ranging general list including art, photography and popular culture.

Manchester University Press
Oxford Road, Manchester, M13 9NR
T 0161 2752310
F 0161 2743346

E mup@manchester.ac.uk
W www.manchesteruniversitypress.co.uk
Includes a programme of paperbacks in art history and design.

Marston House
Marston Magna, Yeovil, BA22 8DH
T 01935 851331
F 01935 851372
Publishes on fine art, architecture and ceramics.

Merrell Publishers
42 Southwark Street, London
SE1 1UN
T 020 74032047
F 020 74071333
E mail@merrellpublishers.com
W www.merrellpublishers.com
Publishers of books on all aspects of visual culture, from key titles on major artists to surveys of international architecture and explorations of cutting-edge developments in world design.

National Portrait Gallery Publications
St Martins Place, London, WC2H 0HE
T 020 73060055
F 020 73216657
E sellis@npg.org.uk
W www.npg.org.uk/live/pubs.asp
Aims to support the work of the gallery and to increase visitors' knowledge and enjoyment of its collections.

NMS Publishing Ltd
Royal Museum, Chambers Street, Edinburgh
EH1 1JF
T 0131 2474026
F 0131 2474012
E ltaylor@nms.ac.uk
W www.nms.ac.uk
Publishes non-fiction related to the National Museums of Scotland collections.

Octopus Publishing Group
2–4 Heron Quays, London
E14 4JP
T 020 75318400
F 020 75318650
E firstnamelastname@octopus-publishing.co.uk
W www.octopus-publishing.co.uk
Contact Derek Freeman or Henri Masonlel
Imprints include Cassell Illustrated (illustrated books for the international market) and Conran Octopus (quality illustrated books).

Oxford University Press

Great Clarendon Street, Oxford, OX2 6DP
T 01865 556767
F 01865 556646
E WebEnquiry.UK@oup.com
W www.oup.com
Founded in the sixteenth century, producing
scholarly and reference works.

Pavilion

The Chrysalis Building, Bramley Road
London, W10 6SP
T 020 73141400
F 020 73141594
E sales@chrysalisbooks.co.uk
W www.chrysalisbooks.co.uk
Contact Laura Brudenell
A Chrysalis Books Group imprint. Publishes
quality art books. Published artists include Jack
Vettriano.

Phaidon Press Ltd

Regent's Wharf, All Saints Street, London, N1 9PA
T 020 78431234
F 02078431111
W www.phaidon.com
A publisher on the visual arts since 1923. Offices
in New York, London, Paris and Berlin.

Philip Wilson Publishers Ltd

109 Drysdale Street, The Timber Yard
London, N1 6ND
T 020 70339900
F 020 70339922
E pwilson@philip-wilson.co.uk
W www.philip-wilson.co.uk
Contact Philip Wilson
Publishers of art books, museum and exhibition
catalogues, monographs of contemporary artists
and complete catalogues of twentieth-century
artists.

Prestel Publishing Ltd

4 Bloomsbury Place, London, WC1A 2QA
T 020 73235004
F 020 76368004
E sales@prestel-uk.co.uk
W www.prestel.com
Contact Andrew Hansen
Established in Germany in 1923. A leading
publisher of high-quality, illustrated books on art,
architecture, design and photography. The London
office opened in 1997 and has its own publishing
programme.

Primrose Hill Press Ltd

Stratton Audley Park, nr Bicester, OX27 9AB
T 01869 278000
F 01869 277820
E info@primrosehillpress.co.uk
W www.primrosehillpress.co.uk
Specializes in the art of wood-engraving.

Reaktion Books Ltd

33 Great Sutton Street, London, EC1V 0DX
T 020 7253 1071
F 020 7253 1208
E info@reaktionbooks.co.uk
W www.reaktionbooks.co.uk
Founded in 1985. Publishing programme includes
titles on art history, architecture, design and
photography.

RotoVision

4th Floor, Sheridan House, 112–116A Western
Road, Hove, BN3 1DD
T 01273 727268
F 01273 727269
E sales@rotovision.com
W www.rotovision.com
For over 30 years, publisher of illustrated books on
all aspects of design, photography and the
performing arts.

Routledge Publishers

2 Park Square, Milton Park, Abingdon
OX14 4RN
T 020 70176000
F 020 70176708
E tom.church@tandf.co.uk
W www.routledge.com
Publishers in the fields of art, art history, design,
visual culture and aesthetics.

Royal Jelly Factory

11 Kemp House, 103 Berwick Street, London
W1F 0QT
T 020 77346032
F 0870 0549832
E info@royaljellyfactory.com
W www.royaljellyfactory.com
Publishers of New Art Up-Close, a series of pocket-
sized books on living artists. Also offers web-
design services to artists and small arts
organizations.

Sangam Books Ltd

57 London Fruit Exchange, Brushfield Street,
London, E1 6EP

T 020 73776399
F 020 73751230
Traditionally a publisher of textbooks but with some art titles.

Search Press Ltd
Wellwood, North Farm Road, Tunbridge Wells
TN2 3DR
T 01892 510850
F 01892 515903
E searchpress@searchpress.com
W www.searchpress.com
A specialist art and craft publisher for thirty-five years. Series include leisure arts, watercolour tips and techniques, design source books and handmade greetings cards.

Seren
57 Nolton Street, Bridgend, CF31 3AE
T 01656 663018
F 01656 649226
E general@seren-books.com
W www.seren-books.com
An independent literary publisher, specializing in English-language writing from Wales. Publishes on art and photography produced in Wales, both historical and contemporary. Seren's list includes David Jones, Josef Herman, Peter Prendergast, Iwan Bala and David Hurn.

Taschen UK Ltd
1 Heathcock Court, 5th Floor, 415 Strand
London, WC2R ONS
T 020 7845 8585
F 020 7836 3696
E contact-uk@taschen.com
W www.taschen.com
Contact Christa Urbain
Founded in 1980 by Benedict Taschen in Cologne, Germany. All editorial submissions are handled by the German office.

Tate Publishing
Millbank, London, SW1P 4RG
T 020 78878869
F 020 78878878
E tp.enquiries@tate.org.uk
W www.tate.org.uk/publishing
Publishing since 1932, including scholarly works, series and exhibition catalogues.

Textile & Art Publications
12 Queen Street, Mayfair, London, W1J 5PG
T 020 74997979

F 020 74092596
E post@textile-art.com
W www.textile-art.com
Publishes a limited number of titles each year, covering a variety of subjects from Oriental and Islamic art to Pre-Columbian and medieval art.

Thames & Hudson
181A High Holborn, London
WC1V 7QX
T 020 78455000
F 020 78455050
E editorial@thameshudson.co.uk
W www.thamesandhudson.com
Founded in 1949. An international publisher of books on visual culture throughout the world, from prehistory to the twenty-first century. Art titles include the *World of Art* series, monographs, artists' books (collaborations with David Hockney, Lucian Freud and many others), art theory, practical instruction and art history (all periods). Target audiences include students, professionals and the general public.

TownHouse Dublin
Trinity House, Charleston Road, Ranelagh
Dublin 6
T 01 4972399
F 01 497 0927
E books@townhouse.ie
W www.townhouse.ie
Founded in the early 1980s, publishing extensive list of art and architecture titles.

V&A Publications
Victoria and Albert Museum, South Kensington,
London, SW7 2RL
T 020 79422966
F 020 79422967
E vapubs.info@vam.ac.uk
W www.vandabooks.com
Publishers of popular and scholarly illustrated books on fashion and interior design, fine and decorative arts, architecture and photography.

Worple Press
Achill Sound, 2b Dry Hill Road, Tonbridge
TN9 1LX
T 01732 368958
E theworpleco@aol.com
W www.worplepress.co.uk
Contact Amanda Knight or Peter Carpenter
Founded in 1997, specializing in poetry and alternative arts titles. Four to five titles per year.

Submissions welcome. Authors include Iain Sinclair, Kevin Jackson, Elizabeth Cook and Peter Kane Dufault.

Yale University Press
47 Bedford Square, London, WC1B 3DP
T 020 70794000
F 020 70794901
E sales@yaleup.co.uk
W www.yalebooks.co.uk
The London headquarters were established in 1967. Publishes scholarly books in the humanities, with a particular emphasis on art history.

Art bookshops

1853 Gallery Shop
Salts Mill, Victoria Road, Saltaire, Shipley, Bradford, BD18 3LB
T 01274 531163

Arnolfini Bookshop
16 Narrow Quay, Bristol, BS1 4QA
T 0117 9172304
F 0117 917 2303
E bookshop@arnolfini.org.uk
W www.arnolfini.org.uk
Arts centre with a high-quality specialist arts bookshop.

Art Books Etc
81 Westwater Way, Didcot, Oxon, OX11 7TY
T 01235 812834
F 01235 813535
E sales@artbooksetc.co.uk
W www.artbooksetc.co.uk
Specialist art and design bookseller catering for students and lecturers as well as libraries at schools and colleges. Special emphasis on contemporary titles on fine art, graphics, product and interior design, fashion, animation, advertising and architecture. Sales either through the website or a site visit can be arranged, setting up a bookshop for direct sales to students at discount prices.

Art Books International
Unit 14 Groves Business Centre, Shipton Road, Milton-under-Wychwood, Chipping Norton OX7 6JP
T 01993 830000
F 01993 830007
E sales@art-bks.com
W www.art-bks.com

Art Data
12 Bell Industrial Estate, 50 Cunington Street London, W4 5HB
T 020 87471061
F 020 87422319
E orders@artdata.co.uk
W www.artdata.co.uk

Arts Bibliographic
37 Cumberland Business Park, Cumberland Avenue, London, NW10 7SL
T 020 89614277
F 020 89618246
E sales@artsbib.com
W www.artsbib.com
Library suppliers, founded in 1978, specializing in books and catalogues on art and design, and supplying university and public libraries in the UK and abroad.

Artwords
65a Rivington Street, London EC2A 3QQ
T 020 77292000
F 020 77294400
E shop@artwords.co.uk
W www.artwords.co.uk

Artwords at the Whitechapel
Whitechapel Art Gallery, 80 Whitechapel High Street, London, E1 7QX
T 020 72476924
F 020 77294400
E shop@artwords.co.uk
W www.artwords.co.uk

Ashmolean Museum Shop
Beaumont Street, Oxford, OX1 2PH
T 01865 288070
E publications@ashmus.ox.ac.uk
W www.ashmolean.org/shop

BALTIC Shop
South Shore Road, Gateshead, NE8 3BA
T 0191 440 4947
F 0191 478 1922
E shop@balticmill.com
W www.balticmill.com

Bircham Gallery Shop
14 Market Place, Holt, NR25 6BW
T 01263 713312
E Birchamgal@aol.com
W www.birchamgallery.co.uk

Attached to the Bircham Gallery, a light and spacious art gallery in the centre of Georgian Holt specializing in contemporary British paintings, sculpture, original prints, studio glass, ceramics, and designer jewellery. Selected for the Crafts Council list of craft shops and galleries, and is approved by Arts Council England for the 'Own Art' interest free purchase scheme. The gallery shop sells art books and specialist magazines, crafts and cards.

Blackwell Art & Poster Shop
27 Broad Street, Oxford, OX1 3BS
T 01865 333641
F 01865 794143
E art@blackwell.co.uk
W www.blackwell.co.uk
Contact Alan Pointer
A specialist art bookshop including sections on fine art, architecture, photography, fashion, design, cinema, art techniques and decorative arts. Art prints, posters and frames are also available. Part of the Blackwell's chain, originally founded in Oxford in 1879

Blenheim Books
11 Blenheim Crescent, London, W11 2EE
T 020 77920777
E sales@blenheimbooks.co.uk
W www.blenheimbooks.co.uk
Founded in 1996 as Garden Books when it specialized only in books on this subject. Success encouraged the owner to enlarge on the titles held and in 2000 the shop name was changed to Blenheim Books. Since then it has served architects, and interior, fashion, landscape and graphic designers. Also well stocked photography, wildlife and childrens sections.

British Bookshops and Sussex Stationers
Unit 6, Crowhurst Road, Hollingbury Industrial Estate, Brighton, BN1 8AF
T 01273 507999
F 01273 502630
E tclark@britishbookshops.co.uk
A bookseller and retailer of artists' materials. More than fifty stores throughout south-east England.

British Museum Bookshop
British Museum, Great Russell Street, London, WC1
T 020 73238587
F 020 74367315
E customerservices@britishmuseum.co.uk
W www.britishmuseum.co.uk

Charles Vernon-Hunt Books
Geoffrey Van Arcade, 107 Portobello Road, London W11 2QB
T 0208 854 1588
F 020 8854 1588
E c.vernonhunt@btinternet.com
W Books listed on www.abebooks.com
Bookseller specializing in non-Western art reference books (African, Oceanic, Indian, Islamic, Chinese and Japanese). Sells latest publications and exhibition catalogues from around the world and out of print books. Mail order service available. Book stall open Saturdays only.

Chester Beatty Library Shop
Dublin Castle, Dublin 2
T 01 4070750
E abarbati@cbl.ie
W www.cbl.ie

Claire de Rouen Books
First Level, 125 Charing Cross Road, London WC2H 0EA
T 020 72871813
F 020 72871925
E clairederouen@sohobooks.co.uk
Bookshop with particular reputation for fashion photography titles.

Cornerhouse Shop
70 Oxford Road, Manchester M1 5NH
T 0161 2287621
E info@cornerhouse.org

Courtyard Shop
The Fitzwilliam Museum, Trumpington Street, Cambridge, CB2 1RB
T 01223 764399
F 01223 764406
E shops@fitzwilliammuseum.org
W www.fitzwilliammuseum.org
Offers a large selection of books, stationery, gifts and jewellery in relation to the museum's collections and temporary exhibitions.

Coutauld Gallery Bookshop
Somerset House, The Strand, London WC2R 0RN
T 020 78482579
F 020 78482417
E shop@sctenterprises.com
W www.courtauld.ac.uk/gallery/furtherinfo.html

De La Warr Pavilion Shop
Marina, Bexhill-on-Sea, TN40 1DP
T 01424 787900
E info@dlwp.com
W www.dlwp.com

Dean Gallery Shop
73 Belford Road, Edinburgh, EH4 3DS
T 0131 6246272
F 0131 6237126
E deanshop@nationalgalleries.org
W www.nationalgalleries.org
A wide selection of art books, NGS publications, prints, cards and posters from the NGS's collections. Also sells educational toys and books for children.

Design Museum Shop
Shad Thames, London, SE1 2YD
T 0870 9099009
F 0870 9091909
E shop@designmuseum.org
W www.designmuseum.org

The Dover Bookshop
18 Earlham Street, London, WC2H 9LG
T 020 78362111
F 020 78361603
E images@doverbooks.co.uk
W www.doverbooks.co.uk
Founded in 1986, specialists in copyright free, permission free and royalty free images, engravings, patterns, designs and clip art. Also a selection of related art books. Images contained in sourcebooks and CD-Roms.

Dundee Contemporary Arts Shop
152 Nethergate, Dundee, DD1 4DY
T 01382 909900
F 01382 909221
E mail@dca.org.uk
W www.dca.org.uk

Foyles Bookshop
113–119 Charing Cross Road, London
WC2H 0EB
T 020 74375660
E orders@foyles.co.uk
W www.foyles.co.uk
Founded in 1903 and situated at the heart of Soho, Foyles is amongst the world's most famous bookshops. The shop is divided into fifty-six subject areas over five floors and has its own gallery space and specialist art department on the second floor. Customers can expect to find an extensive range of art, architecture, photography and design titles.

Fruitmarket Gallery Bookshop
45 Market Street, Edinburgh, EH1 1DF
T 0131 2252383
F 0131 2203130
E info@fruitmarket.co.uk
W www.fruitmarket.co.uk/bookshop.html
The gallery also has its own publishing programme.

Grenville Books – The Book People Ltd
Bryn Derwen, Parc Menai, Bangor
LL57 4FB

Hatchards
187 Piccadilly, London, W1J 9LE
T 020 74399921
F 020 74941313
E books@hatchards.co.uk
W www.hatchards.co.uk

Hayward Gallery Shop
Belvedere Road, London, SE1 8XZ
T 020 79283144
E hginfo@hayward.org.uk
W www.hayward.org.uk

Heffers Academic & General Books
20 Trinity Street, Cambridge, CB2 1TY
T 01223 568568
F 01223 568591
E heffers@heffers.co.uk
W www.heffers.co.uk

Hodges Figgis
56–58 Dawson Street, Dublin 2
T 01 6774754
E books@hodgesfiggis.ie
W www.waterstones.co.uk

Ian Shipley Books Ltd
70 Charing Cross Road, London
WC2H 0BQ
T 020 78364872
F 020 73794358
E enquiries@shipley.co.uk
W www.artbook.co.uk

ICA Bookshop
The Mall, London, SW1Y 5AH
T 020 77661452

F 020 78730015
E bookshop@ica.org.uk
W www.ica.org.uk/bookshop
Contact Russell Herron (Manager)
Stockists of books on cultural theory, philosophy, art, art theory and new media. Also has a range of hard-to-find magazines and art dvds.

John Sandoe (Books) Ltd
10 Blacklands Terrace, London, SW3 2SR
T 020 75899473
F 020 75812084
E sales@johnsandoe.com
W www.johnsandoe.com
An independent bookshop in Chelsea, founded in 1957. Stocks a wide range of art titles covering individual artists, the decorative arts and architecture.

Koenig Books Ltd.
At the Serpentine Gallery, Kensington Gardens, London, W2 3XA
T 020 77064907
F 020 77064911
E info@koenigbooks.co.uk
W www.koenigbooks.co.uk
Contact Franz Koenig (Bookshop Manager and Company Director)
An independent bookshop in the Serpentine Gallery with a wide range of stock on modern and contemporary art, photography, architecture and art theory. Specializes in artists' books, monographs and catalogues. Has full access to the stock and services of Buchhandlung Walther Koenig in Cologne.

Leeds City Art Gallery Shop
Headrow, Leeds, LS1 3AA
E info@bridgeman.co.uk

MAGMA Covent Garden
8 Earlham Street, Covent Garden, London WC2H 9RY
T 020 72408498
E enquiries@magmabooks.com
W www.magmabooks.com
Branches: MAGMA Manchester, 22 Oldham Street, Northern Quarter, Manchester M1 1JN
T 0161 2368777

Magma Design Ltd
117–119 Clerkenwell Road, London EC1R 5BY
T 020 72429503

F 020 72429504
E enquiries@magmabooks.com
W www.magmabooks.com

Manchester City Gallery Shop
Mosley Street, Manchester, M2 3JL
T 0161 2358888
F 0161 2358899

Marcus Campbell Art Books
43 Holland Street, Bankside, London SE1 9JR
T 020 72610111
F 020 72610129
E info@marcuscampbell.co.uk
W www.marcuscampbell.co.uk
Specializes in out-of-print, second-hand and rare books on twentieth-century and contemporary art. Focus on individual artists' monographs and catalogues, important movements and artists' books.

Modern Art Oxford Shop
30 Pembroke Street, Oxford, OX1 1BP
T 01865 722733
F 01865 722573
W www.modernartoxford.org.uk/Visit/shopandcafe.php

National Gallery of Ireland Shop
Merrion Square West, Dublin 2
T 01 6633518
E bookshop@ngi.ie
W www.nationalgallery.ie
Contact Lydia Furlong (Manager)

National Gallery of Scotland Shop
The Mound, Edinburgh, EH2 2EL
T 0131 6246567
F 0131 6237126
E ngshop@nationalgalleries.org
W www.nationalgalleries.org
A wide selection of art books, NGS publications, prints, cards and posters from the NGS's collections. Also sells educational toys and books for children.

National Gallery Shop
National Gallery, Sainsbury Wing, London WC2H
T 020 77472461
E help@nationalgallery.co.uk
W www.nationalgallery.co.uk
Holds a comprehensive range of art books

covering Western European art from around 1250 to 1900, an extensive range of gifts and souvenirs and a print-on-demand service, allowing customers to print high quality, full-colour, prints of any painting in the gallery's collection.

National Portrait Gallery Shop
2 St Martin's Place, London, WC2H 0HE
T 020 73122463
F 020 73060056

Oriel Mostyn Art Gallery Shop
12 Vaughan Street, Llandudno, LL30 1AB
T 01492 879201
F 01492 878869
E post@mostyn.org
W www.mostyn.org

Pennies from Heaven
Osierbed House, Hall Road, Little Bealings, Woodbridge, IP13 6NA
T 01473 612800
F 01473 612800
E sales@penniesfromheaven.org.uk
W www.penniesfromheaven.org.uk
Contact John or Stephanie Simmonds
Art, design and architecture bookseller since 1985. Specializes in the sale of current issue, remainder and publishers' returns direct to educational establishments throughout the UK and abroad. Contact to arrange a visit/presentation of 1,500 titles at discounted prices.

Photographers' Gallery Shop
8 Great Newport Street, London WC2H 7HY
T 020 78311772 ext. 3
F 020 72400591
E bookshop@photonet.org.uk
W www.photonet.org.uk

RIBA Bookshop
66 Portland Place, London, W1B 1AD
T 020 72567222
F 020 76377185
W www.ribabookshops.com
Other branches Manchester CUBE, 113–115 Portland Street, Manchester M1 6DW T 0161 236 7691; West Midlands Region, Margaret Street, Birmingham B3 3SP T 0121 233 2321; Yorkshire Region, The Centre for Design, 8 Woodhouse Square, Leeds LS3 1AD T 0113 245 6250; Royal Society of Ulster Architects, 2 Mount Charles, Belfast BT7 1NZ T 028 90323760.

Royal Academy of Arts
Unit C Elm Village, 114 Camley Street, London NW1 0PS
T 0800 6346341
E mailorder@royalacademy.org.uk

Royal Kilmainham Bookshop
Irish Museum of Modern Art, Royal Hospital, Kilmainham, Dublin 8
T 01 6770783
E rkbook@iol.ie
Contact Michael Corcoran (Manager)

Scottish National Gallery of Modern Art Shop
75 Belford Road, Edinburgh, EH4 3DR
T 0131 6246307
F 0131 6237126
E gmashop@nationalgalleries.org
W www.nationalgalleries.org
A wide selection of art books, NGS publications, prints, cards and posters from the NGS's collections. Also sells educational toys and books for children.

Scottish National Portrait Gallery Shop
1 Queen Street, Edinburgh, EH2 1JD
T 0131 6246418
F 0131 6237126
E pgshop@nationalgalleries.org
W www.nationalgalleries.org
A wide selection of art books, NGS publications, prints, cards and posters from the NGS's collections. Also sells educational toys and books for children.

Selfridges Book Department
400 Oxford Street, London, W1A 1AB
T 08708 377377
W www.selfridges.co.uk

Tate Britain Shop
Millbank, London, SW1P 4RG
T 020 78878000
E info@tate.org.uk

Tate Modern Shop
Bankside, London, SE1 9TGT
T 020 74015167
E info@tate.org.uk

Tate St Ives Shop
Porthmeor Beach, St Ives, TR26 1TG
T 01736 791110
F 01736 794480

E shop.stives@tate.org.uk
W www.tate.org.uk

Thomas Heneage Art Books
42 Duke Street, St James's, London
SW1Y 6DJ
T 020 79309223
F 020 78399223
E artbooks@heneage.com
W www.heneage.com
Founded in 1977 and among the UK's largest art
bookshops, selling art reference books, catalogues
raisonnés, monographs and exhibition catalogues
worldwide. Shop policy is to stock the most
authoritative book on any subject and in any
language, irrespective of it being new or
secondhand.

Three Counties Bookshop
6 High Street, Ledbury, HR8 1DS
T 01531 635699
E threecountiesbookshop@supanet.com
Contact Alan Cowan
Stockists of artists' materials by leading
manufacturers as well as books.

Trinity College Library Shop
College Street, Dublin 2
T 01 6081171
E paul.corrigan@tcd.ie
Contact Paul Corrigan (Manager)

V&A Shop
Victoria & Albert Museum, Cromwell Road,
London, SW7 2RL
T 020 79422696
W www.vandashop.co.uk

Walker Art Gallery Shop
William Brown Street, Liverpool, L3 8EL
T 0151 478 4199
E thewalker@liverpoolmuseums.org.uk

Wallace Collection Shop
Hertford House, Manchester Square, London
W1U 3BN
T 020 75639522
F 020 75639566
E shop@wallacecollection.org
W www.wallacecollection.org/s/index_shop.htm

The Watermill
Mill Street, Aberfeldy, PH15 2BG
T 01887 822896

E info@aberfeldywatermill.com
W www.aberfeldywatermill.com

Waterstone's
9–13 Garrick Street, London
WC2E 9BA
T 020 78366757
E manager@covent-garden.waterstones.co.uk
W www.waterstones.co.uk
Branches: 203/206 Piccadilly, London SW1Y 6WW
T 020 78512400; 82 Gower Street, London
WC1E 6EQ, T 0207 636 1577.

Whitworth Gallery Shop
The University of Manchester, Oxford Road,
Manchester, M15 6ER
T 0161 2757450
F 0161 2757451
E Whitworth@man.ac.uk

Zwemmer Art
24 Litchfield Street, London, WC2H 9NJ
T 020 72404158
F 020 78367049
E enquiries@zwemmer.com
W www.zwemmerbooks.co.uk
Opened in 1983, specializing in books on art
and architecture, with a gallery upstairs.
Books and journals on contemporary art and
architecture are held on the ground floor while the
basement is dedicated to pre-20th century art and
architecture, non-western arts, and out-of-print
and remaindered books. Also has an on-line
service.

Conservators

Allyson Rae
Peacehaven, Long Stratton Road, Forncett St Peter,
Norwich, NR16 1HT
T 01953 788 544
E allysonrae@btinternet.com
Contact Allyson Rae
Allyson Rae is an ICON-accredited conservator
with 28 years experience, latterly as head of
organic artefacts conservation at the British
Museum. Specializing in ethnography, feather-
work, textiles and organic artefacts, services
include all aspects of collection assessment and
care, conservation treatment and advice on insect
pest management for heritage organizations and
private clients. Recent clients include the Royal
Ontario Museum, Canterbury Cathedral Archive
and Norwich Castle Museum.

C.S. Wellby

The Malt House, 4 Church End, Haddenham
Aylesbury, HP17 8AH
T 01844 290036
E candm@wellby.plus.com
Contact Christopher Wellby
Practising since 1973. Specializes in the
conservation and restoration of oil paintings on
canvas and panel. Also provides reports and
surveys of collections. Fellow of the British
Association of Paintings Conservator Restorers.

Christine Bullick

5 Belford Terrace, Edinburgh, EH4 3DQ
T 0131 3326948
F 0131 3326948
E mail@bullickconservation.com
W www.bullickconservation.com
Contact Christine Bullick, painting conservator
An accredited painting conservator with thirty
years' experience in the conservation of paintings
on panel, canvas and metal supports. Works for
public collections and private clients.

Ciara Brennan Conservation of Fine Art

Terenure Enterprise Centre, 17 Rathfarnham Road
Terenure, Dublin 6W
T 01 4903237
F 01 4903238
E brennan.ciara@gmail.com
Contact Ciara Brennan
Specializing in easel paintings; oil, acrylic and
tempera on canvas, wood and metal supports. Also
offers advice on environmental monitoring and
storage for works of art.

Clare Finn & Co. Ltd

38 Cornwall Gardens, London
SW7 4AA
T 020 79371895
F 020 79374198
E FinnClare@aol.com
Contact Clare Finn
Founded in 1983, offering a full range of
conservation services for paintings, including
consolidation, tear repair, cleaning, lining, filling,
retouching and varnishing. Clare Finn herself has
wide-ranging specialist knowledge of different
periods and styles from Old Masters through to
contemporary painting techniques. Additional
services offered include scientific examination of
paintings, mounting, framing, and treatment of
existing frames. Advice to purchasers and research
projects are undertaken.

Conservation Studio

59 Peverells Wood Avenue, Chandler's Ford
SO53 2FX
T 023 8026 8167
F 023 8026 8267
E winstudio@aol.com
W www.conservationstudio.org
Contact Paul Congdon-Clelford
A specialist studio workshop that provides a
complete restoration and conservation service for
paintings, specializing in oils and works of art on
paper. Home and business consultations available,
together with collection and delivery nationwide.
Clients include museums, institutions, dealers
and private individuals.

Consultant Conservators of Fine Art

North Staffordshire
T 01538 702928 / 07974 791627
F 01538 703714
E huonweaver@aol.com
Contact Marilyn Jackson-Mooney or Ian Mooney
Founded in 1974, providing conservation and
restoration of paintings, prints and watercolours
by qualified conservation graduates of Gateshead
Conservation College. Undertakes work for
museums, church dioceses and private clients.
Relining, wood panel and miniatures repairs, and
large paintings are specialities.
Price range Subject to an hourly rate or quote.

Eddie Sinclair

10 Park Street, Crediton, EX17 3EQ
T 01363 775552
E eddie@sinclair-polychromy.co.uk
Operating since 1979, conserving and researching
medieval materials and techniques in historic
buildings such as Exeter and Salisbury Cathedrals.
Has published and lectured widely on aspects of
historical painting techniques and has acted as a
consultant to the BBC.

Egan, Matthews & Rose

12 Douglas Court, West Henderson's Wynd
Dundee, DD1 5BY
T 01382 229772
F 01382 229772
E eganmatthewsrose@ecosse.net
Carries out all aspects of structural work,
cleaning and restoration of easel paintings,
including works on fabric, wood and metal
supports. Experienced in working on site, on
collections and on outsized paintings. Also
undertakes collection surveys and loan reports.

Welcomes enquiries seeking advice on any aspect of the care of easel paintings.

Ellen L. Breheny
10 Glenisla Gardens, Edinburgh, EH9 2HR
T 0131 6672620
E ellen@breheny.com
Contact Ellen L Breheny
Founded in 1988 for the conservation and restoration of ceramics, vessel glass and related materials, e.g. enamels, jade, plastics and non-architectural plaster.

Fitzgerald Conservation
The Rise, Sevenoaks, TN13
T 01732 460096
E julie.fitzgerald1@virgin.net
W www.paperconservation.org.uk
Specializes in the conservation of works of art on paper, including prints and drawings, watercolours, photographs, parchment, pith and wallpapers. Conservation assessments and treatments carried out. Consultations, surveys, preservation programmes and environmental advice and disaster advice given. Also offers training seminars and workshops.

Graham Bignell New North Press & Paper conservation
Standpoint Studios, 45 Coronet Street, London N1 6HD
T 020 77293161
F 020 77293161
E graham.bignell@talk21.com
Contact Graham Bignell
Founded in 1980 and specializes in the conservation of prints, drawings, posters, watercolours and all archive material.

Halahan Associates
38 Kitson Road, London, SE5 7LF
T 020 77030806
F 020 77030806
E frances.halahan@halahan.co.uk
W www.halahan.co.uk
Contact Frances Halahan
Offers pragmatic advice on collection care issues. Specializes in exhibition work, condition surveys, audits of collections, advising on storage and display solutions and environmental regulation and pest control for museums, galleries, historic houses and collectors. Also undertakes remedial conservation work for museums and galleries and private collections. Over fifteen years of experience in the museum sector.

Hamish Dewar Ltd
14 Mason's Yard, Duke Street, St James's
London, SW1Y 6BU
T 020 79304004
F 020 79304100
E hamish@hamishdewar.co.uk
Contact Hamish Dewar
Established in 1980, specializing in the conservation and restoration of paintings.

Ines Santy Paintings Conservation and Restoration
15 Leopold Place, Edinburgh
EH7 5LB
T 0131 5565002
F 0131 5565002
E isanty@btinternet.com
Established in 1998, specializing in conservation and restoration of oil paintings on canvas and panel. Accredited since 1993. Undertakes interventive treatment (e.g. surface cleaning, varnish removal, retouching) and structural work (consolidation of paint or ground layers, strip-lining, lining, replacement of stretchers, conservation framing). Small repairs may be undertaken to accompanying frames.

Institute for the Conservation of Historic and Artistic Works in Ireland
1 Lower Grand Canal Street, Dublin 2
T 01 6030904
E ichawi@eircom.net
W www.irelandconservation.org
Established in 1991 'to promote for the benefit of Ireland the preservation and conservation of historic and artistic works'. Membership is exclusive to accredited conservator/restorers. Institute organizes courses for heritage sector and awards bursaries to conservation students.

International Fine Art Conservation Studios Ltd
43–45 Park Street, Bristol, BS1 5NL
T 0117 9293480 / 020 85491671
F 0117 9225511
E enquiries@ifacs.co.uk
W www.ifacs.co.uk
Contact Richard Pelter ACR FBAPCR
Established in 1969 and has been involved in conservation projects throughout the UK and overseas. A fully-qualified team can accommodate paintings of any size, period or contemporary. Other services include technical research and paint analysis schemes.

Jane McAusland Ltd
Flat 3, 41 Lexington Street, Soho, London
W1F 9AJ
T 020 74371070
F 01449 770689
E janemca@globalnet.co.uk
A large, well-equipped studio founded in 1970.
Conserves fine art on paper from any period,
including pastels and Oriental works. Also offers
advice on general conservation of paper-supported
art through storage and display.

Judith Gowland
Leases Barn, Braiseworth, Eye, IP23 7DS
T 01379 871556 / 07714 895916
E paperdoc@madasafish.com
Established in 1992, specializing in conservation
of works of art on paper.

Judith Wetherall (trading as J.B. Symes)
28 Silverlea Gardens, Horley, Surrey, RH6 9BB
T 01293 775024
F 01293 775024
E judith@thewetheralls.org.uk
Contact Judith Wetherall
A studio set up in 1977. Conservation, restoration
and new work undertaken. Expert knowledge of
gilding and paint history and techniques.

Julian Spencer-Smith
The Studio, 30a College Road, Woking
GU22 8BU
T 01483 726070
F 01483 726070
E jupastudio@btconnect.com
W www.picturerestorer.com
Contact Julian Spencer-Smith
Founded in 1982. Restorers and conservators of oil
paintings. Cleaning and restoration work uses
minimal intervention and follows ethical
restoration standards in reversibility. Does all
lining and structural work in-house.

Julie Crick Art Conservation
The Old Laboratory, Anstey Hall, Maris Lane
Trumpington, Cambridge, CB2 2LG
T 01223 846699
E julie@crickcollins.com
W painting-conservation-restoration.co.uk
Contact Julie Crick (Dip.Con.)
Founded in 1984. Undertakes the conservation
and care of easel paintings on canvas or wood for
museums, churches and collections large and
small. Also offers advice on packing and

transportation of paintings, on the best methods of
protecting works of art and on repairing paintings
if they become damaged. Will work on extremely
large paintings down to very small ones.

Lesley Bower Paper Conservation
34 Park House Gardens, Twickenham
TW1 2DE
T 020 88929391
E bower@blueyonder.co.uk
W www.westlondonartists.co.uk
Provides surveys for small museums and
undertakes preventive conservation including
environmental control. Offers advice on storage
and display and provides staff training.

Life – A New Life for Old Documents
87 St Georges Road, Great Yarmouth
NR30 2JR
T 01493 854395
E lorraine.finch@paperconservation.fsnet.co.uk
W www.paperconservation.fsnet.co.uk
Has over a decade of experience in providing
conservation and preservation services to
institutions and individuals. All aspects of archives
and art on paper conservation and preservation are
undertaken, from large-scale projects to single
items, as well as photographic conservation.

Lucia Scalisi
13 Burnsall Street, London, SW3 3SR
T 020 7351 6112
E luciascalisi@ukonline.co.uk
Conservation of easel paintings. Formerly Senior
Conservator of Paintings, Victoria & Albert
Museum. Accredited Conservator, Institute of
Conservation and Fellow of the International
Institute of Conservation.

Rachel Howells
61 Geraints Way, Cowbridge, CF71 7AY
T 01446 773038
F 01446 773038
E Rachel@RachelHowells.co.uk
Working on a freelance basis since 1990. Main
activities include conservation and restoration,
including structural work, tear repair, linings, and
also surface treatments, cleaning and
consolidation. Work with artists in the past has
included giving advice on materials and
techniques, treating accidental damages, treating
mould growth, improving structural conditions of
canvases and accessory supports, and offering
advice on framing.

Ronald Moore Fine Art Conservation
Upper Sydcombe, Dorstone, Hay-on-Wye
HR3 6BA
T 01497 831566
E moorerestoration@aol.com
Thirty years' experience, with particular expertise
in fire, water, bomb and structural damage to oil
paintings and works on paper. Also offers
consultation and valuation services.

Rupert Harris Conservation
Studio 5c, Block A, No 1 Fawe Street, London
E14 6PD
T 020 75152020
F 020 79877994
E enquiries@rupertharris.com
W www.rupertharris.com
Contact Rupert Harris
Established in 1982 and appointed metalwork
conservation adviser to the National Trust in the
same year. Work covers bronze, lead, zinc and
electrotype sculpture, modern and contemporary
art, historical lighting, casting and replication,
gilding, consultancy and maintenance. Can advise
artists on the use of materials and paint finishes,
security fixings and maintenance of public
sculpture.

Simon Gillespie Studio
16 Albemarle Street, London, W1S 4HW
T 020 74930988
F 020 74930955
E info@simongillespie.com
W www.simongillespie.com
Founded in 1982, specializing in restoring
paintings. Advice on techniques and conservation
given.

Siobhan Conyngham Fine Art Conservation
Dundrocken, Carrick Macross, County Monaghan
T 042 9661734
E pconyngham@eircom.net
Carries out conservation and restoration of oil
paintings.

Sophia Fairclough Ltd
10 Redland Terrace, Redland, Bristol, BS6 6TD
T 0117 973 9800
E info@fairclough-harrison.co.uk
Established in 1980. Specializes in the
conservation of works of art on paper, particularly
twentieth-century and contemporary work. Works
for many West-End galleries. Also gives advice and
consultation on materials for contemporary artists.

Price range Varies according to the nature of the
work. Estimates are always given before starting
work.

Taylor Pearce Ltd
Fishers Court, Besson Street, London
SE14 5AF
T 020 72529800
F 020 72778169
E admin@taylorpearce.co.uk
Founded in 1986. Sculpture conservators by
appointment to the Queen. Lists all major public
galleries and collections on client list. Carries out
restoration and conservation to sculpture, ranging
from classical to medieval to contemporary.
Also makes and installs (mainly stone)
sculpture for prominent contemporary artists and
acts as consultant exhibitions conservators to
institutions such as the Royal Academy and
National Gallery.

Textile Conservancy Company Ltd
3A Pickhill Business Centre
Smallhythe Road, Tenterden
TN30 7LZ
T 01580 761600
F 01580 761600
E alex@textile-conservation.co.uk
W www.textile-conservation.co.uk
Contact Alexandra Seth-Smith
Founded in 1998, providing the cleaning and
repair of historical textiles, rugs and tapestries.
Clients include English Heritage, the National
Maritime Museum, the Wellcome Trust Library
and a variety of private collectors.

Valentine Walsh
3 Whitehorse Mews, London
SE1 7QD
T 020 72611691
F 020 74019049
E valentine@valentinewalsh.co.uk
W www.valentinewalsh.co.uk
Contact Valentine Walsh
Over twenty years' experience of conservation
of easel paintings and polychrome sculpture
and works for West End dealers and national
museums on pieces from all art periods.
Works to museum standards and advises on
transport, insurance, care and maintenance and
preventive conservation. Services include disaster
response, collection surveys, condition reporting
and scientific analysis. All work is fully
documented.

Consultants

Artquest
University of the Arts London, 65 Davies Street, London, W1K 5DA
T 020 75146493
F 020 75146211
E info@artquest.org.uk
W www.artquest.org.uk
Contact Stephen Beddoe (Programme Manager)
Provides advice and information to London's visual arts sector. The programme responds to the professional needs of artists in the region throughout their careers by providing a website, telephone and email helpline, advisory sessions, and training and seminars. Support covers areas such as presenting and selling work, research and development of new work practices and techniques, financial advice and ongoing professional-development and training opportunities. Also provides a comprehensive legal advice archive and advice service for visual artists. The programme is funded by Arts Council England and University of the Arts London.

Bridgeman Art Library
17–19 Garway Road, London, W2 4PH
T 020 77274065
F 020 77928509
E adrian.gibbs@bridgeman.co.uk
W www.bridgemanart.co.uk
Contact Adrian Gibbs
A commercial picture library established in 1972 by Harriet Bridgeman and specializing in images of art, history and culture. The archive holds approximately one million images from collections around the world, covering every aspect of art and including works by over five hundred artists in copyright. Operates a no-fee service for contemporary artists to administer their copyright and to sell reproduction licences in their work. Accepts 5 x 4 colour transparencies or digital files of 50-megabyte RGB tiffs.

Business Art Galleries
Curwen & New Academy Gallery, 34 Windmill Street, London, W1T 2JR
T 020 73234700
F 020 74363059
E gallery@curwengallery.com
W www.curwengallery.com
Among Britain's most established art consultancies, having been set up in 1978 as part of the Royal Academy to provide art to businesses.

In 1988 the company moved premises and set up the New Academy Gallery in Fitzrovia. In the following years the company purchased the Curwen Gallery at 4 Windmill Street, originally set up in the area by the famous Curwen Studio in 1958. At the start of 2005, the galleries combined in one space at 34 Windmill Street.

Business2Arts
44 East Essex Street, Temple Bar, Dublin 2
T 01 672 5336
F 01 672 5373
E info@business2arts.ie
W www.business2arts.ie
Started in 1988 to promote the benefits to businesses of supporting Irish arts.

Central House
Unit 12.1, 29 Fashion Street, London, E1 6PX
T 07973 439026
E elle@thecentralhouse.com
W www.thecentralhouse.com
Contact Elyse Eales
Founded in 2002, representing young contemporary British artists. Acts as consultants for developers, interior designers and corporate clients.

Corman Arts
24 Daleham Gardens, London, NW3 5DA
F 02074331339
E tca@btinternet.com
W www.thomascormanarts.com
Contact Ruth Corman
Specializes in consultancy for both corporate and private clients. Clients can choose from over three hundred artists and makers producing paintings, prints, photography, textile art, wall hangings, contemporary ceramics, metalwork and sculpture.

Davidson Arts Partnership
34 Quinton Street, Neasden Village, London NW10 0BE
T 020 8900 0880
F 020 8900 0880
E phil@davidsonarts.com
W www.davidsonarts.com
Contact Philomena Davidson
Formed in 1999, an independent consultancy, specializing in the field of public art, managing projects involving all forms of art. Experienced in providing services to a wide range of clients, guiding them through the process of programming, selection, planning and

implementation, and project managing major corporate and civic art commissions and events.

Dickson Russell Art Management

23 St Peter's Square, Hammersmith, London
W6 9NW
T 020 87419577 / 020 77337137
F 020 85639249
E dickson.russell@ntlworld.com
W www.dicksonrussell.co.uk
Contact Emma Russell and Rachel Dickson
Established in 1992 to offer comprehensive art-management and consultancy services to public, corporate and private clients. Deals with acquisition, exhibition curation, management of existing collections and commissioning of artworks, across a wide range of media to include painting, works on paper, sculpture, installation, photography and film-based work. Contemporary and period work sourced according to client requirements. Additional services include shipping, art handling, framing, restoration, valuation and catalogue preparation.

east73rd

19 Tintern Close, London, SW15 2HF
T 020 82465821
F 020 82465821
E info@east73rd.com
W www.east73rd.com
Contact Nicki Makris
Established in 2000, has recently started concentrating solely on consultancy work, offering corporate and private clients a cross-section of contemporary art, ranging from highly representational to completely abstract. Artists supported are up-and-coming painters, photographers and sculptors with work at affordable prices.

Enso

7/8 Addley Park, Liosban Industrial Estate, Galway
T 087 7435660
E ensoart@yahoo.ie
W www.ensoart.com
Contact Kevin Flanagan
An artist-led initiative founded in 2004, a platform for live art and collaborative initiatives in the West of Ireland. Develops projects of artistic and cultural significance, dealing with contemporary issues in Irish culture , and develops its members' personal artistic concerns. Supports a wide variety of artistic practices, including experimental music, contemporary dance, video and film installation,

and live art performance in multidisciplinary exhibtions and events.

FotoLibra

The Saint Line House, Tiger Bay, Cardiff
CF10 5LR
E info@fotoLibra.com
W www.fotoLibra.com
Licenses usage rights on copyright pictures to publishers, splitting the fee with the artist. Also provides secure digital storage for images.

Getty Images

101 Bayham Street, London, NW1 0AG
T 0800 3767977
W www.getty-images.com
The world's foremost provider of visual content to communication professionals.

HS Projects

51 Balcombe Street, London
NW1 6HD
T 020 7487 5448
E info@hsprojects.com
W www.hsprojects.com
Over ten years' experience working with artists and businesses. Work undertaken includes exhibitions, commissions, project management, contracts, workshops and advice. Does not represent artists except on a project basis when retained by the artist. Arrange appointment to visit office.

Impact Art

The Lodge, Warren Cottage, Station Road, North Chailey, BN8 4HQ
T 01444 473878
E art@impactart.co.uk
W www.impactart.co.uk
An independent art consultancy that delivers professionally managed programmes of site-specific art and built environment art works involving artists from a broad spectrum of disciplines. Projects range from large-scale public commissioning programmes to commercial headquarters and smaller-scale projects sourcing art works. Notice of open-competition projects are through the national art press. However, as commissioners they will view new work for consideration. Initial contact via email.

International Art Consultants Ltd

The Galleries, 15 Dock Street, London, E1 8JL
T 020 74811337
F 020 74813425

W www.afo.co.uk
Established in 1979, a consultancy sourcing and
commissioning art from around the globe. Works
with clients in the corporate, hotel, healthcare and
urban regeneration sectors, with budgets ranging
from very little to £1 million+.

International Intelligence on Culture
4 Baden Place, Crosby Row, London
SE1 1YW
T 020 74037001
F 020 74032009
E enquiry@intelculture.org
W www.intelculture.org
International Intelligence on Culture is an
independent company specializing in policy
analysis and intelligence, consultancy, research,
project management, training and advisory
services with an international dimension.

Mac Medicine Ltd
90 Elmore Street, London, N1 3AL
T 07968 271048
E help@macmedicine.net
W www.macmedicine.net
Offers web design advice to artists.

Modus Operandi Art Consultants
4th Floor, 2–6 Northburgh Street, London
EC1V 0AY
T 020 74900009
F 020 74900018
E mail@modusoperandi-art.com
W www.modusoperandi-art.com
Independent art consultancy, providing artistic
direction and a commissioning service to a range
of clients. Client base includes regenerative
agencies, developers, architectural practices, local
authorities, private sector companies, transport
authorities, educational establishments,
environmental and arts organizations. Particular
emphasis on urban and rural regenerative
projects.

nobleART
63 Stanley Road, Cambridge
CB5 8LF
T 01223 306298
E nobleart@nobleart.plus.com
W www.noble-art.co.uk
Contact Guy Noble
Founded in 2000. An art consultancy for homes
and businesses offering contemporary art at
affordable prices.

Pilot
The Old Limehouse Townhall, 646 Commercial
Road, London, E14 7HA
T 07906 181774
W www.pilotlondon.org
An independent not-for-profit initiative led by
artists and independent curators to provide
ongoing support for emerging artists who do not
have commercial representation. Project is
designed to be a platform, and catalyst, where
information is exchanged and contacts made
between artists, curators, collectors and gallerists.
One hundred curators choose one hundred
suitable artists for an annual event.

plan art consultants
63 Squirries Street, Bethnal Green, London
E2 6AJ
T 020 77393007
F 020 77393189
E art@plan-art.co.uk
W www.plan-art.co.uk
Contact Ivan Tennant
Founded in 1997. Includes a multidisciplinary
team of consultants who advise on all aspects of
the development and implementation of public,
corporate and hotel art strategies.

Royal Jelly Factory
11 Kemp House, 103 Berwick Street, London
W1F 0QT
T 020 77346032
F 0870 0549832
E info@royaljellyfactory.com
W www.royaljellyfactory.com
Web-design and coding services aimed primarily at
those involved in the arts, particularly individual
artists and small-scale organizations.

Sheeran Lock Ltd
The Mansion House, Church Lane, Market Hill,
Framlingham, IP13 9EQ
T 01728 621126
E imogenlock@sheeranlock.com
W www.sheeranlock.com
Contact Imogen Lock
Founded in 1990 by John Sheeran, an art curator,
and Imogen Lock, a specialist in communications.
Creates art exhibitions, competitions, events and
education programmes, and is best known for the
ways it cross-fertilizes art, education and business.
Helps artists maximize their potential and develop
their careers through its artist consultancy service,

as well as by organizing retrospective and thematic exhibitions, publishing catalogues and monographs, and creating websites for artists. Also generates cultural projects commissioned and sponsored by the corporate sector.

Snowgoose
12 Chaytor Terrace South, Craghead
DH9 6AZ
T 01207 290639
F 01207 299791
E info@snowgoose.co.uk
W www.snowgoose.co.uk
Designs and builds websites for artists and designers.

Wetpaint Gallery
The Old Chapel, 14 London Road, Cirencester
GL7 1AE
F 01285 644990
E cah@contemporary-art-holdings.co.uk
W www.contemporary-art-holdings.co.uk
Contact Celia Wickham
A corporate art consultancy established in 1990. Specializes in providing art work for offices and commercial environments such as conference centres, hotels and exhibition spaces. Pieces range from original prints and paintings to fabric wall hangings, tapestries, contemporary glass and site specific sculpture. The consultancy also operates an art rental scheme. Artists wishing to submit their work for consideration should send images on disk together with an sae for returns.

Workplace Art Consultancy
12 Adderley Grove, London, SW11 6NA
T 020 77397500
F 020 77298170
E enquiries@wacart.com
W www.wacart.com
Contact Michael Boitier
A corporate, residential, healthcare and digital-art consultancy established in 1990. Clients include the Bank of England, the Ministry of Defence, the Bank of New York, Reuters and the Institute of Directors. Also works extensively with architects and designers both in the UK and abroad.

Founders and art manufacturers

AB Fine Art Foundry Ltd
1 Fawe Street, London, E14 6PD
T 020 75158052
F 020 79877339
E enquiries@abfineart.com
W www.abfineart.com
Contact Henry or Jerry

Art Bronze Foundry (London) Ltd
1–3 Michael Road, Kings Road, London
SW6 2ER
T 020 77367292
F 020 77315460
E service@artbronze.co.uk
Contact Philip Freiensener

Art Cast
36 Southwell Road, London, E5
T 020 77338424

Art Founders Ltd
9 Swinborne Drive, Springwood Industrial Estate, Braintree
CM7 2YP
T 01376 343222
F 01376 341793
E info@artfounders.co.uk
W www.artfounders.co.uk

Bronze Age Sculpture Casting Foundry Ltd and Limehouse Gallery
272 Island Row, Basin Approach, Limehouse, London, E14 7HY
T 020 75381388
F 020 75389723
E info@bronzeage.co.uk
W www.bronzeage.co.uk
Contact Susan Rolfe (Production and General Manager)
Established for over fifteen years, offering a full service to artists looking to cast their sculpture into bronze. Service includes scaling-up and on-site moulding.

Cast Iron Co. Ltd
8 Old Lodge Place, Twickenham
TW1 1RQ
T 020 87449992
F 020 87441121
E info@castiron.co.uk
W www.castiron.co.uk
Contact Gary Young
Founded in 1987, specializing in casting in iron, bronze, etc. and in fabrication. Specialists in architectural metalwork and restoration. Able to work with sculptor to produce patterns, moulds and castings in any metal type.

Castle Fine Art Foundry
Tanat Foundry, Llanrhaeadr Ym MoChnant
Oswestry, SY10 OAA
T 01691 780261
F 01691 780011
E castlefinearts@btconnect.com
W www.sculpture.gb.com
Contact Chris Butler or Paul Daiton
Established in 1990, producing quality bronze
castings. Specialists in casting both public art and
gallery pieces. Provide an enlarging facility and
project management to their clients.

Dublin Art Foundry
3a Rostrevor Terrace, Dublin 2
T 01 6760690
F 01 6760690
E info@dublinartfoundry.com
W www.dublinartfoundry.com
Opened in 1970 and now one of the most
important and respected foundries in Ireland.

Lakeland Mouldings
Soulby, Pooley Bridge, Penrith, CA11 0JF
T 017684 86989
F 017684 86989
E anne@lakelandmouldings.co.uk
W www.lakelandmouldings.co.uk
Contact Anne Woods
A freelance mouldmaking and resin casting
company with over fifteen years' experience.
Offers a professional service to individual
sculptors, businesses, galleries and giftware
manufacturers. Able to produce silicone moulds
and resin casts from original pieces of work.

Livingstone Art Founders
Maidstone Road, Matfield, Tonbridge, TN12 7LQ
T 01892 722474
Foundry specializing in the 'Lost Wax' process of
bronze casting in the traditional plaster and grog
investment and ceramic shell coatings. Operate a
weekly delivery and collection service to London.

LS Sculpture Casting
367 Westcott Venture Park, Westcott, Aylesbury
HP18 0XB
T 01296 658884
F 01296 658882
E david@lssculpturecasting.com
W www.lssculpturecasting.com
Contact David Challis
Operating for over 21 years, specializing in bronze
resin casting, although they do have foundry

connections. Run by experienced team of
moulders, casters and finishers.

Lunts Castings Ltd
Unit 7, Hawthorns Industrial Estate, Middlemore
Road, Birmingham, B21 0BJ
T 0121 5514301
F 0121 5237954
E info@luntscastings.co.uk
W www.luntscastings.co.uk
Contact Tony Limb
Cast in bronze, brass, silver and gold, primarily for
the sculptural trade.

MFH Art Foundry Ltd
Project Workshops, Quarley
SP11 8PX
T 01264 889544
F 01264 889898
Contact Roger Squires
Founded 1980. Specialist silver and bronze
sculture foundry, offering complete service
including mould making, casting, fabrication and
patination.

Mike Smith Studio
Unit 4, 709 Old Kent Road, London
SE15 1JZ
T 020 72775377
F 020 72775420
E mail@mikesmithstudio.com
W www.mikesmithstudio.com
The studio was started in 1989 by Michael Smith.
Works with all materials and processes appropriate
to realizing a project, with the exception of metal
casting. Studio occupies 10,000 sq. ft and is fully
equipped to handle projects of any scale. Works
with artists, architects, designers and other clients
in a variety of ways, including fabricaton,
consultancy, design development, production,
installation and project management. Has a
worldwide client base.

Milwyn Casting
Old Brook Farm, Murthering Lane, Navestock, nr
Romford, RM4 1HL
T 01277 373779
E mwcast@artistsfolio.com
Contact Alex Davies
A fine-art foundry offering bronze-casting, steel
fabrication and a silicon mouldmaking service.

Morris Singer Ltd
Highfield Site, Church Lane, Lasham, GU34 5SQ

T 01256 381033
F 01256 381565
E info@morrissinger.co.uk
W www.morrissinger.co.uk
Contact Chris Boverhoff
A sculpture-casting foundry, founded in 1848. Services include art-work enlarging, lost wax and sand casting, installation and restoration.

Pangolin Editions

Unit 9, Chalford Industrial Estate, Chalford GL6 8NT
T 01453 886527
F 01453 731499
E sales@pangolin-editions.com
W www.pangolin-editions.com
Foundry casting on a scale ranging from miniature to monumental for an international clientele. One of the last foundries still practising the traditional skills of lost wax block investment alongside the latest casting technologies. Specializes in a wide specturm of patinas from traditional shades to unusual colours.

Powderhall Bronze

21 Graham Street, Edinburgh, EH6 5QN
T 0131 5553013
F 0131 5553013
E kerryhammond@caster.worldonline.co.uk
W www.powderhallbronze.co.uk
Founded in 1989 and offering a full casting service to sculptors in bronze, lead and aluminium using ceramic shell, grog investment and sandcasting techniques. Other services include enlarging and conservation works. The Foundry Gallery at Powderhall Bronze is open weekdays from 10am to 4pm and at other times by appointment, showing bronze sculptures by a wide selection of artists. All works are for sale. Group tours can be arranged. A variety of sculpture classes are held in the foundry classroom throughout the week.

Framers

A. Bliss

5 Bakers Yard, Bakers Row, London, EC1R 3HF
T 020 78374959
F 020 78378244
E edward@abliss.co.uk
W www.abliss.co.uk
Contact Edward Mawby
Specialist fine-art dry-mounters of photographs and digital prints on to many surfaces, including aluminium and glass.

Absolute Framing

54 Rathfarmham Wood, Rathfarmham, Dublin 14
T 01 4936205
E sales@pictureframing.ie
W www.pictureframing.ie
Offers wide range of framing sevices.

Acacia Works

20 Gayal Croft, Shenley Brook End, Milton Keynes MK5 7HX
T 01908 501268
E trudy@acaciaworks.co.uk
W www.acaciaworks.co.uk
Contact Trudy Phillips
Offers picture-framing and mount-cutting up to museum standard. Art commissions also undertaken and full consultancy service available. Original art and prints available.

Alec Drew Picture Frames Ltd

7 Cale Street, Chelsea Green, London SW3 3QT
T 020 73528716
F 020 73528716
E framing@alec-drew.demon.co.uk
W www.alec-drew.co.uk
Founded in 1977. A bespoke framer, mainly catering to the local area. Offers a full framing service from simple certificates to Gesso and gilded frames via perspex or hand-laid veneer. Can also recommend restorers or picture-hangers.

Art & Frame

35 South Parade, Yate Shopping Centre, Yate BS37 4BB
T 01454 327010
E info@artandframe.co.uk
W www.artandframe.co.uk
Contact John Evans
Offers a full range of framing services, with a wide selection of frames to choose from in both contemporary and traditional styles. Mounts are only cut from conservation- and museum-quality boards, with a choice of many colours and textures. Also stocks a large range of artist materials, readymade frames and mounts.

Art and Soul

G14 Belgravia Workshops, 157 Marlborough Road London, N19 4NF
T 020 72630421
E becxb@hotmail.com
W www.artandsoulframes.com
Contact Rebecca Bramwell

A framing service with a wide range of mouldings, box-frames, acid-free mounts, etc. Established in 1989 by St Martin's graduate Rebecca Bramwell. Happy to offer advice to artists.

Art of Framing
26 Albert Avenue, Bray, County Wicklow
T 01 2828967
Offers range of framing services.

Artisan for Unusual Things
80 London Road, Teynham, Sittingbourne ME9 9QH
T 01795 522121
F 01795 520744
Contact Melanie Clews
Established in 1983. A retail shop and workshops specializing in design-led miscellanea for contemporary and classic interiors. Offers bespoke on-site framing for two- and three-dimensional items, whenever possible utilizing recycled materials.
Price range Negotiable

Artlines
Unit 9 Europark, Lathaleere Industrial Estate, Baltinglass, County Wicklow
T 059 6482132
E info@artlines.ie
W www.artlines.ie
Contact Helen Blake
Founded in 2001, a creative picture framers offering over 60 colours of mountboard and over 250 mouldings. Also stocks extensive range of ready-made frames and artists' materials.

Artworks
Port Road, Letterkenny, County Donegal
T 074 9125073
Specialist picture framers.

Attic Picture Framing Supplies
11 Boulton Industrial Centre, Hockley, Birmingham, B18 5AU
T 0121 5515454
F 0121 2135072
E frame.tec@virgin.net
Contact Peter Frith
Supplies framing materials to the trade and public. A large range of mouldings in stock and a full range of mounting boards, along with all the sundries required for framing. Can either frame art work from start to finish or supply kits that include frame rims, pre-cut mounts, glass and backing. Will send samples of frames on request.

Barbers
18 Chertsey Road, Woking, GU21 5AB
T 01483 769926
Contact Stuart Herring
Under present management since 1985. Offers a full bespoke and contract picture-framing service. Stocks a wide range of artist materials and houses a modern gallery providing exhibition possibilities.

Bourlet Fine Art Frame Makers
32 Connaught Street, London, W2 2AF
F 020 77244837
E gabrielle@bourlet.co.uk
W www.bourlet.co.uk
Contact Gabrielle Rendell
Founded in 1838. Gilders, carvers and restorers specializing in making fine-art frames for period and contemporary art. Clients include museums in the UK and overseas, interior designers, West End galleries, artists and private collectors.
Price range From £150

Caffrey's Gallery & Framing Studio
Garden Street, Ballina, County Mayo
T 096 22352
Offers range of framing services.

Campbell's of London
1–5 Exhibition Road, London, SW7 2HE
T 020 75849268
F 020 75813499
E wendel.clement@campbellsoflondon.co.uk
W www.campbellsoflondon.co.uk
Contact W. Clement
Founded in 1966, stocking one of the largest collections of handmade frames in the UK. Campbell's gallery (£1,000 to £3,000 per week) also carries a range of original paintings and signed limited-edition prints. Consultancy service available.

Darbyshire Frame Makers
19–23 White Lion Street, London, N1 9PD
T 020 7812 1200
F 020 7812 1201
E enquiries@darbyshire.uk.com
W www.darbyshire.uk.com
Contact Dan Edwards or Laura Beveridge
Founded in 1992. A leading framer and art fabricator to the contemporary art world. Aims to provide the right creative solution through a process of collaborative consultation.

Dealg Design Ltd
Deeside Industrial Estate, Irish Street, Ardee
County Louth
T 041 6853338
F 041 6856280
E dealgdesign@iol.ie
Over twenty-five years experience in the bespoke
and contract framing market. Clients include
National Gallery of Ireland and leading hotels and
offices.

Fairgreen Picture Framing
Old Barrack Road, Collooney, County Sligo
T 086 3818829
Picture framers founded in 2002.

Fastnet Framing
Coorydarrigan, Schull, County Cork
T 028 28404
E framer@iol.ie
Contact Geoff or Martina McCarthy
Founded 1985. All forms of picture framing and
canvas stretching undertaken. Specialists in
individual one-off frames for artists. Large variety
of finishes and woods.

Fine Art Framing Studio
12 Main Street, Midleton, County Cork
T 021 4631540
F 021 4631540
E 1goldframe@eircom.net
Fine art framers.

Frame Tec
8 Greenfield Road, Harborne, Birmingham
B170EE
T 0121 4281038
E frame.tec@virgin.net
Contact Peter Frith
Founded in 1988, a picture-framer and art gallery
specializing in original art exhibited on a sale-or-
return basis. Although art work is vetted, it is not
necessary that it is framed as the gallery can
undertake this and add the cost onto the selling
price. Charges a commission on sales of thirty-
three per cent plus VAT, but does not charge for
hanging space.

Framemaker (Cork) Ltd
Carrigaline Industrial Park, Carrigaline
County Cork
T 021 4376008
E theframemaker@eircom.net
W www.theframemaker.ie

Contact Paddy Costigan
Founded 1987, principally undertaking picture
framing and large-format giclée printing. Also
offers image capturing service, artists' studios and
a gallery space. Branches: 36 Cook Street, Cork T
021 4276008.

Frames of Mind
Townsend Street, Birr, County Offaly
T 00353 5791 20035
E framesofmind@eircom.net
Contact Robert Alexander
Founded 1990. Qualified as a Fine Art Trade
Guild-commended framer since 1997. All types of
work undertaken, including hand finishing of
mouldings.

Framework
Tullyval, Knockvicar, Boyle, County Roscommon
T 071 9667063
F 071 96 67063
E michael.ewing@o2.ie
Specialists in conservation framing and hand-
finished timber mouldings. Many different woods
and profiles. Unlimited range of colours and
finishes and an artists' discount of 20% offered.

Framework & Co
2 Castle Street, Mullingar, County Westmeath
T 044 42332
Range of framing services offered.

Framework Picture Framing
5–9 Creekside, Deptford, London, SE8 4SA
T 020 86915140
F 020 86915140
E enquiries@frameworkgallery.co.uk
W www.frameworkgallery.co.uk
Contact Adrian Morris-Thomas
Founded in 1988. A specialist bespoke picture-
framer with a large range of mouldings. All
materials used are of conservation quality. Acrylic
frames and dry-mounting available. A large
workshop and experienced team of framers can
accommodate most framing requirements. Free
consultation. Also available are exhibition-standard
readymade frames. Premises include the
Framework Gallery, showing contemporary fine art.

Framing Fantastic
149 Sevenmile Straight, Muckamore, Antrim
BT41 4QT
T 028 94439287
F 028 94439287

E info@framingfantastic.com
W www.framingfantastic.com
Contact Shane Noble
Bespoke picture framing and computerised mount cutting service. Online ordering of conservation and white core mounts cut to order for delivery throughout UK and Ireland. Member of the Fine Art Trade Guild. Also runs online gallery of Irish and Ireland-related art and prints.

Framing Loft

Terryland Retail Park, Headford Road, Galway
T 091 562462
F 091 562462
E s-mloftus@yahoo.com
W www.framingloft.com
Offers professional picture framing service.

The Framing Workshop

80 Walcot Street, Bath, BA1 5BD
T 01225 482748
F 01225 422910
E framing@theframingworkshop.com
W www.theframingworkshop.com
Offers a comprehensive framing service. Expertise in hand-finishing skills including gilding, painting, liming and staining. Stocks over 120 plain wood and five hundred finished mouldings including swept, oval and circular frames. Also home to art work by established local artists including Peter Brown and Nick Cudworth.

Frandsen Fine Art Framers Ltd

7 Lillie Yard, Fulham, London, SW6 1UB
T 020 73859930
F 020 76101404
E frandsenframes@msn.com
Contact Derek Tanous
Handmade picture frames, period and modern style, gilded and decape finishes. Established for nearly a hundred years.

Frank B. Scragg & Co.

68 Vittoria Street, Birmingham
B1 3PB
T 0121 2367219
F 0121 2363633
E sales@frankscragg.co.uk
W www.frankscragg.co.uk
Contact John Lewis
A long-established company distributing a wide range of items for framing and hanging pictures, including the Gallery Hanging System of rods and sliding hooks. Free catalogue on request.

Fringe Arts Picture Framers

'Great Down', Hog's Back, Seale, Farnham
GU10 1HD
T 01483 810555
F 08707482254
E lyn@fringearts.co.uk
W www.fringearts.co.uk
Contact Lyn Hall
Run by Lyn Hall, with over twenty-two years of bespoke framing experience. Offers a wide range of specialisms, including handling textiles (modern and traditional), conservation framing, specialist mount-cutting skills, and canvas-stretching. Currently working for a large number of well-known and amateur artists.

Gallery 2000

11–13 Windle Court, Clayhill Park, Neston
CH64 3UH
T 0151 3531522
F 0151 3531300
E art@gallery2000.co.uk
W www.gallery2000.co.uk
Contact Jenny Holland
A family business founded in 1986 by resident artist Jenny Holland. Prints and originals, watercolours and oils. Local scenes, Lake District, North Wales and Anglesey, Isle of Man, Ireland, Wirral, Liverpool and Chester. Specialist framer of pictures and all memorabilia. Readymade frames and decorative mounts, 'while-you-wait' service. Comprehensive stock of artists' materials. In-house, scanning and wide-format giclée printing. Illustrated website with international shopping basket for UK local scenes, dispatched worldwide.

Geoghegans Picture Framing Service

Rathkeale, Limerick, County Limerick
T 069 64286
Extensive range of framing services offered.

Goslings

50 Station Road, Sudbury, CO10 2SP
T 01787 371932
Contact Miss W. Allen
In business for over twenty-five years, offering a full picture-framing service and stocking art materials. Accompanying gallery holds exhibitions throughout the year.

Graham Harrison Framing Ltd

Studio 5 & 6, 81 Southern Row, London
W10 5AL
T 020 89694599

F 020 89640238
E graham@ghframing.com
Contact Graham
Founded 1994, offering a bespoke framing service
to artists, galleries, corporate and private clients.
Specializes in hand finishes and gilding for
contemporary and traditional frames. Also offers
conservation and restoration services. Quotes
provided free of charge.

Ian Dixon GCF Bespoke Framers

White Timbers, Forest Road, East Horsley
KT24 5ER
T 01483 282059
F 01483 282059
E dixonframes@btinternet.com
Contact Ian Dixon GCF
All types of framing undertaken including
originals, photographs, prints, needlework,
medals, memorabilia and sports equipment.
Conservation framing and repairs. Computerized
mount-cutting service (single or multi-aperture).
Corporate work welcomed. Giclée printing of
artists' work and greetings card printing. National
Award Winners six times (including Framing
Business of Distinction).

J&M Framework

5 Station Parade, Woodthorpe Road, Ashford
TW15 2RX
T 01784 258800
F 01784 250503
E info@jandmframework.com
W www.jandmframework.com
Contact Jim Cowell
Established for over twenty years, specializing in
readymade picture frames and mounts. Can also
make frames to size from an extensive range of
mouldings.

J.A. & G.J. Cowell (trading as Thomas Ellis)

7 Beaumont Street, Hexham, NE46 3LZ
T 01434 602050
Established 1829. Picture-framing (tapestries,
needleworks, etc.). Artists' supplies by Daler-
Rowney. Picture sales, including local artists.

Largs Hardware Services & Gallery Eight

3–11 Stanlane Place, Largs, KA30 8DA
T 01475 672634
F 01475 672634
Founded in 1888, offering a picture-framing
service in an on-site workshop. Also houses a
gallery and sells artists' materials.

Leighswood Art and Publishing

Unit 10, Lion Industrial Park, Northgate Way,
Aldridge nr Walsall, WS9 8AY
T 01922 458424
E duncan@leighswoodart.com
W www.leighswoodart.com
Founded in 1996 as a picture-framing business
alongside selling local artists' works. Specializes in
all aspects of framing and also produces giclée
prints. Recently started publishing fine-art prints
and marketing them to galleries throughout the
UK. Currently represents seven artists, covering all
styles and subjects. New artists and all quality
submissions will be considered.

Loft Frames & Gallery

4 Western Road, Clonakilty, County Cork
T 023 35625
Specialist framers.

Michael Hackman

Kite Hill Studios, Kite Hill, Selborne, Alton
GU34 3LA
T 01420 511524
F 01420 511491
E frames@kitehill.biz
Contact Michael Hackman
Has been producing frames for clients including
designers, hotels, artists and retail stores for the
past fifteen years. Specializes in hand-finished
frames using gesso, oil and water gilding, and a
variety of paint finishes to client's specification.
Works in solid woods, producing frame widths of
up to 180mm in one section.

Millennium Fine Art & Framing Ltd

43 Drury Lane, Solihull, B91 3BP
T 0121 7053323
E solihull@millenniumfineart.co.uk
W www.millenniumfineart.co.uk
Offers framing service and range of fine art and
sculpture.

Old Church Galleries

98 Fulham Road, Chelsea, London, SW3 6HS
T 020 75918790
F 020 75918791
E sales@oldchurchgalleries.com
W www.oldchurchgalleries.com
A bespoke picture-framing and mounting service,
from conservation to museum standards. Offers a
large choice of handmade and manufactured
frames and decorative mounts, as well as
stretching and oil and paper restoration services.

Paul Mitchell Ltd
17 Avery Row, Brook Street, London, W1K 4BF
T 020 7493 8732
F 020 7409 7136
E admin@paulmitchell.co.uk
W www.paulmitchell.co.uk
Contact Paul Mitchell or Mary Ross-Trevor
Provides a comprehensive framing and
conservation service. From an extensive inventory
of antique European frames, the company is able
to supply dealers, auctioneers, museums and
private collectors worldwide with expertly
researched framing proposals.

Paul Treadaway
Field Cottage, North Road, Widmer End
HP15 6ND
T 01494 713918
F 01494 713918
E paul@fineartframes.co.uk
W www.fineartframes.co.uk, www.verre-
eglomise.com
Founded in 1970. A maker and gilder of replica
antique frames for drawings, watercolours and
prints. Also offers restoration and gilding of
antique picture frames. A maker of verre-eglomise
glass mounts for antique and contemporary art
work.

Pendragon Frames
1–3 Yorkton Street, London, E2 8NH
T 020 77290608
F 020 77297711
E sales@pendragonframes.com
W www.pendragonframes.com
Dedicated to producing fine handmade frames
using conservation techniques. Has undertaken
much work in the museums and galleries sector.
Portfolio of clients also includes photographers,
artists, private collectors, consultants and
companies.

pictureframes.co.uk
Unit 22d, Wincombe Business Park, Shaftesbury
SP7 9QJ
T 0845 2267249
E mail@pictureframes.co.uk
W www.pictureframes.co.uk
Contact Hope Elletson GCF
Professional framers since 1989, offering full
bespoke framing up to museum standard
including gilding etc. Website offers custom-made
picture frames direct to the door as well as ready-
made frames and other goods and services for

artists. Since 2007 has marketed and reproduced
artists' work using modern printing technology
and provided internet-based framing technology to
work on the artist's website.

Railings Gallery
5 New Cavendish Street, London, W1G 8UT
T 020 79351114
F 020 74869250
E artists@railings-gallery.com
W www.railings-gallery.com
Contact Geihle Sander
Founded in 1980. An in-house framing workshop
offering artists and photographers advice and
competitive prices for framing for exhibitions and
one-off bespoke frames, using conservation
materials. Also stocks contemporary limited-
edition original prints and paintings with a
figurative or abstract feel.

Rebecca's Picture Framing
Cara Main Street, Leap, County Cork
T 028 33332
Provides wide selection of framing services.

Reeves Art Studio
33 Church Street, Athlone, County Westmeath
T 090 6478507
Offers variety of framing services.

Renaissance 2
36 Town End, Golcar, Huddersfield
HD7 4NL
T 01484 659596
E info@renaissance2.co.uk
W www.renaissance2.co.uk
Contact Diane Myzak
Offers bespoke and small-run picture-framing
services to artists and photographers with an
emphasis on innovative design. Also produces and
sells limited-edition giclée prints. Can produce fine
art prints from artists' own work at economical
prices.

Riccardo Giaccherini Ltd
39 Newman Street, London, W1T 1QB
T 020 75801783
F 020 76375221
E louise.liddell@riccardogiaccherini.co.uk
Contact Louise Liddell
A traditional Florentine-style workshop,
specializing in handmaking, joining, carving and
gilding mirror and picture frames. Old Master and
contemporary works framed by international staff.

Riverside Gallery
4 Popes Quay Cork, County Cork
T 021 4502730
Offers extensive framing service.

Simon Beaugie Picture Frames Ltd
Manor Farm Workshops, Hamstreet Rd
Shadoxhurst, Ashford, TN26 1NW
T 01233 733353
F 01233 732354
E framing@simonbeaugie.com
Established for over ten years, offering a
comprehensive conservation picture-framing
service for the trade. Free consultation, collection
and delivery service in Central London.

Vereker Picture Framing
Cork Road, Mallow, County Cork
T 022 22384
E derriveri@eircom.net
Founded in 1992, undertaking framing for private
individuals, commercial enterprises and artists.
Also carries out conservation work, including acid-
free mountboard, backing board and tape.

Wallace Brown Studio
10 Duke Street, Bedford, MK40 3HR
T 01234 360237
F 012234 360237
Contact Wally Greenaway
Founded in 1960. Framing studio offering a
complete bespoke and ready-made contract service
to the trade, industry and professionals alike. The
modern studio incorporates up-to-date equipment
together with an experienced workforce.

Art insurance

Aon Artscope
8 Devonshire Square, Cutlers Gardens, London
EC2M 4PL
T 020 78820470
F 020 78820383
E artscope@aon.co.uk

AUA Insurance
De Vere House, 90 St Faiths Lane, Norwich
NR1 1NL
T 01603 628034
F 01603 761384
E sales@aua-insurance.com
W www.aua-insurance.com
Specialist provider of insurance facilities for
individuals and businesses involved in

photography and other creative arts. Cover can
include liability and professional negligence.

AXA Art Insurance Ltd
106 Fenchurch Street, London
EC3M 5JE
T 020 72654600
F 020 77020016
E info@axa-art.co.uk
W www.axa-art.co.uk
Contact Helen George
Specialists in art and antiques for over 40 years,
from single objects to high-risk commercial
proposals. Offers detailed advice on risk
management, protection, conservation and
recovery. Clients include private and corporate
collectors, museums, galleries and dealers.

Carroll & Partners
2 White Lion Court, Cornhill, London
EC3V 3NP
T 020 76232228

Golden Valley Insurance Services
The Olde Shoppe, Ewyas Harold, HR2 0ES
T 0845 2261303
F 0845 2261304
E gvinsurance@aol.com
Offers specialist insurance for photographers.

Gwennap Stevenson Brown Ltd
1 Tomlins Corner, Queen Street, Gillingham
SP8 4DJ
T 01747 821188
F 01747 821177

Hallett Independent Ltd
Asset House, 7–9 Quay Street, Lymington
SO41 3AS
T 01590 672888
F 01590 673222
E info@hallettindependent.com
W www.hallettindependent.com
Provides specialist art insurance for both UK and
international galleries dealing in contemporary art,
and for collectors of contemporary art and artists.
Also advises on installation, transport, framing,
storage, security, maintenance, valuations,
photography, management computer software etc.

Heath Lambert Group
133 Houndsditch, London, EC3A 7AH
T 020 75603000
E rnorthcott@heathlambert.com

W www.heathlambert.com
Contact Richard Northcott
One of the largest brokers in the London market for fine art, collectibles and private jewellery. Caters for clients ranging from galleries and museums to individual private collectors, corporate collectors, art and antique dealers and shippers. Acts for many major museums and galleries in the UK and Europe as well as arranging exhibitions worldwide.

Hiscox PLC

1 Great St Helen's, London, EC3A 6HX
T 020 74486000
F 020 74486797
E enquiry@hiscox.co.uk
W www.hiscox.com

HSBC Insurance Brokers Ltd

Fine Arts and Antiques Section, Bishops Court, 27–33 Artillery Lane, London, E1 7LP
T 020 7661 2474
F 020 7661 2175
E peterclifford@hsbc.com
W www.insurancebrokers.hsbc.com/hsbc/jewellery/services
Contact Peter Clifford
A leading independent specialist with one of the most experienced and knowledgeable teams in the London market dedicated to the insurance needs of the art and related risks market.

Insurancenow Services Ltd

1st Floor, 413a Chingford Road, Walthamstow, London, E17 5AF
T 020 85315336
F 020 85274527
E paul@insurancenow.co.uk
W www.insurancenow.co.uk
Contact Paul
Established in 1999, incorporating an insurance directory website that provides links to specialist fine-art insurers.

Masterpiece

Chubb Insurance Company of Europe S.A., 106 Fenchurch Street, London, EC3M 5NB
T 0800 111511
W www.chubb.com/international/uk/personal/jewellery.html

Phillippa Levy & Associates

19 Louisa Street, London, E1 4NF
T 020 77901963

F 020 77904100
E leavypitt@aol.com
Contact Phillippa Levy
Established in 1981, offering insurance to artists and craftspeople (public/employers' liability, exhibitions, studio contents). All policies are tailormade to individual needs. Exhibitions covered worldwide, including transit to and from venue. Personal accident cover also available.

Photoguard

Pavilion Insurance Management Ltd, Pavilion House, Mercia Business Village, Coventry CV4 8HX
T 02476 851000
F 02476 851080
E admin@Photoguard.co.uk
W www.Photoguard.co.uk
Insurance for photographers and their equipment.

Society for All Artists (SAA)

P.O.Box 50, Newark, NG23 5GY
T 01949 844050
F 01949 844051
E info@saa.co.uk
W www.saa.co.uk
Provides free public liability and exhibition insurance for affiliated art groups and individual members as a benefit of membership. Ideal for those wishing to exhibit, teach, run courses, workshops or painting holidays (UK only). Applies only to two-dimensional works of art.

T.H. March & Co. Ltd

Hare Park House, Yelverton Business Park Yelverton, PL20 7LS
T 01822 855555
F 01822 855566
E insurance@thmarch.co.uk
W www.thmarch.co.uk

Willis

Fine Art, Jewellery and Specie Division
10 Trinity Square, London, EC3P 3AX
T 020 74888111
E molloyl@willis.com

Windsor Insurance Brokers Ltd

Fine Art and Antiquities Division, Lyon House 160–166 Borough High Street, London SE1 1JR
T 020 74077144

Packers and shippers

01 Art Services Ltd
Unit 2, Towcester Road, London
E3 3ND
T 020 75157510
F 020 75382479
E info@01artservices.co.uk
W www.01artservices.co.uk
Contact Liz Cooper
Founded in 1992, specializing in the
transportation, installation and storage of fine art
within the UK. Can cater for all types of project,
from the carriage or hanging of a single art work to
the management and coordination of whole
exhibitions and collections. Client base includes
leading artists, galleries, museums, consultants,
fine framers, designers, and corporate and private
collectors.

3 Lanes Transport Ltd
5 Albany Terrace, St Ives
TR26 2BS
T 07970 948324
F 01736 798400
E info@3lanes.com
W www.3lanes.com

Anglo Pacific
Units 1 & 2 Bush Industrial Estate
Standard Road, North Acton
London
NW10 6DF
T 020 89651234
F 020 89654954
E info@anglopacific.co.uk
W www.anglopacific.co.uk

Art Move Ltd
Unit 3, The Arches, Grant Road
London, SW11 2NU
T 020 75851801
F 020 72230241
E mail@artmove.co.uk
W www.artmove.co.uk
Contact Alistair Adie
Founded in 1983. Transports, stores and installs art
works, from single pieces to whole shows. Also
provides an export packing service and ships
worldwide. Has regular (weekly) run between
London and Scotland at part-load prices from £70
plus VAT (also the minimum charge for work
around London).

C'Art Art Transport Ltd
Unit 7, Brunel Court, Enterprise Drive, Four
Ashes, Wolverhampton
WV10 7DF
T 01902 791797
F 01902 790687
E info@cart.uk.com
W www.cart.uk.com
Specialists in art transportation, packing and
shipping. Climate-controlled storage. Also offer
public sculpture installation, exhibition hanging
and courier services.

Cadogan Tate Fine Art Logistics
6–12 Ponton Road, London
SW8 5BA
T 020 78196611
F 020 78196601
E c.evans@cadogantate.com
W www.cadogantate.com
Contact Chris Evans
Professional packers and shippers of art. Offices in
London, New York and Paris. Weekly shuttle
service to Paris, Geneva and Zurich. London
warehouse is bonded allowing art to be stored in
bond VAT unpaid. Private temperature-controlled
vaults also available.

Constantine Ltd
Constantine House, 20–26 Sandgate Street
London
SE15 1LE
T 020 77328123
F 020 77322631
E reception@const.co.uk
W www.const.co.uk

Damon Bramley
Box Cottage, Viney Woodside, Lydney
GL15 4LX
T 01594 510365
F 01594 510365
E damon@boxcottage.plus.com
Founded in 1998, specializing in the transport and
installation of sculpture and similar 3-D artwork.
Four-wheel drive lorry equipped with six-tonne
crane enables access to almost any site. Large van
also in fleet for smaller pieces. All aspects of
installation undertaken from foundations to fixing.
Contact for obligation-free quote.

Davies Turner Worldwide Movers
49 Wates Way, Mitcham
CR4 4HR

T 020 76224393
F 020 77203897
E T.Hutchison@daviesturner.co.uk
W www.daviesturner.com

Gallery Support Group

Elder Farm, West End Lane, Heathrow
T 0788 6754123
E info@gallerysupportgroup.com
W www.gallerysupportgroup.com
A group of experienced professionals in art
moving and hanging. Operating in central London
with clients including private individuals, artists,
galleries and museums.

Hedley's Humpers

3 St Leonard's Road, North Acton, London
NW10 6SX
T 020 89658733
F 020 89650249
E london@hedleyshumpers.com
W www.hedleyshumpers.com

HMC Logistics Ltd

Unit 21, Newington Industrial Estate, Crampton
Street, London
SE17 3AZ
T 020 77031666
F 020 77036999
E info@hmclogistics.com
W www.hmclogistics.com
Contact Andy Keir

Kent Services Ltd

Unit 3 Phase 2, Grace Road, Sheerness
ME12 1DB
T 01795 660812
F 01795 669906
E ksl@kent-services.com
W www.kent-services.com
Contact Sheila Amey (Director)
Provides economical and ready access to a large
quantity of high-standard containers for safe and
secure transportation of art objects. Containers
also for sale. Small-quantity materials service.
Transportation and storage of cases for temporary
exhibitions.

Lockson UK

Unit 1, Heath Park Industrial Estate, Freshwater
Road, Chadwell Heath
RM8 1RX
T 020 85972889
F 020 85975265

E shipping@lockson.co.uk
W www.lockson.co.uk

M&G Transport & Technical Services

18 Maple Crescent, Rishton, Blackburn
BB1 4RJ
T 01254 884244
F 01254 884244
E enquiries@museumtransport.co.uk
W www.museumtransport.co.uk
Contact Karen Yates
Founded in 1997, providing transport and
technical services to museums, galleries, artists,
collectors, etc. Also offers picture-hanging,
exhibition installation, mounting and framing
services.

Martinspeed Ltd

Albert Yard, 7 Glasshouse Walk, London
SE11 5ES
T 020 77350566
F 020 77930137
E richard.chapman@martinspeed.com
Established in 1975 to provide specialized art
handling services for artists, collectors, dealers,
commercial galleries, public museums and
galleries world-wide. Specializes in the storage,
packing, casing, installation, transport, import and
export of individual works and whole exhibitions.
Martinspeed's facilities include a fleet of climate
controlled air-ride fine art vehicles, indemnity
approved storage warehouses, case making to all
specifications and an airport office, all staffed by
fully trained, experienced and knowledgeable
people.

Maxtrans London

Unit 7, Heathrow International Trading Estate
Green Lane, Hounslow
TW4 6HB
T 0870 2245555
F 0870 2245556
E info@maxtrans.com
W www.maxtrans.com

Momart Limited

199–205 Richmond Road, London
E8 3NJ
T 020 89863624
F 020 85330122
E enquiries@momart.co.uk
W www.momart.co.uk
Fine art handling, including transportation, case
making and packing, import/export services,

exhibition installation, preventive conservation and storage.

Moving Experience
19A Alexandra Road, St John's Wood, London
NW8 0DP
T 020 74832501
F 020 74834088
E roberto@movexp.co.uk
W www.movexp.com
In business since 1997, offering picture-hanging and art-installation services. Clients include private individuals, artists, galleries, museums and commercial companies. Charges are per art installer and are for half a day (up to four hours) or a full day (four to eight hours). Only installs and hangs pictures; does not supply hanging systems.

MTec Freight Group
Unit 10, Gentlemans Field, Westmill Road, Ware
SG12 0EF
T 01920 461800
F 01920 466606
E info@mtechfreightgroup.com
W www.arttransport.com

Oxford Exhibition Services Ltd
Station Road, Uffington, Faringdon, SN7 7QD
T 01367 820713
F 01367 820504
E enquiries@oxex.co.uk
W www.oxex.co.uk
Contact Michael Festenstein (Managing Director)
Established in 1986. Provides safe packing, secure domestic (air-suspension, climate controlled vehicles) and international shipping, specialist temperature and humidity controlled storage and installation of museum objects and works of art to the highest standards of conservation and security. (International and London office: 2 Sandgate Trading Estate, Sandgate Street, London, SE15 1LE; T 020 7732 7610).

Seabourne Mailpack Worldwide
13 Saxon Way, Moor Lane
Harmondsworth
UB7 0LW
T 020 83221700
F 020 83221701
E info@seabourne-mailpack.com
W www.seabourne-mailpack.com
Founded in 1962, offering a specialist collection, packing and delivery service worldwide. In conjunction with parent company Seabourne

Express Courier Ltd, any transit time can be catered for. Services are often tailormade.

Sovereign International Freight Ltd
Sovereign House, 8–10 St Dunstans Road
Feltham, TW13 4JU
T 020 87513131
F 020 87514517
E info@sovereignlondon.co.uk
W www.sovereignlondon.co.uk

T. Rogers & Co. Ltd
P.O. Box 8, 1a Broughton Street, London, SW8 3QL
T 020 76229151
F 020 76273318

Team Relocations
Drury Way, London
NW10 0JN
T 020 87840100
F 020 84510061
W www.teamrelocations.com

Transeuro (Fine Art Division)
Drury Way, London, NW10 0JN
T 020 87840100
F 020 84593376
E Richard.Edwards@transeuro.com
W www.transeuro.com
Collections throughout the UK and Europe, packing and casing to museum standard. Air-ride transport with full 'climate control' and experienced staff of fine art handlers. Secure storage in North West London on demand. World-wide shipments by sea and air, with all export documentation, including carnets and insurance if necessary. Also exhibition handling and installation.

Printers, print publishers and printmakers

Abacus (Colour Printers) Ltd
Lowick House, Lowick, nr Ulverston, LA12 8DX
T 01229 885361
F 01229 885348
E sales@abacusprinters.co.uk
W www.abacusprinters.co.uk
The company has been established in Cumbria for twenty years. Specializes in turning artists' images into print. Offers high-quality 'waterless' offset printing of postcards, greetings cards, folders, posters, catalogues, calendars, limited-edition

prints and giclée prints. Potential customers should contact for a free sample pack.

Advantage Printers
Unit C3, Newtown Estate, Coolock Industrial Estate, Dublin 17
T 01 8476711
F 01 8484433
E artroom@advantageprinters.ie
W www.advantageprinters.ie
Established in 1969, offering wide range of printing services, including digital and screen printing.

Art Marketing Ltd
Unit 3, Redbourn Industrial Park, High Street, Redbourn, nr St Albans, AL3 7LG
T 01582 794541
F 01582 792664
E sales@artmarketing.co.uk
W www.artmarketing.co.uk
Contact The Design Manager
A family company formed in 1980, developing trading relationships with major high-street retailers as well as 1,500 independent galleries and lifestyle and home-interior stores. Employs and publishes artists working on open edition, original or limited-edition bases and supplies products in many formats. Aims to develop and encourage artists to identify popular furnishing colour trends and themes to maximize their success.

ArtChroma
P.O.Box 627, Portsmouth, PO6 2WZ
T 023 92387831
E info@artchroma.com
W www.artchroma.co.uk
Contact Roland Clarke
A UK giclée printer providing services for artists, photographers, galleries and fine-art publishers. Specializes in giclée printing onto fine-art paper or canvas, and large-format poster printing.

Artline Media
Gloucester Place, Briston, Melton Constable NR24 2LD
T 01263 860103
F 01263 860138
E phillip@artlinemedia.co.uk
W www.artlinemedia.co.uk
Contact Phillip Round
A division of a company established for thirty years. Original roots were in the photographic industry before moving over completely to digital

technology. For many years it has been supplying high-quality prints, up to A3-size and, with a recent investment in new equipment, it has expanded range to include low runs of calendars,greetings cards, postcards, notelets and up to A1-size giclée prints. Also has an online art gallery where customers can sell cards, prints and original art work. Fine art calendars available in low-run quantities (minimum 5).

Beaver Lodge Prints Ltd
Units 25–26 Broomhills Industrial Estate, Braintree, CM7 2RW
T 01376 552558
F 01376 553881
E sales@beaverlodgeprints.co.uk
W www.beaverlodgeprints.co.uk
Contact James Arnold
A print-distribution company for over twelve years, sourcing artists of modern and contemporary art work to be published. Works on behalf of publishers in Germany, Italy and the USA.

Black Church Print Studio
4 Temple Bar, Dublin 2
T 01 677 3629
F 01 677 3676
E info@print.ie
W www.print.ie
Non-profit fine art print studios, established in 1982. Dedicated to the provision of a professional workspace for its members. The studio provides facilities for artists working in intaglio, lithography, screenprint, relief and digital media. Also offers a regular schedule of print-making courses for both beginner and advanced students in all areas of printmaking.
Price range Full membership costs €484.

Broad Oak Colour Ltd
Units A&B, 254 Broad Oak Road, Canterbury CT2 7QH
T 01227 767856
F 01227 762593
E enquiries@broadoakltd.co.uk
W www.broadoakltd.co.uk
Contact Simon Young or Terry Tilbury
Colour printers for twenty-three years, producing limited-edition prints on Bockingford paper, etc.

CanvasRus
Ladds House, Old Otford Road, Sevenoaks TN14 5EZ
T 01732 454092

E sales@canvasRus.co.uk
W www.canvasRus.co.uk
A leading specialist in the manufacture and supply of contemporary digital printed canvas art.

Colorworld Imaging
PO Box 2, Norham Road, North Shields, NE29 0YQ
T 0191 2596926
F 0191 2576948
E enquiries@colorworldimaging.co.uk
W www.colorworldimaging.co.uk
Offers wide range of film processing and printing services, both traditional and digital.

Cork Printmakers
Wandesford Quay, Crosses Green, Cork
T 021 4322422
E info@corkprintmakers.ie
W www.corkprintmakers.ie
Set up in 1991, to support artists working in the medium of print. Offers open access workshop (equipment and materials) to artists specializing in fine art printmaking, extensive education programme and promotion of artists' work through sales and exhibitions.

Dayfold Solvit
27 Black Moor Road, Ebblake Industrial Estate Verwood, BH31 6BE
T 01202 827141
F 01202 825841
E mark@dayfold.com
W www.dayfold.com
Contact Mark Smith
Founded in 1979. A fine-art lithographic printer specializing in the production of high-quality limited-edition prints and promotional material, including show catalogues and leaflets.

DesignerPrint
8 Stafford Road, Southampton, SO15 5EA
T 023 80333564
F 023 80333564
E info@designerprint.co.uk
W www.designerprint.co.uk
Contact Peter Horner
Company specializing in printing images onto canvas, block-mounting and poster-printing.

Digital Print Studio
The Finsbury Business Centre, 40 Bowling Green Lane, London, EC1R 0NE
T 0779 0368554
E info@dprints.co.uk
W www.dprints.co.uk
Contact Andrew Turnbull MA (RCA)
Digital print studio run by artist Andrew Turnbull MA (RCA), who has over ten years' experience in digital and traditional printmaking. Produces high quality, archival giclée digital prints for artists and photographers using the latest large format printers and visual software.

Dolphin Fine Art Printers
37 Nuffield Road, Nuffield Estate, Poole, BH17 0RA
T 01202 673048
F 01202 661500
E info@dolphin-printers.co.uk
W www.dolphin-printers.co.uk
Founded in 1970, producing open- and limited-edition prints and giclée. Specializes in offering guidance for those starting out.

East London Printmakers
SPACE, The Triangle, 129 Mare Street, Hackney, London, E8 3RH
T 020 85254330 (SPACE Studios)
E info@eastlondonprintmakers.co.uk
W www.eastlondonprintmakers.co.uk
Contact Nick Morley (Studio Manager)
A group of artist-printmakers, formed in 1998, running a spacious, modern and newly equipped printmaking studio with open access. Equipment for water-based screenprinting, etching copper and zinc, intaglio printing, rosin aquatint, relief printing and fabric printing. The studio is used by rent-paying keyholders, who have twenty-four-hour access, and by open-access users who pay per session. ELP run workshops in various printmaking techniques at all levels. Non-studio members (£24 per year) can attend talks and meetings and participate in exhibitions.
Price range £60 per month for 24-hour access and £12 or £15 for 3- or 4- hour open access sessions

Eyes Wide Digital Ltd
The Old Coach House, Unit 1, Charman Road, Redhill, RH1 6AH
T 01737 780789
F 01737 780987
E info@eyeswidedigital.com
W www.eyeswidedigital.com
Contact Ian Ingle
Specializes in bespoke canvas printing. Reproduces fine art onto canvas or art paper for artists and galleries throughout Europe. Images can be supplied in print format, as negatives or transparencies, or as a digital file through email or on CD.

Gemini Digital Colour Ltd
North Road, Bridgend Industrial Estate, Bridgend
CF31 3TP
T 01656 652447
F 01656 661266
E info@geminidigitalcolour.co.uk
W www.geminidigitalcolour.co.uk
Contact Dominic Lee
Fine-art printers, specializing in print-on-demand,
giclée and short-run printing from postcards to
limited-edition canvases and prints. Offers
personal advice and assistance to the amateur and
professional artist alike.

Genesis Imaging Chelsea Ltd
Unit D2, The Depot, 2 Michael Road, Fulham,
London, SW6 2AD
T 020 7731 2227
F 020 7731 8778
E lynad@genesisimaging.co.uk
W www.genesisimaging.co.uk
Contact Lynda Blackwell
A photographic processing and printing company
offering a range of digital services, large format
display exhibition printing, scanning and
retouching. **Branch** Genesis Imaging City Ltd, 80
Kingsland Road, London, E2 8DP **T** 020 77297140
F 020 77292080 **Contact** Mark Foxwell.

Graal Press
Eskhill Cottage, Roslin, Midlothian, EH25 9QW
T 0131 440 2589
E graalpress@btinternet.com
W www.graalpress.com
Contact Robert Adam or Carol Robertson
A fine-art print studio founded in 1998 in a rural
location eight miles from Edinburgh city centre.
Specializes in collaborative projects and innovative
approaches to printmaking using media such as
artist's water-based paints for screenprinting,
acrylic-resist etching and recently developed
tusches for light-sensitive processes. Courses are
available in progressive and safer printmaking
methods as well as in personal and artistic
development. Robert Adam and Carol Robertson
are the authors of *Screenprinting: the complete water-
based system* (Thames & Hudson 2004) and
*Intaglio: The Complete Safety-First System for
Creative Printmaking* (Thames & Hudson 2007).

The Hermit Press
Liverpool
T 0778 0605178
E info@thehermitpress.com
W www.thehermitpress.com
Produces prints for artists, photographers,
galleries, artist's agents etc. with no restriction
on the size of order. Uses digital technology
coupled with light fast pigment inks and
natural, acid-free papers or canvas for long-lasting,
high-quality prints up to 44 inches wide and
any length.

Hole Editions
Unit 12, Mushroom Works, St Lawrence Road,
Newcastle-upon-Tyne, NE6 1AR
T 0191 2243449
E info@holeeditions.co.uk
W www.holeeditions.co.uk
Contact Lee Turner
Founded in 2005 by Master Printer Lee Turner,
specializing in collaborative hand lithography.
Producing original lithographs from stones, plates
and photo plates. Work undertaken either in the
capacity of publisher or as contract printer.
Monotype sessions are available.

Hot Chilli Studio
Cockport Farm, Otterham, Camelford, PL32 9SS
T 0845 2269331
E info@hotchillistudio.co.uk
W www.hotchillistudio.co.uk
Contact Julia Phillips
Supplier of high quality wide-format fine art
printing, postcards, business cards and stationery.
Uses fine art papers and lightfast, pigment based
inks. Latest digital print technology allows
reproduction of images to any size (dependent on
image quality) up to 44" wide x 100' long.
Extensive range of quality media from fine art
papers to canvas. All work is quoted for on an
individual basis.

Hudson Killeen
130 Slaney Road, Dublin Industrial Estate,
Glasnevin, Dublin 11
T 01 8306128
F 01 8306993
E print@hudsonkilleen.ie
W www.hudsonkilleen.ie
A fine lithographic printers.

imagiclee.com
48 Wynford Terrace, Leeds, LS16 6HY
T 0113 274 4954
E printit@imagiclee.com
W www.imagiclee.com
Contact Peter Learoyd

Produces museum-quality fine art giclée prints from original artwork, scans, photographs and digital files. Prints only with light-fast archival pigmented inks on to a wide range of materials from watercolour papers and canvases to poster and photographic papers. Also helps customers to sell their prints by providing space in an online gallery at shopforprints.com

J. Thomson Colour Printers Ltd
14 Carnoustie Place, Glasgow, G5 8PB
T 0141 4291094
F 0141 4295638
E production@jtcp.co.uk
W www.jtcp.co.uk
Specialists in lithographic fine-art reproduction and high-quality scanning from transparencies. Over fifty years' experience in the production of fine-art prints, catalogues, brochures, fine-art books and fine-art cards.

Kustom
76 Clerkenwell Road, London, EC1M 5TN
T 020 78650000
F 020 78650001
E comments@metroimaging.co.uk
W www.metroimaging.co.uk
Contact Michael Mardon
Specializes in professional hand prints and digital photographic prints.

Leicester Print Workshop
50 St Stephen's Road, Highfields, Leicester, LE2 1GG
E info@leicesterprintworkshop.com
W www.leicesterprintworkshop.com
Contact Angela Harding (Director)
Artist-led organization, providing facilities and equipment to artists and those interested in printmaking. Equipped for etching lithography, screenprinting, relief printing, framing and mounting. There is also studio space available on the upper levels.
Price range £60–£120

Limerick Printmakers
4 Robert Street, Limerick
T 061 311806
E limprintmakers@eircom.net
W www.limerickprintmakers.com
Fine art printmaking studio and gallery.

London Print Studio
425 Harrow Road, London, W10 4RE
T 020 89693247

F 020 89640008
E info@londonprintstudio.org.uk
W www.londonprintstudio.org.uk
An independent, not-for-profit arts organization providing low-cost training and access to artists' print and graphic arts facilities. The studio has a printmaking studio with facilities for screenprinting, etching, blockprinting and lithography, a computer facility with computers, scanners and printers, and a large-format digital printing service. Also incorporates gallery with a changing programme of exhibitions and events. Services offered include an MA in Printmaking & Professional Practice, various education and training programmes, and editioning. Use of facilities open to artists, community organizations, members of the general public and anyone interested in art.
Price range Studio hire from £1.56 per hour.

Loudmouth Art Printing
5 Hendon Street, Sheffield, S13 9AX
T 0845 2309805
F 0114 2880044
E info@loudworld.co.uk
W www.loudworld.co.uk
Contact Paul Jenkinson
Design-led printer specializing in producing sumptuous quality print to the arts and crafts industries for over twenty years. Business cards, artists cards, private view cards, leaflets, brochures. No minimum quantity. 1,000 postcards from £62.00. Turnaround from 3 days. Call for a free pack or visit website

Mark Harwood Photography
12 The Waterside, 44–48 Wharf Road, London N1 7SF
T 020 74908787
F 020 74901009
E mail@markharwood.plus.com
W www.markharwoodstudio.co.uk
Contact Mark Harwood
A multi award winning photographer offering original photography, in-house scanning and fine-art printing to very large sizes. Photographic tuition and support for artists and creative projects also available.
Price range Studio rented out on daily basis for photographers. See www.locamotive.co.uk

Mat Sant Prints – (Formerly Digital Fine Art & Print)
47 Great Western Studios, Paddington (New) Yard,

Great Western Road, London, W9 3NY
T 07754 702090
E mat@matsant.com
W www.matsant.com
Contact Mat Sant
With ten years experience in producing large-format digital giclée prints on artists' papers and canvas. Specializes in printing limited editions for artists, publishers and galleries.

New North Press
Standpoint Studios, 45 Coronet Street, London N1 6HD
T 020 77293161
F 020 77293161
E graham.bignell@talk21.com
Contact Graham Bignell
Founded in 1985, specializing in the editioning of linocuts, woodcuts and wood engravings and editions of letter press artist's books. The studio has a broad range of types available for small editions.

Newnum Art
29 Oxford Road, Worthing, BN11 1UT
T 01903 821191
F 01903 820507
E enquiries@newnumart.co.uk
W www.newnumart.co.uk
Contact Mandy Newnum
Founded in 2001 as an offshoot of a litho and digital-printing company and consequently has considerable print expertise. Specializes in giclée printing as well as conventional litho and waterless litho using a Heidelberg DI press.
Price range Studio of 600 sq. ft available for hire from £75.

Oberon Art Ltd
67 High Street, Burnham, SL1 7JX
T 01628 600500
E sales@oberonart.co.uk
W www.oberonart.co.uk
Contact Susie Lipman
An artist-run fine-art publishing company, supplying limited-edition prints by selected artists. Provides a high-quality, giclée printing service where time will be taken to accurately match colour and texture to mimic the original piece. The ethos of the company is that it is run by an artist for artists, craftsmen and art-lovers for the enjoyment and celebration of art and crafts. Also runs a gallery exhibiting original paintings and prints by local and national artists alongside hand-made ceramics, sculpture, blown and cast glass, and greeting cards. A bespoke picture framer is resident in the workshop at the rear and is a member of the Fine Art Trade Guild.

Paulsharma.com
91 Blackheath Park, London, SE3 0EU
E enquires@paulsharma.com
W www.paulsharma.com
Contact Paul Sharma
Founded in 2002. Offers high-quality limited-edition prints for the home or office.

Peak Imaging
FREEPOST RLSY-YZJX-SLXC, Sheffield, S20 3PP
T 0870 126 6100
F 0114 2243205
E info@peak-imaging.com
W www.peak-imaging.com
Contact Wayne Gledhill
A full service lab, with twenty-five years in the industry. Leading mail order pro-am photographic laboratories. From film processing to digital printing, mounting and framing. Call for a welcome pack.

Pratt Contemporary Art and Pratt Editions
The Gallery, Ightham, Sevenoaks, TN15 9HH
T 01732 882326
F 01732 885502
E pca@prattcontemporaryart.co.uk
W www.prattcontemporaryart.co.uk
Contact Bernard Pratt or Susan Pratt
Printers, publishers and dealers, founded in 1977. Alongside a regular publishing programme, the studios also provide an editioning service to artists and galleries. Working in close collaboration with a master printer, artists are given time to fully explore and experiment with the various processes available, including screenprinting, intaglio, relief and large-format digital printing. Gallery open by appointment.

Press On Digital Imaging
Unit 17 Lakeside Park, Neptune Close, Medway City Estate, Rochester, ME2 4LT
T 01634 294942
F 01634 716604
E info@presson.biz
W www.presson.biz
Specialists in large format digital printing.

Primary Colour
80 Kingsland Road, London, E2 8DP

T 020 77297140
F 020 77292080
E sales@primary-colour.com
W primary-colour.com
Contact Mark Foxwell
Specialists in large-format Lambda display prints, drum and volume scanning, and mounting and laminating.

Printmaker Studio
Manton, Bath Road, Padworth
Reading, RG7 5HR
T 0118 9712896
E enquiries@printmaker.co.uk
W www.printmaker.co.uk
Contact Chris Mercier
A silkscreen and giclée editioning studio founded in 1990. Specializes in screenprinting projects and editioning for artists and printmakers. Also offers a large-format digital giclée printing service for digital art work and reproductions.

Prism
Unit 28 School Close, Chandlers Ford
Eastleigh, SO53 4RA
T 023 80266256
F 023 80266256
E stewart.goldsmith@ntlworld.com
Contact Ian Goldsmith
A lithographic reprographics and printing company founded in 1991. Reproduces originals from A5 cards up to large B1 posters. Sample pack available and advice given.

Redfoxpress
Dugort, Achill Island, County Mayo
E info@redfoxpress.com
W www.redfoxpress.com
Specializes in screen printing and artist's books.

Reggie Hastings
Grennan Mill, Mill Street, Thomastown
County Kilkenny
T 056 7754050
F 087 2236376
E cartoltd@eircom.net
Founded in 2000 as a large format giclée printing facility for artists wanting to edition their prints. Artists include Gottfried Heluwein, Peter Curling and Francis Tansey. Offers full photographic and printing services.
A full graphic design service is also provided, plus a library of imaging for clients to draw from.

Reprotech Studios Ltd
22 Trinity Lane, Micklegate, York, YO1 6EL
T 01904 644006
F 01904 611264
E repstudios@aol.com
Contact John Hall
Founded in 1986, specializing in digital printing and fine-art reproduction. Produces limited-edition giclée prints onto watercolour, paper and canvas.

St Ives Printing & Publishing Co.
High Street, St Ives, TR26 1RS
T 01736 795813
F 01736 795813
E toni@stivesnews.co.uk
W www.stivesnews.co.uk
Contact Mr Toni Carver (Proprietor)
A printer and publisher of a local newspaper and books, founded in 1951. Offers a range of services for artists, including fine-art lithographic prints and photo-litho reproductions, private-view invitations, greeting cards, catalogues and fine-art photographs.

Stoney Road Press
Stoney Road, Dublin 3
T 01 8878544
E info@stoneyroadpress.com
W www.stoneyroadpress.com
A fine art publishing and editioning house, collaborating with artists on limited edition prints in traditional and experimental media. Also provides editioning services to professional printmakers.

Terracotta Press Ltd
273 Abbeydale Road, Wembley, HA0 1QE
T 020 89974655
F 020 89987842
E print@terracotta-press.co.uk
W www.terracotta-press.co.uk
Contact Karen Low
Established in 1995. A commercial printer of brochures, postcards, posters, fine art prints, etc. Has undertaken work for some of the biggest galleries and studios in London.

Think Ink Ltd
11–13 Philip Road, Ipswich, IP2 8BH
T 01473 400162
F 01473 400163
E charles@think-ink.co.uk
W www.think-ink.co.uk
Specializes in the production of printing for artists,

e.g. greeting cards, postcards, private view cards, giclée prints.

Wall Candi Ltd

High Street, Lane End, High Wycombe, HP14 3JG
T 01494 883250
F 01494 881826
E info@wallcandi.com
W www.wallcandi.com
Contact Jonathan Burns
Specializes in giclée digital fine-art reproduction. Uses state-of-the-art giclée and colour management technology and prints onto a variety of media, producing archival quality prints. Other services include a professional in-house photographic studio for capturing original art work digitally or on to traditional transparency film. Member of the Fine Art Trade Guild.

Studio space

107 Workshop

The Courtyard, Bath Road, Shaw, Melksham
SN12 8EF
T 01225 791800
F 01225 790948
E 107w@shirrett.demon.co.uk
Established in 1976, with 7,000 sq. ft of fully equipped studio space designed to enable artists to create an environment suitable to their own individual specifications. Processes available include multiplate-printing using copper, carborundum, liftground, aquatint, handpainting, relief woodcut and mono-printing. Artists include Ayers, Hodgkin, Hughes, Aitcheson, Heindorf and Ackroyd. Livres d'artiste by Howard Hodgkin, Kidner and Hayter.
Price range £800–£15,000

36 Lime Street Ltd

36 Lime Street, Ouseburn Valley
Newcastle-upon-Tyne, NE1 2PQ
E limest36@yahoo.co.uk
W www.36limestreet.co.uk
Founded in 1984, a tenants' cooperative and the largest artists' studio group in the north-east, representing an eclectic mix of artists, designers, makers, performers and musicians in the region.
Price range Low-cost studio space. Purchase of a lease for each studio is required.

Acme Studios

44 Copperfield Road, Bow, London, E3 4RR
T 020 89816811
F 020 89830567
E mail@acme.org.uk
W www.acme.org.uk
A charity formed in 1972 to provide artists with low-cost studio and living space. Provides 380 studios (over 170,000 sq. ft) throughout east and south-east London, as well as twenty-five accommodation units. Active in other residency and studio and accommodation programmes. Also offers free advice on property issues to artists.
Price range £6.50–£8.50 per sq. ft per year, inclusive.

Amberney Studio

32A Goldney Road, Maida Vale, London
W9 1JR
T 020 72891122
F 0871 2426134
E amberneystudio@tiscali.co.uk
W www.amberneystudios.co.uk
Contact Kathy Roche
Light day studio (60ft x 20ft x 25ft) available for hire, complete with equipment, catering and other services.
Price range £200 per day.

Art Space Portsmouth Ltd

27 Brougham Road, Portsmouth, PO5 4PA
T 02392 874523
E marcia@artspace.co.uk
W www.artspace.co.uk
Contact Marcia Allen (Studio Manager)
Formed in 1980, providing affordable studio space for artists working in a wide range of art forms and media. Aims to encourage the widest audience for the visual arts through education workshops, residencies, open studios and exhibitions.
Price range From £46.66 to £223 per month, inclusive of heat and light.

artists @ redlees

Redlees Studios, Redlees Park, Worton Road
Isleworth, TW7 6DW
E artists@redlees.org
W www.redlees.org
Contact John Carbery
A diverse group of artists formed to organize and promote the collective and individual work of the residents of Redlees Studios. Members' work includes jewellery, glass, ceramics, painting, sculpture and mixed media. Works closely with the Community Initiative Partnership, who maintain the buildings, to organize shows of members' creations.
Price range £100–£200 per month.

Artists and Restorers (A&R) Studios
7 Farm Mews, Farm Road, Hove, BN3 1GH
T 01273 207470
F 01273 207470
E artistandrestorer@fastmail.com.uk
Contact Caroline
Founded in 1996, with the aim of giving artists
and craftspeople an affordable place to practice
their craft in an art environment. Members include
artists, jewellers, textile makers and designers, and
picture-restorers.
Price range £100–£130 per month.

Artspace Studios
7/8 Addley Park, Liosban Industrial Park, Galway
T 091 773046
E artspacegalway@eircom.net
W www.artspacegalway.com
Formed as an artist's collective by a group of
Galway-based artists in 1986 to develop studio
space for professional artists and support group
and individual work and exhibitions. Strives to
upgrade working conditions, and develop
employment, educational and exhibition potential.
Price range €90–€100 per month per studio.

ASC
3rd Floor, 246 Stockwell Road, Brixton, SW9 9SP
T 020 72747474
F 020 72741744
E info@ascstudios.co.uk
W www.ascstudios.co.uk
Contact Lisa Wilson
A London-based registered charity that provides
studio and exhibition space to visual artists and not-
for-profit arts organizations. Currently manages
350 artists' studios across six buildings.
Registration is free and there is a waiting list for
most studios. There is studio space available in
Bethnal Green, E2, Newcross, SW14, Brixton, SW9,
and Camberwell, SE5. Exhibition space is offered
free of charge to visual artists and not-for-profit arts
organizations. Selection is through a committee of
ASC artists. The organization also provides free
advice on all matters relating to studio development
and can help with property negotiation.
Price range Rents are inclusive of building
insurance, service charges, heating and electric
and are based on £9.50–£12 per sq. ft per year.

Ashley Studios
19 Staithe Street, Wells-next-the-Sea, NR23 1AG
T 01328 710923
F 01328 710923

Contact Hazel Ashley
Founded in 1979. A small studio with a
comprehensive range of artists materials. Contacts
with local artists and Wells's thriving art group.
Open all year round.

Association for Cultural Advancement through Visual Art (ACAVA)
54 Blechynden Street, London, W10 6RJ
T 020 89605015
F 020 89609269
E post@acava.org
W www.acava.org
Contact Duncan Smith
Founded 1984. Provides three hundred studios for
artists and arts organizations throughout London.
Associate members have access to facilities and
projects and are able to apply for studios. ACAVA
also provides professional development training,
educational and public art services, and
consultancy on studio development, regeneration
and arts for health and sustainable communities.
Price range £7.50–£12.50

BAKERY Photographic Foundation
Advance Park, Rhosymedre, Wrexham, LL14 3YR
T 01978823000
E bakery@cefn-mawr.com
W www.bakerystudios.com
Contact M. Briggs
6,500 sq. ft of photographic studio space available
for rental. Fully-equipped with equipment for
indoor photographic work.
Price range £50 per day to £25 per hour.

Bedford Hill Gallery and Workshops, Chelsea Bridge Studios
1 The Field, 103 Prince of Wales Drive, London
SW11 3UN
T 020 74988730
F 020 74988730
E chelseabridge.studios@btinternet.com
Contact Roy Woods
Managing and letting artist studios since 1979, the
Bedford Hill Gallery currently manages twelve
exclusive artist studios in a Victorian mansion house,
which stands in its own grounds near Chelsea
Bridge. All studios have high ceilings, and come
equipped with 'natural daylight' secondary lighting.
Price range Around £130 per week for 200 sq. ft
studios.

Bladon Studios Limited
52 High Street, Harrow On The Hill

Harrow, HA1 3LL
T 0845 1082237
E stevebarby@bladonstudios.com
W www.bladonstudios.com
Includes professional fully-equipped photographic
studio facility.

Bow Arts Trust and Nunnery Gallery
183 Bow Road, London, E3 2SJ
T 020 89807774
F 020 89807770
E jclarke@bowarts.com
W www.bowarts.org
Contact Jeremy Clarke
Founded in 1995. Designed to provide long-term
affordable workspace for artists and to operate as an
arts conduit for local communities, and national
and international audiences. Offers space for
approximately one hundred artists, open studios,
employment and training. Nunnery Gallery is a
contemporary project space for national and
international shows. Education at Bowarts runs an
outreach programme across London.
Price range Approx £6.75 per sq. ft per annum eg.
£182.50pcm for 300 sq. ft (including insurance,
education levy, open studios).

Broadstone Studios
Hendron Building, 36–40 Upper Dominick Street
Dublin 7
T 01 8301428
F 01 8301950
E contact@broadstonestudios.com
W www.broadstonestudios.com
Artist-led studio group creating projects and
putting on shows.

The Camera Club
16 Bowden Street, London, SE11 4DS
T 020 75871809
E info@thecameraclub.co.uk
W www.thecameraclub.co.uk
Founded in 1885. Offers high quality studio and
darkroom facilities, a programme of group
workshops and club events, and members' gallery
exhibitions.

Can Studios
4th Floor, Oldknows Factory, St Anns Hill Road,
Nottingham, NG3 4GP
T 0115 9588601
W www.nottinghamstudios.org.uk/can
Contact Stephen Butler
Founded in 1988 and situated on the top floor of

an old textile factory. Has eleven studio spaces
offering only minimal facilities. Artists in the
group participate in the annual open-studio event.
Price range £44 per month, all-inclusive.

cell project space
4–8 Arcola Street, London, E8 2DJ
T 020 72413600
E info@cell.org.uk
W www.cell.org.uk
Studio space for over one hundred visual artists in
four buildings in east London.

Chocolate Factory
Haringey Arts Council, Unit 104, Building B
Clarendon Road, London, N22 6XJ
T 020 83657500
F 020 83658686
W www.chocolatefactory.org.uk
Seventy-five studios in north London for artists
and designers in the areas of sculpture, film, crafts,
fashion and photography.

Clevedon Craft Centre
Moor Lane, Clevedon, BS21 6TD
T 01275 872149
Contact Mr D.A. Stear or Mr J.J. Bright
Established in 1971, the ten craft design studios
and artspace workshops are housed in the
outbuildings of a seventeenth-century Somerset
'long farm', which was once part of the Clevedon
Court Estate.
Price range £20–£75 per week, exclusive of rates,
etc.

Coin Street Community Builders
Oxo Tower Wharf, Barge House Street, London
SE1 9PH
T 020 74013610
F 020 79280111
E info@coin-street.org
W www.oxotower.co.uk
A social enterprise and development trust
responsible for thirteen acres on the South
Bank of London. Includes design studios,
shops and galleries for hire to designers
and artists at Oxo Tower Wharf and
Gabriel's Wharf.
Price range From £400 per month.

Creekside Artists Studios
Units A110, A112 and A114 Faircharm Trading
Estate, Creekside, Deptford, London, SE8 3DX
E info@creeksideartists.co.uk

W www.creeksideartists.co.uk
Contact Mauricio Vincenzi (Chairman)
Not-for-profit artist-led studios founded in 2000.
There are several 250 sq. ft units in an open-plan
setting, with skylights throughout. The
membership of twenty-four artists includes
photographers, painters, printmakers, filmmakers,
sculptors, and textile and installation artists. The
studios have a communal 'chillout' area, as well as
a workbench supplied with basic tools for
communal use. Twenty-four-hour access. Two
open studios a year, as well as exhibitions in
London and abroad. Founding members of
Deptford Arts Network, a network of artists based
in the Creative Hub of Deptford/Greenwich in
London, who work together to share resources
and ideas.
Price range Visit website for more information

Cuckoo Farm Studios

Boxted Road, Colchester, CO4 5HH
T 01206 843530
E info@cuckoofarmstudios.org.uk
W www.cuckoofarmstudios.org.uk
An artist-run studio group consisting of over thirty
studios for artists and craftspeople. Set in a rural
location, two miles from Colchester train station.
Includes gallery, print workshop and outside
space.
Price range £50–£90 per month, inclusive of all
bills.

Custom House Studios Ltd

The Quay, Westport, County Mayo
T 098 28735
F 098 28735
E customhouse@eircom.net
Contact John McHugh
Opened in 2002. Provides 7 studio spaces, a fully
equiped printmaking studio and a gallery. Operated
on a not-for-profit basis by local artists in
conjunction with the local authority, the Department
of Arts, and the Arts Council of Ireland. Gallery
hosts 13 exhibitions each year, selected by panel of
artists. To apply for a studio and exhibition send
letter of interest and examples of work.
Price range 25 per week including utilities for
studio space. 25% commission on all gallery sales.

Dalston Underground Studios

The Basement, 28 Shacklewell Lane, Dalston,
London, E8 2EZ
T 07941 715888
E info@dalstonunderground.org.uk

W dalstonunderground.org.uk
Contact Calum F. Kerr
Established in 2000, providing workspace for
contemporary fine artists and offering long-term
studio space. Currently has space for ten to twelve
artists. Practice is varied and includes painting,
film and performance. Examples of work can be
viewed through website. Provides a space from
which artists can develop projects and exhibit in a
national and international context. A second studio
building housing seven artists opened in 2005 at
Unit B, Leswin Place, off Leswin Road, Stoke
Newington, N16 7NJ.
Price range £90–£180 per month.

Diesel House Studios

Kew Bridge Steam Museum
Green Dragon Lane, Brentford, TW8 0EN
T 020 85698780
F 020 85698781
E thedieselhouse@aol.com
W www.dieselhousestudios.com
Contact Elizabeth Rollins-Scott
Founded in 2001. Specializes in studio rental and
consultancy for private and local government arts
projects. Currently manages thirty studios in
Chiswick, Richmond and Brentford in west
London (expected to rise to fifty). All artists are
provided with a free website, marketing support,
art library and access to digital media as well as
advice on commercial career development. Two
major exhibitions each year (summer and
Christmas), with up to fifty artists and over five
hundred works on show.
Price range £100–£525 per calendar month,
including all bills.

The Drill Hall

16 Chenies Street, London, WC1E 7EX
T 020 73075061
F 020 73075062
E admin@drillhall.co.uk
W www.drillhall.co.uk
Operates a fully-accessible photographic darkroom
suite.

Fire Station Artists Studios

9–11 Lr. Buckingham Street, Dublin 1
T 01 8556735
F 01 8555632
W www.firestation.ie
Established by the Arts Council in 1991 to assist
the needs of practising visual artists, and officially
opened in 1993. Independent since 1997, it now

houses residential studios and the headquarters of the North Centre City Community Training Workshop. Although primarily a studio facility, the Fire Station has developed its activities beyond provision of studios and workshop spaces.

Flameworks Creative Arts Facility
7 Richmond Walk, Devonport, Plymouth, PL1 4LL
T 01752 559326
E flameworks@tiscali.co.uk
W www.flameworks.co.uk
Contact Katie Lake
Founded in 1999, providing artists' workspaces and specialist equipment and services. Group activities include exhibitions, commissions, public-art schemes, newsletter production, marketing and schools residencies. Artist workshops and taster sessions available in metalwork, jewellery, ceramics, mosaic, glass, painting, stone- and wood-carving, printmaking and sculpture.
Price range £40–£150 per month.

Flax Art Studios
44–46 Corporation Street, Belfast, BT1 3DE
An artist-run organization founded in 1989 by a group of Belfast-based artists who were looking for space to make large sculptural and installation works. Runs an artist-in-residence scheme for four international artists each year and also a graduating student residency. Has initiated a community outreach project in partnership with five community groups.

Florence Trust Studios
St Saviour's, Aberdeen Park, London, N5 2AR
T 020 73544771
E info@florencetrust.org
W www.florencetrust.org
Contact Paul Bayley (Director)
Founded in 1989, providing up to twelve studios for one year from August in a grade 1-listed church. An in-house project/gallery space and director are on hand to offer guidance, ensuring artists receive 'much more than just a studio space'. Annual selection process.
Price range Studios cost approximately £200 per calendar month.

Framework Studios
5–9 Creekside, Deptford, London, SE8 4SA
T 020 8691 5140
F 020 8691 5140
E admin@frameworkgallery.co.uk

Contact Adrian or Debbie
Contemporary fine art and applied arts in large studio complex with 24-hour access, situated in South London's Creative Hub area. Good working facilities and exhibitions available.
Price range £55 to £95 per week inclusive.

Gasworks
155 Vauxhall, London, SE11 5RH
T 020 75875202
F 020 75820159
E info@gasworks.org.uk
W www.gasworks.org.uk
Contact Anna Vass
A contemporary arts organization housing twelve artists' studios and presenting a programme of exhibitions, residencies, international fellowships and educational projects.
Price range £200–£300. Studio spaces rarely available. No waiting list. Enquiries to Anna Vass.

Great Western Studios
Great Western Road, London, W9 3NY
T 020 72210100
F 020 72210200
E office@greatwesternstudios.com
W www.greatwesternstudios.com
Founded in 1994, providing workspace for over 140 artists and craftspeople. Each space has good natural light, interesting views and high ceilings. Communal facilities include a café, project spaces and general business services.
Price range £7.50–£10 per sq. ft per year.

Green Door Studios
112 Highgate, Kendal, LA9 4HE
T 01539 721147
E artists@greendoorkendal.fsnet.co.uk
W www.greendoorstudios.co.uk
Contact Rosie Wates (Administrator)
Formed in 1995. Currently has sixteen artists in twelve studio spaces and a further seventy associate members who form part of the Green Door organization/network. All members are equally entitled to participate in the exhibitions, open studios, studio trails, educational activities and professional-development workshops that are undertaken. Members receive regular email communications with news, opportunities, offers and requests.
Price range Twelve studio spaces ranging in price from £119–£257 per quarter or £476–£1028 per year.

Hereford Road Studios
12–14 Hereford Road, London, N1
T 020 72410651
Twenty studio spaces available. Artists should send slides of their work, a CV and an sae.

Holborn Studios
49/50 Eagle Wharf Road, London, N1 7ED
T 020 74904099
F 020 72538120
E studiomanager@holborn-studios.co.uk
W www.holborn-studios.co.uk
One of Europe's largest photographic studio complexes, renting studio space in London for over twenty-five years.

Hoxton Street Studios
12–18 Hoxton Street, London, N1 6NG
T 020 70331984
F 020 70331985
E info@hoxtonstreetstudios.co.uk
W www.hoxtonstreetstudios.co.uk
Photographic studio hire company established in 2004.

Islington Arts Factory
2 Parkhurst Road, Islington, London, N7 0SF
T 020 76070561
E IAF@islingtonartsfactory.fsnet.co.uk
W www.islingtonartsfactory.org.uk
Founded in 1977, complete with dance, music and art studios, three galleries and a professional darkroom. After school and evening classes for children and adults.

JAM Studios
Lews Castle Grounds, Stornoway, HS2 0XR
T 01851 643261
E info@jam-studios.org
W www.jam-studios.org
Contact Emma Drye
Independent artists' studios running courses including a portfolio course, short courses and evening classes on the Isle of Lewis in the Outer Hebrides. Hosts contemporary art exhibitions and events throughout the year and is always open to artists, musicians, film makers, poets and performance artists with ideas for using the studio or exhibition space
Price range studio space is free subject to availability

Kaz Studio
Unit 2, Plot 11, Rawreth Industrial Estate
Rayleigh, SS6 9RL
T 01268 782582
E photos@kazstudio.co.uk
W www.kaz-studio.co.uk
Contact Clive Austen
Established in 1988, specializing in commercial photography. Holds teaching sessions for amateur photographers.

Kingsgate Workshops Trust and Gallery
110–116 Kingsgate Road, London, NW6 2JG
T 020 73287878
E mail@kingsgateworkshops.org.uk
Around fifty arts and crafts studios available. Email for advice on availability.

London Studio Hire
LCA Studios, Studio 1 Cuba Street, London, E14 3RS
T 077 93081068
E studiohire@londonstudiohire.co.uk
W www.londonstudiohire.co.uk
Offers studio and equipment hire for photographers.

Maryland Studios
2nd Floor, 80 Wallis Road, Hackney Wick
London, E9 5LW
T 020 89862555
Contact Thomas Helyar-Cardwell
Established in 1995 to provide a secure, affordable and professional environment for the production of art. Architect-designed studios give good light, access and maximum space. Studio members are expected to participate in annual open studios and contribute to educational workshops.
Price range £150–£300 (£6.75 per sq. ft).

Mivart Street Studios
Epstein Building, Bristol, BS5 6JF
T 0117 3305209
E info@mivartists.co.uk
W www.mivartists.co.uk
Contact Barbara Orme
Home to over fifty artists, makers and performers. Hosts an annual open studios event.
Price range £17–£50 per week.

Mother Studios
D-F 9 Queens Yard, White Post Lane, Hackney Wick, London, E9 5EN
T Studio space 07968 760550. Mother Exhibition and Project space 07968760550
E info@motherstudios.co.uk
W motherstudios.co.uk
Contact Joanna Hughes

A non-profit-making studio founded in 2001 by artist Joanna Hughes for fine artists, designers and makers. There are thirty-four studios with twenty-four-hour access and parking. Mother, a 2,000 sq. ft exhibition space on site is available free to all Mother artists. Send proposals for projects and exhibitions to Joanna Hughes – rates on an indidviual basis.
Price range From £90 per calendar month, inclusive of electricity, water and service charge.

No 19 Cataibh, Dornoch Studio
19 Achavandra Muir, Dornoch, IV25 3JB
T 01862 811099
E sue@cataibh.fsnet.co.uk
Contact Sue Jane Taylor or Ian Westacott
An open-access etching studio located in the north-east Highlands, four miles from the coastal town of Dornoch. The studio has two presses, one 800mm wide and one 400mm wide, and uses non-toxic methods. Artists who have no experience of the etching process are welcome and offered technical assistance. Accommodation available for one to two people (own transport required).
Price range Studio rent per day (plus sundries) £25; accommodation £15 per person; technical assistance £20. Rates vary according to season and availability.

Nottingham Artists' Group
32–36 Carrington Street, Nottingham, NG1 7FG
T 0115 9581450
W www.nottinghamstudios.org.uk/nag
Contact Geoffrey Grant
Founded in 1982 Nottingham Artists Group was the first studio group to be established in Nottingham. Currently provides studio space to nine artists working independently. Work includes oil and acrylic paintings, ceramics, sculpture, photography and prints.
Price range £60–£80

Oldknows Studio Group
3rd Floor, Old Knows Factory Building, St Anns Hill Road, Nottingham, NG3 4GP
T 0115 9413160
E denisecweston@hotmail.com
W www.oldknows.co.uk
Contact Denise Weston or Simon Withers
Founded in 1987, aiming to provide inexpensive and spacious studios for artists. Studio group produces contemporary visual art, from the traditional through to the avant-garde.
Price range £54 per month.

Open Hand Open Space
571 Oxford Road, Reading, RG30 1HL
T 0118 9597752
E info@ohos.org.uk
W www.ohos.org.uk
Contact Emily Smeaton (Administrator)
Founded in 1980. An artist-led organization providing affordable artists' studios and facilities for the production of contemporary visual art. Also runs an exhibitions and education programme to promote public access to contemporary visual art and artists.
Price range £40–£100 per month, inclusive.

Optima Photographic Studios
The Chocolate Factory, 1st Floor, Building D, Clarendon Road, London, N22 6JX
T 020 88810064
F 020 88815756
E mail@optima-studios.co.uk
W www.optima-studios.co.uk
Photographic studios for hire along with darkrooms and processing facilities.

Opus Studios
Unit B3, The Oldknows Factory, St Ann's Hill Road, Nottingham, NG3 4GP
E charlottesmith24@hotmail.com
W www.nottinghamstudios.org.uk/opus
Contact Charlotte Smith
Founded in 1999. A group of ten artists displaying varied creative practices including painting, installation, sculpture, photography and community arts projects. Has exhibited locally, nationally and internationally.
Price range £45–£85

Pallas Studios
17 Foley Street, Dublin 1
T 01 8561404
E info@pallasstudios.org
W www.pallasstudios.org
Pallas Studios was born in Dublin's inner city in 1996. A multi functional artist-run space, presenting exhibitions of contemporary works and offering studio space and other services.

Pavilion Studios
Market Drive, Chiswick, W4 2RX
T 020 87422225
E info@fodm.org.uk
W www.fodm.org.uk
Contact Kathleen Healy
Founded in 2002, offering private lockable spaces to ten artists in a converted farm building on the edge

of a park. Twenty-four-hour access, free parking, central heating and use of a shared kitchen. Spaces vary in size, but most are around 100 sq. ft.

Phoenix Art Studios

c/o Castleforbes Business Park, Upper Sheriff Street, Dublin D1
T 087 2753944
E phoenixartstudios@yahoo.com
Offers studio space in a converted warehouse in the docklands of Dublin.

Phoenix Arts Association

10–14 Waterloo Place, Brighton, BN2 9NB
T 01273 603700
E info@phoenixarts.org
W www.phoenixarts.org
Contact Belinda Greenhalgh (Office Manager)
Established in 1992, providing over one hundred high-quality studios for individual artists as well as larger workspaces for short-term projects. Also a gallery presenting exhibitions of contemporary visual art in all media with an integrated education programme.

Red Gate Gallery & Studios

209a Coldharbour Lane, London, SW9 8RU
T 020 73260993
E info@redgategallery.co.uk
W www.redgategallery.co.uk
Offers studio spaces at £120 per month (fully inclusive) as well as internships for artists who are interested in gaining work experience within a gallery environment. Also hires the gallery space at student-friendly fees. Other services include press mailings, posting of press release on various art related event sites, and invigilation as well as curation of the booked exhibitions. The weekly package is £250, the 2-weekly package £500.
Price range £120–£200

Rogue Artists' Studios

2nd Floor, Crusader Works, 66–72 Chapeltown Street, Manchester, M1 2WH
T 0161 2737492
W www.rogueartistsstudios.org.uk
Contact Martin Nash, David Gledhill
Founded in 1995. Active in painting, textiles, construction, graphics, photography, performance, video, installation and furniture. Offers an annual platform for artists to exhibit their work to the public. Weekly life-drawing class for studio members and general public. Equipped workshop area and computer suite available.

Price range £44–£95 per calendar month all-inclusive.

Southgate Studios

2–4 Southgate Road, London, N1 3JJ
T 020 72546485
E adrian@adrianhemming.com
W www.adrianhemming.com
Contact Adam Gray or Adrian Hemming
Founded in 1990, providing approximately ten studio spaces (average size 400 sq. ft).
Price range On application. Two months' deposit required.

SPACE

129–131 Mare Street, London, E8 3RH
T 020 85254330
F 020 85254342
E mail@spacestudios.org.uk
W www.spacestudios.org.uk
Founded in 1968, SPACE is a charitable organization providing affordable studios across London, currently serving over five hundred artists. SPACE also runs professional development courses and projects for artists as well as a range of media courses and hosts an active exhibitions programme.
Price range £70–£600 per month.

SPACE Place

Fish Island, 43–45 Dace Road, London E3 2NG
T 020 89865998
F 020 89866887
E spaceplace@spacestudios.org.uk
W www.spacestudios.org.uk
Contact Virginia Simpson
A media arts resource centre in Hackney Wick. Offers access to digital-art and video-editing facilities, project space and exhibition space. Also runs a wide variety of courses utilizing two fully equipped editing suites.
Price range £30 per day for Moving Image Suite; £20 per day for Digital Art Suite. £20–£30 for one-day courses.

Spotlight Studios

Canonbury Yard, 202 New North Road, London N1 7BJ
T 020 73549955
F 020 73548333
E info@spotlightstudios.co.uk
W www.spotlightstudios.co.uk
Well-equipped photograhic studio for hire.

Stu-Stu-Studio
10 Gate Street, London, WC2A 3HP
T 020 72421919
E louise@warwickworldwide.com
W www.stu-stu-studio.com
Contact Louise Durham
A daylight studio based in the heart of central
London, suitable for portraiture, still photography,
video etc. Use of the lighting system is included in
the hire charge.
Price range £250 full day, £150 half day

Studio Voltaire
1A Nelsons Row, Clapham, London, SW4 7JR
T 020 76221294
E info@studiovoltaire.org
W www.studiovoltaire.org
Contact Joe Scotland
Founded in 1994. The first and only artist-run
gallery and studio complex in south-west London,
offering a service for local residents, schools and
community groups. Actively promotes access to
and participation in contemporary-art practice with
its exhibition, education and studio programmes.
Price range £60–£250 per calendar month.

Viking Studios and Bede Gallery
4 Viking Precinct, Jarrow, NE32 3LQ
T 0191 4200560
Contact Vince Rea
Founded in 1996, providing ten artists' studios.
Small window space on ground floor used to
display work, situated in Jarrow Shopping Centre.

Visual Arts Centre
32 North Brunswick Street, Dublin 7
T 01 6337937
F 01 6337937
E info@visualartscentre.com
W www.visualartscentre.com
Eight affordable studio spaces for professional
visual artists at various stages of their careers.

Wakefield Artsmill
Rutland Mills, Kirkgate Bridge, Wakefield, WF1 5JR
T 01924 215873
E w-artsmill@pop3.poptel.org.uk
Contact Ian Smith
Incorporated as a company limited by guarantee in
1997. Provides low-cost studio accommodation, an
exhibition space and production facilities for up to
forty artists at all stages of their careers.
Price range Spaces are charged at £3.50 per sq. ft
per year (£24–£114 per month).

Wasps Artists' Studios
77 Hanson Street, Dennistoun, Glasgow, G31 2HF
T 0141 5548299
F 0141 5547330
E info@waspsstudios.org.uk
W www.waspsstudios.org.uk
Contact Helen Moore (Administration Assistant)
Over the last twenty-five years, Wasps has grown to
become the largest visual arts organization in
Scotland, providing low-cost studio space to over
650 artists each year at sixteen locations
throughout Scotland. Aims to sustain and develop
Scotland's visual artist community, provide a
network of working spaces and other low-cost
services to artists and arts organizations.
Price range Current rental rates are between £3.35
and £5.85 per sq. ft per year, fully inclusive. This
translates to between £55 to £100 per month, with
£75 being the average rental for a 200 sq. ft studio.

Waygood Gallery and Studios
548–560 Shields Road, Byker
Newcastle-upon-Tyne, NE6 2UT
T 0191 2656857
F 0191 2244187
E art@waygood.org
W www.waygood.org
Contact Alex Evans
Founded in 1995 with the aims of providing a
place of practice for artists and engaging audiences
with contemporary art. Its site on High Bridge is
currently being redeveloped into new, state-of-the-
art accommodation and will include a gallery with
an international programme of contemporary
visual art and live art, fully accessible studios, a
visual arts learning centre, workshop facilities and
an international residency programme. Until
completion, Waygood will be based at Harkers
Building in Byker, Newcastle.
Price range £30–£150 per month for studio rent,
depending on size of space.

West Walls Studios
53 West Walls, Carlisle, CA3 8UH
T 01228 515127
E west.walls@virgin.net
W www.westwallsstudios.com
Contact Paul Taylor
Established in 1993, an artists' cooperative
working collaboratively and individually on
projects, community activities and exhibitions.
Twelve artists' spaces and small gallery/project
space are available to hire, subject to application.
Studios open to public by appointment and on

annual open weekend.
Price range £60–£150 per month for studios; £150 per month for gallery/project space.

Westbourne Studios
242 Acklam Road, London, W10 5JJ
T 020 75753000
F 020 75753001
E events@westbournestudios.com
W www.westbournestudios.com
Contact Natalie Westhorpe
Situated underneath the Westway, ninety-two studios are available to hire as well as a space for gallery exhibitions, a screening room and a project space.
Price range On application

Widcombe Studios Ltd
The Old Malthouse, Comfortable Place, Upper Bristol Road, Bath, BA1 3AJ
T 01225 482480
E admin@widcombestudios.co.uk
W www.widcombestudios.co.uk
Contact Claire Loder (Studios Administrator)
Founded in 1996, comprising forty-five studios. Also runs courses and has a gallery space available for hire.
Price range £10.50 per square metre per calendar month. Average studio is 10m2, but in reality are all different sizes.

Wimbledon Art Studios
Riverside Yard, Riverside Road, London, SW17 0BA
T 020 89471183
F 020 89445162
E wimbledonartstudios@yahoo.co.uk
W www.WimbledonArtStudios.co.uk
Contact Jane Cavanagh (Art Studio Coordinator)
Established ten years ago and now one of the largest art studios in Europe, with over one hundred artists, sculptors, ceramacists, photographers, jewellers and costume designers under one roof. There are two open-studio shows each year. Twenty-four-hour access, seven days a week, and a good community atmosphere.
Price range From £2 for rental space.

Wollaton Street Studios
179 Wollaton Street, Nottingham, NG1 5GE
E bobrobinsonrig@hotmail.com
W www.nottinghamstudios.org/wollaton
Contact Bob Robinson or Rob Hart
Formed in 1985 and located close to the city centre. Six separate studios arranged around a central

stairwell, with two studios to each floor. Completely artist-run and predominantly encouraging the activity of painting.
Price range £65–£100 per month, inclusive.

The Worx
10 Heathmans Road, Fulham, London, SW6 4TJ
T 020 73719777
F 020 73719888
E enquiries@theworx.co.uk
W www.theworx.co.uk
Photographic, film and tv studios offered for hire.

Yorkshire Artspace Society
Persistence Works, 21 Brown Street, Sheffield S1 2BS
T 0114 2761769
F 0114 2761769
E info@artspace.org.uk
W www.artspace.org.uk
Contact Viv Mager
Established in Sheffield in 1977. Based in a purpose-built studio complex for artists and craftspeople (seventy spaces). Offers business support and training to visual artists and a wide-ranging community outreach programme to schools, community groups and the public.
Price range £88–£240 per month, all-inclusive.

Zoom In Ltd
Clapham Leisure Centre, Clapham Manor Street, London, SW4 6DB
T 020 77207437
E enquiries@zoom-in.org
W www.zoom-in.org
Contact Course Administrator
Exists to provide education and services through photography. Provides part-time evening and weekend photography courses from beginners to advanced levels. All proceeds are committed to providing workshops with community groups aimed at those who may not otherwise have access to photography such as excluded young people, refugees and asylum seekers.
Price range £120–£175 per day.

05

Art
education

Why art school?
Options and approaches for training as an artist

Janet Hand and Gerard Hemsworth

You may want to be an artist and are therefore seriously considering how to turn wanting into doing, and doing into an abiding practice; in this case you may well be asking what art school can offer you. You might already have an involvement in the arts and are at a time in your career when you are considering further study, or you may want to shift the emphasis of your practice. In any case, your first questions will be 'Where do I start?', 'Whom do I approach?' and 'Do I have what it takes?'

Like any practice, art requires commitment and hard work. If you are just starting out, you will need to consider your education and the specific approach to art or design that suits you; this is the first difficult choice on your career path.

Solid foundation
The conventional starting point is a foundation course, which will introduce you to a variety of media and career options, from product design to fashion, textiles and fine art. The availability of courses varies from one institution to another: Byam Shaw School of Art, for example, only offers a foundation in fine art; Central St Martins, on the other hand, has a vast foundation programme with a range of choices across art and design.

This kind of study lasts for a year and aids in choosing the degree that suits your interests and abilities best. Foundation courses are by nature 'diagnostic', so you need not be too concerned that you have not yet come to a decision about which area of art you might wish to pursue eventually. They are geared towards entry into art-school degree courses and will nurture your strengths while guiding you in basic technical requirements. The teaching staff will advise you on which BA programme they think will be most appropriate for the development of your work. Since portfolios need to be ready by Easter, you may consider taking a year out to develop work rather than accepting a place at a college that is not your first choice.

First degree inspection
At BA level, there are numerous art schools vying for your attention through their prospectuses, websites, admissions tutors and admissions offices – all potential first points of contact with colleges on your shortlist. Remember, art schools need your potential as much as you need their expertise, so you will have to identify preferred institutions on your shortlist and visit them on organized open days. Talk to the students who are currently studying there to get a flavour of what is going on, so that you can make an informed choice about which is the right place for you. On college open days you can ask all the questions you need in order to make an appropriate application. A phone call to the admissions office will tell you when and how often these occur.

It is not necessary to have done a foundation course when applying for a degree, although it does give applicants a distinct advantage; some colleges will not interview a student who has not. When making a decision about which BAs to apply for, you should consider the nature of the overall programme in relation to your own aspirations within art practice. Not all applicants to art degrees aspire to be practising artists and many courses offer transferable skills that can be applied in a broader context of art culture.

Consider, also, the ethos of the art school. These generally fall into two categories: the first is interdisciplinary and enables you to move from one medium to another; the second is media-led and will have, for example, a painting department or a stand-alone photography course. Colleges that are media-led may advertise to applicants that you can still make video work within, say, the sculpture department, but make sure this will not be a problem by asking current students.

When you initially visit colleges you are thinking of applying to, you will get a general feel of this ethos. You will also see the size of studio spaces, discover the technical facilities and hear how current students describe the quality of the teaching and learning environment. Students will often volunteer other practical information about their experiences that will help you make a decision. They may tell you how often they get tutorials and from whom. If there are regular visiting tutors to the college, it is worth asking about their involvement in the arts. Are they artists, writers, curators, educationalists?

Students will also give an account of their contextual studies and how these help develop their art practice. Find out if there are separate or integrated history of art or critical studies courses. The way programmes are organized and the courses they offer are not necessarily better or worse from college to college, but they are different. Your understanding of the differences and their appropriateness to you is the basis of making a good choice.

Furthering your education

Some BA graduates acquire professional success as practising artists within months of completion. At Goldsmiths, for example, Damien Hirst, Sarah Lucas, Gary Hume and others had no need for postgraduate studies, but they are the exception and not the rule. In most cases, students who are committed to becoming full-time artists start thinking of applying for postgraduate study after completing their BA.

Postgraduate study is usually when art students begin to consider their practice alongside contemporary artists working in the field. This doesn't mean you have to get to postgraduate level to become a professional artist, but most BA graduates will tell you that the discipline of their profession and their sense of maintaining a serious practice only begins after graduation, and that it is a hard apprenticeship to build a portfolio of interest by working on your own. If you

want or need to continue your study at postgraduate level, you can expect exacting criticism as well as a level of support that artists rarely get otherwise. Remember that your colleagues and fellow students are not only your closest allies but also an embryonic professional network, so it is important that you choose a place to study where you can share ideas and expectations, and most importantly begin to put them into practice through exhibition.

When applying for a postgraduate degree, consider whether or not it is the right time in the development of your career to take full advantage of further study. In the majority of cases, it is worth taking some time between BA and MA in order to develop your concerns and a 'professional practice'.

Generally, you will be asking similar questions of postgraduate programmes as applicants ask of BA programmes. You may also want to know if the MA has an international profile and whether applicants apply from around the world. Again, students are the best people to let applicants know how the college works day to day.

One thing current students may not be able to ascertain is the standard of their programme in comparison to other postgraduate courses. A way to assess the teaching and learning environment of a college is to ask about recent alumni. Is the programme enabling graduates to have careers as practising artists? Is it offering a platform for them to operate? Does it have a network of alumni that can be of help and support?

Recent alumni from the Fine Art MA at Goldsmiths, for example, include many who have gained international recognition, along with many who have been shortlisted for and won the Turner Prize. These include Mark Wallinger, who also represented Great Britain at the Venice Biennale, Yinka Shonibare, who was shortlisted for the 2004 Turner Prize, and Glenn Brown, who had a solo exhibition at the Serpentine in London in 2004. Other major luminaries include Jane and Louise Wilson,

Bob and Roberta Smith, Thomas Demand, David Thorpe, Gillian Wearing, Michael Raedecker and many more.

These days, you can go on to PhD study in art practice – the highest degree of attainment in academic terms, although many colleges also offer fellowships for professional artists and academics. Artists who study towards a PhD often have a commitment to teaching alongside their professional practice, or wish to vitalize their work in a sustained way through research. PhD study is designed for artists and curators who also wish to write a research project proposed and developed by them in support of their practice. Artists pursuing this level of research are most often already exhibiting, curating or working within the profession and continue to do so throughout their course of study. Research students at Goldsmiths, past and present, are working nationally and internationally and have exhibited in venues such as the Whitechapel and Tate galleries.

Status report

Some art schools have independent college status and others operate within a university setting, as is the case with the Department of Visual Arts at Goldsmiths. Goldsmiths is part of the University of London and so has access to the activities, open lectures, libraries and other facilities of the college and university more widely. Independent art schools will organize lectures and talks geared to their student cohort, often in conjunction with galleries.

The learning and teaching environment at any reputable college is as important as its alumni network, with one feeding into the other at all levels. Staff who have contributed significantly in building and maintaining Goldsmiths' reputation have included Professor Nick de Ville, who currently directs our research programme, and Professor Victor Burgin, the current Millard Professor of Fine Art; Peter Creswell, John Thompson and Michael Craig-Martin have also made noteworthy contributions along the way. The department offers programmes in fine art, textiles and curating, as well as a joint BA in art and art history in collaboration with the Department of Visual Culture.

Whatever level of study you wish to pursue, it is always worth asking yourself what kind of support and facilities you will need in the continuation and development of your work. It is then a question of best matching your potential and demonstrable abilities with the most appropriate environment and expertise.

Janet Hand and Gerard Hemsworth are Assistant Director of Research and Director of Postgraduate Studies in Fine Art, respectively, of the Visual Arts Department at Goldsmiths College.

Further, higher and adult education

East Anglia

Cambridge School of Art, Anglia Ruskin University
East Road, Cambridge, CB1 1PT
T 0845 2713333
E answers@anglia.ac.uk
W www.anglia.ac.uk
In 1858 John Ruskin opened a school of art in Cambridge and the School now has over 500 students. The studios and workshops cluster in the distinctive Ruskin Building close to the centre of Cambridge. Public exhibitions are held throughout the year in the Ruskin Gallery and the annual Ruskin lecture takes place each October. Retaining its traditional strengths in illustration and the graphic arts, the School now also extends its activities into the contemporary media arts. Film and video benefit from a close relationship with the Cambridge Arts Picturehouse, and computer games design from a location at the heart of Silicon Fen.
Degrees offered BA (Hons): Fine Art, Illustration, Graphic Design, Photography, Fashion Design, Computer Games, Film & TV Production. FdA: Professional Photography. MA and PgDip: Children's Book Illustration; Printmaking.
Admissions Policy Applicants for practice-based single honours degrees will normally have taken an art and design foundation, BTEC ND, A-levels, level 3 GNVQ or AVCE. While academic qualifications are taken into consideration, admission is also based upon the portfolio of work presented at interview. Applications from those offering other qualifications and/or relevant professional experience are welcomed.

Colchester Institute
Sheepen Road, Colchester, C03 3LL
T 01206 518000
E info@colchester.ac.uk
W www.colchester.ac.uk
Over ten thousand students at two main campuses: Sheepen Road in Colchester and Church Road in Clacton.
Degrees offered BA (Hons): Art and Design.
Other Fine Art courses BTEC FD: Art and Design. Dip. in Foundation Studies: Art and Design (full- and part-time). HND: Art and Design (full- and part-time). ND: Graphic Design; Digital Media.
Admissions Policy For BA (Hons) Art and Design: appropriate ND, Dip. in Foundation Studies or

Advanced GNVQ in Art and Design. Mature students do not need formal qualifications but are considered on merit. Entry requirements vary depending on degree.

College of West Anglia
King's Lynn Centre, Tennyson Avenue
King's Lynn, PE30 2QW
T 01553 761144
F 01553 815555
E enquiries@col-westanglia.ac.uk
W www.col-westanglia.ac.uk
Contact Mike Williams
Founded in 1893
Degrees offered BA: Fine Art.
Other Fine Art courses HND: Fine Art. ND: Fine Art. Access to Art foundation diploma: Art and Design.
Admissions Policy Entry requirements: a substantial portfolio; four GCEs A to C for ND; four GCEs A to C plus at least one A-level for foundation; no formal qualifications for Access diploma; four GCSEs A to C, at least one A-level and foundation diploma or equivalent for BA.

Dunstable College
Kingsway, Dunstable, LU5 4HG
T 01582 477776
F 01582 478801
E enquiries@dunstable.ac.uk
W www.dunstable.ac.uk
Degrees offered BA (Hons) in Graphic Design for Print & New Media. Foundation Degrees: Creative and Editorial Photography; Contemporary Fine Art Practice; Graphic Design & Advertising; Fashion & Surface Pattern Design.
Other Fine Art courses Other fine-art courses: BTEC 1st Dip.: Media; Performing Arts. BTEC National Diploma: Performing Arts; Art and Design; Photography. BTEC ND: Media. BTEC Foundation Dip.: Art and Design.

Norwich School of Art & Design
Francis House, 3–7 Redwell Street, Norwich
NR2 4SN
T 01603 610561
F 01603 615728
E info@nsad.ac.uk
W www.nsad.ac.uk
The only specialist art and design institution in the east of England. Provision ranges from foundation degree to PhD level.
Degrees offered BA (Hons): Fine Art; Contemporary Textile Practices; Visual Studies.

MA: Design and Education; Digital Practices; Fine Art; Textile Culture; Photographic Studies. FdA: Arts and the Community.

South East Essex College
Luker Road, Southend-on-Sea
SS1 1ND
T 01702 220400
F 01702 432320
E learning@southend.ac.uk
W www.southend.ac.uk
Contact Admissions Department
Degrees offered BA (Hons): Fine Art. Other HE courses: Digital Animation; Ceramics; Three-Dimensional Product Design; Fashion; Graphic Design; Interior Design; Photography.
Other Fine Art courses A wide range of arts courses at FE level, and adult courses in the daytime, evenings and weekends, including oil painting, screenprinting and watercolour classes.
Admissions Policy For degrees: 160 UCAS points or mature-entry portfolio. Refer to HE prospectus for full details (phone to request copy).

Suffolk College
Rope Walk, Ipswich, IP4 1LT
T 01473 255885
F 01473 296352
E info@suffolk.ac.uk
W www.suffolk.ac.uk
Contact Sheila Thomas
Has run art and design courses for over one hundred years.
Degrees offered BA (Hons): Fine Art (full- and part-time); Fine Art combined with other subjects such as Psychology, Media Studies, and Early Childhood Studies.
Admissions Policy Normal entry requirements: two A-level passes or equivalent; foundation or ND in related subject. All applicants normally interviewed with their portfolios.

University of Hertfordshire
Faculty for the Creative and Cultural Industries, College Lane, Hatfield, AL10 9AB
T 01707 285300
F 01707 285312
E ad.information@herts.ac.uk
W www.herts.ac.uk or
perseus.herts.ac.uk/uhinfo/courses/art/artanddes ign_home.cfm
Contact David McGravie
Well-resourced faculty contains two schools, Art and Design and Film, Music and Media, which

grew out of the original St Albans School of Art, founded around 1880. Students have access to staff who are practising artists, purpose-built studios and workshops, two professional galleries and modern learning-resource centres.
Degrees offered BA (Hons): Fine Art; Fine Art with Marketing (subject to validation); Applied Art; Applied Art with Marketing (subject to validation); Digital and Lens Media; Digital and Lens Media with Marketing (subject to validation). MA: Fine and Applied Arts Practice.
Other Fine Art courses All degrees are offered on a part-time basis. Autumn-, spring- and summer-term courses: Drawing and Painting; Photography; Printmaking; Sculpture; Digital Photography; Glass; various design subjects. Sixth-form class: Life Drawing.
Admissions Policy Normally foundation diploma. Access certificate, VCE Double Award or BTEC ND/NC in Art and Design, plus GCSE English at grade C or above.

University of Luton
Park Square, Luton, LU1 3JU
T 01582 734111
F 01582 743400
E enquiries@luton.ac.uk
W www.luton.ac.uk
Degrees offered BA (Hons): Art and Design; Digital Photography and Video Art; Fashion Design (top-up); Fine Art. MA: Art and Design.
Other Fine Art courses A range of practical courses and workshops such as Painting, Drawing, Graphic Design, Web Design, Printmaking and Illustration.

East Midlands

Bishop Grosseteste University College Lincoln
Newport, Lincoln, LN1 3DY
T 01522 527347
F 01522 530243
E info@bishopg.ac.uk
W www.bishopg.ac.uk
Contact Victoria Hind
A small University College, established in 1862 with a campus in uphill Lincoln. Subjects within the art curriculum are painting, drawing, printmaking, textiles, ceramics, sculpture, glass and computer-manipulated imagery.
Degrees offered BA (Hons): Education Studies and Art & Design (three years); Primary Education and QTS (three years) with specialization in Art.
Admissions Policy Applicants should apply

through the UCAS system. Entry requirements for the course are 2 A levels at grades C or above, one to be in a relevant subject. Alternative qualifications such as BTEC, GNVQs, etc. are considered in Art and Design. GCSEs in English Language and Mathematics are also required. For further clarification, contact the Registry on 01522 583658.

Chesterfield College

Infirmary Road, Chesterfield, S41 7NG
T 01246 500562 / 500563
E advice@chesterfield.ac.uk
W www.chesterfield.ac.uk
Contact Education Helpline on 01246 500562 or Training Helpline on 01246 500553 for short courses, Saturday college and summer college. Started life in 1841 as the Chesterfield and Brampton Mechanics' Institute, and went through various incarnations, including a merger in 1984 of Chesterfield Art College and Chesterfield College of Technology, before becoming Chesterfield College. Over 21,000 students (around 3,600 full-time).
Degrees offered The programmes of the Department of Art and Design centre around dedicated studios and workshops. Courses include: Fine Art; Photography; Ceramics and Silversmithing; Three-Dimensional Design; Fashion and Textiles; Illustration and Graphics.
Other Fine Art courses Introductory and Intermediate Access to HE: Art and Design. HNC/HND: Fine Art (Book Arts). BTEC level 1 Introductory Dip.: Art, Design and Media. BTEC FD: Art and Design. BTEC ND: Art and Design. Dip. in Foundation Studies: Art and Design. OCN Photography levels 1 and 2. Drawing for Beginners.
Admissions Policy Requirements vary. See website.

De Montfort University

The Gateway, Leicester
LE1 9BH
T 0116 2577570
F 0116 2506281
E artanddesign@dmu.ac.uk
W www.dmu.ac.uk/artanddesign
School of Fine Art established in 1897. The course is studio-based and students can specialize in one discipline, or opt for a broad-based pattern of study across the range of disciplines.
Degrees offered BA (Hons): Fine Art; Design; Crafts.

Other Fine Art courses Fashion; Contour Design; Textile Design; Architecture; Graphic Design; Multimedia Design; Interior Design; Photography and Video; Footwear Design; Product, Furniture and Industrial Design.
Admissions Policy All offers dependent on interview with portfolio. For further information contact Student Recruitment on 0116 2577555.

Grimsby Institute of Further and Higher Education

Nuns Corner, Grimsby
DN34 5BQ
T 01472 311222
E headmissions@grimsby.ac.uk
Contact Helen Geer
Offers an interdisciplinary, contemporary approach. Close links are established between theory and practice. Students benefit from designated studio space and a range of appropriate facilities and workshops. First-year students work across painting, printmaking, sculpture, ceramics, art metalwork and textiles, visual language and critical studies. Contemporary practice is introduced through workshops in film, sound, performance and light. Second- and third-year students confirm choice of discipline culminating in the final degree show.
Degrees offered BA Hons: Fine and Applied Arts (three years full-time; six years part-time).
Admissions Policy Foundation or AVCE Art and Design required. Exceptions may be made for mature applicants. UCAS route B.

Loughborough University

School of Art & Design, Loughborough
LE11 3TU
T 01509 263171
E R.Turner@lboro.ac.uk
W www.lboro.ac.uk
Contact Rebecca Turner
Has twelve thousand students and a 410-acre campus. In 1966, the College obtained a Royal Charter to become the first University of Technology in the country.
Degrees offered BA (Hons): Fine Art (Painting, Printmaking, Sculpture); Visual Communication (Graphic Communication, Illustration); Three-Dimensional Design (Ceramics, Furniture Design, Silversmithing and Jewellery); Textile Design (Printed Textiles, Multi-Media Textiles, Woven Textiles); History of Art and Design. MA: Art and Design (Studio Practice).
Admissions Policy For BA: through UCAS. For

MA: candidates are normally expected to have obtained a good honours bachelor degree or equivalent in an art and design discipline or a closely related subject. A lower-level qualification with appropriate professional or industrial experience may also be considered.

New College Nottingham

P.O. Box 6598, Nottingham, NG1 1NS
T 0115 9 100100
E headmissions@ncn.ac.uk
W www.ncn.ac.uk
Contact Central Admissions
One of the largest colleges of further education in the UK with a wide range of full and part-time study programmes.
Degrees offered FdA: Digital Arts.
Other Fine Art courses BTEC FD: Art and Design. BTEC ND: Fine Art. Dip. in Foundation Studies: Art and Design.

Nottingham Trent University

Burton Street, Nottingham, NG1 4BU
T 0115 9418418
E reg.web@ntu.ac.uk
W www.ntu.ac.uk
Total student population of around 26,000.
Degrees offered BA (Hons): Decorative Arts; Fine Art; Graphic Design; Photography/Photography in Europe; Textile Design. MA: Art and Design, Language and Culture Bridging Programme; Decorative Arts; Fine Art; Graphic Design; Textile Design and Innovation. MPhil/PhD studies and an art and design international access programme also offered.
Admissions Policy For undergraduate: through UCAS, plus other requirements.

South Nottingham College

West Bridgford Centre, Greythorn Drive Nottingham, NG2 7GA
T 0115 9146400
F 0115 9146444
E enquiries@south-nottingham.ac.uk
W www.south-nottingham.ac.uk
Other Fine Art courses BTEC FD: Design. BTEC ND: Art and Design; Three-Dimensional Design; Textile Design. Foundation diploma: Art and Design (post-A-level). HND: Design; Three-Dimensional Design; Graphic Design; Fine Art.
Admissions Policy For HND: through UCAS.

Stamford College

Drift Road, Stamford, PE9 1XA

T 01780 484300
F 01780 484301
E enquiries@stamford.ac.uk
W www.stamford.ac.uk
Contact Jayne Olney
The Visual Arts Centre has specifically equipped life-drawing room, photographic studio, 3-D workshops and Apple Macintosh suites. Degrees are validated by Anglia Poytechnic University.
Degrees offered BA (Hons): Fine Art; Graphic Design.
Other Fine Art courses Foundation diploma: Art and Design.
Admissions Policy All applicants are interviewed. Mature students are encouraged to apply and are considered on a portfolio of work.

University of Derby

Faculty of Arts, Design and Technology, Britannia Mill Campus, Derby, DE22 3BL
T 01332 594008
F 01332 597760
E adtenquiry@derby.ac.uk
W vertigo.derby.ac.uk
Contact Jas Dhillon on 01442 594058.
Courses in fine art date back to the beginning of the nineteenth century. Recent alumuni include Nisha Dougal (Artists' Newsletter) and Sarah Key (studying for PhD in painting at Loughborough). Was scheduled to move to a new campus at Markeaton Street in Sept. 2007.
Degrees offered BA (Hons): Fine Art; Photography; Film and Video; Illustration. MA: Advanced Art and Design Theory and Practice (ADAPT).
Other Fine Art courses PgCert: Arts Practice.
Admissions Policy Applications are invited from students who are studying art and design subjects at A2 level. Application can be through UCAS routes A or B. There will be a portfolio interview for each applicant.

University of Lincoln

Brayford Pool, Lincoln, LN6 7TS
T 01522 882000
E enquiries@lincoln.ac.uk
W www.lincoln.ac.uk
The Art, Architecture and Design Faculty's three schools provide undergraduate, taught postgraduate and postgraduate research programmes. The Hull and Lincoln Schools of Art and Design were both founded in the 1860s while the School of Architecture was established in the 1930s.

Degrees offered BA (Hons): Fine Art; Animation; Conservation and Restoration; Contemporary Decorative Crafts; Contemporary Lens Media; Fashion Studies; Furniture Design and Practice; Graphic Design; Heritage Investigation; Illustration; Museum and Exhibition Design. MA: Fine Art; Design; Art, Architecture and Design. Fine-art research opportunities (MRes/MPhil/PhD) also offered.

University of Northampton

School of the Arts, St George's Avenue
Northampton, NN2 6JD
T 01604 735500 / 893210
F 01604 717813
E christine.midgley@northampton.ac.uk
W www.northampton.ac.uk
Contact Lisa Goalby
A college of art was first established in the 1800s and is now, as the School of the Arts, a part of the new University of Northampton. Offers specialist facilities and studios and flexible programmes of study where students are encouraged to work within and across diciplinary boundaries. Alumni include Will Alsop, Andrew Collins and the X Foundation,
Degrees offered BA (Hons): Fine Art; Fine Art Painting and Drawing; Photographic Practice; Illustration. MA: Fine Art; Curatorial Studies .
Other Fine Art courses Joint Honours: Fine Art Painting & Drawing; History of Art and Design.
Admissions Policy Via UCAS routes A and B. Normally Foundation Art and Design or equivalent. Applicants interviewed. Non-standard applications welcome.

London

The Art Academy

201 Union Street, Southwark, London
SE1 0LN
T 020 74016539
F 020 74016541
E info@artacademy.org.uk
W www.artacademy.org.uk
Contact Isabella Byerley (Course Administrator)
Founded in 2000, aiming to train artists to the highest standard and to provide access to the arts for the community through a wide range of short course, lectures and exhibitions. Have had over two-thousand enrolled students.
Degrees offered Offers an intensive, three-year, in-house Fine Art Diploma for students specializing in either sculpture or painting. The course is

predominately practice based and offers an average of thirty tutored hours per week (one of the highest levels of contact hours in the country for a fine arts course). Twenty places available each year.
Other Fine Art courses Part-time, evening, short and weekend courses in painting, drawing and sculpture.

Byam Shaw School of Art

2 Elthorne Road, Archway, London, N19
T 020 72814111
W www.csm.arts.ac.uk/csm_byam_shaw.htm
Contact John O'Sullivan
A small school founded in 1910, focusing on the study of fine art. Joined Central Saint Martins College of Art and Design in 2003.
Degrees offered BA (Hons) Fine Art; PG Diploma Fine Art; MA Fine Art; Foundation Degree in Fine Art Skills and Practices (2 year degree).
Other Fine Art courses Fine Art Foundation.

Camberwell College of Arts

Peckham Road, London
SE5 8UF
T 020 75146302
F 020 75146310
E enquiries@camberwell.arts.ac.uk
W www.camberwell.arts.ac.uk
Over a hundred years old. Alumni includes Howard Hodgkin, Maggi Hambling, Tom Phillips, Gillian Ayres, Richard Long and Cathy de Monchaux.
Degrees offered BA (Hons): Drawing; Painting; Sculpture; Ceramics. MA: Printmaking; Book Arts; Drawing; Digital Arts; Digital Arts (online).
Other Fine Art courses An extensive programme of short courses, tailormade courses and summer schools offered in conjunction with Chelsea College of Art and Design. For further details contact Short Course Unit on 020 7514 6311 or email shortcourses@camberwell.arts.ac.uk.
Admissions Policy For undergraduate: through UCAS and completion of a foundation year or related qualifications and/or experience (particularly for mature students). For postgraduate: direct to the college, accompanied by a project proposal. Deadline for AHRB funding: mid-February.

Central St Martins College of Art & Design

Southampton Row, London
WC1B 4AP
T 020 75147000
F 020 75147024

E info@csm.arts.ac.uk
W www.csm.arts.ac.uk
Founded in 1989 by the merger of Central School of Art & Crafts (1869) and St Martin's School of Art (1854). St Martin's was particularly well known for fashion and fine art and the Central School for a wide range of design and art, including theatre design, industrial design and graphic design. In 2003 the Byam Shaw School of Art joined Central St Martins. Alumni include Lucian Freud and Frank Auerbach.
Degrees offered BA (Hons): Fine Art; Art, Design and Environment; Criticism, Communication and Curation: Arts and Design; Ceramic Design. FdA: Fine Art Skills and Practice. PgCert: Drawing; Glass; Printmaking; Photography; Fine Arts. MA: Fine Art. PhD programmes.
Other Fine Art courses Fine-art foundation and Foundation Studies in Art and Design. Short courses (summer school, Christmas school, Easter school and evening and weekend courses) and study-abroad courses.

Chelsea College of Art & Design

John Islip Street, London, SW1
T 020 75147751
F 020 75147778
E enquiries@chelsea.arts.ac.uk
W www.chelsea.arts.ac.uk
Degrees offered BA (Hons): Fine Art; Textile Design; Interior and Spatial Design; Graphic Design Communication. MA: Fine Art; Textile Design; Interior and Spatial Design. PgDip: Fine Art. Foundation Studies: Art and Design.
Other Fine Art courses Art foundation: Interior Design. Graduate Dip.: Interior Design (subject to validation). Short course programme, including evening, Saturday and summer schools.
Admissions Policy UCAS route B. Portfolio. Two GCE A-levels and three GCSEs (grade C or above). IELTS 6.5. Although most applicants to BA courses have completed foundation studies, Chelsea welcomes applications from a wide range of people with differing qualifications.

Croydon College

College Road, Croydon
CR9 1DX
T 020 87605914
E info@croydon.ac.uk
W www.croydon.ac.uk
Established for over one hundred years. Strong African, Caribbean and Asian influences and links with many other ethnic communities. Two main

sites, Fairfield and the adjacent dedicated Higher Education Centre.
Degrees offered BA (Hons): Fine Art (Combined Media) (also Dip./Cert. of HE); Fine Art (Combined Media with Digital Art) (also Dip. of HE); Fine Art (Combined Media with Print and Book) (also Dip. of HE); Photomedia (also Dip./Cert. of HE).
Other Fine Art courses BTEC Dip. in Foundation Studies: Art and Design. BTEC FD: Art and Design. All courses offered part-time.
Admissions Policy Dependent upon portfolio work and UCAS points.

Goldsmiths College

New Cross, London, SE14 6NW
T 020 79197171
E admissions@gold.ac.uk
W www.goldsmiths.ac.uk
Founded in 1891 and part of the University of London since 1904. Almost 5,400 undergraduates and 3,000 postgraduates. Alumni in art and design include Lucian Freud, Antony Gormley, Damien Hirst, Margaret Howell, Gary Hume, Steve McQueen, Mary Quant, Bridget Riley, Sam Taylor-Wood, Gillian Wearing, Jane and Louise Wilson.
Degrees offered BA (Hons): Fine Art (Studio Practice and Contemporary Critical Studies); Fine Art (extension degree); Fine Art and History of Art; Fine Art and History of Art (extension degree); Design. MA: Design (Critical Theory and Practice); Fine Art. PgDip: Fine Art.
Admissions Policy Admission is based on the UCAS system for undergraduates. Postgraduate admission is normally by interview and portfolio inspection. Entrance requirements are normally a first degree of at least second-class standard in Fine Art or the equivalent; or Goldsmiths' PgDip in Fine Art; or a proven record of experience as a practising artist.

Kingston University

River House, 53–57 High Street, Kingston-upon-Thames, KT1 1LQ
T 020 85472000
E admissions-info@kingston.ac.uk
W www.kingston.ac.uk
17,500 students over four campuses.
Degrees offered BA (Hons): Fine Art; Graphic Design; Photography with Graphic Design. MA: Communication Design.
Other Fine Art courses Edexcel Dip. in Foundation Studies: Art and Design.

Admissions Policy For undergraduate: through UCAS. Requirements vary depending on degree.

London College of Communication
Elephant and Castle, London, SE1 6SB
T 020 75146853
F 020 75146848
E media@lcc.arts.ac.uk
W www.lcc.arts.ac.uk
Founded in 1883 as St Bride Foundation and the North-western Polytechnic. Formerly known as the London College of Printing. Granted university status in 2003. Around nine thousand students.
Degrees offered Digital Media; Film and Video; Photography; Surface Design.
Other Fine Art courses FE, Young at Art and professional training courses.

London Metropolitan University
31 Jewry Street, London, EC3N 2EY
T 020 74230000
E admissions@londonmet.ac.uk
W www.londonmet.ac.uk
Can trace its roots back to 1848 with the establishment of the Metropolitan evening classes for young men. Ranks as London's largest unitary university with over 35,000 students.
Degrees offered BA (Hons): Design; Design (Graphics); Fine Art; Fine Art (specialist route); Fine Art Contemporary Theory and Practice. MA by project: Applied Art; Art, Design and Visual Culture; Design; Drawing; Fine Art; Visual Culture.
Other Fine Art courses Dip. in Foundation Studies: Art and Design.
Admissions Policy See the university's standard entry requirements (for both postgraduate and undergraduate). In addition, students should have undertaken an art foundation course. Students are selected by portfolio inspection and interview.

London South Bank University
103 Borough Road, London, SE1 0AA
T 020 79288989
E enquiry@lsbu.ac.uk
W www.lsbu.ac.uk
Founded in 1892 as the Borough Polytechnic and amalgamated with four other colleges in 1970 to become South Bank Polytechnic. Granted university status in 1992. Nearly eighteen thousand students.
Degrees offered BA (Hons): Digital Media Arts; Digital Photography.
Admissions Policy See website.

Middlesex University
North London Business Park, Oakleigh Road South, London, N11 1QS
T 020 84115000
E admissions@mdx.ac.uk
W www.mdx.ac.uk
Degrees offered BA (Hons): Fine Art; Applied Arts; Design; Graphic Design; Illustration; Photography. MA: Fine Art Practice and Theory. MFA: Graphic Design.
Other Fine Art courses FdA: Graphic Design; Fine Art Practice and Theory. Edexcel Dip. in Foundation Studies: Art and Design. Dip. of HE: Three-Dimensional Design; Visual Communication Design (Graphic Design). HND/HNC: Fine Art; Graphic Design; Public Art.
Admissions Policy For undergraduate: UCAS (requirements depend on degree). For full- and part-time postgraduate programmes, normally apply direct to the university. See website.

Prince's Drawing School
19–22 Charlotte Road, London, EC2A 3SG
T 020 76138527
F 020 76138599
E enquiry@princesdrawingschool.org.uk
W www.princesdrawingschool.org.uk
An independent educational organization that enables artists to broaden and extend their drawing practice. Founded by the Prince of Wales in 2000. Initially a part of the Prince's Foundation, the Drawing School became a charity in its own right in 2004. Over four hundred students attend classes run by the school each term.
Other Fine Art courses Runs twenty-six courses over each ten-week term, during the daytime from Monday to Saturday and most evenings. Geared mainly for students with some experience of drawing, enrolment is open and students don't need to submit a portfolio.

Richmond, The American International University in London
Richmond Hill Campus, Queen's Road Richmond-upon-Thames, TW10 6JP
T 020 83329000
F 020 83321596
E enroll@richmond.ac.uk
W www.richmond.ac.uk
Attended by students from over one hundred countries. Degrees recognized in the UK and USA.
Degrees offered BA: Art, Design and Media. Offers a range of contemporary, cross-disciplinary, multimedia core courses dealing with concepts in

art, design and media, and the interfaces between them. Students also schooled in professional skills and techniques and appropriate theory.
Admissions Policy See website.

Roehampton University
School of Arts, Erasmus House, Roehampton Lane, London, SW15 5PU
T 020 83923000
W www.roehampton.ac.uk
Degrees offered Undergraduate courses: Art Practice and Critical Skills; Childhood and the Arts; Painting and Printmaking. Postgraduate courses: Art Studies.

Royal Academy Schools
Burlington Gardens, Piccadilly, London W1J 0BD
T 020 73005650
F 020 73005856
E schools@royalacademy.org.uk
W www.royalacademy.org.uk
Contact The Schools Administrator
A small independent institution offering the only three-year full-time postgraduate course in Britain. Traces its routes back to 1768. No fees charged and every effort made to support students with bursaries, awards and grants for materials, albeit at a modest level. Many students need to take some part-time work – often in the Royal Academy itself – to offset the high cost of living and studying in London.
Degrees offered Postgraduate Diploma in Fine Art
Admissions Policy Looks for artists who show complete commitment to their work, a potential for creative growth and a passionate and obsessive desire to discover an original and personal vision.

Royal College of Art
Kensington Gore, London, SW7 2EU
T 020 75904444
F 020 75904500
E admissions@rca.ac.uk
W www.rca.ac.uk
Contact Assistant Registrar
The world's only wholly postgraduate university of art and design, specializing in teaching and research. Alumni include James Dyson, Ridley Scott, Robin Day, Zandra Rhodes, Philip Treacy, Tracey Emin, David Hockney and Henry Moore.
Degrees offered MA, MPhil and PhD degrees. School of Fine Art: Painting; Printmaking; Photography; Sculpture. School of Applied Arts: Ceramics and Glass; Goldsmithing;

Silversmithing; Metalwork; Jewellery. School of Communications: Animation; Communication; Art and Design. School of Humanities: Conservation; Curating; Contemporary Art; History of Design. School of Fashion and Textiles: Fashion Menswear; Fashion Womenswear; Constructed Textiles; Printed Textiles. School of Architecture and Design: Architecture and Interiors Design; Products; Industrial Design; Engineering; Interaction Design; Vehicle Design.
Admissions Policy Entry requirements and application deadlines all listed on website.

Slade School of Fine Art (UCL)
Gower Street, London WC1E 6BT
T 020 76792313
F 020 76797801
E slade.enquiries@ucl.ac.uk
W www.ucl.ac.uk/slade
Contact Caroline Nicholas
Concerned with contemporary art and the practice, history and theories that inform it. Provides for the education of professional artists by professional artists and scholars of the history and theory of art. Founded in 1871 as a department of UCL. Located in the centre of London close to many important galleries, museums and theatres.
Degrees offered BA: Fine Art. MA: Fine Art. MFA: Fine Art. MPhil/PhD: Fine Art.
Other Fine Art courses Summer, Easter and Saturday classes. Continuing education opportunities including a specialist research development programme.
Admissions Policy For BA: UCAS route A. For graduate taught programmes: direct application. Email for further details.

Thames Valley University
Ealing Campus, St Mary's Road, Ealing, London W5 5RF
T 020 85795000
W www.tvu.ac.uk
Campuses in Ealing, Slough and Reading.
Degrees offered BAs and MAs in fine art, design, digital arts and photography.

University of East London
Longbridge Road, Dagenham RM17 6UG
T 020 82233333
F 020 82232900
E admiss@uel.ac.uk
W www.uel.ac.uk

Degrees offered BA (Hons): Fine Art (three years full-time; five years part-time); Fine Art with foundation year (four years full-time). MA/PgDip: Fine Art (MA: one year full-time or two years part-time; PgDip: one year part-time with the option of a second year to complete the MA). Professional Doctorate: Fine Art (three years full-time or four to five years part-time).
Admissions Policy Contact Beryl Watson on 020 82233400 for details on admission to all fine-art programmes.

University of the Arts London
See entries under: Byam School of Art; Camberwell College of Arts; Central St Martins College of Art and Design; Chelsea College of Art and Design; London College of Communication; Wimbledon School of Art.

University of Westminster
309 Regent Street, London, W1B 2UW
T 020 79115000
W www.wmin.ac.uk
Founded in 1838 as Britain's first polytechnic.
Degrees offered BA (Hons): Animation; Mixed Media Fine Art (full- and part-time); Ceramics; Photographic Arts; Photography (part-time); Digital and Photographic Imaging.
Admissions Policy Online for part-time and postgraduate courses. For BA (Hons): through UCAS.

West Thames College
London Road, Isleworth
TW7 4HS
T 020 83262000
E info@west-thames.ac.uk
W www.west-thames.ac.uk
Contact Siobhan Fitzgerald
HND programmes have been running at West Thames since 1985.
Other Fine Art courses HND: Graphics and Advertising; Fine Art; Fashion. Foundation diploma: Art and Design. ND: Art and Design. Various part-time classes.
Admissions Policy ND, AVCE, foundation or A-levels. Mature students with relevant experience welcomed. Portfolio required at interview. Applications accepted from January to September. Enrolment from late August.

Wimbledon School of Art
Merton Hall Road, Wimbledon, London
SW19 3QA

T 020 84085000
F 020 84085050
E info@wimbledon.ac.uk
W www.wimbledon.ac.uk
Contact Linda Tinsley, Admissions Officer
Founded in 1890, a specialist art and design school. Staff are all practising artists, designers and scholars within their specialist fields. Current students show work in exhibitions, performances and costume parades at key venues in London. Alumni include Anthony Cragg, Kenny Ho, Raymond Briggs and Jeff Beck.
Degrees offered BA (Hons): Fine Art (Painting); Fine Art (Sculpture); Fine Art (Graphic Media); Theatre (Costume Design); Theatre (Costume Interpretation); Theatre (Set Design for Stage and Screen); Theatre (Design for Performance); Theatre (Technical Arts and Special Effects). MA: Fine Art (Painting); Fine Art (Drawing); Fine Art (Sculpture); Fine Art (Graphic Media); Theatre (Visual Language of Performance). MPhil and PhD programmes of research.

Working Men's College
44 Crowndale Road, London
NW1 1TR
T 020 72554700/ 0800 3581854 (freephone)
F 020 73835561
E info@wmcollege.ac.uk
W www.wmcollege.ac.uk
Founded in 1854 to provide a liberal arts education for the Victorian skilled artisan class and was associated with the Cooperative Movement. Among the first adult education institutes in the country. Caters for both women and men.
Other Fine Art courses Foundation course: Art and Design.
Admissions Policy By completion of enrolment form. Concessionary fees for some students.

North-east

City of Sunderland College
Bede Centre, Durham Road, Sunderland
SR3 4AH
T 0191 5116260 / 5116060
W www.citysun.ac.uk
Approximately 24,000 students at five main college centres. Courses also offered by distance learning and at community centres.
Other Fine Art courses Art and Design Cert. in Advanced Studies: Calligraphy; Digital Imaging and Photography. FdA: Applied Art; Life Drawing; Oil Painting; Painting and Drawing; Photography;

Printed Textiles; Silk Painting; Stained Glass; Watercolours.

Admissions Policy Entry requirements vary depending upon the course and level of study. Contact the college for individual fact sheets.

Cleveland College of Art & Design

Green Lane, Linthorpe, Middlesbrough
TS5 7RJ
T 01642 288888
F 01642 288828
E studentrecruitment@ccad.ac.uk
W www.ccad.ac.uk
A specialist art and design college; one of four nationally, offering further, higher and continuing education courses in the creative professions. Has roots that go back to 1880 and was formed by the merger of Teesside and Hartlepool Colleges of Art.
Degrees offered BA (Hons): Fine Art.
Other Fine Art courses BTEC Dip.: Fine Art.
Admissions Policy Full-time applications through UCAS routes A and B.Part-time direct to college.

Newcastle College

Rye Hill Campus, Scotswood Road
Newcastle-upon-Tyne, NE4 5BR
T 0191 2004000
F 0191 2004517
E enquiries@ncl-coll.ac.uk
W www.newcastlecollege.co.uk
Four hundred staff and thirty thousand students.
Degrees offered BA (Hons): Fine Art. FdA: Contemporary Ceramic Practice; Fine Art Practice; Photographic Practice; Textile Design and Practice.
Other Fine Art courses HNC: Photography.

Northumbria University

Division of Visual Arts, School of Arts and Social Sciences, Room 123, Lipman Building, Newcastle-upon-Tyne, NE1 8ST
T 0191 2274444
E ar.admissions@unn.ac.uk
W www.northumbria.ac.uk
Contact Liz Candlish
The BA (Hons) Fine Art was established in 1969 and recruits 60–70 students per year. The Fine Art programmes offer specialist and cross disciplinary teaching in all areas of contemporary art practice, including painting, print, sculpture, photography and time-based media. A visiting programme of artists offer talks on their work and tutorial advice. Galleries such as the BALTIC Centre for Contemporary Art and Waygood Gallery collaborate with the university to offer educational opportunities. The University Gallery has an ongoing programme of exhibitions and Gallery North, in the Division of Visual Arts itself, is a research and teaching resource administered by Fine Art. Alumni include Jane Wilson, Louise Hopkins, Matthew Higgs, Daphne Wright and Richard Grayson.
Degrees offered BA (Hons): Fine Art; Contemporary Photographic Practice. MA: Art Practices (Fine Art); Art Practices (Media); Fine Art and Education; Fine Art (part-time).
Other Fine Art courses Portfolio foundation course. Foundation diploma: Art and Design (overseas).
Admissions Policy At undergraduate level applicants will normally have satisfactorily completed a foundation course in art and design. For entry to MA programmes a good degree in visual arts is required.

University of Newcastle-upon-Tyne

Fine Art, School of Arts & Cultures
The Quadrangle, Newcastle-upon-Tyne
NE1 7RU
T 0191 222 6047
F 0191 2228013
E fineart@ncl.ac.uk
W www.ncl.ac.uk/sacs/about/fineart
Contact Nigel Villalard
Distinguished history dating back to its its foundation as the King Edward VII School of Art over a hundred years ago. Since the 1950s it has been associated with artists and teachers including Richard Hamilton, Victor Pasmore, Sean Scully and Susan Hiller. Housed in purpose-built accommodation which includes studios, workshop facilities and the University's Hatton Gallery.
Degrees offered BA (Hons): Fine Art (UCAS codes: W150 route A; E100 route B) – 4-year undergraduate programme with studio practice studied alongside the history of art. MFA: Fine Art – 2-year full-time postgraduate programme.
Other Fine Art courses Fine art drawing and history of art modules can be taken as part of the BA Hons Combined Studies programme. Studio-based and history of art research degree programmes.
Admissions Policy Selection for both BA and MA is made principally on consideration of examples of studio work and interview.

University of Sunderland

Edinburgh Building, City Campus, Chester Road, Sunderland, SR1 3SD

T 0191 5153154
W www.welcome.sunderland.ac.uk
Degrees offered BA (Hons): Art and Design; Fine
Art; Glass, Architectural Glass and Ceramics;
Photography, Video and Digital Imaging.
Admissions Policy For degree, foundation degrees
and HND programmes applicants need to be at
least 18 years of age on 31 December in the
proposed year of entry.

University of Teeside
Middlesbrough, TS1 3BA
T 01642 218121
F 01642 342067
E registry@tees.ac.uk
W www.tees.ac.uk
Originally founded as Constantine College, the
institution was officially opened in 1930. Has
twenty thousand students.
Degrees offered BA (Hons): Fine Art;
Contemporary Three-Dimensional Design;
Design; Graphic Design. MA: Design. Art
foundation: Design for Exhibition and Display;
Graphic Design.

Northern Ireland

Ulster University
Belfast Campus, York Street, Belfast
BT15 1ED
T 0870 0400700
E online@ulster.ac.uk
W www.ulst.ac.uk
School of Art and Design located at both York
Street campus in Belfast city centre and at the
Foyle Arts Centre at the Magee campus. The
largest art and design education centre on the
island of Ireland. INTERFACE is a new research
centre based in the School of Art and Design, part
of a multi-million-pound redevelopment of the
Belfast campus.
Degrees offered BA (Hons): Art and Design; Fine
and Applied Arts; Textiles and Fashion Design.
Other Fine Art courses Foundation Studies: Art
and Design.

North-west

Blackpool and the Fylde College
School of Art and Design, Palatine Road, Blackpool
FY1 4DW
T 01253 352352
E mp@blackpool.ac.uk
W www.art-design.ac.uk

Contact Malcolm Pearson
Offers recently created fine-art course, covering the
specialist disciplines of drawing, painting,
printmaking and digital imaging. Has evolved
from the grade-1 foundation course.
Degrees offered BA (Hons): Fine Art: Profesional
Practice (subject to validation by Lancaster
University). MA: Visual Design as Creative
Practice.
Admissions Policy Fine art applications through
UCAS for BA and direct to the institution for MA.

City College Manchester
Abraham Moss Campus, Crescent Road,
Crumpsall, Manchester, M8 5UF
T 0161 6148000 / 0800 0130123 (freephone)
E admissions@ccm.ac.uk
W www.ccm.ac.uk
Over 29,000 students and 1,200 staff.
Other Fine Art courses NVQ level 3, Foundation
and Intermediate: Photography; Black and White
Photography Introduction; Digital Photography
Introduction. NCFE levels 1 and 2: Ceramics
Introduction; Life Drawing.

Cumbria Institute of the Arts
Brampton Road, Carlisle
CA3 9AY
T 01228 400300
F 01228 514491
E info@cumbria.ac.uk
W www.cumbria.ac.uk
Contact Admissions Officer
Around 1,200 full-time students. Founded in the
1820s. Delivers a variety of courses at FE and HE
levels in the visual, performing and media arts,
crafts, design and cultural heritage.
Degrees offered BA (Hons): Fine Art;
Contemporary Applied Arts; Graphic Design;
Multimedia Design and Digital Animation. MA:
Contemporary Fine Art; Contemporary Applied
Arts. Research degrees up to PhD level.
Other Fine Art courses Some evening classes.
Phone for part-time brochure.
Admissions Policy Entry to undergraduate
programmes through UCAS routes A and B. Most
applicants will have completed a BTEC ND, Dip. in
Foundation Studies, Access to HE course,
Advanced GNVQ or equivalent course, and have
two grade C passes at A2 or, for Scottish students,
three Highers at grades BBC. Applicants for MAs
will normally have a first degree at 2:1 or above.
However, applicants with equivalent professional
experience are invited to contact the institute.

East Lancashire Institute of Higher Education

Blackburn College, Feilden Street, Blackburn
BB2 1LH
T 01254 292594
W www.elihe.ac.uk
Contact Carla Patchett
Offers a range of art and design provision through
full- and part-time study routes.
Degrees offered BA (Hons): Fine Art (Integrated
Media). FdA: Multimedia.
Other Fine Art courses HND: Photography; Textile
Design.
Admissions Policy All candidates applying to the
school are interviewed for places. For details of
admission requirements see website.

Frink School of Figurative Sculpture

Cross St Mill, Leek, ST13 6BL
T 01538 399210
E info@frinkschool.org
W www.frinkschool.org
Set up to preserve and continue the teaching of
figurative sculpture. Established in 1996 and
named after the sculptor Elisabeth Frink
(1933–93). Operates from the Moorland Arts
Centre in Leek on the edge of the Peak District.
Other Fine Art courses Offers a mix of part-time
weekday, weekend and one-week courses, covering
aspects of sculpture and also drawing and
painting, including: Life and Portrait Modelling;
Life Drawing and Painting; Wood Carving; Stone
Carving; Related Modelling and Casting Processes;
Welding; Terracotta Firing.

Lancaster University

Bailrigg, Lancaster, LA1 4YW
T 01524 65201
E ugadmissions@lancaster.ac.uk
W www.lancs.ac.uk/depts/art/
Art is a part of the new Lancaster Institute for the
Contemporary Arts that also includes Music and
Theatre Studies. The BA Fine Art degree nurtures
the 'informed practitioner' and comprises two-
thirds studio practice (painting, drawing, digital,
installation options or hybrids) and one-third art
history/professional practice. The MA continues
the notion of the 'informed practitioner'.
Degrees offered BA (Hons): Fine Art. MA: Art
(Studio Practice). MPhil/PhD: Fine Art; Art
History.
Admissions Policy Takes 35 students a year.
Normally looks for a good portfolio plus
academic grades of BCC. A foundation year is not
essential.

Liverpool Community College

Bankfield Road, Liverpool
L13 0BQ
T 01512 523214
E enquiry@liv-coll.ac.uk
W www.liv-coll.ac.uk
Other Fine Art courses AVCE in Art & Design;
BTEC First Diploma in Design; BTEC GNVQ
Intermediate in Art and Design; BTEC HNC/HND
in Fine Arts; BTEC National Diploma in
Foundation Art & Design; Graphic Design;
3–Dimensional Design; GNVQ Foundation Art &
Design.

Liverpool Hope University College

Hope Park, Liverpool
L16 9JD
T 0151 2913000
F 0151 2913444
E admission@hope.ac.uk
W www.hope.ac.uk
Tradition stretching back over 150 years, when the
Church of England Diocese of Chester and the
Roman Catholic Sisters of Notre Dame established
separate teacher education colleges for women. An
ecumenical Christian foundation.
Degrees offered BA (Hons): Design. BA
(Combined Hons): Fine Art and Design (with
another subject of your choice). BA, QTS: Fine Art
and Design with Teacher Training.
Other Fine Art courses Cert. of HE (Combined
Hons): Fine Art and Design (with another subject).
Admissions policy.
Admissions Policy Applications should be made
through UCAS.

Liverpool John Moores University

Rodney House, 70 Mount Pleasant, Liverpool
L3 5UX
T 0151 2312121
E artadmissions@livjm.ac.uk
W www.livjm.ac.uk
Contact Karen Davis
University took its name from Sir John Moores,
the founder of the Littlewoods empire. Originally a
small mechanics institution (Liverpool Mechanics'
School of Arts). Now has over 24,000 students
studying over two hundred courses at
undergraduate and postgraduate level.
Degrees offered BA (Hons): Fine Art; Graphic
Arts; Fashion and Textile Design. PGCE: Art and
Design.
Admissions Policy Looks for evidence of creative
ability and motivation regardless of entry route.

Applications through UCAS system and portfolio interview.

Manchester Metropolitan University
Faculty of Art and Design, Ormond Building
Lower Ormond Street, Manchester, M15 6BY
T 0161 2471705
F 0161 2476393
E artdes.fac@mmu.ac.uk
W www.mmu.ac.uk
Contact Faculty Office
The faculty has a distinguished history dating back over 150 years. The painter Adolphe Valette, a contemporary of L.S. Lowry, was both a student and a teacher at the faculty.
Degrees offered BA (Hons): Fine Art; Interactive Arts. MA: Fine Art.
Admissions Policy For BA: 160 tariff points plus foundation course. For MA: good undergraduate fine-art degree.

Mid-Cheshire College
Hartford Campus, Chester Road, Northwich
CW8 1LJ
T 01606 74444
E info@midchesh.ac.uk
W www.midchesh.ac.uk
Around ten thousand students.
Other Fine Art courses BTEC FD: Art and Design. BTEC Introductory Dip.: Art and Design. BTEC ND: Graphic Design; Photography. Edexcel Dip. in Foundation Studies: Art and Design. HND: Photography; Graphic Design. Various part-time courses.
Admissions Policy In general, a number of GCSEs at a certain grade or above, portfolio and interview.

Oldham College
Rochdale Road, Oldham, OL9 6AA
T 0161 6245214
F 0161 7854234
E info@oldham.ac.uk
W www.oldham.ac.uk
Contact Patricia Walkenden
Other Fine Art courses HND: Fine Art (two years); Multimedia (two years). ND: Art and Design (one year). Adult Access to Art and Design (two years).
Admissions Policy All students receive a one-to-one interview for advice and guidance with an experienced member of teaching staff. Students can apply at any time of year.

Runshaw College
Euxton Lane, Chorley, PR7 6AD
T 01772 642040
E justask@runshaw.ac.uk
W www.runshaw.ac.uk
Established as a sixth-form college in 1974.
Other Fine Art courses Foundation Studies: Art and Design. HND: Graphic Design; Fine Art.
Admissions Policy Apply through UCAS.

Southport College
Mornington Road, Southport, PR9 0TT
T 01704 500606
F 01704 392794
E guidance@southport-college.ac.uk
W www.southport-college.ac.uk
All foundation-degree programmes are offered in conjunction with either the University of Central Lancashire in Preston or Liverpool John Moores University. Around twelve thousand students (two thousand studying on full-time or modular courses).
Other Fine Art courses Dip. in Foundation Studies: Art and Design. ND: General Design and Art.
Admissions Policy Entry requirements for ND in General Design and Art: four GCSE passes at grade C or above (three if the portfolio presented at interview is exceptionally good). A good standard of Intermediate GNVQ in Art and Design is also acceptable. For Dip. in Foundation Studies (Art and Design), candidates are expected to: possess at least two AS levels supported by a minimum of three GCSEs grades A to C, or equivalent; exhibit a portfolio that shows a satisfactory standard of work, particularly in the area of objective drawing; project a high level of commitment and enthusiasm. If an applicant's work exhibits exceptional ability, the need for minimum number of formal academic qualifications may be waived. Mature students with a good portfolio may be accepted without academic qualifications.

St Helens College
Brook Street, St Helens, WA10 1PZ
T 01744 733766
F 01744 623400
E enquire@sthelens.ac.uk
W www.sthelens.ac.uk
Founded as the Gamble Institute in 1896
Degrees offered FdA: Photography and Digital Imaging; Multimedia Arts and Animation.
Other Fine Art courses Access, BTEC, HND and foundation courses in a wide range of subjects including calligraphy, ceramics, digital video production, painting and drawing, photography,

textiles, visual studies, oil and watercolours.
Admissions Policy For all HND and degree programmes: through UCAS. For all FE programmes (including part-time HNC): apply directly to the college's admissions unit.

St Martin's College
Bowerham Road, Lancaster
LA1 3JD
T 01524 384384
E admissions@ucsm.ac.uk
W www.ucsm.ac.uk
Founded in 1963 by the Church of England as a College of Education to train teachers. Over ten thousand students (28% being mature students).
Degrees offered BA (Hons)/Dip. of HE: Fine Art (part-time studies available).
Admissions Policy See website.

Stockport College of Further and Higher Education
Wellington Road South, Stockport
SK1 3UQ
T 0845 2303107
F 0161 9583452
E enquiries@stockport.ac.uk
W www.stockport.ac.uk
Founded in 1887. Has fifteen thousand students enrolled within twelve vocational areas offering qualifications from GCSE to degrees validated by local universities.
Degrees offered BA (Hons): Documentary and Fine Art Photography.
Admissions Policy Five GCSE passes and two A-levels or satisfactory completion of art and design foundation, Access course, BTEC ND or Advanced GNVQ.

University College Chester
Parkgate Road, Chester, CH1 4BJ
T 01244 375444
E enquiries@chester.ac.uk
W www.chester.ac.uk
Contact For undergraduate admissions, email enquiries@chester.ac.uk or telephone 01244 375444 / 392780. For postgraduate admissions, email postgrad@chester.ac.uk or telephone 01244 392780. For enquiries about course content, contact Pete Turnbull, Head of Fine Art.
Housed in a modern, custom-built facility, part of the main campus. Aims of the programme are to develop practical skills and creative potential relevant to fine-art practice, and to provide a theoretical framework that allows students to engage in informed discourse and constructive self-evaluation of work.
Degrees offered BA (Single and Combined Hons): Fine Art; New Media. PgDip/MA: Fine Art.
Admissions Policy See website.

University of Bolton
Deane Road, Bolton, BL3 5AB
T 01204 900600
E enquiries@bolton.ac.uk
W www.bolton.ac.uk
Contact Art and Design Admissions, phone 01204 903367.
Formerly known as Bolton Institute. Won university status in 2005. Of eight thousand students, approximately 72% are from the north-west.
Degrees offered BA (Hons): Art and Design; Textile/Surface Design.
Other Fine Art courses Art and design foundation.
Admissions Policy For BA Art and Design: art foundation course; or four GCSE passes and two A-levels including Art; or Intermediate or Advanced GNVQ in Art and Design or related subjects; or BTEC ND in Art and Design subjects; or Access to HE Programme in Art and Design subjects. For two-year foundation: four GCSEs at grade C or above. For one-year foundation: five GCSEs at grade C or above and one A-level, preferably in Art. Special consideration given to candidates over 21 without these qualifications.

University of Central Lancashire
Department of Art and Fashion, Victoria Building Room VB338, Preston, PR1 2HE
T 01772 893182
F 01772 892921
E omwells@uclan.ac.uk
W www.uclan.ac.uk/facs/destech/artfash/index.htm
Contact admissions@uclan.ac.uk
Degrees offered BA (Hons): Fine Art; Photography; Art and Design. MA: Fine Art: Archive Interventions; Fine Art: Curatorial Initiatives; Fine Art: Painting and Printmaking; Fine Art: Site and Place; Fine Art: Time-Based Media and Photography.

University of Salford
School of Art and Design, Irwell Valley Campus, Blandford Road, Salford, M6 6BD
T 0161 2952604
F 0161 2952605
E j.howarth@salford.ac.uk

W www.artdes.salford.ac.uk
Contact Julie Howarth
The BA (Hons) in Visual Arts offers a broad-based fine-art course, which encourages self-directed study in the studio across any chosen media. The students' individual personal development and study is supported by relevant theory, studio tutorials and peer learning events. There is an emphasis on contextualization and a high degree of freedom in the studio. The Masters in Contemporary Fine Art is located in studios alongside and there is a strong community of learning encouraged from foundation level through to postgraduate.
Degrees offered BA (Hons): Visual Arts. PgDip: Contemporary Fine Art. MA: Contemporary Fine Art.
Other Fine Art courses A range of continuing professional-development courses for postgraduates or mid-career practitioners.
Admissions Policy Normal entry requirements: foundation diploma in art and design or 160 tariff points. All applicants are interviewed. Mature students welcomed. At postgraduate level applicants will normally hold an upper second class degree with honours. However, all applicants are interviewed with portfolios.

Wirral Metropolitan College

Conway Park Campus, Europa Boulevard
Conway Park, Birkenhead, CH41 4NT
T 0151 5517777
F 0151 5517001
W www.wmc.ac.uk
Degrees offered BA (Hons): Fine Art (full- or part-time).
Other Fine Art courses Foundation diploma: Art and Design. BTEC FD: Art and Design. BTEC: Introduction to Art, Design and Media. BTEC ND: Art and Design.

Scotland

Duncan of Jordanstone College of Art and Design

School of Fine Art, University of Dundee
Perth Road, Dundee, DD1 4HT
T 01382 343291
F 01382 200983
E j.a.ritchie@dundee.ac.uk
W www.dundee.ac.uk/fineart/
Contact Tracey Drummond
College founded in 1892 and merged with the university in 1994. Fine Art is one of four schools

in the faculty (the others being Architecture, Design and Television & Imaging). Fine Art students work across the full range of contemporary media, including painting, sculpture, printmaking, photography, video and digital, performance, installation and artists' publication. Staff are all practising artists working at national and international levels.
Degrees offered BA (Hons): Fine Art; Art and Philosophy; Contemporary Practices. Also MFA programmes.
Admissions Policy See website for details of level 1 (general course) and level 2 entry requirements and dates of application.

Edinburgh College of Art

74 Lauriston Place, Edinburgh
EH3 9DF
T 0131 2216000
F 0131 2216000
E m.wood@eca.ac.uk
W www.eca.ac.uk
The College traces its routes back to 1760, the oldest established drawing academy in Britain. Founded on its present site in 1907 in a beaux arts' building. The building includes a Sculpture Court built on Palladian principles and has a complete cast (made in situ) of the Parthenon Frieze. Alumni include: Dame Elizabeth Blackadder, Sir Eduardo Paolozzi, Alan Davie, John Bellany, Sir Basil Spence, John Arden, Sir Nicholas Grimshaw and Barbara Rae.
Degrees offered BA (Hons): Painting; Design and Applied Arts; Visual Communication; Sculpture. BA: Combined Studies (part-time).
Other Fine Art courses ECA Summer School Centre of Continuing Studies offers part-time courses.
Admissions Policy Entry through UCAS for all full-time undergraduate courses. Interview and portfolio information is specific to different courses.

Glasgow School of Art

167 Renfrew Street, Glasgow, G3 6RQ
T 0141 3534500
F 0141 3534746
E info@gsa.ac.uk
W www.gsa.ac.uk
Founded in 1845 as one of the first government schools of design. Now a leading institution for the study and advancement of fine art, design and architecture. International community of over 1,600 (primarily undergraduate) students studying

in ten specialist fine art or design departments, or within the Mackintosh School of Architecture. Growing postgraduate community studying for taught and research degrees. The history of the GSA is inextricably linked to Charles Rennie Mackintosh, who graduated from the School in 1896 and went on to design the School of Art building. Graduates include the Turner Prize winners Simon Starling and Douglas Gordon and the Beck's Futures Winners Roderick Buchanan, Toby Paterson and Rosalind Nashashibi.

Degrees offered BA (Hons): Fine Art (Painting and Printmaking, Photography, Sculpture and Environmental Art); Design (Ceramics, Interior Design, Silversmithing and Jewellery, Textiles, Visual Communication); Product Design; Product Design Engineering. MA: Fine Art; 2D/3D Motion Graphics; Design Textiles as Fashion; Art, Design and Architecture in Education; Architecture; Research. Mphil. PhD.

Other Fine Art courses Continuing education programme including portfolio preparation, weekend and evening classes, summer schools and Easter vacation courses in art design and architecture.

Admissions Policy Entry through UCAS for all undergraduate programmes. Postgraduate applications direct to the School. Scholarships available.

Heriot-Watt University

Edinburgh, EH14 4AS
T 0131 4495111
E edu.liaison@hw.ac.uk
W www.hw.ac.uk
More than 6,300 students on campus in Scotland plus over 9,500 on external programmes in 140 countries worldwide. The eighth oldest HE institution in the UK. Established by Royal Charter in 1966, its origins date back to 1821 through the School of Arts of Edinburgh.

Degrees offered BA (Hons): Design for Textiles. Taught courses at postgraduate level are either MA, PgDip or PCert courses.

Other Fine Art courses Part-time study is available.

Admissions Policy For undergraduate: through UCAS. For PgDip: applicants need a first degree.

Robert Gordon University

Gray's School of Art, Garthdee Road, Aberdeen AB10 7QD
T 01224 263600
F 01224 263636
E a.young@rgu.ac.uk
W www2.rgu.ac.uk
Gray's School of Science and Art was founded in 1885. It later merged with Robert Gordon's Technical College and became the Robert Gordon University in 1992

Degrees offered BA (Hons): Design and Craft; Fine Art; Design for Digital Media. MA: Fine Art.

Admissions Policy For admission requirements for specific courses see website.

Studio Art School

St Leonard's House, Lasswade Road, Loanhead EH20 9SD
T 0131 4402754
E info@studioartschool.co.uk
W www.studioartschool.co.uk
Contact Arlene Stewart
The Studio Art School was established in 2004 and provides practical, online art and design tuition for those who wish to progress to degree level programmes at art collge or university and those who wish to develop their skills through certified and non-certified vocational courses. Online teaching and learning environment allows students complete flexiblity in their studies.

Other Fine Art courses City & Guilds level 1: Drawing & Painting; Introduction to Sketchbooks; Introduction to Fashion Design and Illustration. City & Guilds level 2: Creative Sketchbooks; Fashion Design and Illustration; Drawing & Painting; Art Appreciation. Preparation for Higher Education: Undergraduate Bridging Course. Level 3 Diploma in Foundation Studies: Art & Design. Pre-Masters Diploma in Art and Design.

Admissions Policy There are no specific entry requirements although the School offers a free portfolio appraisal and study advice service, 'Which Course?'.

UHI Millennium Institute

Executive Office, Ness Walk, Inverness, IV3 5SQ
T 01463 279000
F 01463 279001
E EO@uhi.ac.uk
W www.uhi.ac.uk
Granted status of HE Institute in 2001, providing university-level courses throughout the Highlands and Islands of Scotland. Partnership of fourteen colleges and research institutions in the region, coordinated by UHI executive office based in Inverness.

Degrees offered BA: Creative Media; Fine Art.

Other Fine Art courses HND: Art and Design. HNC: Fine Art.

University of Edinburgh

History of Art, 20 Chambers Street
Edinburgh, EH1 1JZ
T 0131 6504124
F 0131 6508019
E histart@ed.ac.uk
W www.arts.ed.ac.uk/fineart
Contact Lisa Kendall (Arts Admissions)
Founded in 1880, History of Art at the University
of Edinburgh has the oldest chair of Art History in
Britain. A leading centre for the discipline, in a city
with world-class art collections.
Degrees offered MA: Fine Art (five years), jointly
run with Edinburgh College of Art.
Admissions Policy UCAS requirements –
minimum BBB at 'A' level. Portfolio to be
submitted to Edinburgh College of Art in January.

University of Paisley

Ayr Campus, Beechgrove, Ayr
KA8 0SR
T 01292 886388
F 01292 886387
E william.strachan@paisley.ac.uk
Contact William Strachan
Degrees offered BA (Hons): Digital Art. Aims to
unite 'traditional' art skills to skills in digital
technologies. The routes to specialism are digital
media, creative video and filmmaking, and
animation. Some academic study as well as work
in art and digital contexts.
Admissions Policy Entry requirements involve
three parts: (1) three SQA Highers (BBC) (or
equivalents), including English; (2) an art and
design portfolio; (3) a brief interview based on (2).

South-east

Bedford College

Cauldwell Street, Bedford, MK42 9AH
T 01234 291000
F 01234 342674
E info@bedford.ac.uk.
W www.bedford.ac.uk
Contact Enquiries and Admissions at Bedford
College, FREEPOST BF 356, Bedford MK42 9BR,
or phone 0800 0740234.
Courses for all levels of ability, both in art and
design and in the more specialist disciplines of
fine art, graphic design, multimedia, three-
dimensional design and textiles. Provides practical
sessions and projects to help develop artistic skills,
and academic study into the social, cultural and
historical development of chosen media.

Other Fine Art courses GNVQ in Art & Design
Level 1 & 2; BTEC Diploma in Foundation Studies;
BTEC National Diploma in Fine Art; BTEC
National Diploma in Photography; BTEC National
Diploma in Textiles; BTEC HNC/D in Fine Art;
BTEC HNC/D in Textiles.
Admissions Policy For requirements see website.
Students with no previous qualifications can take
an Access to Art and Design course.

Brighton University

68 Grand Parade, Brighton, BN2 2JY
T 01273 600900
E postmaster@brighton.ac.uk
W www.brighton.ac.uk
Brighton School of Art opened in the Royal
Pavilion Kitchens in 1859. It merged with Brighton
Technical College in 1970 to form Brighton
Polytechnic. The Polytechnic became Brighton
University in 1992. The School of Arts and
Communication encompasses painting, sculpture,
printmaking, critical fine-art practice, dance,
music and theatre with visual practice, graphic
design, illustration and editorial photography.
With 30 staff and 400 students; the school has an
international profile and student exchanges links
are established with art schools in Bordeaux,
Limoges, Chicago, Kansas, New York and Warsaw.
Degrees offered BA (Hons): Art and Design;
Illustration; Painting; Printmaking; Sculpture.
MA/PgDip: Fine Art Printmaking; Printmaking
and Professional Practice; Fine Art; Photography.
New route PhD: Art and Design.
Other Fine Art courses HNC and HND: Fine Art.
For part-time evening and Saturday classes contact
arthouse@brighton.ac.uk or 01273 643015.
Admissions Policy UCAS routes A or B.
Candidates are interviewed and should bring a
portfolio of work. For MA courses apply by 1 July.

Buckinghamshire Chilterns University College

Faculty of Design, Queen Alexandra Road
High Wycombe, HP11 2JZ
T 01494 603054
F 01494 461196
E desenq@bcuc.ac.uk
W www.bcuc.ac.uk
There has been a School of Art and Design in High
Wycombe for over 100 years. Over 1,300 students
studying at all levels from Foundation to PhD.
Degrees offered BA (Hons): Fine Art (full- and
part-time); Textiles and Surface Design. MA: Art
and Design: Illustration; Ceramics with Glass;
Printmaking.

Other Fine Art courses Edexcel Dip. in Foundation Studies: Art and Design. Part-time drawing course.

Canterbury Christchurch University College

Department of Media and Art, North Holmes Road, Canterbury, CT1 1QU
T 01227 767700
F 01227 782888 / 470442
E M.S.Holt@cant.ac.uk
W www.cant.ac.uk
Contact Department of Admissions,
Founded by the Church of England in 1962, built on what was the old orchard ground of St Augustine's Abbey. Welcomes students from all faiths and none. The Department of Media and Art is located on the Canterbury campus.
Degrees offered BA: Digital Culture, Arts and Media; Ceramics; Fine Art; Painting; Sculpture. Also teacher training with art and design. MA: Ceramics; Fine Art.
Admissions Policy All college students must be at least 17 years of age by 1 October in the year of admission and fulfil the minimum entry requirements. Offers will be made in terms of grades rather than points. Candidates who have not had the opportunity to take a recognized qualification in key skills will not be disadvantaged in terms of their application. See website.

Northbrook College Sussex

Littlehampton Road, Goring-by-Sea, Worthing BN12 6NU
T 01903 606060
F 01903 606073
E enquiries@nbcol.ac.uk
W www.northbrook.ac.uk
Formed in 1987 when three local colleges merged, including the West Sussex College of Design.
Degrees offered BA (Hons): Fine Art (Painting); Fine Art (Sculpture); Fine Art (Printmaking). All courses run full- and part-time.
Other Fine Art courses Cert./Dip. of HE: Fine Art.
Admissions Policy Applicants should have two A-levels/BTEC ND/GNVQ. All applicants will be interviewed with a portfolio that should include drawing and demonstrate creative, technical, written and visual abilities.

Oxford and Cherwell College

Oxpens Road, Oxford, OX1 1SA
T 01865 550550
F 01865 248871
E enquiries@oxford.occ.ac.uk
W www.occ.ac.uk

Degrees offered BA (Hons): Graphic Design and Illustration; Fine Art.
Other Fine Art courses Foundation Studies: Art and Design. HND: Graphic Design; Illustration; Advertising and Multimedia.
Admissions Policy See website.

Oxford Brookes University

Department of Arts, Richard Hamilton Building, Headington Campus, Oxford, OX3 0BP
T 01865 484995
F 01865 484952
E lisa.atkinson@brookes.ac.uk
W www.ah.brookes.ac.uk/art
Contact Lisa Atkinson
Degrees offered BA (Hons): Fine Art. MA: Contemporary Arts and Music; Social Sculpture; Composition and Sonic Art; Contemporary Art.
Other Fine Art courses Foundation Diploma in Art and Design
Admissions Policy CCD at A level (or equivalent) and successful completion of foundation or access course in Art and Design is normally required. Applicants with alternative qualifications welcomed. UCAS routes A and B.

Oxford University

University Offices, Wellington Square Oxford, OX1 2JD
T 01865 270000
E undergraduate.admissions@admin.ox.ac.uk
W www.ox.ac.uk
Oxford is the oldest university in the English-speaking world and lays claim to nine centuries of continuous existence. More than 130 nationalities represented in student population of over sixteen thousand.
Degrees offered BFA: Fine Art. MFA: Fine Art.
Admissions Policy Undergraduate: UCAS system. All candidates are required to submit a portfolio of their work (see the Ruskin School of Drawing and Fine Art prospectus for further information). The School is not looking for a particular style or skill, although it is generally felt that a foundation course can be beneficial to a candidate. Should be a sufficient amount of work to demonstrate real commitment and interests, with a good selection of drawings. Must be sent or delivered in a strong standard type portfolio (A1). Postgraduate: Entry requirements as outlined in Applications and Admissions procedure (completion of a bachelor's degree with a first or upper second-class honours or the international equivalent). Additional: Applicants will be expected to have completed or

be about to complete a good Honours Degree which would normally be in Fine Art.

Reigate School of Art, Design and Media (East Surrey College)

Gatton Point North, Claremont Road, Redhill
RH1 2JX
T 01737 788391
F 01737 788392
E afowler@esc.ac.uk
W www.esc.ac.uk
Contact Allison Fowle (Art School Administrator).
Celebrated its 110th anniversary in 2005
Other Fine Art courses Level 4 BTEC HND/HNC:
Fine Art; Graphic Design and Illustration; Digital
Photography; Textile Design; Modelmaking and
Special Effects; Lettering, Calligraphy and Heraldic
Art. Level 3 BTEC ND: Fine Art; Graphic Design;
Photography; Fashion and Clothing; Multimedia.
Level 3 BTEC foundation diploma: Art and Design.
Admissions Policy For ND: four GCSEs, grade C
and above. For HND: ND in Art or A-level Art.
Mature students – acceptable portfolio.

Southampton Solent University

East Park Terrace, Southampton
SO14 OYN
T 023 80319000
F 023 80334161
E enquiries@solent.ac.uk
W www.solent.ac.uk
Origins can be traced back to a private school of art
founded in 1856. More recently Southampton
Institute became Southampton Solent University
in July 2005, with 16,000 students. Also at the
University is the Millais Gallery, which celebrated
its 10 year anniversary in 2006. The Millais
Gallery is situated on the main campus at
Southampton Solent University in the John Everett
Millais Building. It is a public art gallery
committed to the exhibition of mainly
contemporary visual arts which addresses issues of
relevance to culturally diverse communities locally,
regionally, nationally and internationally.
Degrees offered BA (Hons): Fine Art; Fine Arts
Valuation; Fine Art Media; Illustration;
Photography; Animation; Computer & Video
Games; Digital Media; Performance; Comedy,
Writing & Performance; Design Studies; Graphic
Design; Multimedia Design; Product Design &
Marketing; Film Studies; TV & Video Production.
Foundation: Art, Design & Media.
Admissions Policy Admission to all undergraduate
courses is via UCAS.

University College Chichester

Bishop Otter Campus, College Lane, Chichester
PO19 6PE
T 01243 816000
E C.Ferguson@ucc.ac.uk
W www.ucc.ac.uk/arts/fineart/index.html
Contact Admissions Office at
admissions@ucc.ac.uk or 01243 816002
Bishop Otter College was established in 1839 to
train schoolmasters. In 1946 Bognor Regis
Emergency Training College was founded in 'an
emergency' effort to staff the nation's schools in
the aftermath of the Second World War. In 1977
the two colleges merged and became known as the
West Sussex Institute of Higher Education. In
1999 it became University College Chichester.
Broad artistic interdisciplinarity welcomed as part
of fine-art practice.
Degrees offered BA (Hons): Fine Art. Minor: New
Media Arts. MA: Fine Art.
Admissions Policy Qualifications recommended:
Art Foundation Course with Pass. Basic
Requirement: Advanced GNVQ Art with Merit, or
Pass in approved Access course, or 2–3 A-level
passes, including Art A-level grade C/B, or
equivalent mix of A-levels and AS levels, or
equivalent. Applicants must also present a
portfolio.

University College for the Creative Arts at Maidstone

Maidstone Campus, Oakwood Park
Maidstone, ME16 8AG
T 01622 620000
F 01622 621100
E info@ucreative.ac.uk
W www.ucreative.ac.uk
Formed through the merger of the Surrey Institute
of Art & Design, University College and the Kent
Institute of Art & Design. As well as Maidstone,
there are four other campus sites: Canterbury
(New Dover Road, Canterbury, CT1 3AN; T 01227
817302); Epsom (Ashley Road, Epsom, KT18 5BE:
T 01372 728811); Farnham (Falkner Road,
Farnham, GU9 7DS; T 01252 722441); Rochester
(Fort Pitt, Rochester, ME1 1DZ; T 01634 888702).
Degrees offered BA (Hons): 3D Design: Ceramics
or Glass or Metalwork & Jewellery; Animation;
Applied Arts; Arts & Media; Design, Branding &
Marketing; Digital 3D Design; Digital Screen Arts;
Fashion; Film Production; Fine Art; Graphic
Communication; Graphic Design; Illustration;
Interior Design; Modelmaking; Photography;
Photography & Media Arts; Design or Graphic

Design; Printmaking; Product Design; Silversmithing, Goldsmithing & Jewellery; Textile Design; Video & Photography; Video Media Production. MA: Animation; Artists' Film, Video & Photography; Contemporary Crafts (Ceramics, Glass, Jewellery; Textiles); Creative Enterprise; Curating Contemporary Craft; Design; Fashion; Fashion; Film & Video; Fine Art; Graphic Design & Communication; Graphic Design & New Media; Interior Design; Museums & Contemporary Curating; Photography; Spatial Practices: Art, Architecture & Performance; Sustainable Product Design; Urban Design.
Other Fine Art courses A wide range of foundation, access and part-time courses (including evening, and summer school courses) are available.

University of Kent
The Registry, Canterbury
CT2 7NZ
T 01227 764000
E recruitment@kent.ac.uk
W www.kent.ac.uk
The school consists of thirty-three academic staff, supported in their work by two administrators, four secretaries and six technicians. Over eight hundred students from the UK, Europe and beyond. Many programmes involve practical creative elements, some involve work placements, and some allow students to spend a year abroad, in Europe or the USA.
Degrees offered BA (Hons): Contemporary Art; Fine Art (one year top-up at South Kent College).
Other Fine Art courses HND: Fine Art.

University of Portsmouth
University House, Winston Churchill Avenue
Portsmouth, PO1 2UP
T 023 92848484
F 023 92843082
E info.centre@port.ac.uk
W www.port.ac.uk
Inaugurated in 1992. The former polytechnic grew from the Portsmouth and Gosport School of Science and Arts, founded in 1869
Degrees offered MA: Art, Design and Media.
Other Fine Art courses Dip. in Foundation Studies: Art and Design; Art, Design and Photography.
Admissions Policy Applications through UCAS where applicable. All other applications by university application form.

University of Reading
Department of Fine Art, 1 Earley Gate
Reading, RG6 6AT
T 0118 3788050 / 3788051
F 0118 9262667
E FineArt@reading.ac.uk
W www.rdg.ac.uk/fineart/index.htm
Contact Jean Butler
Constituted by Royal Charter in 1926. Has its origins in the union of the Schools of Art and Science in 1892, forming a university extension college of Oxford ten years later. Distinguished visitors and teachers include Walter Crane, Roger Fry, Robert Gibbings, Walter Sickert, Claude Rogers, Sir Terry Frost and Martin Froy.
Degrees offered Four-year BA (Hons): Art (also available as a joint subject with Psychology, Philosophy, History of Art and Film, Theatre and Television). Three year BA (Hons): Fine Art. MFA: Fine Art.
Admissions Policy For BA: UCAS route A. For foundation, BTEC or GNVQ: UCAS route B. For MFA: application forms available from university.

Winchester School of Art
University of Southampton, Park Avenue
Winchester, SO23 8DL
T 023 80596900
F 023 80596901
E ij@soton.ac.uk
W www.wsa.soton.ac.uk
Originally founded in 1872, Winchester School of Art joined the University of Southampton in 1996. Offers opportunitites for interdesciplinary research and study combined with excellent facilities.
Degrees offered BA (Hons): Graphic Arts (pathways in Graphic Design, Advertising Design Management, Photography and Digital Media, Digital Animation); Fine Art (pathways in Painting, Printmaking, Sculpture, New Media); Textiles, Fashion and Fibre (pathways in Textile Design, Fashion, Textile Art); Heritage Studies: Museums & Galleries. MA: Fine Art (pathways in Painting, Sculpture, Printmaking, Fine Art by Project); Design (pathways in Fashion Management; Fashion Design; Fashion and Design Journalism; Communication Design; Advertising Design; Design Management; Textile Design; Textile and Fibre Art); Museums and Galleries (pathways in Culture, Collections and Communications; Collections Management; History of Textiles and Dress; Interpreting Historic Interiors; Access and Learning; Archives in

Museums); Textile Conservation; Organics Conservation. MRes Programmes. MPhil and PhD opportunities. Note that the only studio-based part-time course now on offer is the MA Fine Art. The Textile Conservation, Organics Conservation and Museums and Galleries programmes can all be taken on a part-time or full-time basis.
Admissions Policy Refer to website for latest information.

South-west

Arts Institute at Bournemouth
Wallisdown, Poole, BH12 5HH
T 01202 533011
F 01202 537729
E general@aib.ac.uk
W www.aib.ac.uk
Contact Alison Aspery
Established in 1883.
Degrees offered BA (Hons): Fine Art (full- and part-time). FdA: Printmaking (part-time).
Other Fine Art courses NCFE Cert.: Art and Design (part-time). Institute Cert.: Fine Art; Life Drawing; Printmaking (part-time plus short Easter and summer courses).
Admissions Policy Full-time: through UCAS. Part-time: direct to institute (forms available through Short Course Department).

Bath School of Art and Design
Bath Spa University College, Sion Hill, Lansdown Bath, BA1 5SF
T 01225 875875
F 01225 875666
E enquiries@bathspa.ac.uk
W www.bathspa.ac.uk/schools/art-and-design
Contact enquiries@bathspa.ac.uk
Founded in 1898, becoming Bath College of Higher Education in 1975 and granted degree-awarding powers in 1992. Became Bath Spa University in 1999. About 4,500 students in total.
Degrees offered BA (Hons): Fine Art (Painting/Sculpture/Media); Creative Arts. MA: Fine Art. PgCert: Fine Art. PgDip: Fine Art.
Admissions Policy For undergraduate courses, a foundation course in art and design or appropriate BTEC course plus five subjects at GCSE level (or one subject at GCE/VCE A-level with three different subjects at GCSE level; or other qualifications considered equivalent). If applying to study Art and Design, looking above all for creative ability and suitability for chosen course. Entry also possible via Access courses.

Bristol School of Art, Media and Design
University of the West of England, Bower Ashton Campus, Kennel Lodge Road, Bristol, BS3 2JT
T 0117 3284716
F 0117 3284745
E amd.enquiries@uwe.ac.uk
W www.uwe.ac.uk
Founded in 1853. More than 1,600 students studying at all levels.
Degrees offered BA (Hons): Art and Visual Culture; Drawing and Applied Arts; Fine Art; Fine Art in Context; Illustration; Illustration with Animation; Textile Design. MA: Fine Art (Research); Illustration (Research); Illustration with Animation (Research); Interactive Media; Interactive Media (Research); Multidisciplinary Printmaking. PhD and New Route PhDs.
Other Fine Art courses Foundation Studies: Art and Design. Short courses: Animation; Applied Arts; Computing for Artists; Drawing; Photography; Printmaking. Also runs Easter courses, evening classes, Saturday workshops and summer schools.

Dartington College of Arts
Dartington Hall Estate, Dartington, Totnes TQ9 6EJ
T 01803 862224
F 01803 861666
E enquiries@dartington.ac.uk
W www.dartington.ac.uk
Contact Margaret Eggleton
Founded in 1961, having evolved as part of a rural regeneration experiment. Situated on a private estate with approximately 850 acres on the outskirts of Totnes in South Devon. Has an international reputation for experimental arts practices within a close-knit community of 500+ undergraduates and 100+ postgraduate students. Degrees are validated in partnership with the University of Plymouth. Alumni include Josie Lawrence, Verity Sharp, Matthew Linley, Marcus Davey and Matthew Strachan.
Degrees offered BA (Hons): Fine Art (Contemporary Practices); Fine Art (with Digital Arts Practices/ Choreographic Practices/ Cultural Entrepreneurship/ Textual Practices/ Theatre Practices/ Sound Practices/ Community Practices); Art and Performance; Art and Performance (with Digital Arts Practices/ Choreographic Practices/ Cultural Entrepreneurship/ Textual Practices/ Theatre Practices/ Sound Practices/ Community Practices).

Admissions Policy A foundation course in art and design and/or Art A-level/AS or vocational A-level (160 UCAS points). Minimum 140 points from six- or twelve-unit awards. Equivalent experience also taken into consideration. Selection based on presentation of a portfolio and interview.

Exeter College
Victoria House, 33–36 Queen Street, Exeter
EX4 3SR
T 01392 205232
E admissions@exe-coll.ac.uk
W www.exe-coll.ac.uk
The tertiary college for the City of Exeter and surrounding parts of Mid-, East and South Devon. Victoria Yard Studios is the college's centre for higher-level study in art and design. The fully equipped premises have light and spacious studios, facilities for printmaking, photography, wood, metal workshops and IT. Nearby are various gallery venues including the Phoenix Arts Centre and Spacex Gallery.
Degrees offered BA (Hons): Fine Art.
Other Fine Art courses Foundation Studies: Art and Design. HND: Three-Dimensional Applied Arts.

Filton College
Filton Avenue, Bristol, BS34 7AT
T 0117 9092324
F 0117 9312233
E admin@filton.ac.uk
W www.filton.ac.uk
Large range of art and design courses across three sites: Bristol School of Art in the city centre; Western Institute of Specialist Education (WISE); and Filton College at Filton, north Bristol.
Other Fine Art courses HND: Fine Art; Graphic Design. Bristol School of Art offers a wide range of open-access part-time courses (varying length across the year): Life Drawing; Ceramics; Painting; Stained Glass; Jewellery; Enamelling; Printmaking; Sculpture; Digital Imaging.
Admissions Policy For HND: apply through UCAS. For other courses: apply directly. Phone, email or fax the college for further information.

Plymouth College of Art and Design
Tavistock Place, Plymouth, PL11 2QP
T 01752 203434
F 01752 203444
E enquiries@pcad.ac.uk
W www.pcad.ac.uk
Contact Jean Edmonds

Originally founded as an art school in the nineteenth century and now one of the few remaining specialist art colleges in the country providing both FE and HE. Composed of four subject areas: Three-Dimensional Design; Media and Photography; Design Communications; and Fine Art, Diagnostic Drawing and Painting. The Viewpoint Gallery allows students and local artists to exhibit work.
Degrees offered BA (Hons): Applied Arts; Fine Art.
Other Fine Art courses FdA: Fine Art; Applied Arts; Spatial Design. ABC Dip. in Foundation Studies. BTEC ND: Fine Art.
Admissions Policy For all HE courses: through UCAS. Selected applicants will then be invited to attend an interview and present a portfolio of work. For FE courses: apply direct to the college.

Somerset College of Arts and Technology
Wellington Road, Taunton
TA1 5AX
T 01823 366366
E enquiries@somerset.ac.uk
W www.somerset.ac.uk
Contact Admissions Office
Formed in 1974 from the Taunton Technical College and Somerset College of Art, institutions with histories going back over a century.
Degrees offered Fashion; Fashion and Textiles; Interior Textiles; Surface Design; Interior Textiles and Surface Design; Graphic Design (top-up year); Packaging Design (top-up year); Advertising Design (top-up year); Fine Art (top-up year; awaiting validation). Foundation: Graphic Design; Fine Art; Three-Dimensional Design (Product); Interior Spatial Design.
Admissions Policy UCAS routes A and B. Art-related ND, Advanced GNVQ, A-levels or foundation year. Five GCSEs grade C or above (including English Language). Top-ups require relevant art foundation or HND.

Swindon College
Department of Fine Art, School of Art and Design, Phoenix Building, North Star Avenue, Swindon
SN2 1DY
T 01793 498989
E fineart@swindon-college.ac.uk
W www.scsa.swindon-college.ac.uk
Contact Swindon College Student services on 01793 498308 / admissions@swindon-college.ac.uk
Offers a wide range of art and design programmes at HND, BA and MA levels.

Degrees offered BA (Hons) Fine Art: Drawing for Fine Art Practice.
Other Fine Art courses Foundation Diploma: Art and Design; Access Art and Design.
Admissions Policy UCAS routes A or B. Students should have: Foundation or Access (Art and Design); or ND (Art and Design); or two A-levels and five GCSEs at grade C or above; or entry to year two with HND in appropriate subject; or other equivalent qualifications or experience.

University College Falmouth

Woodlane, Falmouth, TR11 4RH
T 01326 211077
F 01326 213880
E admissions@falmouth.ac.uk
W www.falmouth.ac.uk
Founded as an art school in 1902. Now a leading specialist university college for art, design and media at undergraduate and postgraduate level, having been granted the power to award its own degrees in 2004. An award-winning design centre and broadcast-industry-standard media centre at Tremough in Penryn complement the College's specialist studios in Falmouth.
Degrees offered BA (Hons): Fine Art. MA: Contemporary Visual Arts. (Full- and part-time.)
Other Fine Art courses Dip. in Foundation Studies (full- or part-time): Art and Design. Annual printmaking summer school.
Admissions Policy For BA: foundation, ND, AVCE/Advanced GNVQ, qualifications or experience. For MA: degree or relevant qualifications or experience.

University of Bath

Claverton Down, Bath, BA2 7AY
T 01225 383019
E admissions@bath.ac.uk
W www.bath.ac.uk
Received Royal Charter in 1966 but can trace its history back to the Bristol Trade School founded in 1856.
Degrees offered FdA: Digital Media Arts (Multimedia); Digital Media Arts (Moving Image Production).
Other Fine Art courses Workshops include: Contemporary Ceramics; Painting in the Twenty-First Century; Drawing in the Twenty-First Century; Contemporary Flat Glass; Digital Video; Ceramics: Throwing on the Wheel; Ceramics: Figurative Sculpture; Ceramics: Raku Digital Art.
Admissions Policy For foundation degree programmes: apply through UCAS. Minimum

entry requirements will normally be at least four GCSE passes (at grades C or above), including Maths and English together with one or more of the following: UCAS tariff of 80; one pass at Advanced GCE level; one pass in a six-unit vocational A-level; a broader base of studies incorporating AS level; success in an Access to HE course; formally assessed outcomes acquired by dint of APEL. There may be additional entry requirements for each specific foundation degree programme.

University of Gloucestershire

Pittville Campus, Albert Road
Cheltenham, GL52 3JG
T 01242 714929
F 01242 714949
W www.glos.ac.uk
Contact Bob Davison
Art education began in Cheltenham 150 years ago and became part of the University of Gloucestershire in 2001. Pittville Campus specializes in courses in art, media and design. The fine-art courses build on strong theoretical and practical foundations, incorporating new media and contemporary practices.
Degrees offered Fine Art: Painting and Drawing; Fine Art: Photography.
Admissions Policy Applicants interviewed through UCAS routes A and B would normally have completed a foundation course or equivalent.

University of Plymouth

Faculty of Arts, 2 Endsleigh Place
Plymouth, PL4 8AA
T 01752 238106
F 01752 238102
E arts.admissions@plymouth.ac.uk
W www.plymouth.ac.uk
Founded as Exeter School of Art over 150 years ago. Formerly on Exeter campus of the university but moved to Plymouth in 2007
Degrees offered BA (Hons): Fine Art (full- and part-time). MA: Fine Art (full- and part-time).
Admissions Policy For BA (Hons): through UCAS routes A and B. Portfolio required.

Weston College

Knightstone Road, Weston-super-Mare
BS23 2AL
T 01934 411411
F 01934 411410
E enquiries@weston.ac.uk
W www.weston.ac.uk

Can trace its origins to private drawing and painting classes provided by Henry Stacy in Oriel Terrace in 1859. The School of Art was opened in 1865 and since 1993 the college has been an autonomous public body.
Degrees offered BA (Hons): Fine Art (in association with Bath Spa University College).
Other Fine Art courses HND: Fine Art (three years part-time or two years full-time).

Wales

Cardiff School of Art and Design
University of Wales Institute Cardiff
Howard Gardens, Cardiff, CF24 0SP
T 029 20416647
F 029 20416944
E artdesign@uwic.ac.uk
W www.uwic.ac.uk/csad
There has been a college of art in Cardiff for over 130 years. School located on two campuses. The Howard Gardens campus in the city centre houses the Howard Gardens Gallery, a public gallery and community resource with a continuous programme of curated and touring exhibitions. The second campus is at Llandaff on the northern edge of the city centre, with purpose-built studios and a student learning resource.
Degrees offered BA (Hons): Art and Theory Matrix; Broadcast Media & Popular Culture; Ceramics; Contemporary Textile Practice; Design for Interactive Media; Fine Art; Graphic Communication; Interior Architecutre. MA: Ceramics; Fine Art. Foundation Dip.: Art & Design.
Other Fine Art courses Cardiff Open Art School: Evening classes and short summer courses (Painting; Life Drawing; Printmaking; Photoshop).
Admissions Policy Refer to website.

North Wales School of Art and Design
North East Wales Institute of Higher Education, Regent Street, Wrexham, LL11 1PF
T 01978 293502
F 01978 310060
E d.loonie@newi.ac.uk
W www.newi.ac.uk/nwsad
Founded as School of Science and Art in 1887. Full member of the University of Wales since 2002.
Degrees offered BA (Hons): Applied Arts; Fine Art. MA: Animation; Contemporary Applied Arts.

Swansea Institute
Faculty of Art & Design, Dynevor Centre for Art,
Design and Media, De-La-Beche Street
Swansea, SA1 3EU
T 01792 481285
F 01792 470385
E artanddesign@sihe.ac.uk
W www.sihe.ac.uk
A member of the University of Wales. Faculty of Art and Design, founded over 150 years ago, is now housed in a new multi-million pound city-centre complex.
Degrees offered BA (Hons): Design for Advertising; Fine Art (Ceramics); Fine Art (Combined Media); Fine Art (Painting and Drawing); General Illustration; Graphic Design. Joint Honours: Art History; Art History and Visual Arts Practice; Photography in the Arts; Photojournalism; Video; Documentary Video; Video Arts; Surface Pattern Design (Contemporary Applied Arts Practice); Surface Pattern Design (Textiles for Fashion); Surface Pattern Design (Textiles for Interiors). MA: Fine Art; Photography; Visual Arts Enterprise; Visual Communication. MPhil and PhD research degrees.

Trinity College
School of Creative Arts and Humanities
Carmarthen, SA31 3EP
T 01267 676767
F 01267 676766
E registry@trinity-cm.ac.uk
W www.trinity-cm.ac.uk
Degrees offered BA (Hons): Fine Art.
Admissions Policy Via UCAS.

University of Glamorgan
Pontypridd, CF37 1DL
T 0800 716925
F 01443 822055
E enquiries@glam.ac.uk
W www.glam.ac.uk
Over twenty thousand students.
Degrees offered BA (Hons): Art Practice; Media Studies and Art Practice. MA: Art in the Community.
Other Fine Art courses Foundation certificate: Visual and Community Art.

University of Wales, Aberystwyth
School of Art, Buarth Mawr, Aberystwyth
SY23 1NG
T 01970 622460
F 01970 622461
E cpw@aber.ac.uk
W www.aber.ac.uk/art

Contact Chris Webster
Founded in 1872. The first university institution to be established in Wales. Over 7,000 registered students, including over 1,100 postgraduates across 18 academic departments. The School of Art is unusual in the traditional British university context as one of the few places where art practice can be studied along with art history or another subject as part of a university degree.
Degrees offered BA (Hons): Art; Art History; Art with Art History. MA: Art; Art and Art History. MPhil and PhD: Art; Art History. Art Practice may be taken in Drawing and Painting, Printmaking, Photography, and Book Illustration with Typography.
Other Fine Art courses Degree courses also available on a part-time basis.
Admissions Policy Entry onto all art practice courses will only be considered in conjunction with the submission of a portfolio.

University of Wales, Bangor
Bangor, LL57 2DG
T 01248 382016 / 382017
E Admissions@bangor.ac.uk
W www.bangor.ac.uk
Opened in 1884 in an old coaching inn with fifty-eight students and ten members of staff. In 1893 it became one of the three constituent colleges of the University of Wales.
Degrees offered HE Cert. in Fine Art (part-time).
Other Fine Art courses Part time courses: Colour in Fine Art; Explorations in Fine Art Drawing and Painting; Drawing and Painting from Life; Fine Art Challenge (Module 2); Modernism; Painting and Composition; Exploring Three-Dimensional and Sculpture; Life, Costume and Portrait Study; Working from Nature; Atelier Life Class; Fine Art Printmaking.
Admissions Policy No particular academic qualifications required for the certificate. However, it is only suitable for those with some competence in art e.g. experienced amateur artists, or those who have previously attended an art foundation course. Expects to offer a place to anyone it feels would benefit from studying for the certificate. Prospective students with no foundation experience may be offered direct entry if they can produce a satisfactory portfolio of work.

University of Wales, Newport
Caerleon Campus, P.O. Box 101, Newport
NP18 3YH
T 01633 432432

F 01633 432046
E uic@newport.ac.uk
W www.newport.ac.uk
Degrees offered BA (Hons): Animation; Fine Art; Documentary Photography; (Contemporary Media); Photographic Art; Photography. BScEd (Hons): Design and Technology. Dip. in Foundation Studies: Art and Design.
Admissions Policy For BA (Hons): through UCAS.

West Wales School of the Arts
College of Carmarthenshire/Coleg Sir Gar
Graig Campus, Sandy Road, Llanelli, SA15 4
T 01554 74800
F 01554 756088
E admissions@colegsirgar.ac.uk
W www.colegsirgar.ac.uk
Coleg Sir Gar has five campuses spread throughout Carmarthenshire, offering courses from GCSE up to postgraduate-degree level.
Degrees offered BA (Hons): Three-Dimensional Art in the Landscape; Fine Art Sculpture; Fine Art Painting; Art and Design Multidisciplinary; Graphic Design (including pathways in Illustration and Computer Arts); Contemporary Textiles (including interpretive pathway in Surface Decoration); Ceramics; Photography. Many BA degrees can be taken part-time.
Other Fine Art courses Part-time courses in ceramics, drawing and painting, textile printing, figurative sculpture, fine art, life drawing, photography (beginner and advanced). FD: Art, Design and Craft; Advanced Art; Design and Craft. ND: Ceramics.

West Midlands

Birmingham Institute of Art and Design
Department of Art, University of Central England
Margaret Street, Birmingham, B3 3BX
T 0121 3315970
F 0121 3316970
E art@students.uce.ac.uk
W www.biad.uce.ac.uk/home.htm
Contact General admissions enquiries: info@ucechoices.com. International admissions: Pauline Burke, pauline.burke@uce.ac.uk.
Provides education for nearly 4,000 students on 5 campuses located in the centre and to the north and south of the centre of Birmingham. The faculty offers a comprehensive portfolio of courses at all levels from FE to higher research. The Department of Art is located in Margaret Street in a newly refurbished grade 1-listed building, where

it first opened in 1885
Degrees offered BA (Hons): Art and Design by Negotiated Study; Fine Art; Fine Art (Painting and Sculpture); Textile Design; Visual Communication; Multimedia Art. PgCert: Research Practice in Art, Design and Media. PGCE: Art and Design. MA: Art and Education; Fine Art; Textiles, Fashion and Surface Design; Visual Arts: Critical and Contextual Practices; Multimedia Art; Artist/Teacher Scheme. MPhil and PhD degrees.
Other Fine Art courses BTEC foundation diploma: Art and Design. HND: Fine Art; Visual Communication; Textiles. Cert. or Dip.: Art and Design by Negotiated Study; Fine Art. Short and leisure courses: Art Club; Watercolour Painting.
Admissions Policy See website.

Coventry University
Priory Street, Coventry, CV1 5FB
T 024 7688 8248
F 024 7688 8667
E afuture.ad@coventry.ac.uk
W www.coventry.ac.uk
Founded in 1843. Expertise is wide-ranging, including practising artists, designers, leading researchers and scholars.
Degrees offered BA: Fine Art; Illustration; Graphic Design; Applied Arts; Fashion; Fine Art and Illustration; Graphic Design and Illustration. MA: Design and Digital Media; Media Arts; Fine Art; Contemporary Crafts; Performance and Media Arts.
Admissions Policy Undergraduate: 200–220 tariff points, GCSE English Language, plus portfiolio review. Postgraduate: relevant undergraduate degree and portfolio.

Dudley College of Technology
The Broadway, Dudley, DY1 4AS
T 01384 363000
E admissions@dudleycol.ac.uk
W www.dudleycol.ac.uk
Other Fine Art courses Art and Design (levels 1 to 3); Three-Dimensional Design; Graphic Design; Photography; Sculpture; Glass Design.
Admissions Policy Depends on the course but generally a portfolio is required.

Herefordshire College of Art & Design
Folly Lane, Hereford, HR1 1LT
T 01432 273359
F 01432 359615
E hcad@hereford-art-col.ac.uk
W www.hereford-art-col.ac.uk

Contact Fiona Watkins
A small specialist arts college, founded 150 years ago. Offers a range of courses in art, design and the performing arts – from entry level including GCSEs or A-levels, through to foundation and honours degrees, or part-time courses for those returning as a mature student.
Degrees offered FDA/BA (Hons): Fine and Applied Arts; Illustration.
Other Fine Art courses Portfolio course (part-time). Many short/evening courses.
Admissions Policy All applicants will need to provide a portfolio of work and attend an interview.

North East Worcestershire College
Slideslow Drive, Bromsgrove
B60 1PQ
T 01527 570020
F 01527 572900
E admissions@ne-worcs.ac.uk
W www.ne-worcs.ac.uk
Contact Susan Greetham
Other Fine Art courses BTEC HND: Fine Art. Set up in 2001 and aims to offer a broad-based fine art programme of study. BTEC HNC: Fine Art.
Admissions Policy For HND: applications can only be accepted through UCAS (either Route A or B). For HNC: apply direct to College. All applicants are interviewed and a portfolio of artwork is required.

North Warwickshire & Hinckley College
Hinckley Road, Nuneaton, CV11 6BH
T 024 76243000
E the.college@nwhc.ac.uk
W www.nwhc.ac.uk
Degrees offered BA (Hons) in Negotiated Studies: Art and Design.
Other Fine Art courses BTEC FD: Design. BTEC Introductory Dip.: Art, Design and Media. Certified Dip. in HE: Art and Design. Edexcel foundation diploma: Art and Design. Edexcel ND: Fine Art; Graphic Design. HND: Visual Communication; HND: Three-Dimensional Design Practice. Also adult education classes.

Solihull College
Art and Design, Blossomfield Road, Solihull
B91 1SB
T 0121 6787006
F 0121 6787200
E tammy.dennis@solihull.ac.uk
W www.solihull.ac.uk
Contact Tammy Dennis (HE Admissions Officer)
Opened in 1993, the college has purpose-built

painting and sculpture studios.
Degrees offered BA (Hons): Fine Art (three years full-time or six years part-time; validated by UCE).
Admissions Policy Full-time applications via UCAS. 20 places per year. Part-time applications direct to the college. 5 places per year.

Staffordshire University
Faculty of Arts, Media and Design, College Road
Stoke-on-Trent, ST4 2XW
T 01782 294552
F 01782 294760
E n.a.powell@staffs.ac.uk
W www.staffs.ac.uk
Contact Neil Powell
School of Art established in 1876
Degrees offered BA (Hons): Fine Art. MA: Fine Art. Full- or part-time.
Admissions Policy Portfolio interview plus 160 points. UCAS routes A and B. Requires English GCSE at grade C or above. Applications welcome from those who wish to experience a broad-based art course and who may already have an established area of practice and wish to deepen their knowledge of a particular specialism.

Stourbridge College
Longlands Centre, Brook Street
Stourbridge, DY8 3XB
T 01384 344600
F 01384 344601
W www.stourbridge.ac.uk
Contact Elaine Dunn
Other Fine Art courses HND: Fine Arts (full- or part-time). Course provides a progression route to either the second or third year of BA (Hons) in Fine Art or employment in related areas. Emphasis on the vocational nature of fine art and students gain an understanding of professional practice.
Admissions Policy Art and design qualifications in either a foundation diploma, ND, AVCE Double Award or a high level of skill. UCAS route B.

Sutton Coldfield College
34 Lichfield Road, Sutton Coldfield
B74 2NW
T 0121 3555671
F 0121 3550799
E heenquiries@sutcol.ac.uk
W www.sutcol.ac.uk
Other Fine Art courses BTEC Dip. in Foundation Studies: Art and Design. BTEC HND: Three-Dimensional Design (Crafts); Fine Art; Graphic Design; Textiles.

Telford College of Arts & Technology
Haybridge Road, Wellington, Telford
TF1 2NP
T 01952 642200
F 01952 642263
E studserv@tcat.ac.uk
W www.tcat.ac.uk
Established over one hundred years ago. Over 16,000 students (1,200 full-time). Courses include NVQs, professional, preparatory degrees and tailor-made programmes.
Other Fine Art courses GNVQ Foundation in Art. Art & Design Diploma in Foundation Studies. Foundation Diploma in Art & Design. Encaustic art workshop.

University College Worcester
Henwick Grove, Worcester, WR2 6AJ
T 01905 855000
F 01905 8555132
E registry@worc.ac.uk
W www.worc.ac.uk
Contact Francesca Fairhurst
Worcester College of Higher Education was founded in 1947 as an emergency teacher training college. Began to offer a wider curriculum in the early 1990s, when degrees in art and design and other subjects were added to the portfolio. Won degree-awarding powers in 1997 and has a strong strategic partnership with Birmingham University. Has eighteen thousand students. Awarded £1m in 2002 from HEFC to develop a digital arts centre.
Degrees offered BA (Hons): Art and Design (Single honours); Visual Arts (Major honours); Communication Design (Major honours); Creative Digital Media (Single honours); Interactive Media (Major honours); Communication Design (Major honours).
Other Fine Art courses Three modules available for both part- and full-time students at Malvern Hills and Evesham College, one of which is available as a three-week summer school. These are all level 1 courses and include: Fine Art Practice and Theory; Landscape and Visual Identity; Textile Design.
Admissions Policy Grades CC or equivalent. UCAS routes A and B. Portfolio interviews in the spring.

University of Wolverhampton
Wulfruna Street, Wolverhampton, WV1 1SB
T 01902 321000
E enquiries@wlv.ac.uk
W www.asp.wlv.ac.uk

Four campuses covering the West Midlands and
Shropshire.
Other Fine Art courses Various foundation
degrees.

Walsall College of Arts & Technology
St Paul's Street, Walsall, WS1 1XN
T 01922 657000
F 01922 657083
E info@walcat.ac.uk
W www.walcat.ac.uk
Contact Alan Tyler
Other Fine Art courses Edexcel Foundation
Studies: Art and Design (post-A-level).
Admissions Policy Apply November/December for
admission the following September.

Warwickshire College
Warwick New Road, Leamington Spa
CV32 5JE
T 01926 318207
F 01926 319025
E jherbert@warkscol.ac.uk
W www.warkscol.ac.uk
Contact John Herbert
The School of Art in Leamington was founded in
1866 and is now a part of Warwickshire College.
Alumni include Sir Terry Frost. The Dip. of HE
fine-art course is run in conjunction with the
Birmingham Institute of Art and Design at the
University of Central England.
Other Fine Art courses Diploma of Higher
Education in Fine Art. A wide range of full-time
courses include BTEC Diploma in Foundation
Studies (Art & Design) and ND Art & Design,
which include studies in fine art plus a variety of
short courses in life drawing, painting and
sculpture.
Admissions Policy Applicants to be at least 18 years
old at entry. A comprehensive portfolio of work
plus one of the following: successful completion of
a foundation course in Art & Design; a merit
profile at National Diploma in a relevant subject; a
merit at Advanced VCE in a relevant subject; A-
Levels (180 points); equivalent qualifications and
experience. Apply through UCAS Route A or
Route B.

Yorkshire and Humberside

Barnsley College
P.O. Box 266, Church Street, Barnsley
S20 2YW
T 01226 216216

F 01226 216553
E programme.enquiries@barnsley.ac.uk
W www.barnsley.ac.uk
Offers courses from AS, HNC and HND to degree
level. Most students come from Barnsley and
surrounding areas of Yorkshire. Access courses for
mature students with few or no qualifications.
Degrees offered BA: Art and Design (Fine Art).
Other Fine Art courses Intermediate and
foundation certificates: Art and Design; Ceramics;
Drawing and Painting; Photography; Textiles.

Bradford College
Great Horton Road, Bradford
BD7 1AY
T 01274 433333
F 01274 741060
E admissions@bilk.ac.uk
W www.bradfordcollege.ac.uk
Origins go back to 1863 when the School of
Industrial Design and Art was formed. Runs
courses through to postgraduate level. Past
students include David Hockney and Andy
Goldsworthy.
Degrees offered BA (Hons): Art and Design;
Fashion Design; Fine Art; Graphic Media
Communication (Graphic Design, Moving Image,
Interactive Multimedia, Illustration); Textile
Design; Photography (stage 3, top-up).
PgCert/PgDip/MA: Photography; Politics of Visual
Representation; Representation in Film;
Printmaking.
Other Fine Art courses Most full-time courses may
be taken on a part-time basis. HND: Spatial Design
(Interior Design); Photography (Editorial,
Advertising and Fine Art).
Admissions Policy Entry normally based on
portfolio and interview. Entry requirements for
full-time undergraduate courses published in
college prospectus or on UCAS site. Encourages
applications from potential students who can
demonstrate suitable qualifications or experience
in an appropriate area of study.

Craven College, Skipton
School of Art and Media, Aireville Campus,
Skipton, BD23 1US
T 01756 693855
F 01756 797047
E enquiries@craven-college.ac.uk
W www.craven-college.ac.uk
Contact Christine Bailey
Housed in a custom-built centre opened in 2001.
There are fifteen specialist studios including

Three-Dimensional Design, Graphic Design, Photography, Textiles, Ceramics, Fine Art and Printmaking.
Other Fine Art courses Dip. in Foundation Studies: Art and Design. HNC: Three-Dimensional Design (Jewellery); Fine Art. HNC/HND: Graphic Design; Textiles. Range of full- and part-time art courses.

Dewsbury College
Halifax Road, Dewsbury, WF13 2AS
T 01924 465916
F 01924 457047
E info@dewsbury.ac.uk
W www.dewsbury.ac.uk
The main campus on Halifax Road hosts the majority of general courses, while the Batley and Wheelwright campuses (Batley School of Art and Design) deliver mainly art and design courses.
Degrees offered BA (Hons): Contemporary Photographic Arts; Creative Imaging; Fine Art and Design. FdA: Applied Arts; Digital Arts; Graphic Design.

Doncaster College
Waterdale, Doncaster, DN1 3EX
T 01302 553610
E he@don.ac.uk
W www.don.ac.uk
Contact Joanne Crapper
Degrees offered BA (Hons): Visual Communication; Combined Design; Art & Associated Crafts; Art & Design (1 year top-up).
Admissions Policy 100 tariff points. Applications accepted through UCAS right up to clearing.

Hull School of Art and Design
Queens Gardens, Wilberforce Drive, Hull HU1 3DG
T 01482 490970
F 01482 480971
E rmoore@artdesignhull.ac.uk
W www.artdesignhull.ac.uk
Contact Carol Morgan
Situated close to the city centre, the school has been reformed, with BA Hons courses transferring from the University of Lincoln to Hull College to form Hull School of Art and Design.
Degrees offered BA Hons: Contemporary Fine Art Practice (subject to validation for Sept 07). This programme offers specialisms in Painting, Sculpture, Printmaking and Mixed Media, including lens-based and digital work. FdA: Creative Arts. Commits students to two years of

degree study with option of third-year honours top-up. The programme encourages work across traditional and non-traditional media boundaries. Students are able to progress to the new BA Hons Contemporary Fine Art Practice programme for a one-year top up.
Other Fine Art courses National Diploma in Fine Art. A two-year programme for people aged 16 and above. OCN Drawing and Painting courses. Part time day and evening options. Fine Art one-week summer school, usually run in July and with painting and/or printmaking options
Admissions Policy FdA Creative Arts applications are via UCAS for full-time and direct for part-time. For the BA Hons: Contemporary Fine Art Practice, applications are directly to the School. All other courses apply directly to the College.

Leeds College of Art & Design
Blenheim Walk, Leeds, LS2 9AQ
T 0113 2028000
F 0113 2028001
E info@leeds-art.ac.uk
W www.leeds-art.ac.uk
Contact Student Advice Team
Founded over one hundred years ago. Past students include Henry Moore, Barbara Hepworth and Damien Hirst.
Degrees offered BA (Hons): Art and Design (interdisciplinary); Fine Art (part-time).
Other Fine Art courses HND: Photography. Dip. in Foundation Studies: Art and Design. College diploma: Design. ND: Art and Design. College certificate: Art and Design. Access to Art and Design A2 levels: Fine Art; Sculpture and Ceramics; Photography. Also a selection of part-time courses both in the day and evening.
Admissions Policy Apply through UCAS for BA (Hons) Art & Design (interdisciplinary) and HND Photography. All other applications should be made on a College application form.

Leeds School of Contemporary Art and Graphic Design
Leeds Metropolitan University, Calverley Street Leeds, LS1 3HE
T 0113 2833108
F 0113 2833094
E t.gray@leedsmet.ac.uk
W www.leedsmet.ac.uk/as/cagd/
Contact Tracy Gray
Evolved from the Leeds College of Art.
Degrees offered BA (Hons): Fine Art; Contemporary Creative Practice.

Admissions Policy Admission is by direct entry and UCAS routes A and B. Preference is given to applicants with pre-degree experience of study at FE level.

Park Lane College
Park Lane, Leeds, LS3 1AA
T 0113 2162000
F 0113 2162020
E course.enquiry@parklanecoll.ac.uk
W www.parklanecoll.ac.uk
Runs art-based courses across a range of levels.
Admissions Policy See website for details.

Sheffield College, Hillsborough Centre
Livesey Street, Sheffield, S6 2ET
T 0114 2602248
F 0114 2602201
E sheila.smith@sheffcol.ac.uk
W www.sheffcol.ac.uk
Contact Sheila Smith
Other Fine Art courses HND/Foundation Degree: Fashion.
Admissions Policy UCAS routes A or B.

Sheffield Hallam University
Faculty of Arts, Computing, Engineering and Sciences, Psalter Lane Campus
Sheffield, S11 8UZ
T 0114 2252607
F 0114 2252603
E cultural@shu.ac.uk
W www.shu.ac.uk
Contact Jane Leadston
Founded as Sheffield School of Design in 1843, name changed to Sheffield School of Art some years later. At present location since 1950
Degrees offered BA (Hons): Fine Art. MA: Fine Art. Part- and full-time.
Admissions Policy BA: Diploma in Foundation Studies in Art and Design plus portfolio preferred; application through UCAS Route A and Route B.

University of Huddersfield
School of Art and Design, Queensgate
Huddersfield, HD1 3DH
T 01484 422288
E admissions@hud.ac.uk
W www.hud.ac.uk
Degrees offered BA (Hons): Fine Art Painting and Drawing; Fine Art with Community Education; Fine Art with Contemporary Writing.

University of Hull
School of Arts, Scarborough Campus, Filey Road, Scarborough, YO11 3AZ
T 01723 362392
E ssa@hull.ac.uk
W www.hull.ac.uk
Contact admissions@hull.ac.uk
Degrees offered BA: Digital Arts; Design For Digital Media.

University of Leeds
The School of Fine Art, History of Art and Cultural Studies, Old Mining Building
Leeds, LS2 9JT
T 0113 3435192
F 0113 2451977
E fine.art.enquiries@leeds.ac.uk
W www.leeds.ac.uk
Almost one hundred years old. 31,500 students.
Degrees offered BA (Hons): Fine Art; Art History; Art History with Museum Studies. MA: Fine Art; Art History; Country House Studies; Feminism and the Visual Arts; Feminist Theory and Practice in the Visual Arts; Sculpture Studies.

York St John College
Lord Mayor's Walk, York
YO31 7EX
T 01904 624624
F 01904 716931
W www.yorksj.ac.uk
Contact Fiona Coventry
Founded in 1841.
Degrees offered BA (Hons): Art and Design; Design and Technology.
Admissions Policy UCAS routes A or B applicants. Minimum entry is 140 to 160 points plus portfolio.

Yorkshire Coast College
Lady Edith's Drive, Scarborough
YO12 5RN
T 01723 372105
F 01723 501918
E admissions@ycoastco.ac.uk
W www.yorkshirecoastcollege.ac.uk
Over ten thousand students.
Degrees offered BA (Hons): Fine Art. FdA: Applied Digital Media (Design).
Other Fine Art courses BTEC Dip. in Foundation Studies: Art and Design (from level 3). BTEC HNC: Graphic and Multimedia Design. ND: Art and Design (level 3).

Ireland

Burren College of Art
Newtown Castle, Ballyvaughan, County Clare
T 065 7077200
F 065 7077201
E admin@burrencollege.ie
W www.burrencollege.com
Contact Anna Downes (Director of
Communications and Admissions)
Founded in 1993 by Michael Greene and Mary
Hawkes-Greene, a not-for-profit charitable
foundation that offers graduate, undergraduate
and artist residency programmes to students and
artists from around the world. The college is set in
the grounds of a sixteenth-century castle on the
Atlantic coast of Ireland. Facilities include studios,
photography studio and dark room, sculpture
workshop, gallery, library, art supplies shop,
lecture theatre and seminar rooms, cafeteria and
accommodation.
Degrees offered Master of Fine Art.
Other Fine Art courses Post-Baccalaureate,
individual and group study abroad programmes,
summer school, artist residencies and five day
courses.
Admissions Policy For the MFA, a BA with Hons
or a Major in Fine Arts, or evidence of equivalent
achievement. Applicants should normally have
either first class or upper second class honours or a
grade point average of 3.50 or above. Portfolio and
supporting statement also required. In the case of
an outstanding portfolio, 2.2 honours standing or
GPA of 3.0 may be considered. For the Post Bac, a
BA with Hons. Applicants should normally have
either first class or upper second class honours or a
grade point average of 3.50 or above. Portfolio and
supporting statement also required.

Crawford College of Art and Design
Cork Institute of Technology, Sharman
Crawford Street, Cork
T 021 4966777
F 021 4962267
W www.cit.ie
Has provided education in the arts for over 200
years, with a strong tradition in the fields of fine
art, ceramic design, art teacher training and adult
education in the creative arts. There are
departments of fine art, design, art and design
education, and art therapy and adult education.
The college is sited in its own campus in Sharman
Crawford Street, approximately four miles from
the main CIT campus in Bishopstown.

Degrees offered Offers full-time courses to
Bachelors Degree, Masters and Advanced Diploma
levels, all validated by the Cork Institute of
Technology and/or the Higher Education and
Training Awards Council. BA (Hons): Ceramic
Design; Fine Art. BA: Ceramic Design; Fine Art.
Higher Dip. in Arts: Art & Design Teachers. MA:
Art Therapy; Fine Art.
Admissions Policy Entry Requirements: Leaving
Certificate Grade D3 in five subjects at Ordinary or
Higher Level, plus Portfolio. A pass in Foundation
Level Mathematics is recognised as a subject for
courses in Crawford College of Art & Design but
carries a maximum 25 CAO points.

Dublin Institute of Technology, Faculty of Applied Arts
Mountjoy Square, Dublin
T 01 402 4138 / 4181
F 01 402 4297
E artdesignprinting@dit.ie
W www.dit.ie
Contact Vincent O'Hara, Admissions Officer
The largest provider of multi-disciplinary and
professional-level education across the visual and
performing arts and media in Ireland. The School
of Art, Design and Printing offers undergraduate
and graduate qualifications. Approximately 35
students per year are admitted to the BA Fine Art
course, combining studio practice with critical
theory.
Degrees offered BA: Fine Art; Photography. MA:
Digital Media Technology (full-time and part-time).
Admissions Policy Six subjects with a minimum of
two at honours level. Applicants must submit a
portfolio and for the BA Fine Art must
demonstrate drawing, practical and conceptual
abilities.

Dun Laoghaire Institute of Art, Design & Technology
Carraiglea Park, Kill Avenue, Dun Laoghaire
County Dublin
T 01 214 4600
F 01 214 4700
E celine.blacow@iadt.ie
W www.iadt.ie
Contact Celine Blacow (Administrator, School of
Creative Arts)
With 1,500+ students, IADT is Ireland's only
Institute of Art, Design and Technology. Organized
in three schools (Creative Arts, Creative
Technologies and Business and Humanities), it is
home to the National Film School. The School of

Creative Arts runs programmes in makeup for film, TV and theatre, radio, visual arts practice, photography, visual communications, production design, animation and modelmaking. Students in the School of Creative Arts can undertake cross-programme projects with the School of Creative Technologies.

Degrees offered BA (Hons): Fine Art; Photography; Film & TV Production; Visual Arts Practice; Animation; Visual Communications. MA: Visual Art Practice; Screenwriting. Full-time and modular part-time courses are available.

Other Fine Art courses Summer School and Autumn School (for information contact ptc@iadt.ie).

Admissions Policy For entry and portfolio requirements see the 'all courses' section of the IADT website.

Galway-Mayo Institute of Technology

Dublin Road, Galway
T 091 753161
E info@gmit.ie
W www.gmit.ie

Founded in 1972 as a regional technical college, the college became an Institute of Technology in 1992. Enrolment is almost 9,000. Has five specialized schools, with the art and design department part of the School of Humanities. Courses are given at the Galway and Castlebar campuses.

Degrees offered BA (Hons): Fine Art; Textiles; Art & Design (full-time and part-time); Film and Television.

Admissions Policy Minimum requirements for full-time courses are a pass in portfolio assessment and a pass in six Leaving Certificate subjects. Mature applicants may be exempted from the Leaving Certificate requirement and attend an interview instead. For course and admission details see website.

Gorey School of Art

Railway Road, Gorey, County Wexford
T 055 20585
F 055 20585
E gsa@itcarlow.ie
Contact Declan Doyle

Gorey School of Art is a small scale school offering a BA in Fine Art. The school is committed to providing courses taught by artists for the education of artists. It was founded in 2003 and offers electives in painting and sculpture.

Degrees offered BA in Art

Admissions Policy Portfolio and CAO application – portfolios can be submitted in the second week of March, April and May.

Institute of Technology, Tallaght

Baile Aitha Cliath 24
Tamlacht
T 01 4042000
F 01 4042700
E info@it-tallaght.ie
W www.it-tallaght.ie

Established in 1992.

Degrees offered BA (Ordinary and Honours): Audio Visual Media.

Other Fine Art courses Higher Certificate: Audio Visual Media.

Admissions Policy Applications for Higher Certificate and BA degrees are made through the Central Applications Office in Galway. Minimum of five grades D3 in the Leaving Certificate at ordinary or higher level, including English or Irish and Mathematics. Comparable qualifications from other EU countries are accepted. For part-time courses apply direct to the Institute. For details see website.

Institute of Techonology Sligo

Ballinode, Sligo
T 071 9155222
F 071 9160475
E info@itsligo.ie
W www.itsligo.ie

Contact Admissions Office: 071 9155379 or admissions@itsligo.ie.

Degrees offered BA: Fine Art (Ordinary and Honours).

Admissions Policy Applicants for BA Fine Art must successfully complete a portfolio assessment prior to offer of a place. Applicants for admission to the first year of the Institute's full-time courses should apply to the Central Applications Office in Galway. International students from non-EU countires apply direct to the Institute. Normal minimum entry requirements for Higher Certificate and Ordinary Degree courses are 5 grade Ds in Leaving Certificate Examinations ordinary level including English or Irish and Mathematics. For UK students the normal minimum entry requirements are 2 A-levels at Grade D or better and 4 GCSEs to gain entry to a degree course or a minimum of 1 A-level at Grade E or better and 4 GCSEs to gain entry to certificate/ diploma courses.

Limerick Institute of Technology
Moylish Park, Limerick
T 061 208208
F 061 208209
E Information@lit.ie
W www.lit.ie
Contact 061 208262 / 208263
Dates back to 1852 when the Athenaeum Society started a School Of Arts and Fine Crafts in Limerick. Has over four-thousand full-time students and sixteen-hundred part-time. Institute tooks its current form in 1992.
Degrees offered BA: Fine Art in Painting; Fine Art in Printmaking; Fine Art in Sculpture & Combined Media. BA (Hons): Fine Art (in Painting, Printmaking, Sculpture & Combined Media); Graphic Design, Ceramic Design and Fashion Design. MA and PhD by Research: Art and Design.
Other Fine Art courses Higher Dip. in Arts for Art & Design Teachers. Accumulation of Credits and Certification of Subjects (ACCS) courses enable students to take single subject courses to obtain a certificate. There is an adult education course in Portfolio Preparation.
Admissions Policy All undergraduate applications should be made to the Central Applications Office in Galway. This includes NCVA applicants who also use the CAO form to apply for an Institute place. Students for other years apply direct to the Institute. For ACCS courses application forms are available from the admissions office and the closing date is in September.

National College of Art and Design
100 Thomas Street, Dublin 8
T 01 6364200
F 01 6364207
E fios@ncad.ie
W www.ncad.ie
Founded in 1746 by Robert West as a private drawing school. The school was given its current name in 1971. Alumni include W.B. Yeats, A.E. Russell and teachers include Sir William Orpen, Sean Keating, Harry Clark and Maurice MacGonigal. Current enrolment of day and evening students is over 1,500. The Faculty of Fine Art consists of departments of Media, Painting, Fine Print and Sculpture.
Degrees offered BA: Fine Art (Media; Painting; Fine Print; Sculpture; History of Art; Fine Art; Crafts Design [Ceramics, Glass and Metals]; Textile Design). BdeS: Textile Design. Graduates may apply for Higher Dip. in Art and Design

Education. MA: Fine Art (Media; Painting; Fine Print; Sculpture; Virtual Realities; Ceramics; Glass and Metals and Textiles). PhDs also offered.
Other Fine Art courses The centre for continuing education in art and design promotes a broad selection of art, craft and design classes. Also run autumn evening classes and day-time courses at Easter and in the summer months.
Admissions Policy Applicants must be seventeen years or older. All students must submit portfolios and for some courses interviews are required. Portfolio should contain notebooks and sketchbooks showing research, school and personal drawings and ideas, together with no more than ten finished pieces of recent two-dimensional work. Photographs of three-dimensional and very large two-dimensional items may also be included. Applications for first year courses are processed through the Central Applications Office in Galway. Applicants for other courses are made directly to NCAD.

Waterford Institute of Technology
School of Humanities, College Street Campus
Waterford
T 051 302251
F 051 302800
E mhowlett@wit.ie
W www2.wit.ie
Contact Dr Michael Howlett (Head of Department of Applied Arts)
A university-level institution with over 10,000 students and almost 1,000 staff. WIT offers tuition and research programmes in many areas up to doctoral level and is the largest of the Institutes of Technology outside Dublin. Established as Waterford Regional Technical College in 1970, its current designation was awarded in 1998.
Degrees offered BA in Art (WD 022) and BA (Hons) in Art and Society (WD 072).
Other Fine Art courses Part time courses: Introduction to Photography, Digital Photography, Drawing and Painting, Life Drawing, Art Mixed Media.

Foundation studies in art and design

East Anglia

Barking College
Dagenham Road, Romford, RM7 0XU
T 01708 770000
F 01708 770007
Contact Matthew Brown

Barnfield College
New Bedford Road, Luton, LU2 7BF
T 01582 569637
F 01582 572264

Bedford College
Cauldwell Street, Bedford, MK42 9AH
T 01234 291000
F 01234 342674

Braintree College
Church Lane, Braintree, CM7 5SN
T 01376 321711
F 01376 340799

Cambridge Regional College
Kings Hedges Road, Kings Hedges
Cambridge, CB4 2QT
T 01223 418518
F 01223 418519

Chelmsford College
Moulsham Street, Chelmsford
CM2 0JQ
T 01245 265611
F 01245 266908

Colchester Institute
Sheepen Road, Colchester, CO3 3LL
T 01206 518000
F 01206 763041

College of West Anglia
Fennyson Avenue, Kings Lynn
PE30 4EW
T 01553 761144 ext.319

Dunstable College
School of Art and Design, Kingsway
LU5 4HG
T 01582 477776 ext.314
F 01582 478801

E thecorns@talk21.com
Contact Rachel Joy

Epping Forest College
Borders Lane, Debden, Loughton
IG10 3SA
T 020 8508 8311
F 020 8502 0186

Great Yarmouth College
Southtown, Great Yarmouth, NR31 0ED
T 01493 655261
F 01493 653423

Harlow College
Visual Arts, Velizy Avenue, Harlow
CM20 3LH
T 01279 868000
F 01279 868260

Havering College of Further and Higher Education
Ardleigh Green Road, Hornchurch
RM11 2LL
T 01708 462801
F 01708 462736
Contact Jane Norris

Hertford Regional College
Ware Centre, Scotts Road, Ware
SG12 9JF
T 01992 411776
F 01992 411885

Isle College
Ramnoth Road, Wisbech, Cambridge
PE13 0HY
T 01945 582561
F 01945 582706

Lowestoft College
St Peters Street, Lowestoft, NR32 2NB
T 01502 583521
F 01502 500031
E info@lowestoft.ac.uk

Luton Sixth-Form College
Bradgers Hill Road, Luton, LU2 7EW
T 01582 877500
F 01582 877501

North Hertfordshire College
Centre for the Arts, Willian Road, Hitchin
SG4 0LS

T 01462 424242
F 01462 471054

Oaklands College
St Albans City Campus, St Peter's Road
St Albans, AL1 3RX
T 01727 737000
F 01727 737272
E help.line@oaklands.ac.uk

Peterborough Regional College
Creative Studies, Park Crescent
PE1 2QU
T 01733 767366
F 01733 767986
E info@peterborough.ac.uk
W www.peterborough.ac.uk

South East Essex College
Carnarvon Road, Southend-on-Sea
SS2 6LS
T 01702 220400
F 01702 432320

Suffolk College
Rope Walk, Ipswich, IP4 1LT
T 01473 296318
F 01473 343657
E cam@suffolk.ac.uk

Thurrock and Basildon College
Woodview Campus, Woodview, Grays
RM16 2YR
T 01375 391199
F 01375 373356

University of Hertfordshire
Faculty of Art and Design
College Lane, Hatfield
AL10 9AB
T 01707 285347
F 01707 285350

Uxbridge College
Uxbridge Campus, Park Road, Uxbridge,
UB8 1NQ
T 01895 853333
F 01895 853377

West Herts College
Hempstead Road, Watford
WD17 3EZ
T 01923 812674
F 01923 812667

West Suffolk College
Out Risbygate, Bury St Edmunds
IP33 3RL
T 01284 701301
F 01284 750561

East Midlands

Boston College
De Montford Campus, Mill Road
PE21 0HF
T 01205 365701

Castle College Nottingham
Maid Marian Way, Nottingham
NG1 6AB
T 0845 845 0500
E learn@castlecollege.ac.uk
W www.castlecollege.ac.uk

Burton College
Lichfield Street
Burton-on-Trent
DE14 3RL
T 01283 494400
F 01283 494800

De Montfort University
Faculty of Art and Design
The Gateway, Leicester
LE1 9BH
T 0116 2506370
F 0116 2506281
Contact Lulu Hancock

Gateway College
The Newarke, Leicester
LE2 7BY
T 0116 2553079
F 0116 2549857

Grantham College
Stonebridge Road
Grantham
NG31 9AP
T 01476 400200
F 01476 400291
E enquiry@grantham.ac.uk

Grimsby College
Nuns Corner, Grimsby
DN34 5BQ
T 01472 311231
F 01472 315507

Huntingdonshire Regional College
California Road, Huntingdon
PE29 1BL
T 01480 379180
F 01480 379127

Leicester College
St Margaret's Campus
Grafton Place, Leicester
LE1 3WL
T 0116 2242002
F 0116 2242150

Loughborough University
School of Art and Design
12 Frederick Street, LE11 3BJ
T 01509 228941
F 01509 231174
E j.tormey@lboro.ac.uk
Contact Jane Tormey

Mackworth College Derby
Prince Charles Avenue, Mackworth
DE22 4LR
T 01332 519951
F 01332 510548

New College Nottingham
25 Stoney Street, The Lace Market
Nottingham, NG1 1LP
T 0115 9554131
F 0115 9553710

North Lindsey College
Kingsway, Scunthorpe
DN17 1AJ
T 01724 281111
F 01724 294020
E info@northlindsey.ac.uk
W www.northlindsey.ac.uk

South East Derbyshire College
Cavendish Site, Cavendish Road
Ilkestone
DE7 5AN
T 0115 8492111
F 0115 8492148

South Nottingham College
Charnwood Centre
Farnborough Road, Clifton
Nottingham, NG11 8LU
T 0115 9146300
F 0115 9146333

Stamford College
Visual Arts Centre, Drift Road
Stamford, PE9 1XA
T 01780 484300
F 01780 484301

Tresham Institute of Further and Higher Education
Windmill Avenue Campus
Windmill Avenue, Kettering
NN15 6ER
T 01536 410252
F 01536 524965

University College Northampton
St Georges Avenue, Northampton
NN2 6JD
T 01604 735500
F 01604 717813

University of Lincoln
School of Art and Design
Chad Varah House
Wordsworth Street
Lincoln, LN1 3BP
T 01522 882000
F 01522 886041

West Notts College of Further Education
Derby Road, Mansfield
NG18 5BH
T 01623 627191
F 01623 623063

London

Barnet College
Wood Street, Barnet
EN5 4AZ
T 020 84406321
F 020 84415236

Bexley College
269 Woolwich Road
Abbey Road, London, SE2 0AR
T 01322 404280
F 020 83107298

Blake College
162 New Cavendish Street, London
W1W 6YS
T 020 76360658
F 020 74360049
E study@blake.ac.uk

Camberwell College of Arts
Peckham Road, London
SE5 8UF
T 020 75146328
F 020 75146310
E enquiries@camberwell.art.ac.uk

Central St Martins College of Art & Design
Southampton Row, London
WC1B 4AP
T 020 75147000
F 020 75147024
E info@csm.arts.ac.uk
Contact Cally Saunders

Chelsea College of Art & Design
Bagley's Lane, London
SW6 2QB
T 020 75147941
F 020 75147944
E enquiries@chelsea.arts.ac.uk
Contact Philippa Tunstill

City and Guilds of London Art School
124 Kennington Park Road
London, SE11 4DJ
T 020 77352306
F 020 75825361
E info@cityandguildsartschool.ac.uk
Contact Keith Price

City and Islington College
383 Holloway Road, London
N7 0RN
T 020 77009259
F 020 77004268

City Literary Institute
16 Stukeley Street, London
WC2B 5LJ
T 020 74922700
E infoline@citylit.ac.uk

City of Westminster College
Paddington Centre
25 Paddington Green
London
T 020 77238826
F 020 72582700

College of North East London
High Road, Tottenham
London, N15 4RU
T 020 88024352

Community College, Shoreditch
Falkirk Street, London, N1 6HQ
T 020 76139123

Croydon College
Fairfield Campus, College Road
Croydon, CR9 1DX
T 020 86865700
F 020 876 5880

Enfield College
73 Hertford Road, Enfield
EN3 5HA
T 020 84433434

Greenwich Community College
95 Plumstead Road, London
SE18 7DQ
T 020 84884873
F 020 84884899

Hammersmith and West London College
Gliddon Road, Barons Court, London
W14 9BL
T 020 87411688
F 020 85638247

Kensington and Chelsea College
Hortensia Road, London
SW10 0QS
T 020 75735258

Kingston College
55 Richmond Road
Kingston-upon-Thames, KT2 5BP
T 020 89394601 / 89394618 (direct line)
F 020 89394628

Kingston University
Knights Park, 53–57 High Street
Kingston-upon-Thames
KT1 2QJ
T 020 85472000

Lewisham College
2 Deptford Church Street, Lewisham, London
SE8 4RZ
T 020 86943497
F 020 86943408

London College of Communication
Elephant and Castle, London
SE1 6SB
T 020 75146500

London College of Fashion
182 Mare Street, London
E8 3RE
T 020 75147400
F 020 75147484
Contact Sarah Atkinson

London Metropolitan University
Central House, 59–63 Whitechapel High Street
London, E1 7PF
T 020 71334200

Newham College of Further Education
East Ham Campus
High Street South
London, E6 6ER
T 020 82574205
F 020 8254308

Richmond-upon-Thames College
Egerton Road, Twickenham
TW2 7SJ
T 020 86078307
F 020 87449738

South Thames College
Wandsworth High Street
London, SW18 2PP
T 020 89187092
F 020 89187132

Southgate College
High Street, Southgate
London
N14 6BS
T 020 8982 104
F 020 89825051

Southwark College
Surrey Docks Centre
Drummond Road
London, SE16 4EE
T 020 78151526

Tower Hamlets College
Poplar Centre, Poplar High Street
London, E14 0AF
T 020 75107510
F 020 75389153

Waltham Forest College
Forest Road, Walthamstow
London
E17 4JB

T 020 85018217
F 020 85018001

West Thames College
Art, Design and Engineering, London Road,
Isleworth, TW7 4HS
T 020 83262000
F 020 85699314

Westminster Kingsway College
Kentish Town Centre, 87 Holmes Road
London, NW5 3AX
T 020 75568001
F 020 75568003

Wimbledon School of Art
Palmerston Road, London
SW19 1PB
T 020 84085030
F 020 84085050
E foundation@wimbledon.ac.uk
Contact Simon Betts

North-east

City of Sunderland College
Shiney Row Centre
Houghton-le-Spring
Tyne and Wear, DH4 4TL
T 0191 5116113
F 0191 5116380

Cleveland College of Art & Design
Church Square, Hartlepool
TS24 7EX
T 01642 288000

Cleveland College of Art & Design
Green Lane, Linthorpe
Middlesbrough, TS5 7RJ
T 01642 288000
F 01642 288828

Derwentside College
Park Road, Consett
DH8 5EE
T 01207 585900
F 01207 502434

Gateshead College
Durham Road, Low Fell
Gateshead, NE9 5BN
T 0191 4902308
F 0191 4902313

New College Durham
Framwellgate Moor Centre
Durham, DH1 5ES
T 0191 3754325
F 0191 3754222

Newcastle College
Rye Hill Campus, Scotswood Road
Newcastle-upon-Tyne
NE4 7SA
T 0191 2004000
F 0191 2004517

North Tyneside College
Embleton Avenue, Wallsend
NE28 9NJ
T 0191 2295000
F 0191 2295301

Northumberland College
College Road, Ashington
NE63 9RG
T 01670 841200
F 01670 841201

Queen Elizabeth Sixth-Form College
Vane Terrace, Darlington, DL3 7AU
T 01325 465602
F 01325 361705

South Tyneside College
St Georges Avenue, South Shields
NE34 6ET
T 0191 4273535 / 4273500 (direct line)

University of Sunderland
Ashburne House, Ryhope Road
Sunderland, SR2 7EF
T 0191 5152142

Northern Ireland

Armagh College of Further Education
Lonsdale Street, Armagh
BT61 7HN
T 01861 522205
F 01861 526011

Belfast Metropolitan College
T 028 90265327
E chsadmissions@belfastinstitute.ac.uk
W www.belfastmet.ac.uk
Contact Eilish Murray-Bergin

East Tyrone College of Further and Higher Education
Circular Road
Dungannon
BT71 6BQ
T 028 87722323
F 028 87722323
E etyronecolfe@campus.bt.com

Limavady College of Further and Higher Education
Main Street, Limavady
BT49 0EX
T 028 77762334
F 028 77761018
E dhanna@limavady.ac.uk
Contact David Hanna

Newry and Kilkeel Institute of Further and Higher Education
Patrick Street, Newry
BT35 8DN
T 028 30261071
F 028 30259662
E fmccartney@nkifhe.ac.uk
Contact Fiona McCartney

North Downs and Ards Institute
Castle Park Road, Bangor
BT20 4TF
T 028 91276600
F 028 91276601
W www.ndai.ac.uk

North East Institute of Further and Higher Education
Ballymena Campus
Trostan Avenue
Ballymena, BT43 7BN
T 028 25652871 / 2563625 (direct line)
F 028 25659245

North West Institute of Further and Higher Education
Arts Department, Strand Road
Londonderry, BT48 7BY
T 028 71266711
F 028 71260520

Omagh College
2 Mountjoy Road, Omagh
BT79 7AH
T 028 82245433
F 028 82241440

Upper Bann Institute of Further and Higher Education
2–8 Kitchen Hill, Lurgan
Craigavon
BT66 6AZ
T 028 38326135
F 028 38322762
E bradyde@ubi.ac.uk
Contact Dermot Brady

North-west

Barrow Sixth-Form College
Rating Lane, Barrow-in-Furness
LA13 9LE
T 01229 828377
F 01229 836874

Blackburn College
Feilden Street, Blackburn
BB2 1LH
T 01254 55133

Blackpool and the Fylde College
Palatine Road, Blackpool, FY1 4DW
T 01253 352352
F 01253 291627
E visitors@blackpool.ac.uk

Bolton University
Chadwick Street Campus
Bolton, BL2 1JW
T 01204 903903
Contact Ruth Yates

Burnley College
Shorey Bank, Ormerod Road
Burnley, BB11 2RX
T 01282 711200
F 01282 415063

Bury College
Woodbury Centre, Market Street
Bury, Manchester
BL9 0BG
T 0800 0925900
F 0161 2808228

Carmel College
Prescot Road, St Helens
Merseyside, WA10 3AG
T 01744 22876
F 01744 453843
Contact Steve Bonati

Chesterfield College
Infirmary Road, Chesterfield
S41 7NG
T 01246 500609

City College Manchester
The Arden Centre, Sale Road
Northenden, Manchester
M23 0DD
T 0161 9571757
F 0161 9459488

City of Liverpool Community College
The Arts Centre, Myrtle Street
Liverpool, L7 7JA
T 0151 2524354

Cumbria Institute of the Arts
Brampton Road, Carlisle
CA3 9AY
T 01228 400300
E info@cumbria.ac.uk
Contact Martin Fowler

Deeside College
Kelsterton Road, Connah's Quay
Deeside, CH5 4BR
T 01244 831531
F 01244 814395
E enquiries@deeside.ac.uk

Hugh Baird College
Balliol Road, Bootle
L20 7EW
T 0151 3534419
F 0151 3534420

Isle of Man College
Homefield Road, Douglas
Isle of Man, IM2 6RB
T 01624 648206
F 01624 648201

Kendal College
Milnthorpe Road, Kendal
LA9 5AY
T 01539 814700
E enquiries@kendal.ac.uk

Knowsley Community College
Rupert Road, Roby
L36 9TD
T 0151 4775793
F 0151 4775703

Lancaster and Morecambe College
Morecombe Road, Lancaster, LA1 2TY
T 01524 382257

Leek College
Stockwell Street, Leek, ST13 6DP
T 01538 398866
F 01538 399506

Macclesfield College
Park Lane, Macclesfield
SK11 8LF
T 01625 410000
F 01625 410001
E info@macclesfield.ac.uk

Manchester College of Arts and Technology
MANCAT Openshaw Campus
Ashton Old Road, Openshaw
Manchester, M11 2WH
T 0161 9535995
F 0161 9533909

Manchester Metropolitan University
Grosvenor Building, Cavendish Street
Manchester, M15 6BR
T 0161 2471705
F 0161 2476393
Contact Joan Beadle

Mid-Cheshire College
Hartford Campus, Northwich
CW8 1LJ
T 01606 74444
F 01606 720700

Nelson and Colne College
Scotland Road, Nelson
BB9 7YT
T 01282 440267
F 01282 440274

Oldham College
Rochdale Road, Oldham
OL9 6AA
T 0161 6245214
F 0161 6244234

Preston College
The Park School, Moor Park Avenue
Fulwood, Preston
PR1 6AS
T 01772 225604
F 01772 225007

Priestley College
Loushers Lane, Warrington
WA4 6RD
T 01925 633591
F 01925 413887

Runshaw College
Langdale Road, Leyland
PR25 3DQ
T 01772 622688 ext.2128

Salford College
Worsley Campus, Walkden Road
Worsley, Manchester
M28 7QD
T 0161 2115159

South Cheshire College
Creative Arts Department
Dane Bank Avenue
Crewe
CW2 8AB
T 01270 654654
F 01270 651515

South Trafford College
Manchester Road
Altrincham
WA14 5PQ
T 0161 9524733
F 0161 9524672

Southport College
Mornington Road, Southport
PR9 0TT
T 01704 500606
F 01704 392794

St Helens College
School of Arts, S.K.B. Building
Water Street, St Helens
WA10 1PP
T 01744 623221
F 01744 623400

**Stockport College of Further
and Higher Education**
Foundation Art and Design
Wellington Road South
Stockport
SK1 3UQ
T 0161 9583507
F 0161 4806636
E foundidea@hotmail.com

Tameside College
Beauford Road, Ashton-under-Lyne
OL6 6NX
T 0161 9086763
F 0161 9086611

Warrington Collegiate Institute
School of Art and Design
Padgate Campus, Crab Lane
Fearnhead, Warrington
WA2 0DB
T 01925 494494
F 01925 816077

West Cheshire College
Grange Centre, Regent Street
Ellesmere Port, L65 8EJ
T 01244 670359
F 01244 670380

Wigan & Leigh College
School of Art and Design
 Parsons Walk, Wigan
WN1 1RS
T 01942 761811
F 01942 761812

Winstanley College
Winstanley Road, Billinge
WN5 7XF
T 01695 633244
F 01695 633409

Wirral Metropolitan College
12 Quays Campus, Shore Road
Birkenhead
CH41 1AG
T 0151 5517777
F 0151 5517401

Xaverian College
Lower Park Road, Manchester
M14 5RB
T 0161 2241781
F 0161 2489039

South-east

Abingdon & Witney College
Northcolt Road, Abingdon
OX14 1NN
T 01235 555585
E enquiry@abingdon-witneycollege.ac.uk
Contact Hannah Kinch

Alton College
Old Oldham Road, Alton
GU34 1NX
T 01420 592200 ext.235
F 01420 592253

Amersham & Wycombe College
Amersham Campus, Stanley Hill
HP7 9HN
T 01494 735555
F 01494 735566

Ashford School of Art & Design
Tufton Street, Ashford
TN23 1RJ
T 01233 655555
E asad@southkent.ac.uk

**Basingstoke College of
Technology (BCOT)**
Worting Road, Basingstoke
RG21 1TN
T 01256 306221
F 01256 306444

Bracknell & Wokingham College
Church Road, Bracknell
RG12 1DJ
T 01344 460200
F 01344 460360
E study@bracknell.ac.uk

Brooklands College
Heath Road, Weybridge
KT13 8TT
T 01932 797700
F 01932 797800

**Buckinghamshire Chilterns
University College**
Queen Alexandra Road
High Wycombe
HP11 2JZ
T 01494 522141
E swilke01@bcuc.ac.uk
W www.bcuc.ac.uk
Contact Sarah Wilkes

**Chichester College of Arts, Science
and Technology**
Westgate Fields, Chichester
PO19 1SB
T 01243 539481
E info@chichester.ac.uk

City College Brighton & Hove
Pelham Street, Brighton
BN1 4FA
T 01273 667788
F 01273 667703
E info@ccb.ac.uk

Cricklade College
Charlton Road, Andover
SP10 1EJ
T 01264 360000
F 01264 360010
E info@cricklade.ac.uk

East Berkshire College
Station Road, Langley
SL3 8BY
T 01753 793000
F 01753 793316

East Surrey College
Claremont Road, Redhill
RH1 2JX
T 01737 772611
F 01737 768641

Fareham College
Bishopsfield Road, Fareham
PO14 1NH
T 01329 815372
F 01329 822483

**Guildford College of Further and
Higher Education**
School of Art, Design and Media
Stoke Park, Guildford
GU1 1EZ
T 01483 448500 ext.4877
F 01483 448603
E info@guildford.ac.uk

Hastings College of Arts & Technology
Archery Road, St Leonards-on-Sea
TN38 0HX
T 01424 442222
F 01424 71797

Henley College
Deanfield Avenue
Henley-on-Thames
RG9 1UH
T 01491 579988
F 01491 410099
Contact Julian Brinsford-Webb

Isle of Wight College
Medina Way, Newport
PO30 5TA
T 01983 526631
F 01983 521707

**Medway Adult and Community
Learning Service**
Green Street, Gillingham
ME7 5TJ
T 01634 850235
F 01634 500297

Milton Keynes College
Bletchley Centre, Sherwood Drive
Milton Keynes
MK3 6DR
T 01908 684444
F 01908 684399
Contact Adrian Pinkard

NESCOT
Reigate Road, Ewell, Epsom
KT17 3DS
T 020 83943261
F 020 83943030

Newbury College
Oxford Road, Newbury
RG14 1PQ
T 01635 845243
F 01635 845312

Northbrook College
Union Place Campus
Union Place, Worthing
BN11 1LU
T 01903 606124 / 606133
F 01903 606125

Oxford & Cherwell Valley College
Broughton Road, Banbury
OX16 9QA
T 01865 551667
E enquiries@ocvc.ac.uk
W www.ocvc.ac.uk
Contact Chris Roberts

Oxford Brookes University
School of Art, Publishing and Music
Oxford
T 01865 484848
E art@brookes.ac.uk
Contact Lisa Atkinson

**Ravensbourne College of Design
and Communication**
Walden Road
Chislehurst
BR7 5SN
T 020 82894900
F 020 83258320
E info@rave.ac.uk

Reigate School of Art and Design
127 Blackborough Road, Reigate
RH2 7DE
T 01737 766137
F 01737 768643

Richmond Adult Community College
Park Shot Centre
Parkshot, Richmond
TW9 2RE
T 020 89400170
F 020 83326560

Rycotewood College
Priest End, Thame
OX9 2AF
T 01844 212501
F 01844 218809
Contact Chris Hyde

South Downs College
College Road, Waterlooville
PO7 8AA
T 023 92797979
F 023 92364578

Southampton City College
St Mary Street, Southampton
SO14 1AR
T 023 80577324
F 023 80577473

Sussex Downs College
Eastbourne Campus
Cross Levels Way
Eastbourne
BN21 2UF
T 01323 637504
F 01323 637523

Sussex Downs College
Mountfield Road, Lewes
BN7 2XH
T 01273 483188
F 01273 478561

Thames Valley University
Reading Campus, Kings Road
Reading, RG1 4HJ
T 0118 9675000
E learning.advice@tvu.ac.uk
W www.tvu.ac.uk

Thanet College
Ramsgate Road, Broadstairs
CT10 1PN
T 01843 605040
F 01843 605031
E staff-pds@thanet.ac.uk

Totton College
Water Lane, Totton
Southampton
SO40 3ZX
T 023 80874874
F 023 80874879

**University College for the Creative
Arts at Canterbury**
New Dover Road
Canterbury
CT1 3AN
T 01227 817302
E admissions@ucreative.ac.uk
W www.ucreative.ac.uk
Contact Mary Stockton-Smith

**University College for the Creative
Arts at Epsom**
Ashley Road, Epsom
KT18 5BE
T 01372 728811
E admissions@ucreative.ac.uk
W www.ucreative.ac.uk
Contact Ian Parker

**University College for the
Creative Arts at Farnham**
Falkner Road, Farnham
GU9 7DS
T 01252 722441
E admissions@ucreative.ac.uk
W www.ucreative.ac.uk
Contact Jane Cradock-Watson

**University College for the Creative
Arts at Maidstone**
Oakwood Park, Maidstone
ME16 8AG
T 01622 620000

E admissions@ucreative.ac.uk
W www.ucreative.ac.uk
Contact Mike Addison

University College for the Creative Arts at Rochester
Fort Pitt, Rochester
ME1 1DZ
T 01634 888702
F 01634 820300
E admissions@ucreative.ac.uk
W www.ucreative.ac.uk
Contact Gary Clough

University of Portsmouth
School of Art Design and Media
Eldon Building
Winston Churchill Avenue
Portsmouth, PO1 2DJ
T 023 92848484
F 023 92843808

West Kent College
Brook Street, Tonbridge
TN9 2PW
T 01732 358101
F 01732 771415

Winchester School of Art
University of Southampton New College
The Avenue, Southampton, SO17 1BG
T 023 80597440
F 023 80597341
E rn1@soton.ac.uk

South-west

The Arts Institute at Bournemouth
The School of Art, Wallisdown
Poole, BH12 5HH
T 01202 363283
F 01202 537729
E a.scott@arts-inst-bournemouth.ac.uk
Contact Mark Orton

Bournemouth & Poole College
North Road, Poole
BH14 0LS
T 01202 205205

Bridgwater College
Bath Road, Bridgwater, TA6 4PZ
T 01278 441292
F 01278 441232

Camborne Poole Redruth College
Trevenson Road, Poole
TR15 3RD
T 01209 611611
F 01209 616168

City of Bath College
Avon Street, Bath
BA1 1UP
T 01225 312191
F 01225 444213

City of Bristol College
College Green Centre
St Georges Road, Bristol
BS1 5UA
T 0117 9072858
F 0117 9045139

Cornwall College
Trevarthian Road
St Austell
PL25 4BU
T 01726 67911
F 01726 67911
E info@st-austell.ac.uk

Exeter College
Victoria Yard Studios
Queen Street, Exeter
EX4 3SR
T 01392 205290

Ferndown Upper School
Cherry Grove
Ferndown
BH22 9EY
T 01202 871243
F 01202 893383
E school@fernup.dorset.sch.uk

Filton College
Filton Avenue, Bristol
BS34 7AT
T 0117 9092324

Gloscat
Centre for the Arts
Brunswick Road
Gloucester
GL1 1HS
T 01452 426602
F 01452 426601
W www.gloscat.ac.uk

Highlands College
P.O. Box 1000, St Saviour
Jersey
JE4 9QA
T 01534 608620
F 01534 608600

North Devon College
Old Sticklepath Hill, Sticklepath
Barnstaple, EX31 2BQ
T 01271 338107
F 01271 338121

Plymouth College of Art and Design
Tavistock Place, Plymouth, PL4 8AT
T 01752 203434
F 01752 203444
E enquiries@pcad.ac.uk

Salisbury College
Southampton Road, Salisbury
SP1 2LW
T 01722 344344
F 01722 344345

Somerset College of Arts & Technology
Wellington Road, Taunton, TA1 5AX
T 01823 366366
F 01823 366357

South Devon College
Newton Road, Torquay
T 01803 400700
F 01803 400701

Strode College
Church Road, Street
BA16 0AB
T 01458 844444
F 01458 844411

Stroud College
Stratford Road, Stroud
GL5 4AH
T 01453 763424
F 01453 753543
E enquire@stroudcol.ac.uk

Swindon School of Art & Design
Euclid Street
Swindon
SN1 2JQ
T 01793 498490
F 01793 422102

Truro College
College Road, Truro, TR1 3XX
T 01872 267000
F 01872 267100

University College Falmouth
Woodlane, Falmouth
TR11 4RA
T 01326 211832
F 01326 211205

University of Gloucestershire
Park Campus, P.O. Box 220
The Park, Cheltenham
GL50 2QF
T 01242 532700
F 01242 532810

University of the West of England
Faculty of Art, Media and Design
Kennel Lodge Road
off Clanage Road
Bower Ashton
Bristol, BS3 2JT
T 0117 3444768
F 0117 3444765

Weston College
Knightstone Road
Weston-super-Mare
BS23 2AL
T 01934 411411
F 01934 411410

Weymouth College
Cranford Avenue
Weymouth
DT4 7LQ
T 01305 764707
F 01305 208752

Wiltshire College Trowbridge
College Road
Trowbridge
BA14 0ES
T 01225 766241 ext.304
F 01225 777148

Yeovil College
Mudford Road
Yeovil
BA21 4DR
T 01935 423921
F 01935 429962

Wales

Barry College
Colcot Road, Barry
CT62 8YJ
T 01446 725000
F 01446 732667

Bridgend College
Cowbridge Road, Bridgend
CF31 3DF
T 01656 302302
F 01656 663912
E admissions@bridgend.ac.uk

Coleg Gwent
Crosskeys Campus, Risca Road
Crosskeys, NP11 7ZA
T 01495 333456
F 01495 333386

Coleg Llandrillo College
Llandudno Road, Rhos-on-Sea
Colwyn Bay, LL28 4HZ
T 01492 546666

Coleg Meirion-Dwyfor
Barmouth Road, Dolgellau
LL40 2SW
T 01341 422827
F 01341 422393

Coleg Menai
Llys Y Wernen, Ffordd Y Llyn
Parc Menai, Bangor, LL57 4DF
T 01248 370125

Coleg Powys
Llanidloes Road, Newtown
SY16 4HU
T 01686 622722
F 01686 622246

Glamorgan Centre for Art & Design
Glyntaff Road, Glyntaff
Pontypridd, CF37 4AT
T 01443 663309
F 01443 663313

Pembrokeshire College
Merlins Bridge, Haverfordwest
SA61 1SZ
T 01437 765247
F 01437 767279

Swansea Institute of Higher Education
Alexandra Road, Swansea
SA1 6ED
T 01792 481161
F 01792 481161

University of Wales College, Newport
Allt-Yr-Yn Campus
P.O. Box 180, Newport
NP20 5XR
T 01633 432681
F 01633 432682

University of Wales Institute, Cardiff
Western Avenue, Cardiff
CF5 2YB
T 029 20416689
F 029 20416640

West Wales School of the Arts
Faculty of Art/Design
Jobswell Campus
Carmarthen
SA31 3HY
T 01554 748204
F 01267 221515

Yale College of Wrexham
Grove Park Road
Wrexham
LL12 7AA
T 01978 311794
F 01978 291569 / 364254

West Midlands

Cannock Chase Technical College
Progres Centre, Walsall Road
Bridgetown, WS11 1UE
T 01543 462200

City College, Birmingham
Heartlands Art College
St Peters Urban Village, B8 3TE
T 0121 3273608
F 0121 3285884
E darkinstall@citycol.ac.uk

City of Wolverhampton College
Wulfrun Campus, Paget Road
Wolverhampton, WV6 0DU
T 01902 746800
F 01902 423070

Coventry University
School of Art and Design
Priory Street, Coventry
CV1 5FB
T 024 7688248
E h.cannatecca@coventry.ac.uk
Contact Howard Cannatecca

Dudley College of Technology
The Broadway, Dudley
DY1 4AS
T 01384 363000
F 01384 363311

**Herefordshire College of
Art & Design**
Folly Lane, Hereford
HR1 1LT
T 01432 273359
F 01432 341099
E head@hereford-art-col.ac.uk

Hereward College
Bramston Crescent
Tile Hill Lane, Coventry
CV4 9SW
T 024 76461231
F 024 76694305

**Kidderminster College
of Further Education**
Art and Design Department
Hoo Road, Kidderminster
DY10 1LX
T 01562 820811 / 732224 (direct line)
F 01562 748504

Malvern College
College Road, Malvern, WR14 3DF
T 01684 581500

**Matthew Boulton College of Further
and Higher Education**
Jennens Road, Birmingham, B4 7PS
T 0121 5038590
F 0121 4463105
E ask@matthew-boulton.ac.uk
W www.matthew-boulton.ac.uk

Newcastle-under-Lyme College
Liverpool Road, Newcastle-under-Lyme
ST5 2DF
T 01782 254357
F 01782 254281

North Birmingham College
Aldridge Road, Great Barr
Birmingham
B44 8NE
T 0121 3603543
F 0121 3250828

North East Worcestershire College
Bromsgrove Campus
Blackwood Road, Bromsgrove
B60 1PQ
T 01527 585041
F 01527 572900
E info@ne-worcs.ac.uk

North Warwickshire & Hinckley College
Hinchley Road
Nuneaton
CV11 6BU
T 024 76343000
F 024 76328376
E the.college@nwarks-hinckley.ac.uk

Rugby College School of Art
Lower Hamilton Road, Rugby
CV21 3QS
T 01788 338601
F 01788 338575
E info@rugbycoll.ac.uk

Sandwell College
High Street, West Bromwich
B70 8DW
T 0121 2536648

**Shrewsbury College of Arts
and Technology**
London Road, Shrewsbury
SY2 6PR
T 01743 342342
F 01743 342509
E prospects@shrewsbury.ac.uk

Solihull College
Blossomfield Road
Solihull
B91 1SB
T 0121 6787001
F 0121 6787200

Stafford College
Earl Street, Stafford
ST16 2QR
T 01785 223800
F 01785 259953

Staffordshire University
School of Art and Design
College Road
Stoke-on-Trent
ST5 4HL
T 01782 294625
F 01782 294873
E artkm@staffs.ac.uk
Contact Keith Malkin

Stourbridge College
The Longlands Centre
Brook Street
Stourbridge
DY8 3XB
T 01384 344616 / 344600
F 01384 344601

Sutton Coldfield College
Design Centre
90 Upper Holland Road
B72 1RD
T 0121 3621158
F 0121 3213180

Tamworth & Lichfield College
Lichfield Campus
The Friary, Lichfield
WS13 6QG
T 01543 301100
F 01543 301103

**University of Central England
in Birmingham**
BIAD, Linden Road
Birmingham
B30 1JX
T 0121 3315775
F 0121 3315779
E foundation.com@students.uce.ac.uk
W www.biad.uce.ac.uk

Walford and North Shropshire College
College Road, Oswestry
SY11 2SA
T 01691 688000
F 01691 688001

Walsall College of Arts & Technology
St Pauls Street, Walsall
WS1 1XN
T 01922 657000
F 01922 657083

Warwickshire College
Leamington Centre
Warwick New Road
Leamington Spa, CV32 5JE
T 01926 318118
F 01926 318111

Worcester College of Technology
School of Art and Design, Barbourne
Worcester, WR1 1RT
T 01905 725631
E ask@art.wortech.ac.uk
W www.wortech.ac.uk
Contact Sandra Maund

Yorkshire and Humberside

Barnsley College
P.O. Box 266, Church Street
Barnsley
S70 2YW
T 01226 730191
F 01226 298514
Beverley College
Gallows Lane, Beverley
HU17 7DT
T 01482 868362
F 01482 866784

Bradford College
Great Horton Road, Bradford
BD7 1AY
T 01274 433333

Calderdale College
School of Integrated Arts
Francis Street, Halifax
HX1 3UZ
T 01422 357357
F 01422 399320

Craven College, Skipton
Gargrave Road, Skipton
BD23 1US
T 01752 799637
F 01756 794872
E enquiries@craven-college.ac.uk

Dewsbury College
Batley School of Art and Design
Wheelwright Campus
Birkdale Road, Dewsbury
WF13 4HQ

T 01924 451649
F 01924 469491
E info@dewsbury.ac.uk
W www.dewsbury.ac.uk

Doncaster College
Waterdale, Doncaster, DN1 3EF
T 01302 553553
F 01302 553559

Hopwood Hall College
Rochdale Campus, St Marys Gate
Rochdale, OL12 6RY
T 01706 345346 ext.2214
F 01706 41426

Huddersfield Technical College
New North Road
Huddersfield
HD1 5NN
T 01484 536521
F 01484 511885

Hull School of Art and Design
Queen's Gardens, Hull
HU1 3DG
T 01482 480970
E info@artdesignhull.ac.uk
W www.artdesignhull.ac.uk

Keighley College
Cavendish Street, Keighley
BD21 3DF
T 01535 618662
F 01535 618665

Leeds College of Art and Design
Blenheim Walk
Leeds, LS2 9AQ
T 0113 2028000
F 0113 2028001
E info@leeds-art.ac.uk
W www.leeds-art.ac.uk
Contact Elspeth Hodson

Leeds Metropolitan University
City Campus, Calverley Street
Leeds, LS1 3HE
T 0113 2832600

**Rotherham College of Arts
and Technology**
Eastwood Lane, Rotherham
S65 1EG

T 01709 362111
F 01709 373053
E info@rotherham.ac.uk
W www.rotherham.ac.uk

Selby College
Abbots Road, Selby
YO8 8AT
T 01757 211011
F 01757 213137

Sheffield College
Hillsborough Centre
Livesey Street
Sheffield
S6 5ET
T 0114 2602248
F 0114 2602201
E john.milner@sheffcol.ac.uk
Contact John Milner

Wakefield College
Thornes Park Centre
Thornes Park
Wakefield, WF2 8QZ
T 01924 789855
E m.grant@wakcoll.ac.uk
Contact Mandi Grant

Wyke College
Grammar School Road
Hull, HU5 4NX
T 01482 346347
F 01482 473336
E office@wyke.ac.co.uk

York College
Art, Design and Craft
Tadcaster Road, York
YO24 1UA
T 01904 770200
F 01904 770499
Contact Angela Newdick

Yorkshire Coast College
School of Art and Design
Westwood Campus
Valley Bridge Parade
Scarborough
YO11 2PF
T 01723 361960
F 01723 366057
E enquiries@ycoastco.ac.uk
W www.ycoastco.ac.uk

Art Libraries

East Anglia

Albert Sloman Library
University of Essex
Wivenhoe Park
Colchester
CO4 3SQ
T 01206 873192
E libcomment@essex.ac.uk
W libwww.essex.ac.uk

Anglia Polytechnic University
Cambridge Campus Library
East Road, Cambridge
CB1 1PT
T 01223 363271 x2301
W libweb.apu.ac.uk

Colchester Institute
Sheepen Road, Colchester
CO3 3LL
T 01206 518642
E philip.smith@colch-inst.ac.uk
W www.colch-inst.ac.uk

Fitzwilliam Museum
Trumpington Street, Cambridge
CB4 1SL
T 01223 332900
W www.fitzmuseum.cam.ac.uk

Henry Moore Foundation Library and Archive
Dane Tree House, Perry Green
Much Hadham
SG10 6EE
T 01279 843333
E library@henry-moore-fdn.co.uk

Norwich School of Art & Design Library
St George Street, Norwich
NR3 1BB
T 01603 610561 x3073
E info@nsad.ac.uk
W www.nsad.ac.uk

Sainsbury Research Unit Library
Sainsbury Centre, University of East Anglia,
University Plain, Norwich
NR4 7TJ
T 01603 592659
E sru.library@uea.ac.uk
W www.uea.ac.uk/art/sru/library/library.htm

Southend-on-Sea Borough Libraries
Victoria Avenue
Southend-on-Sea
SS2 6EX
T 01702 612621
W www.southendlibrary.com

Suffolk College Library
Rope Walk, Ipswich
IP4 1LT
T 01473 255885
E info@suffolk.ac.uk
W www.suffolk.ac.uk/content/supp_learn/
library.htm

University of Cambridge
Faculty of Architecture & History of Art Library
1 Scroope Terrace
Cambridge, CB2 1PX
T 012 2333 2950
W www.arct.cam.ac.uk/coursebase/resources/lib

University of East Anglia Library
Norwich, NR4 7
T 01603 592421
E library@uea.ac.uk
W www.lib.uea.ac.uk

University of Hertfordshire Learning & Information Services
College Lane, Hatfield
AL10 9AB
T 01707 284678
W www.herts.ac.uk/lis

University of Luton
Learning Resources
Park Square, Luton
LU1 3JU
T 01582 743262
W lrweb.luton.ac.uk

East Midlands
Kimberlin Library, De Montfort University
The Gateway, Leicester
LE1 9BH
T 0116 257 7042
W www.library.dmu.ac.uk

Loughborough University
Pilkington Library, Loughborough
LE11 3TU
T 01509 222360
W www.lboro.ac.uk/library

Nottingham Arts Library
Angel Row, Nottingham
NG1 6HP
T 0115 915 2811
E arts.library@nottinghamcity.gov.uk
W www.nottinghamcity.gov.uk/libraries

Nottingham Trent University
The Boots Library, Goldsmith Street, Nottingham
NG1 5LS
T 0115 848 2175
W www.ntu.ac.uk/lis

University College Northampton
Learning Resources Avenue Campus, St George's
Avenue, Northampton
NN2 6JD
W www.library.northampton.ac.uk

University of Derby
Britannia Mill Learning Centre, Mackworth Road,
Derby
DE22 3BL
T 01332 594050
W www.lib.derby.ac.uk/library/homelib.html

University of Leicester Library
PO Box 248 University Road, Leicester
LE1 9QD
T 0116 252 2042
E libdesk@le.ac.uk
W www.le.ac.uk/li/index.html

University of Nottingham
Hallward Library, University Park, Nottingham
NG7 2RD
T 0115 951 4561
E library-arts-enquiries@nottingham.ac.uk
W www.nottingham.ac.uk/
librarycheesypeaswww.nottingham.ac.uk/library

London

Africa Centre
38 King Street, London
WC2E 8JT
T 020 7836 1973
E info@africacentre.org.uk
W www.africacentre.org.uk

**Anthroposophical Society in Great Britain
Library**
Rudolf Steiner House, 35 Park Road
London

NW1 6XT
T 020 7224 8398
E RSH-Library@anth.org.uk

Archbishops' Council
Council for the Care of Churches, Church House
Great Smith Street, London
SW1P 3NZ
T 020 7898 1884
E enquiries@ccc.c-of-e.org.uk

Arts Council of England
14 Great Peter Street, London
SW1P 3NQ
T 020 7973 6517
E enquiries@artscouncil.org.uk
W www.artscouncil.org.uk

Austrian Cultural Forum
28 Rutland Gate, Knightsbridge, London
SW7 1PQ
T 020 7584 8653
E andrea.rauter@bmaa.gv.at
W http:www.austria.org.uk/culture

Back Hill Library
School of Media, London College of Printing
10 Back Hill, Clerkenwell, London
EC1R 5LQ
T 020 7514 6882
E initial.surname@lcp.linst.ac.uk
W www.linst.ac.uk/library

BFI National Library
21 Stephen Street, London
W1T 1LN
T 020 7255 1444
E information@bfi.org.uk
W www.bfi.org.uk/nationallibrary

Birkbeck College Library
Malet Street, London
WC1E 7HX
T 020 7631 6239
E library-help@bbk.ac.uk
W www.bbk.ac.uk/lib

Bridgeman Art Library
17–19 Garway Road, London
W2 4PH
T 020 7727 4065
E london@bridgeman.co.uk
W www.bridgeman.co.uk

British Architectural Library (RIBA Library)
66 Portland Place, London
W1B 1AD
T 090 6302 0400
E info@inst.riba.org
W www.riba-library.com

British Council
Visual Arts Library, 10 Spring Gardens
London
SW1A 2BN
T 020 7389 3008
W www.britishcouncil.org/arts/vad

British Library (Scholarship & Collections)
96 Euston Road, London
NW1 2DB
T 020 7412 7676
E reader-services-enquiries@bl.uk
W www.bl.uk

British Library Map Library
96 Euston Road, London
NW1 2DB
T 020 7412 7702
E maps@bl.uk
W www.bl.uk/collections/maps

British Museum
Anthropology Library, Dept. of Ethnography
6 Burlington Gardens, London
W1S 2EX
T 020 7323 8031
E ethnography@thebritishmuseum.ac.uk

British Museum
Department of Prints and Drawings
Great Russell Street, London
WC1B 3DG
T 020 7323 8408
E prints@thebritishmuseum.ac.uk
W www.thebritishmuseum.ac.uk/
pd/pdhome.html

British Universities Film & Video Council
77 Wells Street, London
W1T 3QJ
T 020 7393 1500
E ask@bufvc.ac.uk
W www.bufvc.ac.uk

Byam Shaw School of Art
2 Elthorne Road, London
N19 4AG

T 020 7281 4111
E info@byam-shaw.ac.uk
W www.byam-shaw.ac.uk

Camberwell College of Arts Library
Peckham Road, London
SE5 8UF
T 020 7514 6349
W www.arts.ac.uk/library

Central Saint Martins College of Art & Design
Charing Cross Road Library, 107–109 Charing
Cross Road, London
WC2H 0DU
T 020 7514 7190
E a.huxstep@csm.linst.ac.uk
W www.linst.ac.uk/library (for Library & Learning
Resources)

Central Saint Martins College of Art & Design
Drama Centre London Library, 176 Prince of Wales
Road, London
NW5 3PT
T 020 7267 1177
E c.barontini@csm.linst.ac.uk
W www.linst.ac.uk/library (for Library & Learning
Resources)

Central Saint Martins College of Art & Design
Southampton Row Library, Southampton Row,
London
WC1B 4AP
T 020 7514 7037
E e.powis@csm.linst.ac.uk
W www.linst.ac.uk/library (for Library & Learning
Resources)

Chelsea College of Art and Design
Hugon Road Library, Hugon Road, Fulham,
London, SW6 3ES
T 020 7514 7901/2
W www.linst.ac.uk/library

Chelsea College of Art and Design
Lime Grove Library, Lime Grove, Shepherds Bush,
London
W12 8EA
T 020 7514 7833
E lg-lib@linst.ac.uk
W www.linst.ac.uk/library

Chelsea College of Art and Design
Manresa Road Library, Manresa Road, London
SW3 6LS

T 020 7514 7773
W www.linst.ac.uk/library

Cinema Theatre Association
44 Harrowdene Gardens
Teddington, Middlesex
TW11 0DJ
T 020 8977 2608
W www.cinema-theatre.org.uk

Courtauld Institute of Art Library
Somerset House, Strand
London, WC2R 0RN
T 020 7848 2701
E booklib@courtauld.ac.uk
W www.courtauld.ac.uk

Crafts Council
44a Pentonville Road
Islington
London
N1 9BY
T 020 7806 2501
E reference@craftscouncil.org.uk
W www.craftscouncil.org.uk

English Heritage Library
23 Savile Row
London
W1S 2ET
T 020 7973 3001
E library@english-heritage.org.uk

English Heritage Photo Library
23 Savile Row
London
W1S 2ET
T 020 7973 3338/9
E celia.sterne@english-heritage.org.uk

Fine Art Trade Guild Archive
16–18 Empress Place
London
SW6 1TT
T 020 7381 6616
E info@fineart.co.uk
W www.fineart.co.uk

Fulham Reference Library
598 Fulham Road
London
SW6 5NX
T 020 8753 3876
E info@haflibs.org.uk

Geffrye Museum Archive
Kingsland Road
London
E2 8EA
T 020 7739 9893
E info@geffrye-museum

Getty Images
Hulton Archive
Unique House
21–31 Woodfield Road
London
W9 2BA
T 0207 579 5768
E sarah.mcdonald@getty-images.com

Goethe-Institut Inter Nationes Library
50 Princes Gate
Exhibition Road
London
SW7 2PH
T 020 7596 4044
E library@london.goethe.org
W http//www.goethe.de/gr/lon/enindex.htm

Goldsmiths College Library
Lewisham Way
New Cross, London
SE14 6NW
T 020 7919 7150
E library@gold.ac.uk
W www.gold.ac.uk/infos/lib

Guildhall Library (Print Room)
Aldermanbury, London
EC2P 2EJ
T 020 7332 1839
E prints&maps@corpoflondon.gov.uk

Hayward Gallery Library
Belvedere Road, London
SE1 8XX
T 020 7921 0854
E pgriffin@hayward.org.uk
W www.haywardgallery.org.uk

Historical Manuscripts Commission
Quality House, Quality Court
Chancery Lane
London
WC2A 1HP
T 020 7242 1198
E nra@hmc.gov.uk
W www.hmc.gov.uk

Horniman Museum Library
100 London Road
Forest Hill, London
SE23 3PQ
T 020 8291 8681
E Enquiry@horniman.ac.uk
W www.horniman.ac.uk/visiting/library.cfm

Hyman Kreitman Research Centre for the Tate Library & Archive
Millbank, London
SW1P 4RG
T 020 7887 8838
E research.centre@tate.org.uk
W www.tate.org.uk/researchservices/researchcentre

Imperial College of Science, Technology and Medicine
Central Library
Exhibition Road, London
SW7 2AZ
T 020 7594 8820
E libhelp@ic.ac.uk
W www.lib.ic.ac.uk

Imperial War Museum, Photographic Archive
All Saints Annexe
Austral Street, London
SE11 4SL
T 020 7416 5338
E photos@iwm.org.uk

Inchbald School of Design Library
32 Eccleston Square, London
SW1V 0NR
T 020 7630 9011
E info@inchbald.co.uk

Institute of International Visual Arts Library
6–8 Standard Place
Rivington St, London
EC2A 3BE
T 020 7729 9616
E ariede@iniva.org
W www.iniva.org

Lambeth Palace Library
Lambeth Palace Road, London
SE1 7JU
T 020 7898 1400
W www.lambethpalacelibrary.org

London College of Communication
Elephant & Castle, London
SE1 6SB
T 020 7514 6527/8026
E libraryenquiries@lcp.linst.ac.uk
W www.arts.ac.uk/library

London College of Fashion
20 John Princes Street, London
W1G 0BJ
T 020 7514 7453/7455
W www.arts.ac.uk/library

London Metropolitan University
Learning Centre
North Campus
236–250 Holloway Road
London, N7 6PP
T 020 7753 5170
W www.unl.ac.uk/library

London Metropolitan University
Library and Learning Resource Centre
City Campus
41–71 Commercial Road
London, E1 1IA
T 020 7320 1869
W www.lgu.ac.uk/as/library/ilrc/index.htm

London Metropolitan University
The Women's Library
Old Castle Street
London, E1 7NT
T 020 7320 3515/3516
E enquirydesk@thewomenslibrary.ac.uk
W www.thewomenslibrary.ac.uk

London Transport Museum Reference Library
39 Wellington St, London
WC2E 7BB
T 020 7379 6344
W www.ltmuseum.co.uk/collections/reference.html

Main Library Queen Mary, University of London
Mile End Road, London
E1 4NS
T 020 7882 3300
E library-enquiries@qmul
W www.library.qmul.ac.uk

MAKE, the organisation for women in the arts
Central St. Martins College of Art, 107–109

Charing Cross Road, London
WC2H 0DU
T 020 7514 8869
E womensart@csm.linst.ac.uk
W www.womensart.org.uk

Mary Evans Picture Library
59 Tranquil Vale
Blackheath, London
SE3 0BS
T 020 8318 0034
E Lib@mepl.co.uk
W www.mepl.co.uk

Middlesex University
Art & Design Learning Resources
Cat Hill, Barnet, Herts, EN4 8HT
T 020 8411 5111
W www.ilrs.mdx.ac.uk

Museum of Domestic Design & Architecture (MODA)
Cat Hill, Barnet, Herts
EN4 8HT
T 020 8411 5244
E moda@mdx.ac.uk
W www.moda.mdx.ac.uk

Museum of London Library
150 London Wall, London
EC2Y 5HN
T 020 7814 5605

National Maritime Museum
Caird Library, Park Row
Greenwich, London
SE10 9NF
T 020 8312 6673
E library@nmm.ac.uk
W www.nmm.ac.uk/cmr/index.html

National Portrait Gallery
Heinz Archive & Library
Orange St, St Martin's Place
London, WC2H 0HE
T 020 7306 0055 x 257
E archive@npg.org.uk
W www.npg.org.uk/live/research.asp

Natural History Museum Library
Cromwell Road, London, SW7 5BD
T 020 7942 5460
E library@nhm.ac.uk
W www.nhm.ac.uk/library

Paul Mellon Centre for Studies in British Art
16 Bedford Square, London
WC1B 3JA
T 020 7580 0311
E info@paul-mellon-centre.ac.uk
W www.paul-mellon-centre.ac.uk

Roehampton Learning Resources Centre
University of Surrey Roehampton
Roehampton Lane, London
SW15 5SZ
T 020 8392 3770
E enquiry.desk@roehampton.ac.uk
W www.roehampton.ac.uk/support/infoserv/index.asp

Royal Academy of Arts
Burlington House
Piccadilly, London
W1J 0BD
T 020 7300 5737
E library@royalacademy.org.uk
W www.royalacademy.org.uk

Royal Borough of Kensington & Chelsea Central Reference Library
Hornton Street, London
W8 7RX
T 020 7937 2542
E information.services@rbkc.gov.uk
W www.rbkc.gov.uk

Royal College of Art Library
Kensington Gore, London
SW7 2EU
T 020 7590 4224
E library@rca.ac.uk
W www.rca.ac.uk

School of Oriental & African Studies Library, University of London
Art Section, Thornhaugh Street
Russell Square, London
WC1H 0XG
T 020 7898 4163
E libenquiry@soas.ac.uk
W www.soas.ac.uk/library

Society for the Protection of Ancient Buildings
37 Spital Square, London
E1 6DY
T 020 7377 1644
E info@spab.org.uk
W www.spab.org.uk

Society of Antiquaries of London
Burlington House, Piccadilly
London, W1J 0BE
T 020 7479 7084
E library@sal.org.uk
W www.sal.org.uk

Sotheby's Institute of Art
30 Oxford Street
London
W1D 1AU
T 020 7462 3240
E sothebys.com

St Bride Printing Library
Bride Lane, Fleet St
London
EC4Y 8EE
T 020 7353 4660
E stbride@corpoflondon.gov.uk
W www.stbride.org/index.htm

Swiss Cottage Library
88 Avenue Road, London
NW3 3HA
T 020 7974 6528

The National Gallery, Libraries & Archive Department
Trafalgar Square
London
WC2N 5DN
T 020 7747 2542
E lad@ng-london.org.uk
W www.nationalgallery.org.uk/about/history/library

The National Gallery, Technical Library Scientific Department
Trafalgar Square
London
WC2N 5DN
T 020 7747 2829
E jo.kirby@ng-london.org.uk

University College London
Folklore Society Library
University College London
Gower Street
London
WC1E 6BT
T 020 7862 8564
E folklore.society@talk21.com
W www.folklore-society.com

University College London Library
Gower St, London
WC1E 6BT
T 020 7679 7700
E library@ucl.ac.uk
W www.ucl.ac.uk/library

University of East London
African and Asian Visual Artists Archive
4–6 University Way, London
E16 2RD
T 020 8223 7561
E j.e.conley@uel.ac.uk
W www.uel.ac.uk/aavaa

University of East London
Docklands Learning Resources Centre
University Way, London
E16 2RD
T 020 8223 3434
W www.uel.ac.uk/lss

University of East London
Holbrook Learning Resources Centre
Holbrook Road, London
E15 3EA
T 020 8223 3251
E s.p.lyes@uel.ac.uk
W www.uel.ac.uk/lss

University of London Library
Senate House
Malet Street, London
WC1E 7HU
T 020 7862 8461
W www.ull.ac.uk

University of Westminster
Marylebone Campus Library
35 Marylebone Road
London
NW1 5LS
T 020 7911 5000 x 3171
W www.wmin.ac.uk/mrdlib

Victoria and Albert Museum
Archive of Art and Design
Word & Image Department
Blythe House, 23 Blythe Road
London
W14 0QX
T 020 7603 1514
E archive@vam.ac.uk
W www.vam.ac.uk/resources/archives/aad

Victoria and Albert Museum
National Art Library
Word & Image Department
Cromwell Road, London
SW7 2RL
T 020 7942 2400
E nal.enquiries@vam.ac.uk
W www.vam.ac.uk/nal

Victoria and Albert Museum
Prints, Drawings, Paintings and Photographs
Collection, Word & Image Department
Cromwell Road, London, SW7 2RL
T 020 7942 2563
E pdp@vam.ac.uk
W www.vam.ac.uk/resources/print_study_reading

Victoria and Albert Museum
Theatre Museum, Archive of Art and Design,
Word & Image Department
Blythe House, 23 Blythe Road
London
W14 0QX
E tmenquiries@vam.ac.uk
W www.vam.ac.uk/vastatic/theatre/
researching.html

Wallace Collection Library
Hertford House
Manchester Square, London
W1U 3BN
T 020 7563 9528
E gpt88@dial.pipex.co.uk
W www.the-wallace-
collection.org.uk/i_s/library_and_archives/library
_archives_index.htm

**Warburg Institute (School of Advanced Study,
University of London)**
Woburn Square
London
WC1H 0AB
T 020 7862 8935
E warlib@sas.ac.uk
W www.sas.ac.uk/warburg

**Wellcome Library for the History and
Understanding of Medicine**
183 Euston Road
London
NW1 2BE
T 020 7611 8582
E Library@wellcome.ac.uk
library.wellcome.ac.uk

William Morris Gallery
Lloyd Park, Forest Road
Walthamstow
London
E17 4PP
T 020 8527 3782
W www.lbwf.gov.uk/wmg

William Morris Society
Kelmscott House
26 Upper Mall
Hammersmith, London
W6 9TA
T 020 8741 3735
E william.morris@care4free.net
W www.morrissociety.org

Wimbledon College of Art
Merton Hall Road, London
SW19 3QA
T 020 8408 5027
E p.jennett@wimbledon.ac.uk
W www.arts.ac.uk/library

Worshipful Company of Goldsmiths
Goldsmiths' Hall
Foster Lane, London
EC2V 6BN
T 020 7606 7010
E the.library@thegoldsmiths.co.uk
W www.thegoldsmiths.co.uk

North-east

Ashburne Library (University of Sunderland)
Ashburne House
Ryhope Road, Sunderland
SR2 7EF
T 0191 515 2119
W www.library.sunderland.ac.uk

Newcastle College
School of Art & Design Library
Rye Hill Campus, Scotswood Road
Newcastle-upon-Tyne
NE4 7SA
T 0191 200 4000

Newcastle Libraries
Princess Square, Newcastle-upon-Tyne
NE99 1DX
T 0191 2774100
E information@newcastle.gov.uk
W www.newcastle.gov.uk/libraries

Northumbria University
Library and Learning Services
City Campus, Ellison Terrace
Newcastle-upon-Tyne
NE1 8ST
T 0191 227 4125
E need@northumbria.ac.uk
northumbria.ac.uk/sd/central/library

Robinson Library
University of Newcastle-upon-Tyne
Newcastle-upon-Tyne
NE2 4HQ
T 0191 222 7662
E library@ncl.ac.uk
W www.ncl.ac.uk/library

University of Teesside
Library & Information Services
Borough Road, Middlesbrough
TS1 3BA
T 01642 342100
W www.tees.ac.uk/lis

Northern Ireland

Architecture & Planning Library,
Queen's University Belfast
Lennoxvale, Belfast
BT9 5EQ
T 028 90 335459
E k.latimer@qub.ac.uk
W www.qub.ac.uk/lib

Centre for Migration Studies at the Ulster-
American Folk Park
2 Mellon Road, Castletown
Omagh, Co. Tyrone
BT78 5QY
T 028 8225 6315
E uafp@ia.ie
W www.qub.ac.uk/cms

University of Ulster Library
York Street, Belfast
BT15 1ED
T 028 9026 7270
W www.ulster.ac.uk/library

North-west

Chester College Learning Resources
Parkgate Road, Chester
CH1 4BJ

T 01244 375444
E enquiries@chester.ac.uk
W www.chester.ac.uk/smilne

Cumbria Institute of the Arts Library
Brampton Rd, Carlisle
CA3 9AY
T 01228 400312
W www.cumbriacad.ac.uk

John Rylands University Library
of Manchester
Burlington Street, Manchester
M13 9PP
T 016 1275 3738
E libtalk@man.ac.uk
ryliweb.man.ac.uk

Lancaster University Library
Bailrigg, Lancaster
LA1 4YH
T 01524 592516
E library@lancs.ac.uk
libweb.lancs.ac.uk

Liverpool John Moores University
Aldham Robarts Learning Resource Centre
Mount Pleasant, Liverpool
L3 5UZ
T 0151 231 3701
E cwis.livjm.ac.uk/lea/aldham

Manchester Central Library
Arts Library
St Peter's Square, Manchester
M2 5PD
T 016 1234 1974
E arts@libraries.manchester.gov.uk
W www.manchester.gov.uk/libraries/central/arts

Manchester Metropolitan University
All Saints Library, Oxford Road, Manchester
M15 6BH
T 0161 247 6108/6116
E artdesign-lib-enq@mmu.ac.uk
W www.mmu.ac.uk/services/library

Museum of Science & Industry
in Manchester
Liverpool Road, Castlefield
Manchester
M3 4FP
T 0161 606 0127
W www.msim.org.uk

Ruskin Library
Library Avenue
Lancaster University
Lancaster
LA1 4YH
T 01524 593587
E ruskin.library@lancaster.ac.uk
W www.lancs.ac.uk/users/ruskinlib

Sheppard Worlock Library
Liverpool Hope
Hope Park
Taggart Avenue
Liverpool
L16 9JD
T 0151 291 2001
W www.hope.ac.uk/lib/lrd.htm

Southport College Library
Mornington Road, Southport
PR9 0TT
T 01704 500606
E library@southport.ac.uk

Sydney Jones Library
University of Liverpool
Chatham Street, Liverpool
L69 3DA
T 0151 794 2679
E ql10@liverpool.ac.uk
W www.liv.ac.uk/library

**University of Central Lancashire Library &
Learning Resources Services**
St. Peter's Square
Preston
PR1 2HE
T 01772 892269
W www.uclan.ac.uk/library/libhom1.htm

Walker Art Gallery Library/Archive
William Brown Street
Liverpool
L3 8EL
T 0151 478 4199
W www.nmgm.org.uk

Whitworth Art Gallery
University of Manchester
Oxford Road, Manchester
M15 6ER
T 0161 275 7450
E whitworth@man.ac.uk
W www.whitworth.man.ac.uk

Scotland

Aberdeen University Library
Meston Walk, Aberdeen
Aberdeenshire
AB24 3UE
T 01224 272590
W www.abdn.ac.uk/diss/library

**Duncan of Jordanstone College
of Art & Design Library**
Perth Road, Dundee
DD1 4HT
T 01382 345255
E dojlib@dundee.ac.uk
W www.dundee.ac.uk/library

Dundee City Library
Art and Music Department
Wellgate Centre, Dundee
DD1 1DB
T 01382 434326
E Arts.video@dundeecity.gov.uk
W www.dundeecity.gov.uk

Edinburgh College of Art Library Service
Lauriston Place, Edinburgh
EH3 9DF
T 0131 221 6034
W www.lib.eca.ac.uk

Edinburgh University Library
George Square, Edinburgh
EH8 9LJ
T 0131 650 1000
E Library@ed.ac.uk
W www.lib.ed.ac.uk

Fine Art Library
George IV Bridge, Edinburgh
EH1 1EG
T 0131 242 8040
E central.fineart.library@edinburgh.gov.uk
W www.edinburgh.gov.uk/CEC/Recreation/
Libraries/FineArtLibrary/GuidetoFineArtLibrary/
fineartintro.html

Glasgow School of Art Library
167 Renfrew Street
Glasgow
G3 6RQ
T 0141 353 4551
E j.mckay@gsa.ac.uk
W www.gsa.ac.uk/library

Glasgow University Library
Glasgow University Library
Hillhead Street, Glasgow
G12 8QE
T 0141 330 6704/5
E library@lib.gla.ac.uk
W www.lib.gla.ac.uk

Mitchell Library
North Street, Glasgow
G3 7DN
T 0141 287 2933
E arts@gcl.glasgow.gov.uk
W www.mitchelllibrary.org

Napier University
Merchiston Learning Centre
10 Colinton Road, Edinburgh
EH10 5DT
T 0131 455 2582
E nulis.enquiry@napier.ac.uk
W www.nulis.napier.ac.uk

National Gallery of Scotland Library
The Mound, Edinburgh
EH2 2EL
T 0131 624 6501
W www.nationalgalleries.org

National Library of Scotland
George IV Bridge, Edinburgh
EH1 1EW
T 0131 226 4531
E enquiries@nls.uk
W www.nls.uk

National Monuments Record
of Scotland
John Sinclair House
16 Bernard Terrace
Edinburgh
EH8 9NX
T 0131 662 1456
E nmrs@rcahms.gov.uk
W www.rcahms.gov.uk

National Museums of Scotland
Library
Chambers Street
Edinburgh
EH1 1JF
T 0131 247 4137
E library@nms.ac.uk
W www.nms.ac.uk

Robert Gordon University
Georgina Scott Sutherland Library
Garthdee Road, Aberdeen
AB10 7QE
T 01224 263475
W www2.rgu.ac.uk/library

Royal Scottish Academy Collections
The Dean Gallery
73 Belford Road
Edinburgh
EH4 3DS
T 0131 624 6277
E info@royalscottishacademy.org

Scottish Arts Council
12 Manor Place, Edinburgh
EH3 7DD
T 0845 603 6000
E help.desk@scottisharts.org.uk
W www.scottisharts.org.uk

Scottish National Gallery of Modern
Art Archive and Library
Dean Gallery, Belford Road
Edinburgh
EH4 3DS
T 0131 624 6252/3
E gmarchive@nationalgalleries.org (archive)
gmalibrary@nationalgalleries.org (gallery)
W www.nationalgalleries.org

Scottish National Portrait Gallery
1 Queen Street
Edinburgh
EH2 1JD
T 0131 624 6420
E pginfo@nationalgalleries.org
W www.nationalgalleries.org

St Andrews University Library
North Street, St Andrews, Fife
KY16 9TR
T 01334 462281
E library@st-and.ac.uk
W www-library.st-and.ac.uk

University of Strathclyde Library
101 St James' Road
Glasgow
G4 0NS
T 0141 548 4620
E libray@strath.ac.uk
W www.lib.strath.ac.uk

South-east

Amersham & Wycombe College Learning Resources Centre
Stanley Hill, Amersham
HP7 9HN
T 01494 735553

Bate Collection of Musical Instruments
University of Oxford
St Aldate's, Oxford
OX1 1DP
T 01865 276139
E Bate.Collection@music.ox ac.uk
W www.ashmol.ox.ac.uk/BCMIPage.html

BBC Written Archives Centre
Caversham Park, Reading
RG4 8TZ
T 0118 948 6281
E wac.enquiries@bbc.co.uk
W www.bbc.co.uk/thenandnow

Bodleian Library
Broad Street, Oxford
OX1 3BG
T 01865 277162
W www.bodley.ox.ac.uk

Brighton Public Library
Vantage Point
New England Street
Brighton
BN1 2GW
T 01273 296961/57/69
E blibrary@hotmail.com
W www.brighton-hove.gov.uk/bhc/libraries

Buckinghamshire Chilterns University College
High Wycombe Campus Learning Resources
Centre, Queen Alexandra Road
High Wycombe
HP11 2JZ
T 01494 605107
E hwlib@bcuc.ac.uk
W www.bcuc.ac.uk/main.asp?page=400

Canterbury Christ Church University College Library
North Holmes Road
Canterbury
CT1 1QU
T 01227 767700 x 2514
W www.library.cant.ac.uk

Centre for the Study of Cartoons & Caricature
Templeman Library, University of Kent at
Canterbury, Canterbury
CT2 7NU
E library.ukc.ac.uk/cartoons

Edward Barnsley Furniture Archive
Cockshott Lane, Froxfield
GU32 1BB
E enquiries@barnsley-furniture.co.uk
W www.barnsley-furniture.co.uk

Embroiderers' Guild Library
Apt.41 Hampton Court Palace
East Molesey
KT8 9AU
T 020 8943 1229
E administrator@embroiderersguild.com
W www.embroiderersguild.org.uk/eglibrary/index.html

Epsom Library
6 The Derby Square, Epsom
KT19 8AG
T 01372 721707
E epsom.information@surreycc.gov.uk

Gayton Library
Harrow Library Services
Gayton Road, Harrow, Middlesex
HA1 2HL
T 020 8427 6012/6986
E Gayton.library@harrow.gov.uk
W www.harrow.gov.uk/council/departments/libraries/libraryhome.asp

Hampshire County Council Museums Service Library
Chilcomb House, Chilcomb Lane
Winchester
SO23 8RD
T 01962 846304
E gill.arnott@hants.gov.uk
W www.hants.gov.uk/museums

High Wycombe Reference and Business Library
Queen Victoria Road
High Wycombe
HP11 1BD
T 01494 510241
E hwrlib@hotmail.com
W www.buckscc.gov.uk/libraries/lima_lib_hwr.stm

Kingston University
Knights Park Learning Resources Centre
Knights Park, Kingston upon Thames
KT1 2QJ
W www.kingston.ac.uk/library_media/index.html
T 020 8547 7057
library@kingston.ac.uk

Northbrook College Library
Littlehampton Road, Durrington
Worthing
BN12 6NU
T 01903 606213
E a.torley@nbcol.ac.uk

Open University Library
Walton Hall, Milton Keynes
MK7 6AA
T 01908 659001
E Lib-help@open.ac.uk
W www.oulib1.open.ac.uk

Oxford Brookes University Library
(Headington Library)
Gipsy Lane, Headington
Oxford
OX3 0BP
T 01865 483156
W www.brookes.ac.uk/services/library

**Ravensbourne College of Design
and Communication**
Walden Road
Chislehurst
BR7 5SN
T 020 8289 4919
E s.hocking@rave.ac.uk
W www.rave.ac.uk

Reading University Library
Whiteknights
PO Box 223
Reading
RG6 6AE
T 0118 378 8770
E library@reading.ac.uk
W www.reading.ac.uk/library

**Reigate School of Art, Design
& Media Library**
Claremont Road
Redhill
RH1 2JX
T 01737 772611 x 1253

Sackler Library
University of Oxford
1 St John Street, Oxford
OX1 2LG
T 01865 278092
W www.saclib.ox.ac.uk

Southampton City Libraries
Civic Centre, Southampton
SO14 7LW
T 023 8083 2462
E reference.library@southampton.gov.uk
W www.southampton.gov.uk/education/libraries

Southampton Institute
Mountbatten Library
East Park Terrace, Southampton
SO14 0YN
T 02380 319249
W www.solent.ac.uk/library

Sutton Library
St Nicholas Way, Sutton
SM1 1EA
T 0208 770 4765
E sutton.music@sutton.gov.uk
W www.sutton.gov.uk/lfl/librarie/index.htm

Templeman Library
University of Kent at Canterbury
Canterbury
CT2 7NU
T 01227 764000 x 3570
E library-enqiry@ukc.ac.uk
W www.ukc.ac.uk/library

University College for the Creative Arts
Epsom Library and Learning Centre
Ashley Road, Epsom
KT18 5BE
T 01372 202460
W www.ucreative.ac.uk

University College for the Creative Arts
Canterbury Library
New Dover Road
Canterbury
CT1 3AN
T 01227 817514
W www.ucreative.ac.uk

University College for the Creative Arts
Maidstone Library, Oakwood Park
Maidstone, ME16 8AG

T 01622 620120
W www.ucreative.ac.uk

University College for the Creative Arts
Rochester Library, Fort Pitt, Rochester
ME1 1DZ
T 01634 888734
W www.ucreative.ac.uk

University Library
University of Surrey, Guildford
GU2 7XH
T 01483 683325
E library-enquiries@surrey.ac.uk
W www.surrey.ac.uk/library

University of Brighton
Aldrich Library, Cockcroft Building,
Moulsecoomb, Brighton
BN2 4GJ
T 01273 642760
E AskAldrich@brighton.ac.uk
W www.brighton.ac.uk/studentlife/libraries.php

University of Brighton
Design History Research Centre Archives
including the Design Council Archive, Grand
Parade, Brighton
BN2 2JY
T 01273 643219/09
E dhrc@brighton.ac.uk
W www.brighton.ac.uk/descoarchive

University of Brighton
St Peter's House Library
16–18 Richmond Place, Brighton
BN2 9NA
T 01273 643221
E Asksph@brighton.ac.uk
W www.brighton.ac.uk/is/lstpeter.html

University of Sussex Library
Falmer, Brighton
BN1 9QL
T 01273 678163
E library@sussex.ac.uk
W www.sussex.ac.uk/library

University of Westminster
Harrow Learning Resources Centre
Watford Road, Northwick Park, Harrow
HA1 3TP
T 020 7911 5885
W www.wmin.ac.uk/harlib

Winchester School of Art Library
Park Avenue, Winchester
SO23 8DL
T 023 8059 6982/4
E wsaenqs@soton.ac.uk
W www.library.soton.ac.uk/wsal/index.shtml

Worthing Reference Library
Richmond Road, Worthing
BN11 1HD
T 01903 212060
W www.westsussex.gov.uk/Li/home.htm

South-west

American Museum in Britain Library
Claverton Manor, Bath
BA2 7BD
E amibbath@aol.com

Arts Institute at Bournemouth Library
Wallisdown, Poole
BH12 5HH
T 01202 363308
E library@aib.ac.uk
W www.aib.ac.uk

Bath Spa University College
Sion Hill Library, 8 Somerset Place
Bath
BA1 5HB
T 01225 875648
W www.bathspa.ac.uk/library

**Bournemouth & Poole College Learning
Resources Centre**
North Road Parkstone, Poole
BH14 0LS
T 01202 205681
W www.thecollege.co.uk

Bournemouth University Library
Fern Barrow, Poole
BH12 5BB
T 01202 595083
W www.bournemouth.ac.uk/library

Bristol Art Library
College Green, Bristol
BS1 5TL
E anthony_beeson@bristol-city.gov.uk
W www.bristol.gov.uk/ccm/navigation/leisure-
and-culture/libraries

Cheltenham Art Gallery & Museum
Clarence Street, Cheltenham
GL52 6DS
T 01242 237431
W www.cheltenhammuseum.org.uk

Cheltenham Library
Clarence Street, Cheltenham
GL50 3JT
T 01242 532585/6
E cheltref@gloscc.gov.uk

Dartington College of Arts
Library and Learning Resources Centre
Dartington Hall Estate, Totnes, TQ9 6EJ
T 01803 861651
E Library@dartington.ac.uk
W www.dartington.ac.uk/studentsup/llrc.htm

Frewen Library
University of Portsmouth, Cambridge Road,
Portsmouth
PO1 2ST
T 02392 843228
E library@port.ac.uk
W www.libr.port.ac.uk

**Information and Learning Services, University
of Plymouth (Exeter Campus)**
Earl Richard Road North, Exeter
EX4 6HU
T 01392 475049
W www.plymouth.ac.uk

Museum of Costume
Fashion Research Centre, 4 Circus
Bath, BA1 2EW
T 01225 477752
E costume_enquiries@bathnes.gov.uk
W www.museumofcostume.co.uk

National Monuments Record
Kemble Drive, Swindon
SN2 2GZ
T 01793 414600
E nmrinfo@english-heritage.org.uk
W www.english-heritage.org.uk/knowledge/
nmr/index.asp

Plymouth College of Art and Design Library
Tavistock Place, Plymouth
PL4 8AT
T 01752 203412
W www.pcad.ac.uk/library.htm

Russell-Cotes Art Gallery & Museum
East Cliff, Bournemouth
BH1 3AA
T 01202 451858
E diane.edge@bournemouth.gov.uk
W www.russell-cotes.bournemouth.gov.uk

University of Bath Library & Learning Centre
Claverton Down, Bath
BA2 7AY
T 01225 388388
E Library@bath.ac.uk
W www.bath.ac.uk/libary

**University of Bristol Information Services,
Arts & Social Sciences Library**
Tyndall Avenue, Bristol
BS8 1TJ
T 0117 928 8017
E library@bristol.ac.uk
W www.bris.ac.uk/is

**University of Exeter Library & Information
Service**
Stocker Road, Exeter
EX4 4PT
T 01392 263873
E library@ex.ac.uk
W www.ex.ac.uk/library

University of Gloucestershire
Pittville Learning Centre Learning and
Information Services, Pittville Campus
Albert Road, Pittville, Cheltenham
GL52 3JG
T 01242 532254
W www.glos.ac.uk

**University of the West of England
Bristol (UWE)**
Faculty of Art, Media & Design Library, Bower
Ashton Campus, Kennel Lodge Road, Bristol
BS3 2JT
T 0117 344 4750
E Geoff.Cole@uwe.ac.uk
W www.uwe.ac.uk/library

Wales

Architecture Library, Cardiff University
Bute Building, King Edward VII Avenue
Cardiff
CF10 3NB
T 029 2087 5975

E harriss@cf.ac.uk
W www.cardiff.ac.uk/infos/centres/architecture

Cardiff County Libraries & Information Service
Central Library/Humanities Library
St David's Link, Frederick Street, Cardiff
CF10 2DU
T 029 2038 2116
E enquiry@libraries.cardiff.gov.uk
W www.cardiff.gov.uk/libraries

Museum of Welsh Life/Amgueddfa Werin Cymru
St Fagans/Sain Ffagan, Cardiff, CF1 3NP
T 029 2057 3500
E mwl@nmgw.ac.uk
W www.nmgw.ac.uk/mwl/index.en.shtml

National Museums & Galleries of Wales Library
Cathays Park, Cardiff, CF10 3NP
T 02920 573202
W www.nmgw.ac.uk

University of Wales College, Newport
Library & Information Services Caerleon Campus
PO Box 179, Newport, NP18 3YG
T 01633 432294
E llr@newport.ac.uk
lis.newport.ac.uk

University of Wales Institute, Cardiff (UWIC)
Howard Gardens Library
Howard Gdns, Cardiff, CF2 1SP
T 0292 041 6243
W www.uwic.ac.uk/library

West Midlands

Barber Fine Art Library
University of Birmingham, Edgbaston
Birmingham, B15 2TT
T 0121 414 7334
E bblib@bham.ac.uk
W www.is.bham.ac.uk/barberart

Bournville Centre for the Visual Arts
University of Central England, Ruskin Hall,
Lindon Road, Bournville, Birmingham, B30 1JX
T 0121 331 5756
E sue.o'sullivan@uce.ac.uk
W www.uce.ac.uk/library/public

College of Art Library
University of Central England, Margaret Street
Birmingham, B3 3BX

T 0121 331 5977
W www.uce.ac.uk/library/public

Coventry University
Lanchester Library, Frederick Lanchester Building
Gosford Street, Coventry, CV1 5DD
T 02476 887542
W www.library.coventry.ac.uk

Gosta Green
University of Central England
Corporation Street, Birmingham, B4 7DX
T 0121 331 5860
E library.uce.ac.uk

Harrison Learning Centre
St Peters Square, Wolverhampton
WV1 1RH
T 01902 322300
W www.wlv.ac.uk/lib

Herefordshire College of Art & Design Library
Folly Lane, Hereford, HR1 1LT
T 01432 273357
W www.hereford-art-col.ac.uk

Keele Information Services Library
Keele University, Keele, ST5 5BG
T 01782 583535
E libhelp@keele.ac.uk
W www.keele.ac.uk/depts/li

Kidderminster Library
Market Street, Kidderminster
DY10 1AD
T 01562 824500
E kiddersminsterlib@worcestershire.gov.uk
W www.worcestershire.gov.uk/libraries

Lace Guild
The Hollies, 53 Audnam, Stourbridge
DY8 4AE
T 01384 390739
E hollies@laceguild.org
W www.laceguild.orgcheesypeaswww.laceguild.org

School of Jewellery Library
University of Central England, Vittoria Street,
Birmingham, B1 3PA
T 0121 331 6470
W www.uce.ac.uk/library/public

Shakespeare Centre Library
Henley Street, Stratford-upon-Avon, CV37 6QW

T 01789 201813
E library@shakespeare.org.uk

Staffordshire University
Thompson Library, College Road
Stoke-on-Trent, ST4 2XS
T 01782 294771
E LLRS@staffs.ac.uk
W www.staffs.ac.uk/services/library_and_info/
library.html

Stoke-on-Trent Libraries Information & Archives
Bethesda Street, Hanley
Stoke-on-Trent, ST1 3RS
T 01782 238420
E stoke.archives@stoke.gov.uk (archives section)
hanley.ref@stoke.gov.uk (reference section)
W www.stoke.gov.uk/council/libraries

University of Warwick Library
Gibbet Hill Road, Coventry, CV4 7AL
T 024 7652 4103
E library@warwick.ac.uk
library.warwick.ac.uk

Worcester College of Technology
School of Art & Design, Barbourne Road
Worcester, WR1 1RT
T 01905 725631
E smaund@wortech.ac.uk
W www.wortech.ac.uk

Yorkshire and Humberside

Art & Design Library
Grimsby College Libraries
Westward Ho, Grimsby, DN34 5AQ
T 01472 311231 x 372

Bowes Museum
Newgate, Barnard Castle, DL12 8NP
T 01833 690606
E info@bowes.org.uk
W www.bowesmuseum.org.uk

Bradford Central Library
Prince's Way, Bradford, BD1 1NN
T 01274 753688
E bradford.libraries@bradford.gov.uk
W www.bradford.gov.uk/council/libraries/
frames.html

Doncaster College
Church View Learning Resource Centre

Church View, Doncaster, DN1 1RF
T 01302 553816
W www.don.ac.uk/facilities/lrc.htm

Grove Library, Bradford College
Great Horton Road, Bradford
BD7 1AY
T 01274 753156
W www.bradfordcollege.ac.uk/college/facilities/
collfac/libraries

Henry Moore Institute
74 The Headrow, Leeds, LS1 3AH
T 0113 246 9469
E library@henry-moore@ac.uk

Leeds Art Library
Calverley Street, Leeds
LS1 3AB
T 0113 247 8247
E artandmusic@leeds.gov.uk

Leeds College of Art & Design
Vernon Street, Leeds
LS2 8PH
T 0113 202 8096
E chris.graham@leeds-art.ac.uk
W www.leeds-art.ac.uk

Leeds Metropolitan University
Learning Centre, Leslie Silver Building
Woodhouse Lane, Leeds
LS1 3HE
T 0113 283 5968
E infodesk.lc@leedsmet.ac.uk
W www.leedsmet.ac.uk/lis/lss

Leeds University Library
Leeds
LS2 9JT
T 0113 233 5513
E library@library.leeds.ac.uk
W www.leeds.ac.uk/library

National Arts Education Archive (Trust)
University of Leeds
Bretton Hall Campus
Wakefield, WF4 4LG
T 01924 832020
E skielty@leeds.ac.uk
naea.leeds.ac.uk/cheesypeasnaea.leeds.ac.uk

National Museum of Film & Photography
Pictureville, Bradford, BD1 1NQ

T 01274 203377
E b.binder@nmsi.ac.uk
W www.nmpft.org.uk

Royal Armouries Library
Armouries Drive, Leeds
LS10 1LT
T 0113 220 1832
E enquiries@armouries.org.uk
W www.armouries.org.uk/leeds/library.html

Sheffield Arts & Social Sciences Central Library
Surrey Street, Sheffield
S1 1XZ
T 0114 2734747
E Sheffield.cas@dial.pipex.com

Sheffield Hallam University Learning Centre
Psalter Lane Campus, Psalter Lane
Sheffield, S11 8UZ
T 0114 225 2727
E lc-psalter@shu.ac.uk
W www.shu.ac.uk/services/lc/psalter/index.html

University of Huddersfield Learning Centre
Queensgate
Huddersfield
HD1 3DH
T 01484 472040
E lc@hud.ac.uk
W www.hud.ac.uk/tlc/index.html

University of Sheffield Main Library
Western Bank, Sheffield
S10 2TN
T 0114 222 7200
E library@sheffield.ac.uk
W www.shef.ac.uk/library

University of York
J B Morrell Library, Heslington, York
YO10 5DD
T 01904 3969
E libraryk-m@york.ac.uk
W www.york.ac.uk/services/library

Ireland

Burren College of Art Library
Newtown Castle
Ballyvaughan,Co Clare
T 353 65 7077200
E Admin@burrencollege.com
W www.burrencollege.com

Crawford College of Art & Design Library
Sharman Crawford St, Cork
T 353 214 966 777 x251
W www.cit.ie

Dublin City Central Library
ILAC Centre, Henry Street, Dublin 1
T 01 873 4333
E dubcilib@iol.ie
W www.iol.ie/dublincitylibrary

Dublin Institute of Technology Library
40–45 Mountjoy Square, Dublin 1
T 353 1 402 4108
E mjs.library@dit.ie
W www.dit.ie/library/index.html

National College of Art & Design Library
100 Thomas Street, Dublin 8
T 353 1 6364347
E romanod@ncad.ie
W www.ncad.ie/library/library.html

National Gallery of Ireland Library
Merrion Square West, Dublin 2
T 353 1 6633543/6
E alydon@ngi.ie
W www.nationalgallery.ie/html/library.html

National Library of Ireland
Department of Prints & Drawings
Kildare Street, Dublin 2
T 353 1 6030207
E jfinegan@nli.ie
W www.nli.ie/co_print.htm

Trinity College Library
College Street, Dublin 2
351 1 6081657
W www.tcd.ie/Library

University College Dublin
Richview Library, Richview
Clonskeagh, Dublin 14
T 353 1 7162741
E richview.library@ucd.ie
W www.ucd.ie/~library/branches/arch/index.html

06

Art fairs and festivals

Fair's fare: Negotiating market value for the British artist

Louisa Buck

Making money and the trickle-down effect

Only a decade ago London was a relatively minor art market player – albeit one with a clutch of interesting artists and galleries – but now this former backwater has expanded to become the second largest marketplace for contemporary art in the world (after New York) and the undisputed centre of the European art market. As this market is unregulated and essentially global, it is notoriously difficult to estimate exactly how much revenue it generates in the UK, but it is likely to be well in excess of £500 million every year. However, the main beneficiaries of this shift in art market status are the top-end dealers and their prize artists – those who have already achieved a degree of exposure, can command high sums and whose work is innately 'market friendly'. It also has to be stressed that this dramatic market expansion is restricted to London alone, and has not yet manifested itself anywhere else in the UK.

At the same time, the ever-increasing number of galleries, both large and small, which continue to open up in London's East and West Ends acts to enrich the art ecosystem and also provide unprecedented opportunities to show and see a wide range of new work. Although the rewards may not be immediately evident for artists at the beginning of their careers, being invited to exhibit in one of the smaller spaces which blur the boundaries between project space and commercial gallery can provide crucial exposure and a potential entry point into the wider art market. An encouraging tendency among London's burgeoning collector base is that it is just as likely to seek out some of the newer art showcases – even at art college degree shows – as to beat a path to the more established galleries.

Frieze ends commercial chill

Undoubtedly the most dramatic manifestation of London's evolution into a global art market contender has been the arrival and year-on-year success of the Frieze Art Fair, London's first international contemporary art fair held in Regent's Park. It immediately established itself as a major annual event when it was inaugurated in October 2003, attracting collectors, curators, critics and artists from across the world. It has also spawned a host of simultaneous activities and special exhibitions, as every element of the London art world strives to take advantage of this international influx. Frieze is organized by the eponymous British art magazine, and is at pains to promote an edgy, maverick image that sets it apart from other art fairs. Certainly it is the only one housed in a specially designed, tented structure by architect David Adjaye (which is put up and taken down every year) and boasts an impressive programme of newly commissioned artist's projects.

Nonetheless, for all its cultural aspirations, Frieze is a nakedly commercial enterprise. Artists and art lovers should never forget that its primary purpose is to sell as much top-end art as possible in its four-day run. As such, it provides a fascinating snapshot of the international market at work: who the main players are, what they are selling, and to whom. Here it is possible to assess the commercial flavours of the moment and to be entertained by the sight of the art market's major dealers – whether Marian Goodman, Nicholas Logsdail or Jay Jopling – strutting their stuff and delivering their sales pitches. Also, there's always some great new art to be seen, even if a maze of booths does not present the most conducive of surroundings (although many galleries want to make a good impression by curating or presenting their stands in interesting ways). For an artist, being shown at Frieze guarantees exposure to all the major international art world players – and inclusion is not necessarily contingent on being signed up to a major gallery. In order to keep its line-up fresh, Frieze also makes a point of allowing a handful of edgy younger spaces to set up shop alongside the big names.

Zoo: New is Improved

The host of satellite events that are timed to coincide with Frieze, and which vary from year to year, are also often worth investigating. In 2004 and 2005 the most interesting of these was Zoo, an alternative mini-fair of young, challenging and mainly London-based galleries and project spaces – and indeed some artists without any representation at all – many of whom are destined for participation in Frieze in the future. Zoo, which lives up to its name by being inspirationally situated in two parts of London Zoo, is backed by a consortium of dealers and collectors as well as receiving some public funding from the Arts Council – and judging by the commercial and critical success of its first two years seems set to continue unabated. The general consensus is that Zoo is the perfect youthful counterpoint to its big sister on the other side of Regent's Park, and being selected to show work there has provided a crucial boost to young artists and galleries alike.

More mixed in quality is Scope, the contemporary art fair based in various hotels in London, which also piggybacks on the interest generated by Frieze, just as it coincides with other major fairs in New York, Miami and Los Angeles. Here each hotel room is taken over by individual galleries – mainly from the US but also increasingly from Europe – but only on rare occasions is a display imaginative enough to hold its own against the hotel décor.

Faithful forerunners

The triumph of Frieze has inevitably eclipsed the other art fairs taking place across the UK, especially The London Art Fair, which, since 1988, has been held every year in the Business Design Centre in Islington. But even in its heyday The London Art Fair never managed to attract galleries from overseas and always contained many of the UK's more conservative galleries as well as those showing more historical British art. Now it has officially repositioned itself as a fair which specializes in Modern British Art, signifying anything produced over the past hundred years from L.S. Lowry to Gavin

Turk, while also attempting to introduce a more experimental element with a special subsidized Art Projects section in which approximately twenty galleries are invited to adopt a more radical approach, whether by showing young artists or established artists working in new ways.

For a more thoroughgoing historical approach, the 20/21 British Art Fair at the Royal College of Art presents top-notch British art from 1900 to the present day, from classic pieces at Agnew's and the Marlborough Gallery to Alan Cristea's works on paper. The other high-profile art fair presence in the UK comes in the form of the various Affordable Art Fairs which, as their title suggests, sell a wide range of art most of which is not usually especially avant-garde in nature but which is reasonably priced, accessible in style and aimed at a wide market. Artists showing at the Affordable Art Fairs often achieve good sales but at the expense of generally being outside the critical loop.

Quality not quantity

More modest and selective, but also more progressive, is the Contemporary Art Society's annual ARTfutures fair in London which features work by recent graduates as well as more established names, all of which have been picked by the CAS. In its time the CAS has provided an early marketplace for some of the art world's biggest names: in the early 1990s, for example, works by the likes of Mona Hatoum, the Chapman brothers and Cornelia Parker could be purchased for hundreds rather than thousands of pounds. ARTfutures remains a popular destination for young collectors and artists, especially since its move in 2005 to the swanky Bloomberg Space in Finsbury Square.

In the case of art fairs and events, size isn't necessarily everything; and this is especially true in the case of the various unofficial, ad-hoc, artist-run events which crop up at regular intervals, and which combine the chance to buy with the chance to have a good time. Following in the footsteps of the legendary 'Fêtes Worse than Death' organized by the late, lamented Joshua

Compston in and around Hoxton in the early 1990s, there have been more recent occurrences such as the Art Car Boot Sale and the Art Bring and Buy, all of which have featured various permutations of artist-run stalls where prizes can be won and/or purchases made of art works and objects for often ludicrously low amounts of money. £1 Bob and Roberta Smith 'concrete rubbing' or £5 Abigail Lane set of Fly stickers, anyone? By organizing their own events, unknown artists can draw attention to themselves, by-pass any reliance on dealers and make some money in the process. At the same time, more established names often enjoy the energy and informality of these events and, by taking part, help to raise the overall profile of the occasion.

Biennial: boom or bust?

On a more sober, less commercial note, an air of general artistic vibrancy, if not direct sales, can be whipped up by the timely appearance of an art festival. These generally take place outside the metropolitan art centres and tend to focus on the site-specific and the temporary. Here size usually does matter. A case in point was the 1998 Art Transpennine, an ambitious one-off exhibition stretching across the Pennines in the North of England, consisting of a series of temporary works of art and shows commissioned from thirty-five artists, a third of them British and the rest from abroad, along a 130-mile corridor from Liverpool to Hull. Then there is also the now-established Liverpool Biennial, an international series of exhibitions and events that colonizes a wide variety of locations, both official and unorthodox, throughout Liverpool, with work by both British and international artists (Liverpool Biennial 2006 included publicly sited works by Vong Phaophanit, Tracey Emin, Jorge Pardo and Antony Gormley). Alternating with the Liverpool Biennial is Art Sheffield, another city-wide contemporary art event which takes place in a range of venues both public and commercial, large and small, conventional and unexpected.

However, while these events can give rise to some extraordinary projects and often attract a temporary flurry of attention to an area and maybe even some of its artists, they are primarily for the benefit of the international art world and have little lasting impact on the local scene. Curators and artists may focus on the characteristics of a region, but the engagement rarely does more than scratch the surface, and within a few days of its opening, the art band wagon moves on, its attention fixed on the next event. If there is not a proper infrastructure within a region for the making, the showing and the selling of art, then no amount of subsidized temporary activities, however well-intentioned, can hope to make a significant impression.

The diaspora effect

Yet all is not gloom and there are encouraging signs that the frequency of these regional arts festivals is giving rise to a more sympathetic climate for contemporary art nationwide, with local artists becoming increasingly savvy at timing their activities to coincide with larger events and taking advantage of the pre-publicity and press coverage that surrounds them. Although London dominates the UK market, this has not prevented communities of artists and young galleries from making their presence felt elsewhere in the UK, especially in Bristol, Manchester, Sheffield, Newcastle-upon-Tyne and Liverpool, not to mention the well-established art scene in Glasgow. For what these individuals realize is that the art world – and its market – is an international as well as a national entity of which London is just one, albeit highly significant, element. Overall, therefore, the boom in the London art market and the exponential increase in sales and events can only be to the benefit of the artistic community at large. It is just up to the artists to negotiate this complex territory and to put themselves in a position to seize opportunities as they present themselves.

Louisa Buck is a writer, contemporary art correspondent for The Art Newspaper and author of Market Matters: the dynamics of the contemporary art market and Moving Targets: A User's Guide to British Art Now.

Art fairs and festivals

20/21 British Art Fair
Royal College of Art
Kensington Gore, London
SW7 2EU
T 020 87421611
F 020 89955094
E info@britishartfair.co.uk
W www.britishartfair.co.uk
Founded in 1988. The only event to showcase
British art from 1900 to the present day. Sixty of
the UK's leading dealers exhibit a wide range of
painting and sculpture featuring all the great
names of twentieth- and twenty-first-century
British art up.
Submission Policy The fair is only open to dealers
and galleries.
Frequency Annual.

20/21 International Art Fair
Royal College of Art
Kensington Gore, London
SW7 2EU
T 020 87421611
F 020 89955094
E info@20-21intartfair.com
W www.20-21intartfair.com
Featuring modern and contemporary art from
around the world: Asia, Australia, Europe, the US
plus a strong British content. Some fifty dealers
and galleries taking part.
Frequency Annual.

Affordable Art Fair
Sadler's House, 180 Lower Richmond Road
Putney, London, SW15 1LY
T 020 8246 4848
F 020 8246 4841
E enquiries@affordableartfair.com
W www.affordableartfair.com
Founded in 1999 with the aim of making original
art work more accessible. The ceiling on price is
currently £3,000 but prices are as low as £30.
Attracts not only first-time buyers but also
collectors in search of work by emerging artists.
Submission Policy The fair is for dealers and
galleries (rather than independent artists) that
represent living artists producing contemporary,
original paintings, prints, sculpture and
photography.
Frequency Twice a year in London (March and
October) and annual in Bristol, New York, Sydney
and Melbourne.

Appledore Visual Arts Festival
3 Marine Parade, Appledore, EX39 1PJ
T 07900 212747
E fionasmermaids@netzero.net
W www.appledorearts.org
Contact Jane Bartlett
Founded in 1997. Includes exhibitions, artist talks,
open studios, workshops and residencies. Events
for adults and children of mixed ages and abilities.
Several further education establishments involved,
including SCATS, Falmouth, Plymouth and North
Devon College.
Submission Policy Artists from all art forms are
encouraged to submit proposals for inclusion in
the festival. Stalls allocated by selection.
Frequency An annual four-day festival (on the
weekend after the spring bank holiday).

Art Fortnight London Ltd
44 Duke Street, St James's, London
SW1Y 6DD
T 020 78398139
F 020 79252903
E sophie@artfortnightlondon.com
W www.artfortnightlondon.com
For a fortnight every summer and throughout the
year, a programme of events, exhibitions, private
views, master classes, VIP art tours, and art
parties. Aims to bring together galleries, auction
houses and museums.

Art in Action
96 Sedlescombe Road, Fulham, London
SW6 1RB
T 020 73813192
E info@artinaction.org.uk
W www.artinaction.org.uk
Contact Patricia Prendergast
Exhibition of over 250 participating artists and
craftsmen. Over a four-day period in the grounds
of Waterperry House near Oxford. 25,000 visitors
come to watch and speak to working
demonstrators.
Submission Policy Application details available
from the above address. Applications are invited in
September and October.
Frequency Annual.

Art Ireland
Unit 29, 17 Rathfarnham Road
Terenure, Dublin 6W
T 01 4992244
E maria@eriva.com
W www.artireland.ie

Ireland's largest and best attended art fair. Hosts exhibitions from over 190 artists and galleries.
Submission Policy Artists are invited to submit work for vetting process. There is a cost for exhibition spaces.

Art Ireland Spring Collection

RDS, Ballsbridge, Dublin 4
T 01 4992244
F 01 4903238
E maria@eriva.com
W www.artireland.ie
An annual art fair hosting exhibitions from eighty artists and galleries from Ireland and abroad. Particularly known for modern, contemporary work from up-and-coming artists.
Submission Policy There is a vetting process for all new exhibitors. Welcomes applications from artists, artist groups and galleries. There is a charge to exhibit (€1,650 for an eight sq. metre space).
Frequency Annual in March/April.

Art London

Burton's Court, St Leonard's Terrace
Chelsea, London, SW3
T 020 72599399
E ralph@eburyevents.co.uk
W www.artlondon.net
Over seventy-five UK and international galleries showing twentieth-century and contemporary art (paintings, sculpture, photography, works on paper and ceramics), priced from £300 to over £100,000.

Art Sheffield

Sheffield Contemporary Art Forum
P.O. Box 3754, Sheffield, S1 9AH
T 0114 2812013
E contact@artsheffield.org
W www.artsheffield.org
Biennial festival of contemporary art held in venues throughout the city.

ARTfutures

Contemporary Art Society, Bloomsbury House, 74–77 Great Russell Street, London, WC1B 3DA
T 020 76120730
F 020 76314230
E cas@contempart.org.uk
W www.contempart.org.uk
Organized by the Contemporary Art Society, with a track record of recognizing emerging talent. Past exhibitors include Damien Hirst, Sam Taylor-Wood and Douglas Gordon.
Submission Policy Entry to the festival is free and selection of work is by invitation only.

Artists & Makers Festival

RAG, 35 Lanfranc Road, Worthing, BN14 7ES
T 01903 526268
E rag@artistsandmakers.com
W www.artistsandmakers.com
An independent festival that takes place across West Sussex every July, featuring artists' open houses and studios alongside a programme of live literature and music.
Submission Policy Application details are posted on the website.

ArtsFest

10th Floor, Alpha Tower, Suffolk Street
Queensway, Birmingham, B1 1TT
T 0121 6852605
F 0121 6852606
E mail@artsfest.org.uk
W www.artsfest.org.uk
Contact Sabra Khan
The UK's largest free arts festival, attracting audiences in excess of 100,000. Over three hundred performances take place over the weekend across arts venues and the streets and squares of Birmingham.
Submission Policy West Midlands-based, or performing in West Midlands in months following the event.
Frequency Annual.

Asian Art in London

32 Dover Street, Mayfair
London, W1S 4NE
T 020 74992215
F 020 74992216
E info@asianartinlondon.com
W www.asianartinlondon.com
Contact Virginia Sykes-Wright (PR Marketing) or Antonia Howard-Sneyd (Company Secretary)
Established in 1997, bringing together London's leading Asian art dealers, major auction houses and societies in a series of gallery selling exhibitions, auctions, receptions, lectures and seminars. These are complemented by exhibitions at leading museums. Prices range from £5 to over £500,000. Works span all media and ages.
Submission Policy Participants must be dealing within Central London. Does not personally handle submissions from artists.
Frequency Annual.

Battersea Contemporary Art Fair

Mollington House, Homelands
Midhurst Road, Haslemere, GU27 3LL
T 0870 2860066
E maria@bcaf.info
W www.bcaf.info
Contact Maria Scaman
Founded in 1991 and bought by current directors
on previous organizers' retirement in 2001. Held
at the Battersea Arts Centre in Lavender Hill,
SW11. Features 150 artists, sculptors, printmakers
and photographers. Works priced from £25 to
£4,000.
Submission Policy Send CV with four examples of
work in hard copy or jpegs. Artists only – no
galleries or agents.
Frequency Twice a year, in May and November.

Belfast Festival at Queen's

8 Fitzwilliam Street, Belfast, BT9 6AW
T 029 90971034
E festival@qub.ac.uk
W www.belfastfestival.com
Every year since 1963, the largest festival of its kind
in Ireland has celebrated the best of international
art and culture. Runs for three weeks.
Frequency Annual.

The Big Draw

The Campaign for Drawing, 7 Gentleman's Row
Enfield, EN2 6PT
T 020 8351 1719
E info@drawingpower.org.uk
W www.drawingpower.org.uk
Contact Sue Grayson Ford (Campaign Director)
Includes over 1,000 events held throughout the
UK each October to promote the art of drawing for
all. Quentin Blake is campaign patron.

Bow Festival

Space, 129–131 Mare Street, London, E8 3RH
E melanie@spacestudios.org.uk
W www.spacestudios.org.uk
A fortnight of collaborative public-art projects that
engage with the community and built
environment of Bow. Space project-manages and
produces the festival on behalf of the Roman Road
Revel Group, which is made up of local volunteers.

Brighton Art Fair

P.O. Box 73, Hove, BN3 1ZE
E info@brightonartfair.co.uk
W www.brightonartfair.co.uk
Now in its third year Brighton Art Fair is an

opportunity for art buyers to meet with and
purchase work direct from the artists. Works range
from traditional to contemporary and prices are
generally from £50 to £2000.
Submission Policy Open to all artists in the UK
and beyond, artists groups and Sussex-based
galleries. Interested in painting, photography,
sculpture and original prints.
Frequency Annual.

Brighton Craft Fair

PO BOx 73, Hove, BN3 1ZE
E info@brightoncraftfair.co.uk
W www.brightoncraftfair.co.uk
A new high quality applied arts fair, selling direct
to the public and galleries. Organized by the same
team as the Brighton Art Fair.
Submission Policy Makers and designers in the
UK and beyond, artists groups and Sussex based
galleries are welcome to apply for space.
Applications can be downloaded from the website;
deadline for applications – 1st May.
Frequency Annual.

Brighton Festival

Festival Office
12a Pavilion Buildings
BN1 1EE
T 01273 700747
F 01273 707505
E info@brighton-festival.org.uk
W www.brighton-festival.org.uk
Started in 1966, one of the UK's largest
international arts festivals.

Brighton Photo Biennial

University of Brighton, Grand Parade
Brighton, BN2 0JY
T 01273 643052
F 01273 643052
E mail@bpb.org.uk
W www.bpb.org.uk
A celebration of international photographic
practice committed to stimulating critical debate
on photography in all its forms. Bringing together
known and unknown bodies of work, new
commissions and previously unseen images, BPB
aims to reach the widest possible audience. Runs a
continuous education programme that is active
during and between biennials, creating grass roots
projects with local communities, artists and
individuals.
Frequency Every two years (next edition
in 2008).

Celf Caerleon Arts Festival

c/o Hambrook Cottage, Isca Road, Caerleon
Newport, NP18 1QG
T 01633 423354
E editor@caerleon-arts.org
W www.caerleon-arts.org
A two-week summer festival started in 2003.
The main event is an international sculpture
symposium in which around ten sculptors are
selected to create new works from wood in public.
Sculptors are paid a fee and their work is
afterwards sited around the town.
Submission Policy Applications from sculptors
working in wood are usually invited towards the
end of the year for selection in January and
February. See website for details.
Frequency Annual.

Ceramic Art London

Royal College of Art
Kensington Gore, London, SW7 2EU
T 020 74393377
F 020 72879954
E organiser@ceramics.org.uk
W www.ceramics.org.uk
Contact Tony Ainsworth
The festival's vision is to be the national focus for
studio ceramics. Components include a selling fair
of ninety of the best potters worldwide (prices
range from £30 to £30,000); a major, free events
programme; an exhibition of student work; major
prizes for potters; full-colour catalogue. Presented
by the Craft Potters Association of Great Britain
and Ceramic Review Magazine, in association with
the Arts Council.
Submission Policy Open to all working studio
potters (not students) worldwide, in any ceramic
form. Selection of exhibitors is by independent
selection panel. Applications via website.
Frequency Annual.

Chelsea Arts Fair

Penman Antiques Fairs
Widdicombe
Bedford Place
Uckfield, TN22 1LW
T 01825 744074
F 01825 744012
E info@penman-fairs.co.uk
W www.penman-fairs.co.uk
Over forty British and international galleries
display contemporary and twentieth-century works
of art in a relaxed atmosphere. Held in Chelsea Old
Town Hall.

Cheltenham Artists Open Houses

59 Cirencester Road, Charlton Kings
Cheltenham, GL53 8EX
T 01242 580506
E robertfreeman3@compuserve.com
W www.artistsopenhouses.org.uk
Contact Bob Freeman
Founded 2000 to promote local artists and to
provide the public with an opportunity for closer
contact with artists and their creative processes in
their studios and homes.
Submission Policy Open to artists in Cheltenham
and 10-mile radius. Subscription £30. Application
form on website.
Frequency Biannual.

Cork Art Fair

Cork City Hall, Cork
T 01 4992244
F 01 4903238
E maria@eriva.com
W www.thecorkartfair.com
Contact Maria McMenamin
The second annual fair took place in 2007, with
nearly twice as many exhibitors as 2005. Over sixty
artists and galleries exhibited a wide range of
painting, sculpture and prints. Prices range from
€500 upwards.
Submission Policy Always looking for new artists,
groups and galleries to exhibit. Post or email a
selection of images and a list of previous
exhibitions to maria@eriva.com or Maria
McMenamin, Unit 19, 17 Rathfarnham Road,
Terenure, Dublin 6W.
Frequency Annual in August.

Deptford X

c/o Creative Lewisham Agency, 1 Resolution Way
Deptford, London, SE8 4NT
E info@deptfordx.org
W www.deptfordx.org.uk
A programme of integrated exhibitions for
different sites and venues in and around Deptford.

Dorset Art Weeks

1 Cross Tree Close, Broadmayne
Dorchester, DT2 8EN
T 01305 853100
E admin@dorsetartweeks.co.uk
W www.dorsetartweeks.co.uk
Contact Peter Lightfoot
Hosts a biennial open-studios event showing the
work of artists and makers across the county.
Artists exhibiting in their own workplaces and

homes sell work and receive feedback directly from visitors. Held over sixteen days in May/June. The event does not at present operate a selection policy but this is under constant review. In future years, the newly formed organization (charitable trust status applied for), Dorset Visual Arts, will organize visual arts events of which Dorset Art Weeks will remain at the core.
Frequency Biennial.

Dulwich Art Fair
Penman Antiques Fairs, Widdicombe, Bedford Place, Uckfield, TN22 1LW
T 01825 744074
F 01825 744012
E info@penman-fairs.co.uk
W www.penman-fairs.co.uk
Held at Dulwich College and aimed at art-lovers who live in south London. Features galleries from London and across the UK offering contemporary art from £50 to over £10,000.

Dumfries & Galloway Arts Festival
Gracefield Arts Centre, 28 Edinburgh Road Dumfries, DG1 1JQ
T 01387 260447
F 01387 260447
E info@dgartsfestival.org.uk
W www.dgartsfestival.org.uk
Contact Annette Rogers
Started in 1979. Presents a wide range of art forms, including jazz, folk and classical music, drama, literature, children's events, films and exhibitions, in various venues located between Langholm in the east to Gatehouse of Fleet in the west of the region.
Frequency Annual.

Earagail Arts Festival
Unit B6, Donegal County Enterprise Fund Business Centre, Lisneannan, Letterkenny County Donegal
T 074 9168800
F 074 9168490
E info@eaf.ie
W www.eaf.ie
Annual festival of contemporary and traditional arts, held throughout Donegal.

Edinburgh Art Fair
Arte in Europa, 77 Poplar Park, Port Seton East Lothian, EH32 0TE
T 01875 819 595
F 01875 819857

E enquiries@arteineuropa.com
W www.artedinburgh.com
Inaugural festival held in 2005. Over seventy exhibitors from throughout Europe and the UK, showcasing over five hundred artists, sculptors and photographers, from recent graduates and self-taught artists to established names.
Frequency Every November.

Edinburgh International Festival
Hub, Castlehill, Edinburgh, EH1 2NE
T 0131 4732001
W www.eif.co.uk
Founded over fifty years ago and one of the world's leading festivals of the arts. Held in locations throughout Edinburgh.

Euroart Live Festival
Euroart Studios & Gallery, Unit 22F @ N17 Studios, 784–788 High Road, London, N17 0DA
W www.euroart.co.uk
A festival of live-art performances drawn from a diversity of cultures. Aims to instigate dialogue and debate across art forms and cultural borders and, by presenting work from both mature and emerging artists, across generations.

ev+a – Limerick Biennial
69 O'Connell Street, Limerick
T 087 9477042
E info@eva.ie
W www.eva.ie
Major festival of contemporary art.

FRED
3 Walton's Yard, Market Square Kirkby Stephen, CA17 4QT
T 017683 71561
E info@fredsblog.com
W www.fredsblog.com
Founded in 2004, now Europe's largest annual festival of site-specific work. 40–50 artists' projects are shown in largely rural locations across Cumbria.
Submission Policy Work must demonstrate innovation in its delivery. Submission details are published on the website.

Free Range
The Old Truman Brewery
91 Brick Lane, London, E1 6QL
T 020 7770 6003
F 020 7770 6005
E tamsin@trumanbrewery.com

W www.free-range.org.uk
Contact Tamsin O'Hanlon
Annual festival, bringing together fresh talent from the UK's premier art and design courses. The largest of its kind in Europe, with exhibitions covering a range of disciplines focused into three categories – Art, Design and Photography. Now in its seventh year.
Submission Policy Submissions welcome from graduate art and design colleges and courses.
Frequency Every summer over two months.

Frieze Art Fair
3–4 Hardwick Street, London, EC1R 4RB
T 020 7833 7270
E info@friezeartfair.com
W www.frieze.com
London's largest international art fair launched in 2003 by the publishers of frieze magazine. Takes place in Regent's Park, London and features over 150 of the most exciting contemporary art galleries in the world. As well as these exhibitors, the fair includes specially commissioned artists' projects and a talks programme.
Submission Policy Accepts gallery applications only.
Frequency Annual.

Galway Art Fair
Radisson Hotel, Galway
T 01 4992244
F 01 4903238
E maria@eriva.com
W www.galwayartfair.com
Contact Maria McMenamin
New fair with exhibitions from fifty artists and galleries. Work from up-and-coming artists and established artists exhibited. Prices range from ?500 upwards.
Submission Policy Accepts applications from artists, groups and galleries to exhibit. There is a vetting process and a cost to exhibit.
Frequency Annual.

Glasgow Art Fair
UZ Events, 125–129 High Street, Glasgow, G1 1PH
T 0141 5526027
F 0141 5526048
E artfair@uzevents.com
W www.glasgowartfair.com
Contact Cristina Armstrong
Scotland's national art fair brings together 43 selected galleries from Scotland, the UK and Europe to offer over 16,000 visitors the opportunity to invest in a wide range of quality

contemporary art under one roof, in the UK, outside of London. Representing work by over a thousand artists and attracting dedicated art collectors and occasional buyers alike.

Glasgow International
125/129 High Street, Glasgow, G1 1PH
T 0141 5526027
F 0141 5526048
E info@glasgowinternational.org
W www.glasgowinternational.org
Contact Francis McKee (Head Curator)
Glasgow's curated and commissioning festival of contemporary visual art, established in 2005. Hosts new work and commissions by Scottish and international artists across key venues and spaces throughout the city. Attracts some 28,000 visitors.
Submission Policy Proposals are considered but not the primary means of curation.
Frequency Biennual from 2008.

Inspired Art Fair
Christchurch, Commercial Street, Spitalfields, London, E1
T 020 83747318
F 020 83744566
E jo@inspiredartfair.com
W www.inspiredartfair.com
Contact Charles Schultz
Established in 2003, showcasing up to fifty independent emerging artists. Held at Christchurch Spitalfields, London. 'Where the city meets the East End.'
Submission Policy Go to website to view cost and stand sizes. Two methods of submitting images: by post or email. A selection committee chooses all the artists taking part on the quality, technical ability and originality of artists' work.
Frequency Annual.

International Ceramics Fair and Seminar
Haughton International Fairs, 31 Old Burlington Street, London, W1S 3AS
T 020 77345491
F 020 74944604
E info@haughton.com
W www.haughton.com
Founded in 1982, bringing together leading international ceramics dealers from around the world to display and sell European pottery, porcelain, glass and enamels. Includes lecture series.

Inverness Art Fair
Old High Church Halls

45 Milton Crescent, Inverness, IVU
T 01463 220802
E lwjohnson@zoom.co.uk
Contact Len W. Johnson
Founded in 2004 by the Old High St Stephen's
Church of Scotland to increase church funds and
to create a marketing opportunity for artists of all
abilities throughout the Highlands and Islands of
Scotland. Selling prices of paintings vary from
£100 to over £1,000.
Submission Policy Visual arts in most media are
acceptable with a restriction on size over 100cm2
(except under previous agreement).
Frequency Annual, running for the first week in
June each year.

Leeds Art Fair

61a Weetwood Lane, Leeds, LS16 5NP
T 0113 2425242
E info@ytb.org.uk
W www.leedsartfair.org.uk
A contemporary visual arts event, with preference
given to artists with ties to or living and working in
the local area.

Liverpool Biennial

P.O. Box 1200, The Tea Factory, 82 Wood Street
Liverpool, L69 1XB
T 0151 7097444
F 0151 7097377
E info@biennial.com
W www.biennial.com
Established in 1998. A major international festival
of contemporary art.

London Art Fair

Business Design Centre
52 Upper Street
London, N1 0QH
T 020 72886736
F 020 72886446
E laf@upperstreetevents.co.uk
W www.londonartfair.co.uk
Contact Sarah Monk
Features the best of Modern British and
contemporary art in a spectacular venue in the
heart of Islington by one-hundred leading UK
galleries.
Submission Policy UK Galleries dealing in Modern
British and contemporary art welcome to apply.
Frequency Annual.

London Design Festival

56 Kingsway Place, Sans Walk, London, EC1R 0LU

T 020 70145313
F 020 70145301
E info@londondesignfestival.com
W www.londondesignfestival.com
Has grown quickly from 40 partner events in 2003
to 170 in 2005 reflecting the breadth and depth of
design in London. Seeks to celebrate excellence in
every design discipline. In 2006 over 40 more
retailers took part for first time, ensuring an
expanding audience. 150,000 people attended
events in 2004.
Submission Policy Partners stage eclectic range of
events and activities all over London, including
seminars or exhibitions, film screenings,
competitions and awards, receptions, private views
and parties. Brings together people with a range of
interests from lifestyle to urban regeneration to
trends to digital special effects.
Frequency Annual, though dates vary from year to
year.

The London Original Print Fair

T 020 7439 2000
E info@londonprintfair.com
W www.londonprintfair.com
First held in 1985. Now at the Royal Academy of
Arts (Burlington House, Burlington Gardens,
London W1). Features 45 international dealers,
showing prints from Dürer to Hockney and Hirst.

Manchester Art Show

P.O. Box 512, Altrincham, Cheshire, WA15 9WL
T 0161 9287353
F 0161 9291537
E info@engagingarts.co.uk
W www.manchesterartshow.co.uk
Contact Valerie McNamara
Founded in 2002 and now established as the
north's largest selling contemporary art fair. The
show takes place in the MICC-GMEX in the heart
of Manchester city centre. No price limit on work
exhibited.
Submission Policy Applications from artists in all
forms of visual arts are welcome.
Frequency Annual.

Margate Rocks

P.O. Box 373, Birchington, CT7 9WY
E info@margaterocks.co.uk
W www.margaterocks.co.uk
Established in 2001. An eclectic mix of
contemporary art, using alternative venues and
existing businesses as exhibition spaces. Centred
around the Old Town and Harbour area of Margate,

with other events happening throughout Thanet. Artists' open-studio programme began in 2005.
Submission Policy Work must be inventive, interesting and able to engage the public.
Frequency Annual, in July.

Museums and Galleries Month (MGM)
The Campaign for Museums, 35–37 Grosvenor Gardens, London, SW1W OBS
T 020 72339796
F 020 7 2336770
E info@campaignformuseums.org.uk
W www.mgm.org.uk
Celebration of the UK's museums and galleries, with special events, workshops and exhibitions in museums and galleries around the country. Organized by the Campaign for Museums, MGM is an opportunity for museums and galleries to try out new events to attract visitors.
Frequency Annual, in May.

National Review of Live Art
New Moves International Ltd, P.O. Box 25262 Glasgow, G1 1YW
T 0141 3575538
E admin@newmoves.co.uk
W www.newmoves.co.uk
Europe's longest-running festival of live art.

Nine Days of Art
T 01803 868805
E anneward@onetel.net.uk
W www.ninedaysofart.co.uk
Contact Anne Ward (Secretary)
A festival organized in the south-west of England by the Skills Training and Rural Arts Week (STRAW) Project.

On The Wall Art Fair
Upper Street Events, Business Design Centre 52 Upper Street, Islington, London, N1 0QH
T 020 72886191
F 020 72886446
E elliotg@upperstreetevents.co.uk
W www.on-the-wall.co.uk
Contact Elliot Gard (Sales Manager)
A major London-based fair providing independent professional artists and artist studios with direct routes to consumer and trade buyers.
Submission Policy Event open to two-dimensional originals, limited editions, three-dimensional sculpture and applied-art objects in traditional or new media. Vetted.
Frequency Annual.

Open Studios Northamptonshire
P.O. Box 7139, Kettering, NN16 6BR
T 01536 741493
E info@openstudios.org.uk
W www.openstudios.org.uk
Contact Emma Davies
An annual visual arts event since 1996 where artists from Northamptonshire and the borders of surrounding counties open up their studios to the public. Normally held in August or September. Also exhibitions in alternative venues such as churches, pubs and cafes, and heritage buildings. A year round colour directory is also produced and participating artists' events and exhibitions are posted onto the website throughout the year.
Submission Policy Open to all visual artists at any stage of their career from Northamptonshire and the surrounding county borders. Year-round enquiries welcome but applications received between January and March.

Oxfordshire Artweeks
P.O. Box 281, Oxford, OX2 9FX
T 01865 861574
F 01865 861574
Contact Caryn Paladina
First held in 1981. Now the largest open-studio festival of visual art in the country. Artists invite the public into their homes and studios. Run by a board comprising artists as well as other professionals who volunteer time and expertise. There is also one part-time paid coordinator.
Submission Policy The festival operates a no-selection policy and welcomes all artists, commercial galleries, public-art spaces, schools and any other organization wishing to take part. To take part, artists must either be a member, or be part of a larger group that has membership. Welcomes artists working in all media and styles. It is up to each participant to find their own venue and to organize their exhibition.

Photo-London
2nd Floor, 13 Mason's Yard, St James's London, SW1Y 6BU
T 020 7839 9300
E info@photo-london.com
W www.photo-london.com
Began in 2004 as London's first international photography fair. Around fifty exhibitors from ten countries showing photography, film and video from throughout the history of the art form. Takes place in the Royal Academy of Arts' Burlington Gardens.
Frequency Annual.

Raw Arts Festival

E rawartsfestival@yahoo.co.uk
W www.raf2007.com
Contact Piers Midwinter
Began life in London in 2004 and has since
travelled to Valencia and New York. Aims to
provide a patform for 'raw artists' (folk/intuitive/
marginalized/self-taught/visionary art etc).
Submission Policy Artists should submit pictures
and information about themselves. Please check
the website for details of entry fee etc.

Redbridge Arts Festival

London Borough of Redbridge Leisure Services
8th Floor, Lynton House, 255–259 High Road,
Ilford, IG1 1NY
E jacqueline.eggleston@redbridge.gov.uk
A showcase of artistic disciplines held at a range of
locations throughout Redbridge.

Rhubarb-Rhubarb – The UK's International Festival of the Image

212 The Custard Factory, Gibb Street, Digbeth
Birmingham, B9 4AA
T 0121 773 7889
F 0121 773 7888
E info@rhubarb-rhubarb.net
W www.rhubarb-rhubarb.net
Contact Lorna-Mary Webb
Works to build the confidence of photographers by
supporting mentoring courses, events, portfolio
sessions and the International Festival of the Image,
a three-day portfolio review established in 2000. It
draws international curators, gallery directors,
publishers, agents and picture editors, to advise and
inform photographers on portfolio content,
opportunities for becoming more visible and future
sector developments. Prices vary each year but can
be viewed on the website. Supported by exhibitions,
seminars, portfolio promenade and events.
Submission Policy Photographers wishing to show
folios should have experience of an exhibition,
publication or commission.
Frequency Annual.

Rye Festival

P.O. Box 33, Rye
TN31 7YB
T 01797 224442
E info@ryefestival.co.uk
W www.ryefestival.co.uk
Contact Pat Field
A festival of the arts founded in 1971 and now
including more than fifty events over two weeks.

Scope Art Fair (London)

521 West 26th Street, New York
NY 10001, USA
T +1 212 2681522
F +1 212 2680123
E info@scope-art.com
W www.scope-art.com
Aims to demystify the buying process of
contemporary art by producing international art
fairs of cutting-edge art and emerging culture. The
fairs bring together up-and-coming dealers,
curators and artists in a relaxed atmosphere.
Founded in 2002 and currently producing fairs in
the USA and London.
Submission Policy The fair is vetted for exhibitors.
Interested artists should work through an exhibitor.

Somerset Art Weeks

SAW Ltd, Dillington House, Ilminster, TA19 9DT
T 01460 259324
F 01460 259324
E arts@somersetartweek.freeserve.co.uk
W www.somersetartweek.org.uk
A biennial showcase of open studios and
exhibitions, residencies, installations and special
events.
Submission Policy £15 for artist members; £25 for
organizations; £7 to £15 for Friends.

St Ives International

1 Queen's Chambers, 38–40 Queen Street
Penzance, TR18 4BH
T 01736 333024
F 01736 333074
E info@stii.co.uk
W www.stii.co.uk
A partnership organization founded by Falmouth
College of Arts, Newlyn Art Gallery, South West
Arts and Tate St Ives to present major arts projects
in Cornwall.

Zoo Art Fair

164 Fernhead Road, London, W9 3EL
T 00 44 (0)208 964 3272
E info@zooartfair.com
W www.zooartfair.com
Founded in 2004, identifying and supporting
emerging commercial and non-commercial art
organizations on an international platform.
Exhibitors include galleries, project spaces, artist
collectives, curatorial groups and publications. Zoo
Art Fair is a non-profit enterprise, sponsored by
established collectors, galleries, arts businesses
and public funders.

Being an artist

Susan Jones

In the 21st century, there is much more to 'being an artist' than just making works of art. Although your art work may be good, this is not any guarantee of commercial success. Manoeuvring yourself into a position to be selected or commissioned requires the 'good art' to be presented by an artist with well-honed skills in areas such as negotiation, communication and management – of themselves and their professional arrangements. As artist Mark Gubb advises: 'Don't be afraid to call yourself an artist and be professional in everything you do'.[i]

The reasons people choose to be an artist continue to be as many and varied as they have ever been. They encompass everything from the need for pure freedom of artistic expression to expanding a well-loved hobby post retirement. With perhaps as many as 60,000 people already describing themselves as artists and over 3,700 joining the profession annually as they graduate from art and design courses, it goes without saying that competition is fierce for gaining status and recognition within the art world's hierarchies.[ii]

Artists in the 21st century have ever more diverse contexts and audiences for their work. Process-based and socially engaged artists must balance their own aspirations with the desires of commissioners to employ art to ameliorate social problems – such as poor education, housing and mental health. And, as artist Becky Shaw has commented: 'While I will always value the energy of working to commission or on a residency, it has dawned on me that this often makes me feel powerless. I work if the phone rings, apply to things – I never know when I will be working and when I won't.'[iii]

Sales of artists' skills and services play a major role in enabling professional artists to make a living. Commissions make up around 23% of the value of openly-advertised opportunities to artists published by a-n[iv], with an average value of £17,796. Artists' residences amount to 9% of the total value and average out at £4,768 each, which can be significantly less than public art commissions which may offer over £250 a day to artists experienced in this field[v], in addition to budgets for materials, fabrication and support. Exhibition offers make up a quarter of the opportunities and although the vast majority offer little or no financial return for the artists selected, these are nevertheless considered to be what validates an artists' work and widens their career options.[vi] Forty-one percent of artists see selling their work as a priority, although the markets for art beyond London are clearly ripe for development.[vii] The Own Art scheme[viii] operated by Arts Council England and Scottish Arts Council aims to widen sales of contemporary art to private and domestic collectors by providing interest-free credit to purchasers at selected galleries. The Arts Council of Wales runs the Collectorplan scheme. However, as our research[ix] reveals, it is through a portfolio of opportunities, including income from sales, that most artists maintain an artistic livelihood.

So within this complex and diverse environment for contemporary visual arts practice, what are the common concerns among all who would describe themselves as an artist, whatever the medium or genre they employ, their cultural background, their career stage or the kinds of audiences they seek for their work? The answer might be a desire to experience good practice: to be treated fairly by employers and commissioners, to be respected and valued for the contribution they make to society as a whole and a requirement to have their professional status recognized.

These needs are encapsulated within *The Code of Practice for the Visual Arts*.[x] This takes commonly-agreed principles and demonstrates through the experiences of artists, arts commissioners and employers why and how they should be applied. In short, it explains that good practice prevails when artists and their collaborators:

Contribute confidently – engaging with the development of ideas and solutions to problems, challenging stereotypes and assumptions about who knows what, being generous with knowledge and skills and knowing their worth.

Prepare thoroughly – researching the context, legislative implications and environmental factors as well as the interests of partners and colleagues.

Collaborate creatively – establishing mutual respect by identifying shared goals and welcoming discussion and debate.

Aim high – aspiring to bring quality to everything they do, from the work and the presentation of their ideas, to negotiating projects or managing professional relationships.

Although at first glance these principles may appear to be too simply expressed to carry any weight, many artists are reporting that having taken responsibility to define their professional practices themselves, both their artistic status and employment prospects have improved as a result. As Carey Young comments: 'The more you are seen as an independent specialist...the more respect you will get'.[xi]

The Code of Practice and sister publication *Establishing a charge rate for a working artist* also available as *The artist's fees toolkit*[xii] forms one part of a matrix of support structures available to visual artists nowadays. Over 85% of artists recognize the value of networking with like-minded people. As artist Mark Gubb has commented: 'Attending conferences, exhibition openings and having a drink in the pub with friends are all part of building networks and support structures. For all the slide banks and databases that exist actually and ephemerally, taking to people about what you do is always going to be the primary way of getting your work about'.[xiii] Initiatives such as a-n's AIR (Artists' Interaction & Representation)[xiv] scheme that support practitioners through a combination of professional benefits, including

face-to-face discussions as well as lobbying, play their part within this.

All professions are dependent on such peer networks, which provide the basic mechanism for sharing contacts and knowledge, exchanging advice and lifting spirits when you're downhearted. The growth of artists' networks over the last ten years has been considerable, aided in part by artists' increased access to email and the internet. While some artists' networks are built around open studio events, with websites promoting the artists and their work throughout the year, others are based on specific artistic media or specialist 'interest groups' and, increasingly, these stretch way beyond the UK, generating exchange between artists and collaborations for new, global art projects. a-n's UK-wide Networking Artists' Networks (NAN) initiative[xv] aims to provide greater visibility for such activity and to support it through events, research visits and bursaries.

Although successful artists – 2005 Turner prizewinner Simon Starling included – tend to claim they have just 'been lucky', such a throw-away remark generally belies a far more complex set of contributing circumstances and recognition factors. Brian Eno, renowned first because of his key role in Roxy Music and later as an artist working with Laurie Anderson and others, says that luck is more about 'being ready', that is being aware of the art world ladders and seeking them out. Look at the cv of an up-and-coming artist and it usually reveals that somewhere along their career path they have been 'spotted' by a respected curator, selected for a notable open submission show, or been reviewed in a well-respected art magazine.

Similarly, most artists who are invited to show at a gallery will already have an exhibiting track record or a recommendation from another gallery or artist already represented there. Artist-curator Gavin Wade calls this: 'The organic process of relationships with other people, and development of your work over a period of time. You have to meet and talk to other people. It's as simple and as difficult as that. You are only going to be invited, introduced or recommended by being seen.'[xvi]

So, the attitudes of *other people* make up the final part of the jigsaw that is 'being an artist'. When asked about the role and impact of artists, key personalities in public life offer differing perspectives. Shreela Ghosh of the Louise T Blouin Foundation says: 'I'm on artists' side, to be convinced by their ideas and at the same time offering constructive feedback'. Yvette Vaughan-Jones of Visiting Arts recognizes that: 'Artists are fundamental to my work: without them, I wouldn't have a job'. Significantly, Guardian columnist Jonathan Freedland notes that: 'If art continues to be a largely minority interest, one that is the province of a small group of the economically comfortable cognoscenti, then its relevance will be limited.'[xvii]

Susan Jones, formerly an artist, is Director of Programmes, a-n The Artists Information Company, publishers of www.a-n.co.uk, a comprehensive UK and international resource that exposes the diversity and complexity of artists' practice and provides a context for good practice. She also works as an arts consultant and artists' adviser and provides evidence to arts policy-making including to the Commons Select Committee 2005 enquiry into the Market for Art and Arts Council England's Turning Point visual arts strategy in 2006.

[i] Signpost, www.a-n.co.uk

[ii] Research papers, www.a-n.co.uk

[iii] Evidence by Becky Shaw to Future Forecast: Social space think-tank on www.a-n.co.uk

[iv] Daily-updated Opportunities and jobs service with News feeds on www.a-n.co.uk

[v] The artist's fees toolkit on www.a-n.co.uk provides a framework to calculate day rates against overheads and experience level

[vi] Art work analysed on www.a-n.co.uk, drawn from all opportunities in 2005

[vii] Report published on www.artscouncil.org.uk

[viii] See www.artscouncil.org.uk/ownart/

[ix] Research paper: Making a living as an artist on www.a-n.co.uk

[x] *The Code of Practice for the Visual Arts* with versions for artists and arts organizers is freely available on www.a-n.co.uk

[xi] Artist's profile on www.a-n.co.uk

[xii] This provides a very useful framework for artists to work out what they need to earn annually, taking into account their career stage and overheads such as studio, travel, research, insurance, etc.

[xiii] Networker, report on the Networking artists' networks initiative in Reflections on networking on www.a-n.co.uk

[xiv] Practising visual and applied artists can sign up for AIR with an a-n Artist subscription through www.a-n.co.uk/subscribe

[xv] See Networking on www.a-n.co.uk for background and opportunities

[xvi] Approaching galleries on www.a-n.co.uk

[xvii] Extracts from interviews in Future Forecast: Outer space, published on www.a-n.co.uk

07

Competitions, residencies, awards and prizes

Studying abroad

Tim Braden

Jumping ship
Amsterdam, 15 February 2005

'Hey Nat, can you do me a favour when you come over and bring me a packet of razor blades from Boots? I need the old-fashioned double-sided blades (like razors in cartoons, a rectangular plate, sharp on the 2 long edges with a jagged shape punched out of the centre). I think they come in packs of 10 by Wilkinson Sword. I use them to prepare canvas so need 2 or 3 packs if possible. Eternally grateful etc...'

(An email to a friend during my first month in Holland: I was clearly not as adaptable to life abroad as I thought.)

There are so many artists from around the world working in London that you can get lazy and kid yourself that you are being international just by going to an exhibition by a friend who may have been born in Mexico.

Unless you are invited, or already have friends to introduce you, it can be pretty hard to go abroad and meet local artists. Residencies provide that introduction: the quick answer to the inevitable 'so, what are you doing here?' question.

I have friends who went to London, expecting a warm greeting from the 'art scene' and were shocked by the level of indifference to outsiders. Smaller towns might have less going on, but they are much more accessible. Go to New York as a young artist and, like an aspiring actress in Hollywood, you're unlikely to cause much of a stir. In Amsterdam, you're allowed to feel part of things from the first weekend. It's also good to shake off the 'Europe-is-something-that-happens-in-Brussels' indoctrination fed to us by the English press and realize that art is being made outside of East London.

Help is at hand
Amsterdam, 2 October 2006

To: residents@rijksakademie.nl
Dear all, Next week, 5 and 6 October, Philippe Pirotte

is coming for studio visits and a workshop/seminar (details to come). David Claerbout will be here for studio visits 20 and 21 October. Please let me know if you would like an appointment with either of them. Thank you! Mirella

I had just finished a two-year residency at the Rijksakademie, a fine art programme in Amsterdam. It takes around 50 artists – half from Holland and the other half from the rest of the world – and the average age is 30. You are given a healthy stipend, a flat and a studio and access to a lot of technical assistance. Every week or so, a group of interesting artists, curators or theoreticians are paid to come and spend time with you to talk about your work for hours.

A residency can take some getting used to. After years in a lonely studio wishing for more attention, it can feel pretty strange being looked at so much; in fact, I slightly resented it at times. I always used to like working when nobody expected me to (or cared). On a residency, nobody is going to tell you *what* to make, but there is a lot of healthy expectation. With hindsight, this is probably the closest thing to 'professional training' that an artist could ever hope for. As the academy took care of almost everything else – from housing, to grants, to a canteen and a bicycle repair shop – this left me feeling strangely disempowered. But I soon got over it and remembered that I didn't have to think about gas bills and I could get on with making art. Although with all the other artists around, you can't stay locked away for too long because it is like being part of one big, happy family.

14 April 2006

To: residents@rijksakademie.nl
Subject: good intentions

Evi's birthday
Bradley goes USA
Helen shipped her paintings and goes to the USA
Inti in cuba
Vincent back from Poland
Chiara and Peggy still didn't start exercise

Kuang-Yu goes Miami-Vice
Dachi in the house
Tomoko happy
Stephanos back from Athens.
Welcome back Hala!
Goodbye Sasha Korea!
Is Cevdet back?
Gal's new residency card.
Nicolas in the house
Karina happy
Mu going to China for the sake of love
Brody leaving the rijks soon
Easter!
Special act: 'Brody and the hula hoop'

Monday April 17
Party in smoking room under the canteen.
Starts at 9 pm.
Please bring your own drinks!

A residency is a time to experiment and a rare second chance to do the kind of things you're supposed to do at art school (like learn to weld, or try out lithography). And, perhaps more importantly, that sense of disorientation of being somewhere new can be a great way to get some distance from your own work.

Don't feel rejected
I applied to the Rijksakademie in 2003 and was rejected after the first interview, which was painful (and expensive as I had flown over with a number of paintings and put myself up in a hotel). Foreign residencies are often prepared to pay, or help, with the airfare if you ask (I discovered later), although this has no bearing on whether or not you are likely to succeed in the interview. I know people who were given the money to fly over from South America for the interview, and then didn't get in (which must have hurt too).

Unlike art schools, residency programmes tend to be much more open and treat you more like a real, adult person. There is no mystique about the selection procedure, they will happily tell you why you did or didn't get in. It is always worth calling back after the interview or after

you receive a letter. You might as well get some good advice out of the whole ordeal. Call, say that you are disappointed, and ask how you could have presented yourself better. Ask if it is worth applying again. They are usually pretty straight with you and, if you think about it, it is almost strange not to call.

A letter of recommendation always helps, either by an ex-resident artist, or just someone who knows you and the place (I'm sure this applies to any institution/competition/grant application) and goes much further than a boring letter from your old art teacher.

Get out there
25 May 2005
'...just got back from a great trip to Iceland for 10 days, have you ever been there? A mad place...really tiny scene. We were in Reykjavik for an arts festival, then travelling round in a tour bus with 18 of us from the Rijks. Snowing one minute and desert-like the next with hot steam blasting out of the ground all over the place, and glaciers melting into the sea. Seals swim around in bright sunshine, we went whale watching wrapped in fisherman's thermals and all of us sat in a 30-foot long old cheese-making tub full of hot water on a hilltop 35 kilometres from the Arctic Circle watching the sun (which never really set) come up at 3 in the morning. Still on a bit of a high from lack of sleep, I think...'

So, studying abroad is great for getting out of your own environment for a bit, great if you want to experiment for a while in a new system, great for making new friends from around the world, and not great if you are in a serious relationship back home. It's not going to solve all your problems, but I can assure you, you will miss it when it's finished.

Tim Braden is an artist who lives and works in London and Amsterdam. He was on the residency program at the Rijksakademie 2005–06. He is represented by Timothy Taylor Gallery, London and Galerie Arquebuse, Geneva

Competitions, residencies, awards and prizes

1871 Fellowship
Ruskin School of Drawing and Fine Art
74 High Street, Oxford, OX1 4BG
T 01865 276940
F 01865 276949
E vanda.wilkinson@ruskin-school.ox.ac.uk
W www.ruskin-sch.ox.ac.uk/lab
Established in 2001 by the Laboratory at the Ruskin School of Drawing and Fine Art and the San Francisco Art Institute to help artists make new work by spending periods of time in Oxford and San Francisco. The fellow devotes two months to research-related activities in England before travelling to San Francisco for up to four months of intensive studio-based production. The fellowship was implemented in 2001. Current value of award is £18,000.
Frequency One award annually.
Entry Policy The award is by nomination only.

Abbey Awards in Painting and Abbey Scholarship in Painting
Abbey Council, P.O. Box 5
Rhayader, LD6 5WA
T 01597 810704
E faithclark@netmatters.co.uk
W www.bsr.ac.uk
Contact Faith Clark (Administrator)
Awards enable artists to work in the British School at Rome for two to three months. Exhibition of scholars' and awardees' work held at the end of each academic year. The British School has a Curator (Contemporary Arts Programme) to assist with exhibitions and in making contact with an artistic community in Rome, and an Arts Adviser responsible for direct support of painters.
Frequency Normally at least two to three awards. Abbey Council also offers a yearly scholarship tenable at British School at Rome.
Entry Policy Open to mid-career painters who are UK, Commonwealth or US citizens with an established record of achievement. No age limit.

ACE Award for Art in a Religious Context
All Hallows on the Wall, 83 London Wall
London, EC2M 5ND
T 020 7374 0600
F 020 7374 0600
E awards@acetrust.org
W www.acetrust.org
Contact Laura Moffatt

Presented by the Art and Christianity Enquiry (ACE) in association with the Michael Marks Charitable Trust. The commissioned work, in any visual medium, must be within the building or grounds of a worship space of any faith group; it may be permanent or a temporary, completed and in situ before or by the time of the entry deadline. £2,000 of the prize goes to the artist and £1,000 to the client as well as a specially commissioned artwork to display for a period of six weeks.
Frequency One award of £3,000 every two years.
Entry Policy Entries should reflect both theological insight and aesthetic excellence.

ACE/MERCERS International Book Award
All Hallows on the Wall, 83 London Wall
London, EC2M 5ND
T 020 7374 0600
F 020 7374 0600
E awards@acetrust.org
W www.acetrust.org
Contact Laura Moffatt
Given by the Art and Christianity Enquiry (ACE) in association with the Mercers' Company for a book that makes an outstanding contribution to the dialogue between religious faith and the visual arts. The subject matter may relate to any major faith tradition, and to any visual medium (including film, performance arts, design and architecture). Entries should be written in or translated into English.
Frequency One award of £3,000 every two years.

ACE/REEP Award
17 Allan House, 55 Saffron Hill, London
EC1N 8QX
T 020 74046859
F 020 74046859
E gardenawards@reep.org
W www.reep.org
Contact Diana Lazenby
Given jointly by the Religious Education and Environment Programme (REEP) and the Art and Christianity Enquiry (ACE) to an artist working with a school to design a garden that includes an art work incorporating text. First presented in 2003 and runs every two years. Artists working on community projects are encouraged to work with a primary or secondary school to design a school garden. This should involve cross-curricular work, especially RE and Spirituality. A specific theme for the artwork varies each time. £2,500 goes to the winning artist and £500 to the school.
Entry Policy Visit website to register and view curriculum and practical advice. Only submit plans and a proposal for this award.

Adolph & Esther Gottlieb Foundation Grants

Adolph & Esther Gottlieb Foundation
380 West Broadway, New York, NY 10012, USA
T +1 212 2260581
F +1 212 2260584
Contact Jenny Gillis (Grants Manager)
Ten individual support grants available through an annual juried competition. Grant amounts are determined each year (typically US$20,000 each, awarded end March). The foundation also administers a year-round emergency assistance grants programme, which assists artists suffering from recent catastrophic circumstances such as fire, flood, medical emergency, and who have worked for a minimum of ten years in a mature phase of their art. Grant amounts range from US$1,000 to US$10,000.
Entry Policy Open to painters, sculptors and printmakers who have been working for minimum twenty years in a mature phase of their art and have financial need. Application forms available by post in early September. Only written requests for application forms honoured; none sent out in response to telephone/fax requests.

AiR Creative Programme

The Media Centre, 7 Northumberland Street, Huddersfield, HD1 1RL
T 0870 9905007
F 0870 9905000
E info@druh.co.uk
W www.druh.co.uk
Contact Tom Holley (Creative Director)
Focus on digital and interactive media. Programme comprises Medialounge exhibition space, international artist residency programme, commissions, Speaker's Corner and Ultrasound festival (experimental and electronic music). Emphasis is on knowledge sharing, collaboration and partnerships between artists, academics and creative networks regionally, nationally and internationally.
Frequency Four residencies per year.
Entry Policy Open submission process. Artists are requested to make initial contact before submitting CVs, as programme encompasses diverse range of interests.

Akademie Schloss Solitude

Stiftung des öffentlichen Rechts, Solitude 3
Stuttgart, 70197, Germany
T +49 711996190
F +49 7119961950
E mail@akademie-solitude.de
W www.akademie-solitude.de
A public foundation, the Akademie Schloss Solitude operates an international artist programme awarding live/work fellowships to artists working in the disciplines of architecture, the visual arts, the performing arts, design, literature, music/sound and video/film/new media. Also awards fellowships to emerging scientists and managers to work on collaborative projects with artistic fellows at the Akademie. Fellows from the seven art disciplines can participate in the programme but only scientists and managers can apply for a fellowship within the programme. The Akademie was opened in 1990 and is subsidized by the state of Baden-Württemberg. A total of 45 furnished live/work studios are available to fellows and guests.
Frequency Grants awarded every two years.
Entry Policy General age limit 35, or studies should be completed within the past five years. Application forms by request only.

Alexander Graham Munro Travel Award

The Royal Scottish Society of Painters in Watercolour, 29 Waterloo Street, Glasgow G2 6BZ
T 01355 233725
Contact Roger Frame (Secretary)
An award of £3,500 to an artist under 30 years of age, to be used in conjunction with travel. Council to be informed of proposed itinerary and benefits to artist.
Entry Policy Only work in a water-based medium.

Arcimboldo Award

W www.arcimboldo-award.com
Each year the Fondation d'entreprise HP France awards a prize of €10,000 to a digital artist. Established in 1999. Winner chosen on basis of artistic merit of the contest entry, calibre of the creative approach and contribution of digital technology.
Entry Policy Closing date: March. Works must be printed on paper. Candidates must certify that they hold moral and legal rights to the photographs submitted.

Arles Photography Book Prize

RP, 10 Rond-point des Arènes, Arles, BP 96–13620, France
Reinstated in 2000 and awarded to the best photography book published in the previous year (from July to June). Shared between publisher and photographer and awarded in July each year at the

Recontres Internationales de la Photographie in Arles.
Frequency Annual prize.
Entry Policy Closing date: June.

Artes Mundi Prize

Room A2.10, UWIC Llandaff Campus
Western Avenue, Cardiff, CF5 2YB
T 02920 555300
F 02920 555800
E info@artesmundi.org
W www.artesmundi.org
Contact Tessa Jackson
First awarded in 2004 to celebrate artists who have gained recognition in their own country and are emerging internationally. Focuses upon those who discuss the human form, the human condition and add to our understanding of humanity. A shortlist is drawn up by two international selectors; the shortlisted artists exhibit a body of work at the National Museum of Wales in Cardiff; and a panel of curators and artists award the £40,000 prize to the artist who consistently makes work of note and quality, and is thought-provoking within the criteria of the prize.
Frequency Every two years (even-numbered years).
Entry Policy Artists considered through nomination process only. See website for details.

Artist of the Year by the Society for All Artists (SAA)

AOY SAA, P.O. Box 50, Newark
NG23 5GY
T 01949 844050
F 01949 844051
E AOY@saa.co.uk
W www.saa.co.uk
Contact Susan Caughtry
The SAA exists to inform, encourage and inspire all who want to paint, from beginners to professionals. This competition is open to all, with SAA members benefitting from free unlimited entries.
Frequency One main competition per year.
Entry Policy Open to paintings (not previously published) in the main categories of landscape, seascape, flowers, still life, abstract and figure, with prizes for Artist of the Year, Young, Junior, Beginner, Amateur and Professional.

Artist-in-Residence, Durham Cathedral

41 Ellerby Mews, Thornley, County Durham
DH6 3FB
T 01429 820869
E billhalluk@yahoo.co.uk
W www.artschaplaincy.org.uk
Contact Canon Bill Hall
Founded in 1983, the residency offers an artist time and space to assess their practice and development while responding to the cathedral as a powerful creative statement. Should the artist wish, currently there is also the offer of a short-term collaboration with another artist, perhaps from another art form.
Frequency Twelve-month residency beginning each year in October, £17,000 fee + teaching fee.
Entry Policy A good first degree/MA. Artists should be over 25 years old and be able to demonstrate a continuous theme of exploration.

Artists in Berlin Programme (DAAD)

Deutscher Akademischer Austauschdienst
Berlinner Kunstlerprogramm
Jagerstrasse 22–23
Berlin 10117, Germany
T +49 302312080
F +49 302292512
To promote the exchange of artists' experiences and the concern for current cultural issues in other countries. Each year fifteen to twenty artists of international reputation are invited to live and work in Berlin for twelve months to present their work to the Berlin public. Invitations issued with grants to allow adequate standard of living and rental of apartments/workrooms.
Entry Policy No application process for visual arts; a commission issues invitations.

Artists Residences (Cyprus)

Cyprus College of Art
7 Leonard Street
London, EC2A 4AQ
T 020 8676 4610
F 07092 194514
E enquiries@artcyprus.org
W www.limassolstudios.org
Contact Michael Paraskos
Has offered since 1969 British artists the opportunity to spend an extended period of time living and making art on the island of Cyprus. Residencies are from one month upwards and can happen in either Limassol or Paphos. Facilities are geared towards painters and hands-on sculptors, although other practitioners are welcome to apply providing they can supply any specialist equipment themselves. Living accommodation can be arranged upon request.

Frequency Up to ten at any one time. Artists must be self-funding.
Entry Policy Artists should apply directly via the online form on the website. Any additional information required will be requested after this.

Arts and Crafts in Architecture Awards
The Saltire Society, 9 Fountain Close
22 Hugh Street, Edinburgh, EH1 1TF
T 0131 5561836
F 0131 5571675
E saltire@saltire.org.uk
W www.saltiresociety.org.uk
Contact Kathleen Munro
Exists to promote art and culture of Scotland. Awards made for works of art and craft designed to enhance and enrich buildings. Examples include sculpture, painting, tilework, mosaic, tapestry, textile hangings, glass, plaster, metalwork and enamel. Artists and craftsmen working in any suitable medium are invited to enter the competition. The society may arrange for members of the panel to inspect selected entries on site. Adjudication will take place as soon as possible after closing date. Awards or commendations, each in the form of a certificate, will be made to the artist or craftsman and commissioning body or person.
Entry Policy Work must: (1) be located in Scotland; (2) have been completed the previous year within the period 1 April to 31 March inclusive; and (3) be an intrinsic part of a building or group of buildings. Each entry must be accompanied by a fee of £35.

Arts Awards
The Wellcome Trust, 215 Euston Road
London, NW1 2BE
T 020 76117222
F 020 76118269
E arts@wellcome.ac.uk
W www.wellcome.ac.uk/funding/
publicengagement/arts
Contact Marie-Lise Sheppard
The Arts Awards support arts projects which stimulate interest and debate in biomedical science, encourage new ways of thinking and foster high quality practice and collaborative partnerships across the arts, science and/or education. Supports a range of projects working in any art form and any area of biomedical science. Encourages collaboration between professionals from different disciplines, between adults and young people and between experts and the public.

Aims to support projects that ask difficult questions and give fresh perspectives on science and its role in our lives.
Frequency Deadlines throughout the year.

Arts Council England – Helen Chadwick Fellowship
Ruskin School of Drawing and Fine Art
74 High Street, Oxford
OX1 4BG
T 01865 276940
F 01865 276949
E vanda.wilkinson@ruskin-school.ox.ac.uk
W www.ruskin-sch.ox.ac.uk/lab
Contact Paul Bonaventura
Established by the Laboratory at the Ruskin School of Drawing and Fine Art and the British School at Rome to help artists make new work by spending periods of time in Oxford and Rome. After visiting Italy for a one-month reconnaissance period, the fellow devotes two months to research-related activities in England before returning to Italy for three months of intensive studio-based production. The fellowship was implemented in 1997 and the current value of the award is £7,500.
Frequency One award annually.
Entry Policy The award is advertised in the specialist press. Applicants must be British nationals or have been continuously resident in the UK since March 2002. It is expected that the fellowship will attract visual artists who have established their practices in the years following graduation and who have identified a project that could be made possible or enhanced by spending periods of time both in Oxford and Rome.

Arts Council England – Oxford-Melbourne Fellowship
Ruskin School of Drawing and Fine Art
74 High Street, Oxford
OX1 4BG
T 01865 276940
F 01865 2276949
E vanda.wilkinson@ruskin-school.ox.ac.uk
W www.ruskin-sch.ox.ac.uk/lab
Contact Paul Bonaventura
Established by the Laboratory at the Ruskin School of Drawing and Fine Art and the Victorian College of the Arts to help artists make new work by spending periods of time in Oxford and Melbourne. The fellow devotes two months to research-related activities in England before travelling to Melbourne for up to four months of intensive studio-based production. The fellowship

was implemented in 2002. The current value of the award is £7,500.

Frequency One award biannually.

Entry Policy The award is advertised in the specialist press. Applicants must be British nationals or have been continuously resident in the UK since March 2002. It is expected that the fellowship will attract visual artists who have established their practices in the years following graduation and who have identified a project that could be made possible or enhanced by spending periods of time both in Oxford and Melbourne.

Arts Council of Northern Ireland International Residencies

MacNiece House, 77 Malone Road, Belfast
BT9 6AQ
T 028 9038 5200
F 028 9066 1715
E info@artscouncil-ni.org
W www.artscouncil-ni.org
The Banff Residency offers two funded residencies for established Irish artists, one from Northern Ireland and one from the Republic, for 8–10 weeks at the Leighton Studios in Banff, Canada. The Winnipeg Residency is a four-week funded placement at the Platform Centre for the Photographic and Digital Arts at Winnipeg, Canada, for a photographer or lens-based or digital artist. The St James Cavalier, Malta residency is a three-week placement to work on a specific project in Valletta, Malta. There is also a British School of Rome Fellowship providing a visual artist with a nine-month residency to work on a project of their choosing. Scholars are encouraged to use the time to work on ideas in sketch or maquette form.

Arts Council of Northern Ireland Support for Individual Artists Programme

MacNiece House, 77 Malone Road, Belfast
BT9 6AQ
T 028 9038 5200
F 028 9066 1715
E info@artscouncil-ni.org
W www.artscouncil-ni.org
Offers a portfolio of awards. The General Arts Award is given for specific projects, specialized research, personal artistic development and certain materials/equipment. The Major Individual Award aims to help established artists develop extended or ambitious work, and are awarded annually for a specific discipline. There are also Travel Awards to allow individual artists to travel from Northern Ireland to assist their development. Applicants

must have been invited by a host organization in the destination country. The International Awards enable individual artists working internationally (including GB and Ireland) to arrange exchanges or take up self-arranged residencies. The New York Residency Award allows an artist the opportunity to take up a self-arranged residency in the city. The Council also offers the International Artists Profile service, offering assistance with profiling and international marketing material.

Arts Grant Committee (Sweden)

Konstnärsnämnden
P.O. Box 1610
Stockholm 11186, Sweden
T +46 84023570
F +46 84023590
E info@konstnarsnamnden.se
Contact Nils Johansson (Director)
The Visual Arts Fund, part of the Arts Grant Committee, runs a programme called Artists in Residence in Sweden (AIRIS). Offers an opportunity for Swedish artists to invite foreign artists with whom they wish to work/collaborate to Sweden to participate in workshops, symposia or to work towards an art exhibition.

Frequency Grants are issued four times a year and range from £3,500 to £20,000 to cover the costs of travel, accommodation, fees, materials, premises and documentation.

Entry Policy Approach must be made by Swedish artists.

Arts/Industry Artist-in-Residency

John Michael Kohler Arts Center
608 New York Avenue
P.O. Box 489, Sheboygan
WI 53082-0489, USA
T +1 920 4586144
E kcridler@jmkac.org
W www.jmkac.org
Contact Kim Cridler (Arts/Industry Coordinator)
Provides artists worldwide with access to plumbingware firm Kohler Co., through two six-month residencies. Artists-in-residence are provided with studio space in the factory, accessible twenty-four hours a day, seven days a week. Additionally, they receive free materials, use of equipment, technical assistance, photographic services, housing, round-trip transportation within continental USA from their home to the site, and weekly honoraria. Available media are vitreous china, iron, enamel and brass.

Entry Policy Emerging and established artists in

any discipline are invited to apply for arts/industry residencies. Closing date: August for the following year. Send sae for application form or visit website.

Association of Photographers (AOP) Open
The AOP, 81 Leonard Street, London
EC2A 4QS
W www.the-aop.org
Open to professional and amateur photographers, with a mission to celebrate the diversity of photography as an artistic medium. The AOP also administers a Bursary (£15,000), an Assistant Photographer's Award, Document (awarded for documentary photography) and Zeitgeist (to provide an overview of trends and fashions in published photography).
Entry Policy Membership of the AOP is not necessary and no set themes or categories are imposed for the open.

Balmoral Scholarship for Fine Arts
Künstlerhaus Schloss Balmoral
Villenpromenade 11, Bad Ems
56130, Germany
T +49 260394190
F +49 2603941916
E info@balmoral.de
W www.balmoral.de
Contact Dr Sabine Jung
An international institution for fine arts. Allocates grants to qualified artists of all ages in fields of painting, drawing, sculpture, installation, graphics and design, photography and art theory. Not an art college, but a meeting place where gifted artists can widen their horizons by meeting colleagues from various art sectors and from different parts of the world. Eight apartments and eight studios available.
Frequency Monthly grant given for eleven-month residency.
Entry Policy Applicants should have relevant training/study or degree followed by at least 3 years experience. Knowledge of at least one language (German, English or French) is requested.

Beck's Futures Exhibition and Award
W www.becksfutures.co.uk
A total of £45,000 prize money awarded (£20,000 to the winner and the remainder between five others). Nominations are by professional exhibition curators, museum directors, critics and artists from Britain and Ireland, who propose three artists each. Run in conjunction with the ICA.

Bellagio Individual, Collaborative and Parallel Residencies
The Rockefeller Foundation, 420 Fifth Avenue, New York, NY 10018–2702, USA
E bellagio@rockfound.org
W www.rockfound.org
Provides a stimulating international environment for month-long study residencies for scholars, scientists and artists. Scholars, artists and others may apply as individuals or with one collaborator who is also qualified for the residency.
Entry Policy Applicants must be scholars, scientists, policymakers, practitioners or artists who expect their work at the centre to result in publication, exhibition, performance or other concrete product. Request application one year in advance of residency period.

Best of Digital Arts
Jenoptik L.O.S.GmbH – Digital Cameras
Oskar-Von-Miller-Str. 1a, Munich-Eching
85386, Germany
T +49 816577475
F +49 816577503
E info@eyelike.com
W www.eyelike.com
A showcase for creativity and design in all areas of photography. The website has a facility for simple submission of images.
Frequency Certificates for US$2,000, US$1,500 and US$500 for the first three winners, which can be used against purchases of equipment/services from Jenoptik.
Entry Policy Check website for applications. Closing date to upload images: January.

Bloomberg New Contemporaries
Studio I, Rochelle School, Arnold Circus
London, E2 7ES
T 07785 706227
E ncinfo2004@yahoo.co.uk
W www.newcontemporaries.org.uk
Contact Bev Bytheway (New Contemporaries Administrator)
An annual exhibition of work by students and recent graduates from the UK's art colleges. Tours major UK arts venues each year. First established in 1949 and much-respected, New Contemporaries helps support emerging artists at the start of their careers.
Entry Policy New Contemporaries is open to all final year undergraduates and current postgraduates of Fine Art at UK colleges and those artists who graduated in the previous 12 months.

Selection by an invited panel of artists, initially from slides through to a final selection from actual work from a shortlist. Submission forms are available from the website from October-January.

BOC Emerging Artist Award

International Art Consultants/Art for Offices
The Galleries, 15 Dock Street, London
E1 8JL
E laura@afo.co.uk
W www.boc.com
Launched in 2002. Supports promising young artists based in the UK with a grant of £20,000 to the winner, with additional discretionary awards of £1,000 each to runners-up. The winner's award also includes ongoing support from BOC and its art consultant, Art for Offices/International Art Consultants. The award is designed to cover a year's studio rental and materials, a travel bursary and the costs of a London-based exhibition at the end of the award period.
Entry Policy Open to suitably qualified UK-based artists working in two dimensions who are under 30 years of age at the award's closing date.

BP Portrait Award

National Portrait Gallery, St Martin's Place
London, WC2H 0HE
T 0870 1126772
W www.npg.org.uk
Contact Beatrice Hosegood
An annual event aimed at encouraging young artists to focus on and develop the theme of portraiture within their work. Many artists shown have gained commissions as a result of interest in the award and resulting exhibition.
Entry Policy Four annual prizes. First prize of £25,000 in 2005, plus at the judges' discretion, a commission worth £4,000 to be agreed between the National Portrait Gallery and the artist.

Braziers International Artists Workshop

c/o 164 Swaton Road, London
E3 4ER
T 020 75154798
F 020 73893101
E info@braziersworkshop.org
W www.braziersworkshop.org
Contact Bernadette Moloney
An artist-led initiative, providing opportunities for international exchange and dialogue between professional artists. Founded in 1995, the annual residential workshop takes place in rural Oxfordshire for 16 days each August. The

workshop provides a rich and challenging environment that encourages artists to experiment and try new ideas. The rural location encourages site-specific, installation collaborative projects as well as new media, painting and sculpture. The organization also manages a number of longer term residencies for overseas artists in the south-east and an Arts Council England International Fellowship for a UK artist overseas.
Frequency 1 International Fellowship and 3 regional residencies awarded annually
Entry Policy Open to visual artists across all disciplines. Recent graduates should not apply. Deadline: February/March. See website for details.

British Journal of Photography

Incisive Media, Haymarket House
London, SW1Y 4RX
T 020 74849944
F 020 74849989
E bjp.endframe@bjphoto.co.uk
W www.bjp-online.com/endframe
Contact Mick Moore
The BJP/Nikon Endframe Award began four years ago. Entrants must submit a portfolio of photographs and supplementary material, including a 'dream project' proposal (see website) to be published in BJP. From the 51 published each year, eight finalists are chosen, interviewed and given £300 to develop their proposal idea with full costings. A winner is then chosen, who must then use the bursary to complete their project and then present it at the annual Vision event in November.
Frequency £5,000 awarded annually as a bursary.
Entry Policy This is a photographic competition, and entrants must be living in the UK and be available for interview if they are selected as a finalist.

Byard Art Open Competition

Byard Art, 4 St Mary's Passage
Cambridge, CB2 3PQ
T 01223 464646
F 01223 464655
E info@byardart.co.uk
W www.byardart.co.uk
Contact Ruth Hawkins
Established 1993. Annual competition with winners selected by professional panel of judges. General public invited to vote for 'The People's Prize'.
Entry Policy Open to professional artists living or working within a 25-mile radius of Cambridge. Acceptable media: painting, printmaking, photography, sculpture, ceramics, textiles and glass.

Calouste Gulbenkian Foundation Awards

98 Portland Place, London, W1B 1ET
T 020 76365313
F 020 79087580
The work of the foundation is divided into programmes in arts, education and social welfare, with a separate programme for Anglo-Portuguese cultural relations. The arts programme is principally for professionals or individual professional artists working in partnerships or groups. It aims to support the development of new art-making in any form, though activities must not be linked to mainstream education. There are also grants available for non-professional participants outside the formal education and community sectors for the research and development of unusual experimental projects.
Entry Policy Open to UK and Irish organizations. Closing date: at least three months before project starting date.

Celeste Art Prize

28 Vestry Road, London, SE5 8NX
T 020 7252 6240
E info@celesteartprize.co.uk
W www.celesteartprize.co.uk
Contact Sara Pearce
Founded in 2005. Aims to encourage excellence in painting in its widest possible sense from the traditional to works that push the boundaries of painting. Initial selection by Goldsmiths College Curatorial Programme. The finalists vote for winner and give prize money. Awards: £10,000 for professional artist, £5,000 for student artist, exhibition for finalists and catalogue for short-listed artists.
Frequency Annual: 1 x £10,000 for professional artist, 1 x £5,000 for student artist.
Entry Policy Open to UK citizens and anyone living and working in the UK at time of submission. No age limit.

The Cill Rialaig Project Artists Retreat

Cill Rialaig, Ballinskelligs, County Kerry
T 066 9479297
F 066 9479324
E cillrialaig@esatclear.ie
Contact Mary O'Connor
Founded in 1991 the Cill Rialaig Artists Retreat is situated on a remote Cliffside in County Kerry, consisting of six renovated cottages (soon to be seven, with a meeting house and composer's house soon to be completed also), each self-contained with kitchen, bedroom, bathroom and studio. One- to six-week residencies are awarded free of charge (donations while welcomed are not obligatory). Cill Rialaig is a registered charity, founded with the intention of maintaining and developing the arts in both Ireland and abroad. International applications welcomed.
Frequency Up to 12 residencies awarded monthly.
Entry Policy Submit via email or post, CV, artist statement, and 10–12 copies of recent work (hard copies prefereble).

Clark Digital Bursary

Watershed, 1 Canon's Road
Harbourside, Bristol
BS1 5TX
E info@watershed.co.uk
W www.watershed.co.uk/bursary
Awarded annually for the creative development and production of new work in digital media. These awards can be for any stage of development and/or completion of new digital work. Technical support on the winning project can be arranged at either Watershed Media Centre in Bristol or PVA Media Lab in Bridport.
Entry Policy Open to artists and multimedia producers working in the south-west.

Commonwealth Arts and Crafts Award

The Commonwealth Foundation, Marlborough House, Pall Mall, London
SW1Y 5HY
T 020 79303783
F 020 78398157
W www.oneworld.org/com_fnd/
Contact Andrew Firmin
An award to enable young artists and craftspeople to learn new techniques or enhance existing skills, work with more established artists and mount an exhibition of their work in another region of the Commonwealth. Seeks to encourage sharing of artistic traditions within the Commonwealth and promote excellence in arts and crafts in Commonwealth countries. Each award covers airfares, living expenses for up to nine months and expenses of mounting an exhibition in the host country. Preference given to talented individuals showing promise of artistic initiative, merit and achievement in their own countries and who seek opportunities for creative work with other artists and craftspeople. Participants are expected to plan, organize and manage their awards.
Frequency Biennial prize worth £6,000.
Entry Policy Open to anyone aged between 22 and 25 who is a citizen of a Commonwealth country.

CORE Program

The Glassell School of Art, 5101 Montrose
Boulevard, Houston
TX 77006, USA
T +1 713 6397500
W core.mfah.org/home.asp
Awards one- and two-year residencies to highly
motivated, exceptional visual artists and art
scholars who have graduated but have yet to
develop a professional career. Established in 1982
within Glassell School of Art, the teaching wing of
Houston's Museum of Fine Arts. Residents engage
in ongoing dialogue with each other and with
invited guests. Each artist-resident is given
approximately 450 sq. ft of private studio space,
twenty-four-hour access to school facilities and
equipment, and a US$9,000 annual stipend.
Entry Policy Send twelve slides of work (include
name of artist and practical details of each piece)
completed in previous two years. The selection
jury views six slides from each applicant in first
elimination round. The remaining six slides will
only be viewed in the second round. Applicants are
encouraged to number their slides 1 to 12, in order
of priority. Also include a CV, statement of intent,
three letters of recommendation and an sae for
return of slides.

Cove Park Residency Programme

Peaton Hill, Cove
Argyll and Bute
G84 0PE
T 01436 850123
F 01436 850445
E information@covepark.org
W www.covepark.org
Contact Alexia Holt
Founded in 1999. Located on a fifty-acre site
overlooking Loch Long on the west coast of
Scotland. Organizes residencies for national and
international artists working in all art forms. Up to
ten residencies at any one time, lasting from one
week to three months. The programme runs from
May to October. Artists receive a fee (determined
by the duration of the residency), accommodation
and, when appropriate, studio space.
Frequency Up to fifty residencies each year.
Entry Policy Selection is by both invitation and
application. When applications are required, the
residency is advertised nationally and
internationally and on Cove Park's website.
Requirements vary following open submission and
application, depending on the form of the
residency itself.

Crafts Council Development Award

44a Pentonville Road, Islington, London
N1 9BX
T 020 72787700
F 020 78376891
E maker@craftscouncil.org.uk
W www.craftscouncil.org.uk
For makers who are about to set up their business,
or who are within three years of doing so. The
award includes: an equipment grant of up to
£5,000, which must be matched by the recipient; a
maintenance grant of £2,500; a residential course
in business training aimed specifically at small
creative practices; provision of 1,000 promotional
postcards; one-to-one support from a Crafts
Council Professional Development Officer, which
includes two studio visits; four years
representation on Photostore, the Crafts Council's
visual database.
Entry Policy Applicants must have completed their
studies, be about to or have practised as
craftsperson for no more than three years, live and
work in England and be resident for tax purposes.
(The Award is open to non-UK nationals as long as
they fulfill this condition.) Annual deadlines for
the award are 1 March, 1 June, 1 September and 1
December.

Crafts Council Next Move Scheme

44a Pentonville Road, Islington, London
N1 9BY
T 020 78062504
F 020 78376891
E makerdev@craftscouncil.org.uk
W www.craftscouncil.org.uk
A setting-up scheme designed to put new
designer-makers on the fast track. Placements
include rent-free studio space in a college
department over a two-year period, maintenance
grant of £6,000, business/equipment grant of
£1,000, in depth support and business training
and access to specialist equipment.
Entry Policy Open to MA or BA applied arts and 3D
design graduates wanting to develop their practice
and business.

Creekside Open

APT, 6 Creekside, Deptford, London
SE8 4SA
E enquiry@creeksideopen.org
W www.creeksideopen.org
Contact Liz May
Launched in 2005 to celebrate the tenth
anniversary of the Art in Perpetuity Trust.

A bi-annual competition for inclusion in an exhibition at the APT Gallery. Awards of £500 are given. Open to all visual/fine artists living or working in greater London.
Entry Policy Entry by slide submission.

David Canter Memorial Fund
c/o Devon Guild of Craftsmen, Riverside Mill Bovey Tracey, TQ13 9AF
T 01626 832223
F 01626 834220
E jenny@crafts.org.uk
W www.crafts.org.uk
Contact Jenny Plackett (Secretary)
Provides support for special projects, such as setting up a workshop, buying materials and equipment or for research and travel. Grants usually range between £500 and £1,000.
Entry Policy Open to artists who have finished formal training, working full- or part-time. Awards are usually made in the autumn, and the selection process falls into two stages: (1) preliminary application using the application form, for shortlisting; and (2) shortlisted applicants are asked to send further information about their work, together with six slides of recent pieces for final selection.

De Ateliers
Stadhouderskade 86, Amsterdam
1073 AT, Netherlands
T +31 206739359
F +31 206755039
E office@de-ateliers.nl
W www.de-ateliers.nl
Founded in 1963. An international studio programme run by artists at a postgraduate level. Offers twenty young artists at the beginning of their professional career the opportunity to develop their work in a private studio during a maximum of two years, supported with a stipend and the critical guidance from prominent artists who do weekly individual studio visits. Tutors include Rob Birza, Dominic van den Boogerd, Marlene Dumas, Ceal Floyer, Willem de Rooij, Marien Schouten, Didier Vermeiren and Marijke van Warmerdam.
Frequency Some ten studios available annually.
Entry Policy Application is possible at any time and open to young artists from Holland and abroad at the beginning of their professional career. Ability to speak English is required. Apply by sending documentation of work (slides, CDs, videotapes) and application form to be found on the website.

Applications are selected by tutors. Main criteria are visual qualities, artistic ambitions and prospects for future development.

Dedalo Painting Award
Loc., Greppolungo 43–44, Camaiore (LU)
55041, Italy
T +39 347 740 4236
E info@dedaloarte.org
W www.dedaloarte.org and www.artcoursestuscany.com
Contact Sarah Baker
Founded by artists in 1996, Dedalo Arte offers residencies primarily to painters, although equipment for ceramics and bronze sculpture is also available for use. The artists chosen will be present during a season of courses and invited to talk about their work and way of working during informal discussions with fellow participants. The award has a value of around £900 and consists of a fourteen-day stay in Castelfalfi in Tuscany, with full board and shared use of a studio. Materials are not included. The artist is asked to leave behind a piece of work of their own choice.
Entry Policy To apply send one photo of a recent work, a 1–2 page CV, and short artist statement. Applications accepted in either English or Italian.

Delfina Studio Trust
50 Bermondsey Street, London
SE1 3UD
T 020 73576600
E admin@delfina.org.uk
W www.delfina.org.uk
The largest residency programme in the UK, awarding studio space to as many as eighteen artists each year for periods ranging from two months to two years. Set up in 1988 as a registered charity with the aim of providing high-quality studio space and related facilities for visual artists. Housed in a renovated factory in the Bankside area of central London, it provides thirty studios in total.
Submission Policy Applications should be mailed between 1 and 31 January each year for artists from abroad, and during the same period every other year for British artists. Artists should send eight slides of recent work and/or VHS/DVDs, a CV, and sae. For further information visit the website. Grants awarded:6 international residencies awards every year and 6 British residency awards every two years. The Trust does not provide stipends or grants, and does not provide for everyday costs.

Derek Hill Foundation Scholarship in Portraiture

The British School at Rome, at the British
Academy, 10 Carlton House Terrace
London, SW1Y 5AH
T 020 79695202
F 020 79695401
E bsr@britac.ac.uk
W www.bsr.ac.uk
Contact Dr Gill Clark (The Registrar)
Founded in 2004 and funded by the Derek Hill
Foundation. Aims to encourage painters to focus
upon and develop the theme of portraiture within
their work. Offers full board and lodging at the
British School at Rome for three months, with a
grant of approximately £950 per month.
Frequency One each year.
Entry Policy Applicants must be of British or Irish
nationality and aged 24 or over on 1 September of
the academic year in which the scholarship will be
held. An application form must be completed.
Closing date: mid-December.

Deutsche Börse Photography Prize

5 & 8 Great Newport Street, London
WC2H 7HY
T 020 78311772
F 020 78369704
E info@photonet.org.uk
W www.photonet.org.uk
Aims to reward a living photographer of any
nationality who has made the most significant
contribution to the medium of photography
during the past year. Photographers are nominated
for a significant exhibition or publication that took
place in that year. Nominations are made by an
academy, a diverse group of people invited by the
Photographers' Gallery from photography
institutions throughout Europe. From these, four
shortlisted photographers are selected by a jury
and invited to present their work in an exhibition
at the Photographers' Gallery. The winner receives
£30,000; three runners-up each receive £3,000.
Frequency An annual exhibition and award.

Deveron Arts Residency Programme

The Studio, Brander Building
The Square, Huntly, AB54 8BR
T 01466 794494
F 01466 794494
E info@deveron-arts.com
W www.deveron-arts.com
Contact Claudia Zeiske
Founded in 1995 to engage artists for short- and
long-term residency programmes to work within

the community, bringing contemporary art to a
wide audience. Aims to work within a theme that
is of local significance but also of national and even
global concern. Deveron Arts has no dedicated
gallery space as 'the town is the venue'.
Frequency Average of three residencies per year.
Entry Policy Artists are advised to write or email
for further information before submitting CVs.

Djerassi Resident Artists Program

2325 Bear Gulch Road, Woodside
CA 94062-4405, USA
T +1 650 7471250
F +1 650 7470105
W www.djerassi.org
Based in the foothills of Santa Cruz Mountains of
Northern California. Visual arts studios and living
quarters are located in a twelve-sided barn. The
Artists' Barn also houses a choreography studio,
darkroom and composers' studio. Artists pay for
travel, personal needs, materials and supplies.
Frequency Residencies last for four to six weeks,
from April through to October. No residency fee
and all meals are provided.
Entry Policy Application deadline is February for a
residency in the following year. Instructions and
forms available from the website.

EAC Over 60s Art Awards

Art Awards, PO Box 279, Esher
KT10 8YZ
T 01372 462190
F 01372 460032
W www.artawards.eac.org.uk
Annual open competition for amateur artists over
the age of 60 living in the UK. Created by the
Elderly Accomodation Counsel, this competition
celebrates the talent and creativity of older artists.
Around 120 artists are selected for exhibition in
the prestigious Mall Galleries, and prizes are
awarded in a range of categories.

East End Academy

Whitechapel Art Gallery
80–82 Whitechapel High Street
London, E1 7QX
E info@whitechapel.org
W www.whitechapel.org
Showcases new work from emerging artists living
and working in east London. Works on show range
from pencil-and-ink drawings to room-sized
environments, and include painting, photography,
video and installation. First launched in 1932 as an
open-submission exhibition for 'all artists living

and working east of the famous Aldgate Pump'.
There are also off-site commissions. Admission is
free and most works are for sale.

East International
Norwich School of Art and Design, St George
Street, Norwich, NR3 1BB
T 01603 610561
F 01603 615728
E nor.gal@nsad.ac.uk
W www.nsad.co.uk/gallery
An exhibition open to visual artists working in any
medium. Each year one artist is given £5,000.
Takes place at Norwich Gallery, the Fine Art
Studios of Norwich School of Art and Design and
the Sainsbury Centre for Visual Art at the
University of East Anglia. Emphasis is on choosing
artists from work submitted on slide. Now a major
international open exhibition held every summer,
selected by a number of distinguished curators and
artists including David Tremlett, Helen Chadwick,
Konrad Fischer, Marian Goodman, Rudi Fuchs and
Richard Long.
Entry Policy No rules of age, status, place of
residence or medium to limit those who may enter.
For entry form and further information contact
above address.

Elephant Trust Award
512 Bankside Lofts, 65 Hopton Street
London, SE1 9GZ
T 020 79221160
F 020 79221160
E ruth@elephanttrust.org.uk
W www.elephanttrust.org.uk
Contact Ruth Rattenbury
Founded in 1975. Aims to make it possible for
artists and those presenting their work to complete
projects when frustrated by lack of funds. Bias
towards the visual arts; particularly interested in
funding projects that depart from the routine and
signal distinct and imaginative sets of possibilities.
Value of awards usually about £2,000.
Frequency The trustees meet four times a year to
consider applications and decide on awards.
Entry Policy Grants not available for students or for
educational and other study purposes.

Elizabeth Foundation for the Arts
P.O. Box 2670, New York
NY 10108, USA
T +1 212 5635855
F +1 212 5631875
E grants@efa1.org

Offers a grants programme for individuals in the
visual arts. Selection is based on quality of work,
financial need, background and dedication to
career, and proposals for use of grant. Grant
amounts range from US$2,500 and US$12,000
and are targeted to assist artists in creating new
work and/or gaining recognition for work. Twelve
to fifteen grants awarded per year. Applicant pool
averages one thousand applications. Previous
grantees not eligible to apply for five years
following their grant periods.
Entry Policy Open to artists in all media except
photography, video/film and crafts. Must be over
30 or have been working for at least six years since
completing formal schooling. Closing date: 1 May.

Elizabeth Greenshields Foundation Grants
1814 Sherbrooke Street West, Suite #1, Montreal,
Quebec
H3H 1E4, Canada
T +1 514 9379225
F +1 514 9370141
E egreen@total.net
Contact Micheline Leduc (Administrator)
Grants for artists in early stages of career, working
in painting, drawing, printmaking and sculpture.
Work must be representational or figurative. The
award of C$10,000 is tenable anywhere in the
world and may be used for any art-related purpose.
Entry Policy Applicants must have started or
already completed art-school training and/or
demonstrate through past work and future plans a
commitment to making art a lifetime career.

Erna & Victor Hasselblad Foundation Awards and Bursaries
Ekmansgatan 8, Göteborg
SE-412 56, Sweden
An international photography award selected by
jury (no applications accepted). Also stipends and
research grants for photographic research and
scholarly projects. Bias towards research in
photographic theory and history, scientific
photography, conservation and restoration of
photographic material and experimental projects.
Entry Policy Open to photographers, researchers
and other professionals working primarily within
the field of still photography. Open to all
nationalities. Closing date: usually March.

European Association for Jewish Culture Grants
London Office, 79 Wimpole Street, London
W1G 9RY
T 020 79358266

F 020 79353252
E london@jewishcultureineurope.org
W www.jewishcultureineurope.org
Contact Lena Stanley-Clamp
Founded in 2001, the EAJC awards grants for new work in performing and visual arts with a Jewish dimension. The value of grants is from €5,000€10,000.
Frequency Grants awarded annually
Entry Policy Priority given to individual artists, playwrights, choreographers and curators. Applicants must be European nationals or long-term residents. Record of artistic or scholarly achievement must be appended to application. Application forms and guidelines available on website.

European Award for Women Photographers
Dryphoto, CP 1024, Via Pugliese 23, Prato
I-59100, Italy
T +39 574604939
F +39 574444508
E dryphoto@po-net.prato.it
Started in 1995 and open to all females resident in Europe who use the photographic medium as an expressive instrument of artistic research. Prize worth €2,500.

Federation of British Artists (FBA)
Mall Galleries, 17 Carlton House Terrace
London, SW1Y 5BD
T 020 79306844
F 020 78397830
E info@mallgalleries.com
W www.mallgalleries.org.uk
Of nine member art societies, eight hold their annual open exhibitions in the Mall Galleries. Any artist may submit work for selection. Work for exhibition is selected by a committee of members from the society where work has been submitted.
Entry Policy See website or send sae to Mall Galleries for full details. Indicate the relevant society and address to 'Entry Details' at the above address. A maximum of six works may be entered.

Feiweles Trust
Yorkshire Sculpture Park, West Bretton
Wakefield, WF4 4LG
Established in 1989, supporting work in schools and the community by artists at the beginning of their careers. A sculpture bursary in the region of £10,000 is awarded to a sculptor to work with schools and the community for approximately one hundred days. Some preliminary planning work

will need to be undertaken before the bursary begins. It is expected that the appointed artist will use this bursary experience to develop their own artistic practice.

Florence Trust Residencies
St Saviour's, Aberdeen Park, London
N5 2AR
T 020 73544771
E info@florencetrust.org
W www.florencetrust.org
Contact Paul Bayley (Director) or Lea O'Loughlin (Studio Manager)
Founded in 1988, offering 10–12 twelve-month studio residencies (July–August) and career development support. Artists benefit from one-to-one sessions, an open studios event and a summer exhibition with full-colour catalogue. For artists' professional development (including business planning, marketing, interview and presentation skills and applying to other trusts and foundations for funding) and production of new work. Housed in grade-1-listed Victorian church.
Entry Policy Send application form (available from website), artist's CV, 10–15 examples of work (slides or CD-Rom), an sae and application fee. Rolling submissions accepted, closing 1 June each year.

Franklin Furnace Fund for Performance Art and Franklin Furnace Future of the Present
80 Hanson Place #301, Brooklyn
NY 11217, USA
T +1 212 3987255
F +1 212 3987256
E mail@franklinfurnace.org
W www.franklinfurnace.org
Contact Dolores Zorreguieta
An avant-garde arts organization founded in 1976. The Fund for Performance Art (supported by Jerome Foundation and the New York State Council on the Arts) awards grants of between US$2,000 and US$5,000 to emerging performance artists, allowing them to produce major works in the New York area. Artists from all areas of the world are invited to apply. The Future of the Present awards artists an honorarium and offers its resources to facilitate the creation of 'live art on the Internet'. Open to artists worldwide.
Frequency Around ten awards per year.
Entry Policy See website for full details.

Friends of Israel Educational Foundation
P.O. Box 42763, London, N2 0YJ

T 020 4440777
F 020 84440681
E info@foi-asg.org
W www.foi-asg.org
Contact John D A Levy
The award consists of return air passage to Israel, a minimum of six weeks' work on a kibbutz with time for painting/art instruction by the award winner, a ten-day placement at the Bezalel School of Art in Jerusalem, and free time to travel around the country and an exhibition.
Entry Policy Open to British students graduating from art school: painters, printmakers and illustrators are invited to apply. Send a CV, academic letter of reference, statement of reasons for wishing to visit Israel and a representative selection of work (transparencies to be submitted initially). Closing date: 1 May each year.

Friends of the Royal Scottish Academy Artist Bursary
The RSA, The Mound, Edinburgh, EH2 2EL
T 0131 2253922
F 0131 2206016
E friends@royalscottishacademy.org
W www.royalscottishacademy.org
Founded in 1995 to enable artists to continue and extend their creative development. The bursary will assist in the cost of a specific developmental project such as travel or research, attending a course or workshop, or to supplement or replace income in order to permit a period of exploration and experimentation. Worth £2,000.
Frequency Annual.
Entry Policy Applications invited from artists permanently resident in Scotland, qualified and working within the disciplines of the RSA (painting, drawings, sculpture, architecture and printmaking). Must have completed full-time education (including postgraduate study) at least three years beforehand. Strong preference to those over 35 years old or working professionally for ten years or more. Closing date: 1 July.

Gallery 1839
London, SW15 5LS
T 020 83928557
E kevin@lpa-management.com
W www.gallery1839.com
Contact Kevin O'Connor
Founded in 2007, Gallery 1839 specializes in the sale of twentieth- and twenty-first-century photographs. Competitions (approximately nine per year) are on an ongoing basis.

Entry Policy All entries should be sent as jpegs through website.

Gen Foundation
45 Old Bond Street, London, W1X 2AQ
T 020 74955564
F 020 74954450
E info@genfoundation.org.uk
Provides substantial scholarships and grants to students and scholars from a broad cross-section of fields. Aims to further academic research in both the humanities and natural sciences by awarding grants to candidates from a variety of disciplines. In recognition of the importance of crosscultural exchange in today's global society, also aims to deepen understanding between Japan and the rest of the world. Scholarships are one-off, non-renewable grants of approximately £2,000.
Entry Policy The foundation will make preliminary selection of candidates on the basis of submitted application forms, then conduct interviews. Scholarships are awarded annually to candidates mainly from the UK and Japan.

The Getty Foundation
1200 Getty Center Drive, Suite 800, Los Angeles CA 90049–1685, USA
T +1 310 4407320
F +1 310 4407703
W www.getty.edu
Provides support to institutions and individuals throughout the world for projects that promote the understanding of art and its history and the conservation of cultural heritage. Projects are sought that set high standards and provide opportunities for collaboration.

Gilchrist-Fisher Memorial Award
c/o Rebecca Hossack Gallery
35 Windmill Street, London
W1P 1HH
T 020 74364899
F 020 73233182
E rebecca@r-h-g.co.uk
W www.r-h-g.co.uk
Established in 1987 in memory of Alasdair Gilchrist-Fisher who died of cancer in December 1986 at the age of 24. For work with landscape art as the broad theme. First prize of £3,000; £1,000 for runner-up. Winner's work is also exhibited at the Rebecca Hossack Gallery.
Entry Policy Applications are invited from artists under 30 years of age, particularly graduates. Closing date: usually June.

Global Arts Village

Utsav Mandir, Ghitorni, Mehrauli-Gurgoan Road
110030, India
T +91 1155657265 / 1126804790
E info@globalartsvillage.com
W www.globalartsvillage.com
Contact Julie Upmeyer
Residencies offered at the Village, an emerging art
centre in New Delhi. Open to emerging, mid-
career and established artists. Encourages diversity
and multicultural exchange among creative people
of all kinds. Practices community living, sharing
meals and evening activities on a three-acre
property that includes: gardens; ceramics,
sculpture and two-dimensional studios; a
meditation hall; a common building; dance studio;
performance spaces; and accommodation. Caters
for studio ceramics, sculpture, photography,
Ikebana, digital arts, arts management, land art,
fibre arts, installation art and public art. Offers five
different types of residency; details on website.
Entry Policy Applications to include: a completed
residency application; documentation of creative
work in the form of digital photos attached to an
email; thin frame slides or photographs (twelve
maximum); a brief description of the project (two
hundred words maximum); a brief explanation of
why the project is especially suited to the Village
and India (two hundred words maximum).

Gunk Foundation Grants for Public Arts Projects

P.O. Box 333, Gardiner
NY 12525, USA
T +1 914 2558252
F +1 914 2558252
E gunk@mhv.net
W www.gunk.org
Contact Nadine Lemmon
Provides grants to individuals and organizations as
well as national and international projects. At
present, concentrating on supporting production
of non-traditional public-art projects. Interested in
supporting projects that move out into the spaces
of daily life. Also favours projects that reach a non-
traditional art audience. Likely range of grants is
between US$1,000 and US$5,000.
Entry Policy Applications in writing. Hesitant to
fund production of video or film unless specifically
earmarked for public space (such as public-access
television or outdoor screenings).

Inches Carr Trust Craft Bursaries

The Inches Carr Trust, 2 Blacket Place
Edinburgh, EH9 1RL

T 0131 6672906
W www.inchescarr.org
Annual awards to craft workers based in Scotland
with a minimum of five years' experience in their
craft. Each award is £5,000 to enable the applicant
to develop a specific aspect of their work or to
undertake a specific project.
Frequency Annual. Maximum of three awards
per year.
Entry Policy Provide a description of current work,
the specific project or aspect for development
proposed and a CV. Closing date: end April.

ING Discerning Eye

P.O. Box 279, Esher, KT10 8YZ
T 01372 462190
F P.O. Box 279
E DE@parkerharris.co.uk
W www.discerningeye.org or
www.parkerharris.co.uk
Annual open competition for artists born or
resident in the UK, working in any media,
including moving image. Works to be no larger
than 20 x 20 inches. A selection panel of six well
known figures from the art world each curate their
own section, inviting well known artists to exhibit
alongside lesser known artists selected from the
open competition. Prizes awarded in a range of
categories. Winning entries will be exhibited at
The Mall Galleries, London. Launched 1990.

International Artists' Centre, Poland (Miedzynarodowe Centrum Sztuki)

ul.Jackowskiego 5/7, Poznan
60–508, Poland
T +48 618483777
E artistscentre@dialcom.com.pl
W www.dialcom.com.pl/artistscentre
Residencies open to all artists from various
disciplines and cultural backgrounds. Usually last
three months.

J.D. Fergusson Arts Award

The Fergusson Gallery, Marshall Place, Perth
PH2 8NS
T 01738 441944
F 01738 621152
E museum@pkc.gov.uk
W www.perthshire.com
Contact Jenny Kinnear
Inaugural award presented in 1997. Aims to
support artists who have shown a high level of
commitment but have not yet received any awards
or recognition. Artists working in any medium

considered. Value in the region of £2,000.
Frequency Annual award, alternating year-on-year between an exhibition award and a travel bursary.
Entry Policy Must be Scottish by birth or lived in Scotland for more than 50% of their life. Closing date: 31 October.

James Milne Memorial Trust
Scottish Trade Union Congress, Middleton House 333 Woodlands Road, Glasgow, G3 6NG
T 0141 3378100
F 0141 3378101
Grants open to Scots aged 26 and under of outstanding talent, based in Scotland and who will be able to extend their skills by a period of study out of the UK. Study may be formal or informal.

Jerwood Applied Arts Prize
Crafts Council, 44a Pentonville Road, London N1 9BY
T 020 7278 7700
F 020 7837 6891
E reference@craftscouncil.org.uk
W www.craftscouncil.org.uk
Contact Aravec Clarke (Exhibitions Officer - Touring)
Founded in 1995 and presented in collaboration with the Crafts Council and the Jerwood Charity. The most prestigious and significant prize in the applied and decorative arts. Now in its twelfth year, it covers six categories: metal, jewellery, ceramics, textiles, glass and furniture. Prize worth £30,000.
Frequency Annual: textiles 2008, glass 2009, furniture 2010.
Entry Policy Entry requirements on website from November/December. Shortlisting in February and exhibition in September. Award presented end September. The exhibition then tours the UK for one year (four venues plus Crafts Council Gallery in London). Open to artists, makers and designers.

Jerwood Contemporary Painters
P.O. Box 279, Esher, KT10 8YZ
T 01372 462190
F 01372 460032
E jcp@parkerharris.co.uk
W www.jerwoodvisualarts.org
An exhibition of works by thirty emerging artists. Created by the Jerwood Charitable Foundation, this exhibition promotes the work of those who have moved on from student status but have not yet attained recognition as artists. It also presents a perspective on the concerns and debates in contemporary painting, particularly among artists in the early stages of their careers.

Jerwood Drawing Prize
Wimbledon College of Art, Merton Hall Road London, SW19 3QA
T 020 7514 9709
F 020 7514 9642
E jerwood@wimbledon.arts.ac.uk
W www.wimbledon.arts.ac.uk/jerwood
Contact Clare Mitten or Rose Heelas
Aims to promote and reward talent and excellence in contemporary drawing. Every year, a changing panel of distinguished artists, writers, critics, collectors and curators select the show independently, defining their own priorities for an exhibition of current drawing practice.
Frequency Prizes awarded yearly. First Prize: £6,000; Second Prize: £3,000; Student Awards: £1,000 each.
Entry Policy Open to artists resident or domiciled in the UK. Application forms available from the end of May.

Jerwood Sculpture Prize
P.O. Box 279, Esher, KT10 8YZ
T 01372 462190
F 01372 460032
E jsp@parkerharris.co.uk
W www.jerwoodvisualarts.org
Biennial prize promoting excellence in sculpture. Artists within 15 years of graduation submit a proposal to create a large scale outdoor sculpture. Short list is awarded with a £1,000 commission to create small scale maquettes, and the winner is awarded a £25,000 commission to create their proposal, which will go on display in Jerwood Sculpture Park at Ragley. Closing date: Autumn 2008. Launched 2001.

John Moores 24 Exhibition of Contemporary Painting
Walker Art Gallery, William Brown Street, Liverpool, L3 8EL
T 0151 478 4121
F 0151 478 4190
E johnmoores24@liverpoolmuseums.org.uk
W www.thewalker.org.uk
Contact Lisa Baker
A major exhibition of contemporary paintings selected through open competition. First prize of £25,000 in cash; ten smaller prizes also awarded. Founded by the late Sir John Moores, the exhibition continues to be supported by the Moores family. Has a track record for spotting rising talent. The exhibition also plays a major part in the Liverpool Biennial, the only biennial of

contemporary art in the UK. Supported by John Moores Liverpool Exhibition Trust and the aFoundation.
Submission Policy Entries must be original new paintings, by someone who is based in the U.K. Full conditions on website.
Entry Policy For entry form and further information send sae. Handling fee payable on request of an entry form. First phase judged on slides and second phase on actual work.

Kettle's Yard Open and occasional residency opportunities
Castle Street, Cambridge, CB3 0AQ
T 01223 352124
F 01223 324377
E mail@kettlesyard.cam.ac.uk
W www.kettlesyard.co.uk
Contact Elizabeth Fisher
Every two years there is an exhibition open to artists in the east of England. Currently rethinking the nature of the artists fellowship and residency opportunities. Contact Kettle's Yard directly as the nature of the opportunities can vary greatly. All media is eligible for the open and the residencies programme.

Künstlerinnenhof Die Höge
Högenhausen 2, Bassum
D - 27211, Germany
T +49 424993030
F +49 4249930344
E info@hoege.org
W www.hoege.org
Launched an artist-in-residence programme in June 2000, the first of its kind in Europe. Women scholars as well as women artists from all areas of the arts are invited to work experimentally in multimedia. A former farmstead serves as an atelier, forum and common stage for women artists working professionally in the areas of the fine arts, music, literature, multimedia, performance, theatre and dance, and a field station for academic research by women scholars.
Entry Policy A jury of three to four members choose the participants, who receive grants to reside at the Höge for one to nine months.

Lady Artists Club Trust Award
McGrigor Donald Solicitors, 70 Wellington Street, Glasgow, G2 6SB
T 0141 2486677
E enquiries@mcgrigors.com
W www.mcgrigors.com

For women artists who either live within thirty-five miles from Glasgow city centre or were born, educated or trained in Glasgow. Students not eligible to apply.

Laing Solo
Laing Art Gallery, New Bridge Street
Newcastle-upon-Tyne, NE1 4JA
T 0191 2327734
F 0191 2220952
E laing@twmuseums.org.uk
W www.twmuseums.sorg.uk/laing
Contact Natalie Frost
A national competition for emerging artists.

Leverhulme Trust Grants and Awards
1 Pemberton Row, London
EC4A 3BG
T 020 78225220
F 020 78225084
E gdupin@leverhulme.ac.uk
W www.leverhulme.org.uk
Established in 1925 at the wish of William Hesketh Lever, the first Viscount Leverhulme. The trust provides academic and education research grants across the UK. In the area of performing and fine arts, there are grants available in the following schemes: artists-in-residence; training and professional development; education.
Entry Policy New guidelines published annually accompanied by new application forms and all applicants need to ensure that they use both. Closing dates: vary from scheme to scheme. Study website before applying.

London Photographic Association
23 Roehampton Lane, London, SW15 5LS
T 020 8392 8557
E kevin@london-photographic-association.com
W www.london-photographic-association.com
Contact Kevin O'Connor
The principal objective of the Association is to give photographers and photography international exposure through its awards structure, online exhibitions, portfolio and essay space, public space exhibitions and relationships with other members of the media, creative and photographic communities worldwide.
Frequency Competitions run throughout the year.
Entry Policy See website for up-to-date information.

Lynn Painter-Stainers Prize
P.O. Box 279, Esher, KT10 8YZ

T 01372 462190
F 01372 460032
E lps@parkerharris.co.uk
W www.painter-stainers.org or
www.parkerharris.co.uk
Annual prize for representational painting. Total prize money: £22,500. Open to artists born or resident in the UK. Winning entries will be exhibited in the Painters' Hall in London in November. Launched 2005.

Manchester Academy of Fine Arts Open

c/o The Portico Library & Gallery, 57 Mosley Street
Manchester, M2 3HY
E secretary@mafa.org.uk
W www.mafa.org.uk
The Academy holds Members Only Exhibition whilst seeking a venue for its previous annual open exhibition which invited submissions from painters, sculptors and printmakers and had prizes ranging up to £2,000.
Entry Policy No restriction on style or subject.

Mark Tanner Sculpture Award

Standpoint, 45 Coronet Street, Hoxton
London, N1 6HD
W www.standpointlondon.co.uk/mta.html
Established in 2001, the largest sculpture prize of its kind in the UK, offering financial support towards the production of new work (£6,000) and a solo exhibition (£4,000) to an exceptional emerging sculptor. The exhibition is held at the Standpoint Gallery. Founded in memory of the sculptor Mark Tanner, one of the first artists to show at Standpoint who died in 1998 after a long illness.
Entry Policy Aimed at sculptors based in Greater London who are making ambitious, outstanding work within fine art practice. Particularly interested in work that demonstrates a commitment to process and material. Applications must include: a Mac-friendly disc with up to 10 images as jpeg files at 72dpi, maximum width/height for images 20cm (all other information should be sent as hard-copy); a separate sheet listing the details of each work corresponding to the numbered image: title, date, materials, dimensions, process; a CV (max. 2 sides A4) including contact details and studio address; an artist statement up to 500 words; a summary of how the award would be used and how it would benefit the applicant's work and professional development (up to 500 words); a professional reference; and an sae.

Max Mara Art Prize for Women

Stephanie Churchill PR, 15–17 Huntsworth Mews
London, NW1 6DD
T 020 72986530
F 020 77064730
A prize for female artists, sponsored by the Italian fashion house.

Monagri Foundation Residency

Archangelos Monastery, Monagri
CY-4746, Cyprus
T +357 5434165
F +357 5434166
E info@mongri.org.cy
W www.monagri.org.cy
The Monagri Foundation invites artists from all disciplines and nationalities to apply for a residency. Artists should be prepared to make an appropriate contribution to the development of the arts in Cyprus by giving lectures, holding workshops or other communal activities. Typically residencies last from two weeks to a year.

Montana Artists' Refuge Residency Program

Box 8, Basin, Montana
MT 59631, USA
T +1 406 2253500
F +1 406 2259225
E mtrefuge@earthlink.net
An artist-run residency programme located near the Continental Divide. Founded in 1993 by four local artists and area residents to provide living and work space to artists in all media. Mission is to further the creative work of artists, to create residencies for artists, and to provide arts programmes and art education for both artists and community members.
Frequency Residencies last three months to one year (year-round). Only two artists present at a time.
Entry Policy Accepts applications from visual artists in arts and crafts, book art, ceramics, clay/pottery, drawing, fibre/textile, film-/video-making, folk art, installation, jewellery, mixed media, painting, paper art, photography, and sculpture. To request application form, send sae. Closing date: August for winter residencies (January to March). Applications for other months accepted on ongoing basis.

Mostyn Open

12 Heol Vaughan, Llandudno, LL30 1AB
T 01492 879201
F 01492 878869

E post@mostyn.org
W www.mostyn.org
Open to artists working in any medium. There is a prize of £6,000 but selectors reserve the right to split the prize money if appropriate.
Entry Policy No geographical or age restrictions; size limitations depend on available gallery space.

National Endowment for Science, Technology and the Arts (NESTA)

Fishmongers' Chambers, 110 Upper Thames Street, London, EC4B 4AQ
T 020 76459638
F 020 76469501
E nesta@nesta.org.uk
W www.nesta.org.uk
NESTA's purpose is to support and promote talent, innovation and creativity in the fields of science, technology and the arts. Primary activity is the support of individuals, rather than organizations, existing businesses or projects. Each fellow is supported for between three to five years and receives a support package of between £25,000 to £75,000 over the term of the fellowship.
Frequency Fifty to a hundred projects funded each year.
Entry Policy Open to UK residents or organizations (registered in the UK for three years). Under-18s must be sponsored by an adult. Applications assessed throughout year. Forms available on website or on disk.

National Museum of Women in the Arts (NMWA) Library Fellows Programme

Library and Research Centre
National Museum of Women in the Arts
1250 New York Avenue
NW, Washington
D.C., USA
T +1 202 7837365
F +1 202 3933234
E library@nmwa.org
W www.nmwa.org
Established in 1989 to encourage the creation of quality book art and to support the NMWA's Library and Research and book art programmes. Fellows provide up to $12,000 annually for the production of an artist's book in an edition of 125. Winning artist is selected at Fellows' annual meeting in Spring.
Frequency One annually.
Entry Policy Only women may apply. Artists must complete application available from the library or on the website. Deadline is 31 January.

Paisley Art Institute Annual Exhibition Prizes and biennial Scottish Drawing Competition

c/o 4 Mount Charles House, 36 Mount Charles Crescent, Ayr, KA7 4NY
E gesso.clark@btinternet.com
W www.paisleyartinstitute.org.uk
Paisley Art Institute was founded in 1876. The present Galleries were built by Sir Peter Coats and presented to the Institute in 1915. In turn the Institute made a gift of them to the the town of Paisley. There is an annual exhibition each Spring and also a Biennial Scottish Drawing Competition. Open entrants are eligible for prizes at both exhibitions.
Submission Policy:No performance art.
Frequency Drawing competition held every two years (prizes over £1,000). Numerouus prizes awarded at the annual exhibition for painting and sculpture.
Entry Policy Annual exhibition is held in the Spring. Write to the Secretary, Michael Clark.

Paul Hamlyn Foundation

Sussex House, 12 Upper Mall, London
W6 9TA
T 020 72273500
F 020 72220601
E phf@globalnet.co.uk
Grants usually awarded to large national institutions, tending not to exceed £25,000. Categories covered by the foundation are: General Arts Grants; Increasing Awareness of the Arts; Art in Education; and Individual Artists.
Entry Policy Open to UK citizens. Apply in writing. Also by nomination.

Pepinières Europennes Pour Jeunes Artistes

Patrice Bonnaffé, BP 13 9/11 rue Paul Leplat
Marly le Roi cedex
78164, France
T +33 139171100
F +33 139171109
E info@art4eu.net
W www.art4eu.net
Contact Andrea Cooke, 62 Gabriels Road, London NW2 4SA; T 020 84508257 or F 020 84508257. Running for ten years. Offers residencies for emerging artists to aid advancement and professional development. The Map Programme is intended for emerging artists between 20 and 35 years old who are starting their career. The artist is associated with a professional organization, a city representative and a coordinator and stays for a period of three to nine months in a hosting

organization of their choice. Artists in Context – Artists against Exclusion is intended for artists aged 18 to 25, taking place in the framework of European voluntary service. Allows for an artistic project focused on social realities to be carried out during a six-month period.

Entry Policy Open to artists between 18 and 35 living in a country hosting a Pepinière. Send sae (A4 size) to request application form.

The Pilar Juncosa & Sotheby's Awards

Fundació Pilar I Joan Miró a Mallorca, Joan de Saridakis 29, Palma, Mallorca
07015 Spain
T 0034 71 701420
F 0034 71 702102
E premibeques@fpjmiro.org
W miro.palmademallorca.es
Annual prize for works of art/installations created for the area of Fundació Pilar i Joan Miró a Mallorca, known as the 'Cubic Space'. Jury gives priority to artistic value of projects entered, technical skills and any other innovative or experimental aspect they deem important. Total of €24,000 awarded to winning project (€12,000 for the project itself, which must later be mounted in the 'Cubic Space' during the following 12 months, and up to €12,000 for the actual creation of the project, following the presentation of a cost estimate). There are also Pilar Juncosa Grants for training, experimentation and creative work in the Foundation's Graphic Art Workshops and other grants available (see website).

Entry Policy Artists may present one creative project or work designed for the 'Cubic Space'. The project/work must be original and the only one of its kind. Works previously exhibited or entered in other competitions will not be admitted.

Polish Cultural Institute

34 Portland Place, London,
W1N 4HQ
T 020 76366032
F 020 76372190
E pci-lond@pcidir.demon.co.uk
Contact Mrs Aleksandra Czapiewska
The Polish Minister of Culture, in association with the British Council, offers two-week study visits to Poland for people in the field of theatre, dance, music, visual arts, literature, literary translation, conservation of cultural heritage, architecture, musicology, film and photography. Successful applicants are provided with accommodation, per diems and local transportation. The sending

country or visitor is expected to pay travel expenses to and from both capitals.

Entry Policy Open to UK citizens and residents. Apply in writing. Proposals to be made at least eight weeks in advance to the institution in their own country.

Pollock-Krasner Foundation

863 Park Avenue, New York
NY 10021, USA
T +1 212 5175400
F +1 212 2882836
E grants@pkf.org
W www.pkf.org
Contact Caroline Black (Program Officer)
Established in 1985 to provide financial assistance to individual artists of established ability (painters, sculptors and artists who work on paper). Grants range from US$1,000 to US$30,000.

Entry Policy Applications from commercial artists, photographers, video artists, filmmakers, craftsmakers or any artist whose work primarily falls into these categories will not be accepted. The foundation does not make grants to students nor fund academic study. No grants to pay for past debts, legal fees, purchase of real estate, moves to other cities or installation costs, commissions or projects ordered by others. With few exceptions, will not fund travel expenses. Dual criteria for grants are recognizable artistic merit and financial need, whether professional, personal or both. Applications encouraged from artists with genuine financial needs, not necessarily catastrophic. Grants intended for one-year period. Will consider need of applicant for all legitimate expenditures relating to their professional work, personal living and medical expenses. Size and length of grant determined by individual circumstances. Applications year-round.

Purchase Prize BlindArt Permanener Collection

P.O. Box 50113, London
SW1X 9EY
T 020 72459977
F 020 72451228
E info@blindart.net
W www.blindart.net
An innovative, all-inclusive charity founded in 2004, promoting contemporary works of art that can be explored through all five senses, especially touch. The BlindArt Permanent Collection is the world's first permanent showcase of visual art accessible to visually impaired people, and includes paintings, sculpture, installations and other works

of art. Organizes the multi-sensory, interactive Sense & Sensuality exhibitions that break down traditional artistic barriers by helping to dispel the notion that sight is essential to creating or enjoying exceptional art. The overall message is artistic excellence regardless of visual ability.
Frequency Annually and by commission and donations.
Entry Policy Submissions are welcome. Contact info@blindart.net for further details.

Queen Elizabeth Scholarship Trust
The Secretary, No.1 Buckingham Place, London SW1E 6HR
W www.qest.org.uk
Makes annual craft awards to fund further study, training and practical experience for men and women who want to improve their craft or trade skills. Grants between £2,000 and £15,000. Winners also receive emblazoned certificate and engraved sterling silver medal. The trust looks for well-thought-out proposals that will contribute to excellence in modern and traditional British crafts.
Frequency Scholarships awarded twice a year, in spring and autumn.
Entry Policy No age limit. Need to be able to demonstrate a high level of skill and show firm committment to craft or trade. Scholarships not awarded for buying or leasing equipment or premises or for funding courses in general further education. Must live and work in UK to be eligible for a scholarship. Forms downloadable from website or send A4 sae.

Rencontres d'Arles Awards
10 Rond-Point des Arenes, Arles
13200, France
T +33 490967606
F +33 4900499439
E prix@rencontres-arles.com
W www.rencontres-arles.com
Contact Prune Blachere
Founded in 2002. Five €10,000 awards per year: Book Award, Discovery Award, Outreach Award, Project Assistance Grant, No Limit Award.
Entry Policy Qualified international jury determines an artist in each category except for the Book Award, which is open to all-comers.

Rootstein Hopkins Foundation Grants
Rootstein Hopkins Foundation, P.O. Box 14720, London, W3 7ZG
T 020 73812557
E info@rhfoundation.org.uk

W www.rhfoundation.org.uk
The foundation offers financial support to artists, art students, lecturers and designers in the form of travel grants, support grants, sabbatical awards, mature student grants and exchanges. The trustees will choose candidates who they feel will make the best use of the grants to further their careers, and who can present a plan that seems likely to be realized within the grant period.
Entry Policy Open to British passport-holders only.

Royal British Society of Sculptors
108 Old Brompton Road, London, SW7 3RA
T 020 73738615
F 020 73703721
E info@rbs.org.uk
W www.rbs.org.uk
The Royal British Society of Sculptors exists to promote and advance the practice and art of sculpture. It has professional members throughout the UK and internationally, offers bursary memberships on a regular basis and runs an open National Register of Sculptors. Hosts annual bursary and bronze-casting award exhibitions.
Entry Policy Applications for full membership are considered every two months, on average. The non-selective National Register of Sculptors can be joined at any time during the year.

Royal Scottish Academy Alastair Salvesen Art Scholarship
The Competitions Office, Royal Scottish Academy, The Mound, Edinburgh
EH2 2EL
T 0131 2256671
F 0131 2206016
E info@royalscottishacademy.org
W www.royalscottishacademy.org
Contact Pauline Costigane (Assistant Administrative Secretary)
A major initiative intended to encourage young professional painters. Alastair Salvesen is one of Scotland's foremost benefactors and has offered a three- to six-month travel scholarship in association with the RSA since 1989. The £10,000 scholarship is accompanied by a solo exhibition at the RSA.
Frequency Annual.

Royal West of England Academy (RWA) Student Bursaries
Queens Road, Clifton, Bristol, BS8 1PX
T 0117 9735129

F 0117 9237874
E rwa@rwa.org
The council of the RWA offers two bursaries of
£1,000 each to students in the final year of their
degree course in painting, printmaking, sculpture
or architecture. Postgraduate students in their first
year are also eligible to apply.
Entry Policy Closing date: March.

RSA John Kinross Scholarships
The Royal Scottish Academy, The Mound
Edinburgh, EH2 2EL
T 0131 225 6671
E press@royalscottishacademy.org
W www.royalscottishacademy.org
The £2,000 scholarship is intended to assist
students in Scotland within the disciplines of
painting, sculpture, printmaking and architecture
to live and study in Florence for a period of up to
three months. The RSA also arranges a galleries
and museums pass for the students allowing them
free access to the city's artistic and historical
treasures.
Frequency Up to twelve scholarships annually
Entry Policy Painting, sculpture and printmaking:
applications are invited from students in their final
or post-graduate years of study at one of the four
Scottish Colleges of Art. Architecture: applicants
must be senior students at one of the six Scottish
Schools of Architecture presenting work which
would normally be related to the requirements of
the RIBA Part 1 or Part 2 Syllabus. Group work is
not admissible and only one project may be entered
by any one student. All applications must be
supported by not more than eight digital images of
current work on CD and an A4 statement setting
out their reasons for wishing to study in Florence.

Ruth Davidson Memorial Scholarship
RDAM – Elphinstone Institute
Taylor Building
University of Aberdeen, Regent Walk
Aberedeen
AB24 3UB
T 01224 272996
E elphinstone@abdn.ac.uk
Offers the successful applicant three months'
rent-free accommodation in the Languedoc
Roussillon region of the south of France to
develop/express new ideas in their work. Also
provides £3,000 to cover all costs associated with
residency including return travel to France, travel
in local area (driving licence essential), materials
and living expenses.

Entry Policy Open to a painter currently living and
working in Scotland of at least four years'
experience since graduation or since beginning to
exhibit. Students are not eligible. Key criteria used
in selecting artists are quality of work, as shown in
a selection of slides, and the nature of the proposal
for residency period.

Sainsbury Scholarship in Painting and Sculpture
The British School at Rome at the British
Academy, 10 Carlton House Terrace, London
SW1Y 5AH
T 020 79695202
F 020 79695401
E bsr@britac.ac.uk
W www.bsr.ac.uk
Contact Dr Gill Clark (The Registrar)
Founded in 2001 and funded by the Linbury Trust,
open to painters and sculptors who can
demonstrate a commitment to drawing within
their artistic practice and who can present a well-
argued case for the continuation of their studies in
Italy and in particular Rome. Offers full board and
lodging at the British School at Rome for twelve
months (with, at the discretion of the selection
committee, an opportunity for a further nine
months in the following academic year). There is a
grant of approximately £750 per month, plus a
one-off travel grant of £1,000.
Frequency One per year.
Entry Policy Applicants must be: of British
nationality or have been working professionally or
studying at postgraduate level for at least the last
five years in the UK; under 30 on 1 October of the
academic year in which the scholarship will be
held; have graduated or expect to graduate before 1
October of the academic year in which the
scholarship would commence. An application
form must be completed. Closing date for
applications: mid-December.

Sargant Fellowship
The British School at Rome at the British
Academy, 10 Carlton House Terrace, London
SW1Y 5AH
T 020 79695202
F 020 79695401
E bsr@britac.ac.uk
W www.bsr.ac.uk
Contact Dr Gill Clark (The Registrar)
Founded in 1990, one of the senior and most
prestigious residencies offered by the British
School at Rome. Open to distinguished artists and
architects to enable them to research and make

new work within the historical context of Rome. Offers full board and lodging in a residential studio at the school, a grant of £2,000 per month, and a one-off travel allowance of £500.
Frequency Each year or every other year.
Entry Policy Applicants must be of British or Commonwealth nationality, or have been living in the UK or Commonwealth for at least the last three years. An application form must be completed. Closing date: usually early to mid-December or early to mid-January.

Scottish Sculpture Workshop Programme
1 Main Street, Lumsden
Huntley
AB54 4JN
T 01464 861372
F 01464 861550
W www.ssw.org.uk
The Scottish Sculpture Workshop has initiated a programme of fellowships funded by the Scottish Arts Council and the PF Charitable Trust.

Singer & Friedlander/Sunday Times Watercolour Competition
PO Box 279, Esher
KT10 8YZ
T 01372 462190
F 01372 460032
E ksf@parkerharris.co.uk
W www.parkerharris.co.uk
Annual open competition for UK artists working in any water-based media. Now in its twentieth year. 2007 judges included Peter Blake, Frank Whitford and Dr Joanna Selborne. Prize money totalling £30,000.

Skopelos Foundation for the Arts
P.O. Box 56, Skopelos Island
37003, Greece
T +30 2424024143
F +30 2424024143
E info@skopart.org
W www.skopart.org
Contact Jill Somer (Associate Director)
Founded in 1999. Committed to honouring and sharing the Greek artistic tradition while fostering innovative artistic expression and development. The foundation offers residencies in ceramics, painting, printmaking and screenprinting, from September through to May.
Entry Policy An application is required and reviewed by the board of directors. Experience is necessary and college graduates are preferred.

Soros Centres for Contemporary Arts (SCCA) Network Residencies
Bolyai u.14, Budapest 1023, Hungary
T +36 13150303
F +36 13150201
E office@soros.hu
The SCCA is a network of nineteen offices devoted to development of contemporary arts in central and eastern Europe and the former Soviet Union. Runs a residencies scheme. Apply in writing.

St Hugh's Fellowship
The Administrator, The St Hugh's Foundation, Andrew & Company Solicitors, St Swithin's Square, Lincoln
LN2 1HB
E sthughesfoundation@lineone.net
To assist established arts practitioners and animators to develop their careers in the arts and to contribute their knowledge and experience to the wider growth and dissemination of arts practice in the region. Proposals should be for a substantial and sustained programme of work, to be carried out over a period of at least 6 months (2 years maximum). The average grant is up to £10,000.
Entry Policy Open to individuals working as practitioners in any field of arts (under 30 years old on 1 May); resident and working full- or part-time in Lincolnshire or former Humberside area. Application cover sheet and application requirements should be completed and returned by noon on 1 May. Obtain leaflet by sending sae.

Stockport Art Gallery Annual Open Exhibition
Wellington Road South, Stockport
SK3 8AB
T 0161 4744453
F 0161 4804960
E stockport.artgallery@stockport.gov.uk
W www.stockport.gov.uk
Contact Andy Firth
An annual event with four prizes of £100 each.
Entry Policy Information and application forms available in May each year by sending an A5 sae.

Straumur International Art Commune
v/Reykjanesbraut, P.O. Box 33.222
Hafnarfjordur
Iceland
T +354 5650128
F +354 5650655
E solar@tv.is
Contact Sverrir Olafsson (Director)

Established in 1988, since when more than eight hundred artists have visited from twenty-nine countries and all fields of media and art. Funded by the city of Hafnarfjordur and Sol-Art, a private non-profit organization that handles daily operations in close cooperation with the city's cultural committee. The commune consists of five spacious studios of various sizes. Residencies are one to five months, with a maximum of twelve months under special circumstances. The artist has to pay all living and working expenses.
Entry Policy Applications are accepted from all professional artists regardless of artistic media, citizenship, nationality, sex or race.

Summer Exhibition – Royal Academy of Arts
Burlington House, Piccadilly, London, W1J OBD
T 020 7300 5929/5969
F 020 7300 5812
E summerexhibition@royalacademy.org.uk
W www.royalacademy.org.uk
Contact Chris Cook
Founded in 1768. The largest open contemporary-art exhibition in the world encompassing all styles and media. Over a thousand works, the majority of which are for sale. Over 150,000 visitors.
Frequency Annual. Over £70,000 in prize money awarded.
Entry Policy Maximum of three works in any media (£18 per work, non-refundable).

Swansea Open
Glynn Vivian Art Gallery, Alexandra Road, Swansea, SA1 5DZ
T 01792 516900
F 01792 516903
E glynn.vivian.gallery@swansea.gov.uk
W www.glynnviviangallery.org
Open to professional artists as well as to those who have never had the opportunity to show their work in a public art gallery. Three winners are selected from all the entries, with a first prize of £250, second prize of £150 and third prize of £100. These are announced at the beginning of the exhibition, usually held from July to September.

Turner Prize
Tate Britain, Millbank, London, SW1P 4RG
T 020 78878000
F 020 78878007
W www.tate.org.uk/britain/turnerprize
An annual contemporary art award founded in 1984. Considered among the most prestigious and influential awards available. Worth £40,000.

Entry Policy Nominated artists must be under the age of 50 and British, which includes artists working in the UK and British-born artists who may be working abroad. Need to have had an outstanding exhibition or display in the twelve months preceding the competition.

UNESCO Grants Scheme for Young Artists
UNESCO Division of Arts and Cultural Life, Bureau B10.29, rue Miollis, Paris Cedex 15 75732, France
T +33 145684328
F +33 142730401
W www.unesco.org
Contact Madeleine Gobeil (Director)
A limited number of grants for young artists in the field of performance and creation, made for short study tours or projects. Each grant of approximately US$2,000 is intended to cover, for example, the travel costs of the artist. Applicants must organize their own project or course and obtain agreement of the host institution.
Entry Policy Candidates' applications must include the following documents: CV, study plan and dates, letters of agreement from the institution where study will take place, estimation of costs.

V&A Illustration Awards
Victoria & Albert Museum, Cromwell Road, London, SW7 2RL
T 020 79422392
E villa@vam.ac.uk
W www.vam.ac.uk/illustrationawards
Contact Annemarie Bilclough
The V&A Museum has offered awards for professional illustration since 1972. Originally called the Francis Williams Awards (1972–1982) after their benefactor, they became annual in 1987. Prizes up to £2,500 in three categories: Book Illustration; Book Cover and Jacket Illustration; Editorial Illustration. Separate Student Illustrator of the Year category with top prize £1,300. Display of the winning entries hosted at the V&A.
Entry Policy Illustration published in UK in previous twelve months; unpublished work by illustration students. Closing dates: students March; other categories July.

Virginia A. Groot Foundation
P.O. Box 1050, Evanston
IL 60204–1050, USA
Offers a grant of up to US$20,000 to an artist of exceptional talent with a demonstrated ability in the areas of ceramic sculpture or sculpture.

Wingate Rome Scholarship in the Fine Arts
The British School at Rome at the British
Academy, 10 Carlton House Terrace
London, SW1Y 5AH
T 020 79695202
F 020 79695401
E bsr@britac.ac.uk
W www.bsr.ac.uk
Contact Dr Gill Clark (The Registrar)
Founded in 1998 and funded by the Harold Hyam
Wingate Foundation. Open to painters, sculptors
and mixed-media artists who can demonstrate that
they are establishing a significant position in their
chosen field. Offers full board and lodging in a
residential studio at the school for five months,
plus a grant equivalent to £500 per month.
Frequency One each year.
Entry Policy Applicants must be: able to satisfy the
selection panel that they need financial support to
undertake the work projected; living in the British
Isles during the period of application; citizens of
the UK or other Commonwealth country, Ireland
or Israel – or citizens of another EU country
provided that they are and have been for the last
three years resident in the UK; aged 24 or over on 1
September of the academic year in which the
scholarship will be held. An application form must
be completed. Closing date: mid-December.

Women's Studio Workshop Fellowship Grants
P.O. Box 489, Rosendale
New York 12472, USA
T +1 914 6589133
F +1 914 6589031
E wsw@ulster.net
W www.wsworkshop.org

Designed to provide concentrated work time for
artists to explore new ideas in dynamic and
supportive community of women artists. Facilities
feature complete studios in intaglio, silkscreen,
hand papermaking, photography, letterpress and
clay. 2–6 week sessions available each year from
September to June. Fellowships awarded through
jury process. Cost to Fellowship recipients is $200
per week plus materials (approximately one fifth
the cost of actual residency). The award includes
on-site housing and unlimited access to studios.
Artists given studio orientation but should be able
to work independently. Technical assistance
available for additional fee.
Entry Policy Open to women artists. Fellowship
grants applicants should submit an application
form, a resume, six to ten slides, letter of interest
that addresses the purpose of the residency
(explaining areas of proficiency and studio skills)
and sae for return of material.

Woo Charitable Foundation Arts Bursaries
The Administrator, Arts Bursaries
277 Green Lanes, London, N13 4XS
The foundation offers arts bursaries for artists who
have finished their formal education.
Approximately ten bursaries of £5,000 are
awarded to artists working in the visual arts sector
(fine and applied).
Entry Policy Open to artists who have finished
formal education. All applications must include a
CV, ten 35mm slides or colour photos, a short A4
written critique, details of a professional referee,
and a brief summary of how the bursary would
benefit the applicant.

08

Arts boards, councils, funding and commissioning organizations

Where do I stand? A guide to public funding and artists' rights

Tim Eastop

The boundaries of contemporary art are fluid. Artists need time and space in which to fly, to search and to research. Art cross-fertilizes as never before. Artists are curators and critics as well as makers of film and video, crafts, live art, photography and new media. There is vibrant interplay between fine art, design and architecture, music, media, fashion and games. For artists to realize their potential in this expanded field it is essential that they have appropriate professional guidance and support. Through the lens of a public patron this section offers a brief look at the problems artists face and gives some practical tips on studio space, how to apply for funding, and the labyrinth that is the contemporary art market.

Artists don't need to be poor

A recent survey showed that the average gross weekly earnings for visual artists in 2000 was £401, the lowest average earnings for all cultural occupations. Further research in 2004 by the University of Newcastle-upon-Tyne, commissioned by a-n The Artists Information Company, has highlighted that many artists' earnings are substantially lower than those in comparable professions such as teachers, who have similar skills and levels of education. In response, a-n The Artists Information Company, supported by the Arts Council England (ACE), has produced a valuable toolkit for calculating professional fees for artists, now available through its website. The guidance suggests that artists with upwards of ten years' experience could be aiming to earn the annual salary of a mid-career teacher (approximately £34,299 in 2004) or more. A graduate could aim for around £21,090 per annum, a daily rate of £176 to £204.

ACE research into artists' working lives raises significant issues. In terms of taxation, there is a need for increased flexibility in reporting both income and employment status. There are inconsistencies in the level of understanding of artists' lives between tax and benefit offices, and regulations need to be applied in a more coherent and sympathetic way. A useful exemplar under examination is the approach taken by the Australian Tax Office, which, after extensive lobbying by artists' organizations, now distinguishes between professional artists and those who are simply making art for their own enjoyment. If this approach were to be adopted in the UK it would make a huge difference to artists' earning patterns.

ACE is intensifying its commitment to the financial wellbeing of artists under a new activity entitled 'Artists: Time Space Money'. Artists' workspaces pensions, tax, benefits and earnings are being closely studied to inform new investments, partnerships and improvements in the way artists work and make their living.

There needs to be acknowledgment of the significant proportion of time that artists spend on research and development, which is rarely paid for. They therefore have reduced income for long periods. As a result, an artist's career is often characterized by multiple job holding, short-term contracts and under-employment. This can fortunately have beneficial effects for the arts community, as many artists use these periods of time to undertake teaching, outreach and educational work, giving value through their experience and skills.

Applying for funding

The Arts Council welcomes applications from individual artists to its new, open application programme called 'Grants for the Arts'. This funding stream is for individuals, arts organizations and other people who use the arts in their field of work. The funds are for activities that benefit people in England or that help artists and arts organizations from England to carry out their work.

As an artist you can apply for grants for arts-related activities that might include: projects and events; commissions and productions; research and development; capital items (such as equipment); professional development and training, including travel grants; bursaries; residencies; and touring exhibitions or events.

It is crucial that you set aside the time to read and fully understand the guidance notes and application form before you start writing. The most common mistake among applicants is not reading this guidance thoroughly. You can download the form you need to make an application from the Arts Council website or call the number listed in this section of the directory for an application pack. It is strongly recommended that, before you apply, you contact and get advice from the Arts Council Office for the region in which you are based.

When assessing applications, the Arts Council uses five criteria that can be seen in more detail in a document entitled *Grants for the Arts, Understanding the Assessment Criteria*. It is important to note that not all these factors will apply to every application, but they are the type of thing the assessors may look at, so you should read this information carefully.

Assessing officers use their judgment as to what issues are relevant in each case, depending on the type of activity and how much you are applying for. The assessments examine: the artistic quality of the activity; how the activity will be managed; how feasible the activity is financially; how the public will benefit from the activity, immediately or in the long term; and the contribution of the activity to meeting the aims of Grants for the Arts.

You only have a limited number of words to describe your proposal, so the more clearly you express your project and how you will meet the stated funding criteria, the more likely your bid will be to succeed. You must make sure you allow plenty of time to receive a decision before your activity starts. Currently you have to allow six working weeks for applications under £5,000 and twelve working weeks for applications over £5,000.

Understanding funding criteria and writing project proposals concisely are necessary skills for most applications to other trusts, foundations and even commercial sponsors. Where possible, make direct contact to clarify anything you are unsure about. A useful starting point to find the best funding organization for you is the 'Money Map' available on the website of the Department for Culture, Media and Sport (www.culture.gov.uk/moneymap).

Arts Council England and the public purse
As the national arts development agency, ACE is responsible for developing and implementing arts policy and funding on behalf of taxpayers via financing from the Department for Culture, Media and Sport. It makes strategic use of both National Lottery and Treasury grant-in-aid funding, aiming to place the arts at the heart of national life. ACE is placing greater emphasis than ever before on direct support for artists and on helping to enhance the conditions that allow them and their creativity to thrive. ACE not only provides core funding to established venues for presenting contemporary art, but also establishes strategic partnerships further 'up-stream' at the point of production: in the art school; the studio complex; in new media companies; through artist-run projects and socially engaged practices. The ACE collection of modern and contemporary British art directly supports artists and the market. This collection began with the foundation of the Arts Council of Great Britain in 1946. Since then, over 7,000 works have been acquired from artists and commercial galleries and the collection is now the largest national loan collection of modern and contemporary art in the world, and the largest loan collection of British contemporary art. It is highly regarded for its quality and range.

The Arts Council has increased its funding and support to individual artists in England and for international activity both for artists coming into the country and for those going abroad.

Through its Grants for the Arts programme, Arts Council England is investing £25 million in individual artists between 2003 and 2004 and 2005 and 2006. The programme has already allocated £6 million for 852 grants to individual visual artists for work ranging from animation, graphic design and new media to fine art, photography, crafts and live arts. In 2002 and 2003[1], 73 organizations regularly funded by ACE commissioned 854 works from 1,217 individual visual artists. The total expenditure for art commissions in the Arts Council's Capital Programme was nearly £70 million by the time of completion of most projects in 2004; over £2 million was allocated to visual artists' development initiatives in 2004 and 2005, compared with £450,000 in 1999.

These figures demonstrate the scale of public investment in artists by Arts Council England and the returns are being seen countrywide. Innovative practice in the commissioning of new work is exemplified through the work of organizations such as Artangel, IXIA (the lead national public art body), Locus Plus and Modus Operandi. New and improving relationships are growing between artists and local authority planners, developers and other regeneration agencies.

The impact of new investment has an international reach. In 2002, ACE entered into a major partnership with the British Council in China to establish an artist's exchange programme supporting up to thirty artists each year across the art forms to develop new work in China. The programme also funds Chinese contemporary artists to visit, research and present work in this country, using a range of venues and artist-run organizations as their creative base. The International Artists Fellowships Programme, run directly by ACE, awards special research fellowships to high-achieving artists within different geo-cultural contexts. The programme has provided 175 fellowships in 30 countries within 72 different host institutes. Eighty-three of these fellowships were visual artists including those specializing in architecture, craft, new media, photography, moving images and live art.

Artists' workspaces

Many artists have difficulties in finding and affording workspaces with any degree of permanence or reliability. Artists have helped inner city regeneration but ultimately, as in Hoxton in East London, their presence has increased property prices and forced them out. Through its capital grants, ACE is helping more artists and craft-makers to secure their futures by acquiring the freeholds of properties, and creating safer, stimulating workspaces. Over £69 million[2] has been invested through its capital funds. Open studios, where artists group together to show their work, have become a cultural attraction. In 2001, for instance, 32 open-studio events across England represented 3,000 artists and attracted 250,000 visitors, turning over £1.5 million in sales. These events are a celebration of creativity among the artistic grass roots, bringing many more artists to a larger and wider public at a time when art and creativity are assuming a new importance within the economy. Again, a-n The Artists Information Company provides vital advice and toolkits for artists seeking to set up studios. In 2006, ACE will embark on an unprecedented strategic development of artists' workspaces. It plans to work with major housing, regeneration and corporate partners to develop innovative investments in artists' workspaces. The aim is to upgrade the overall quality of workspaces in England, leading to new stocks of specialist live-work accommodation and low-cost, temporary studios.

The market for art

The art market is a broad ecology that includes the ways in which works of art are commissioned, researched, produced, promoted, presented, bought and sold, and how creativity is converted into commercial value. Visual art contributes significantly to the UK economy and in recent years London has become the largest market in Europe and the second largest in the world after New York. The total sales for the UK in 1998 were £3,287 million or €4,765.1 million, representing over 60 per cent of the European Union art trade[3]. The estimated value of sales through contemporary commercial galleries and open studios in England was worth £354.5million in 2003[4], while a recent ACE publication[5] suggested that the international sales of London-based commercial galleries and agents are likely to be at least double this figure.

To enable more people to enter the art market, Arts Council England launched 'Own Art' in November 2004. The Own Art scheme is currently available through 250 regional galleries and outlets, making it more affordable for the public to buy original contemporary art and craft, through point-of-sale interest-free loans.

Despite considerable resistance from the UK art market, a new European Union directive enables visual artists to receive a percentage of the revenue from the resale of their works in the art market. In January 2006, The Artist's Resale Right (or 'droit de suite') was introduced as law in the UK. For the first time in Britain artists are entitled to a percentage share of the price each time their work is resold by a gallery, dealer or auction house. The right is applicable to all professional resales and can be transferred to heirs for up to seventy years after the artist's death. It sends a key signal that all the member states in the EC are committed to the rights and long-term welfare of visual artists. For further details see the Design and Artists Copyright Society (DACS) website: www.dacs.org.uk.

Dream on!

Artists depend on contact. Contact with art world professionals, academics, curators, dealers, critics, other artists and buyers who collectively provide advocacy and endorsement for their work. But when the artist is alone, that is the most important contact of all.

Tim Eastop is Head of Visual Artists Development, Arts Council England National Office

[1]   Joy, A. et al. *A statistical survey of regularly funded organisations 2002–03*, Arts Council England, 2005
[2]   Based on all ACE capital awards to visual arts projects over the past ten years to artists' studios/workspaces
[3]   Market Tracking International Company Limited (MTIC), *The European Art Market 2000*, London, The European Fine Art Foundation (TEFAF), 2000
[4]   Morris, Hargreaves and McIntyre, *Taste buds: how to cultivate the art market: executive summary*, London, Arts Council England, 2004
[5]   Louisa Buck, *Market Matters: The Dynamics of the Contemporary Art Market*, Arts Council England, 2004

Arts boards, councils, funding and commissioning organizations

'A' Foundation
c/o MacFarlane & Co.,
Cunard Building, Water Street
Liverpool, L3 1DS
T 0151 7097444
Contact Paul Kurthousen
Established in 1998 with principal aim of 'helping
Liverpool to establish itself as a centre being at the
cutting edge of the art world'.
Grants awarded Three art-related grants: Liverpool
Biennial Trust, Liverpool Biennial of
Contemporary Art Ltd and Liverpool Biennial
Fringe.

Arcadea
MEA House, Ellison Place
Newcastle-upon-Tyne, NE1 8XS
T 0191 2220708
W www.arcadea.org
A development agency for art, culture and
disability equality. Aims to promote the artistic and
cultural equality of disabled people in the
Northeast region.

Art Consultants Ltd – Art For Offices
15 Dock Street
London, E1 8JL
T 020 74811337
F 020 74813425
E enquiries@afo.co.uk
W www.afo.co.uk
Established in 1979, specializing in sourcing and
commissioning art. Works with developers,
architects and interior designers to provide art
work for the corporate, hotel and leisure sectors.
Can advise on a consultancy basis through
International Art Consultants Ltd or supply art
directly through Art For Offices.

Art Point Trust
2 Littlegate Street
Oxford, OX1 1QT
T 01865 248822
F 01865 248899
E info@artpointtrust.org.uk
W www.artpointtrust.org.uk
A creative company working with artists to support
new thinking and practice for the built
environment and public space. Advocates and
establishes opportunities for artists to create new
work within public contexts. This includes public-
art commissioning, consultancy, research projects
and audience engagement activities. Based in
Oxford and works throughout the south-east of
England.
Grants awarded Has delivered sixty projects worth
£2.5m in the past five years.

Art Projects Network
174 Charlotte Quay Dock
Ringsend Road, Dublin
Dublin 4
T 086 2471114
E art.info@artprojectsnetwork.net
W www.artprojectsnetwork.net
Contact Noel Kelly
Founded in 2003, an independent network of
professional curators and art critics specializing in
the exhibition and exchange of artistic practice and
process across Europe.
Submission Policy Does not accept open
submissions from artists.

ART.e @ the art of change
6 Container City
Trinity Buoy Wharf
64 Orchard Place, London
E14 0JW
T 020 79879921
F 020 79879922
E pete@artofchange.demon.co.uk
W www.arte-ofchange.com
Contact Peter Dunn
Founded 2001. A visual arts organization
concerned with issues of change and, particularly,
the transformation of the urban environment and
its impact upon quality of life and cultural identity.
The practice ranges from strategy through creative
development to production. The core team is a
combination of visual arts practitioners and
strategists, resourced with new technology and
administrative backup. Produces art works in the
public domain in all its aspects, be they physical,
virtual or social, through a process of working with
communities of interest and location.

Artangel
31 Eyre Street Hill, London
EC1R 5EW
T 020 77131400
F 020 77131401
E info@artangel.org.uk
W www.artangel.org.uk
Has pioneered a new way of collaborating with

artists and engaging audiences in a series of commissions since the early 1990s. Previous projects include Rachel Whiteread's House, Janet Cardiff's The Missing Voice, Michael Landy's Break Down and Jeremy Deller's The Battle of Orgreave.

Artists' General Benevolent Institution
Burlington House
Piccadilly, London
W1J 0BB
T 020 77341193
F 020 77349966
Founded in 1814. Aids professional artists whose work has been known to the public for some time and who, through accident, old age or illness, are unable to support their families.

Arts & Disability Forum
Ground Floor, 109–113 Royal Avenue
Belfast, BT1 1FF
T 028 9023 9450
F 028 9024 7770
E info@adf.ie
W www.adf.ie
Contact Kim Andrews
The ADF was formed in 1993 and, as a cross-community charity, aims to provide information to disabled people and organizations. Administers the Arts & Disability Awards Ireland Scheme, distributing over £50,000 each year to artists with disabilities working in all art forms. A gallery was launched in 2002 which hosts monthly exhibitions, showcasing disabled artists works. There are no media exclusions.
Submission Policy Applicants must 1) be a disabled artist; 2) have ADF membership; 3) complete a proposal form and submit artwork.
Grants awarded Total value: £50,000.

Arts and Humanities Research Council
Whitefriars, Lewins Mead
Bristol
BS1 2AE
T 0117 9876500
F 0117 9876600
W www.ahrc.ac.uk
Various schemes funded, including Core Funding Scheme for Higher Education Museums, Galleries & Collections, Postgraduate Awards in the Arts and Humanities, and Advanced Research Awards in the Arts and Humanities.

Submission Policy See website for details of schemes and funding available.

Arts Council England
National Office
14 Great Peter Street
London, SW1P 3NQ
T 0845 3006200
E tim.eastop@artscouncil.org.uk
W www.artscouncil.org.uk
The national development agency for the arts, founded in 1946. Supports artists and organizations working professionally in the contemporary arts. 'Visual arts' is an inclusive term to represenat a range of practices including architecture, craft, fine art, live art, moving image, new-media art, public-art and socially engaged practice, including education. Will invest £1.1billion of public money between 2006 and 2008.
Submission Policy Grants for the Arts are for individuals, arts organizations, national touring companies and other people who use the arts in their work. They are for activities that benefit people in England or help artists and arts organizations from England to carry out their work. Organizations and national touring are funded by the National Lottery. The application season runs from 31 October to 31 August. Application packs become available in the late summer. See website for more detailed instructions.
Grants awarded Grants for the Arts worth approximately £50m a year.

Arts Council England – East England Arts
Eden House, 48–49 Bateman Street
Cambridge, CB2 1LR
T 0845 300 6200
F 0870 2421271
E aileen.muir@artscouncil.org.uk
W www.artscouncil.org.uk
Areas covered Bedfordshire, Cambridgeshire, Essex, Hertfordshire, Norfolk, Suffolk and unitary authorities of Luton, Peterborough, Southend-on-Sea, Thurrock.

Arts Council England – East Midlands Arts
St Nicholas Court
25–27 Castle Gate
Nottingham, NG1 7AR
T 0845 3006200
F 0115 9502467
E fiona.mitchell-innes@artscouncil.org.uk

W www.arts.org.uk
Areas covered Derbyshire, Leicestershire,
Lincolnshire (excluding North and Northeast
Lincolnshire), Northamptonshire,
Nottinghamshire; unitary authorities of Derby,
Leicester, Nottingham, Rutland.

Arts Council England – London Arts
2 Pear Tree Court, London
EC1R 0DS
T 0845 3006200
F 020 76084100
E enquiries@artscouncil.org.uk
W www.arts.org.uk
Area covered: Greater London.

Arts Council England – North East Arts
Central Square, Forth Street
Newcastle-upon-Tyne
NE1 3PJ
T 0845 3006200
F 0191 2301020
E susan.mckeon@artscouncil.org.uk
W www.arts.org.uk
Areas covered Durham, Northumberland;
unitary authorities of Darlington, Hartlepool,
Middlesbrough, Redcar and Cleveland, Stockton-
on-Tees; metropolitan authorities of Newcastle-
upon-Tyne, Gateshead, North Tyneside,
Sunderland and South Tyneside.

Arts Council England – North West Arts
Manchester House
22 Bridge Street, Manchester
M3 3AB
T 0845 3006200
F 0161 8346969
E enquiries@artscouncil.org.uk
W www.arts.org.uk
Areas covered Cheshire, Cumbria and Lancashire;
unitary authorities of Blackburn with Darwen,
Blackpool, Halton and Warrington; metropolitan
authorities of Bolton, Bury, Knowsley, Liverpool,
Manchester, Oldham, Rochdale, St Helens,
Salford, Sefton, Stockport, Teeside, Trafford,
Wigan and Wirral.

Arts Council England – South East Arts
Sovereign House, Church Street
Brighton, BN1 1RA
T 0845 3006200
F 0870 2421257
E enquiries@artscouncil.org.uk
W www.arts.org.uk

Areas covered: Kent, Surrey, East Sussex, West
Sussex, Buckinghamshire, Hampshire, Isle of
Wight, Oxfordshire; unitary authorities of
Bracknell Forest, Brighton and Hove, the Medway
towns, Milton Keynes, Portsmouth, Reading,
Slough, Southampton, West Berkshire, Windsor
and Maidenhead, Wokingham.

Arts Council England – South West Arts
Senate Court, Southernhay Gardens, Exeter
EX1 1UG
T 0845 300 6200
F 01392 229229
E enquiries@artscouncil.org.uk
W www.artscouncil.org.uk
Areas covered Cornwall, Devon, Dorset,
Gloucestershire, Somerset and Wiltshire; unitary
authorities of Bath and North-east Somerset,
Bournemouth, Bristol, North Somerset, Plymouth,
Poole, South Gloucestershire, Swindon and
Torbay.

Arts Council England – West Midlands Arts
82 Granville Street
Birmingham, B1 2LH
T 0845 3006200
F 0121 6437239
E enquiries@artscouncil.org.uk
W www.arts.org.uk
Areas covered Shropshire, Staffordshire,
Warwickshire, Worcestershire; metropolitan
districts of Birmingham, Coventry, Dudley,
Sandwell, Solihull, Walsall and Wolverhampton;
unitary authorities of Hereford, Stoke-on-Trent,
Telford and Wrekin.

Arts Council England – Yorkshire Arts
21 Bond Street, Dewsbury, WF13 1AX
T 0845 300 6200
F 01924 466522
E enquiries@artscouncil.org.uk
W www.artscouncil.org.uk
Areas covered North Yorkshire; unitary authorities
of East Riding, Kingston-upon-Hull, North-East
Lincolnshire, North Lincolnshire and York;
metropolitan districts of Barnsley, Bradford,
Calderdale, Doncaster, Kirklees, Leeds,
Rotherham, Sheffield and Wakefield.

Arts Council Ireland
70 Merrion Square
Dublin, Dublin 2
T 01 6180200
F 01 6181302

E info@artscouncil.ie
W www.artscouncil.ie
Contact Stephanie O'Callaghan (Arts Development Director)
The Arts Council is the Irish government agency for developing the arts. It provides financial assistance to artists, arts organizations, local authorities and others for artistic purposes. It offers advice and information on the arts to government and to a wide range of individuals and organizations. As an advocate for the arts and artists, the Arts Council undertakes projects and research, often in new and emerging areas of arts practice, and increasingly in co-operation with partner organizations.
Grants awarded Funding from government for 2007 was €80m.

Arts Council of Northern Ireland
MacNeice House
77 Malone Road, Belfast
BT9 6AS
T 028 90385200
F 0661715
E info@artscouncil-ni.org
W www.artscouncil-ni.org
Contact Iain Davidson
Under the current five-year arts plan, priority has been given to extend opportunities for artists to develop their work and practice. Many employment possibilities are available for artists under, for example, the Access Programme. There are also major commissioning opportunities across all art forms under the New Work Scheme in areas such as public art, musical composition, script writing, etc. As an expansion of the Arts Council's systems of support for the individual artist, a number of other specific schemes have been developed including: Support for the Individual Artist Programme; Travel Awards Scheme; General Art Awards Scheme; Major Individual Awards Scheme; Artists in the Community Scheme; the Arts and Disability Awards Ireland; Arts and Artists Abroad; Arts and Disability Networking Abroad; International Artists' Profile Scheme Residencies; the British School at Rome Fellowship; self-arranged residencies.
Submission Policy Specific criteria vary according to scheme but for all schemes, applicants must satisfy the following criteria: (1) have made a contribution to artistic activities in Northern Ireland for a minimum period of one year; and (2) be domiciled (as distinct from a national or

resident) in Northern Ireland. Priority is given to practising individual artists.
Grants awarded Annual awards totalling around £1.05m.

Arts Council of Wales
9 Museum Place, Cardiff
CF1 3NX
T 029 20376500
F 029 20221447
E information@ccc-acw.org.uk
W www.ccc-acw.org.uk
Contact Angela Blackburn (Communications Officer)
A national organization with specific responsibility for the funding and development of the arts in Wales. Main sources of funds are an annual grant from the Welsh Assembly and its share of the 'good causes fund' for the arts from the National Lottery. Also receives funds from other sources, including local authorities.

Arts Foundation
2nd Floor, 6 Salem Road, London
W2 4BU
T 020 82293813
F 020 82299410
E artsfound@hotmail.com
Contact Shelley Warren (Director)
Funds artists living and working in England, Scotland or Wales who have demonstrated commitment to and proven their ability in their chosen art form. A minimum of five annual fellowships awarded, worth £10,000 each, in five specific art forms that change every year.
Submission Policy Programme not open to applications. Seventy established artists and other professionals nominate individual artists who are then invited to make an application.

Artsadmin
Toynbee Studios, 28 Commercial Street
London, E1 6AB
T 020 7247 5102
F 020 7247 5103
E admin@artsadmin.co.uk
W www.artsadmin.co.uk
Contact Artists' Advisory Service
A creative organization that produces, resources and promotes contemporary theatre, visual arts, dance, live art and performance. Artsadmin has established Toynbee Studios as a centre for the development and presentation of new work, where it offers a range of opportunities for emerging and

unfunded artists including bursaries, rehearsal spaces, a free advisory service, mentoring schemes, education programme, residencies and showcases.

Submission Policy Each scheme has different requirements and deadlines. See website for specific application criteria.

Grants awarded Grant schemes include: non-studio based bursaries; residencies; awards for artists and curators; subsidized mentoring schemes and performance workshops

Awards for All
T 0845 6002040
W www.awardsforall.org.uk
A grants programme for small groups involved in arts, sports, heritage, education, environment, health and voluntary and community activities that need grants of between £50 and £5,000. Criteria include increasing skills and creativity and improving quality of life. Operates through a series of regional offices.

Submission Policy Open to small, non-profit organizations and some statutory bodies such as parish town councils, schools and health bodies, but not to fund statutory responsibilities. Priority given to groups with a lower income. Groups must spend the money within twelve months of receiving the grant. No requirement for match funding.

Belfast Exposed Photography
The Exchange Place
23 Donegall Street, Belfast
BT1 2FF
T 028 90230965
F 028 90314343
E info@belfastexposed.org
W www.belfastexposed.org
Contact Karen Downey (Exhibitions Director)
A photographic resource, archive and gallery which commissions new work and runs an annual programme of exhibitions. By developing a policy of project origination, placing its main emphasis on the commissioning of new work, producing publications and generating discussion through seminars and talks around projects, it aims to aid the development of an infrastructure in which the photographic arts can flourish.

Submission Policy Only exhibits and supports photographic projects. To submit work for consideration, post samples of work (not more than 20 images) either on disk (Mac-compatible) or printed, along with a statement about the work,

a CV and project proposal. Also include an sae for the return of all work. All submissions should be made for the attention of Karen Downey (Exhibitions Director). Submissions are looked at twice a year, at the end of January and June.

Bloomberg
City Gate House
39–45 Finsbury Square
London, EC2A 1PQ
T 020 73307500
F 020 73926000
W www.bloomberg.com/uk
Contact Jemma Read (Head of Arts Sponsorship and Charitable Investment)
Handles sponsorships and donations together, with no stated preference between them or for any particular art form. Policy is to 'support contemporary arts projects that enrich the community and involve our employees in new and challenging cultural areas'. Has a commitment to the arts and young people.

British Council Arts Group
11 Portland Place, London
W1N 4EJ
T 020 73893194
F 020 73893199
E artweb@britishcouncil.org
W www.britcoun.org/arts/index.htm
Contact Kate Smith
Reinforces the UK's role in the international community through cultural, scientific, technological and educational cooperation, working with partners in the UK and overseas (represented in 110 countries). The principal aims of the council's work in the arts, literature and design are to demonstrate the innovation and excellence of British arts to overseas audiences, to promote intercultural dialogue and exchange, and to stimulate the export of British cultural goods and services. Also runs the Grants to Artists Scheme, designed to help promote British art by assisting professional British artists to exhibit overseas in public or commercial spaces.

Business2Arts
44 East Essex Street
Temple Bar, Dublin 2
T 01 6725336
F 01 6725373
E info@business2arts.ie
W www.business2arts.ie
Contact Rowena Neville

Founded in 1988 as a business council for the arts. With over 130 business members, aims to promote and encourage partnerships between business and the arts, whether through promoting the value of corporate art collections, encouraging companies to use the arts as a tool for client entertainment, or informing business about the marketing benefits of sponsoring the arts. Also has over 120 affiliated arts organizations who make use of a range of programmes, including a Training Programme for the Arts. Also provides advice on approaching companies for sponsorship, writing proposals and marketing an organization. Carries out a national arts sponsorship survey, runs an annual arts showcase for business, and a successful mentoring programme, matching senior arts managers with their peers in the arts.

Submission Policy The Awards are open to arts organizations who have received sponsorship from business in the last year. Call for entries is made in February every year, with a one month application time-frame.

Grants awarded Arts Sponsor of the Year Awards runs annually in May.

Calouste Gulbenkian Foundation

98 Portland Place, London
W1B 1ET
T 020 76365313
F 020 79087580
E info@gulbenkian.org.uk
W www.gulbenkian.org.uk
Contact Sian Ede (Assistant Director, Arts Programme)
The Arts Programme is principally for professional arts organizations or individual professional artists working in partnerships or groups. Its purpose is to support the development of new art-making in any art form. It excludes activities which are linked to mainstream education. The Foundation welcomes applications from British-based organizations involving collaborations with international artists. Grants are available for early research and development activities leading to particularly imaginative and unusual projects devised for urban or rural landscapes, the built environment and the countryside, and to be led by artists, curators or arts organizations. The Foundation also has a reputation for promoting encounters between the Arts and Sciences. It initiates a limited number of arts programmes run by science organizations, arts and science programmes run by arts agencies or museums and galleries, and a small number of

projects where artists undertake initial research in science, including environmental science.
Submission Policy For detailed information on grant programmes and exclusions see the foundation's website or free 'Advice to Applicants for Grants' leaflet.

CBAT – The Arts and Regeneration Agency

123 Bute Street, Cardiff
CF10 5AE
T 029 20488772
F 029 20472439
E info@cbat.co.uk
W www.cbat.co.uk
Has been commissioning and managing public art works for both private- and public-sector clients since 1990. Originally worked as the retained consultants to Cardiff Bay Development Corporation but has been working as an independent public art consultancy across the UK since 1998. Initiates approximately ten projects per year.
Submission Policy Application forms for registration or artist database on request.

Commissions East

St Giles Hall
Pound Hill, Cambridge
CB3 0AE
T 01223 356882
F 01223 356883
W www.commissionseast.org.uk
A visual arts development agency that works with artists and commissioners to create innovative visual arts projects that place artists' work at the heart of everyday life.

Common Ground

Gold Hill House
21 High Street, Shaftesbury
SP7 8JE
T 01747 850820
F 01747 850821
E info@commonground.org.uk
W www.commonground.org.uk and www.england-in-particular.info
Contact Sue Clifford (Director)
Plays a unique role in the arts and environmental fields, distinguished by the linking of nature with culture, focussing upon the positive investment people can make in their own localities and championing popular democratic involvement. Provides information and inspiration through publications and projects such as Parish Maps,

Apple Day, Community Orchards, Tree Dressing Day, New Milestones (sculpture and the land), Confluence (making music for a river) and the Campaign for Local Distinctiveness.
Submission Policy Only occasionally commissions artists but welcomes contact from artists and also facilitators who work directly with communities.

Crafts Council
44a Pentonville Road, Islington
London, N1 9BY
T 020 72787700
F 020 78376891
E reference@craftscouncil.org.uk
W www.craftscouncil.org.uk
The UK development agency for contemporary crafts. An independent organization offering a range of services to makers and the public.

Creative Skills
The Old Grammar School, West Park
Redruth, TR15 3AJ
T 01209 218879
F 01209 219145
E admin@creativeskills.org.uk
W www.creativeskills.org.uk
Contact Jane Sutherland
The professional-development organization for all creative industries practitioners in Cornwall. Set up in 2001 to equip creative practitioners in Cornwall with the skills, knowledge and opportunities to develop and share their creativity and increase their prosperity. Grants depend on funding available.
Submission Policy Professional practitioners working within the creative industries who live in Cornwall.

Cywaith Cymru Artworks Wales
Crichton House
11–12 Mount Stuart Square
Cardiff, CF10 5EE
T 029 20489543
F 029 20465458
E info@cywaithcymru.org
W www.cywaithcymru.org
The national organization for public art in Wales. Established in 1981 to encourage the placing of art in the environment. Regularly gives artists opportunities in public art commissions and artist-in-residence projects. It also offers an artist-initiated residency programme, as well as a mentoring scheme, enabling less established artists to gain experience in residencies.

Submission Policy To register to receive details of Cywaith Cymru opportunities, or for further information on artist-initiated projects or mentoring, contact Cywaith.

Elephant Trust
P.O. Box 5521, London
W8 4WA
Aims to 'advance public education in all aspects of the arts and to develop artistic taste and the knowledge, understanding and appreciation of the fine arts'. Support principally given to individuals, art galleries and other organizations in furtherance of these aims. Various grants awarded.
Submission Policy Excludes students and any other study-related funding. Send applications in writing together with sae. Guidelines are issued. Trustees meet quarterly.

Jewish Association for Jewish Culture
79 Wimpole Street, London
W1G 9RY
T 020 79358266
F 020 79353252
E london@jewishcultureineurope.org
W www.jewishcultureineurope.org
Contact Lena Stanley-Clamp
Established in 2001 with mission to foster and support artistic creativity and achievement, and to promote access to Jewish culture in Europe. Grant programmes include visual arts, performing arts and documentary films.
Grants awarded Approximately twenty grants annually. Total value approx €100,000

Federation of British Artists (FBA)
17 Carlton House Terrace, London
SW1Y 5BD
T 020 7930 6844
F 020 7839 7830
E info@mallgalleries.com
W www.mallgalleries.org.uk
Contact John Deston (Gallery Manager)
The Federation of British Artists was founded in 1961 and is the umbrella organization for nine of the countries leading art societies. The FBA offers open art exhibitions and competitions, gallery tours and workshops, gallery hire, a portrait and fine art commissions service and life-drawing classes.
Submission Policy The FBA runs many open exhibitions, which are open to all artists. Election to membership of art socieities is by merit.

Freeform
Hothouse, 274 Richmond Road
London Fields, London
E8 3QW
T 020 72493394
F 020 72498499
E contact@freeform.org.uk
W www.freeform.org.uk
Active in urban renewal and regeneration through
art- and design-led solutions to humanize the
social and physical environment locally, nationally
and internationally. Combines the skills of artists,
architects and local people on urban regeneration
projects.

Helix Arts
2nd Floor, The Old Casino
1–4 Forth Lane, Newcastle-upon-Tyne
NE1 5HX
T 0191 2414931
F 0191 2414933
E info@helixarts.com
W www.helixarts.com
Specializes in the development of projects and
initiatives, including artist residencies and
commissions, which explore the role and potential
of the arts in a social context.

Henry Moore Foundation
Dane Tree House, Perry Green
Much Hadham
SG10 6EE
T 01279 843333
F 01279 843647
E curator@henry-moore-fdn.co.uk
W www.henry-moore-fdn.co.uk
Contact Timothy Llewellyn (Director)
Established to 'advance the education of the public
by the promotion of their appreciation of the fine
arts and in particular the works of Henry Moore'.
Concentrates its support on sculpture, drawing
and printmaking. Promotes exhibitions and
publications about Henry Moore, both nationally
and internationally.
Submission Policy Does not give grants to
individual applicants, nor provide revenue
expenditure. Apply in writing covering the
following: aims and functions of organization;
precise purpose for which grant is sought; amount
required and details of how figure arrived at;
details of efforts made to find other income,
whether firm commitments have been received
and what others are hoped for; details of budget for
scheme and how scheme will be monitored.

Applications considered at quarterly meetings of
the foundation's grants committee.
Grants awarded Grants towards: exhibitions
around the world (at established galleries only);
conferences, workshops and symposia; museum
and gallery acquisitions of sculpture; conservation
work and research; publications which encourage
public interest in sculpture.

Impact Arts
The Factory, 319 Craigpark Drive
Dennistoun, Glasgow
G31 2TB
T 0141 5753001
F 0141 5753009
E mairi@impactarts.co.uk
W www.impactarts.co.uk
Contact Mairi Sanders
A leading community arts company committed to
involving people of all ages and abilities in
innovative, arts-based activities across Glasgow,
Scotland and the UK. Established in 1994, the
company works in partnership with a variety of
community groups, schools, housing associations
and funding agencies, developing and delivering
tailored long- and short-term projects and events.

International Intelligence on Culture
4 Baden Place, Crosby Row, London
SE1 1YW
T 020 74037001
F 020 74032009
E enquiry@intelculture.org
W www.intelculture.org
Contact Sheena Barbour (Information Officer)
Brings together an experienced multinational
group of experts to work with and for the
international culture sector. Undertakes a range of
activities for public bodies in the UK and overseas,
including policy intelligence, research,
consultancy, project management, training and
information services. Runs tailormade workshops
for cultural organizations, local government,
policy-makers and practitioners on themes such as
European funding, networking, cultural exchange
and cultural politics worldwide.

iris
Faculty of Arts Media and Design
Staffordshire University
Staffordshire, ST4 2DE
T 01782 294721
E info@irisphoto.org
W www.irisphoto.org

IRIS is a research centre within the Faculty of Arts, Media and Design at Staffordshire University, with a focus on the initiation of conferencing, publishing, exhibiting and educational projects within the field of contemporary women's' photographic practice, and broadening access to the medium through books, exhibitions and educational activities.

Submission Policy Information on application for membership can be found at www.irisphoto.org/live/membership.asp

ISIS Arts

1st Floor, 5 Charlotte Square
Newcastle-upon-Tyne
NE1 4XF
T 0191 2614407
F 0191 2616818
E isis@isisarts.org.uk
W www.isisarts.org.uk
Initiates and manages productions, exhibitions and artist residencies, and works with artists on collaborative projects and events. Track record of providing quality arts projects to benefit individual artists, schools and communities alike, while promoting the professional status of the artist. Has a digital facility serving artists in the region and promotes an interdisciplinary approach to the use of new media in the arts. Works with around seventy artists a year on residencies programmes and a further forty as part of training programmes.

J. Paul Getty Jr. Charitable Trust

1 Park Square West, London
NW1 4LJ
T 020 74861859
W www.jpgettytrust.org.uk
Contact Bridget O'Brien Twohig (Administrator)
Aims to fund projects to do with poverty and misery in general, and unpopular causes in particular, within the UK. With regard to the arts grants only the following will be considered: therapeutic use of the arts for the long-term benefit of groups under social welfare (people with mental illness, communities that are clearly disadvantaged, offenders, the homeless, the unemployed and ethnic minorities); projects that enable people in these groups to feel welcome in arts venues, or that enable them to make long-term constructive use of their leisure. Has made total grants worth over £26m since 1986.

Submission Policy Only accepts applications by post. Send a letter no more than two sides long in the first instance, giving an outline of the project and who will benefit, a detailed costing, the existing sources of finance of the organization, and what other applications have been made, including those to statutory sources and the National Lottery. Applicants should disclose if they have applied to or received a grant previously from the trust.

Jerwood Charitable Foundation

22 Fitzroy Square, London
W1P 5HQ
T 020 73886287
F 020 73886289
E info@jerwood.org
W www.jerwood.org.uk
Contact Roanne Dods (Director)
Dedicated to rewarding excellence in the visual and performing arts, and to education. Supports 'outstanding national institutions', along with projects in their early stages which are unable to secure funding from other sources.

Submission Policy Applications should be by letter, outlining the aims and objectives of the organization and those of the specific project or scheme for which assistance is sought. Also include a detailed budget for the project.

Grants awarded Various grants, varying from up to £10,000 in the lower range to £50,000.

Lime

St Mary's Hospital
Hathersage Road
Manchester, M13 0JH
T 0161 2564389
F 0161 2564390
E lime@limeart.org
W www.limeart.org
Contact Brian Chapman
Founded (as Hospital Arts) in 1974. Works to initiate and deliver arts projects within the arena of health and well-being through collaborative and consultative arts practice. The aim is to develop sustainable artistic initiatives in healthcare through embedding the expertise of artists and the cultural industries into care planning and delivery and into the social fabric of hospitals. Commissions around 30 artists per year.

Submission Policy Send CV and examples of current work for consideration. From this, selected artists will be invited to present to the team.

Grants awarded Ten to fifteen grants worth £450,000.

Locus+

17, 3rd Floor Wards Building
31–39 High Bridge
Newcastle-upon-Tyne
NE1 1EW
T 0191 2331450
F 0191 2331451
E locusplus@newart.demon.co.uk
W www.locusplus.org.uk
Formally established in 1993 but preceded by the Basement Group (1979–1984) and Projects UK (1982–1992). A visual arts commissioning agency that works with artists on the production and presentation of socially engaged, collaborative and temporary projects, primarily for non-gallery locations. In each project, place or context is integral to the meaning of the art work. To date, the organization has completed over fifty projects touring to a further twenty-five other venues, and produced over twenty publications and nine artists multiples.

Mid Pennine Arts

Yorke Street, Burnley
BB11 1HD
T 01282 421986
F 01282 429513
E info@midpenninearts.org.uk
W www.midpenninearts.org.uk
A north-west arts agency with a diverse variety of projects running at any one time.

National Endowment for Science, Technology and the Arts (NESTA)

Fishmongers Chambers
110 Upper Thames Street, London
EC4R 3TW
T 020 76459500
F 020 76459501
E nesta@nesta.org.uk
W www.nesta.org.uk
Set up by an Act of Parliament in 1998 to help maximize the country's creative and innovative potential. Funded by an endowment from the National Lottery, using the interest to back people of exceptional talent and imagination. Offers support to explore new ideas, develop new products and services, or experiment with new ways of nurturing creativity in science, technology and the arts.

Nigel Moores Family Charitable Trust

c/o Macfarlane & Co.
2nd Floor, Cunard Building
Water Street, Liverpool, L3 1DS
Aims to raise the artistic taste of the public 'whether in relation to music, drama, opera, painting, sculpture or otherwise in connection with the fine arts'. Also promotes education in fine arts and academic education in general, as well as providing support for environmental causes, the provision of recreation and leisure facilities, and the promotion of religion. Has supported institutions that benefit children and young adults, actors and entertainment professionals, musicians, students, textile workers and designers.
Submission Policy Apply in writing enclosing a synopsis of aims and funds required, together with financial statements. However, the trust has usually committed its funds for designated projects, making unsolicited applications unlikely to succeed. Trustees meet three times a year.

Peter Moores Foundation

c/o Messrs Wallwork, Nelson & Johnson
Chandler House
7 Ferry Road, Office Park
Riversway, Fulwood
Preston, PR2 2YH
W www.pmf.org.uk
Aim is 'the raising of the taste of the public whether in relation to music, drama, opera, painting, sculpture or otherwise in connection with the fine arts'. Causes which promote education in fine arts, academic education or the Christian religion also attract support from the foundation, as does the provision of facilities for recreation and leisure. Activities supported tend to reflect the personal interests of its founder and patron, Peter Moores, a director of The Littlewoods Organisation, the pools and mail order company.
Submission Policy Prospective applicants should note that the foundation will normally support projects that come to the attention of its patron or trustees through their interests or special knowledge. General applications for sponsorship are not encouraged and are unlikely to succeed.
Grants awarded Grants in the following categories: music (performance); music (recording); music (training); fine art; heritage; youth/race relations; social; health; environment.

Picture This

40 Sydney Row, Spike Island
Bristol, BS1 6UU
T 0117 9257010
F 0117 9257040

E office@picture-this.org.uk
W www.picture-this.org.uk
Contact Josephine Lanyon (Director)
A moving-image projects agency that commissions contemporary visual art works and produces exhibitions, publications and touring initiatives. Works in partnership with a range of organizations, from galleries and colleges to public sites. The agency develops a range of projects, residencies, research and presentation opportunities as well as providing creative technology services.
Submission Policy Aims to provide a range of opportunities for artists to produce new work, for audiences to engage with moving-image projects and for individuals to gain the experience necessary to find paid employment. Each year the agency aims to advertise one or two open-submission schemes.

Prince's Trust

Head Office, 18 Park Square East
London, NW1 4LH
T 020 75431234
F 020 75431200
E webinfops@princes-trust.org.uk
W www.princes-trust.org.uk
A charity aiming to offer young people (14 to 30 years old) practical support including training, mentoring and financial assistance. Focuses on those who have struggled at school, been in care, been in trouble with the law, or are long-term unemployed.

Public Art Commissions and Exhibitions (PACE)

7 John Street, Edinburgh
EH15 2EB
T 0131 6200445
E pace@ednet.co.uk
W www.paceprojects.org
Contact Juliet Dean
Established in 1996. A public arts agency dedicated to the integration of art into environmental and building projects. Works in a range of sectors including health, education and the environment. Applies for grants for projects on behalf of the client. Recent awards include £350,000 from the arts lottery for the Royal Aberdeen Children's Project.
Submission Policy Advertizes for artists when opportunities for commissions arise. Works with a range of artists in media such as sculpture, glass, installation, light, photography and new media.

Public Art South West

Arts Council England, South West
Bradninch Place
Gandy Street
Exeter, EX4 3LS
T 01392 229227
E pasw@artscouncil.org.uk
W www.publicartonline.org.uk
Contact Linda Geddes
Recognized as one of the leading public art-development agencies in the UK. Primarily serving the south-west of England, its work extends beyond geographical boundaries in terms of the critical thinking and application of artists' skills and creativity it promotes. Works with artists and national and regional public- and private-sector organizations across Britain, and actively networks with a range of professions within art, design and architecture.
Submission Policy Can advise artists on all aspects of the commissioning process but does not act as a project manager nor recommend artists for individual commissions. Organizes two regional network meetings a year, which have a reduced rate for artists.

Rootstein Hopkins Foundation

P.O. Box 194, Wallington
SM6 0WT
T 020 8773 1919
F 020 8773 1919
E info@rhfoundation.org.uk
W www.rhfoundation.org.uk
Contact Tony Barlow, administrative assistant to the trustees
Founded 1992. Grants once a year, advertized on website and in Artists Newsletter in October/November each year. No correspondence about grants entertained.
Submission Policy Chooses candidates who will make the best use of the grants to further their careers and who can present a plan that seems likely to be realized within the grant period. Looking for recent, strong and consistent work.

Scottish Arts Council

12 Manor Place, Edinburgh
EH3 7DD
T 0131 2266051
F 0131 2259833
E help.desk@scottisharts.org.uk
W www.scottisharts.org.uk
Champions and sustains the arts for Scotland, investing funding from the Scottish Executive and

National Lottery to support and develop artistic excellence and creativity throughout Scotland. **Submission Policy** For detailed guidelines and application forms to each fund and the latest information, contact the help desk from Monday to Friday between 9am and 5pm.

Stanley Picker Trust
1 Warren Park, Kingston Hill
Kingston-upon-Thames
KT2 7HX
T 01722 412412
Primarily supports the arts, giving annual grants and fellowships to the arts faculties at the University of Kingston and bursaries to selected schools of music and drama. The trust-owned Warren Park, Surrey, used as a gallery to display the trust's own art works, is also a major beneficiary, annually receiving the trust's largest grant. Funding is also given in the fields of music, writing, acting, printing and sculpture and a few grants to arts organizations.
Grants awarded Grants total over £250,000.

Vision in Art
44A Halesworth Road, Lewisham
London, SE13 7TN
T 020 83202099
E office@via.demon.co.uk
W www.visioninart.org
Contact Aileen Ryan
A not-for-profit organization facilitating a London-wide network of visual artists in order to raise the profile of the visual arts and of those who practise them. Provides artist-led professional-development services to enable collaborative mentoring, art-work promotion, exchange of relevant information about artistic opportunities, participation in community projects and events, and networking.

Visiting Arts
Units 4.01 & 4.02 Enterprise House
1–2 Hatfields, London
SE1 9PG
T 020 7960 9630
F 020 7960 9643
E information@visitingarts.org.uk
W www.visitingarts.org.uk
Contact John Kundu, Web and Communications Manager
Visiting Arts's purpose is to strengthen intercultural understanding through the arts. It supports artists and arts organizations through

advice, information and awards involving artist residencies, collaborations, presentations and exhibitions, and presenter, promoter and curator development. It delivers training and professional development programmes for overseas arts managers and UK-based cultural attachés, organizes seminars, conferences and networking events to deepen intercultural understanding, provides consultancy and networking services internationally and for the UK, delivers work across the UK and works with an average of forty countries per year.
Submission Policy No open access funding programme.
Grants awarded For details of specific projects visit the website.

Visual Arts Projects
1st Floor, 14 King Street
Glasgow, G1 5QP
T 0141 5526563
F 0141 5530798
Provides arts research fellowships. Also involved in arranging seminars and does some publishing.

VIVID
140 Heath Mill Lane, Birmingham
B9 4AR
T 0121 7667876
F 0871 2510747
E info@vivid.org.uk
W www.vivid.org.uk
Contact Helen Street
Dedicated to the development of contemporary media art and interdisciplinary practice. Supports and commissions research, new works, artists' residencies, events and publications. A project space accommodates the production and exhibition of media arts, bringing together technical resources, support services and presentation facilities.

Voluntary Arts Ireland
12 English Street, Downpatrick
BT30 6AB
T 028 44839327
F 028 44839192
E info@vaireland.org
W www.vaireland.org
Contact Olive Broderick
Seeks to promote participation in the arts and crafts by supporting the development of the voluntary arts sector, primarily by facilitating the

development of a strong infrastructure, strategic thinking and good practice across the sector. Linked to similar bodies in England, Scotland and Wales via the Voluntary Arts Network (VAN).

Wellcome Trust

183 Euston Road, London
NW1 2BE
T 020 76117367
E soss@wellcome.ac.uk
W www.wellcome.ac.uk
A main funder of scientific biomedical research in Britain, with spending on par with the government's Medical Research Council. Within their schemes are the People Awards, a mechanism for funding initiatives up to £30,000 that encourage and support public engagement with biosciences, especially novel and imaginative activities. The scheme is open to academics, mediators and practitioners (including artists).
Submission Policy Applications can be made at any time during the year and will be subject to review by referees.

Winston Churchill Memorial Trust

15 Queen's Gate Terrace
London, SW7 5PR
T 020 75849315
F 020 75810410
E office@wcmt.org.uk
W www.wcmt.org.uk
A living tribute to Churchill, running since 1965, when thousands of people subscribed £3m to provide travelling fellowships. Since then, the net income from investments has been used to fund over three thousand fellowships. Approximately one hundred are awarded annually for projects overseas lasting four to eight weeks on average. The grant awarded covers all fellowship expenses, return airfare, travel within the country(-ies) to be visited, daily living and travel insurance.
Submission Policy British citizens may apply. No formal education or professional qualifications required. No grants awarded for attending courses, academic studies, student grants or gap-year projects.

Woo Charitable Foundation

277 Green Lanes, London
N13 4XS
T 07974 570475
F 020 88863814
Contact John Dowling (Administrator/Secretary)
Established for the advancement of education through supporting, organizing, promoting and assisting the development of the arts in England, together with the specific aim of helping those less able to help themselves. Funding is usually spread over a number of years.
Grants awarded Over £250,000 in 'artistic grants'.

09

Societies and other artists' organizations

Being an artist outside of London

Heather Morison

I think if you make good art, where you live doesn't matter. After all it is your art, not you, that is important. However, your environment does have a huge influence on whether you are able or equipped to make good art, so you should make sure you feel happy with your general situation.

We have lived outside of London for about ten years now and currently reside in Snowdonia, very close to a piece of woodland that we are gradually turning into an arboretum. The UK is a very small place, making it relatively easy to travel about visiting people, seeing shows, doing research and making work. As long as we can do that, we can live anywhere we want. Where we live has a major influence on our work, perhaps more so than for many artists. We make art about where we are. Being somewhat on the edge or the periphery of the art world is a very interesting place to be and gives us a rather unusual view of what is going on. Lots of people come to visit us here and we travel all the time to London and other cities, so we are not cut off, just a little remote. It suits us, but it wouldn't suit everyone.

Advantages to living outside of London
There are lots of advantages to living outside London. We lived there for two years after graduating and then moved to Birmingham. The most obvious benefit for us was that the cost of living was dramatically lower, which meant we could afford the rent on a decent studio. There are fewer artists outside of London and so it is much easier to get to know the arts community and make friends. There are also fewer art events, but this means that everyone always goes and will normally all end up in the same pub afterwards. There are also lots of opportunities outside of London and, quite frankly, not so much competition. Organizations and funding bodies seem much

more willing to help less established artists in order to keep them in the regions and stop them migrating to London.

Support structures
Living next to a mountain, one thing we do miss a bit is having an arts community to mix with readily. I think if we worked alone this might be more of a problem, but we try to keep in regular contact with as many people as possible by email, telephone and on our frequents travels. Having some kind of support structure can be invaluable, especially when you are just starting out after art school. Going to talks, openings and events is a good way to build up a network, while volunteering and looking out for opportunities at your local arts organizations can start to place you in the arts community, even if you aren't yet a successful practitioner.

Showing work
When we arrived in Birmingham we had access to a large, leaky warehouse-sized space, so we started to put on shows. The amazing thing about regional cities is that there always seem to be disused buildings or shops – especially with the amount of regeneration taking place – and they make great temporary exhibition spaces.

The only way to be a successful artist is to show really good work. It is nonsense to be put off if you are finding it difficult to get a gallery show because the only way to show better work is to be showing work in the first place. You can break this vicious circle by showing work anywhere, from disused buildings to billboards and fly posters, and you can do site-specific performances and so on – the list is endless. Invite people, including the press, to come along and just keep doing it, although always remember to document it on the web (this is very important especially when you are outside of London). Make friends with your local contemporary art galleries because when you are ready and your work is good enough, you will have a show there.

Collaborative working

As well as working collaboratively with people in your locale, don't ignore the other cities around you. It is so easy to travel between Bristol and Birmingham, or Swansea and Cardiff, or Manchester and Leeds, so going to events and extending your arts knowledge and community just takes a little bit of effort. Then invite people to see you too.

Don't ignore London

In the UK, London is the centre of the commercial art world and so it would be foolish to ignore it entirely. Making regular visits to London to see all the big shows as well as visiting the smaller galleries in the East End is incredibly important. Be inspired by all the amazing work that is being shown, don't get bitter. Trying to imitate what you see in London, say in Wrexham, may not be appropriate, but it is a good idea to be as professional as if you were trying to be an artist in London. Don't act regional, keep up to date. Read *Frieze*, read *Artforum*, go to the art shows and whenever you can visit the Venice Biennale or Documenta as well as travelling to other regional cities that show amazing art, places such as Berlin and Rotterdam.

Funding

Make friends with your local Arts Council officer. This is easy to do outside of London simply because there are less artists. Look out for funding schemes that are aimed specifically at regional artists (there are many around) and then start to make applications. Don't be put off by rejection; we reckon that you should aim for a one-in-ten success rate. Nearly all the contemporary commercial art galleries are in London and the only way you'll catch their eye is by showing great work in non-commercial shows, so make sure you always invite them to your openings. (And just a quick word about finding a gallery to represent you: wherever you live, research thoroughly and find the right gallery for you before you approach them in any way.)

Having said all this, just live where you feel happiest, and if you make amazing work you'll be a successful artist.

Heather and Ivan Morison have been observing, collecting and documenting their everyday lives – whether tending their garden in Birmingham or travelling across the world – since they left art school. They have exhibited nationally and internationally and represented Wales at the 2007 Venice Biennale. For more information about their work, visit www.morison.info.

Societies and other artists' organizations

a-n The Artists Information Company / a-n Magazine

1st Floor, 7–15 Pink Lane, Newcastle-upon-Tyne
NE1 5DW
T 0191 2418000
F 0191 2418001
E info@a-n.co.uk
W www.a-n.co.uk

A leading UK organization for supporting contemporary visual arts practice. Its publications and services meet the professional needs of artists and the visual arts sector, identifying changing trends and new needs. Subscriptions for artists and arts professionals combine a-n Magazine and other a-n publications with access to resources on www.a-n.co.uk including daily updated artists' jobs and opportunities. Also undertakes visual arts research, organizes artists' events and advocates on behalf of professional visual artists to other organizations.
Admissions Policy Subscription packages open to all. AIR (Artists Interaction and Representation) membership is only available to professional artists and is free as part of an artists' subscription.
Subscription rates Annual artists' subscription £30 (£42 for other individuals, £60 for organizations) for twelve issues of a-n Magazine, over £100 of new publications and access to resources on www.a-n.co.uk.

All Arts – The People's Arts Group

52 Toft Street, Kensington, Liverpool
L7 2PS
T 0151 2220532
E allarts@blueyonder.co.uk
W www.allarts.org.uk
Contact Anthony Mantova

Founded in 1998 to promote, support, develop and create art in all its forms and bridge the traditional void between different arts and art organizations. Runs arts, education and employment open days to show the links between these industries, and has performed plays and run workshops to encourage adults and children to participate in the arts. Has a network of national and international contacts. Works with a number of local and national agencies.
Admissions Policy Artists in various disciplines are welcome to become members and all receive a weekly newsletter.
Subscription rates Annual: £10. Under 18s-free.

Alternative Arts

Top Studio, Bethnal Green Training Centre
Hanbury Street, London
E1 5HZ
T 020 73750441
F 020 73750484
E info@alternativearts.co.uk
W www.alternativearts.co.uk
Contact Maggie Pinhorn

Founded in 1971 to invest in new artists and ideas and to make the arts accessible to the public. Produces a wide range of arts events including exhibitions, festivals, dance, music, poetry, mime, theatre, fashion, photography and literature.
Admissions Policy Only invites submissions when necessary.

Anne Peaker Centre for Arts in Criminal Justice (Unit for the Arts and Offenders)

Neville House, 90–91 Northgate, Canterbury
CT1 1BA
T 01227 470629
F 01227 379704
E info@a4offenders.org.uk
W www.apcentre.org.uk
Contact Carol Clewlow

Set up by Anne Peaker and Dr Jill Vincent in 1992 as part of the Centre for Research in Social Policy at Loughborough University. Based in Canterbury since 2000. Supports the development of the arts within criminal-justice settings. Currently its work falls within the following broad objectives: to influence policy; to promote the value of the arts; to provide clear, up-to-date information, advice and support to all those interested or involved in this field of work; to develop a national framework for continuous professional development for artists working or wishing to work in criminal-justice settings; and to put the organization's knowledge and expertise at the service of the sector.

Art and Spirituality Network

c/o 48 Kenilworth Avenue, London
SW19 7LW
E artandspirituality@gmail.com

A small self-run network of artists and non-artists which provides a supportive and challenging space for people to find spiritual fellowship and nourishment through making art. Workshops aim to bring spiritual refreshment and companionship as well as fostering inspiration and creativity and are open to active artists and those of no artistic experience. Welcomes those of all faiths and none, drawing on a variety of wisdom and faith traditions and on the wider world. Occasional electronic

newsletter publicizes events and news.
Subscription rates Free (small donations welcome).

Art Connections
The Art Depot, Asquith Industrial Estate
Eshton Road, Gargrave, Skipton, BD23 3SE
T 01756 748529
F 01756 749934
E info@art-connections.org.uk
W www.art-connections.org.uk
A project initiated and managed by Chrysalis Arts
Ltd, developing and supporting creative businesses
in the visual arts, crafts and public art sectors in
North Yorkshire. Offers professional artists and
makers information, advice, training and
marketing support services. Also coordinates a
county-wide open-studio programme.
Admissions Policy Services only available to
professional North Yorkshire-based artists and
makers.

The Art House
Wakefield College, Thornes Park Campus
Wakefield, WF2 8QZ
T 01924 377740
F 01924 377090
E info@the-arthouse.org.uk
W www.the-arthouse.org.uk
Contact Helen Darlington (Artists Officer)
A national visual arts organization established to
create equality of opportunity for disabled and
non-disabled artists and craftspeople. Founded in
1994 by a group of visual artists, it is an inclusive
organization that believes in enabling all artists to
have access to work, training and exhibition
opportunities in accessible settings. After 10 years
of planning and fundraising the organization is
now in the process of building a fully accesible
visual arts centre in Wakefield. The Art House
building will provide studio space, accomodation
for artists and their carers and project space. It is
due to open in 2008.
Admissions Policy Visual artists and craftspeople
with and without disabilities.
Subscription rates All fees annual: £15 or £7.50
(concessions) per person; £32.50 for group
membership; £20 for two persons in the same
household.

Art in Partnership
34 Blair Street, Edinburgh, EH1 1QR
T 0131 2254463
F 0131 2256879

E info@art-in-partnership.org.uk
W www.art-in-partnership.org.uk
Contact Lesley Woodbridge
An independent visual arts consultancy and public
art-commissioning agency. Provides an advisory,
curatorial and project-management service for
architects, planners, urban designers and public-
and private-sector organizations considering
commissioning works of art or developing a
collection.
Admissions Policy Send current CV and
documentation of work, e.g.CD, DVD or
slides/publications

Art in Perpetuity Trust (APT)
6 Creekside, Deptford, London
SE8 4SA
T 020 86948344
F 020 86948344
E aptlondon@btconnect.com
W www.aptstudios.org
Contact Liz May
APT encourages participation in the visual arts
through creative practice, exhibitions and
education.
Admissions Policy Supports thirty-seven fine-art
studios. Prospective artists should check the
website for availability.

Art Safari
46 Victoria Road, Woodbridge
IP12 1EJ
T 01394 382235
E info@artsafari.co.uk
W www.artsafari.co.uk
Contact Mary-Anne Bartlett
Painting holidays in Africa offer opportunity to
paint and sketch the wildlife and landscapes of
Kenya, Malawi, Zambia and Namibia. The tours
are based in national parks and areas of
outstanding natural beauty as well as giving
insight into African village life and natural
creativity. Visits to arts centres for carving, textiles,
painting and ceramics. Founded in 2003 by travel
artist Mary-Anne Bartlett.
Admissions Policy Open to artists of all standards.
Bursaries available to professional artists on
application. Opportunities to work alongside
artists from the host country.

Artists' Network Bedfordshire
37 Station Road, Flitwick, Bedfordshire
MK45 1JT
T 01525 714943

E karen.cameron@artsnetbeds.org.uk
W www.artsnetbeds.org.uk
Contact Karen Cameron
Founded in 1995 to promote the visual arts in the
county. A voluntary artist-led organization
promoting exhibitions and studio events. An open
studio event is held every year in September over
three weekends, during which artists open their
houses and studios to the public for free.
Admissions Policy Membership of the network is
open to artists living or working in Bedfordshire.
Selection procedure by committee.
Subscription rates £35 showing member; £15
student member; £15 associate member.

Artpoint

2 Littlegate Street, Oxford, OX1 1QT
T 01865 248822
F 01865 248899
E kevin.wilson@artpoint-trust.org.uk
W www.artpoint-trust.org.uk
Contact Kevin Wilson (Director)
Works with artists to support new thinking and
practice for the built environment and public space
across the South East region. Operates as a 'not for
profit' limited company with charitable status. In
the past five years has delivered over sixty projects,
worth over £5 million. Offers specific project
management skills and works on small to multi-
million pound developments. Aims to advocate for,
and establish, opportunities for artists to create
new work within public contexts. This includes
public art commissioning, consultancy, research
projects, audience engagement activities and
education programmes.
Admissions Policy Artists are welcome to submit
their website, CV or contact details.

Arts & Business

Nutmeg House, 60 Gainsford Street
Butler's Wharf, London, SE1 2NY
T 020 73788143
F 020 74077527
E head.office@aandb.org.uk
W www.aandb.org.uk
A creative network that seeks to help business
people support the arts and the arts to inspire
business people. Fosters long-term partnerships
between business and the arts through an
investment programme, New Partners. Runs a
series of professional-development programmes,
which promote the exchange and development of
skills between the two communities. In association
with the Prince of Wales Arts & Kids Foundation, it

helps businesses develop practical ways of helping
children engage with the arts. Also offers advice,
training, networking and consultancy on a wide
range of issues to business and the arts through a
membership programme.

Arts Catalyst

Toynbee Studios, 28 Commercial Street
London, E1 6LS
T 020 73753690
F 020 73770298
E info@artscatalyst.org
W www.artscatalyst.org
Established for over ten years with a mission to
extend, promote and activate a fundamental shift
in the dialogue between art and science and its
perception by the public. Facilitates collaborative
art-science projects, expanding new territories for
artistic practice and setting up multidisciplinary
research laboratories. Particular current concerns
focus on artists' engagement (practical, artistic,
political) with biotechnology, ecology, space
research, micro- and hyper-gravity research,
astrophysics, biodynamics, and remote
independent research in science, art and tactile
media.

Arts Education Development

16a Broad Street, Bath, BA1 5LJ
T 01225 396425
E penny_hay@bathnes.gov.uk
W www.bathnes.gov/arts
Contact Penny Hay
Runs several major research projects in creative
education: 5x5x5=Creativity, researching creative
learning and teaching strategies in the early years
and primary education; Creative Education for
Disaffected and Excluded Students (CEDES),
researching creative learning and teaching
strategies to engage disaffected and excluded
students, and those at risk of disaffection and
exclusion; The Learning Centre (TLC), academic
research into creative learning and teaching
strategies, including teacher training. Also offers
professional-development courses for teachers to
support arts coordination and creative learning
and teaching strategies.
Admissions Policy Open to artists in education.

Arts Project

Northgate Hospital, Morpeth, NE61 3BP
T 01670 394174
E Brian.Scott@nap.nhs.uk
Contact Brian Scott

Operating since 1982. Runs a programme of participatory arts workshops where visual artists, musicians, etc. work primarily with people with learning disabilities. Though based at Northgate Hospital, workshops also take place in community venues throughout the region. Special ad hoc projects offer occasional opportunities for commissioned work.

Admissions Policy Keen to hear from artists of all disciplines who might be able to work in this demanding field.

ARTS UK
71 Westmacott Street, Newburn
Newcastle-upon-Tyne, NE15 8NA
T 0191 2646686
F 0191 2646686
E email@arts-uk.com
W www.arts-uk.com
Contact Steve Chettle
Set up in 2000 as an arts organization to provide commissioning and other services to private, public and voluntary sectors. Specializes in public art commissions.

Admissions Policy Artists interested in being considered for the database should submit a CV and CD of images.

Association of Illustrators
2nd Floor Back Building
150 Curtain Road, London, EC2A 3AT
T 020 76134328
F 020 76134417
E info@theaoi.com
W www.theaoi.com
Contact Derek Brazell
Established in 1973 to promote illustration, advance and protect illustrators' rights and encourage professional standards. A non-profit-making trade association dedicated to its members' professional interests. Membership consists of freelance illustrators as well as agents, clients, students and universities.

Admissions Policy Full members must supply three printed illustrations produced within the last year. Associate membership is for those yet to be commissioned.

Subscription rates £24 joining fee plus: £126 for full members; £100 for associate members; £45 for student members; £185 for corporate members; £96 for college members.

Aune Head Arts
High Moorland Business Centre, Old Duchy

Hotel, Princetown, Yelverton, PL20 6QF
T 01822 890539
F 01822 890539
E info@auneheadarts.org.uk
W www.auneheadarts.org.uk
Contact Nancy Sinclair
A rural-centric arts organization based on Dartmoor. Works with artists and audiences to bring new work to diverse audiences. Aims to: develop projects utilizing traditional and new technologies; engage communities and audiences in aesthetic reflection and debate on issues of rural life; collaborate with organizations engaged in similar work; provide continuing professional development and mentoring to artists within the region; and develop and disseminate models of best practice and innovation for contemporary artists working within a rural context.

Admissions Policy Project artists are generally selected via invitation or a commissioning process. Time permitting, it may review unsolicited project outlines that complement the organization's work.

Subscription rates Membership fees range from £5 to £10; artists need not be members to be involved in projects.

Autograph ABP
74 Great Eastern Street, London, EC2A 3JG
T 020 77299200
E info@auto.demon.co.uk
W www.autograph-abp.co.uk
A non-profit photographic arts organization established in 1988. Primary role is to develop, exhibit and publish the work of photographers and artists from culturally diverse backgrounds and to act as an advocate for their inclusion in all mainstream areas of exhibition, publishing, training, education and commerce. To this end, it produces its own programme of activities, exhibitions, events, residencies, publications, etc. and collaborates with other arts organizations nationally and internationally.

Admissions Policy Email up to 12 jpegs of work (each 100KB or less) plus CV and artist's statement.

Axis
Round Foundry Media Centre, Foundry Street,
Leeds, LS11 5QP
T 0870 4430701
F 0870 4430703
E info@axisweb.org
W www.axisweb.org
Organization which administers a leading online

guide to artists practising in the UK today. Champions the work of artists by presenting authoritative information about their practice (web links, biographies, images, video and audio clips), enabling artists to profile their work to an expanding audience. Also collaborates with a network of advisors (artists, curators, commissioners, academics and visual arts writers) to inform content on the website. The only artist directory funded by Arts Council England, the Arts Council of Wales and the Scottish Arts Council.
Admissions Policy Encourages applications from practising artists living and working in the UK and who demonstrate a critical engagement with contemporary practice.
Subscription rates £20

Bath Area Network for Artists (BANA)
The Old Malthouse, Comfortable Place, Bath BA1 3AJ
T 01225 471714
E enquiries@bana-arts.co.uk
W www.bana-arts.co.uk
Contact Administrator
An artist-led network established in 1998 to address the needs of the large number of visual artists based in Bath and surrounding areas. It is a non-selective, membership-led organization for artists with a commitment to professional practice. Aims to raise the profile of visual arts activity in the Bath area, establish and strengthen links between artists, artists' groups and art promoters, and advocates increased investment in local arts activities. Members' benefits include a website, newsletter, professional-development opportunities and regular events.
Admissions Policy Membership open to visual artists living or working in the south-west region, particularly Bath and North East Somerset.
Subscription rates £18 for individuals; £54 for groups; £12 for full time students/within one year of graduation. Membership including public liability insurance for artists is also available.

Birmingham Artists
Unit 19, Lee Bank Business Centre
55 Holloway Head, Birmingham, B1 1HP
T 0121 6436040
E info@birminghamartists.com
W www.birminghamartists.com
Contact Pamina Stewart
Founded in 1987 and formerly known as Birmingham Art Trust. Committed to the development of its programme. Uses reclaimed

sites and site-specific venues as alternative gallery spaces, and has organized several large-scale international exhibitions, members' shows and open-studio events. 2004 saw the launch of the Periscope project space. 'The Window' is a members' project that exhibits a wide range of artists and projects throughout the year and mentors emerging artists. Studio space costs from £2.50 per sq. ft per year.
Subscription rates £20

Blood
W www.bloodarts.org
Established in 2002, offering art lovers and emerging collectors an insight into the world of contemporary art through tours and talks around London. Now an events-based membership club under the aegis of the Contemporary Art Society. Monthly events are tailored to highlight the diversity of contemporary art practice.

Bonhoga Gallery
Weisdale Mill, Weisdale, Shetland, ZE2 9LW
T 01595 830400
F 01595 830444
E bonhoga-gallery@shetland-arts-trust.co.uk
The visual arts arm of Shetland Arts Trust, which celebrated its 10th anniversary in 2004. Open year-round showing local, national and international exhibitions of art and craft. Has a touring exhibition programme to five satellite venues throughout Shetland, runs an education and outreach programme, community workshops and a successful residency programme at The Booth in the nearby village of Scalloway. Housed in an old converted mill and about 20 minutes to the west of Lerwick, the main town in Shetland. The Booth is available to rent for £250 per month.

British Academy
10 Carlton House Terrace, London, SW1Y 5AH
T 020 79695200
F 020 79695300
E secretary@britac.ac.uk
W www.britac.ac.uk
The national academy for the humanities and the social sciences, established by Royal Charter in 1902. An independent and self-governing fellowship of scholars, elected for distinction and achievement in one or more branches of the academic disciplines that make up the humanities and social sciences, organized in eighteen sections by academic discipline.
Admissions Policy There are Ordinary Fellows,

Senior Fellows (over the age of 70), overseas Corresponding Fellows and Honorary Fellows (whose numbers are limited to twenty). Up to thirty-five new Ordinary Fellows may be elected in any one year.

British Association of Art Therapists (BAAT)

24–27 White Lion Street, London, N1 9PD
T 020 7686 4216
E info@baat.org
W www.baat.org
The professional organization for art therapists in the UK, formed in 1964. Maintains a comprehensive directory of qualified art therapists and works to promote art therapy in the UK.

British Society of Master Glass Painters

6 Queen Square, London, WC1N 3AR
T 01643 862807
E secretary@bsmgp.org.uk
W www.bsmgp.org.uk
Contact Chris Wyard
Founded in 1926. A society for individuals involved in the production of stained and painted glass and other glass treatments (etching, sandblasting, fusing, etc.), both traditional leaded methods and non-leaded, for religious and secular public buildings or private commissions. Members also involved in research, history, recording, photography and sale of glass.
Subscription rates £30 per year. Concessions: £15 for students; £18 for seniors.

Bureau of Freelance Photographers

Focus House, 497 Green Lanes, London, N13 4BP
T 020 8882 3315
F 020 8886 3933
E mail@thebfp.com
W www.thebfp.com
Contact Angela Kidd
Founded in 1965, aiming to help freelance and aspiring freelance photographers to sell their work. Publishes a monthly Market Newsletter for members and an annual Freelance Photographer's Market Handbook. Members also have access to advice and mediation services.
Admissions Policy Membership open to anyone interested in freelance photography.
Subscription rates £49 per annum UK; £65 per annum overseas.

Cambridge Open Studios

12A High Street, Fulbourn, Cambridge, CB21 5DH
T 01223 561192
E info@cambridgeopenstudios.co.uk
W www.cambridgeopenstudios.co.uk
Contact Jane Gaskell (Administrator)
Exists to promote the making of original works of art and craft and to provide an opportunity for the public to become involved by meeting artists in their studios, seeing their work and how it is produced. Started with six artists in 1974 and by 2004 had three hundred.
Admissions Policy Must be makers or designers of original works of art or craft and live and/or have a studio in Cambridgeshire.
Subscription rates 2007 fees: £25 membership fee; £15 joining fee for new or lapsed members; £132 participation fee; £50 non-volunteer fee.

Candid Arts Trust

3 Torrens Street, Angel Islington, London, EC1V 1NQ
T 020 78374237
F 020 78374123
E info@candidarts.com
W www.candidarts.com
Founded in 1980. A thriving arts centre consisting of three galleries (6,000 sq. ft in total), a café and artists' studios, all available for hire. As a self-funded charity, the trust aims to promote the arts, with an emphasis on newly graduated artists and designers through a marketing package providing exhibition space and artist websites, and acting as an agent for sales and commissions. Also runs the Islington Contemporary Art & Design Fair, regular artists' screenings/film events and life-drawing and painting classes.
Admissions Policy Entry requirements for Network AD (Candid's graduate marketing package): a BA or MA certificate; all media and areas are accepted. Welcomes submissions for exhibitions from artists generally.
Subscription rates £60 for annual subscription to Network AD.

Chelsea Arts Club

143 Old Church Street, London, SW3 6EB
T 020 73763311
E secretary@chelseaartsclub.com
W www.chelseaartsclub.com
Contact Dudley Winterbottom
A hundred-year-old members' club for painters, sculptors, architects, designers, photographers and craftsmen. With dining room, bar, garden and thirteen bedrooms (from £38 a night), based in central London.
Admissions Policy Proposer and seconder required. Election by committee.

Chrysalis Arts Ltd

The Art Depot, Asquith Industrial Estate
Eshton Road, Gargrave, BD23 3SE
T 01756 749222
F 01756 749934
E chrysalis@artdepot.org.uk
W www.chrysalisarts.org.uk
An artist-led company that has been creating art in
public spaces since 1987. Besides working in close
collaboration with architects, landscape architects,
planners and developers, Chrysalis has pioneered
techniques for facilitating community involvement
in public art. In 1997, the company built the Art
Depot as its base and established an international
training centre where artists and others involved in
work in public spaces come to learn and work
together.
Admissions Policy Does not have the capacity to
respond to unsolicited applications. See the
website for training opportunities, etc.

Community Arts Forum

5 Church Street, Belfast, BT1 1PG
T 028 90242910
F 028 9031264
W www.community-arts-forum.org
Founded at a meeting of community arts activists
in Belfast in 1993. A membership-based
organization that elects a fifteen-person executive
annually. Currently has over three hundred groups
and over 150 individual artists affiliated,
representing all sections of society in Northern
Ireland and all areas, and whose activities cover all
art forms. Has been at the forefront of the growth
of community arts activity in Northern Ireland
over the last ten years.

Contemporary Art Society

Bloomsbury House
74–77 Great Russell Street
London
WC1B 3DA
T 020 76120730
F 020 76314230
E cas@contempart.org.uk
W www.contempart.org.uk
Founded in 1910. Promotes the collection of
contemporary arts through gifts to public galleries
and guidance to individuals and companies.
Subscription rates £22.50 including VAT for
students; £45 (£40 by direct debit) including VAT
for individuals; £50 (£45 by direct debit) including
VAT for joint membership shared by two people at
the same address.

Contemporary Art Society for Wales – Cymdeithas Gelfydoyd Gyfoes Cymru

1 Court Cottages, St Fagans, Cardiff, CF5 6EN
T 029 20595206
E seccasw@tiscali.co.uk
Founded in 1937. Supports the contemporary
visual-art scene in Wales by: annual art-work
purchases for gifting to Welsh museums, art
galleries and other public institutions; studentship
awards; awards to other arts bodies; an annual
national Eisteddfod purchase prize; publication
awards; lectures and study visits (including
abroad); exhibitions.
Subscription rates £4 for students; £24 for single
membership; £35 for double membership.

Contemporary Glass Society

c/o Broadfield House Glass Museum
Compton Drive, Kingswinford, DY6 9NS
T 01603 507737
F 01603 507737
E admin@cgs.org.uk
W www.cgs.org.uk
Founded in 1997 with the dual objectives of
encouraging excellence in glass as a creative
medium and developing a greater awareness and
appreciation of contemporary glass worldwide.
Admissions Policy Membership is open to anyone
interested in contemporary glass.
Subscription rates £30 for professional members;
£20 for concessions; £80 for corporate members.

Crafts Council

44a Pentonville Road, Islington, London, N1 9BY
T 020 72787700
F 020 78376891
E reference@craftscouncil.org.uk
W www.craftscouncil.org.uk
The UK development agency for contemporary
crafts. An independent organization, funded by
Arts Council England, that offers a range of services
to makers and the public. London base includes an
exhibition space, shop, reference library, the
National Register of Makers, and Photostore, an
online visual database of selected makers.

Create

10–11 Earl St South, Dublin 8
T 01 4736600
F 01 4736599
E info@create-ireland.ie
W www.create-ireland.ie
Contact Katherine Atkinson
(support@artsincontext.com)

Established in 1983, a national development agency for collaborative arts providing services for arts development and practice in Ireland. Services are designed to support arts practitioners and arts organizations irrespective of their area of practice or arts programme.

Admissions Policy Particularly welcomes applications from practitioners involved in collaborative arts.

Subscription rates Membership rates: €30 for individuals and €60 for organizations.

Creative Learning Agency

Abbey Chambers, Kingston Buildings, Off York Street, Bath, BA1 1LT

T 01225 396 392

F 01225 396 442

E info@creativelearningagency.org.uk

W www.creativelearningagency.org.uk

Contact Donna Baber

An arts education agency which was established in 2001. The agency works to broker partnerships between artists, teachers, educators and arts organizations through its core service, a website and increasingly through one-to-one support for funding, continuing professional development, the Artsmark scheme and specialist arts colleges. The agency works across all artforms, age ranges and abilities. It undertakes activity across four local authorities: Bath and North East Somerset, Bristol, North Somerset and South Gloucestershire.

Admissions Policy Current enhanced disclosure from the criminal records bureau, evidence of three creative learning projects in last two years, plus two referees.

Subscription rates Free to join the database.

Creative Partnerships

T 0845 3006200

E info@artscouncil.org.uk

Provides schoolchildren across England with the opportunity to develop creativity in learning and to take part in high-quality cultural activities. Helps schools to identify individual needs and enables them to develop long-term, sustainable partnerships with organizations and individuals including architects, theatre companies, museums, cinemas, historic buildings, dance studios, recording studios, orchestras, filmmakers and web designers.

CreativeCapital

3 Wilkes Street, London, E1 6QF

T 020 73752973

E info@creative-capital.org.uk

W www.creative-capital.org.uk

Promotes professional development for artists and arts practitioners who live and work in London. A network of arts organizations giving expert advice to people looking for career development and information on training, learning and other relevant services and resources in London. Website and ebulletin offer up-to-date details of events and opportunities.

Cultural Co-operation

Seconf Floor, 334–336 Goswell Road London, EC1V 7LQ

T 020 7841 0506

F 020 74560401

E ldc@culturalco-operation.org

W www.culturalco-operation.org

Contact Polly Betton

An independent arts charity that promotes international and intercultural understanding through the arts. Established in 1987, its programme includes the summer Music Village, London Diaspora Capital (an internet-based resource that raises the profile of artists from London's diverse communities), a year-round education programme for schools, regular continuing professional development for artists and a number of related projects.

Admissions Policy Welcomes contact from artists from London's diverse national and faith communities for possible inclusion on its web database.

Design and Artists Copyright Society (DACS)

33 Great Sutton Street, London, EC1V 0DX

T 020 73368811

F 020 73368822

E info@dacs.org.uk

W www.dacs.org.uk

Contact Janet Tod

Established in 1984. A not-for-profit organization promoting and protecting the copyright and related rights of artists and visual artists in the UK and worldwide. Represents 52,000 artists and their heirs, comprising 36,000 fine artists and 16,000 photographers, illustrators, craftspeople, cartoonists, architects, animators and designers.

Admissions Policy Membership is open to any visual creator.

Design Council

34 Bow Street, London, WC2E 7DL

T 020 74205200

F 020 74205300
E info@designcouncil.org.uk
W www.designcouncil.org.uk
Seeks to demonstrate and promote the role of design in a modern economy.
Admissions Policy Does not welcome submissions from artists.

Devon Guild of Craftsmen

Riverside Mill, Bovey Tracey, TQ13 9AF
T 01626 832223
F 01626 834220
E devonguild@crafts.org.uk
W www.crafts.org.uk
Contact Saffron Wynne (Exhibitions Officer)
The largest contemporary crafts venue in the south-west, representing over 240 makers across the range of craft disciplines. A focus on craft culture for the region, including commissioning, education, professional development, workshops and lectures. Contact for free mailing.
Admissions Policy Members and makers living in the south-west are welcome to apply. Benefits include retail sales, exhibition and marketing opportunities.
Subscription rates £92.50 for full members (associate rate also available).

East Street Arts (ESA)

Patrick Studios, St Mary's Lane, Leeds, LS9 7EH
T 0113 2480040
F 0113 2480030
E info@esaweb.org.uk
W www.esaweb.org.uk
Contact Lara Eggleton
Founded in 1993 by two artists and now governed by board of directors/trustees. Promotes visual artists' career development through events and by offering high-quality, well-managed studios and facilities on two sites. Artists' support includes professional development programmes and training sessions tailored to artists' needs. Annual cost of studio space: £9 per sq. ft for Patrick Studios (in city centre); £5.50 per sq. ft for Beaver Studios.

Empowering the Artist (ETA)

11 Markwick Terrace, St Leonards-on-Sea
TN38 0RE
T 01424 461232
F 01424 461232
E info@eta-art.co.uk
W www.eta-art.co.uk
Contact Deborah Rawson (Director)

Established as a limited company in 1998 and now a leading provider of professional-development opportunities for visual artists in the south-east region of England. One of a network of providers of short courses and mentoring schemes for artists at different stages of their careers.
Admissions Policy Any artist can book on the training programme. Access to the mentoring schemes is by application.

Enable Artists

Wayside Cottage, Ffordd Walwen, Lixwm, CH8 8LU
E enableartists@aol.com
W www.enableartists.com
Contact Catherine Taylor Parry (north) or Alice Dass (south)
Started in 2001 to give artists with multiple sclerosis (MS) the opportunity to show their work in a virtual gallery and to exhibit together.
Admissions Policy Artists with MS are welcome to apply, as well as other disabled artists who are interested in showing their work in a group. Artists who would like to be involved in finding and organizing exhibition spaces are particularly welcome. Membership from throughout the UK.
Subscription rates £10 pa for website and postage.

engage – National Association for Gallery Education

Basement, 108 Old Brompton Road, London
SW7 3RA
T 020 72440110
F 020 73737223
E info@engage.org
W www.engage.org
An international association for gallery educators, artist educators and other arts and education professionals. Promotes access to the visual arts through 'gallery education', i.e. projects and programmes that help schoolchildren and the wider community become confident in their understanding and enjoyment of galleries and the visual arts.
Subscription rates From £32.50 for annual membership.

Enterprise Centre for the Creative Arts (ECCA)

London College of Communication
University of the Arts London, Elephant & Castle,
London, SE1 6SB
F info@ecca-london.org
E info@ecca-london.org
W www.ecca-london.org
ECCA (Enterprise Centre for the Creative Arts)

offers one-to-one advice on setting up and running your own business including: assistance with funding / sponsorship proposals, business planning, financial guidance, selling and promotion, and project-, business- and self-management.

Admissions Policy Does not accept submissions but when attending a session with a specialist creative-industry business adviser, it is recommended to bring along any relevant materials such as a portfolio, CV, cards, brochures etc.

Euroart Studios

Unit 22F, 784/788 High Road, Tottenham London, N17 0DA
T 07802 502136
E studios@euroart.co.uk
W www.euroart.co.uk
Contact Nigel Young

A not-for-profit organization providing affordable studio spaces and opportunities for artists and makers. Established in 2002 in an old rag-trade factory by professional artist/curator Lorraine Clarke and space projects quality engineer Nigel Young. Now a complex of 43 studios of various sizes, hosting some 50 artists/creative businesses who are recipient to various business support services, organization of annual open studios events, off-site exhibitions, provision of information on business and network opportunities, and business mentoring. Pro-actively managed, Euroart promotes the work of its resident artists/creative businesses. Studio spaces from £95 to £550 per month.

Admissions Policy Send CV and images of work via email.

European Council of Artists (ECA)

Borgergade 111, DK-1300 Copenhagen, Denmark
DK-1300 Denmark
T +45 35384401 / +45 35384417
E eca@eca.dk
W www.eca.dk
Contact Elisabet Diedrichs

An umbrella for national, interdisciplinary artists' councils and artists' organizations, currently in twenty-five European countries. Aims to safeguard the political and cultural position of the arts and artists in Europe and works for the interests of the professional artists in political, economic, judicial and social contexts.

Admissions Policy ECA is an organization of artists' organizations. Single artists cannot be members.

Fabrica

40 Duke Street, Brighton, BN1 1AG
T 01273 778646
F 01273 778646
E info@fabrica.org.uk
W www.fabrica.org.uk
Contact Lisa Maddigan

An educational charity with a gallery committed to promoting understanding of contemporary visual art and craft. Opened in 1996 in the defunct Holy Trinity Church in the heart of Brighton. Development was led by a group of artists from Red Herring Studios in Hove. Produces four main exhibition projects a year, in contemporary craft, materials-based installation, lens-based media and digital/interactive art. The Artist Resource, a free information centre for artists, is situated at Fabrica.

Admissions Policy Commissions site-specific work. Contact the gallery for more information.

Federation of British Artists (FBA)

17 Carlton House Terrace, London, SW1Y 5BD
T 020 79306844
F 020 78397830
E info@mallgalleries.com
W www.mallgalleries.org.uk

A registered charity and umbrella organization for nine leading art societies. Aims to be the national focal point for contemporary art with timeless values. Has 614 artist-members and over 10,000 artists who submit to open shows. FBA member societies are the Royal Institute of Painters in Watercolours, the Royal Society of British Artists, the Royal Society of Marine Artists, the Royal Society of Portrait Painters, the Royal Institute of Oil Painters, the New English Art Club, the Pastel Society, the Society of Wildlife Artists and the Hesketh Hubbard Art Society.

Admissions Policy Submissions should be made to individual member societies (see above).

Figurative Artist Network (FAN)

Unit 112, 62 Tritton Road, West Norwood London, SE21 8DE
T 020 87613443
E figurativeFAN@aol.com
W www.steveyeates.co.uk

An artist-led network set up with the aim of fighting the idea that figurative art is an outdated art form. Seeks to bring together artists who share the same aspirations to encourage and support, discuss and inspire the promotion of innovative work in contemporary culture. Holds group sessions and encourages the practice and making of figurative art with a view to setting up a collaborative exhibition.

Forma Arts & Media
P.O. Box 637, Newcastle-upon-Tyne, NE99 1JF
T 0191 2304646
F 0191 2306355
E info@forma.org.uk
W www.forma.org.uk
Contact David Metcalfe
One of Europe's leading agencies for interdisciplinary art. Pioneers new projects with artists internationally. Generates, tours and publishes high-quality work, creating dialogues between artists, audiences and places.

Foundation for Women's Art (FWA)
55–63 Goswell Road, London, EC1V 7EN
T 020 72514881
E admin@fwa-uk.org
W www.fwa-uk.org
Contact Monica Petzal Director
A networking, adminstrative and educational organization that has as its core activity the promotion of women artists through exhibitions, events and an education programme. The website is a prime UK source of informaton about and of interest to women artists.
Admissions Policy Send all proposals to office.
Subscription rates Details of Friends scheme on the website.

GLOSS
Colwell Arts Centre, Derby Road, Gloucester GL1 4AD
T 01452 550439
F 01452 550539
E gloss@gloss-aie.co.uk
W www.gloss-artsineducation.co.uk
Gloucestershire's arts education agency. Aims to provide opportunities for children, their carers and teachers to engage with a wide range of quality creative activity. It does this by providing advice, support and information to schools, youth groups, artists and arts organizations. Produces a termly magazine for teachers and artists. Contact the agency to be added to the mailing list.
Admissions Policy See website to register on online artists' database.

Greenwich Mural Workshop
MacBean Centre, MacBean Street, Woolwich London, SE18 6LW

T 020 88549266
F 020 83167577
E steve@greenwichmuralworkshop.com
W www.greenwichmuralworkshop.com
Contact Steve Lobb
Founded in 1975. An artists' cooperative specializing in the design and manufacture of murals, mosaics, banners and in the design and creation of urban parks, gardens and playgrounds. The group works with local authorities, businesses and community groups and has a strong reputation for its collaborative works.
Admissions Policy Artists experienced in drawing and design and interested in working with a variety of clients should send CV, letter and pictures.

Grizedale Arts
Grizedale, Ambleside, LA22 0QJ
T 01229 860291
F 01229 860050
E info@grizedale.org
W www.grizedale.org
Contact Adam Sutherland or Alistair Hudson
An international research and development agency for visual artists based in the Lake District National Park. The programme supports artists in making new works that relate to the context of the area, engaging with local communities and events, integrating artists' thinking and communication into mainstream and traditional activities. The emphasis is on developing new approaches to working and the dissemination of generated ideas. Up to ten research and development grants are awarded annually, to develop projects that may feed into an annual programme of activity. Grizedale Arts was reconstituted in 2001 as a successor to the previous residency programme sited in Grizedale Forest.

Group 75
Tyddyn Squire, Bersham, Wrexham, LL14 4LU
T 01978 757513
F 01978 757513
E m.tietze@btinternet.com
W www.group75.co.uk
Contact Margaret Tietze
A group of professional artists formed in 1975 by Margaret Tietze. Membership has varied over time; currently ten members, of whom seven live in Wales. Work is in mixed media and exhibitions are toured nationally and internationally with guest artists invited to contribute.
Admissions Policy Artists are invited to join only on recommendation of group members. A balance of media and skills is the criterion.

Guild of Aviation Artists

Trenchard House, 85 Farnborough Road,
Farnborough, GU14 6TF
T 01252 513123
F 01252 510505
E admin@gava.org.uk
W www.gava.org.uk
Contact Susan Gardner
Founded in 1971. Aims to promote, foster and
encourage all forms of aviation art by providing a
forum for discussion of ideas between members
through exhibitions, meetings and workshops.
Holds an annual summer exhibition at the Mall
Galleries in London, as well as regional
exhibitions.
Admissions Policy Aviation art in any hand-
applied medium. Computer-generated or
enhanced work excluded.
Subscription rates Entry membership as a Friend
(artists and non-artists) £25 pa. Membership rates
vary according to status.

Guild of Glass Engravers

87 Nether Street, London, N12 7NP
T 020 84464050
F 020 84464050
E enquiries@gge.org.uk
W www.gge.org.uk
Contact Christine Reyland
Founded in 1975 by a small group of British
engravers. The primary aims are to promote the
highest standards of creative design and
craftsmanship in glass engraving, and to act as a
forum for the teaching and discussion of
engraving techniques.
Admissions Policy Membership is worldwide and
open to anyone interested in engraved glass. The
guild welcomes new members, who may or may
not practise engraving. There is a system of
assessment and election within the guild for
practising engravers.
Subscription rates £30 for UK lay members.

here nor there

E info@herenorthere.org
W www.herenorthere.org
Founded in 1998 to facilitate international
collaborations in digital-media and audiovisual
performances and events. Projects are developed
through directly participating in international
residencies, events and exhibitions. Utilizes
internet technology as a resource and as an arena
for project development and creative collaboration.
Admissions Policy Artists are approached through

invitation or project-based calls for submissions
made via the website.

Hesketh Hubbard Drawing Society

Federation of British Artists, 17 Carlton House
Terrace, London, SE5 9AX
E info@mallgalleries.com
Runs regular life drawing sessions at the Mall
Galleries. Three models pose, two life and one
portrait, with a choice of short or long poses.
Although not tutored, participants learn from the
company of fellow artists.
Admissions Policy Membership is by annual
subscription. A free taster session is offered.
Subscription rates £180 per year.

Independent Art School (IAS)

E editor@independent-art-school.org.uk
W www.independent-art-school.org.uk
Contact Pippa Koszerek
An artist-run project set up in 1999, functioning
as a nomadic university. Its online journal contains
writings from past conferences and events. Has
developed as an artistic concept whereby different
artists can take it on.
Admissions Policy Welcomes emails from artists
or organizations wishing to collaborate.

Independent Artists Network (IAN)

23 North Road, Wells
BA52 TL
T 07966 133901 (D.Cameron) / 07775 938500
(C.Black)
E info@independentartists.org.uk
W www.independentartists.org.uk
Contact Duncan Cameron or Carolyn Black
Founded in 1999 by a number of independent
artists in Bristol. Began as a group wishing to
generate new opportunities for exhibiting in the
region. Commissions temporary public art works
on a project basis, both in Bristol and beyond.

Indigo Arts

9 Cole Road, Aylesbury
HP21 8SU
T 01296 423795
F 01296 392404
E antonia@glynnejones.freeserve.co.uk
Contact Antonia Glynne Jones
A group of artists originally founded by the painter
Oliver Bevan. There is no house style but a
commitment to making intense, evocative images,
whether figurative, abstract or poetic in paint,
collage, assemblage and print or drawing media.

Institute of Art & Law
1–5 Cank Street, Leicester
LE1 5GX
T 0116 2538888
F 0116 2511666
E info@ial.uk.com
W www.ial.uk.com
A small independent research and educational
organization founded in 1995 to analyze the
interface between the world of art and antiquities
and that of the law. Main objective is to increase
public knowledge concerning the contribution of
law to the development of cultural tradition.
Organizes seminars and distance-learning
courses, and publishes a quarterly periodical and
several specialist books.

Institute of International Visual Arts (inIVA)
6–8 Standard Place, Rivington Street, London
EC2A 3BE
T 020 77299616
F 020 77299509
E institute@iniva.org
W www.iniva.org
Founded in 1994. Creates exhibitions,
publications, multimedia, education and research
projects designed to bring the work of artists from
culturally diverse backgrounds to the attention of
the widest possible public. Anchored in the
diversity of contemporary British culture and
society, inIVA engages with culturally diverse
practices and ideas, both local and global. Invites
artists and audiences to question assumptions
about contemporary art and ideas, and acts as a
catalyst for making these debates and art works
part of mainstream culture.

Ipswich Art Society
Upland, 31 Upland Road, Ipswich, IP4 5BT
T 01473 717521
E enquiries@ipswich-art-society.org.uk
W www.ipswich-art-society.org.uk
Contact Jacqueline Marks
Founded in 1874. Deals with paint, print, sculpture
and mixed media. Administers an annual open
each May and June, the Anna Airey Award (to
young artists aged 16 to 25 and to a mature
student) and an exhibition held in February each
year.
Admissions Policy Membership decided by an
election panel who look at sketch books, completed
works, work in progress and statement of aims.
Subscription rates £20 for members; £10 for
Friends.

Ipswich Arts Association
The Town Hall, Ipswich, IP1 1BZ
T 01473 836448
F 01473 836448
E secretary@ipswich-arts.org.uk
W www.ipswich-arts.org.uk
Contact Vera Rogers (Secretary)
Founded in 1984. Supports the work of arts
organizations and individual artists in Ipswich and
Suffolk, with over forty member groups. Provides
opportunities to discuss matters of mutual
concern and acts as a coordinating body for
organizations and individuals. Offers advice and
information on arts locally and promotes and gives
help in presenting events related to arts
organizations. Runs talks and workshops, led by
professional and amateur practitioners. Works
with local authorities and campaigns to secure,
maintain and improve facilities for arts
organizations.

ixia
2nd Floor, 321 Bradford Street
Birmingham, B5 6ET
E info@ixia-info.com
W www.ixia-info.com
A think tank for public art practice. Aims to
provide an independent and objective view of the
factors that affect the quality of artists' work in the
public realm by undertaking research and
enabling debate. Works with artists, policy makers
and delivery organizations within the public and
private sectors. Approach is collaborative ensuring
that partners inform its work. Administers
publications, consultancy, conferences and
training.

Kernow Education Arts Partnership (KEAP)
21b Pydar Street, Truro, TR1 2AY
T 01872 275187
F 01872 275182
E hreynolds@cornwall.gov.uk
W www.keap.org
Contact Helen Reynolds
KEAP is Cornwall's development agency for
promoting creativity and arts in education activity
in learning establishments. Its mission is to
engage the whole community in creative learning
through the arts and delivers this through
providing a brokerage between the arts and
cultural sector and the education sector. It
currently works very closely with Creative
Partnerships Cornwall and plays a significant role
in the development of the local programme and

partnership. KEAP supports various networks, is a lead organization for literature development in the south-west and is developing work in the field of Early Years.

Admissions Policy Email Helen Reynolds for a database form. Info required includes a CV with education experience, references, CRB and PLI details. KEAP is not an artist employment agency but will recommend artists to schools.

Learning Stone Portland Sculpture and Quarry Trust

The Drill Hall, Easton Lane, Portland, DT5 1BW
T 01305 826736
F 01305 826736
E psqt@learningstone.org
W www.learningstone.org
Contact Hannah Sofaer MA (RCA) or Paul Crabtree MA (Ed)

Tout Quarry is the first sculpture quarry in the UK with work constructed and carved into the landscape. One week courses in stone carving/sculpture, starting every Monday from May to October, with professional tuition for beginners and all levels of skill. Visual art and landscape projects at the Drill Hall and Independent Quarry integrate the arts with the stone industry, ecology, geology, architecture and landscape and are a key initiative for the Dorset and East Devon World Heritage Coast. Fully equipped indoor studios for stone-carvers, sculptors and painters with accomodation on site. Large exhibition space and technical support for commissions

Admissions Policy Facilities open to established and emerging artists. Initial email then follow up with telephone call for one-to-one discussion.
Subscription rates £20 per year for Friends scheme offers 10% reduction on courses, a newsletter, an annual Friends exhibition, free lectures and events.

Live Art Development Agency

Rochelle School, Arnold Circus, London, E2 7ES
T 020 70330275
F 020 70330276
E info@thisisliveart.co.uk
W www.thisisliveart.co.uk
Contact Lois Keidan or Daniel Brine

Established in 1999. A leading organization for the support of live art in the UK. Provides practical information and advice, offers opportunities for research, training, dialogue and debate, works in partnership with practitioners and organizations on curatorial initiatives, and develops new ways of increasing popular and critical awareness of live art. The Study Room is a free, open-access research facility used by artists, students, curators and academics and houses one of the largest libraries of live-art-related videos, DVDs and publications in the UK.

Admissions Policy Works exclusively with live art.

London Photographic Association

23 Roehampton Lane, London, SW15 5LS
T 020 83928557
E info@london-photographic-association.com
W www.london-photographic-association.com
Contact Kevin O'Connor

A new association, having grown out of the London Photographic Awards. Membership includes UK and overseas photographers. Aims to give photographers and photography international exposure through an awards structure, online exhibitions, portfolio and essay space, public space exhibitions and relationships with other members of the media, creative and photographic community.

Admissions Policy Visit website for further information.

Luna Nera

Unit 37 Canal Buildings, Shepherdess Walk London, N1 7RR
T 07949 051908
E mail@luna-nera.com
W www.luna-nera.com
Contact Gillian McIver or Valentina Floris

An artist-curator group since 1997. Has created a number of large-scale live-, visual- and media-art events in London and around Europe. Also producing video art live events and screenings. Aims to stimulate interest in the environmental and architectural heritage of localities.

Admissions Policy Interested in strongly site-responsive, collaborative practice only. Does not curate shows for individual artists.

Manchester Academy of Fine Arts

c/o The Portico Library, Mosley Street Manchester, M2 3HY
T 01457 875718
E cliff.moorhouse@btinternet.com
W www.mafa.org.uk
Contact Cliff Moorhouse (Honorary Secretary)

Founded in 1859. Approximately 120 members covering a broad range of media and approaches. Committed to a developing exhibition programme of members' work and the continuation of the north-west of England's major open exhibition. **Admissions Policy** £5 registration fee. Submission of up to six works for consideration by council. References and statement also required. **Subscription rates** £30 per year.

Media Art Bath

16a Broad Street, Bath, BA1 5LJ
T 01225 396479 / 296440
E sally_shaw@bathnes.gov.uk
W www.mediartbath.org.uk
Contact Sally Shaw
Founded in 1999. Specializes in artist commissions in public contexts in relation to new-media technologies. Also provides training and development opportunities, exhibition and production equipment, advice and support. **Admissions Policy** Welcomes intelligent, researched, provocative proposals from artists who have a proven capacity to deliver and produce high-quality work. The artist does not have to have prior experience of new-media technologies.

Midwest

P.O. Box 3641, Kidderminster, DY10 2WP
E info@midwest.org.uk
W www.midwest.org.uk
Contact Jason E. Bowman
Since 2003, Midwest has been working with artists, thinkers and organizations in the UK to develop initiatives that encourage artist-led culture on a global level. Hosts an online catalyst project that supports communication and collaboration in the visual arts at a global level. With free membership to date, it allows artists and interested parties to share information and seeks to support artist-led culture. **Admissions Policy** The Midwest online 'Bugle' accepts submissions of critical writing on artist-led culture. **Subscription rates** Free.

Milton Keynes Society of Artists

16 Chalfont Close, Bradville, Milton Keynes MK13 7HS
T 01908 225290
E katlan@tiscali.co.uk
W www.MKSA.org.uk
Contact Kate East
Founded in 1980. Meets on the last Wednesday of the month at the Meeting Place in Westcroft in Milton Keynes. Meetings consist of demonstrations in all media and a critique.

Members can exhibit four to five times a year with the society. Monthly newsletter sent to enrolled members. **Admissions Policy** Only exhibits original art works. No prints, digital work or photographs. **Subscription rates** £17.50 per year.

Momentum Arts

Bolton's Warehouse, Tenison Road, Cambridge CB1 2DG
T 01223 500202
F 01223 576307
E info@momentumarts.org.uk
W www.momentumarts.org.uk
Works with a range of partners in east England to enable the development of best practice in the arts. Formerly the Eastern Touring Agency, it changed its name to Momentum Arts in 2003. Main activities include: networks and forums; training; delivery of information, advice and consultancy; capacity building through specific projects (e.g. in regeneration or in cultural diversity); action-research projects; dissemination of best practice theory and research findings; providing routes to specialist knowledge and funding sources; making connections between companies, artists and promoters; and raising the profile of working partners.

National Association of Decorative and Fine Arts Societies (NADFAS)

NADFAS House, 8 Guilford Street, London WC1N 1DA
T 020 74300730
F 020 72420686
W www.nadfas.org.uk
Launched in 1968 by Patricia Fay with eleven societies. Has expanded to over 330 societies in the UK, nine in Europe, twenty-eight in Australia and two in New Zealand. With ninety thousand members worldwide, NADFAS works towards promoting and preserving the arts. Concerns include voluntary work to maintain historic buildings, recording churches and their contents, working towards developing the arts for the young and maintaining lecture programmes and tours for members.

National Campaign for the Arts (NCA)

1 Kingly Street, London, W1B 5PA
T 020 7287 3777
F 020 7287 4777
E nca@artscampaign.org.uk
W www.artscampaign.org.uk

Contact Louise de Winter (Director)
The UK's only independent lobbying organization representing all the arts. Founded in 1985 to safeguard, promote and develop the arts and win public and political recognition for their importance as a key element in the national culture. Relies on subscriptions to sustain its work and does not receive any public subsidy. Members gain access to the NCA's information and advice, networks, seminars, conferences and publications.
Admissions Policy Membership is open to organizations and individuals working in, or with an interest in, the arts.
Subscription rates £50 for individuals; £25 for the unwaged. Organizational rates vary according to turnover (see website for full details).

National Network for the Arts in Health (NNAH)

The Menier Gallery, 51 Southwark Street
London, SE1 1RU
T 0870 1434555
F 020 72611317
E info@nnah.org.uk
W www.nnah.org.uk
Contact Lara Dose
A membership organization and advocate for the arts in health field.
Admissions Policy To become a member, complete an application form which is available from the NNAH office or online. Membership includes artists across 30 artforms, community arts organizations, hospital arts directors, senior healthcare managers, health and local authority officers, students, funding bodies, policy makers and evaluators. Annual membership fees are renewable in October and new applicants will be invoiced on a pro-rata basis after completion of the membership application form. All information provided on the form is recorded in a specially designed database and used for membership enquiries and requests from the public and press.
Subscription rates £70 for organizations; £30 for individuals.

National Society for Education in Art and Design (NSEAD)

The Gatehouse, Corsham Court, Corsham
SN13 0BZ
T 01249 714 825
F 01249 716 138
E janetpacker@nsead.org
W www.nsead.org
Contact Janet Packer
Offers combined membership of a professional association, a learned society and a trade union. Provides a coherent and comprehensive source of information for art and design teachers and lecturers. Aims to continually define and reassess policies in all areas of art, craft and design education, disseminate new ideas, research and good practice, and provide a forum for discussion. This is achieved through activities such as publishing (on-line, newsletter, journal and books), specialist book-selling, conference organization, and by providing teaching resources and extensive in-service training opportunities. NSEAD also offers support and access to legal advice and assistance in professional matters whenever possible or desirable.
Admissions Policy Some membership categories are only available to those who are employed or resident in the United Kingdom. Corporate memberships and student memberships are available. The Ordinary membership is for those applying for NSEAD membership for the first time.
Subscription rates Ordinary membership is £78; students pay between £8–£24. There are 6 membership categories in total.

National Society of Painters, Sculptors & Printmakers

122 Copse Hill, Wimbledon, London, SW20 0NL
T 020 89467878
W www.nationalsociety.org
Founded in 1930. Holds an annual exhibition in London representing all aspects of art for artists of every creed and outlook. Two newsletters per year for members.
Submission Policy £42.50 for associate members; £85 for full members.
Admissions Policy Submission to Honorary Secretary of six photographs of work and CV plus sae for the council's preliminary consideration. Original work will be requested later.

New English Art Club

Federation of British Artists, 17 Carlton House Terrace, London, SE5 9AX
E info@mallgalleries.com
W www.newenglishartclub.co.uk
Contact Bob Brown
Founded in 1885 in reaction to the academic artistic tradition of the time. Members have included John Singer Sargent, Wilson Steer, Walter Sickert, Augustus John, Stanley Spencer, Paul Nash and Duncan Grant. While still rooted in the figurative tradition, today's membership also

includes artists who have moved towards abstraction and others whose interests are more narrative. All, however, share a belief in the necessity of good drawing. Holds an annual open exhibition in London.

Admissions Policy Membership is by election only but its annual exhibition at the Mall Galleries is open. Details of annual open exhibition are available from Patricia Renny, Federation of British Artists, 17 Carlton House Terrace, London SW1Y 5BD.

New Work Network

Toynbee Studios, 28 Commercial Street
London, E1 6AB
T 020 7539 9373
E info@newworknetwork.org.uk
W www.newworknetwork.org.uk
Contact Hannah Crosson (New Work Network Administrator)

Promotes and supports the development of new performance, live and interdisciplinary arts practice by providing demand-led networking support for artists and by facilitating engagement and collaboration between practitioners nationally and internationally.
Subscription rates £10 membership fee.

North East Wales Artists' Network (NEWAN)

2 Park Place, Wrexham, LL14 3JD
T 07712 230668
E newan@tiscali.co.uk
W www.newan.co.uk
Contact Jim Ducket

An extended network of artists working across the region since 2001, established in order to provide a support network for recent graduates and other emerging creative talent in the region. Currently comprises eighteen members working across a range of media and at various stages in their careers, from recent graduates to internationally exhibited artists. Primary objectives are the establishment of an artist-run space for the creation and promotion of new works, as well as the development of a vital and energized network of contemporary artists across the region.
Admissions Policy Artists must be able to demonstrate a genuine desire to develop their practice. Application is by informal portfolio presentation.
Subscription rates £25 per year.

Organisation for Visual Arts (OVA)

4 Bellefields Road, Brixton, London, SW9 9UQ

T 020 76523937
F 020 76523941
E info@ova-online.org
W www.ova-online.org
Contact Edward Ward

Founded in 1992 as an inIVA franchise, and independent since 1995. A non-venue-based organization that curates exhibitions, conferences and workshops about contemporary art mainly by living artists of non-European descent whose work deals with postcolonial issues. Any medium available for display and presentation in a gallery is suitable. Prefers to work with artists who have some track record but whose work is not part of the European mainstream.
Admissions Policy Artists should first look at the website and see if their works are suitable. Then they should make initial contact, which is generally followed by an appointment to visit the studio.

Out of the Blue Arts and Education Trust

The Drill Hall, 30–38 Dalmeny Street, Edinburgh EH6 8RG
T 0131 5557100 / 5557101
F 0131 5557101
E nicole@outoftheblue.org.uk
W www.outoftheblue.org.uk
Contact Nicole Lambeng

Founded in 1994 as a gallery space for new artists. Provides studio, production and performance space for Edinburgh's cultural community, while fostering innovative and accessible creative projects (e.g. international tours and exchanges, social inclusion projects, a quarterly arts market, exhibitions, events). Studio space from £40 to £500 per month. Main hall/exhibition space and rehearsal space for hire.

Pastel Society

Federation of British Artists, 17 Carlton House Terrace, London, SE5 9AX
E info@mallgalleries.com

Formed in 1898 with founder members and early exhibitors including Brangwyn, Degas, Rodin, Rothenstein, Whistler and G.F. Watts. Aims to promote the best contemporary work by painters who use the medium for its vibrant colour, immediacy and vitality. Also committed to restoring pastels to the levels of popularity they experienced during the seventeenth and eighteenth centuries and during the time of the Impressionists.
Admissions Policy Membership of the society is by election only, but the annual exhibition at the Mall

Galleries is open. Send an sae to 'PS Entry Details', FBA at the above address. Maximum of six works. Acceptable media are pastel, oil pastels, charcoal, pencil, conte, sanguine or any dry medium.

Pavilion

Host Media Centre, 21 Savile Mount, Leeds
LS7 3HZ
T 0113 200 7061
E admin@pavilion.org.uk
W www.pavilion.org.uk
Contact Ruth Haycock
Formally established in 1983, a visual arts organization that engages with photography and lens-based media. Celebrates, develops and promotes the practice of photography as a powerful tool of creative expression and social empowerment.
Admissions Policy Submissions for selected projects only (photography, film, writing). Details on website.

Peacock Visual Arts

21 Castle Street, off the Castlegate, Aberdeen
AB11 5BQ
T 01224 639539
F 01224 627094
E info@peacockvisualarts.co.uk
W www.peacockvisualarts.com
Contact Monika Vykoukal (Curator)
Started out in 1974 as a printmaking studio and has developed over the years into the main contemporary visual arts organization in Aberdeen and the Northeast of Scotland. Neither a conventional gallery nor a traditional artists' media workshop, it seeks to involve people of all ages and abilities in creative activity across all sectors of contemporary art.
Admissions Policy Exhibition proposals (any medium) are accepted by letter or email. Mark for the attention of Monika Vykoukal.

Phoenix Arts Association

10–14 Waterloo Place, Brighton, BN2 2NB
T 01273 603700
F 01273 603704
E info@phoenixarts.org
W www.phoenixarts.org
A charitable, non-profit arts organization, offering studio spaces, a gallery and education programme to bring together professional artists and the general public. Offers affordable studio space to over a hundred visual artists working across a range of fine- and applied-art practice, as well as

short-term project space for community groups. Runs a programme of contemporary visual arts shows in all media. The education programme features workshops in a variety of practices, including life drawing, fine art, art therapy, children's after-school classes, metal jewellery and ceramic sculpture.

photodebut

Hoxton, London, E2
T 07751 212451
E info@photodebut.org
W www.photodebut.org
Contact Jan von Holleben
Founded in 2003 by the photographers Jan von Holleben, Esther Teichmann and Andy Porter to connect and support talented photographers. Promotes the work of emerging photographers drawing on their collective strength to develop group shows, commissions, community projects, portfolio reviews and educational events. All photodebut photographers share a continuing desire to produce critically engaged work within a variety of contexts.
Admissions Policy Send a portfolio, CV and cover letter with detailed statement of intent, plus sae.
Subscription rates Free.

Printmakers Council

Ground Floor Unit
23 Blue Anchor Lane
London, SE16 3UL
T 020 72376789
F 020 72376789
E s.sloss@lcc.arts.ac.uk
W www.printmaker.co.uk/pmc
An artist-run, non-profit-making association founded in 1965. Promotes the art form of printmaking, mostly by exhibitions that show the public good examples of both the innovative and skilled use of print. Several shows per year, selected from the artist members, at different venues throughout the UK and occasionally abroad. Most shows include educational activities. Members receive a newsletter and have the opportunity to enter shows and be on the council's website database.
Admissions Policy Open to anyone interested in printmaking. Artist and student printmakers may enter for selection in shows. Associate members receive information.
Subscription rates £60 for UK artists; £30 for students; £35 for associate members; £65 for EU artists; £70 for non-EU artists.

Prison Arts Foundation (PAF)

Unit 3, Northern Whig House
2–10 Bridge Street, Belfast, BT 1 1LU
T 028 90247872
F 028 90247872
E office@prisonartsfoundation.com
W www.prisonartsfoundation.com
Contact Mike Moloney
The trust was set up in 1996 with the aim of putting artists into prisons to work with prisoners. Works in all art forms that are allowable by prison security in each establishment. Currently has writers, visual artists, three-dimensional artists, musicians, dancers, folklore artists, leathercraft artists, theatre practitioners, filmmakers and cartoonists engaged in various residencies of varying lengths.
Admissions Policy Operates only in Northern Ireland; 'If interested, tell us why.'

proof

Unit 6 The Glass House, Royal Oak Yard
London, SE1 3GE
T 020 74070336
F 020 73781585
E multiples@proof.demon.co.uk
W www.metaproof.com
Contact Sue Withers or Andrew Moller
Founded in 1999. An artist-run organization with three main functions: to create, curate, exhibit, sell and distribute a range of artists' multiples; to curate and organize exhibitions; and to provide technical help and digital-production facilities for fine artists.

Public Arts

The Orangery, Back Lane, Wakefield
WF1 2TG
T 01924 215550
F 01924 215560
E contact@public-arts.co.uk
W www.public-arts.co.uk
Founded in 1986. Offers professional services and programmes in education and training, public art commissioning, consultancy, general project management and conferencing. The Orangery has been owned and occupied by Public Arts since 1996. A heritage and art site, it includes an exhibition and resource area opened in 2004.

Queens Park Arts Centre

Queens Park, Aylesbury, HP21 7RT
T 01296 424332
F 01296 337363

E info@qpc.org
W www.qpc.org
Contact Louise Griffiths-Kimber or Irene Scott
Founded in 1980. Exists to provide participatory arts activities to the community. Runs over fifty arts and crafts workshops per week including painting, drawing, pottery, woodcarving and willow craft. Also hosts one-off workshops with professional artists. Sells a selection of art materials.
Submission Policy £15 for full members; £8 for concessions.
Admissions Policy Open-access policy for professional and amateur artists and community groups to exhibit art work in the centre's gallery spaces.

RAG

35 Lanfranc Road, Worthing, BN14 7ES
T 01903 526268
E rag@artistsandmakers.com
W www.artistsandmakers.com/rag
Contact Dan Thompson
A Sussex-based group of artists, makers and designers. The group focus on professional development, as well as working together to curate exhibitions and stages an annual arts festival.
Admissions Policy All artists, makers and designers are welcome to apply; preference is given to those in Sussex and surrounding counties.
Subscription rates £60–£120

RDS Foundation

Ballsbridge, Dublin 4
T 01 6680866
F 01 6604014
E arts@rds.ie
W www.rds.ie
The Royal Dublin Society was founded in 1731 to promote and develop agriculture, arts, science, and industry in Ireland. The current arts programme includes the RDS National Crafts Competition, RDS Student Art Awards and the RDS Travelling Art & Craft Exhibitions.

Res Artis – International Association of Residential Arts Centres

Keizersgracht 462 sous, Amsterdam
1016 GE, Netherlands
T +31 20 6126600
F +31 20 6126600
E office@resartis.or
W www.resartis.org
An international foundation founded in 1993. The

sole worldwide network of residential arts centres. Represents the interests of more than two hundred centres and organizations that offer art facilities and conditions conducive for making art. Membership includes residential arts centres, individuals, artists' unions and organizations that represent numerous residential arts centres themselves.

Royal Academy of Arts

Burlington House, Piccadilly, London, W1J 0BD
T 020 73008000
E info@royalacademy.org.uk
W www.royalacademy.org.uk
Founded by George III in 1768. Governed by artists to 'promote the arts of design' and the first institution in Great Britain devoted solely to the promotion of the visual arts. Receives no public funding and is completely independent.
Admissions Policy Annual Summer Exhibition (June to August) welcomes applications in February of each year. Details available on the website or on the number above.
Subscription rates £50 per year for Friends.

Royal Birmingham Society of Artists

4 Brook Street, St Paul's, Birmingham, B3 1SA
T 0121 2364353
F 0121 2364555
E secretary@rbsa.org.uk
W www.rbsa.org.uk
Contact Marie Considine
Founded in 1814. Membership now stands at approximately two hundred professional artists. Aims to promote the arts through holding exhibitions by both regional and national artists. Artists have included Millais, Leighton, Burne-Jones and David Cox.
Submission Policy £22 per year for Friends.
Admissions Policy Membership by election.

Royal British Society of Sculptors

108 Old Brompton Road, London, SW7 3RA
T 020 73738615
F 020 73703721
E info@rbs.org.uk
W www.rbs.org.uk
Contact Adele Love
A membership society for professional sculptors, founded in 1904 by a collective of eminent sculptors of the day. First granted royal patronage in 1911. A registered charity that exists to advance the art of sculpture, ensure a widespread understanding and involvement in contemporary

sculpture, and promote the pursuit of excellence in the art form and its practice. Leading sculptors involved over the years include Sir Hamo Thorneycroft, Alfred Gilbert, Ivor Roberts-Jones, Dame Elisabeth Frink, Michael Kenny, Sir Anthony Caro, Eduardo Chillida, Richard Serra, Philip King, Allen Jones and Michael Sandle.
Submission Policy £125 per year.
Admissions Policy Membership categories are: bursary membership (awarded to a recent graduate or artist of potential; after two years, automatically awarded full associate membership); associate membership (awarded to established sculptors); fellowship (awarded to associate members who present a proven track record of distinction and high achivement); non-selective listing (open to all practising sculptors based in the UK).
Subscription rates Varies depending on level of association.

Royal Glasgow Institute of the Fine Arts

5 Oswald Street, Glasgow, G1 4QR
T 0141 2487411
F 0141 2210417
E rgi@robbferguson.co.uk
W www.rgiscotland.co.uk
Contact Mrs Lesley Nicholl
Founded in 1861 to promote art by means of annual exhibitions (in Glasgow) of oils, watercolour, sculpture, etc. Membership of 1,200. Open to all artists and small gallery available for solo or group exhibitions.
Admissions Policy Works in most media acceptable. Information available from June each year. Small gallery also available to rent. Subscription rates £35 for first year; £25 annually thereafter. No differentiation between artist and lay members.

Royal Hibernian Academy

Gallagher Gallery, 15 Ely Place, Dublin 2
T 01 6612558
F 01 6610762
E rhagallery1@eircom.net
W www.royalhibernianacademy.ie
Contact Ruth Carroll, Exhibitions Curator
Established in 1823 to promote the practice and awareness of the visual arts in Ireland. Dedicated to developing, affirming and challenging the public's appreciation and understanding of traditional and innovative approaches to the visual arts. This is acheived through an international exhibition programme, educational courses, tours and studios visits for Friends of the RHA.

Admissions Policy Applications for exhibition proposals to the RHA Director, Patrick T. Murphy.

Royal Institute of Oil Painters

Mall Galleries, 17 Carlton House Terrace, London SW1Y 5BD
T 020 79306844
F 020 78397830
E info@mallgalleries.com
W www.mallgalleries.org.uk
Founded in 1882 and dedicated to promoting the art of painting in oils. Annual exhibition takes place at the Mall Galleries in central London.
Submission Policy Gallery tours are held during the annual exhibition at the Mall Galleries. £2.50 entry fee (£1.50 concessions).
Admissions Policy Open submission to the annual exhibition. A maximum of six works can be submitted, of which a maximum of four will be selected.

Royal Institute of Painters in Water Colours

Federation of British Artists, 17 Carlton House Terrace, London, SW1Y 5BD
T 020 79306844
F 020 78397831
E info@mallgalleries.com
W www.mallgalleries.org.uk
Founded in 1831. A registered charity aiming to encourage diversity and innovation in the use of watercolours and water soluble medium. From its beginning, the society showed non-members' works alongside that of members.
Admissions Policy Artists are invited to submit to its annual open exhibition. Up to six works in a water-soluble medium. No metal frames. Send sae or see website for details.

Royal Photographic Society

The Octagon, Milsom Street, Bath, BA1 1DN
T 01225 462841
F 01225 448688
E reception@rps.org
W www.rps.org
Formed as the Photographic Society in 1853 and granted Royal Decree in 1894. Mission is 'to promote the Art and Science of Photography'.
Admissions Policy Membership open to everyone with a real interest in photography.

Royal Scottish Academy of Art and Architecture (RSA)

The Mound, Edinburgh, EH2 2EL
T 0131 2256671
F 0131 2206016
E info@royalscottishacademy.org
W www.royalscottishacademy.org
Contact Bruce Laidlaw (Administrative Secretary)
Founded in 1826, an independently-funded institution led by eminent artists and architects whose purpose is to promote and support the creation, understanding and enjoyment of the visual arts through exhibitions and related educational events. Core exhibitions include the RSA Annual Exhibition, RSA Students Exhibition and the Alastair Salvesen Scholarship Exhibtion. Also a continuous and changing programme of new shows. The RSA administers scholarships, awards and residencies for artists living and working in Scotland and has an historic collection of important artworks and an extensive archive.
Admissions Policy Offers a number of scholarships and awards. Check the website or contact directly for application details and dates for open exhibitions.

Royal Scottish Society of Painters in Watercolour

5 Oswald Street, Glasgow
G1 4QR
T 0141 2487411
F 0141 2210417
E rsw@robbferguson.co.uk
W www.thersw.org.uk
Contact Mrs Lesley Nicholl
A registered charity founded in 1878 to promote watercolour painting. Currently has 122 members. Holds annual exhibitions (usually in Edinburgh) open to all artists. A major showcase for watercolourists.
Admissions Policy Submissions to exhibitions must be in water-based media and are subject to selection. Information available from October each year. Membership by election.

Royal Society of Arts (RSA)

8 John Adam Street, London, WC2N 6EZ
T 020 79305115
E general@rsa.org.uk
W www.rsa.org.uk
Founded in 1754, today the RSA is an independent, non-aligned, multidisciplinary registered charity with over 22,000 fellows. Encourages sustainable economic development and the release of human potential through a programme of projects and a national lecture programme consisting of over one hundred events every year. The RSA journal is published bimonthly and automatically sent to all fellows.

Royal Society of British Artists (RBA)

Federation of British Artists, 17 Carlton House Terrace, London, SW1Y 5BD
E info@mallgalleries.com
Established in 1823 by a small group of artists who wished to form an alternative to the Royal Academy. Granted Royal Charter in 1887. Society has had 36 Presidents, including James McNeill Whistler, Walter Sickert and Peter Greenham RA. The society has developed a strong commitment to issues of education and in September 1995 supported the foundation of a new fine-art course based around figurative art, run by Northbrook College in Worthing. Annual open exhibition held at the Mall Galleries.
Admissions Policy Send sae to 'RBA Details' at the above address. Maximum of six works in any medium, including sculpture and original prints. The galleries cannot hang works taller than 8ft.

Royal Society of Marine Artists

17 Carlton House Terrace, London, SW1Y 5BD
T 020 79306844
F 020 78397830
E info@mallgalleries.com
W www.mallgalleries.org.uk
A registered charity devoted to the encouragement and display of contemporary marine painting, drawing, sculpture and printmaking of the highest standard. Founded in 1939, but the Second World War curtailed activity and the society's first exhibition took place in 1946. Granted royal title in 1966. Annual exhibition moved to the Mall Galleries in 1981.

Royal Society of Miniature Painters, Sculptors and Gravers

1 Knapp Cottages, Wyke, Gillingham, SP8 4NQ
T 01747 825718
E pamhenderson@dsl.pipex.com
W www.royal-miniature-society-org.uk
Contact Pam Henderson (Executive Secretary)
Founded in 1895. Aims to promote the fine art of miniature painting or any allied art. Seeks to provide facilities for the exhibition of works by artists in these fields.
Submission Policy £90 for associate membership; £100 for full membership.
Admissions Policy Apply to the Executive Secretary for an exhibition and information sheet.

Royal Society of Painter-Printmakers

Bankside Gallery, 48 Hopton Street
London, SE1 9JH

The Society of Painter-Etchers was founded in 1880 and granted its Royal Charter eight years later. It changed its name to the Royal Society of Painter-Printmakers in 1989. Holds an annual exhibition of members' work at Bankside Gallery and is involved in group exhibitions and mixed watercolour and print shows throughout the year. Committed to raising awareness of printmaking as an art through education, demonstrations and talks.

Royal Society of Portait Painters

Federation of British Artists, 17 Carlton House Terrace, London, SW1Y 5BD
E info@mallgalleries.com
A registered charity that seeks to promote, maintain, improve and advance education in the fine arts and in particular to encourage the appreciation, study and practice of the art of portraiture. Founded in 1891 with the principal aim of overcoming the 'uncertainty attending the acceptance of portraits, however well painted, by all but academicians'. Became a Royal Society in 1911. Holds an annual exhibition at the Mall Galleries. Many substantial prizes are awarded through the exhibition, and exhibiting artists frequently receive commissions.
Admissions Policy For the open, artists may submit up to three works in any two-dimensional medium. Send sae to 'RP Entry Details' at the above address.

Royal Watercolour Society

Bankside Gallery, 48 Hopton Street, London SE1 9JH
E aparker@banksidegallery.com
Contact Angela Parker (Director)
Founded over two hundred years ago. The first institution in the world to specialize in watercolours. Members have included John Sell Cotman, David Cox, Edward Burne-Jones, Helen Allingham and currently include Leslie Worth and Ken Howard. Programme of exhibitions at Bankside Gallery includes two members' exhibitions (spring and autumn) and several joint exhibitions. Also runs an open exhibition during February and a series of educational activities.

Scottish Artists' Union

c/o Equity, 114 Union Street, Glasgow
GI 3QQ
T 07849 637546
E info@sau.org.uk
W www.sau.org.uk

Contact Executive Committee
The representative voice for artists in Scotland since 2001. A membership organization representing visual and applied artists in Scotland, run by a voluntary committee. Registered as an official Scottish Trade Union. Involved in lobbying, defending rights, improving working conditions and payments, and speaking up for artists.
Admissions Policy Applicants must meet four criteria for full membership or two criteria for associate membership. Select from a generous list, detailed on the website.
Subscription rates £35 per year.

Scottish Sculpture Trust

6 Darnaway Street, Edinburgh
EH3 6BG
T 0131 2204788
F 0131 2204787
E info@scottishsculpturetrust.org
W www.scottishsculpturetrust.org
An independent trust that aims to offer advice and opportunities to sculptors throughout Scotland. Maintains a database of Scottish artists working in sculpture, provides information on national and international projects and organizations, and advises on funding, copyright, commissioning, purchasing and exhibiting. Also arranges events and conferences, and publishes *Sculpture Matters* magazine.

Society for All Artists (SAA)

P.O. Box 50, Newark
NG23 5GY
T 01949 844050
F 01949 844051
E info@saa.co.uk
W www.saa.co.uk
Founded in 1992 to inform, encourage and inspire all artists. With over thirty-four thousand members in sixty countries. Members range from complete beginners to amateurs, professionals and teachers. Welcomes anyone to join, whatever their ability, and provides benefits including a full art materials catalogue with ten thousand-plus products, the *Paint newsletter*, which appears six times a year, and the chance for artists to promote their work through the website.

Society for Religious Artists (SFRA)

14 Squirrels Way, Badgers, Buckingham
MK18 7ED
T 01280 816828
E whitebird3@mac.com

W www.cosamara.com
Contact Constantina Wood
Founded in 2006, a forum for religious artists of any faith. Encourages interfaith collaboration, open discussion, sharing of ideas and others' beliefs through art, poetry and creative writing. Aims to promote peace through contemporary and traditional religious art.
Admissions Policy Membership is open to anyone interested in religious art.
Subscription rates £10 per annum.

Society of Botanical Artists

1 Knapp Cottages, Wyke, Gillingham
SP8 4NQ
T 01747 825718
E pam@soc-botanical-artists.org
W www.soc-botanical-artists.org
Contact Pam Henderson (Executive Secretary)
Founded 1986 to promote the fine art of botanical painting or any allied art and to provide facilities for the exhibition of works by artists practising such art. Also seeks to promote appreciation and conservation of botanical species.
Admissions Policy Membership by election based on consistent work. Apply to the Executive Secretary for entry schedule for the annual open exhibition.
Subscription rates £120 to members.

Society of Catholic Artists

Garden Flat, 36 Warham Road, South Croydon
CR2 6LA
T 020 86817633 / 07932 764929
F 020 72725458
E mj.sibtain@virgin.net
W www.catholicartists.co.uk
Contact Mary Davey
Founded in 1929. Aims to supply artists and craftsmen for the creation and restoration of church art, and fellowship for Catholics interested in the visual arts. Skills of members include painting, sculpture, stained glass, ceramics, metalware, woodcarving and pottery.
Admissions Policy Membership is open to any Catholic interested in the visual arts, though artists joining for commissions will need assessment.
Subscription rates Annual membership £15 if within 50 miles of London; £11 outside that; full-time students £5.

The Society of Graphic Fine Art

27 Lorne Avenue, Croydon, Surrey, CR0 7RQ
T 020 8655 0221

E rogerlewissgfa@tiscali.co.uk
W sgfa.org.uk
Contact Roger Lewis
Established in 1919 by Sir Frank Brangwyn RA, the SGFA (The Drawing Society) exists to promote and exhibit works of high quality with the emphasis on good drawing and draughtsmanship in pencil, pen, brush, charcoal, conte or any of the forms of original printmaking. Membership numbers around 95. Welcomes artists working in modern or traditional styles in any wet or dry media and printmaking though does not accept oils. Organizes an annual open exhibition of around 170 works and at least one 'members only' event throughout the year.
Admissions Policy Membership submission is four original finished works (mounted but unframed) and folio of up to twelve original drawings (not copies) or an original sketchbook.

Society of Portrait Sculptors

T 01825 750485
F 01825 750411
E sps@portrait-sculpture.org
W www.portrait-sculpture.org
Contact David Houchin (Honorary Secretary)
A representative body of professional sculptors committed to making portrait sculpture accessible to a wider public. Has an annual open exhibition and seeks to encourage education and training in the art through lectures, prizes and events.

Society of Scottish Artists (SSA)

18 Clarence Street, Edinburgh
EH3 5AF
T 0131 2203977
E ssa@soroka.plus.com
W www.s-s-a.org
Contact Joanne Soroka (Secretary)
Founded in 1891. Represents 'the more adventurous spirit in Scottish art'. Welcomes members from every country and in all media. Hosts an annual open exhibition of contemporary art, held in the Royal Scottish Academy building in Edinburgh.
Admissions Policy Anyone may join as an ordinary member. Professional membership is by election.
Subscription rates Ordinary £40; Professional £50.

Society of Wildlife Artists

Federation of British Artists, 17 Carlton House Terrace, London, SE5 9AX
E info@mallgalleries.com
Founded in 1962. A registered charity aiming to foster and encourage all forms of wildlife art. The society's eighty members produce most of the work on display at the annual exhibition at the Mall Galleries, but non-members are invited to submit their work to be judged by the council for inclusion in the exhibition and outstanding artists are put forward as candidates for membership.
Admissions Policy Send sae to 'SWLA Entry Details' at the above address. Maximum of six works in any medium.

Society of Women Artists

1 Knapp Cottages, Wyke, Gillingham
SP8 4NQ
T 01747 825718
E pamhenderson@dsl.pipex.com
W www.society-women-artists.org.uk
Contact Pam Henderson (Executive Secretary)
Founded in 1855. Aims to promote visual arts undertaken by women.
Admissions Policy Acceptable categories: painting, drawing and sculpture in all media; miniature work; engraving, lithography, etc.; ceramics of a non-utilitarian nature.
Subscription rates £110 for associate members; £130 for full members.

Spike Island

133 Cumberland Road, Cumberland Basin
Bristol, BS3 4NZ
T 0117 9292266
F 0117 9292066
E admin@spikeisland.org.uk
W www.spikeisland.org.uk
Combines working and exhibition spaces for the contemporary visual arts. Aims to provide gallery spaces for 'the making and showing of ambitious new work'. Also offers seventy affordable studios and an international programme of residencies.
Admissions Policy Artists are welcome to apply for annual residency programme (see website). Applications for studio space are also welcome (forms and details available online or by post). A selection committee sits four times a year to select artists for the available spaces.

Suffolk Art Society

1 Holly Cottages, Little Bealings, Woodbridge
IP13 6PN
T 01473 624141
F 01473 630451
E ferial.rogers@virgin.net
W www.suffolkartsociety.org
Contact Ferial Rogers

Founded in 1954, with a membership of around 100 from Suffolk and surrounding counties. Both professional and amateur artists, mostly working in watercolour and oils but some three-dimensional work. Holds three to four exhibitions annually, visiting important local churches including Holy Trinity, Long Melford and Sts Peter and Paul, Lavenham. Awards an annual prize at Suffolk College to a Fine Art student on the BA (Hons) course, under 21 years old, showing the most progress in their studies. Regular newsletters, previews of exhibitions and an annual general meeting keep members in touch.
Admissions Policy Membership by selection annually in spring. Applicants (both professional and amateur) should submit three recent works in any medium for consideration.
Subscription rates £10

Suffolk Open Studios
24 The Street, Bawdsey, Woodbridge
IP12 3AH
T 01449 613077
E chair@suffolkopenstudios.co.uk
W www.suffolkopenstudios.co.uk
Contact Alison Calvesbert
Founded sixteen years ago. Attracts over seven thousand visitors to see the work of two hundred artists in studios across Suffolk. Aims to provide an artistic network for artists and public alike, giving opportunities to artists and helping to promote their work through publications, exhibitions and publicity. Studios are open to the public during the weekends of June each year and throughout the year by appointment. Also showcases artsists' work in large venues and gives artists links in order to promote their work through galleries.
Admissions Policy Open to all artists living or working in Suffolk.
Subscription rates A single artists entry into the Suffolk Open Studios directory is £70.

TotalKunst at the Forest
3 Bristo Place, Edinburgh
EH1 1EY
T 0131 2204538
E committee@totalkunst.com
W www.totalkunst.com, www.theforest.org.uk
Started in 2000, the Forest is a not-for-profit, artist-led initiative run by volunteers and financed through a vegetarian café. The funds are committed to providing a free events space, exhibition gallery, resource centre, free broadband,

film nights, workshops, garden, live bands, etc. TotalKunst, the visual-art programme, launched in 2003.
Submission Policy See website for details: groups.yahoo.com/group/totalkunst/.
Admissions Policy Applications are accepted throughout the year. Places an emphasis on risk-taking works, collaborations and site specificity.

Trans Artists
Keizersgracht 462 sous, Amsterdam
1016 GE, Netherlands
E info@transartists.nl
W www.transartists.nl
Contact Director: Maria Tuerlings
An independent information centre for artists, artist-run initiatives and cultural institutions. Offers details of cultural exchanges, artist-in-residence programmes and work opportunities worldwide.

UK Coloured Pencil Society
c/o Pat Heffer (Secretary), White Meadows, Horton, Devizes, SN10 3NB
T 01380 860205
E secretary@ukcps.co.uk
W www.ukcps.co.uk
Contact Pat Heffer (Secretary)
Founded in 2001 to promote the versatile medium of coloured pencils as well as to support and educate all artists who use it.
Submission Policy Within the UK: £25 for full members; £17.50 for associates. Outside the UK: £30 for full members; £22.50 for associates.
Admissions Policy Open membership. Art work submitted for the juried annual exhibition must be 100% coloured pencil; rules vary for other exhibitions.
Subscription rates £25 pa.

Vane
Kings House, Forth Banks
Newcastle upon Tyne, NE1 3PA
T 0191 2618281
F 0191 2618281
E info@vane.org.uk
W www.vane.org.uk
Contact Paul Stone or Christopher Yeats
Founded in 1997. Having worked with over 500 artists from around the world and presented a series of one-off projects in a variety of temporary venues, Vane opened a permanent gallery space in Newcastle city centre in July 2005. Represents the work of a number of artists, both from across the

UK and abroad, as well as showing the work of invited artists in collaboration with other galleries. **Admissions Policy** Exhibitions are by invitation.

Visual Artists Ireland
37 North Great George's Street, Dublin 1
T 01 8722296
E info@visualartists.ie
W www.visualartists.ie
Contact Niamh Looney
An all-Ireland body for professional visual artists. It provides services, facilities and resources for artists, initiates artistic projects and publications and acts as an advocate on behalf of individual artists. The organization was established in 1980 and has a current membership of over 1,400 artists.
Subscription rates €50 (€25 for concessions).

Visual Artists' Association of Northern Ireland
Flaxart Studios, Edenderry Industrial Estate, Crumlin Road, Belfast, BT14 7EE
T 028 90740465
F 028 90740465
A non-sectarian, non-racist lobbying organization for Northern Irish artists. Hosts workshops and meetings and produces a newsletter.

Visual Arts and Galleries Association (VAGA)
The Old Village School, Witcham, Ely CB6 2LQ
T 01353 776356
F 01353 775411
E admin@vaga.co.uk
W www.vaga.co.uk
A membership body open to organizations and individuals concerned with the exhibition, interpretation and development of modern and contemporary visual art on behalf of the public. Functions as a catalyst, sharing expertise and knowledge and campaigning for a healthy visual arts sector fit to meet the needs of audiences, creative practitioners and the broader public agenda.

Visual Arts Scotland (VAS)
c/o 17 Royal Terrace Mews, Edinburgh EH7 5BZ
T 0797 992 47 44
E vasadmin@btinternet.com
W www.visualartsscotland.org
Contact Tamara Ogilvie
Founded as the Society of Scottish Women Artists in the 1920s (evolved to admit men) and became

known as VAS. A rapidly expanding society of 370 artists, 160 of whom have been selected to professional membership. Annual exhibition in the RSA building in Edinburgh.
Submission Policy £10 for associate members (students, students graduated in the last three years and artists under 25); £30 for ordinary members.
Admissions Policy See website, posters or advertisements for annual open exhibition and various awards.

Visual Images Group
6 Dolphin Place, Aylesbury, HP21 7TG
E vi-group@btconnect.com
W www.bucks-open-studios.org.uk
Contact Sally Bulteel (Chairman)
Aims to promote public awareness of the diversity of visual arts and crafts throughout Buckinghamshire and surrounding counties. Representing over four hundred artists, craftspeople and art lovers, the group has run Bucks Open Studios for the past twenty years, when participating artists open their studios to the public.
Subscription rates £12 individual membership; £18 family/joint membership.

Vital Arts
Royal London Hospital, Whitechapel, London E1 1BB
T 020 73777127
F 020 73777317
E info@vitalarts.org.uk
A groundbreaking programme of integrated arts projects for the comfort, healing and well-being of patients, staff and the hospital community. Arts projects are designed to involve and engage hospital staff, patients, relatives and the local community. Develops commissions and residencies, and shows art by artists, staff and community groups at a number of locations.

Voluntary Arts Network
P.O. Box 200, Cardiff, CF5 1YH
T 029 20395395
F 029 20397397
E info@voluntaryarts.org
W www.voluntaryarts.org
The UK development agency for the voluntary arts, working with policy-makers, funders and politicians to improve the environment for everyone participating in the arts. Provides information and training to those who participate

in the voluntary arts sector. Has headquarters in Cardiff and four teams working in England, Ireland, Scotland and Wales.

Wales Arts International
28 Park Place, Cardiff
CF10 3QE
T 029 20383037
F 029 20398778
E info@wai.org.uk
W www.wai.org.uk
Established in 1997. A partnership between the Arts Council of Wales and British Council Wales to promote contemporary culture from Wales and encourage international exchange and collaboration.

Watercolour Society of Wales – Cymdeithas Dyfrlliw Cymru
4 Castle Street, Raglan
NP5 2JZ
T 01291 690260
Formed in 1959 to promote the practice of painting in water-soluble media. Membership of mainly professional artists either living in or from Wales. Members include Ivor Davies, Bert Isaac, Jonah Jones, Mary Lloyd Jones, Richard A.Wills, Des Hawkins and David Tress.

Welfare State International
Lanternhouse, The Ellers, Ulverston
LA12 0AA
T 01229 581127
E claire@welfare-state.com
W www.welfare-state.org
Founded in 1968 by John Fox and Sue Gill. A loose association of freelance artists aiming to pioneer new approaches to the arts of celebration and ceremony in the UK and internationally. Advocates a role for art that 'weaves it more fully into the fabric of everyday life'. Designs and constructs

performances that are specific to place, people and occasion. Artists are involved as members of small creative teams, project directors, associates and as members of the artists' forum.

Westbury Farm Studios
Foxcovert Road, Milton Keynes
MK5 6AA
T 01980 501214
E westburystudios@hotmail.co.uk
Contact Annabelle Shelton or Sally Annett
Formerly the Silbury Group, founded in 1991 as a handful of artists eager to make connections, find studios and have a place to show their work. Has evolved into one of the longest-running artist collectives in the country. Has two gallery/performance spaces, large grounds and a rolling programme of events, exhibitions and residencies.
Admissions Policy As a members-based collective, the group is always looking for inspirational visual artists. Notify interest by email in first instance.

Women's Arts Association
54a Bute Street, Cardiff Bay, Cardiff
CF10 5AF
T 029 20487850
F 029 20487850
E info@womensarts.demon.co.uk
W www.womensarts.demon.co.uk
Contact Rebecca Spooner
Aims to provide opportunities for and increase recognition of women in the arts in south-east Wales. Also seeks to increase awareness of the special needs of women in the arts.
Admissions Policy Any women over 18 who are artists or have an interest in the arts are welcome. Membership is free to any woman over 18. Subscription to the quarterly newsletter is £10 per year.

Diary of discovery: From art school to the real world

Zoë Mendelson

The last term at art school: 2000

With hindsight I remember one particularly abject phrase stalking the studios in my final weeks at the Royal College of Art: 'the real world'. This relatively under-discussed fantasy land featured neither jobs nor plans and, despite being entirely abstract, had a start date which was precise to the second. The notion that we had been trained to be painters (in the broadest sense of the word) but were now to filter off into fast-food kitchens whilst languishing on the waiting lists for cold East End studios was terrifying. I remember wondering how it felt to train to be a dentist, a tree surgeon, a chef and to jump into a 'real world' with clarity and direction.

The real world had, up until this juncture, been presented to us as something unpalatable. What is, after all, the real world of an artist? We were there to think, to subvert, to imagine, to discuss and to play. There was no system into which we would fall post-college, no strategy for becoming an artist and no route that would be any more fruitful than to continue to push ourselves onwards with all of the above. As it turns out, these non-specific and somewhat self-indulgent strategies have been the very best tactics for me.

To some extent the desire to survive as an artist, to make money and to seek representation were all dirty words in art school. The idea of selling, or of seeking to market yourself in some way, inevitably came so low down in the list of reasons for making the work that it was drained out of all discussion. I found myself subscribing to this evasion with enthusiasm. I wanted to talk about art and audience in the widest sense and not find what I made to be influenced by what was considered exhibitable or contemporary. I felt a growing, if misguided, excitement for the romance of the studio outside an institution and for starving in it in a paint-spattered stupor.

At the tail end of the MA course, my peer group had a series of interviews and studio-based advisory discussions with a London gallerist whom I pretended nonchalantly not to want to impress. I have since forgotten anything we talked about so it was either not very useful or I was not very attentive. I fear the latter.

At what seemed like zero hour we were sent off in pairs to teach at various colleges around the country. This for me was a huge turning point in how I saw my own personal direction. Having never been out of education, I had thought I would struggle hugely on leaving art school, but had failed up until this point to imagine a way of staying on while asserting my independence as an artist. During this bite-sized venture into teaching I discovered that I loved it and felt stimulated and capable in this role. I returned from the work experience with a new sense of direction and have continued to teach there, and at other institutions, ever since.

Moving out of education: 2000–01

The academic year has, of course, no corresponding timeline within the nature of art-making and the final show inevitably falls, for some, at a point of flux in their practice. For me this was certainly the case. I enjoyed the experience but felt exposed, as if, despite the unwise attempt to make a grand statement, my earliest unresolved thoughts were on display.

In fact the most incredible encounter that came out of my degree show surfaced a full four years later as the couple that now represent my work in Paris took my details on the opening night, hoping one day to open their own gallery. They promised themselves they would contact me when they did, and hung onto the little business card I had made until May 2004, when they wrote to me. I knew none of this at the time but as this is now one of the most motivating and lively relationships I have surrounding my work it allows me to reclaim my degree show in retrospect with posthumous enthusiasm. It also reminds me that the response to the work is often invisible to the artist.

At the time I was hugely excited by the prospect of conversations and collaborations that might follow the degree show. As a group, my year at the RCA and the corresponding graduating year at Goldsmiths hung a show in an abandoned school in Whitechapel which had a large audience and several small shows came out of it for me. Many of these were curated by other artists in tiny, off-the-beaten-track spaces in London's East End. For months I said 'yes' to any opportunity that came my way, good or bad. No more than a handful of people saw these little exhibitions but they kept me talking about, and making, my work as I eased my way out of being institutionalized.

By now I had found a studio and decided to go it alone. Having worked in communal studios within colleges for years, I wanted the experience of my own space. This seems an odd decision now as I am not particularly hermitic but it suited me and I have not shared a studio since (although the amount of time I spend on the phone with friends and emailing images back and forth does seem to mock this desire for isolation). My first studio was a disused but lockable living room in a council flat in Hackney. The girl who rented the rest of the flat was an acrobat in the show at the Millennium Dome and kept an unimaginably unsanitary home. It was cheap, it was compact and for a year I convinced myself if I crossed my legs enough I wouldn't have to ever see the bathroom.

During the time I rented this space I was responding to a steady trickle of emails generated by my degree show (ignoring the endlessly clawing web galleries) and finding that occasional proposals for inclusion in small group shows would find their way into my inbox. I was entering any competition I was vaguely eligible for (receiving my slides back in

the post a month later with comforting regularity) and continually applying for residencies I saw advertised in *Artists' Newsletter*. I set up an office in my bedroom, subscribed to every art magazine in print and found myself sending slides all over the country and to publications across the world. I may have single-handedly supported the postal service between the years 2001 and 2002. For stamp money, I taught sporadically and managed a restaurant in the evenings.

It never occurred to me to give up making art. I made no money from it and was exhausted most of the time but the process itself has always driven me. There has barely been a day since leaving college that I have not drawn. I can very easily separate the desire to draw from the desire to earn and for a long time didn't feel particularly driven to seek out gallery representation, while being acutely aware that I would one day crave this support and exchange. I did not believe myself or my work to be mature enough to present to a gallery at this stage. Instead, I enjoyed going to shows that motivated me, struggling with my own practice and giving myself the freedom to create horrible, burnable accidents in my smelly room.

When there was no show on the horizon I decided to curate my own and, along with photographer Anne Hardy and a hearty dose of cheap confectionary, went about selecting artists, finding a venue, writing press releases and attempting to print a small catalogue. This was a huge learning curve and helped me locate my practice in a context of its own choosing as well as widen the circle of people with whom I was discussing my work. It was also incredibly refreshing after a year of working alone to instigate a dialogue with other artists' works.

The tide turns: 2002

By 2002 I realized that an odd shift was taking place. I had had a small solo exhibition in a private house in Kennington and another through Bowieart in the window of the Tardis window-gallery in Farringdon, both precipitated by the MA show. There had been a slight smattering of press. I was gaining in confidence and much better at writing and talking about my work.

Looking around, I saw that some of my peer group from the Royal College were flourishing. It was exciting to see that the work we were making two years post-graduation had developed and changed. A few of my friends were showing in major galleries and appearing in the national press. It seemed to me that these successes were driven by the work itself and there was no over-arching strategic secret to doing well. Those who were successful seemed to have exciting practices and were the ones taking risks. Our slides were passing each other in a frenzy in post office sorting rooms across the country. I felt energized by this, frustrated with my night job and ready to take bigger steps.

Everything then happened at once for me. All the applications and slide-mailing I had been doing on the side began to pay off. The French magazine *Purple* decided to run a five-page story of my drawings, I was selected for the Jerwood Drawing Prize and I was invited to make site-specific work for a group show in a stately home. I moved my studio into my flat and worked through the night in the spare room. These relatively small-scale experiences were catalysts for me and, despite the months of rejection letters that preceded them, I have not needed to seek out projects actively since that point.

On one bizarre day in July 2002 I went to an interview for a year's residency at the University of Gloucestershire (then Cheltenham and Gloucester College of Higher Education) where I was already sporadically lecturing. I felt dizzy all day and as if all my senses were heightened. In one life-changing moment that evening I found myself standing in my bedroom, pregnancy test in hand, watching the little stick turn blue as a disembodied voice on the end of the phone simultaneously told me I had got the job.

I write 'artist' in my passport: 2003

The baby-residency combination forced me to give up my restaurant work and, for the first time, allowed me to be a full-time artist. The degree of focus and space the position offered meant I could consolidate what I had previously been attempting to do with the work in a tiny carpeted bedroom over a chip shop in Ruislip. (Yet another olfactory painting experience). For the first time I became aware of how to use a studio. It became clear to me that this is what I had been primarily learning in the years since college: how to manage my time, how to develop my practice and how to set up a studio that suits the work.

In the long hours at home waiting for my baby to wake up I set up my own website at www.zoemendelson.co.uk and have since found it to be the most valuable career move I have made to date. The site allows easy access to images and information about forthcoming projects and its international capacities make it possible to reach people who cannot make it to the shows. As well as proving to be an essential tool for conversations with curators and collectors, it is also a forum for meeting other artists and having conversations about the work that I would never otherwise be exposed to. These discussions have arisen across genres, with two of my most motivating correspondences being with an American rock musician and a South African jazz pianist.

With the time and space, slowly came the beginnings of a career. I began selling my work for the first time (it now supports me) and the shows I was involved in became higher profile and increasingly international. The representation I began to crave eventually found me and has pulled me out of the inevitable vacuum I was starting to work in. I paint through the night and spend a vast amount of time writing letters, but as a single mum enjoying a career that in one year has sent me to Paris, Italy, Copenhagen, Berlin and various parts of the UK, I do feel as though anything is possible. The only working strategy I ever strictly hold myself to, however foolishly romantic it may seem in this context, is just to keep drawing.

In 2005 I was invited to participate in a show at the Fondation Cartier in Paris and had my first experience of working within a museum context. It was also the first time I had exhibited in a space I had been a fan of as a student, thus my inclusion in this show marked a very definite shift in confidence for me. I worked in the space for a week on a site-specific drawing and the level of organization allowed my own focus to remain on the work itself throughout the project.

Subsequent projects have backed up this model and I am enjoying the conversation that builds around the hanging of shows. In recent months I have been invited to make a work for an exhibition in two years' time. There is a window of opportunity for risk and failure that creeps in again as time frames slow. With this comes the luxury of not feeling that deadlines tie me to a formula, something that would have begun to frighten me if life had grown any more chaotic.

Taking part in the installation of projects has been a huge learning curve and I have had both positive and negative experiences of the democracy and collaboration they necessarily involve. It was, initially, bizarre and somewhat laughable to watch my own work being handled with white gloves. I continually clumsily manage to trash my own projects in a thoroughly comedic fashion, while others move them with trepidation and afford them a different kind of value. As an antidote to this, and as an unnecessarily heavy-handed reminder that I care deeply about the works I make, it has been as soul-destroyingly difficult to make sure works in transit arrive in one piece as it has been to ensure temporal works are finally destroyed. I have had to learn the value of my own work through public experience as it is not necessarily something that exists in the workshop or as a by-product of the doubt that fuels the process.

I have, thus far, taken my little son with me everywhere, requiring no little skilled time-management, not-for-profit international baby-sitting (childcare-sans-frontières?) and, more often than not, a wing and a prayer. I have, somehow, maintained my two days a week in the studio, with the occasional late night accompanied by strong coffee. While I wouldn't exactly recommend any of this, I have found it to be hugely enjoyable and often shout at the telly when the family-career conundrum moaners are invited to speak.

Because of the speed at which economics can conceivably catch up with practice or commitment and the ramifications of the, often temporal, projects I want to undertake I am becoming accustomed to applying for funding. It is hard to quantify ideas before they hatch, but is ultimately necessary and a good skill to develop. In all, there has been much writing to do – statements, interviews, catalogue texts, student assessments – and I am amazed at the time I spend typing away out of the studio. Occasionally, a private-view invitation drops into my inbox from an ex-student and I am reminded that some of those I taught in their first year have also finished their MAs and are at the point I was when this diary began. I am then reminded not to feel nostalgic about the waitressing.

Zoë Mendelson's recent exhibitions include solo shows at Rokeby, London (2005); the Millais Gallery, Southampton (2005); Mogadishni, Denmark (2006); Galerie Kapinos, Berlin (2006) and Galerie Schleicher + Lange, Paris (2004, 2006). She has been included in group shows at the Northern Gallery for Contemporary Art, Sunderland (2004); Chapter Gallery, Cardiff (2006) and J'en Rêve at the Fondation Cartier, Paris (2005). Her work was recently commissioned by *Modern Painters* magazine (2005) and will be on the cover of Cartier's 2007 diary. Zoë teaches at the University of Gloucestershire and at Central St Martins College of Art and Design. She lives and works in London.

10

Art magazines and public relations

Pitch perfect: Networking and presentation skills for artists seeking media attention

Ben Rawlingson-Plant and Helen Scott-Lidgett

Many artists are daunted by the thought of public relations, or PR. Not only has the industry come under attack in recent years from certain sectors of the media that view it as 'spin', but many artists are opposed to the thought of selling themselves to the media, seeing it as vulgar to self-promote or open up their practice to a critical public.

Nothing prepares an artist for the glare of the media and unfortunately PR is not part of any art degree curriculum. The life of an artist can be fairly solitary and not everyone is able to articulate the vision or meanings behind their work. As an exercise, however, every artist should consider their creative impulse, the artists or movements that influence them and, if possible, where their work is going. Even a cursory look at how an artist would like to be positioned, through research in art magazines and visits to galleries and exhibitions, can help enormously when it comes to explaining the context of their work. This strategic approach will also aid the artist in working out where they want to be in five years' time, which gallery they would ideally like to show with, and even whether they will eventually walk off with the Turner Prize or the BP Portrait Award. PR is now generally recognized as a vital part of the success of any endeavour, whether it be a creative or business venture, the latest consumer product on the market, or even an artist at the beginning of their career looking to attract a gallery, buyers and positive reviews.

Traditionally, art was a profession or trade learned through skill and apprenticeship, while artists' guilds, the church or nobility provided support and patronage. However, the history of art is also littered with figures who broke away from their workshop or community to establish their individual reputations as artists, often by portraying a certain self-image or targeting a specific audience. While some artists are well practised in spreading the word about an upcoming project or exhibition or just naturally gifted in the art of self-promotion and networking, others are publicity-shy, perhaps fearful that they may be misquoted or misrepresented in some way. Some artists, such as Lucian Freud, make a point of never speaking to the media. While this is a valid option, the artist would have to feel very confident in their work's ability to do the talking for them.

Happily, there is a middle ground in which an artist can feel comfortable explaining his or her practice, without recourse to force-feeding complex meanings underlying their work to anyone prepared to listen. Art is often deeply personal and it is sometimes helpful to have an outside voice to help communicate the messages. This can be in the form of a curator or dealer, or is often told most eloquently through the words of an arts journalist. After all, PR is the communication of messages, not only through various media, but also through people and objects.

Successful PR for an artist could result in glowing accounts of an exhibition by the country's leading art critics. It could also lead to unwanted headlines, so shock tactics are best avoided unless you have a strong constitution for any potential backlash in the media. The tabloid press is particularly cynical and quick to criticize contemporary art, often portraying it as meaningless and talentless.

Many of the larger commercial galleries and most state-funded public galleries will have press officers or work with PR agencies to achieve the desired level of press coverage for an exhibition. For those not fortunate enough to have this support – which accounts for the vast majority of artists – it is worth noting that there is a standard procedure that should be applied to achieving this goal. The seven essential techniques and tools of the trade are as follows.

The press release

Keep it to one side of A4 with a snappy headline and the project title/dates/venue at the top of the page. The first paragraph should be a succinct summary of what the project involves, who the artist is and where the work is being shown. The second paragraph should offer more detail on the work, incorporating names and dates of the pieces to be exhibited. We would advise making the release as factual as possible since descriptions of art works tend to be overly wordy and off-putting. The final paragraph should briefly summarize what the show is trying to achieve. Contact details should follow with a name, phone number (one that is constantly manned) and an email address. Get someone to proofread all written material. A short quote relating to the artist's work by a recognized name could really help. Any complementary or additional information that may be required by a journalist at a later stage, particularly a standard cv or biography, should be prepared before the release is sent out.

Contacts

Contact details for the numerous art magazines can be found in the next few pages and the more general arts press can be contacted by ringing the switchboards of the national, regional and local papers and asking for direct lines and email addresses. Depending on time, resources and language skills, the international press can also be researched, though this is less likely to pay dividends unless the artist is from abroad and targets their country of origin. On national papers it is worth logging the details of the Arts Editor (the person who commissions reviews in the paper), the Art Critic (the person who reviews shows for the paper) and the Arts Correspondent (the person who writes art news stories for the paper). It is also worth contacting the listings pages – some publications use agencies such as PA News to provide details of where an exhibition is taking place but most national papers have in-house teams who compile this information. Regional or local papers sometimes use one person to cover a number of roles but some will have a specially appointed art critic. Local papers often respond well and this can be a useful tool in driving traffic into a gallery or art space.

Images

It is a good idea to have as many images of the art works as possible available before an exhibition opening. Long-lead publications, i.e. all glossy magazines, art magazines and colour supplements, commission articles and art round-ups approximately three to four months in advance and therefore must have access to good quality, high-resolution images. The simplest way of sending these is as a digital image (jpeg) by email. Clear colour shots of the work are preferable and can often be a deciding factor in whether a show is featured. With listings (often working four weeks in advance of an opening) it is advisable to send a couple of images through with the press release. Also, on a practical level, don't send more than two high-resolution jpeg images at one time or you might crash the computer system of whoever is in receipt of them. If a work is really striking and photogenic it may be worth considering inviting picture desks of national, regional and local papers to send a photographer down to photograph the work *in situ*. Monitor the papers and you can then get a good sense of the type of image they go for.

Timing

It is worth keeping abreast of the cultural calendar and making sure that your exhibition, project or opening event does not clash with major events at major museums or galleries. Also, consider other events such as significant anniversaries that could be linked with the exhibition to give the press an extra reason to cover the exhibition. For example, new art works that are based on human relationships and love could be launched on St Valentine's Day for maximum impact. Major cultural events can be used as a platform for the artist's exhibition or project, and many shows are timed to coincide with art fairs or major auctions when lots of international press and collectors are in town.

Follow-up

Once the press releases and images have been sent out it is vital to follow up, by email and phone, to ensure that everything is in the right hands and to find out if more information is required. However, never hassle: this will have an adverse effect and ensure your show is absolutely not reviewed. It might be worth asking a friend (maybe in exchange for a work of art) to follow up. It is much easier and more effective for a third party to chase any potential press coverage, as many people can be daunted by the prospect of having to promote their own show, particularly during the often stressful run-up to opening a new exhibition. On the other hand, direct contact with the media is to be encouraged as relationships fostered with journalists or writers can encourage them to write again or may lead to a contribution to a future catalogue essay. Arts media will often adopt emerging artists and provide support and practical help by spreading the word. If and when articles appear, they should be compiled and put into a cuttings folder that could be useful when approaching galleries or collectors.

Networking

Networking is a slightly unpleasant term but should be thought of as an artist's means of selling ideas or projects to compatible parties. For an artist to realize their dreams, a helping hand from a collector, curator, art critic and other art world insiders can make a huge difference. It is therefore crucial for artists to believe wholeheartedly in their work, to get out and to project this enthusiasm to others. Any gathering of the art world gathering – whether a dinner party or art fair opening – is an opportunity to meet potentially interested parties. Another chance to make one's art accessible, if the artist is comfortable with the idea, is by making their studio available for individual and group visits: these can be arranged via organizations such as The Contemporary Art Society. The art world calendar has evolved dramatically in the last dozen years and artists may find it beneficial, funds permitting, to attend some of the highlights such as the Venice Biennale, Documenta or Art Basel and its sister event in Miami Beach. Hang out, have fun and meet as many useful people as possible.

Vernissages

When it comes to exhibiting, group shows provide a useful platform for the artist but the solo exhibition offers a key moment in the artists' career growth and the chance to engage with as many art world professionals as possible. Make the most of an evening opening or private view by reaching out to new audiences such as collectors, commercial galleries who may be on the hunt for new talent, or curators from national and regional museums and galleries. Busy art world grandees are asked to several events in any one evening but if you have an original, exciting invitation card and can create a buzz of excitement around your project then even the presence of one powerful person on opening night could act as a springboard to greater things.

Ben Rawlingson-Plant and Helen Scott-Lidgett are Senior Arts Manager and Managing Partner, respectively, of Brunswick Arts Consulting, an agency established in 2001 that focuses on the communication needs of arts and cultural organizations and charities.

Art magazines and public relations

Art magazines

a-n Magazine / a-n The Artists Information Company

1st Floor, 7–15 Pink Lane, Newcastle-upon-Tyne
NE1 5DW
T 0191 22418000
F 0191 22418001
E subs@a-n.co.uk
W www.a-n.co.uk
Monthly magazine for professional artists and
their collaborators. Includes extensive UK and
international artists' opportunities and art jobs
listings, news, reviews, arts services directory,
What's on listings and networking information.
Subscribers also get over £100 of new publications
in the a-n Collections, Research Papers and Good
Practice series and access to all resources on
www.a-n.co.uk including daily updated artists' jobs
and opportunities and publications on making a
living, profile and promotion, professional
development and professional practice.
Editor Gillian Nicol

AA Files

Architectural Association, 36 Bedford Square
London, WC1B 3ES
T 020 78874021
F 020 74140783
E publications@aaschool.ac.uk
W www.aaschool.ac.uk
Since 1981, the Architectural Association's (AA)
journal of record, reflecting the current thoughts,
practices and preoccupations of the school's
academic and studio programmes, its tutors and
its students. Published twice a year, containing
articles on architectural theory, history and
criticism, work by contemporary practitioners and
industrial designers, photography, painting,
sculpture and music, and cross-disciplinary
collaborations. Substantially informed by the AA's
lecture and exhibitions programmes, the journal
publishes original scholarship and projects by
those who visit the school over the course of each
year.
Editor David Terrien

Afterall

Central St Martins College of Art & Design
107–109 Charing Cross Road, London
WC2H 0DU
T 020 75147212
F 020 75147166
E london@afterall.org
W www.afterall.org
Founded in 1999. A journal of contemporary art
published twice a year by Central St Martins
College of Art & Design, London and California
Institute of the Arts, Los Angeles, providing
analysis of significant art of our time. Each issue
brings together several international artists whose
work seems pertinent to the wider cultural debates
of the moment, considered through a variety of
texts and accompanied by high-quality
reproductions. Also has an office in Los Angeles.
Since 2006 has also published two series of books
distributed by The MIT Press.
Editor Charles Esche, Thomas Lawson and Mark
Lewis

Another Magazine

112–116 Old Street, London
EC1V 9BG
T 020 73360766
F 020 73360966
E info@anothermag.com
W www.anothermag.com
Founded in 2001, covering art, fashion and
culture.

Apollo Magazine

20 Theobalds Road, London
WC1X 8PF
T 020 74301900
F 020 74047386
E editorial@apollomag.com
W www.apollo-magazine.com
A monthly international fine- and decorative-arts
and antiques magazine. Founded in 1925 and
relaunched in 2004 in full colour, with a more
topical, contemporary flavour. Specializes in the
publication of new scholarly research. Also
publishes book and exhibition reviews, news and
comment. Relaunched in 2006 in a smaller
format.
Editor Michael Hall

Art & Architecture Journal

70 Cowcross Street, London
EC1M 6EJ
T 00 33 145 670334
F 0033145 670334
E editor@artandarchitecturejournal.com
W www.artandarchitecturejournal.com
Specializes in contemporary art and architecture
collaboration, providing professional information

on art commissions and projects in public places. Founded in 1980 and published quarterly.
Editor Jeremy Hunt

The Art Book
Laughton Cottage, Laughton, Nr Lewes
BN8 6DD
T 01323 811759
F 01323 811756
E ed-exec-theartbook@aah.org.uk
W www.blackwell-synergy.com/links/toc/artbook
Published quarterly on behalf of the Association of Art Historians. Details newly published books on decorative, fine and applied art, art history, photography, architecture and design. Includes feature articles, reviews of exhibitions and their catalogues, reviews of artists' books and interviews with key figures in the art world. At least fifty reviews in each issue on art, photography and architecture books.
Editor Sue Ward (Executive Editor)

Art History
c/o AAH, 70 Cowcross Street, London
EC1M 6EJ
E ed-arthistory@aah.org.uk
W www.aah.org.uk/pubs/arthistory.html
The journal of the Association of Art Historians, providing an international forum for original research relating to all aspects of the historical and theoretical study of painting, sculpture, design and other visual imagery.

Art Monthly
4th Floor, 28 Charing Cross Road, London
WC2H 0DB
T 020 72400389
F 020 74970726
E info@artmonthly.co.uk
W www.artmonthly.co.uk
A leading journal of contemporary art, founded in 1976, providing independent and opinionated commentary on emerging issues and trends. Interviews with top international artists and reviews of both British and international exhibitions. Regular columns include editions, artists' books, books, web art, art law and salerooms.
Editor Patricia Bickers

The Art Newspaper
70 South Lambeth Road, London, SW8 1RL
T 020 77353331
F 020 77353332
E contact@theartnewspaper.com
W www.theartnewspaper.com
A leading paper for the international art world.
Editor Cristina Ruiz

Art Quarterly
7 Cromwell Place, London
SW7 2JN
T 020 72254821
F 020 72254807
E info@artfund.org
W www.artfund.org
The magazine of the National Art Collections Fund (Art Fund). Covers all aspects of the visual arts and includes a news section, opinion pieces, features by celebrated art experts, writers and personalities, book reviews, and exhibition listings. Published four times a year.
Editor Caroline Bugler

The Artist
Caxton House, 63–65 High Street, Tenterden
TN30 6BD
T 01580 763673
F 01580 765411
W www.theartistmagazine.co.uk
Founded in 1931. Aims to provide inspiration, instruction and ideas for all artists, professional and amateur. Each monthly issue contains masterclasses and 'in conversation' features with leading artists, reports on materials, events, exhibitions and news relevant to all practising painters.
Editor Sally Bulgin

Artists & Illustrators
226 City Road, London
EC1V 2TT
T 020 77008500
F 020 72534370
E aim@quarto.com
W www.aimag.co.uk
Established in 1986. The UK's best-selling magazine for practising artists. Also organizes Europe's biggest art materials exhibition.

ArtReview
Hereford House, 23–24 Smithfield Street, London
EC1A 9LF
T 020 72364880
E info@art-review.co.uk
W www.art-review.co.uk
A monthly magazine with articles on the visual arts of the twentieth and twenty-first centuries

written by international art critics and writers, novelists and cultural historians including Luc Sante, Geoff Dyer, Gordon Burn, Jonathan Lethem, Matthew Collings and Natasha Walter.

Arts Research Digest

Holy Jesus Hospital, City Road
Newcastle-upon-Tyne, NE1 2AS
T 0191 2333856
F 0191 2333857
E hc.ard@unn.ac.uk
W www.arts-research-digest.com
A specialist journal providing up-to-date details about current and recent research in the arts and cultural sector around the world. Published three times a year and available by subscription only.
Editor Nessa O'Mahony

Aspect Magazine

316 Summer Street, 5th Floor, Boston
MA 02210, USA
E mmittelman@aspectmag.com
W www.aspectmag.com
A biannual DVD magazine of new media art, with a mission to distribute and archive works of time-based art. Each issue highlights 5–10 artists working in new or experimental media, whose works are best documented in video or sound. Each work can be viewed with or without an additional commentator audio track.

Audio Arts

6 Briarwood Road, London, SW4 9PX
T 020 77209129
E editor@audio-arts.co.uk
W www.audio-arts.co.uk
Since 1973, the only art magazine regularly published on audio cassette, bringing listeners into contact with contemporary artists and the critical discourse surrounding contemporary art. Each year there are cassette and CD editions of up to 120 minutes' duration, accompanied by supporting texts and colour images.

Black & White Photography

Guild of Master Craftsman Publications Ltd, 86 High Street, Lewes, BN7 1XN
T 01273 477374
F 01273 402849
E ailsam@thegmcgroup.com
W www.thegmcgroup.com
Published thirteen times per year, aimed at both enthusiast and professional photographers who are passionate about the monochrome medium.

Publishes interviews with known and up-and-coming photographers, as well as technique features and product reviews which cover both traditional and digital.
Editor Ailsa McWhinnie

Blueprint

Wilmington Media Ltd, 6–14 Underwood Street
London, N1 7JQ
T 020 74900049
E vrichardson@wilmington.co.uk
W www.blueprintmagazine.co.uk
A monthly magazine of contemporary architecture, design and culture, with emphasis on high quality photography and illustration.
Editor Vicky Richardson

British Journal of Aesthetics

Department of Philosophy, University of York
York, YO10 5DD
T 01904 433251
E P.V.Lamarque@york.ac.uk
W bjaesthetics.oupjournals.org
Founded in 1960. An international forum for debate in aesthetics and the philosophy of art. Published to promote the study, research and discussion of the fine arts and related types of experience from a philosophical standpoint. Appears quarterly and includes a substantial reviews section.
Editor Professor Peter Lamarque

British Journal of Photography

Incisive Media, Haymarket House, London
SW1Y 4RX
T 020 74849885
F 020 74849989
E bjp.news@bjphoto.co.uk
W www.bjp-online.com
Founded in 1854, BJP is the world's longest-running weekly photography magazine. Focusing on professional photography, the magazine contains international news, listings, reviews and features, including interviews, market reports, book and exhibition reviews and business-related matters. Covers all areas of professional photography, from fine art, advertising and fashion, to editorial, industrial, weddings, scientific and medical.
Editor Simon Bainbridge

The Burlington Magazine

14–16 Duke's Road, London
WC1H 9SZ

T 020 73881228
F 020 7388229
E burlington@burlington.org.uk
W www.burlington.org.uk
Has appeared every month since its creation in
1903. Selects concise, authoritative articles from
internationally renowned scholars presenting new
works, discoveries and fresh interpretations in
painting, sculpture, architecture and the decorative
arts, from antiquity to the present day. Contains
main articles, shorter notices, exhibition and book
reviews, and a calendar of forthcoming
exhibitions. Also contains advertisements with
details of works currently on the market.

Ceramic Review

25 Foubert's Place, London, W1F 7QF
T 020 74393377
E editorial@ceramicreview.com
W www.ceramicreview.com
Founded in 1970, published six times a year.
Illustrated in full colour throughout, it includes
practical and critical features on ceramic works
from the UK and round the world. It also carries
news of events and exhibitions as well as reviews
of exhibitions and books plus a comprehensive
'what's on' listing. Aimed at anyone working or
involved in the world of ceramics and studio
pottery, as well as libraries, collectors, curators and
museums.
Editor Emmanuel Cooper

Circa Art Magazine

43–44 Temple Bar, Dublin 2
T 01 6797388
E info@recirca.com
W www.recirca.com
Ireland's leading magazine of contemporary visual
art and culture. Published quarterly, it includes
news, reviews, previews, interviews, feature
articles and a host of images. Maintains a long
tradition of quality reporting on the innovative
Irish visual arts scene with a fresh, contemporary,
critical perspective.
Editor Peter FitzGerald

Contemporary

K101, Tower Bridge Business Complex, 100
Clements Road, London
SE16 4DG
T 020 77401740
F 020 72523510
E info@contemporary-magazine.com
W www.contemporary-magazine.com

Relaunched in 2002. A monthly magazine with an
estimated readership of over 75,000. Covers visual
arts, books, architecture, design, fashion, film,
music, media, photography, dance and books.
Editor Brian Muller (Publisher); Michele Robecchi
(Senior Editor)

Crafts Magazine

44a Pentonville Road, Islington, London
N1 9BY
T 020 72787700
F 020 78370858
E crafts@craftscouncil.org.uk
W www.craftscouncil.org.uk/crafts/index.htm
Contemporary craft magazine published by the
Crafts Council. The only British magazine to cover
all craft forms, from studio work to public
commissions, and from modern experimental
work to traditional and historic designs. Published
on alternate months.

Dazed & Confused

112–116 Old Street, London
EC1V 9BG
T 020 73360766
F 020 73360966
W www.dazeddigital.com
Monthly magazine founded in 1992, dealing in
cutting-edge art and fashion.

Digital Camera Magazine

Future, 30 Monmouth Street, Bath
BA1 2BW
T 01225 442244
E rob.bowen@futurenet.co.uk
W www.digitalcameramag.co.uk
Founded in 2001, a monthly magazine with strong
reputation for allowing photographs to 'do all the
talking'. Also contains hands-on advice and
practical techniques.
Editor Marcus Hawkins

Foto8

1–5 Honduras Street, London
EC1Y 0TH
T 020 7253 8801
F 020 7253 2752
E info@foto8.com
W www.foto8.com
A picture-led magazine presenting photo
reportages by award-winning photographers and
exclusive essays written by leading journalists.
Published quarterly.
Editor Jon Levy

Flux Magazine

42 Edge Street, Manchester
M4 1HN
T 0161 8320300
F 0161 8191196
E editorial@fluxmagazine.com
W www.fluxmagazine.com
A UK-based bi-monthly magazine covering
national and international fashion, music, art and
culture.
Editor Lee Taylor

frieze

3–4 Hardwick Street, London
EC1R 4RB
T 020 78337238
E admin@frieze.com
W www.frieze.com
Covers all that is vital in contemporary art and
visual culture, featuring emerging artists and
highlighting new currents in art practice as well as
offering a fresh perspective on more established
artists. Includes exhibition reviews, interviews, city
reports and worldwide listings. Published eight
times a year.

Galleries Magazine

Barrington Publications, 54 Uxbridge Road
London, W12 8LP
T 020 8740 7020
F 020 8740 7020
E art@galleries.co.uk
W www.galleries.co.uk
The UK's largest-circulating monthly arts listings
magazine, describing current exhibitions and the
stock of 450–500 commercial and public art
galleries, galleries for hire and art services. New
shows diary, artist index, dealer index, stock index
– all updated monthly. Website carries additional
references and indexes as well as indexed gallery
press releases and topical news.
Editor Andrew Aitken

The Good Gallery Guide

The Art House, Wakefield College
Margaret Street, Wakefield, WF1 2DH
T 01924 377740
F 01924 377090
E feedback@goodgalleryguide.com
W www.goodgalleryguide.com
Aims to make visiting galleries easier for everyone.
Initially started as a guide to help disabled people
plan visits to art galleries but can now be used by
all visitors. For each gallery there are details of how
to get there, what facilities exist and a personal
review of the gallery. Aims to work with galleries to
improve their access.
Editor Stuart Bolton

HotShoe

29–31 Saffron Hill, London, EC1N 8SW
T 020 7421 6000
F 020 7421 6006
E hotshoe@photoshot.com
W www.hotshoeinternational.com
A bi-monthly contemporary photography
magazine that covers all categories including
documentary, photojournalism, art, and creative.
The title has been published for over 30 years, but
was bought by World Illustrated in 2002. It has a
new format (80% of A4) and content that includes
interviews, portfolio features, book and show
reviews, awards, and listings.
Editor Melissa DeWitt

I-D Magazine

124 Tabernacle Street
London, EC2A 45A
T 020 74909710
F 020 72512225
W www.i-dmagazine.com
Began as a fanzine dedicated to the street style of
punk-era London in 1980. Has metamorphosed
into a glossy magazine that documents fashion.
Editor Terry Jones (Editor-in-Chief)

icon

Media 10 Limited
National House, 121–123 High Street, Epping
CM16 4BD
T 01992 570030
F 01992 570031
E info@icon-magazine.co.uk
W www.icon-magazine.co.uk
A major monthly international design and
architecture magazine.

Irish Arts Review

State Apartments, Dublin Castle, Dublin 2
T 01 6793525
E sperkins@irishartsreview.com
W www.irishartsreview.com
Founded in 1984, one of Ireland's leading art
magazines, published four times a year. Each
edition runs to 150 fully-illustrated pages and
features articles on printing, sculpture, design,
architecture, exhibitions and photography.
Editor John Mulcahy

The Jackdaw

88 Leswin Road, London
N16 7ND
T 020 72544027
E dg.lee@virgin.net
W www.thejackdaw.co.uk
Founded in 2000. A newsletter for the visual arts published ten times a year.

Journal of Visual Art Practice

Nottingham Trent University, Nottingham
NG1 4BU
E richard.woodfield@ntu.ac.uk
W www2.ntu.ac.uk/ntsad/nafae/
publications.shtml
Founded by the National Association of Fine Art Education in 2000 and published by Intellect. Aimed at tutors and students in the fine-art sector. Addresses issues of contemporary debate in fine-art studios, in matters of both content and practice. Particularly welcomes contributions from studio tutors and students undertaking the Fine Art PhD.

Journal of Visual Culture

Joanne Morra, Central St Martins College of Art & Design, London, WC1B 4AP
E g.morra@csm.arts.ac.uk
Published three times a year. Aims to promote research, scholarship and critical engagement with visual cultures from a range of methodological positions, at various historical moments, and across diverse geographical locations.
Editorial Group: Marquard Smith (Editor-in-Chief), Raiford Guins (Principal Editor), Joanne Morra (Principal Editor), Mark Little, Vivian Rehberg, Dominic Willsdon, Heidi Cooley, Susan pui san Lok and Rob Stone

Knight's Move

E shoesandtoast@hotmail.com
A quarterly journal of artists' writing, established in 2006. Aims to provide a public space in which visual artists can use the written word as another form of artistic endeavour.
Editor David Howells and Charlie Woolley

Latest Art Magazine

Unit 1, Level 5 North, New England House
New England Street, Brighton, BN1 4GH
W www.latest-art.co.uk
Covers the contemporary art scene in London, Brighton and the southeast. Readership of 100,000.
Editor Colette Meacher

Map Magazine

14 High Street, Edinburgh, EH1 1TE
T 0131 5503095
F 0131 5578500
W www.mapmagazine.co.uk/listings
Launched in 2005, an international art magazine from Scotland. Published quarterly, with the aim of stimulating debate and discussion. Designed to appeal to artists, art professionals and an informed general arts audience. Includes features, artist profiles, reviews and art news. Published February, May, August and November. Also online, with a listings section.
Editor Alice Bain

Marmalade Magazine

Kent House, 14–17 Market Place, London, W1W 8BY
T 020 76121139
F 020 76121112
E mail@marmaladeworld.com
W www.marmaladeworld.com
Aimed at a readership from the creative industries, from art and design, fashion and advertising, to music and the media in general. Carries a mix of new ideas and trends, as well as being a committed showcase for new creative talent.
Editor Kirsty Robinson and Sacha Spencer Trace

Modern Painters

E info@modernpainters.co.uk
W www.modernpainters.co.uk
A monthly art publication founded in 1988. Covers visual and performing arts and culture.

n.paradoxa: international feminist art journal

38 Bellot Street, London
SE10 0AQ
T 020 88583331
F 020 88583331
E k.deepwell@ukonline.co.uk
W web.ukonline.co.uk/n.paradoxa/index.htm
The only international feminist art journal dedicated to contemporary women (visual) artists and feminist theory. Contributions are published by women writers, curators, artists and critics from around the world. In print since 1998. A separate edition started online in 1996. Online and print versions contain different contents. Print editions are organized thematically.
Editor Katy Deepwell

NADFAS Review

NADFAS House, 8 Guilford Street, London
WC1N 1DA

T 020 74300730
F 020 72420686
E nadfasreview@nadfas.org.uk
W www.nadfasorg.uk
The quarterly magazine of the arts-based educational charity, with over 330 member societies and 90,000 members worldwide. Offers in-depth articles on the decorative arts, current exhibtions listings and showcases of many of the volunteer projects that members are involved in.
Editor Judith Quiney and Glyn Wilmhurst

Next Level
95 Greenwood Road, London, E8 1NT
T 020 79232117
F 020 79232117
E sheyi@nextleveluk.com
W www.nextleveluk.com
An independent photography publication launched in 2002 and released twice a year during May and October. Aims to showcase new and established photographic artists from around the world and to bring awareness and debate to contemporary issues from a visual and text-based perspective.
Editor Sheyi Antony Bankale

Object – Graduate Research and Reviews in the History of Art and Visual Culture
History of Art Department, University College London, Gower Street, London WC1E 6BT
T 020 76797545
F 020 79165939
E object@ucl.ac.uk
W ucl.ac.uk/object
Founded in 1998. An annual journal produced and edited by postgraduate students from the History of Art Department at UCL, featuring articles drawn from ongoing research alongside reviews of recent exhibitions and publications. Contents represent the diversity of issues and methodologies with which the postgraduate students in the department are engaged.
Editor Emily Richardson (Editor-in-Chief)

Oxford Art Journal
Mary Hunter, Department of Art History, University College London, Gower Street London, WC1E 6BT
W oaj.oupjournals.org
Has an international reputation for publishing innovative critical work in art history. Committed to the political analysis of visual art and material

representation from a variety of theoretical perspectives, and has carried work addressing themes from antiquity to contemporary-art practice. Also carries extended reviews of major contributions to the field.

Performance Research
Linden Elmhirst (Administrative Assistant), Dartington College of Arts, Totnes, TQ9 6EJ
T 01803 861683
E performance-research@dartington.ac.uk
W www.performance-research.net
Founded in 1995 and published quarterly. A specialist journal that promotes the dynamic interchange between scholarship and practice in the expanding field of performance. Interdisciplinary in vision and international in scope, its emphasis is on research in contemporary performance arts within changing cultures.

Portfolio – Contemporary Photography in Britain
43 Candlemaker Row, Edinburgh, EH1 2QB
T 0131 2201911
F 0131 2264287
E Info@portfoliocatalogue.com
W www.portfoliocatalogue.com
Magazine for innovative photographic art created and shown in Britain. Published in May and November, combining the contemporary interests and current reviews of a magazine with the quality reproductions and detailed information of an exhibition catalogue. Features the work of established photographers and artists accompanied by in-depth essays, a series of portfolios by emerging artists, and reviews from esteemed writers and curators. Large-format publication (295mm high x 245mm wide), containing 96 pages of colour and duotone photographs.
Editor Gloria Chalmers

Preview of the Visual Arts in Ireland
8 Oakley Park, Blackrock, County Dublin
E info@preview.ie
W www.preview.ie
Founded in 1995, Preview is a listing guide to visual art exhibitions in Irish galleries, museums and art centres. The print guide, containing descriptive text and images of upcoming art shows and events, is published six times a year. The website contains listings as well as thumbnail images of artists' works. Listing, advertising and image rates are available on request or can be viewed on the website. Circulation of

approximately 5,000 per issue.
Editor N. D. McCullough

Print Quarterly Publications
52 Kelso Place, London, W8 5QQ
T 020 77954987
F 020 77954988
E admin@printquarterly.co.uk
W www.printquarterly.co.uk
The aim of the charity is to advance, promote and
encourage education and research in the field of
art history and the contemporary arts, in particular
in the medium of prints.
Editor David Landau

Printmaking Today
Cello Press Ltd, Office 18 Spinners Court
55 West End, Witney, OX28 1NH
T 01993 701002
F 01993 709410
E Eds@pt.cellopress.co.uk
W www.printmakingtoday.co.uk
First published in 1990. The authorized journal of
the Royal Society of Painter-Printmakers. Aims to
provide a forum for printmakers, collectors and
curators.
Editor Anne Desmet

RA Magazine
Royal Academy of Arts, Burlington House
Piccadilly, London, W1J 0BD
T 020 73005820
F 020 73005882
E ramagazine@royalacademy.org.uk
W www.ramagazine.org.uk
Founded in 1983. Published quarterly in
association with the Royal Academy of Arts (RA) in
London, and distributed to the ninety thousands
Friends of the RA as part of their membership
benefits. In addition, ten thousand copies of the
magazine sell in the academy shop, on specialist
news stands and by subscription. Editorial covers
art, exhibitions and events at the RA and by Royal
Academicians, as well as art, architecture, books
and culture more broadly in Britain and abroad.
Editor Sarah Greenberg

Raw Vision
1 Watford Road, Radlett, WD7 8LA
T 01923 856644
F 01923 859897
E info@rawvision.com
W www.rawvision.com
Founded in 1989 to bring Outsider art to an

international audience. Has since moved on to
cover subjects that fall into the fields of Art Brut,
Outsider art, contemporary folk art, visionary art
and the marginal arts of the world. Published five
times per year.
Editor John Maizels

Royal Photographic Society Journal
Finsbury Business Centre, 40 Bowling Green
Lane, London, EC1R 0NE
T 020 74157099
F 020 74157133
E mail@rpsjournal.demon.co.uk
The journal of the Royal Photographic Society.
Published ten times a year. Promotes the art and
science of photography, covering all aspects of the
medium, and featuring interviews with key
photographers, equipment and book reviews,
comment and analysis.
Editor David Land

RSA Journal
8 John Adam Street, London, WC2N 6EZ
T 020 74516902
E amanda.jordan@rsa.org.uk
W www.thersa.org/journal/index.asp
The bimonthly journal of the Royal Society for the
Encouragement of Arts.

Sculpture Journal
Liverpool University Press, 4 Cambridge Street
Liverpool, L17 0AB
T 0151 7942234
F 0151 7942235
E lup@liv.ac.uk
W www.liverpool-unipress.co.uk
Founded in 1997. Britain's foremost scholarly
journal devoted to sculpture in all its aspects.
Disseminates information, scholarship and
knowledge in the international field of sculpture
from the late-medieval period to the present day
and provides an international forum for sculptors,
writers and scholars. Published twice a year
(March and October), the journal includes
illustrated scholarly articles on all aspects of
sculpture, and reviews of exhibitions and
publications. Published for and reflects the aims of
the Public Monuments and Sculpture Association.
Editor Katharine Eustace

Selvedge
P.O. Box 40038, London, N6 5UW
T 020 83419721
F 020 83419721

E editor@selvedge.org
W www.selvedge.org
A magazine of textiles in all forms, including fine art, fashion and interiors. Six issues per year.

Source Magazine

P.O. Box 352, Belfast, BT12WB
T 028 90329691
E info@source.ie
W www.source.ie
A quarterly Arts Council-funded magazine providing informed critical debate around contemporary photographic culture. Reproduces portfolios of images from a wide range of contemporary photographers' work alongside exhibition and book reviews, and in-depth essays on photographic culture covering national and international material.

TATE ETC.

20 John Islip Street, London, SW1P 4RG
T 020 78878959
F 020 78878729
E tateetc@tate.org.uk
W www.tate.org.uk/tateetc
Published three times per year, with a circulation of ninety thousand. Features in-depth articles by leading writers in their fields such as Alain de Botton, Paul Farley, Alison Gingeras and Lynne Cooke, and has a strong emphasis on giving a voice to artists. While a certain percentage of the magazine is devoted to exhibitions at the four Tates (Modern, Britain, Liverpool and St Ives) it also includes polemical, thematic features. Within these articles the magazine aims to blend the historical, modern and contemporary.
Editor Simon Grant

things magazine

P.O. Box 35095, London, NW1 7WN
T 020 72675891
E editors@thingsmagazine.net
W www.thingsmagazine.net
Originally founded in 1994 by a group of writers and historians based at the Victoria & Albert Museum and the Royal College of Art in the belief that objects can open up new ways of understanding the world. The magazine is both online and an occasional print publication.
Editor Hildi Hawkins and Jonathan Bell

Third Text

2G Crusader House, 289 Cricklewood Broadway, London, NW2 6NX
T 020 88307803
E thirdtext@btconnect.com
W www.tandf.co.uk/journals/titles/ 09528822.asp
An international scholarly journal dedicated to providing critical perspectives on art and visual culture. Examines the theoretical and historical ground by which the West legitimizes its position as the ultimate arbiter of what is significant in this field. A forum for the discussion and (re-)appraisal of the theory and practice of art, art history and criticism, and the work of artists hitherto marginalized thorough racial, gender, religious and cultural differences.
Editor Rasheed Araeen

Time Out

Universal House, 251 Tottenham Court Road London, W1T 7AB
T 020 78133000
F 020 78136001
W www.timeout.com
A guide to what's happening in London. First published in 1968.

V&A Magazine

V&A, South Kensington, Cromwell Road, London SW7 2RL
T 020 7942 2000
E vanda@vam.ac.uk
W www.vam.ac.uk
The Victoria & Albert Museum's magazine includes subject matter such as contemporary design, interior design, photography, fashion, art, architecture, craft and textiles.

Variant

1/2 189b Maryhill Road, Glasgow
G20 7XJ
T 0141 3339522
E variantmag@btinternet.com
W www.variant.org.uk
An independent critical arts and culture publication published three times a year, with a circulation of 15,000 copies. Aims to widen the involvement of its readership in debate, discussion and awareness of social, political and cultural issues that are otherwise ignored, hidden, suppressed or censored. Looks to its readership to provide, inform and generate content for the magazine. All articles are free on the website.
Editor Daniel Jewesbury and Leigh French

Visual Culture in Britain

University of Northumbria, School of Arts and

Sciences, Squires Building, Sandyford Road
Newcastle-upon-Tyne
NE1 8ST
T 0191 2273235
E ysanne.holt@unn.ac.uk
W www.manchesteruniversitypress.co.uk:
Founded in 2000. Aims to locate the range of
visual culture – art, design, print, photography, the
performing arts, etc. – in relation to the wider
culture (historically and geographically), from the
eighteenth century to the present. The journal
addresses visual culture in the context of debates
such as racial, ethnic and gender identities,
nationality and internationalism, high and low
culture, and models of production and
consumption.
Editor Ysanne Holt

Wallpaper
T 020 73221592
E editor@wallpaper.com
W www.wallpaper.com
A magazine 'for urban modernists and global
navigators'. Aimed at an international audience,
covering interiors, industrial design, architecture,
entertaining, fashion and travel.

Public relations

Arts Marketing Association
7a Clifton Court, Clifton Road, Cambridge
CB1 7BN
T 01223 578078
F 01223 245862
E info@a-m-a.co.uk
W www.a-m-a.co.uk
Supports the professional development of its
members via a range of tools including a
mentoring scheme, an accredited certificate in arts
marketing, publications (many available free to
members), a website, and a broad programme of
events.

artsinform
Farncombe House, 16 Market Street, Lewes
BN7 2NB
T 01273 488996
F 01273 488497
E jessica@mediacontacts.org.uk
W www.mediacontacts.org.uk
A marketing consultancy and public relations
agency working exclusively within the visual arts
sector. Set up in 1994 by arts journalists Jessica
Wood and Rosie Clarke.

The Artspost
Lewisham Library, 199–201 Lewisham High Street
Lewisham
SE13 6LG
A free publicity distribution service available to
arts and community organizations throughout the
borough. Distributes to over ninety venues in
Lewisham.

Bolton & Quinn Ltd
10 Pottery Lane, Holland Park, London
W11 4LZ
T 020 72215000
F 020 72218100
E erica@boltonquinn.com
Offers public relations services in the arts and
culture sector.

Brunswick Arts Consulting
16 Lincoln's Inn Fields, London
WC2A 3ED
T 020 7936 1290
F 020 7936 1299
E bartsinfo@brunswickgroup.com
W www.brunswickgroup.com
Brunswick Arts was founded in 2001 to serve the
specific communication needs of arts, cultural and
charitable organizations in today's challenging
climate. An in-house team craft tailor-made
campaigns for each client, often combining wide-
ranging arts and media experience with that of
external consultants at the top of the arts and
charitable professions. Has clients and offices
around the world, with clients ranging from major
organizations to individuals, and including
festivals and exhibitions, tourism, funding and
capital initiatives. Track record of successfully
matching sponsors with appropriate arts and
charitable organizations.

Cawdell Douglas
10–11 Lower John Street
London
W1F 9EB
T 020 74392822
F 020 72875488
E press@cawdelldouglas.co.uk
W www.cawdelldouglas.co.uk
Offers public-relations services in the arts, heritage
and culture sector.

Hobsbawm Media 1 Marketing Communications Ltd (HMC)
15 Doughty Street, Bloomsbury, London

WC1N 2PL
T 020 74309444
F 020 74309595
E julia@hmclondon.co.uk
W hmclondon.co.uk
An independent London-based communications
consultancy with over a decade of experience.
Editor Julia Hobsbawm (Chief Executive and
Founder)

HQ – International Communications
for the Arts Ltd
11 Savile Row, London
W1S 3PG
T 020 72873060
F 020 72873060
E info@hqcommunications.com
Created in 1998 in response to the demand from
UK art institutions for stronger international
media exposure, and from foreign equivalent
institutions for increased visibility in the UK.
Services are tailored to the clients' requirements by
a small, dedicated and multi-lingual team. UK
clients include the British Museum, the National
Portrait Gallery, the Royal Academy of Arts, the
Saatchi Gallery, Virgile and Stone
(Designers/Architects) and Albion. Foreign clients
include the Fondation Cartier pour l'art
contemporain, Le Printemps de Septembre,
Ambassade de France and Fung Collaboratives
(The Snow Show).
Editor Daniele Reiber

Idea Generation
10 Greenland Street, Camden, London
NW1 0ND
T 020 74284949
F 020 74284948
E frontdoor@ideageneration.co.uk
W www.ideageneration.co.uk
Set up in 2000, specialising in public relations for
the arts and entertainments sectors. Clients have
included Frieze Art Fair, Spruth Magers Lee,
Hauser & Wirth Zurich London, Lisson Gallery,
Manchester International Festival, Amazon.co.uk,
and European Firm Promotion. Check website for
up-to-date client list.

JB Pelham PR
208 Latimer Road, North Kensington, London
W10 6QY
T 020 8969 3959
F 020 8964 4562
E jasmin@jbpelhampr.com

W www.jbpelhampr.com
Works with art galleries, arts organizations, art
fairs and independent artists to provide strategic
public relations campaigns. With over ten years'
experience.

media contacts
Farncombe House, 16 Market Street, Lewes
BN7 2NB
T 01273 488996
F 01273 488497
E info@mediacontacts.org.uk
W www.mediacontacts.org.uk
A press information service in book and online
format, researched specifically for the visual arts.
Provides a continuously updated list of over four
thousand visual-arts journalists working in all
areas of the UK and international press. Also
provides detailed insider information for each
entry, including lead times, deadlines and
preferred method of contact. Online service allows
user to select own press list, paste in a press
release and image and send it out. Published since
1995 by artsinform PR.
Editor Laura Charlton

Parker Harris Partnership
15 Church Street, Esher
KT10 8QS
T 01372 462190
F 01372 460032
E info@parkerharris.co.uk
W www.parkerharris.co.uk
Founded by Emma Parker and Penny Harris in
1990, specializing in the creation, organization,
marketing, press and public relations of fine-art
exhibitions and events.

Pippa Roberts Publicity & Communications
101 Mapledene Road
London Fields, London
E8 3LL
T 020 79233188
E pr@pipparoberts.com
A public relations company founded in 2001,
specializing in press relations, marketing
communications and corporate activity for art and
antiques fairs, events and retailers, art exhibitions,
competitions and shows. Clients since 2001
include Olympia Fine Art and Antiques Fairs, the
London Silver Vaults, Olympia Loan Exhibitions
(Augustus John, Edward Burra, Keith Vaughan,
Graham Sutherland, Prunella Clough, Wyndham
Lewis), Decorative Antiques and Textiles Fairs,

BlindArt (charity) competition and exhibition, HALI Carpet Textile and Tribal Art Fair.

Rebecca Ward

33 Wellington Row, London
E2 7BB
T 020 7613 3306
E press@rebeccaward.co.uk
W www.rebeccaward.co.uk
A freelance public relations consultant with more than twelve years experience of promoting the arts and fashion. Current and past clients include the V&A, Port Eliot Lit Fest, China Power Station Part 1 at Battersea Power Station for the Serpentine Gallery, Crafts Council, SHOWstudio.com, The Women's Library, Thomas Williams Fine Art, University of the Arts, V&A's Museum of Childhood, English Heritage, Heritage Lottery Fund and the Iran Heritage Foundation.

Sue Bond Public Relations

T 01359 271085
F 01359 271934
E info@suebond.co.uk
W www.suebond.co.uk
Established in 1982, specializing in fine arts, antiques and cultural events.

Theresa Simon Communications

Stratton House, 1 Stratton Street, London
T 020 76299645
E pr@theresasimon.com
W www.theresasimon.com
An agency specializing in public relations and marketing for visual and performing arts, design and architecture organizations. Clients have included the Wallace Collection, the London Architecture Biennale, Archives Libraries Museums London, Arts Council England, Zoo Art Fair and Modus Operandi Art Consultants.
Editor Theresa Simon (Director)

General index

Alphabetical index to all entries.
All companies and organizations are listed according to
their full names, e.g. Henry Moore Institute is found under
'H' and Paul Hamlyn Foundation can be found under 'P'.

Subject index

Selected entries by category.